T0189849

Lecture Notes in Computer Science

Lecture Notes in Artificial Intelligence   14017

Founding Editor

Jörg Siekmann

Series Editors

Randy Goebel, *University of Alberta, Edmonton, Canada*
Wolfgang Wahlster, *DFKI, Berlin, Germany*
Zhi-Hua Zhou, *Nanjing University, Nanjing, China*

The series Lecture Notes in Artificial Intelligence (LNAI) was established in 1988 as a topical subseries of LNCS devoted to artificial intelligence.

The series publishes state-of-the-art research results at a high level. As with the LNCS mother series, the mission of the series is to serve the international R & D community by providing an invaluable service, mainly focused on the publication of conference and workshop proceedings and postproceedings.

Don Harris · Wen-Chin Li
Editors

Engineering Psychology and Cognitive Ergonomics

20th International Conference, EPCE 2023
Held as Part of the 25th HCI International Conference, HCII 2023
Copenhagen, Denmark, July 23–28, 2023
Proceedings, Part I

 Springer

Editors
Don Harris
Coventry University
Coventry, UK

Wen-Chin Li
Cranfield University
Cranfield, UK

ISSN 0302-9743 ISSN 1611-3349 (electronic)
Lecture Notes in Artificial Intelligence
ISBN 978-3-031-35391-8 ISBN 978-3-031-35392-5 (eBook)
https://doi.org/10.1007/978-3-031-35392-5

LNCS Sublibrary: SL7 – Artificial Intelligence

This Springer imprint is published by the registered company Springer Nature Switzerland AG
The registered company address is: Gewerbestrasse 11, 6330 Cham, Switzerland

Foreword

Human-computer interaction (HCI) is acquiring an ever-increasing scientific and industrial importance, as well as having more impact on people's everyday lives, as an ever-growing number of human activities are progressively moving from the physical to the digital world. This process, which has been ongoing for some time now, was further accelerated during the acute period of the COVID-19 pandemic. The HCI International (HCII) conference series, held annually, aims to respond to the compelling need to advance the exchange of knowledge and research and development efforts on the human aspects of design and use of computing systems.

The 25th International Conference on Human-Computer Interaction, HCI International 2023 (HCII 2023), was held in the emerging post-pandemic era as a 'hybrid' event at the AC Bella Sky Hotel and Bella Center, Copenhagen, Denmark, during July 23–28, 2023. It incorporated the 21 thematic areas and affiliated conferences listed below.

A total of 7472 individuals from academia, research institutes, industry, and government agencies from 85 countries submitted contributions, and 1578 papers and 396 posters were included in the volumes of the proceedings that were published just before the start of the conference, these are listed below. The contributions thoroughly cover the entire field of human-computer interaction, addressing major advances in knowledge and effective use of computers in a variety of application areas. These papers provide academics, researchers, engineers, scientists, practitioners and students with state-of-the-art information on the most recent advances in HCI.

The HCI International (HCII) conference also offers the option of presenting 'Late Breaking Work', and this applies both for papers and posters, with corresponding volumes of proceedings that will be published after the conference. Full papers will be included in the 'HCII 2023 - Late Breaking Work - Papers' volumes of the proceedings to be published in the Springer LNCS series, while 'Poster Extended Abstracts' will be included as short research papers in the 'HCII 2023 - Late Breaking Work - Posters' volumes to be published in the Springer CCIS series.

I would like to thank the Program Board Chairs and the members of the Program Boards of all thematic areas and affiliated conferences for their contribution towards the high scientific quality and overall success of the HCI International 2023 conference. Their manifold support in terms of paper reviewing (single-blind review process, with a minimum of two reviews per submission), session organization and their willingness to act as goodwill ambassadors for the conference is most highly appreciated.

This conference would not have been possible without the continuous and unwavering support and advice of Gavriel Salvendy, founder, General Chair Emeritus, and Scientific Advisor. For his outstanding efforts, I would like to express my sincere appreciation to Abbas Moallem, Communications Chair and Editor of HCI International News.

July 2023   Constantine Stephanidis

HCI International 2023 Thematic Areas and Affiliated Conferences

Thematic Areas

- HCI: Human-Computer Interaction
- HIMI: Human Interface and the Management of Information

Affiliated Conferences

- EPCE: 20th International Conference on Engineering Psychology and Cognitive Ergonomics
- AC: 17th International Conference on Augmented Cognition
- UAHCI: 17th International Conference on Universal Access in Human-Computer Interaction
- CCD: 15th International Conference on Cross-Cultural Design
- SCSM: 15th International Conference on Social Computing and Social Media
- VAMR: 15th International Conference on Virtual, Augmented and Mixed Reality
- DHM: 14th International Conference on Digital Human Modeling and Applications in Health, Safety, Ergonomics and Risk Management
- DUXU: 12th International Conference on Design, User Experience and Usability
- C&C: 11th International Conference on Culture and Computing
- DAPI: 11th International Conference on Distributed, Ambient and Pervasive Interactions
- HCIBGO: 10th International Conference on HCI in Business, Government and Organizations
- LCT: 10th International Conference on Learning and Collaboration Technologies
- ITAP: 9th International Conference on Human Aspects of IT for the Aged Population
- AIS: 5th International Conference on Adaptive Instructional Systems
- HCI-CPT: 5th International Conference on HCI for Cybersecurity, Privacy and Trust
- HCI-Games: 5th International Conference on HCI in Games
- MobiTAS: 5th International Conference on HCI in Mobility, Transport and Automotive Systems
- AI-HCI: 4th International Conference on Artificial Intelligence in HCI
- MOBILE: 4th International Conference on Design, Operation and Evaluation of Mobile Communications

List of Conference Proceedings Volumes Appearing Before the Conference

1. LNCS 14011, Human-Computer Interaction: Part I, edited by Masaaki Kurosu and Ayako Hashizume
2. LNCS 14012, Human-Computer Interaction: Part II, edited by Masaaki Kurosu and Ayako Hashizume
3. LNCS 14013, Human-Computer Interaction: Part III, edited by Masaaki Kurosu and Ayako Hashizume
4. LNCS 14014, Human-Computer Interaction: Part IV, edited by Masaaki Kurosu and Ayako Hashizume
5. LNCS 14015, Human Interface and the Management of Information: Part I, edited by Hirohiko Mori and Yumi Asahi
6. LNCS 14016, Human Interface and the Management of Information: Part II, edited by Hirohiko Mori and Yumi Asahi
7. LNAI 14017, Engineering Psychology and Cognitive Ergonomics: Part I, edited by Don Harris and Wen-Chin Li
8. LNAI 14018, Engineering Psychology and Cognitive Ergonomics: Part II, edited by Don Harris and Wen-Chin Li
9. LNAI 14019, Augmented Cognition, edited by Dylan D. Schmorrow and Cali M. Fidopiastis
10. LNCS 14020, Universal Access in Human-Computer Interaction: Part I, edited by Margherita Antona and Constantine Stephanidis
11. LNCS 14021, Universal Access in Human-Computer Interaction: Part II, edited by Margherita Antona and Constantine Stephanidis
12. LNCS 14022, Cross-Cultural Design: Part I, edited by Pei-Luen Patrick Rau
13. LNCS 14023, Cross-Cultural Design: Part II, edited by Pei-Luen Patrick Rau
14. LNCS 14024, Cross-Cultural Design: Part III, edited by Pei-Luen Patrick Rau
15. LNCS 14025, Social Computing and Social Media: Part I, edited by Adela Coman and Simona Vasilache
16. LNCS 14026, Social Computing and Social Media: Part II, edited by Adela Coman and Simona Vasilache
17. LNCS 14027, Virtual, Augmented and Mixed Reality, edited by Jessie Y. C. Chen and Gino Fragomeni
18. LNCS 14028, Digital Human Modeling and Applications in Health, Safety, Ergonomics and Risk Management: Part I, edited by Vincent G. Duffy
19. LNCS 14029, Digital Human Modeling and Applications in Health, Safety, Ergonomics and Risk Management: Part II, edited by Vincent G. Duffy
20. LNCS 14030, Design, User Experience, and Usability: Part I, edited by Aaron Marcus, Elizabeth Rosenzweig and Marcelo Soares
21. LNCS 14031, Design, User Experience, and Usability: Part II, edited by Aaron Marcus, Elizabeth Rosenzweig and Marcelo Soares

47. CCIS 1836, HCI International 2023 Posters - Part V, edited by Constantine Stephanidis, Margherita Antona, Stavroula Ntoa and Gavriel Salvendy

https://2023.hci.international/proceedings

Preface

The 20th International Conference on Engineering Psychology and Cognitive Ergonomics (EPCE 2023) is an affiliated conference of the HCI International Conference. The first EPCE conference was held in Stratford-upon-Avon, UK in 1996, and since 2001 EPCE has been an integral part of the HCI International conference series. Over the last 25 years, over 1,000 papers have been presented in this conference, which attracts a world-wide audience of scientists and human factors practitioners. The engineering psychology submissions describe advances in applied cognitive psychology that underpin the theory, measurement and methodologies behind the development of human-machine systems. Cognitive ergonomics describes advances in the design and development of user interfaces. Originally, these disciplines were driven by the requirements of high-risk, high-performance industries where safety was paramount, however the importance of good human factors is now understood by everyone for not only increasing safety, but also enhancing performance, productivity and revenues.

Two volumes of the HCII 2023 proceedings are dedicated to this year's edition of the EPCE conference.

The first volume centers around an array of interconnected themes related to human performance, stress, fatigue, mental workload, and error management. Drawing on the latest research and real-world case studies, works included for publication explore perspectives of stress and fatigue and study mental workload across different tasks and contexts. A considerable number of articles delve into exploring high-pressure environments characteristic of aviation and technology industries, where human error can have severe consequences, aiming to evaluate and enhance performance in such demanding contexts, as well as to understand the competencies and psychological characteristics of professionals in these fields. Furthermore, this volume discusses the topic of resilience to cope with the demands of challenging contexts, exploring facets of resilience engineering in synergy with threat and error management, system safety competency assessment, as well as vigilance and psychological health and safety in these contexts.

The second volume offers a comprehensive exploration of the role of human factors in aviation, operations management, as well as the design of autonomous systems. The prominence of human factors in aviation is addressed in a number of papers discussing research and case studies that investigate the gamut of aviation systems – including the flight deck, training, and communication – and explore pilots' perceptions, perspectives, and psychological aspects. These works also deliberate on issues of safety, efficacy, and usability. Additionally, from the perspective of operations management, a considerable number of papers discuss research and provide valuable insights into the critical role of human factors in enhancing the safety and efficiency of various operational contexts. Finally, a significant proportion of this volume is devoted to understanding the complex interplay between humans and autonomous systems, exploring design processes, human-centered design practices, evaluation perspectives and ethical dilemmas.

Papers of these volumes are included for publication after a minimum of two single-blind reviews from the members of the EPCE Program Board or, in some cases, from members of the Program Boards of other affiliated conferences. We would like to thank all of them for their invaluable contribution, support and efforts.

July 2023

Don Harris
Wen-Chin Li

20th International Conference on Engineering Psychology and Cognitive Ergonomics (EPCE 2023)

Program Board Chairs: **Don Harris,** *Coventry University, UK* and **Wen-Chin Li,** *Cranfield University, UK*

Program Board:

- Gavin Andrews, *HeartMath UK, UK*
- James Blundell, *Coventry University, UK*
- Mickael Causse, *ISAE-SUPAERO, France*
- Wesley Chan, *Cranfield University, UK*
- Maik Friedrich, *German Aerospace Center (DLR), Germany*
- Nektarios Karanikas, *Queensland University of Technology, Australia*
- Hannu Karvonen, *VTT Technical Research Centre of Finland Ltd., Finland*
- Gulsum Kubra Kaya, *Cranfield University, UK*
- Kylie Key, *FAA Flight Deck Human Factors Research Laboratory, USA*
- John Lin, *National Taiwan Normal University, Taiwan*
- Ting-Ting Lu, *Civil Aviation University of China, P.R. China*
- Chien-Tsung Lu, *Purdue University, USA*
- Pete McCarthy, *Cathay Pacific Airways, UK*
- Brett Molesworth, *UNSW Sydney, Australia*
- Jose Luis Munoz Gamarra, *Aslogic, Spain*
- Anastasios Plioutsias, *Coventry University, UK*
- Tatiana Polishchuk, *Linköping University, Sweden*
- Dujuan Sevillian, *National Transportation Safety Board (NTSB), USA*
- Anthony Smoker, *Lund University, Sweden*
- Lei Wang, *Civil Aviation University of China, P.R. China*
- Jingyu Zhang, *Chinese Academy of Sciences, P.R. China*
- Xiangling Zhuang, *Shaanxi Normal University, P.R. China*
- Dimitrios Ziakkas, *Purdue University, USA*

The full list with the Program Board Chairs and the members of the Program Boards of all thematic areas and affiliated conferences of HCII2023 is available online at:

http://www.hci.international/board-members-2023.php

HCI International 2024 Conference

The 26th International Conference on Human-Computer Interaction, HCI International 2024, will be held jointly with the affiliated conferences at the Washington Hilton Hotel, Washington, DC, USA, June 29 – July 4, 2024. It will cover a broad spectrum of themes related to Human-Computer Interaction, including theoretical issues, methods, tools, processes, and case studies in HCI design, as well as novel interaction techniques, interfaces, and applications. The proceedings will be published by Springer. More information will be made available on the conference website: http://2024.hci.international/.

General Chair
Prof. Constantine Stephanidis
University of Crete and ICS-FORTH
Heraklion, Crete, Greece
Email: general_chair@hcii2024.org

https://2024.hci.international/

Contents – Part I

Human Performance and Error Management

Resilience and Performance in Demanding Contexts

Contents – Part II

Human Factors in Operations Management

Human-Centered Design of Autonomous Systems

Stress, Fatigue, and Mental Workload

Suitability of Physiological, Self-report and Behavioral Measures for Assessing Mental Workload in Pilots

Hilke Boumann[1]([✉]) [iD], Anneke Hamann[1] [iD], Marcus Biella[1] [iD],
Nils Carstengerdes[1] [iD], and Stefan Sammito[2,3] [iD]

[1] Institute of Flight Guidance, German Aerospace Center (DLR), Lilienthalplatz 7, 38108 Braunschweig, Germany
Hilke.Boumann@dlr.de
[2] German Air Force Centre of Aerospace Medicine, Linder Höhe, 51147 Cologne, Germany
[3] Occupational Medicine, Faculty of Medicine, Otto-von-Guericke-University of Magdeburg, Leipziger Straße 44, 39120 Magdeburg, Germany

Abstract. Adaptive automation shall support users in a flexible way. One way to achieve this could be by monitoring cognitive states of pilots in order to anticipate an individual's need for support. A special challenge lies in choosing methods that enable a valid measurement of the cognitive state in question since different measures are associated with distinct strengths and weaknesses. For example, practical considerations like environmental factors, wearing comfort and intrusiveness have to be considered. The objective of this paper is to provide a collection of physiological, self-report and behavioral measures that can be applied to assess mental workload in pilots, and to discuss their advantages and disadvantages for this purpose. A targeted literature search was conducted to this end. The comparisons drawn in this paper reveal that a multi-method approach is preferable to relying on a single measure. In this regard, however, there is no one-size-fits-all solution and it is strongly advised to consider the selection of appropriate measures carefully for each specific research question and application context.

Keywords: Mental workload · psychophysiology · aviation · pilots

1 Introduction

Mental workload (MWL) is a key concept in the aviation domain. Flying an aircraft is highly complex, involving tasks like aviation, navigation, communication, and systems management [1]. To achieve better performance, many tasks are already highly automated (e.g. autopilots relieving pilots of many manual aspects of flying an aircraft). In such increasingly automated systems, pilots take on a monitoring role, only taking over if the system fails [2]. This goes along with problems like Bainbridge's well-known ironies of automation [2].

The concept of human-centered automation addresses the new challenges imposed by automated systems [3]. One of the principles of human-centered automation defined by Billings [3] is that both automated systems and human operator shall be aware of each other's state. Adaptive automation could be one way to achieve this. Adaptive automation refers to adaptive aiding of the operator and dynamic allocation of tasks between human and machine [4] depending on the situation at hand and/or the operator state.

A prerequisite for this is the valid measurement of the operator state. A variety of measures has been used in human factors research in order to assess cognitive states (e.g. [5]). At first glance self-report measures like questionnaires have the advantage of face validity: They refer directly to the construct of interest and can obtain subjective insights from individuals. However, measurement in operational settings can be intrusive, even more so if the questionnaire contains multiple items and requires the operator to shift their attention from the task at hand. Measures like performance or eye-tracking data can be used to analyze an individual's behavior while they lack to depict internal processes. Finally, the relation of physiological measures to cognitive states has been researched, see e.g. Charles and Nixon [6]. They can potentially provide objective and real-time measurements of cognitive states. Yet a one-to-one mapping of a physiological correlate to a cognitive state does sometimes not exist as one physiological measure may be sensitive to multiple cognitive states.

Furthermore, cognitive states may covary and confound. For instance, a demanding task may result in an increase of experienced MWL and mental fatigue and a decrease in situation awareness at the same time [7]. Therefore, the challenge for researches is to select measures that fit their research question and application, and to keep in mind possible confounding factors to facilitate a valid measurement of the cognitive state in question. This is further complicated by the lack of precise definitions of some cognitive states [8, 9].

In this paper, MWL is defined as the part of one's cognitive resources that is occupied with the task at hand [10]. If the task demands are low, only few resources are needed to perform it, and, accordingly, MWL is perceived as low. Increasing task demands (in terms of difficulty, temporal demands, secondary or parallel tasks etc.) can increase MWL up to a point at which the task demands exceed the available cognitive resources. As a result, performance declines and errors may occur [11, 12].

MWL is a particularly important concept regarding the boundaries of pilots' cognitive capacity [5]. Hence, the objective of this paper is to provide a collection of physiological, self-report and behavioral measures that can be applied to assess MWL with reference to the cockpit workplace, and to discuss their advantages and disadvantages for this purpose. A targeted literature search was conducted to achieve this. The main focus was given to the most promising methods for future research from the authors' point of view.

2   Overview of Measures

2.1   Physiological Measures

2.1.1   Respiratory Rate

Functioning and Measurement. The respiratory rate (RR) is defined as "the times of respiration observed during a minute (in breaths per minute, or bpm)" [13]. Generally, increases in RR occur due to an increased oxygen demand by the body [14]. This can be associated with physical activity, but also with increased arousal or emotional influences [14]. Commonly used measurement techniques include methods based on airflow and respiratory movements of the chest [14, 15]. Methods based on airflow require subjects to wear a sensor like a thermistor or a facemask [15]. Methods based on respiratory movements include, for example, impedance pneumography (by measuring changes in the resistance between two electrodes placed on the chest) [13, 14], respiratory inductance plethysmography (by placing two wires on chest and abdomen, measuring changes in inductance caused by differences in volume) [13, 15] or strain gauges (a tube filled with mercury, the electrical resistance changing with the tube expanding and contracting with respiratory movements) [14]. Furthermore, RR can also be obtained from ECG data [15].

Assessment of MWL. RR has been shown to be sensitive to task-difficulty for tasks of varying difficulty [16–20] as well as comparisons between task and baseline [17, 21]. RR has been found to achieve an accuracy of 68% in classifying high and low MWL conditions, placing it as third best predictor after EEG and eye movements [22]. However, RR sometimes lacks sensitivity to finer nuances in task difficulty and resulting MWL [17, 19]. There is a number of confounding factors influencing RR, such as time-on-task and learning effects [18] and single- vs. multitasking [23]. In addition, RR is impacted by both physical activity and speech [14, 17].

Conclusion. RR is able to differentiate between low vs. high workload conditions. However, differentiation between more than two difficulty levels is not always possible. Confounding variables should be controlled for to achieve a valid measurement of MWL. Furthermore, RR is not best suited for tasks that require physical effort [6] and all tasks that require the participants to communicate verbally. Regarding speech, it can be imagined that phases of differing MWL also impact the amount of communication required by pilots via radio. Thus, RR is not the most appropriate MWL measure in realistic flight simulations. Regarding pilots' acceptance, wearing facemasks to measure airflow might be perceived as uncomfortable and disruptive, though Charles, Nixon [6] noted that military pilots might be used to wearing oxygen masks.

2.1.2 Blood Pressure

Functioning and Measurement. Blood pressure (BP) is defined as "the force exerted by the blood against the vessel walls" [24] (p. 185). It is measured in millimeters of mercury (mmHg) [24]. The highest level of pressure is called systolic BP and the lowest level is called diastolic BP [24]. Changes in blood pressure are linked to activity of the sympathetic nervous system [25, 26] and psychological stress leads to increases in BP [27]. Non-invasive methods for measuring BP include auscultatory measurements, oscillatory measurements, arterial tonometry, and the volume clamp or Peñaz method

[24]. All mentioned methods require participants to wear either a cuff on the upper arm, wrist and/or finger.

Assessment of MWL. Systolic and diastolic BP was found to be sensitive to differences between task vs. rest conditions [28, 29]. Results regarding its ability to differentiate between varying levels of task difficulty seem to be mixed [28, 29].

Conclusion. The measurement of BP, especially by means of cuffs, can be perceived as uncomfortable by subjects and can only be done in intervals. The interval-only measurements do not allow for the non-invasive detection of short-term changes in BP. Furthermore, the measurements can only be carried out to a limited extent, especially during physical exertion, and are often overlaid with artefacts [30]. Newer technologies also allow continuous measurements, but the validity of these methods still needs to be optimized [31].

2.1.3 Electrodermal Activity

Functioning and Measurement. The term electrodermal activity (EDA) describes autonomic variations in the electrical characteristics of the skin [32]. EDA is linked to activity of the sympathetic nervous system and is related to cognitive and emotional states, attentional processes and arousal [32]. This section discusses two properties of EDA, namely skin conductance level (SCL) and skin conductance responses (SCR). SCL is the slow, tonic component of EDA constituting a continuously shifting baseline within an individual [32]. SCRs are the faster, phasic components of EDA that can either be attributed to the onset of a specific stimulus (event-related SCR) or occur without any attributable stimulus (non-specific SCR) [32]. SCL and SCR can be determined by applying a low voltage and measuring the electrical current between two electrodes placed on the skin [33]. EDA is typically measured in μS (microsiemens) or μmho (micromho) [32]. Electrodes are applied to the palm, fingers or the sole of the foot to achieve reliable and valid recordings [33].

Assessment of MWL. EDA is, amongst other things, used in research regarding habituation and orienting responses due to it responsiveness to new stimuli and reflection of habituation processes [33]. SCL was shown to be sensitive to the difference between baseline vs. task conditions [17, 21] and to some extent to different levels of task difficulty [17]. However, SCL is not sensitive to differences between all nuances of MWL and there is evidence for a ceiling effect for high levels of MWL [17]. Furthermore, time-on-task is a possible confounding factor [21]. EDA is sensitive to temperature, movement, speech and respiratory actions like sighing or coughing [32]. Braithwaite [32] recommend to keep a room temperature of around 22 to 24 °C, give subjects sufficient time to get used to temperature of the experimental environment, to minimize movements and to log events like speech, coughing, sighing or sneezing if they cannot be avoided [32]. Individual differences like gender or age also influence EDA and should be controlled [33]. Finally, about 10% of people are non-responsive with regards to EDA [32].

Conclusion. More research regarding the suitability of EDA in the context of MWL is desirable [6]. In the existing literature, there is evidence that EDA is sensitive to large differences in MWL like baseline vs. task performance but not to differences between all levels of MWL, as well as evidence for a ceiling effect in measuring. Possible confounding factors should be controlled. Furthermore, due to its sensitivity to movement and speech, EDA is not well-suited for realistic contexts.

2.1.4 Electroencephalography

Functioning and Measurement. Electroencephalography (EEG) is a noninvasive method to assess the electrical activity of the brain. The electrical signals of the brain can be detected with electrodes placed on the scalp, usually held in place by a flexible cap, net or helmet-like headpiece. These signals are then amplified, recorded, and processed further (for a thorough explanation of the underlying neuronal processes and operating principles of EEG see [34]). From the frequency composition of the signal (frequency domain) or event-related changes following an external stimulus (time domain), information on the cortical activity can be gained. Over the years, EEG devices have decreased in size, and in addition to conventional wet gel-based electrodes, saline-based sponge electrodes and dry electrodes are available and can achieve sufficient data quality [35]. These technical advances make EEG devices ever more wearable, easier and faster in preparation, and thereby more suitable for applied research [36]. However, EEG data are prone to motion artefacts, eye movement (blinks, saccades) and environmental noise (such as line noise or external power sources), and must be pre-processed to reduce artefacts in the data sets. EEG can achieve high temporal precision with sampling rates up to 1,000 Hz, but somewhat lacks in spatial precision.

Assessment of MWL. Typically, MWL assessment is done using band power analyses, i.e. changes in the frequency composition of the EEG signal. This allows for a continuous assessment without disturbing the pilots in their tasks. Increasing MWL is usually characterized by increasing frontal theta band power [37–39], and decreasing parietal alpha band power [40, 41]. However, changes in alpha activity are also associated with frequent task switching [41] and are not always found with increasing MWL [38]. Furthermore, alpha and theta activity can also be influenced by growing mental fatigue [42]. Under controlled experimental conditions, up to three levels of MWL can be differentiated using frontal theta band power [38].

Conclusion. EEG is a useful and powerful measure for MWL assessment because it directly measures cortical activity. However, EEG is best used in experimental setups as confounding effects of mental fatigue need to be controlled for, and task characteristics considered. Regarding pilots' acceptance, wearing comfort over time is the most important factor, followed by visual aesthetics [43]. The incorporation of dry EEG electrodes into a regularly worn helmet or cap could increase acceptance outside the laboratory.

2.1.5 Functional Near-Infrared Spectroscopy

Functioning and Measurement. Functional near-infrared spectroscopy (fNIRS) is a noninvasive method for the assessment of cortical activity. It relies on cerebral blood flow and oxygenation. When cortical activation increases, so does the oxygen influx into the affected regions [44]. Oxygenated and deoxygenated blood absorb light differently. By emitting light in the near-infrared spectrum into the cortex and measuring the absorption and scattering, information can be gained about the concentration changes in oxygenated and deoxygenated blood in the cortical tissue [45]. An fNIRS setup therefore involves optodes, i.e. light sources (LEDs or lasers) and detectors placed on the scalp or forehead, held in place by a flexible cap or headband. fNIRS measurements are mostly measurements of change, i.e. concentration changes relative to a baseline or different task, while absolute oxygen concentrations cannot be obtained. fNIRS is relatively unaffected by electrical noise [46], but excessive body movement or vibration can result in momentary displacement of the optodes and motion artefacts in the data. Because blood flow is subject to gravity, strong head and body movements as well as g-forces may alter the course of the concentration changes induced by the task. Furthermore, systemic noise from respiration and heartbeat can overlay the fNIRS signal and has to be filtered out or accounted for statistically [45, 47]. fNIRS data are usually sampled at below 10 Hz, but can achieve a high spatial precision of two to three centimeters [45].

Assessment of MWL. Increasing MWL is associated with higher cortical activation, which in turn presents in fNIRS data as higher levels of oxygenated and lower levels of deoxygenated blood [38, 48, 49]. Frontal and prefrontal areas are of the highest interest, and especially the right dorsolateral prefrontal cortex (dlPFC) was found to be sensitive to changes in MWL [38, 49]. However, there is evidence that cortical oxygenation changes do not increase steadily with increasing demand, but reach a plateau [38, 50], and is also affected by other cognitive states such as mental fatigue [51]. Using fNIRS, up to three MWL levels can be differentiated [38].

Conclusion. fNIRS presents a viable option for MWL assessment by means of cortical oxygenation changes. With portable devices and a comparably low susceptibility to movement artefacts and environmental noise, it poses a good opportunity for applied research. However, confounding effects of systemic noise and mental fatigue, amongst others, should be considered when designing experiments. When using full-motion flight simulators or conducting real flights, attention should be paid to excessive motion and g-forces that could momentarily influence the fNIRS signal. Regarding pilots' acceptance, wearing a cap or headband over an extended period of time can elicit discomfort. Similar to EEG, the incorporation of the sensors into a regularly worn helmet or cap could increase acceptance outside the laboratory.

2.1.6 Heart Rate

Functioning and Measurement. Heart rate (HR) is defined as the number of heart actions in one minute. It reflects the individual cardiovascular workload and is influenced by numerous factors [52]. It should be formally distinguished from pulse rate, which is measured peripherally, e.g. at the wrist. In some cardiac arrhythmias, there may be a difference between HR and pulse rate, whereas in healthy individuals, pulse rate and HR are nearly congruent. The difference between the two values is called the pulse deficit [52].

The HR at rest in adults is 60–80 beats per minute and can reach 200 and above under stress. Typically, HR is measured using an electrocardiogram (ECG) or a heart rate monitor like a chest belt. The reliability and validity of these heart rate monitors has been demonstrated in numerous studies [53–56]. Peripheral measurement systems using pulse oximeters formally measure the pulse rate.

HR is influenced by numerous factors at rest that are often difficult to control, such as fatigue, ambient temperature, personal health and fitness level. Therefore, for the basic measurement a light dynamic physical load of 20 watts is recommended [57], which largely eliminates these influencing factors and leads to an increase of approx. 18.5 beats/min for men and approx. 24.5 beats/min for women.

Assessment of MWL. The measurement of HR for physical stresses, especially dynamic stresses, has long been established. The HR increases with increasing load; the increasing course depends essentially on the fitness level and the level of the load [52]. Some studies have investigated the relationship between MWL and the increase in HR and have been able to demonstrate the utility of this physiologically easily elicitable parameter for the assessment of MWL [16, 58].

Conclusion. HR is a simple, collectable physiological parameter for measuring physical exertion, but also for MWL. It has been established for years and, with the expansion of the analysis of heart rate variability, takes on further two very good parameters for analysis significance of MWL. Especially for pilots with low physical loads (UAV or fixed-wing aircraft pilots), HR can therefore be used well as a parameter for MWL.

2.1.7 Heart Rate Variability

Functioning and Measurement. Heart rate variability (HRV) is based on the mathematical analysis of successive intervals between two heartbeats, the so-called NN intervals. HRV is subject to physiological variability at rest or under stress, reflecting the interaction of the sympathetic and parasympathetic nervous systems, and thus the vegetative nervous system [52, 59]. Under resting conditions, the parasympathetic part predominates over the sympathetic part, which leads to a higher variability of the successive heart actions.

For the measurement of the underlying consecutive heartbeats, ECG measurements are the gold standard for subsequent HRV analysis [52]. Heart rate monitors in the form of chest belts can also be used with slight restrictions. Due to the pure recording of the intervals between the cardiac actions without accompanying visible ECG, the artefact correction is only possible to a limited extent [60]. Pulse oxyimetric measurement methods for recording the pulse wave do not represent a valid measurement of the heartbeats and, according to analyses, show a clear shift in the analysed variability measures [61], they are therefore not referred to as HRV but as pulse rate variability.

Assessment of MWL. A large number of different HRV parameters are available for HRV analysis; RMSSD, LF, HF, LF/HF, DQ and SD1 should be used to record MWL

[52]. The relationship between changes in HRV and MWL has been demonstrated in numerous studies (for reviews, see e.g. [6] or [62]).

Conclusion. The HRV analysis is a relatively simple non-invasive method for measuring MWL. However, numerous factors influence HRV like physiological parameters (e.g. age, gender, circadian rhythm), diseases (e.g. heart, lung, renal, metabolic and psychiatric diseases), lifestyle factors (e.g. physical fitness, sporting activity, increased body weight, smoking, alcohol abuse) and external factors (e.g. noise, night shift work, harmful substances, medications) [63], which is why primarily intraindividual comparisons should be used. Because HRV is also influenced by numerous external factors (noise, climate, etc.), a baseline measurement is necessary for measurements in realistic environments.

2.2 Behavioral Measures

2.2.1 Eye-Tracking

Functioning and Measurement. The measurement of eye movements provides an assessment of visual attention [64]. For an overview of different eye-tracking techniques, see Duchowski [64]. While some techniques measure the position of the eyes relative to the subject's head only, other techniques also enable so called point of regard measurements, i.e. they provide information about the point or location a subject is looking at [64]. Video-based techniques tracking corneal reflection and pupil center allowing for point of regard measurement [64, 65]. According to Duchowski [64], video-based eye-trackers are accurate, but the sampling rate is usually limited to 60 Hz. Devices can be table-, monitor or head-mounted [64]. Head-mounted devices can be intrusive, but for tasks involving a lot of movement, they are better suited than fixed mounted devices [65].

MWL Assessment. A multitude of eye-tracking measures has been used in research related to human performance factors. This section discusses selected metrics related to eye movements. We refer to Glaholt [66] to obtain an extensive overview of eye-tracking measures in the cockpit. Dwell time increase with increasing task difficulty [67]. Glaholt [66] defines a dwell as "a set of one or more consecutive fixations on the same area, instrument or display" (p. 9). In contrast to this, increasing temporal demand was shown to be associated with a decrease in average dwell duration [68]. Studies examining overall patterns of scanning behavior resulted in inconsistent findings. Entropy rate, a measure of randomness of scanning behavior, was shown to decrease with task difficulty, i.e. scanning behavior became less random with an increase in task difficulty [67]. On the other hand, Di Nocera et al. [69] computed an index for the distribution of fixations and found evidence that higher workload could be associated with more diffuse fixation patterns. Several eye-tracking measures were shown to be sensitive to pilot expertise (for an overview, see Glaholt [66]). Tole et al. [67] concluded that scanning behavior of pilots with high skill might be less sensitive to variations in task difficulty compared to that of novices.

Conclusion. Eye-tracking is a viable measure for MWL assessment, though there is a multitude of metrics to choose from. Different eye-tracking techniques are associated with different advantages and disadvantages [64] and properties like accuracy and sampling rate have to be appropriate for the research question at hand. Some general methodological disadvantages should be considered in the design of a study. For example, repeating the calibrations of the eye-tracker are usually necessary [65], which might be disruptive to longer tasks and could pose a problem for realistic settings. Contrast and luminance influence pupil size and should be controlled because too small pupil sizes may pose a problem to eye-trackers [65]. Similarly, contact lenses and glasses can be problematic for eye-trackers [65]. Visual distractions should be minimized [65]. Seeing that eye movement measures are sensitive to pilot expertise [66, 67], pilot expertise should be collected as a research variable. Regarding the use of head-mounted vs. table-mounted systems, the trade-off between free movement and intrusiveness [65] should be weighed.

2.2.2 Performance Data

Functioning and Measurement. Performance data can involve measures of primary or secondary task performance. Primary task performance measures can be used as an estimate for MWL and a direct measure of performance at the same time [70]. Possible metrics of task performance are error rates, response times or accuracy [5]. Task performance is assumed to decline when MWL becomes too high [71]. However, subjects may be able to uphold a stable task performance under differing levels of MWL, for example by adjusting strategies or spending more resources on the task [5, 71].

Therefore, a secondary task can be introduced simultaneously to the primary one. In the case of the loading-task technique, subjects are instructed to prioritize the secondary task and MWL is inferred from the primary task performance [5]. In the case of the subsidiary-task paradigm, the primary task obtains priority and changes in MWL should be reflected in secondary task performance [5]. To ensure its sensitivity, the secondary task should draw from the same processing resources as the primary one [71]. This requirement can be derived from Wickens' Multiple Resource Theory, described in detail in Wickens [72]. The theory assumes four dimensions of processing resources and predicts that interference between two tasks is related to the extent that these dimensions overlap between tasks. It should be noted that Multiple Resource Theory predicts performance decrements for cases in which dual-task performance is associated with mental overload, but is less relevant for low MWL situations [73]. A secondary task can either be external to the operational context, i.e. not usually part of the primary task, or an embedded task, i.e. integrated in the operational context [5, 71].

Assessment of MWL. Primary task performance alone can be insensitive to variations in MWL, especially at lower levels of MWL [5, 71]. Additionally, primary task performance measures that reflect changes in MWL are specific for the task hand [74–76]. It was recommended that primary task performance measures should be chosen in a way to reflect strategy adjustments in order to detect variations in MWL [75]. Secondary task performance measures seem to be sensitive to larger differences in MWL [70]. Studies showed that secondary task performance measures can reflect changes in MWL, but sometimes lack sensitivity for differentiating between all MWL levels [75, 76].

Conclusion. Primary and secondary task performance measures are relatively easy to apply and it is convenient that primary task performance data is typically of interest in any case [70]. However, primary task performance alone is not a suitable measure of MWL [70]. Secondary tasks must be designed thoughtfully to ensure overlap between resources [70]. In realistic settings, embedded secondary tasks might be better suited to fit into the operational environment than external ones [5]. While secondary tasks could be used for training and evaluation purposes, this technique is not appropriate in real operations due to its intrusiveness.

2.3 Self-report Measures

Assessment of MWL. Self-report measures come with several advantages: Their application is easy and low in cost, and they directly reflect subjects' perceived MWL [5]. Such measures usually allow for relative comparisons between experimental conditions and a baseline scenario [5]. In order to be good, self-report measures need to be reliable, accepted, non-intrusive, sensitive to variations in MWL and diagnostic of MWL [5].

Well-known examples for self-report measures of MWL are NASA Task Load Index (NASA-TLX) [77, 78] and Instantaneous Self-Assessment (ISA) [79]. NASA-TLX is an example of a multidimensional MWL measure as it quantifies six dimensions of workload: mental demand, physical demand, temporal demand, performance, effort and frustration. Subjects are asked to rate the perceived demand on each of the six scales. In addition to the separate scale scores, an overall workload score is computed. To do so, participants rate the extent to which each scale contributed to overall workload, though this weighting procedure can also be omitted [77]. Due to the six sub-scales, the rating takes time and is thus mostly done after completion of the task or in between tasks. ISA is a unidimensional measure: Subjects are asked to rate their perceived MWL on a scale from 1 (under-utilized) to 5 (excessive). Due to its conciseness and simplicity, ISA can be applied during task execution [79]. The ISA rating can for example be given verbally or by holding up fingers. The scale can also be presented on the same screen the subject is already working on, announced by a signal like an auditory cue, and the rating can be typed in or clicked directly.

However, online application of a questionnaire like ISA can be intrusive to task performance [79]. According to Tattersall and Foord [79], the level of intrusiveness may be reduced when the resources required to rate the task and to perform the primary task are compatible with respect to Multiple Resource Theory by Wickens [73]. Yet, the longer or more complex the questionnaire, the longer the operator will need to shift their attention from the task at hand, risking the loss of situation awareness. Thus, intrusiveness should be avoided especially in realistic contexts. Hence, applying self-report measures after task-execution can sometimes be preferable [79]. The downside of post-hoc applications is that subjects might forget things in retrospect [5].

Further disadvantages of self-report measures are the task variability effect, which describes subjects' tendency to use the entire range of a rating scale regardless of the range of stimuli, and that subjects' answers might be biased [5]. Furthermore, while some self-report measures like ISA enable collection of ratings during task performance, self-report measures do not provide a continuous assessment of MWL.

Conclusion. Self-report measures provide an easy way to obtain insights of subjects' perceived MWL. While these insights are valuable, they can also be prone to bias. Furthermore, self-report measures do not provide a continuous measurement of MWL. If a self-report measure is to be applied during task execution, the level of intrusiveness should be considered. In realistic settings especially, intrusiveness on the primary task should be avoided, which is why post-hoc application may be better suited in this context.

3 Discussion

Self-report, behavioral and physiological measures of MWL are associated with different advantages and disadvantages. It is therefore advisable to combine complementary measures to overcome the drawbacks of each individual measure. In addition, the choice of appropriate measures also depends on the research question, the intended experimental setting, and the tasks.

3.1 Compatibility of Physiological Measures

In order to be used in combination, compatibility of measuring instruments has to be ensured. Especially physiological measurements are associated with high requirements and the risk to interfere with each other. Problems could arise when sensors of two or more measurement methods are applied to the same location. In the following section, some challenges with concurrent physiological measurements are discussed.

Sensors that are placed on the head include EEG, fNIRS, head-mounted eye-tracking devices, and thermistors and facemasks used to obtain RR. EEG and fNIRS can be combined into one montage [38]. Software like the fNIRS Location Decider fOLD can help to choose locations that target the cortical structures involved in the processes of interest [80]. Temporal EEG electrodes will most likely get in the way of eye-tracking glasses. Exclusion of some electrodes is possible, but could impact pre-processing and analysis. If appropriate for the experimental setting, a remote eye-tracking system could be used instead. A facemask for measuring RR that is fastened behind the ears or at the back of the head could also be incompatible with EEG electrode placement or eye-tracking glasses. As an alternative, RR could be measured using sensors that are applied to the chest.

Sensors that are placed on the chest concern HR, HRV and RR. An ECG allows the collection of all three measures at once and would therefore be easiest option.

Other sensors are applied to an arm, wrist, hands or fingers. This concerns the measurement of EDA and BP. If BP sensors on the wrist or fingers are to be used, this could potentially come into conflict with the placement of electrodes for measuring EDA on the palm or fingers. If possible, the other hand or another finger can be used if both measurements shall be obtained at the same time. Alternatively, EDA electrodes can be placed at the sole of the foot.

It is advisable to test the compatibility of sensors for each experimental set-up and the specific devices used in advance. Apart from the placement of the sensors themselves, another factor to keep in mind is the placement of cables and attached devices. Cables of all applied devices should be placed without restricting subjects or being perceived as distracting or intrusive. Additionally, measuring instruments might have to be compatible with operational equipment worn by pilots. It is important to ensure that concurrent measurements are synchronized using matching timestamps.

3.2   Suitability of Measures According to Experimental Setting

The terms low-fidelity and high-fidelity are used here to differentiate between different levels of realism. The term low-fidelity includes laboratory conditions that allow a large amount of control over potential confounding factors, but no realistic representation of an operational environment. Mock-up simulators are closer to reality, but not to full extent. The same applies to so-called demonstrators, which primarily present a new subsystem (e.g. head-up displays) but neglect the other aspects (e.g. lack of overhead panel). High-fidelity environments include full-flight simulators and operational environments like aircraft cockpit. High- and low-fidelity settings are associated with differing prerequisites and technical requirements.

High Fidelity Settings. High-fidelity settings are associated with several requirements and restrictions. While they allow for ecologically valid conclusions, the manipulation of MWL is less controlled than in low fidelity settings. The tasks are more realistic, yet the performance measures are harder to define and interpret. 1) MWL assessment should be as non-intrusive as possible. Secondary tasks should not be used in real operations for this reason, but can still be applied for training or evaluation purposes. Self-report measures should be applied after instead of during the task. With regards to eye-tracking, the need for recalibrations could be intrusive. 2) Pilots should be comfortable even for longer periods of time. This could not be the case if facemasks for measuring RR, cuffs for measuring BP or eye-tracking glasses are worn. EEG and fNIRS sensors should be integrated into helmets or caps that are part of pilots' regular equipment. 3) In real operations, measurement periods might be longer than in low-fidelity conditions. It has to be considered that other states like mental fatigue or time-on-task effects can confound with MWL and thus impair the validity of measurements. 4) Environmental factors are hard to control. This is a problem for measures that are susceptible to factors like temperature, noise or ambient illumination (e.g. EDA, HRV, eye-tracking). Motion and g-forces can impact fNIRS signal. 5) Pilots might move and speak more than in low-fidelity conditions. It needs to be noted that some physiological measures are sensitive to speech and/or movement, e.g. BP and EDA. If physical exertion is expected to occur, this should be kept in mind when HR, HRV or RR are measured.

Furthermore, operational environment, e.g. equipment and gear, can pose limitations to certain measurement methods and real-time measurement might be harder to achieve than in low-fidelity settings.

Low Fidelity Settings. Low-fidelity settings are generally associated with less restrictions than high-fidelity settings. There is a high extent of control regarding environmental and other confounding factors, though this is at the expense of external validity.

For example, intrusiveness is not as critical as in operational contexts, allowing for the use of self-report during the experiments. Primary and secondary tasks can be used to gather insights into the detrimental effects of increasing MWL on performance. If it can be expected that wearing a certain measuring device will become uncomfortable over time, the duration of experiments can be adapted accordingly. Effects of mental fatigue can also be controlled in this way. Finally, participants can be instructed to minimize movements, speech or actions like sighing or coughing.

3.3 Conclusions

The overall conclusion of this paper is that a combination of measures is preferable to relying on a single measure. Thus, it is recommended to use a multi-method approach to obtain valid measurements of MWL. Different measures are associated with distinct strengths and weaknesses and should be combined to be complementary. In this regard, however, there is no one-size-fits-all solution. Therefore, it is strongly advised to consider the selection of appropriate measures carefully for each specific research question and application context.

3.4 Prospects for Future Research

Beyond MWL, there are other human factors that have an impact on human performance. Apart from MWL, Edwards [7] identified the factors situation awareness, attention, vigilance; fatigue, team, communication and trust to be of relevance within the Framework of Human Performance Envelope (HPE). Interactions between these factors should be considered. These basic assumptions have been discussed in the literature on HPE [7, 81].

Furthermore, this paper does not provide a complete overview of measures that can be used for assessing MWL. Other methods that could be further explored for this purpose are for example ocular measures like pupil size or blink rate, expert observations, electromyography, communication and voice analysis, posture or facial expressions.

In addition to the collection of suitable physiological, self-report and behavioral measures for MWL, for each application the most suitable measurement systems and devices need to be identified. For instance, a 32-channel wet-electrode EEG might be a viable option in the laboratory, but not feasible under realistic flight conditions. Similarly, circumstances may be different for civil commercial aviation and military operations. For example, the type of aircraft, G-forces acting on the pilot, space constraints in the cockpit, and worn equipment influence which measurement methods can be used. Therefore, for each research question and setting, the measures and devices should be chosen carefully.

Acknowledgements. DLR's research work was financed with funding from the German Federal Ministry of Defence. Stefan Sammito is an active Bundeswehr Medical Service officer and works for the German Federal Ministry of Defence. This paper reflects the opinion of the authors and not necessarily the opinion of the German Federal Ministry of Defence or the Surgeon General of the German Air Force.

References

1. Wickens, C.D., Dehais, F.: Expertise in aviation. In: Ward, P., Maarten Schraagen, J., Gore, J., Roth, E.M. (eds.) The Oxford Handbook of Expertise. Oxford University Press, Oxford (2019)
2. Bainbridge, L.: Ironies of automation. In: Johannsen, G., Rijnsdorp, J.E. (eds.) Analysis, Design and Evaluation of Man–Machine Systems, Pergamon, pp. 129–135 (1983)
3. Billings, C.E.: Human-centered aviation automation: principles and guidelines. In. Ames Research Center, Moffett Field, California (1996)
4. Parasuraman, R.M., Mouloua, M., Hilburn, B.: adaptive aiding and adaptive task allocation enhance human-machine interaction. In: Paper Presented at the Automation Technology and Human Performance: Current Research and Trends, Norfolk, VA (1999)
5. Martins, A.P.G.: A review of important cognitive concepts in aviation. Aviation 20(2), 65–84 (2016). https://doi.org/10.3846/16487788.2016.1196559
6. Charles, R.L., Nixon, J.: Measuring mental workload using physiological measures: a systematic review. Appl. Ergon. 74, 221–232 (2019). https://doi.org/10.1016/j.apergo.2018.08.028
7. Edwards, T.: Human performance in air traffic control. University of Nottingham (2013)
8. Parasuraman, R., Sheridan, T.B., Wickens, C.D.: Situation awareness, mental workload, and trust in automation: viable, empirically supported cognitive engineering constructs. J. Cogn. Eng. Decis. Mak. 2(2), 140–160 (2008). https://doi.org/10.1518/155534308x284417
9. Dekker, S., Hollnagel, E.: Human factors and folk models. Cogn. Technol. Work 6(2), 79–86 (2004). https://doi.org/10.1007/s10111-003-0136-9
10. O'Donnell, R.D., Eggemeier, F.T.: Workload assessment methodology. In: Boff, K.R., Kaufman, L., Thomas, J.P. (eds.) Handbook of Perception and Human Performance. John Wiley & Sons, New York (1986)
11. Stokes, A., Kite, K.: Flight stress: stress, fatigue, and performance in aviation. Repr ed. Avebury, Aldershot (1997)
12. Fürstenau, N., Papenfuss, A.: Model based analysis of subjective mental workload during multiple remote tower human-in-the-loop simulations. In: Fürstenau, N. (ed.) Virtual and Remote Control Tower: Research, Design, Development, Validation, and Implementation, pp. 293–342. Springer, Cham (2022)
13. Liu, H., Allen, J., Zheng, D., Chen, F.: Recent development of respiratory rate measurement technologies. Physiol. Meas. 40(7), 1–27 (2019). https://doi.org/10.1088/1361-6579/ab299e
14. Roscoe, A.H.: Assessing pilot workload: Why measure heart rate, HRV and respiration. Biol. Psychol. 34(2), 259–287 (1992). https://doi.org/10.1016/0301-0511(92)90018-P
15. AL-Khalidi, F.Q., Saatchi, R., Burke, D., Elphick, H., Tan, S.: Respiration rate monitoring methods: a review. Pediat. Pulmonol. 46(6), 523–529 (2011). https://doi.org/10.1002/ppul.21416
16. Brookings, J.B., Wilson, G.F., Swain, C.R.: Psychophysiological responses to changes in workload during simulated air traffic control. Biol. Psychol. 42(3), 361–377 (1996). https://doi.org/10.1016/0301-0511(95)05167-8
17. Mehler, B., Reimer, B., Coughlin, J.F., Dusek, J.A.: Impact of incremental increases in cognitive workload on physiological arousal and performance in young adult drivers. Transp. Res. Rec. 2138(1), 6–12 (2009). https://doi.org/10.3141/2138-02
18. Fairclough, S.H., Venables, L., Tattersall, A.: The influence of task demand and learning on the psychophysiological response. Int. J. Psychophysiol. 56(2), 171–184 (2005). https://doi.org/10.1016/j.ijpsycho.2004.11.003
19. Backs, R.W., Navidzadeh, H.T., Xu, X.: Cardiorespiratory indices of mental workload during simulated air traffic control. Proc. Hum. Fact. Ergon. Soc. Ann. Meet. 44(13), 89–92 (2000). https://doi.org/10.1177/154193120004401323

20. Backs, R.W., Seljos, K.A.: Metabolic and cardiorespiratory measures of mental effort: the effects of level of difficulty in a working memory task. Int. J. Psychophysiol. **16**(1), 57–68 (1994). https://doi.org/10.1016/0167-8760(94)90042-6
21. Fairclough, S.H., Venables, L.: Prediction of subjective states from psychophysiology: a multivariate approach. Biol. Psychol. **71**(1), 100–110 (2006). https://doi.org/10.1016/j.bio psycho.2005.03.007
22. Hogervorst, M.A., Brouwer, A.-M., van Erp, J.B.F.: Combining and comparing EEG, peripheral physiology and eye-related measures for the assessment of mental workload. Front. Neurosci. **8** (2014). https://doi.org/10.3389/fnins.2014.00322
23. Fournier, L.R., Wilson, G.F., Swain, C.R.: Electrophysiological, behavioral, and subjective indexes of workload when performing multiple tasks: manipulations of task difficulty and training. Int. J. Psychophysiol. **31**(2), 129–145 (1999). https://doi.org/10.1016/S0167-876 0(98)00049-X
24. Berntson, G.G., Quigley, K.S., Norman, G.J., Lozano, D.L.: Cardiovascular psychophysiology. In: Handbook of Psychophysiology. Cambridge Handbooks in Psychology, 4 edn, pp. 183–216. Cambridge University Press, New York (2017)
25. Ayada, C., Toru, Ü., Korkut, Y.: The relationship of stress and blood pressure effectors. Hippokratia **19**(2), 99–108 (2015)
26. Charkoudian, N., Rabbitts, J.A.: Sympathetic neural mechanisms in human cardiovascular health and disease. Mayo Clin. Proc. **84**(9), 822–830 (2009). https://doi.org/10.4065/84.9.822
27. Lundberg, U., et al.: Psychophysiological stress and EMG activity of the trapezius muscle. Int. J. Behav. Med. **1**(4), 354–370 (1994). https://doi.org/10.1207/s15327558ijbm0104_5
28. Veltman, J.A., Gaillard, A.W.K.: Physiological workload reactions to increasing levels of task difficulty. Ergonomics **41**(5), 656–669 (1998). https://doi.org/10.1080/001401398186829
29. Veltman, J.A., Gaillard, A.W.K.: Physiological indices of workload in a simulated flight task. Biol. Psychol. **42**(3), 323–342 (1996). https://doi.org/10.1016/0301-0511(95)05165-1
30. James, G.D., Gerber, L.M.: Measuring arterial blood pressure in humans: auscultatory and automatic measurement techniques for human biological field studies. Am. J. Hum. Biol. **30**(1), e23063 (2018). https://doi.org/10.1002/ajhb.23063
31. Xing, X., et al.: Blood pressure assessment with in-ear photoplethysmography. Physiol. Meas. **42**(10), 105009 (2021). https://doi.org/10.1088/1361-6579/ac2a71
32. Braithwaite, J.J.W., Jones, D.G., Rowe, M.R.: A guide for analysing electrodermal activity (EDA) & skin conductance responses (SCRs) for psychological experiments. In: Behavioural Brain Sciences Centre, p. 43. University of Birmingham, UK (2015)
33. Boucsein, W., et al.: Society for psychophysiological research ad hoc committee on electrodermal measures: publication recommendations for electrodermal measurements. Psychophysiology **49**(8), 1017–1034 (2012). https://doi.org/10.1111/j.1469-8986.2012.013 84.x
34. Jackson, A.F., Bolger, D.J.: The neurophysiological bases of EEG and EEG measurement: a review for the rest of us. Psychophysiology **51**(11), 1061–1071 (2014). https://doi.org/10. 1111/psyp.12283
35. Radüntz, T.: Signal quality evaluation of emerging EEG devices. Front. Physiol. **9**, 98 (2018). https://doi.org/10.3389/fphys.2018.00098
36. Wascher, E., et al.: Neuroergonomics on the go: An evaluation of the potential of mobile EEG for workplace assessment and design. Hum. Fact., 187208211007707 (2021). https://doi.org/ 10.1177/00187208211007707
37. Dussault, C., Jouanin, J.-C., Guezennec, C.-Y.: EEG and ECG changes during selected flight sequences. Aviat. Space Environ. Med. **75**(10), 889–897 (2004)
38. Hamann, A., Carstengerdes, N.: Investigating mental workload-induced changes in cortical oxygenation and frontal theta activity during simulated flights. Sci. Rep. **12**(1), 6449 (2022). https://doi.org/10.1038/s41598-022-10044-y

39. Puma, S., Matton, N., Paubel, P.-V., Raufaste, É., El-Yagoubi, R.: Using theta and alpha band power to assess cognitive workload in multitasking environments. Int. J. Psychophysiol. Off. J. Int. Organ. Psychophysiol. **123**, 111–120 (2018). https://doi.org/10.1016/j.ijpsycho.2017.10.004

40. Dehais, F., et al.: Monitoring pilot's mental workload using ERPs and spectral power with a six-dry-electrode EEG system in real flight conditions. Sensors (Basel, Switzerland) **19**(6), 1324 (2019). https://doi.org/10.3390/s19061324

41. Holm, A., Lukander, K., Korpela, J., Sallinen, M., Müller, K.M.I.: Estimating brain load from the EEG. Sci. World J. **9**, 639–651 (2009). https://doi.org/10.1100/tsw.2009.83

42. Roy, R.N., Bonnet, S., Charbonnier, S., Campagne, A.: Mental fatigue and working memory load estimation: interaction and implications for EEG-based passive BCI. In: Conference Proceedings: Annual International Conference of the IEEE Engineering in Medicine and Biology Society, pp. 6607–6610 (2013). https://doi.org/10.1109/embc.2013.6611070

43. Radüntz, T., Meffert, B.: User experience of 7 mobile electroencephalography devices: comparative study. JMIR Mhealth Uhealth **7**(9), e14474 (2019). https://doi.org/10.2196/14474

44. Huppert, T.J., Franceschini, M.A., Boas, D.A.: Noninvasive imaging of cerebral activation with diffuse optical tomography. In: Frostig, R. (ed.) In Vivo Optical Imaging of Brain Function, pp. 209–238. CRC Press (2009)

45. Huppert, T.J.: Commentary on the statistical properties of noise and its implication on general linear models in functional near-infrared spectroscopy. Neurophotonics **3**(1), 010401 (2016). https://doi.org/10.1117/1.NPh.3.1.010401

46. Liu, T., Pelowski, M., Pang, C., Zhou, Y., Cai, J.: Near-infrared spectroscopy as a tool for driving research. Ergonomics **59**(3), 368–379 (2015). https://doi.org/10.1080/00140139.2015.1076057

47. Barker, J.W., Aarabi, A., Huppert, T.J.: Autoregressive model based algorithm for correcting motion and serially correlated errors in fNIRS. Biomed. Opt. Express **4**(8), 1366–1379 (2013). https://doi.org/10.1364/boe.4.001366

48. Causse, M., Chua, Z.K., Peysakhovich, V., Del Campo, N., Matton, N.: Mental workload and neural efficiency quantified in the prefrontal cortex using fNIRS. Sci. Rep. **7**(1), 5222 (2017). https://doi.org/10.1038/s41598-017-05378-x

49. Geissler, C.F., Schneider, J., Frings, C.: Shedding light on the prefrontal correlates of mental workload in simulated driving: a functional near-infrared spectroscopy study. Sci. Rep. **11**(1), 705 (2021). https://doi.org/10.1038/s41598-020-80477-w

50. Causse, M., Chua, Z.K., Rémy, F.: Influences of age, mental workload, and flight experience on cognitive performance and prefrontal activity in private pilots: a fNIRS study. Sci. Rep. **9**(1), 7688 (2019). https://doi.org/10.1038/s41598-019-44082-w

51. Nguyen, T., Ahn, S., Jang, H., Jun, S.C., Kim, J.G.: Utilization of a combined EEG/NIRS system to predict driver drowsiness. Sci. Rep. **7**, 43933 (2017). https://doi.org/10.1038/srep43933

52. Sammito, S., Thielmann, B., Klussmann, A., Deußen, A., Braumann, K.-M., Böckelmann, I.: S2k-Leitlinie Nutzung der Herzschlagfrequenz und der Herzfrequenzvariabilität in der Arbeitsmedizin und der Arbeitswissenschaft: AWMF-RegNr 002/042 (2021)

53. Kingsley, M., Lewis, M.J., Marson, R.E.: Comparison of Polar 810s and an ambulatory ECG system for RR interval measurement during progressive exercise. Int. J. Sports Med. **26**(1), 39–44 (2005). https://doi.org/10.1055/s-2004-817878

54. Nunan, D., Jakovljevic, D.G., Donovan, G., Hodges, L.D., Sandercock, G.R., Brodie, D.A.: Levels of agreement for RR intervals and short-term heart rate variability obtained from the Polar S810 and an alternative system. Eur. J. Appl. Physiol. **103**(5), 529–537 (2008). https://doi.org/10.1007/s00421-008-0742-6

55. Radespiel-Troger, M., Rauh, R., Mahlke, C., Gottschalk, T., Muck-Weymann, M.: Agreement of two different methods for measurement of heart rate variability. Clin. Auton. Res. **13**(2), 99–102 (2003). https://doi.org/10.1007/s10286-003-0085-7

56. Treiber, F.A., Musante, L., Hartdagan, S., Davis, H., Levy, M., Strong, W.B.: Validation of a heart rate monitor with children in laboratory and field settings. Med. Sci. Sports Exerc. **21**(3), 338–342 (1989)

57. Hettinger, T., Wobbe, G.: Kompendium der Arbeitswissenschaft. Kiehl Verlag, Ludwigshafen (1993)

58. Finsen, L., Søgaard, K., Jensen, C., Borg, V., Christensen, H.: Muscle activity and cardiovascular response during computer-mouse work with and without memory demands. Ergonomics **44**(14), 1312–1329 (2001). https://doi.org/10.1080/00140130110099065

59. Malik, M., et al.: Heart rate variability: standards of measurement, physiological interpretation, and clinical use. Eur. Heart J. **17**(3), 354–381 (1996). https://doi.org/10.1093/oxfordjournals.eurheartj.a014868

60. Nunan, D., Sandercock, G.R.H., Brodie, D.: A quantitative systematic review of normal values for short-term heart rate variability in healthy adults. Pace-Pacing Clin. Electrophysiol. **33**(11), 1407–1417 (2010). https://doi.org/10.1111/j.1540-8159.2010.02841.x

61. Schafer, A., Vagedes, J.: How accurate is pulse rate variability as an estimate of heart rate variability? a review on studies comparing photoplethysmographic technology with an electrocardiogram. Int. J. Cardiol. **166**(1), 15–29 (2013). https://doi.org/10.1016/j.ijcard.2012.03.119

62. Lohani, M., Payne, B.R., Strayer, D.L.: A review of psychophysiological measures to assess cognitive states in real-world driving. Front. Hum. Neurosci. **13**, 57 (2019). https://doi.org/10.3389/fnhum.2019.00057

63. Sammito, S., Bockelmann, I.: Analysis of heart rate variability: mathematical description and practical application. Herz **40**, 76–84 (2015). https://doi.org/10.1007/s00059-014-4145-7

64. Duchowski, A.T.: Eye Tracking Methodology: Theory and Practice, 3rd edn. Springer, Heidelberg (2007)

65. Goldberg, J., Wichansky, A.: Eye tracking in usability evaluation: A practitioner's guide. (2003)

66. Glaholt, M.G.: Eye tracking in the cockpit: a review of the relationships between eye movements and the aviator's cognitive state. In. Defence Research and Development Canada, Toronto, Canada (2014)

67. Tole, J.R., Stephens, A.T., Vivaudou, M., Ephrath, A.R., Young, L.R.: Visual scanning behavior and pilot workload. In. NASA (1983)

68. Faulhaber, A.K., Friedrich, M.: Eye-tracking metrics as an indicator of workload in commercial single-pilot operations. In: Longo, L., Leva, M.C. (eds.) H-WORKLOAD 2019. CCIS, vol. 1107, pp. 213–225. Springer, Cham (2019). https://doi.org/10.1007/978-3-030-32423-0_14

69. Di Nocera, F., Camilli, M., Terenzi, M.: A random glance at the flight deck: pilots' scanning strategies and the real-time assessment of mental workload. J. Cogn. Eng. Dec. Mak. **1**(3), 271–285 (2007). https://doi.org/10.1518/155534307X255627

70. Stanton, N.A., Salmon, P.M., Rafferty, L.A., Walker, G.H., Baber, C., Jenkins, D.P.: Human Factors Methods: A Practical Guide for Engineering and Design, 2nd edn. CRC Press, London (2013)

71. Wierwille, W.W., Eggemeier, F.T.: Recommendations for mental workload measurement in a test and evaluation environment. Hum. Factors **35**(2), 263–281 (1993). https://doi.org/10.1177/001872089303500205

72. Wickens, C.D.: Multiple resources and performance prediction. Theor. Issues Ergon. Sci. **3**(2), 159–177 (2002). https://doi.org/10.1080/14639220210123806

73. Wickens, C.D.: Multiple resources and mental workload. Hum. Factors **50**(3), 449–455 (2008). https://doi.org/10.1518/001872008x288394

74. Casali, J.G., Wierwille, W.W.: A comparison of rating scale, secondary-task, physiological, and primary-task workload estimation techniques in a simulated flight task emphasizing communications load. Hum. Factors **25**(6), 623–641 (1983). https://doi.org/10.1177/001872088 302500602

75. Casali, J.G., Wierwille, W.W.: On the measurement of pilot perceptual workload: a comparison of assessment techniques addressing sensitivity and intrusion issues. Ergonomics **27**(10), 1033–1050 (1984). https://doi.org/10.1080/00140138408963584

76. Wierwille, W.W., Connor, S.A.: Evaluation of 20 workload measures using a psychomotor task in a moving-base aircraft simulator. Hum. Factors **25**(1), 1–16 (1983). https://doi.org/10. 1177/001872088302500101

77. Hart, S.G.: Nasa-task load index (NASA-TLX); 20 years later. Proc. Hum. Fact. Ergon. Soc. Ann. Meet. **50**(9), 904–908 (2006). https://doi.org/10.1177/154193120605000909

78. Hart, S.G., Staveland, L.E.: Development of NASA-TLX (Task Load Index): results of empirical and theoretical research. In: Hancock, P.A., Meshkati, N. (eds.) Advances in Psychology, North-Holland, vol. 52. pp. 139–183 (1988)

79. Tattersall, A.J., Foord, P.S.: An experimental evaluation of instantaneous self-assessment as a measure of workload. Ergonomics **39**(5), 740–748 (1996). https://doi.org/10.1080/001401 39608964495

80. Zimeo Morais, G.A., Balardin, J.B., Sato, J.R.: fNIRS optodes' location decider (fOLD): a toolbox for probe arrangement guided by brain regions-of-interest. Sci Rep **8**(1), 3341 (2018). https://doi.org/10.1038/s41598-018-21716-z

81. Biella, M., Wies, M.: Human performance envelope: overview of the project and technical results. In: Paper presented at the Future Sky Safety Final Conference, FSS on Final Approach, Brüssel, Belgium (2018)

Evaluating the Impact of Passive Fatigue on Pilots Using Performance and Subjective States Measures

Stefano Conte[1]([⊠]) [iD], Donald Harris[1] [iD], and James Blundell[2] [iD]

[1] Faculty of Engineering, Environment and Computing,
Coventry University, Coventry CV1 5FB, UK
stef.conte@outlook.com

[2] Institute of Clean Growth and Future Mobility, Coventry University, Coventry CV1 5FB, UK

Abstract. Fatigue is a serious threat to flight safety, being a contributing factor of many aviation accidents. Sleep-related fatigue has been the most researched; however, fatigue also depends on task-related factors such as time-on-task and workload. Desmond and Hancock [1] theorized two opposite types of task-related fatigue: active fatigue (induced by cognitive overload) and passive fatigue (elicited by prolonged, understimulating and monotonous tasks). Research mainly conducted in the automotive sector demonstrated the existence of these different states and found that passive fatigue is linked to decline in performance and vigilance, together with task disengagement. Automation is extensively used in most flights, and though pilots are particularly vulnerable to passive fatigue due to the nature of their tasks (especially during cruise with autopilot engaged), no specific passive fatigue research involving pilots exist. This study intended to fill that gap, by employing well-rested licensed pilots (N = 26) who underwent an experiment involving the Multi-Attribute Task Battery (MATB) which replicates some of the tasks encountered during flight. Pilots were randomly assigned to either a one-hour very low workload scenario intended to induce passive fatigue, or a one-hour moderate workload control scenario. Pilot performance on the MATB was measured as simple reaction times (SRTs) and the frequency of missed cues on a system-monitoring task. Subjective measures were used to evaluate how task engagement and perceived workload changed over the course of the experiment. Results confirmed that passive fatigue had a detrimental effect on performance as pilots in that scenario showed significantly slower SRTs compared to the control group. Task engagement scores did not decline as predicted, but instead increased significantly more in the passive fatigue scenario, indicating a possible self-assessment inefficacy generated by the monotonous tasks. These findings suggests that wakeful pilots experience performance decline during prolonged monotonous and mostly automated flights, thus a wiser use of automation or the development of appropriate countermeasures is needed.

Keywords: Passive Fatigue · Pilot · Fatigue · Automation · Autopilot · Underload · Workload · Flight Safety · Reaction Time · Task Engagement · Vigilance · MATB

1   Introduction

Fatigue is an acknowledged hazard that degrades various types of human performance and has been identified as a contributing factor for accidents in a wide range of settings, including aviation where the dangers of fatigue have been recognized as early as 1942 [2–4]. In the field of transportation research, the conventional approach to deal with fatigue issues is mostly oriented towards sleep research and its causal factors such as circadian rhythm, sleep debt, and time since awakening. Still, there are several endogenous and exogenous factors that influence the fatigue-related physiological states that impair pilot's performance and vigilance which are not associated with sleep. Among those factors, task-related aspects such as workload and time-on-task have a substantial influence on fatigue [5, 6].

1.1   Active and Passive Fatigue States and Their Origin

In 2001 Desmond and Hancock [1] proposed a new theory to illustrate the adaptive nature of fatigue in the execution of complex tasks. Following the result of their experiments on simulated driving performance under different conditions, they introduced the concept of active and passive fatigue. Active fatigue is the result of prolonged and continuous task-related perceptual-motor adjustments. In contrast, passive fatigue is caused by chronic understimulation that requires little or no perceptual-motor response, when the individual appears to be doing nothing at all. This condition typically occurs when the operator is required to monitor the performance of a highly automated system and provide relatively infrequent system instruction/input. For example, in transportation settings involving highly automated tasks such as long-haul flights [1]. In general, active fatigue and passive fatigue are associated with cognitive overload or underload conditions, respectively. During high workload conditions, the operators continually mobilize their cognitive resources to meet the high task demand, causing active fatigue. In contrast, passive fatigue is induced when automation relegates them to a system-monitoring role with little or nothing to do, such as driving a highly automated car or flying using the autopilot. However, it is important to underline that 'overload and underload conditions are not synonymous with active and passive fatigue, but may provide insight into psychological differences between the two forms of fatigue' (p.17) [7]. Vigilance tasks characterized by boredom and monotony, tend to produce larger reductions in task engagement, which induce passive fatigue [7, 8].

1.2   Passive Fatigue State Indicators

Passive fatigue has detrimental effects on the operator's subjective state, performance, and vigilance. Previous research has presented support in differentiating task engagement, distress, and worry dimensions as subjective indices of the dynamic transaction between the individual and the task environment [9]. Task engagement represents 'a theme of commitment to effort as the person strives to accomplish task goals' (p.3) [9]. When engagement is low, the individual experiences low energy, low motivation, and high distractibility, which corresponds to a fatigued state [9]. Driving simulation experiments by Saxby et al. [10, 11] demonstrated that qualitatively different tasks provoked different active and passive fatigue responses. Active fatigue elicited high distress scores, while passive fatigue caused large-magnitude task engagement decrements and a loss of motivation, indicating that low workload caused by automation produced considerable fatigue. Although perceived workload decreased in the passive condition, lower workload did not translate to higher engagement. In fact, the active fatigue condition, even if more distressing, was the most effective in maintaining task engagement. Therefore Saxby et al.'s [10] findings contested the assertion that automation reduces fatigue by decreasing workload, by demonstrating empirically the induction of passive fatigue under automation.

1.3 Passive Fatigue Effects on Performance and Vigilance

In terms of performance, Saxby et al. [11] found that passive fatigued drivers exhibited slowest brake and swerve reaction times to unexpected events that required emergency intervention to avoid a crash. Consequently, these drivers committed a far greater frequency of crashes compared to drivers within control and active fatigue driving conditions, leading to the realization that passive fatigue is actually a greater threat to safety compared to active fatigue. Corroborating findings by Matthews et al. [12] showed that automation-induced response time slowing was a consistent effect of passive fatigue. Likewise, previous research has revealed that monotonous driving conditions produce larger steering wheel movements, since the fatigued drivers lost perceptual sensitivity to small deviations and their reaction time tended to increase, resulting in larger wheel corrections [13].

Vigilance decrements in a monitoring task is defined as 'a decrease in the number of targets detected that occurs after a short period on the task' [14]. Mathew et al. [15] suggested that drivers experiencing passive fatigue are disinclined to dedicate effort to their task meaning that they may fail to search actively for potential hazards. Schmidt et al. [16] investigated the effects of a 4-h monotonous real-world driving scenario on drivers' vigilance state. Reaction times increased linearly throughout the experiment alongside a continuous reduction in the physiological vigilance EEG and ECG markers. Interestingly, subjective vigilance measures were consistent with performance and physiological data for the first three hours before a sharp dissociation manifested; In the last hour, objective vigilance and performance measures continued to decline whereas the subjective measure indicated an improvement of vigilance. The researchers concluded that drivers misjudged their subjective states towards the end of the drive.

1.4 Passive Fatigue in Aviation

In contrast to the automotive settings, where automation is a relatively recent novelty, aircraft pilots have been using flight automation since 1912 [17]. Pilots using low-level cockpit automation need to manually perform more flight and navigation related tasks compared to those using high-level automation, where they may only need to execute monitoring functions [18]. High-level automation plays a key role in the operation of modern commercial flights, where 80% of flights are typically flown manually for just four minutes [19], and in general aviation flights where the employment of automation has escalated dramatically [20]. Consequently, commercial pilots regularly find themselves in system-monitoring and supervisory roles with minimal direct interaction with the environment; A situation likely to induce passive fatigue. Paradoxically, a large share of pilots reports that 'automation actually increased workloads during phases of flight already characterized by high workload and decreased during periods of low workload' (p.170) [21].

Conventional methods to dealing with fatigue-related problems for pilots is mainly positioned towards sleep-related research. Task-induced fatigue studies in aviation, particularly those concentrating on passive fatigue, are scarce [5]. This is unfortunate as understanding the causal factors of fatigue is essential to deploying appropriate countermeasures, as some of them may simultaneously alleviate one type of fatigue whilst exacerbating the other [6]. Recent passive fatigue aviation research by Wohleber et al. [22] investigated factors influencing sustained performance and fatigue during of multiple Unmanned Aerial Systems (UAS) operations. The research involved a large sample performed surveillance within multi-UAS simulation designed to impose low cognitive demands for 2 h. The underload task configuration produced subjective passive fatigue as shown by large magnitude decline in task engagement scores from pre- to post-task, along with a decrement of performance measured as task accuracy, which were the same subjective state and performance effects of passive fatigue found by Saxby et al. [10, 11]. The last part of their hours experiment showed a pronounced 'end effect' with performance returning to its initial level. This end effect resulting in a recovery of performance was judged as a motivational boost found when participants can anticipate the end of the task, sufficient to compensate for the resource shortfall in the final part of the experiment. The main limitation reported in the experiment was the use of untrained civilian participants (undergraduate students) rather than air real UAS pilots who are trained to manage their vigilance throughout long missions.

The first experiment on active and passive fatigue oriented towards manned flight tasks was conducted in 2019 by Bernhardt et al. [23]. As active and passive fatigue were theorized as general concepts, they should arise across different settings, including complex tasks such as flight tasks. To demonstrate that, this study utilized the NASA's Multi-Attribute Task Battery-II (MATB-II) that replicates the cognitive tasks frequently encounter during flight by pilots. To induce active and passive fatigue, this study developed manipulations similar to those created by Saxby et al. [10, 11] to induce active and passive fatigue states. Their study wanted to expand the understanding of active and passive fatigue states by using continuous electroencephalographic EEG and reaction time measurements. Electroencephalographic indices of task engagement were used to evaluate active and passive fatigue states. Three MATB fatigue induction scenarios were created: active, control, and passive. The first finding of this experiment was that the multivariate task engagement EEG metric in the passive fatigue condition was significantly lower than the EEG engagement in active fatigue. Subjective task engagement scores measured using the Short Stress State Questionnaire did not differ significantly as a function of fatigue condition and time on task from pre to post experiment. All three conditions reported similar reductions in subjective engagement from pre to post MATB, thus failing to replicate the findings by Saxby et al. [10, 11]. Performance data did not reveal any significant differences between the fatigue conditions, in contrast to the results obtained by Saxby et al. [11], as reaction times to respond to radio calls significantly increased in all three conditions. One of the limitations of Bernhardt's [23] study comes from the sample used. Even if the MATB platform mimics the cognitive tasks encountered by pilots during flight, his sample consisted of non-pilot undergraduate students.

2 Aim of This Study

The necessity of this research derives from different factors. Firstly, passive fatigue is a relatively new and not widely investigated concept that is now emerging in the transportation industry [24]. The recent increase in driving automation solutions has sparked the interest in passive fatigue research in the automotive sector, however despite the similarities in the nature of pilots and drivers tasks it is important to establish if the findings of passive fatigue studies from the automotive domain are replicable in aviation settings, especially in terms task engagement, performance, and vigilance effects. Furthermore, the limited number of aviation passive fatigue studies [22, 23] have involved samples made of generic students, instead of using pilot populations. More recently, Wingelaar-Jagt et al. [25] stated that the International Civil Aviation Organization's definition of fatigue identifies workload as a possible cause, and the associate between the two constructs requires greater scrutiny. Furthermore, Matthews et al. [12] suggest that drivers experiencing passive fatigue are disinclined to dedicate effort to their task meaning that they may fail to search actively for potential hazards. In fact, research [15] suggests reduced scanning effort for task-relevant information is linked to periods of automation. Cockpit scanning is a fundamental task that must be continuously performed by pilots to detect potentially fatal malfunctions. Consequently, there is the need to test if passively fatigued pilots are more prone to vigilance error, where they fail to notice a task-critical cues. Understanding how passive fatigue affects pilots could lead to a reconsideration of automation in the flight deck and to the development of specific countermeasures to enhance flight safety when the pilot experience cognitive underload. The current research investigates the effects of passive fatigue experienced by pilots during prolonged periods of low workload and automatic systems monitoring, in comparison to a control group completing a moderate workload version of the same task. The effects of passive fatigue on licensed pilots, in terms of performance (reaction times), vigilance (errors of omission) and subjective states (task engagement and perceived workload), are analyzed and discussed in comparison to research from driving settings.

2.1 Research Questions and Hypotheses

Based on existing literature four research questions and hypotheses are presented:
Research question and hypothesis 1
Do pilots show a significant decline in their performance, manifesting as a slowing of reaction times, when experiencing passive fatigue?
H_1 Reaction times are significantly slower in the passive fatigue group than the control group.
Research question and hypothesis 2

Do pilots show a vigilance decline (in terms of errors of omission) when experiencing passive fatigue?

H_2 The percentage of missed cues is higher among the pilots of the passive fatigue group compared to the pilots in the control group.

Research question and hypothesis 3

Do pilots show a significantly higher loss of task engagement when experiencing passive fatigue as demonstrated by the research in driving settings?

H_3 Task engagement score decline significantly more in the passive fatigue group in comparison to the control group after one hour.

Research question and hypothesis 4

Do pilots report a significantly greater decline of workload when experiencing passive fatigue? This hypothesis aims to verify that pilots that undergo the passive fatigue scenario experience underload.

H_4 Perceived workload score decline significantly more in the passive fatigue group than the control group after one hour.

3   Method

3.1   Participants

Twenty-six licensed pilots (24 males and 2 females) aged between 20 and 51 (M = 29.85, SD = 9.49) volunteered for the experiment. The 26 participants held different types of licenses: 1 Light Aircraft Pilot License, 17 Private Pilot License, 6 Commercial Pilot License, and 2 Airline Transport Pilot License. Experience ranged between 32 and 11,000 flight hours (M = 781, SD = 2156). The research project and protocols were approved by the Coventry University Ethics Department.

3.2   Materials and Instruments

Multi-Attribute Task Battery (MATB).   The experimental platform used in this study was OpenMATB, an open-source version of the NASA's Multi-Attribute Task Battery (MATB) which replicates a set of tasks representative of those performed in aircraft piloting [26]. For this experiment only the tracking, system-monitoring, and resource management tasks were displayed. The tracking task was designed to be automatic, however participants were told to monitor the functioning of the autopilot and to intervene, using a sidestick, if they deemed necessary.

For the system-monitoring task participants monitored four graduated gauges representing the temperatures and fuel pressures of two engines (labelled '1 TEMP', '2 TEMP', 'F1 PRESS' and 'F2 PRESS') and an annunciator panel with two lights (AUX FUEL PUMP that had to always stay on and the GEN FAIL amber light indicating that the generator had failed). The frequency of monitoring task abnormal 'events' was manipulated to produce the two task load conditions (details below). For each event, participants had a maximum of 10 s to detect the abnormality and press an appropriate keyboard key to revert the system to a nominal state.

The resource management task, located in the bottom center, takes the form of a diagrammatic representation of an aircraft fuel system [26]. The participants were asked to transfer fuel through button-activated pumps when needed so that the main tanks would not completely drain. The lead researcher coded the MATB plugins to create a representation of an instrument panel that could be more realistic and reasonable for a real pilot. MATB interface in normal condition is show in Fig. 1 below.

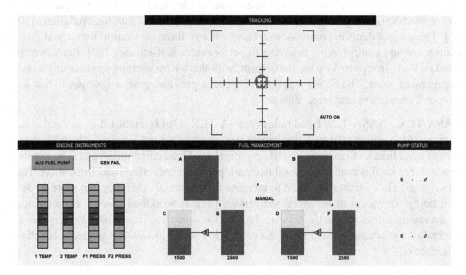

Fig. 1. MATB interface used in this experiment during normal conditions.

Scenarios. Two MATB scenarios (control and passive fatigue) were coded by the researchers. The operating principle of the two main scenarios, in terms of tasks and frequency of events, were based on the methods employed by Bernhardt et al. [23]. The control scenario was designed to be fast-paced in terms of event frequency (1 random event every 10 s) to increase task engagement, but with no more than one event occurring at the same time to keep a nominal moderate task load. The passive fatigue scenario was designed to induce very low task load due to having easy and infrequent tasks (1 random event every 4 to 7 min) that shifted the pilots into a passive monitoring role. In contrast to Bernhardt et al. [23], the system-monitoring task was used for both the modulation of the task load and to assess participant performance.

Reaction Time Measurement. Participant performance was based on simple reaction time (SRT) to generator failure events on the system-monitoring task. It was chosen since the GEN FAIL amber light closely represents the MASTER CAUTION amber indication in real aircraft. Therefore, to pilots, the prompt is highly salient and a semantically associated urgent cue. In both scenarios, the GEN FAIL warning amber light was activated every 15 min.

Vigilance Measurement. Vigilance was measured as error of omission, defined as an occurrence where the participant failed to respond to a system-monitoring event [14].

The rate of missed events (errors of omission) is one of the most common behavioral assessments of vigilance [27]. The percentage of missed events was calculated from the total number of events missed by the participant during the experiment.

SSSQ. Task engagement state of participants was assessed using task engagement indicators from the Short Stress State Questionnaire (SSSQ) [28]. The SSSQ is a short version of the Dundee Stress State Questionnaire (DSSQ) that was developed to measure consciously reportable, transactional stress states. The eight task engagement indicators in the SSSQ have been found to be sensitive to passive fatigue manipulations [10, 11]. These eight items encompass: two energy items, three motivation items, and three confidence and control items referring to performance self-efficacy [29]. Each item is rated on scale from 1 to 5 by the participant, with the 8-item average representing a task engagement score. The SSSQ was administered at pre- and post-task stages to test for temporal changes in task engagement.

NASA TLX. NASA-Task Load Index (NASA-TLX) [30] is a multi-dimensional scale constructed to obtain post-task participant perceived workload estimate. The scale consists of six subscales to support identify principal workload components of a task: mental demand, physical demand, temporal demand, performance, effort, and frustration. The unweighted TLX version was used to increase experimental efficiency, but more so due to it being equivalent to the weighted version [31]. A workload score was calculated by averaging scores across the 6 subscales. TLX scores were taken from participants at the end of the scenarios (including the calibration scenario which provided a baseline reference).

3.3 Procedure

The experiment was conducted on a portable workstation (Fig. 2) Participants were told they were supposed to imagine themselves flying alone during a cruise phase in a large twin piston engine aircraft (e.g., P2012/C404), with no radio communications and with the autopilot engaged. Participants were not told which scenario had been assigned to them, or how long the experiment would last. Moreover, the use of watches, smartphones and any other timekeeping device was forbidden to avoid the 'end effect' that was observed towards the end of other long-lasting experiments [32]. The experiment was performed individually by all participant to investigate how pilots deal with passive fatigue when flying alone, which is a condition frequently experienced by private pilots and a probable future condition in commercial Single Pilot Operations. The participants were asked how many hours of sleep they were able to achieve the night before the experiment to assess if any of them was possibly under the influence of drowsiness, thus altering the impact of the independent variables. Before the start of the actual experiment, participants completed a 5-min calibration scenario with moderate taskload to familiarize them with the controls and to take baseline measurements of reaction times, task engagement and perceived workload. Written informed consent was obtained before the experiment from each pilot who participated in this study. They were debriefed at the end of the experiment to inform them which scenario they had been randomly assigned to.

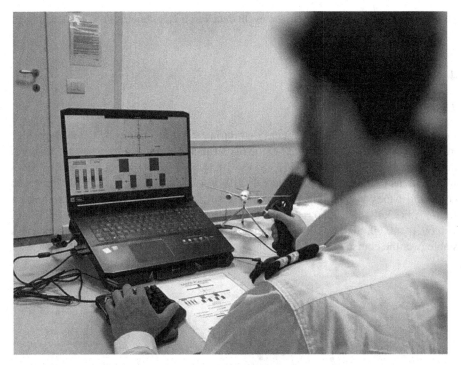

Fig. 2. One of the pilots participating in the experiment.

3.4 Experimental Design

The study used two independent variables (IVs) and four dependent variables (DVs). The first IV was *scenario* (between-group) that represented the control or passive fatigue scenario the participant was assigned to. The second IV was *time* (repeated-measures) that reflected the time passed since the start of the experiment (measured in minutes, at intervals of 15).

The DVs were: simple reaction time (SRT), measured in milliseconds, missed events percentage (representing the error of omission), task engagement score change (post-task minus pre-task) and TLX score change (post-task score minus pre-task).

3.5 Data Analysis

SRT was analyzed using linear mixed models (LMMs) in the SPSS statistical software due to the inclusion of a repeated measures factor in the experimental design. Fixed factors included *scenario* (2 levels: control or passive Fatigue) and *time* (0, 15, 30, 45, 60 min). Random effects were fitted as by-participant intercepts. The Satterthwaite approximation method for the degrees of freedom was used with alpha set to 0.05. 95% confidence intervals are included as estimates of effect size for significant main effects and interactions.

The analysis of *scenario* effects on missed events percentage, task engagement score changes, and TLX score change (post-task score minus pre-task) were analyzed using parametric and nonparametric (in the event data was nonparametric) t-tests. An alpha of 0.05 was used in all comparisons.

4   Results

4.1   SRT

Figure 3 presents the 128 SRTs measured during the study alongside the average SRT mean for the control and passive fatigue (experimental) groups. A significant *scenario* main effect on SRT was found $F(23.85) = 10.34$, $p = 0.004$, indicating that the SRTs were 332 ms (95% Confidence Interval: 119–546) slower in the passive fatigue group compared to the control group. However, the results did not show a significant main effect for *time*, $F(93.40) = 1.05$, $p = 0.38$. The *scenario* by *time* was not significant $F(93.40) = 0.69$, $p = 0.60$. SRT was slower in the passive fatigue group, and this difference was stable over the course of the experiment.

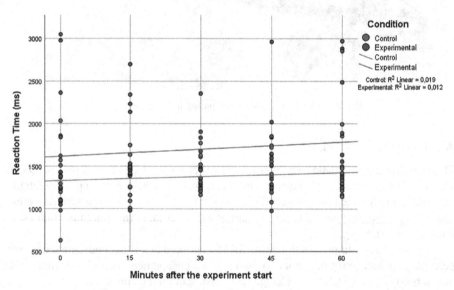

Fig. 3. Grouped Scatter of simple reaction times measured in the experiment.

4.2   Errors of Omission (Missed Events) Difference Between Groups

To answer the second research question, the considered dependent variable was the percentage of the system monitoring task events that were missed by the participants in both groups. The percentages were not normally distributed for both the control and the passive fatigue group therefore, a non-parametric test was performed. A Mann-Whitney U test was conducted to determine whether there is a difference in the percentage of the system-monitoring task events that were missed between the participants of the control group and the experimental group. The results indicate a non-significant difference in the percentage of the system-monitoring task events of control (n = 13, M = 0.32, SD = 0.45, median = 0.28) and passive fatigue (n = 13, M = 2.37, SD = 3.70, median = 0) groups, U = 74.50, z = 0.562, p = 0.614, r = 0.11. Thus, the null hypothesis cannot be rejected.

4.3 Task Engagement Variation Between Passive Fatigue and Control Groups

To answer the third research question, the considered dependent variable was the difference of the task engagement score between post-task score and pre-task score (baseline). Differences were not normally distributed for both the control and the passive fatigue group thus, to compare the statistical significance of the task engagement score differences a non-parametric test was performed. A Mann-Whitney U test was conducted to determine whether there was a significant difference in task engagement score variation after one hour between the control group and the experimental group. The results indicate a statistically significant difference in the task engagement score variation of control and passive fatigue groups after one hour, as task engagement increased more in the passive fatigue group (n = 13, M = 0.17, SD = 0.31, median = 0.25) than the control group (n = 13, M = 0.02, SD = 0.40, median = 0) U = 122.50, z = 1.977, p = 0.050, r = 0.388; Consequently, the null hypothesis was rejected along with the alternate hypothesis H_3 since the task engagement score increased significantly more in the passive fatigue group compared to the control.

4.4 Perceived Workload Variation Between Passive Fatigue and Control Groups

An independent-samples t-test was conducted to compare the TLX scores variation scores after one hour between the control and passive fatigue groups. The TLX scores differences were normally distributed, and the parametric assumptions were met. There was a larger loss of perceived workload in the passive fatigue group (M = -20.90, SD = 12.96) compared to the control group (M = -8.98, SD = 11.79), t(24) = 2.45, p = 0.022. Thus, the null hypothesis that the TLX scores variation would not be significant can be rejected. Cohen's D point estimate of 0.96 indicates a large effect.

5 Discussion

This research explored the effects of passive fatigue on pilots' performance, vigilance and subjective state during flight-related tasks. The results of this study support the first hypothesis: as predicted, the SRTs were significantly higher in the passive fatigue group. In fact, the analysis highlighted that the passive fatigue scenario had a negative effect on the pilot participants' SRTs, as they reacted slower to the GEN FAIL warning compared to the control group. This relationship supports the expected outcome of the initial hypothesis, with passive fatigue having a detrimental effect on reaction times and follows the results obtained in the driving simulations by Saxby et al. [11]. The results also contradict the investigation of Bernhardt et al. [23] who found no performance difference in participants under passive fatigue. These findings imply that a pilot performing flight-related tasks in a passive fatigue state reacts slower to panel indications or visual cues compared to a pilot in nominal conditions.

The second hypothesis was not accepted as results did not provide a clear indication of the effects of passive fatigue on vigilance measurement through the comparison of errors of omission measured through the percentage of missed events by the pilots.

Contrary to the prediction made in the third hypothesis, the task engagement score of pilots increased during the experiment, as both groups manifested a higher task engagement in the post-task SSSQ compared to the pre-task. Furthermore, task engagement scores increased significantly more in the passive fatigue group than the scores of the control group. This finding indicates that the low taskload and monotonous passive fatigue scenario did not induce task disengagement in the same way it occurred in the other research on passive fatigue [8, 10, 23], although Saxby et al. [11] also found no significant difference between DSSQ task engagement score of control and passive fatigue drivers groups. In fact, the pilots of the passive fatigue group displayed higher motivation, energy and confidence (all aspects that constitute task engagement in the SSSQ [29] than the pilots in the control group).

Regarding the fourth research question, the effects of the condition on perceived workload are evident when considering the change in TLX score from pre-task (calibration scenario common for all participants, therefore usable as a baseline) to post-task. In this case the passive fatigue condition generated a significantly larger loss of perceived workload TLX score (M = −20.90, SD = 12.96) compared to the control group (M = −8.98, SD = 11.79). This indicates that each TLX score, calibrated with its baseline reference, dropped significantly more in the passive fatigue scenario which suggests that pilots found themselves experiencing a lower workload in their scenario compared to the control pilots, not in term of absolute TLX, but in terms of relative difference from a common baseline.

The results mentioned above provide contradictory findings on passive fatigue compared to the previous studies. The decline of performance is similar to the findings in the automotive sectors [11, 13, 16, 22], however the task engagement growth in low taskload scenario is in contrast with most passive fatigue studies made so far [10, 13, 22, 23]. However, a similar discrepancy also occurred in the study by Schmidt et al. [16] that reported the effects of monotonous driving on vigilance as in the final part of the experiment the subjective measures dissociated sharply from the performance and physiological indicators. Since all the objective measures consistently pointed to a further decline in vigilance, they concluded that the participants lacked self-assessment in those monotonous condition and hence misjudged their subjective states [16]. Furthermore, the slower SRTs of the passive fatigue scenario represent an objective measure that cannot be consciously altered by participants, while the task engagement score derived from a subjective state questionnaire, which might have been influenced by the experimental design or by a 'make a good impression' bias, resulting in higher rating of some SSSQ items like 'I was committed to attaining my performance goals' or 'I wanted to succeed on the task'.

To sum up, the results have proven that the passive fatigue scenario has generated a qualitatively different state in pilots in terms of performance, task engagement and perceived workload. The passive fatigue group exhibited significantly slower reaction times, relatively greater increases in task engagement, and decrements in perceived worked in comparison to a control group that experienced moderate taskload. The passive fatigue concept is now extended to pilots, who showed a significant decline of performance in the experimental condition. Based on the similarity with the finding from Schmidt et al. [16], it is possible to assume that the experimental scenario succeeded in passive fatigue induction judging the performance results, but also created a flawed self-evaluation in the pilots that resulted in a growth of task engagement in such a monotonous and underload situation.

5.1 Implications

The findings from the present study have important practical implications for pilots. Firstly, we can expect passive fatigue to be frequently encountered by flight crews and single pilots during the cruise phase when the extensive use of automation (e.g. autopilot, autothrottle) relegates pilots to a supervisory role for prolonged time periods. Passive fatigue will contribute to performance decrements, which usually go unnoticed or are attributed to other factors (e.g. sleepiness, mind-wandering, distraction). It is likely to accumulate during cruise resulting in dangerous situations where pilots are required to react to unexpected events that demand immediate actions (e.g. sudden depressurization, uncontained engine failure or fire, TCAS resolution advisory, bird strike for general aviation flights flying at low levels). The reduction in the capacity of self-assessment identified with passive fatigue might also compromise safety, especially in single pilot operations as the pilot might not be able to confidently self-identify performance decrements.

5.2 Limitations and Future Research Recommendations

The main limitation of this study comes from the platform used for the experiment. MATB is an established platform in aviation Human Factors studies, its low physical fidelity presentation might have contributed to the task disengagement of pilot participants as they might have considered the platform as banal compared to the complexity of a real flight deck. Another limitation was the laboratory setting of the experiment which increased participants' expectancy of the investigated abnormal events. In real flight settings, pilots scan the instrument panel for cues, they do not expect to find any abnormality as they assume that the flight will continue uneventfully. In driving settings, more experienced drivers are more capable of compensating fatigue effects during a routine driving task, despite their diminished capacity [33]. It is likely that the same occurs with professional pilots who are more used to fatigue effects and are therefore more skilled in counteracting the detrimental effects on performance. Future research should test the influence of pilots' experience on passive fatigue effects. Future research should also investigate the MATB tracking tasks performance of pilots in a passive fatigue state after an autopilot failure to see if passive fatigue presents the same reductions in the ability to accurately maintain headings, altitudes, airspeeds, bank angles, and vertical velocities like in other sleep-related fatigue investigations [34]. Finally, as May and Baldwin [6] stated that passive fatigue can worsen sleepiness symptoms, future studies should investigate the interaction of passive and sleep-related fatigue, since pilots often experience sleep-related fatigue due to the nature of their job.

6 Conclusion

Fatigue remains a significant threat to flight safety. Task-related fatigue depends on time-on-task and cognitive workload and through the latter factor it was further divided in active and passive fatigue by Desmond and Hancock [1]. Passive fatigue is a consequence of cognitive underload and sustained monotony that usually appears from monitoring a system for a prolonged period [1, 15]. With recent technological advances in avionics, pilots spend most of the flight monitoring the aircraft's systems, with only occasional system interactions. Automation is also spreading to general aviation because it helps in reducing workload, especially for those who fly as single pilots. Concern arises when pilots are assigned the primary role of system monitoring, which may increase suscep-tibility to fatigue and consequently encourage task disengagement and distraction [12]. Pilots may be especially vulnerable to passive fatigue during cruise, which presents the lowest workload. This study was conducted to investigate this topic and fill this research gap. Consistently, with previous studies involving car drivers, this study found that pilots in the passive fatigue condition showed slower reaction times compared to pilots in a control group. These findings indicate that pilots can experience the same passive fatigue performance decrements as the general population while performing monotonous flight-related tasks that involve abundant use of automation and low cognitive workload. The subjective state measure of task engagement increased significantly more in the pilots group that underwent a very low workload and monotonous scenario (verified by the larger decline of workload TLX score), contrary to most of the literature on passive fatigue effects on drivers. The discrepancy between performance decline and increased task engagement can be attributed to a flawed self-assessment capacity that occurred in other passive fatigue studies [16, 23].

This research contributes to the expanding base of knowledge regarding passive fatigue, providing valid findings from a sample of licensed pilots for the first time. These new conclusions, especially in terms of performance variation, provide a picture of what happens in the flight deck during the underloading cruise phase and might be the basis for the development of adaptive automation or countermeasures that prevent passive fatigue.

Acknowledgments. Special thanks to the Coventry University's Human Factors in Aviation MSc academic staff that helped in the realization of this research. Words cannot express our gratitude to all the kind and patient people that helped through the long and complicated process of reaching potential pilot participants and arranging the experiment with them. We would like to particularly thank Marco Frosio, Elena Guardigli, Stefano 'Steve' Caini, Cristian Groff, Pietro Luigi Rinaldi and Damiano Fachiri as this endeavor would not have been feasible without all of you. We would like to extend my sincere thanks to all the staff of Professional Aviation S.r.l., FTO Padova S.r.l. and Aeroclub Ferrara flight schools as well as DastyFlySim Simulation Centre for promoting this research and for offering unrestricted use of their facilities for the experimental needs. Finally, we would like to express our deepest appreciation to all the 26 pilots who took part in the experiment and spent hours of their valuable time to help us out in this project.

References

1. Desmond, P.A., Hancock, P.A.: Active and passive fatigue states. In: Stress, Workload, and Fatigue, pp. 455–465. Lawrence Erlbaum Associates Publishers (2001)
2. Editorial, L.: Fatigue in aircraft pilots. Lancet **239**(6182), 234–235 (1942). https://doi.org/10.1016/S0140-6736(00)57817-9
3. Williamson, A., Lombardi, D.A., Folkard, S., Stutts, J., Courtney, T.K., Connor, J.L.: The link between fatigue and safety. Accid. Anal. Prev. **43**(2), 498–515 (2011). https://doi.org/10.1016/j.aap.2009.11.011
4. ICAO International Civil Aviation Organization. Doc 9966 Manual for the Oversight of Fatigue Management Approaches (2016)
5. Hu, X., Lodewijks, G.: Detecting fatigue in car drivers and aircraft pilots by using non-invasive measures: the value of differentiation of sleepiness and mental fatigue. J. Saf. Res. **72**, 173–187 (2020). https://doi.org/10.1016/j.jsr.2019.12.015
6. May, J.F., Baldwin, C.L.: Driver fatigue: the importance of identifying causal factors of fatigue when considering detection and countermeasure technologies. Transport. Res. F: Traffic Psychol. Behav. **12**(3), 218–224 (2009). https://doi.org/10.1016/j.trf.2008.11.005
7. Saxby, D. J. Active and Passive Fatigue in Simulated Driving (2007).http://rave.ohiolink.edu/etdc/view?acc_num=ucin1195507547
8. Matthews, G., Desmond, P.A.: Task-induced fatigue states and simulated driving performance. Q. J. Exp. Psychol. Sect. A **55**(2), 659–686 (2002). https://doi.org/10.1080/02724980143000505
9. Matthews, G.: Stress states, personality and cognitive functioning: a review of research with the Dundee Stress State Questionnaire. Pers. Individ. Differ. **169**, 110083 (2021). https://doi.org/10.1016/j.paid.2020.110083
10. Saxby, D.J., Matthews, G., Hitchcock, E.M., Warm, J.S.: Development of active and passive fatigue manipulations using a driving simulator. In: Proceedings of the Human Factors and Ergonomics Society Annual Meeting, vol. 51, no. 18, pp. 1237–1241 (2007). https://doi.org/10.1177/154193120705101839
11. Saxby, D.J., Matthews, G., Hitchcock, E.M., Warm, J.S., Funke, G.J., Gantzer, T.: Effect of Active and passive fatigue on performance using a driving simulator. In: Proceedings of the Human Factors and Ergonomics Society Annual Meeting, vol. 52, no. 21, pp. 1751–1755. (2008). https://doi.org/10.1177/154193120805202113
12. Matthews, G., Wohleber, R., Lin, J., Rose Panganiban, A.: Fatigue, automation, and autonomy: challenges for operator attention, effort, and trust. In Human Performance in Automated and Autonomous Systems, pp. 127–150. CRC Press (2019). https://doi.org/10.1201/9780429458330-7
13. Thiffault, P., Bergeron, J.: Monotony of road environment and driver fatigue: a simulator study. Accid. Anal. Prev. **35**(3), 381–391 (2003). https://doi.org/10.1016/S0001-4575(02)00014-3
14. APA American Psychological Association. APA Dictionary of Psychology. https://dictionary.apa.org
15. Matthews, G., Neubauer, C., Saxby, D.J., Wohleber, R.W., Lin, J.: Dangerous intersections? a review of studies of fatigue and distraction in the automated vehicle. Accid. Anal. Prev. **126**, 85–94 (2019). https://doi.org/10.1016/j.aap.2018.04.004
16. Schmidt, E.A., Schrauf, M., Simon, M., Fritzsche, M., Buchner, A., Kincses, W.E.: Drivers' misjudgement of vigilance state during prolonged monotonous daytime driving. Accid. Anal. Prev. **41**(5), 1087–1093 (2009). https://doi.org/10.1016/j.aap.2009.06.007
17. Yathisha, L. Aircraft controlling system using optimal controllers. In: ATMECE (2016)
18. Gil, G.-H., Kaber, D., Kaufmann, K., Kim, S.-H.: Effects of modes of cockpit automation on pilot performance and workload in a next generation flight concept of operation. Hum. Fact. Ergon. Manuf. Serv. Ind. **22**(5), 395–406 (2012). https://doi.org/10.1002/hfm.20377

19. Berry, D.: How long do pilots really spend on autopilot? (2018).https://saiblog.cranfield.ac.uk/blog/how-long-do-pilots-really-spend-on-autopilot

20. Dietrich, A.M.: Unsettled Topics in the General Aviation Autonomy Landscape (2022). https://doi.org/10.4271/EPR2022004

21. Wiener, E.L.: Human factors of advanced technology (glass cockpit) transport aircraft (1989)

22. Wohleber, R.W., et al.: The impact of automation reliability and operator fatigue on performance and reliance. In: Proceedings of the Human Factors and Ergonomics Society Annual Meeting, vol. 60, no. 1, pp. 211–215 (2016). https://doi.org/10.1177/1541931213601047

23. Bernhardt, K.A., Poltavski, D., Petros, T., Ferraro, F.R.: Differentiating active and passive fatigue with the use of electroencephalography. In: Proceedings of the Human Factors and Ergonomics Society Annual Meeting, vol. 63, no. 1, pp. 1285–1289. (2019). https://doi.org/10.1177/1071181319631106

24. Farahmand, B., Boroujerdian, A.M.: Effect of road geometry on driver fatigue in monotonous environments: a simulator study. Transport. Res. F: Traffic Psychol. Behav. **58**, 640–651 (2018). https://doi.org/10.1016/j.trf.2018.06.021

25. Wingelaar-Jagt, Y.Q., Wingelaar, T.T., Riedel, W.J., Ramaekers, J.G.: Fatigue in aviation: safety risks, preventive strategies and pharmacological interventions. Front. Physiol. **12**, 1399 (2021). https://doi.org/10.3389/fphys.2021.712628

26. Cegarra, J., Valéry, B., Avril, E., Calmettes, C., Navarro, J.: OpenMATB: a multi-attribute task battery promoting task customization, software extensibility and experiment replicability. Behav. Res. Methods **52**(5), 1980–1990 (2020). https://doi.org/10.3758/s13428-020-01364-w

27. Larue, G.S., Rakotonirainy, A., Pettitt, A.N.: Predicting driver's hypovigilance on monotonous roads: literature review. In: 1st International Conference on Driver Distraction and Inattention (2010)

28. Helton, W.S.: Validation of a short stress state questionnaire. In: Proceedings of the Human Factors and Ergonomics Society Annual Meeting, vol. 48, no. 11, pp. 1238–1242 (2004). https://doi.org/10.1177/154193120404801107

29. Helton, W.S., Näswall, K.: Short stress state questionnaire. Eur. J. Psychol. Assess. **31**(1), 20–30 (2015). https://doi.org/10.1027/1015-5759/a000200

30. Hart, S.G., Staveland, L.E. Development of NASA-TLX (Task Load Index): results of empirical and theoretical research, pp. 139–183 (1988). https://doi.org/10.1016/S0166-4115(08)62386-9

31. Miller, S.: Workload Measures Literature Review. National Advanced Driving Simulator University of Iowa (2001)

32. Bergum, B.O., Lehr, D.J.: End spurt in vigilance. J. Exp. Psychol. **66**(4), 383–385 (1963). https://doi.org/10.1037/h0044865

33. Belz, S.M., Robinson, G.S., Casali, J.G.: Temporal separation and self-rating of alertness as indicators of driver fatigue in commercial motor vehicle operators. Hum. Fact. J. Hum. Fact. Ergon. Soc. **46**(1), 154–169 (2004). https://doi.org/10.1518/hfes.46.1.154.30393

34. Caldwell, J.A., Caldwell, J.L., Brown, D.L., Smith, J.K.: The effects of 37 hours of continuous wakefulness on the physiological arousal, cognitive performance, self-reported mood, and simulator flight performance of F-117A pilots. Mil. Psychol. **16**(3), 163–181 (2004). https://doi.org/10.1207/s15327876mp1603_2

Cognitive Effort in Interaction with Software Systems for Self-regulation - An Eye-Tracking Study

Gilbert Drzyzga, Thorleif Harder(✉), and Monique Janneck

Institute for Interactive Systems, Technische Hochschule Lübeck, Lübeck, Germany
{gilbert.drzyzga,thorleif.harder,monique.janneck}@th-luebeck.de

Abstract. The importance of digital degree programs has grown increasingly in recent years, due in part to their ability to provide a personalized learning experience for students. However, degree programs in this format have higher dropout rates than traditional degree programs. In the process of a user-centered design approach, a dashboard for the online degree programs of a university network is developed to provide information and recommendations about the learning process based on descriptive analysis and machine learning (ML) methods. For this purpose, ML models are developed, trained and evaluated. The goal of the dashboard is to promote self-regulation among students and reduce dropout rates. It will be set up as a plug-in through the learning management system (LMS) Moodle exclusively for students. In order to understand which aspects are important for users in relation to the cognitive processes involved in interacting with the dashboard, an eye-tracking study was conducted using the thinking aloud technique. The goal of the study was to investigate which cognitive demands are set for the users when interacting with the prototype and how the automatically generated information is perceived. When integrating the LD into the LMS, care should be taken to ensure that all content is realized in an understandable and easy-to-follow manner, due to the fact that otherwise the effort required to focus on the content elements of the LD could become greater - and with it the cognitive requirements.

Keywords: Higher Education · Learning-Management-System · Learners Dashboard · Self-regulation · Motivation · Structuring of Feedback · Usability · User Experience

1 Introduction

The importance of digital degree programs has grown in recent years, in conjunction with the fact that they provide students with personalized learning opportunities [3, p. 17–18]. They give students the opportunity to learn largely independent of time and place and thus organize their study programs more flexibly [8, p. 50]. Most teaching materials are provided in digital form via a learning management system (LMS). However, there are higher dropout rates in degree programs in this format than in traditional degree programs [2, p. 1]. Due to physical distance, students often do not have the opportunity to learn with other fellow students or interact face-to-face with instructors. Within an LMS like Moodle, data accumulates that can be used for evaluation [9]. In the context of a user-centered design approach [5], a learner dashboard (LD) is being developed for the online degree programs of a university network, which provides descriptive analyses and evaluations of the usage behavior within the LMS and additionally information and recommendations on the learning process based on machine learning (ML) methods. For this purpose, ML models are developed, trained and evaluated [6]. The goal of the dashboard is to stimulate and promote self-regulation among students in order to reduce dropout rates in digital degree programs. It is set as a plug-in via the LMS Moodle exclusively for students, teachers will not have access to the compiled information and performed analyses.

The aim of the present study was to determine which cognitive demands are set on the users when interacting with the prototype and how the dynamically generated information for learning support is perceived. One focus was on the perception and attention of students when interacting with the dashboard. It also aimed to identify possible common problems in the interaction in the area of user interface, usability, and user experience (UX), and to gain further information about the presentation of the dashboard elements and content. The research was guided by three main research questions:

Research Questions (RQ)

RQ1: How should an LD be structured so that students are motivated to use it?
RQ2: How should the LD's learner content elements be structured so that it can promote self-regulation?
RQ3: How should LD content elements be organized in relation to cognitive demands?

This study presents the results on the research questions considering the cognitive load students feel when using the LD. Through this study, it is hoped to gain a better understanding of how students perceive the various aspects of the LD and how they interact with the LD. This should result in recommendations for the future organization of the LD. Based on the research questions, a guided interview (see Appendix) was developed to conduct the study.

2   Background

On the basis of previous studies [5], a LD is being developed that provides the information that is essential for students in a clearly arranged manner. The aim is to give students a tool with which they can validate their learning and their commitment to it – and thus self-regulate [12–17]. Self-regulated learning (SLR) is described by Pintrich [10, p. 453] as an "active, constructive process whereby learners set goals for their learning and then attempt to monitor, regulate, and control their cognition, motivation, and behavior, guided and constrained by their goals and the contextual features in the environment". With the LD set, students are able to view and reflect on what they have already achieved in an overview and in detail. There is the opportunity to define their own learning goals and to monitor them independently and self-directedly. A basic feature of the LD is that the information provided is categorized into three main views and is located at different temporal levels. Specifically, these are the overall view, the semester view, and the module view. Figure 1 shows a picture of the developed prototype. It consisted of a total of 14 different views (wireframes) with context-based modals and was presented to the participants as a clickable graphical prototype in an internet browser during the session.

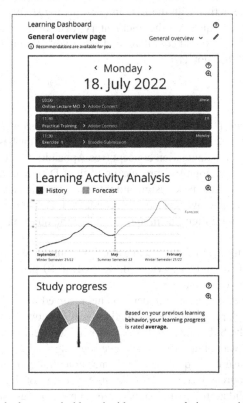

Fig. 1. Prototype of the learners dashboard with recommendations, navigation and three cards

The prototype is structured to enable students to obtain information about their learning progress on three temporal levels: The overall view provides information about the entire course of study. On the next level, the semester view, students are provided with a summary of all information on the modules they have taken in the respective semester. Finally, the module view provides all information about a specific module. The main views are always divided into areas of equal size – so-called "cards" – which differ according to the selected main view on the content level. For each of these cards, further details on the selected context can be displayed on a detail page after selection while the remaining cards are then hidden. Among other things, this is done to present the multitude of information to the students in a compact form to avoid cognitive overload [11]. In Fig. 1, the "Learning Activity Analysis" card shows an analysis of past learning progress to the left of the dashed line labeled "May" which corresponds to the current time, and the forecast based on the ML algorithm to be integrated is shown to the right.

3 Methodical Approach

In order to understand which points – in addition to the general structure and the content and navigation elements used – are important for users in relation to the cognitive processes involved in interacting with the LD, an eye-tracking study was conducted using the Thinking Aloud technique. Another elementary focus of the study was that the LD should present as little additional cognitive load as possible for the learner, otherwise it might be rejected and thus not used.

3.1 Procedure

To investigate interaction behavior, specific tasks and questions were developed for the prototype based on the research questions. They deal with both the basic layout, the structure of the content, and the navigation concept (see Appendix), focusing particularly on the comprehensibility and cognitive processing of the LD content and the content elements used. To make sure the task design and interview questions were appropriate and understandable, three qualitative pretests were conducted. Through these pre-tests, orthographic inaccuracies and difficulties in understanding the questions could be identified and resolved.

As participants students of a 4th-semester UX course were recruited. Thus, the participants already had study experienced. A total of 10 people participated in the study, including 6 women and 4 men.

At the beginning of a session, the participants received a brief introduction to the accompanying research project, the associated university network, and the purpose and procedure of the study. Subsequently, the participants' consent to the anonymous processing of their data was obtained. For the eye-tracking analysis, "Tobii Pro Glasses 3"[1] were used. To ensure the quality of the data, potential confounding factors such as extraneous light sources were avoided. At the beginning of the study, a calibration was performed to validate the participants' gaze points to ensure the highest possible accuracy of the results. Subsequently, the prototype was tested by students in approximately 20-min sessions using the provided guideline. A start and end point for the test was established and clearly announced to the subjects. The basis for the test was the prototype described in Sect. 2, implemented as a high-fidelity prototype.

Both static and dynamic stimuli were recorded during the study. For the static stimuli, dwell time and interaction in views and associated modals were measured, including fixation time for specific elements. For the dynamic stimuli, attention orientation was measured over time during interaction with the prototype [1].

---

[1] https://www.tobii.com/products/eye-trackers/wearables/tobii-pro-glasses-3.

3.2 Data Analysis

The recorded utterings of the participants were transcribed by two research assistants according to predefined transcription rules [19], the statements made by the test persons were coded on the basis of a qualitative content analysis according to Mayring [18]. For this purpose, individual categories were formed and analyzed according to the predefined transcription rules/code definitions. The interviews were first examined individually and the individual paraphrased and text passages were summarized according to the established codes. Subsequently, the uniform code system was generated and applied accordingly to all interviews. In the subsequent processing and documentation, the individual passages in the various categories were considered in an overall context.

4 Results

4.1 Eye-Tracking

Task 1: Opening the Various Higher-level Views (Overall, Semester, Module view) of the Study Program. The task was to name these higher-level views (Fig. 2), to assess whether participants understood the general structure and the information about their learning progress or were missing specific information. In addition to the objectives mentioned in the introduction, the goal was to find out if the different levels could be kept apart and if the participants felt informed by the data presented.

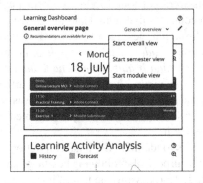

Fig. 2. Crop of the Prototype of the learners dashboard with the main navigation

The recurring and consistent structure was evaluated positively. Some test persons could name the three main views right away. For others, they were shown on the screen or emerged from the conversation with the moderators. Regarding clarity, the headlines were evaluated positively due to their size. The cards were recognized as a unit, were evaluated as not nested and showed clarity. It could be directly recognized *"[...] without thinking too much [...]"* or *"[...] reading through it at all [...]"* what it was about. It was also expressed that the information provided was intuitively recognizable. As disadvantage it was noted that the cards presented and their contents changed only slightly, creating a feeling of *"[...] always being on the same page [...]"*. Therefore, it was necessary to look in the header of the LD to see where one was located. Some indicated in this context that highlighting, for instance in color, could help. With regard to clarity, it was noted that the individual elements were too small and that it was not known *"[...] what exactly was displayed or what one had to click on [...]"*. One test person commented that it was confusing at first *"[...] due to everything changing at the same time [...]"* and then not knowing where exactly to look.

Overall, the test subjects found themselves well informed about the learning progress. It was noted that on the main view of the module view, a larger area would be desirable visualizing current activities and tasks, e.g. concrete deadlines and assignments, rather than general information on the learning process. One person commented negatively on the data preparation and found himself uninformed, due to the fact that only the system data is mapped *"[...] in the application and not at all the state of my head or my analog stuff [...]"*. As a general overview, the presentation was considered useful, while more details would be desirable. Motivating at this point could be a comparison with other students. Regarding the status it was expressed that a daily view with time spent in the LMS could help, with the possibility to compare different days and time spans. The learning activity analysis graph could be presented larger while reducing text. Some participants needed a closer look to assess which information was shown or how the information was scaled.

Regarding missing features or information, various suggestions were made, e.g. the modules one is currently enrolled in should be displayed as well as upcoming deadlines with a countdown, so that it is clear right away how much time is left until submission etc. Several elements were not found right away, for instance information about recommendations, which could be highlighted and integrated, for instance, centrally in the header of the LD or through a message or banner. The recommendations still lack *"[...] concrete values such as grades or learning points, i.e. credit points, because in the learning progress I would find it quite nice to have my total score, i.e. how many credits I need in total and how many I have now. [...]"*. Participants also suggested a possibility to enter additional data themselves, although it was also noted that this might be too much of a hassle for some students. One person noted that he/she was missing something but could not name it.

The goal of the analysis is to identify which gaze directions and areas are important for the test persons. For this purpose, the following heatmaps are showing the dwell time of the gaze over the period of processing the task. Figure 3 shows fixation and Fig. 4 shows attention. It is clear to see that the information is found where it was suspected (in the upper area of the LD). This is also where the menu items for selecting the other main views appear.

The other elements or information that should be used in this task are perceived and recognized accordingly. The test person could solve the task without much effort.

Task 2: Opening the Card for Learning Activity Analysis. In this task, it was observed if the learning activity analysis information presented was recognized or understood.

Presenting the activities in this way can be motivating for students as they can see what they have already accomplished in the LMS in the past (Fig. 5). There were problems

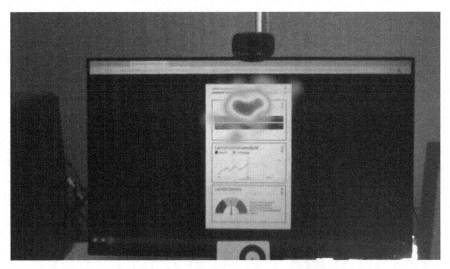

Fig. 3. Visualization heatmap fixation

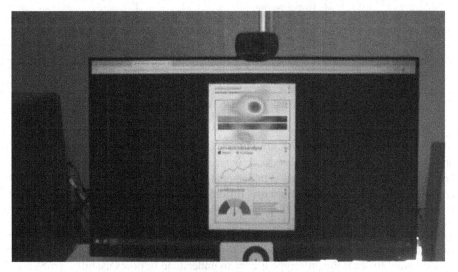

Fig. 4. Visualization heatmap attention

in the presentation related to labeling the axes and understanding the graph presented. In relation to the forecast, there were difficulties in interpreting it imminently and clearly, as well as putting what has been done in relation to what is to be expected from it (forecast). It was commented that more explanations were necessary to understand how the predictions are made – the graph and the coordinate system were viewed as too abstract. However, individually, after some consideration students recognized that actions for possible optimization of one's learning progress can result from the information presented. The cognitive demands are higher at this point, which is reflected by comments such as

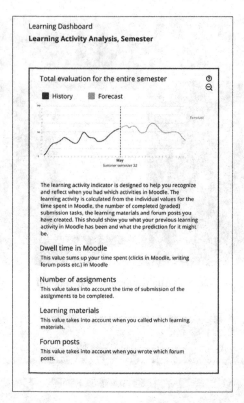

Fig. 5. Detail view of the learning activities

"Well, you can see it relatively quickly, but you still have to think a bit at the beginning." or *"[...] well, then I see the current status, but it doesn't help me personally. I think that's just too abstract for me."* In order to understand if the navigation concept of the present prototype is easy to understand and use, different aspects regarding intuitiveness were identified in the interviews (see chapter "Navigation concept").

Task 3: Editing Function: Adding or Deleting a Card. The goal of this task was to validate the navigation concept for adding/removing cards to see if there is potential for optimization; to see if the prototype is easy to understand or poses usability problems.

In Fig. 6 the process of deleting and adding cards is shown using the calendar card as an example. In step 1, the pencil icon (top right) is selected and leads to the view for deleting cards (step 2). After a card is deleted, it is removed from the LD (step 3). Adding cards works via the lower active (empty) area with the plus icon. When a card is added, the modal for adding it is opened (step 4). At this point, the user selects a card to be added to the LD. Finally, in step 5, the selected card(s) are confirmed. After that, the view shows the initial position from step 1. The test persons stated that they recognized elements from other programs or apps. For instance, the pencil icon was immediately recognized as editing function. In the next dialog, an "X" symbol was displayed at the existing cards (Fig. 6, step 2), whereby the test persons generally immediately recognized

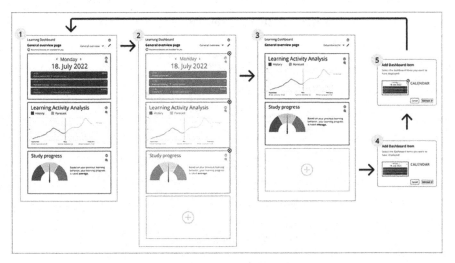

Fig. 6. Process of deleting and adding a card

that a card can be removed from the dashboard. Positive comments were made that this function was kept simple and straightforward. Due to the fact that this functionality was realized in such a way that only the essential opportunities of an editing function were made available during the interaction, the test persons rated this as positive. It was noted that the "X" icon for removing a card could also be positioned elsewhere on the card or that the entire card could be set to be clickable for removal. Among other things, the test persons commented, *"Well, the functionality is intuitive, that's self-explanatory."* Some test persons initially had difficulty recognizing that the cards were interchangeable and needed assistance. During the interviews, it became apparent that there could be an opportunity for the LD to build up gradually to be able to learn this functionality. At some points, it was noted that hints should appear if something wrong was selected by the user. The process of editing, deleting, and adding cards set challenges for some people (*"[...] I say no. One-easy this was not. [...] It's impractical because there is no such thing that tells me I have to scroll now to see this. [...] And in any case, if that's more than three, four, then you don't see the plus at all. [...]"*), this process was not easy to realize and sometimes it took more effort to solve the task.

Task 4: Opening the Help Page. Reading/Recording Content/Texts (Amongst Other Things, Opening the Help Page). The main focus was on the understandability of the help texts for the LD (Fig. 7).

The information presented about the dashboard was sufficient for the test persons, but they wished for a different format. The headline and breakdown of the help texts into individual sections, which was presented in a larger font, was positively emphasized: *"Well, I would say that the layout is quite good, due to the fact that you first look up here at the large headline and then you get general information about the cards and then you see the small sections, I wouldn't say that it's too much text."* However, there were also contrasting opinions that reading too much text is exhausting and that too much text is

Fig. 7. Modal for the help page

not read. It was suggested that instead of text, graphics could be used to explain content. Regarding the segmentation of the several text sections, if the essential information is easy to understand for the test persons it was stated: *"But this is very small! May I make it bigger? So, in that point, if you compare it with the rest of the text, of course already quite exhausting to read in the size [...]"* and that *"[...] would I break off now, due to, I would not want to read, yes exactly, it is too much text, much too small yes.".* It was suggested to summarize the texts in headings and to organize it clickable: *"If I see, ah, here so three facts, ah, that interests me, then I take me now still the minute time and then I would click again and look in. [...]".*

Task 5: Opening the Learning Progress Recommendations Page. The focus of this task was on whether the information was perceived as trustworthy and understandable enough to foster acceptance of the LD (Fig. 8). The recommendations provided will be based on descriptive user data from the LMS on the one hand and generated by machine learning methods on the other hand.

The reference to the recommendations (in the header of the LD) was overlooked by the majority of the test persons. Suggestions were made to display them more prominently (by highlighting them in color, always in the same position). The test persons commented amongst other things: *"[...] Here, for example, I think that somehow it is not really made clear that you can click on it, I think. [...]".*

In some cases, it was difficult to recognize the information at first glance. The test persons therefore needed assistance and support from the moderators. The recommendations should generally be put more in focus, for instance – due to the fact that *"[...] I personally think they help me the most – I'm pretty sure [...]".* Also, the contents of the card to the recommendations was criticized for being too small font and too much text: *"I think this little section is easy to read, the first thing. The second thing, not too much information, if I want to read multiple information now, then I'm supposed to click on something again. But this is enough here, this section, this little text, due to*

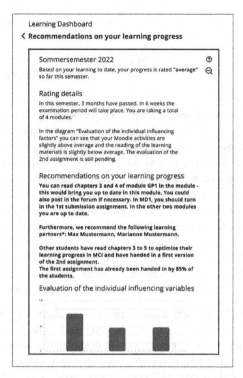

Fig. 8. Detail view for the recommendations page

myself I don't feel like reading long texts for example." Furthermore, it was noted that the concentration for long texts is not sufficient and symbols or colors might work better.

Regarding trustworthiness, test persons stated that they would trust the information, but *"[...] especially if it is below average I would panic so easily. Yes, but maybe if it is above average. I don't know. So, you always actually know better how far you are."* Students stated that they would trust the information because they know it is based on the data entered into the system – but it was not clear if they would take it to heart. There were no objections from the test persons regarding the understandability of the recommendation texts. The selected formulations could be understood.

One test person commented that they could think of using the dashboard to get direct feedback from the person mentoring the module. This could be realized for instance by a button "Request help from the teacher".

In the card with the recommendations, the section for comparison with other students was highlighted: That they can see there how other students are doing in their study program, what they have done so far in comparison, or how far they have come in the degree program or module - that would motivate them to do more themselves.

General Questions. In addition, the test persons were given some further small-scale tasks on how to use the LD to obtain information about their general perception of using and interacting with the LD.

Finding Content/Content Items and Further Assistance. The task focused on two main points: The structure of the LD, if it is understandable, simple and comprehensible or if it is perceived as too convoluted, and on whether additional help is needed. Generally, the test persons did not find the LD convoluted. In this context, it was pointed out that it was not always intuitive to use due to the fact that *"[...] everything was very small and sometimes left, sometimes right. But still, once you looked at it and looked at it once, you found it."* However, when actually integrated in the LMS, students voiced that the LD might not be prominent enough. Overall, the font size and the understandability of the navigation elements were criticized in this conjunction, for instance when opening the detailed views: *"[...] But I wouldn't have expected it to run via this plus magnifying glass. Rather, if you had clicked directly on the card."* With regard to further assistance for finding content elements, it was stated that these would not be needed.

Navigation Concept. In addition to the aspects about the use of navigation elements mentioned in the section "Editing function: adding a new card", specific more general questions about the navigation concept of the dashboard were set at the end of the session. The navigation concept is set up in such a way that the main menu is hidden in the detailed views of the cards. This was not perceived as a disadvantage as such but it was noted that an opportunity to return to the previous view could be made available instead of closing the view with the minus magnifying glass icon. The magnifying glass icon was rated as more of a disadvantage overall *"[...] how do I get back? Hm, but I can, now I realize of course, OK, I have to go back to the magnifying glass here – I had also clicked the plus magnifying glass to get in here - but I had just not remembered that at all. "*, but the meaning behind it was understood by most. Instead of the magnifying glass symbol, the opportunity of an "X" button to close in the upper right corner of a card was mentioned, the help symbol could then be placed one line lower. The help was not found right away, the test persons had to search for the symbol for the most part. Switching between the individual main views did not cause any problems. The paths to the individual content elements were primarily described as intuitive and simple *"Rather too quick to find. [...] Yes, so I think, if that is then also colorful and so. Then actually (...) it's all good to find. Yes, it is. "* The breakdown of the various contents in the cards was also rated primarily positively.

4.2 User Experience Questionnaire (UEQ-S)

As a follow-up to the eye-tracking study, participants rated the usability of the prototype using the short version of the User Experience Questionnaire (UEQ-S) [7]. The pragmatic quality – which describes usability criteria such as reliability, clarity, and efficiency – was rated above average with $M = 1.55$ and thus confirmed the general interaction concept of the dashboard prototype (Fig. 9). In contrast, hedonic quality – which evaluates UX features such as novelty and stimulation – was rated below-average with M = -0.25, which is probably due to the fact that only wireframes were used for the prototype [4]. Therefore, special attention will be paid to user experience when developing further prototypes of the dashboard.

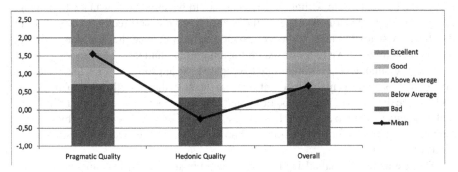

Fig. 9. Benchmark of the evaluated Prototype

5 Summary and Conclusion

The study was segmented into two units: In the first unit, the prototype was evaluated using five concrete tasks and a general section with higher-level questions about LD using an eye-tracking study with Thinking Aloud technique. In the second unit, the prototype was evaluated using the UEQ-S. Here, the five tasks aimed to investigate the cognitive load when operating the LD. The general questions were intended to provide insights into what learners' perceptions were when using the LD.

In relation to RQ1, the results show that learners are motivated to use the LD when it is intuitive to use and the content is easy to understand. The recommendations on learning progress, the calendar with upcoming deadlines, the analysis of learning activities, and the assessment of learning progress can help learners to keep track of their own learning progress when organizing their study programs. With these opportunities, learners are motivated to use the LD to validate and reflect on their learning, which is a key aspect of self-regulated learning [14]. The semester view and module view also provide learners with more detailed information about their current learning progress. It was positively highlighted that they can access this information when needed. The opportunity to compare themselves with other students was particularly emphasized. These results on RQ2 reflect that these opportunities can support students' self-regulation due to the fact that they can find out about their learning progress and process at any time. As a result, they are motivated to engage with the learning content. RQ3 showed that a wide variety of factors play a role, both in terms of content and structure. With regard to the structure of the LD, there were no negative opinions concerning the presentation of the individual cards on the learning progress and process of the learners. On the basis of the navigation it was shown that a coherent navigation concept has to be used. It was shown that known navigation elements lead to a reduction of cognitive effort. For instance, a detailed view of a card can be called up by clicking directly on it instead of using a magnifying glass icon. In this context it was shown that if own navigation elements are used, they should be repeated in the same way. For instance, in the LD prototype used, the plus icon was used to open the detail view, so when closing the detail view, the opposite should be used, in this case a minus magnifying glass icon. Overall, care should be taken to generate as few clicks as possible within the LD. This could be solved for instance by having a navigation bar (breadcrumb) to get to the next higher view or directly to the start of the dashboard. Contextual help in the LD can additionally reduce the load due to the fact that learners do not have to try or search for unfamiliar elements.

On the content level, it is important to prepare texts appropriately, i.e. that the textual information is made available in a font size and quantity that is well suited to the content - a font size that is too small can be tiring and lead to learners not reading it or having to make too much effort to absorb it. It can be beneficial if the text is supported by symbolic language or graphics for explanations and notes. The texts used were understandable in terms of content.

The results reflect that a LD must be prepared in such a way that students are motivated to use it. Therefore, it must be simple in its structure and navigation and not present additional challenges to use. At the content level, care must be taken to ensure that the formulations are understandable and motivating so that learning progress information can be absorbed without difficulty; this applies in particular to the font size and the amount of text.

6 Outlook

The study has shown that several aspects can contribute to the cognitive load of using a software system and their reduction will be considered in the further development of the LD. In addition to the identified issues, other interaction problems have been encountered. These relate in particular to the interruption of activities and partially inconsistent user control. The clickable prototype will be further developed based on the findings and additional evaluations (amongst other things focus group discussions, workshops & user tests) are planned for the coming months. Optional data input for non-existing data (e.g. additional learning effort outside the LMS) should be considered. However, this function should not overburden the students additionally and would still have to be tested accordingly.

Acknowledgements. This work was funded by the German Federal Ministry of Education, grant No. 01PX21001B.

Appendix

Procedure and questions for the usability test.

- **START**

    - **Task: open the different higher-level views on the study program.**

        - Which ones are there?

- How clear do you find the different views?
- Do you feel informed about your learning progress respectively about your current status in the study program?
- Are you missing any information? If yes, which one?

- **Task: Add a new card.**

  - How explanatory/intuitive do you find the handling of this functionality?

- **Task: Open the help page.**

  - Is the content understandable for you?
  - Is all essential information evident to you?

- **Task: Open the page with the recommendations on your learning progress**

  - Would you trust the information/recommendations displayed?

- **END**

  GENERAL QUESTIONS ABOUT THE LOW-FIDELITY PROTOTYPE

- How did you perceive the individual content elements? Rather nested or more intuitive/quicker to find?
- How easy was it to be able to go back to the beginning?
- Did you find the interaction elements well labeled?
- Did you find the navigation elements easy to understand?
- Did you know your position within the Learning Dashboard at all times?
- Did you miss the drop-down menu to overall, semester, and module views in the subviews?
- Do you need more help with the dashboard?

References

1. Carter, B.T., Luke, S.G.: Best practices in eye tracking research. Int. J. Psychophysiol. **155**, 49–62 (2020)
2. Diaz, D.P.: Online drop rates revisited. Technol. Sour. **3**(3), 35–51 (2002)
3. Getto, B., Hintze, P., Kerres, M.: (Wie) Kann Digitalisierung zur Hochschulentwicklung beitragen?, pp. 13–25 (2018)
4. Hassenzahl, M.: The hedonic/pragmatic model of user experience. Towards UX Manifesto **10**, 2007 (2007)
5. Drzyzga, G., Harder, T.: Student-centered development of an online software tool to provide learning support feedback: a design-study approach. In: Proceedings of the 6th International Conference on Computer-Human Interaction Research and Applications, Valletta, Malta, 27–28 October 2022, pp. 244–248. SCITEPRESS - Science and Technology Publications (2022)

6. Janneck, M., Merceron, A., Sauer, P.: Workshop on addressing dropout rates in higher education, online – everywhere. In Companion Proceedings of the 11th Learning Analytics and Knowledge Conference (LAK 2021), pp. 261–269 (2021)
7. Schrepp, M., Hinderks, A., Thomaschewski, J.: Design and evaluation of a short version of the user experience questionnaire (UEQ-S). Int. J. Interact. Multimedia Artif. Intell. 4(6), 103–108 (2017)
8. Wannemacher, K., Jungermann, I., Scholz, J., Tercanli, H., von Villiez, A.: Digitale Lernszenarien im Hochschulbereich (2016)
9. Keller, B., Baleis, J., Starke, C., Marcinkowski, F.: Machine learning and artificial intelligence in higher education: a state-of-the-art report on the German University landscape. Heinrich-Heine-Universität Düsseldorf, pp. 1–31 (2019)
10. Pintrich, P.R.: The role of goal orientation in self-regulated learning. In: Handbook of Self-Regulation, pp. 451–502. Academic Press (2000)
11. Paas, F., Renkl, A., Sweller, J.: Cognitive load theory and instructional design: Recent developments. Educ. Psychol. 38(1), 1–4 (2003)
12. Matcha, W., Uzir, N.A., Gasevic, D., Pardo, A.: A systematic review of empirical studies on learning analytics dashboards: a self-regulated learning perspective. IEEE Trans. Learn. Technol. 13(2), 226–245 (2020). https://doi.org/10.1109/TLT.2019.2916802
13. Chen, L., Lu, M., Goda, Y., Yamada, M.: Design of learning analytics dashboard supporting metacognition, pp. 175–182 (2019). https://doi.org/10.33965/celda2019_201911L022
14. Corrin, L., de Barba, P.: How do students interpret feedback delivered via dashboards?, pp. 430–431 (2015). https://doi.org/10.1145/2723576.2723662
15. Corrin, Linda; de Barba, Paula: Exploring students' interpretation of feedback delivered through learning analytics dashboards (2014). https://www.researchgate.net/profile/Paula-De-Barba/publication/271769111_Exploring_students%27_interpretation_of_feedback_delivered_through_learning_analytics_dashboards/links/54d14ed20cf25ba0f0411598/Exploring-students-interpretation-of-feedback-delivered-through-learning-analytics-dashboards.pdf. Accessed 18 June 2021
16. Farahmand, A., Dewan, M.A.A., Lin, F.: Student-facing educational dashboard design for online learners, pp. 345–349 (2020). https://doi.org/10.1109/DASC-PICom-CBDCom-CyberSciTech49142.2020.00067
17. Schumacher, C., Ifenthaler, D.: Features students really expect from learning analytics. Comput. Hum. Behav. 78, 397–407 (2018). https://doi.org/10.1016/j.chb.2017.06.030
18. Mayring, P.: Qualitative content analysis: demarcation, varieties, developments [30 paragraphs]. Forum Qualitative Sozialforschung/Forum Qual. Soc. Res. 20(3), Art. 16 (2020). https://doi.org/10.17169/fqs-20.3.3343
19. Rädiker, S., Kuckartz, U.: Audio- und Videoaufnahmen transkribieren. In: Analyse qualitativer Daten mit MAXQDA. Springer VS, Wiesbaden (2019). https://doi.org/10.1007/978-3-658-22095-2_4

Comparison of Two Methods for Altering the Appearance of Interviewers: Analysis of Multiple Biosignals

Ziting Gong and Hideaki Kanai[(✉)]

Japan Advanced Institute of Science and Technology, 1-1 Asahidai,
Nomi, Ishikawa 923-1292, Japan
s2120015@jaist.ac.jp, hideaki@acm.org

Abstract. This study uses a simulation of an actual video interview to compare the effects of acquaintance and animated character scenes as interviewers on participants' mental stress and perceptions. The acquaintance group tended to have lower anxiety levels in the self-state anxiety assessment and in the change in nasal tip temperature during the anticipation and presentation phases. Furthermore, the results of eye movements during the presentation showed that the acquaintance group paid more attention to the interviewer and perceived the interviewer with a higher frequency than the animated character group. In addition, we used the functional Near-Infrared Spectroscopy (fNIRS) technique to explore the effects of interview stress on brain activity. The stranger group tended to increase cerebral blood flow in both the left and right prefrontal cortices of the participants within 4 s of meeting the interviewer on the screen. This result may be related to mental stress, which promotes the brain's regulatory function.

Keywords: video interview · fNIRS · mental stress

1 Introduction

Low-cost and convenient video chats are indispensable communication tools. Vision plays a significant role in the formalization of human's perception of things and people [22]. For example, the appearance of an avatar in VR influences the emotions and behaviors of the user. This phenomenon is known as the Proteus Effect [25]. Furthermore, in collaborative virtual environments (CVEs), the avatar's appearance influences the emotions and behaviors of the other participants [18]. The video interview format offers the possibility of changing not only our appearances but also the appearances of other participants shown on the screen. Seeing friends' faces helps the user achieve a deeper level of calm and comfort in a natural setting [17]. Using voice assistants from friends and family increases users' engagement and persuasion [6]. Inspired by their work, we proposed replacing the interviewer's image on the participant's screen with

ⓒ The Author(s), under exclusive license to Springer Nature Switzerland AG 2023
D. Harris and W.-C. Li (Eds.): HCII 2023, LNAI 14017, pp. 53–64, 2023.
https://doi.org/10.1007/978-3-031-35392-5_4

that of a familiar person in a video interview. We explored whether this method could alleviate mental stress to improve the participant's performance. In the preliminary survey, we found that the participants had high expectations of the avatar approach, using animated characters to reduce stress. Therefore, we also set up another experimental condition that replaced the interviewer's image with an animated character to compare with our proposed method for investigating the effects of multiple biosignals on the emotions and visual behaviors of participants.

Thermal infrared imaging (TII) is a non-contact technique for measuring the temperature distribution based on the amount of infrared energy emitted from an object. Studies have shown that decreases in human nose temperature are related to stress and tension [11,14,27]. Therefore, we used a thermal infrared camera to measure the change in temperature of the participant's nose during the interview to speculate on changes in the tension of participants.

Eye tracking is a technology that uses sensors to track a user's visual behavior in real time. Eye movement has been found to have a robust relationship with cognitive behavior [13]. Therefore, our experiment captured information on the eye tracking of participants to infer their perception and interaction with the interviewer during the presentation.

fNIRS is a non-invasive, non-ionizing optical imaging technique that measures hemodynamic changes associated with brain activity [4,12,19,26]. Because it is portable and insensitive to bodily movements, fNIRS is widely used in many fields, such as psychology. The prefrontal cortex (PFC) is a brain region critical for regulating thoughts, behaviors, and emotions [2]. Excessive exercise causes a significant increase in oxygen concentration [10]. The stress of mental arithmetic also increases the change in oxygen-hemoglobin (oxy-Hb) concentration in the bilateral PFC [23]. However, it is still unclear whether mental stress caused by the interview affects the changes in cerebral blood flow. In this study, we used the fNIRS device (HOT-2000) to observe the changes in cerebral blood flow during the presentation in video interviews under different conditions (stranger, acquaintance, and animated character interviewer groups).

In summary, this study focused on the impact of the two methods on users' emotions and perceptions during an interview by analyzing biological signals. In addition, total hemoglobin concentration in the PFC was used as an indicator to explore the effects of interview stress on brain activity. We propose two hypotheses to achieve the above goals:

- Participants in the acquaintance interviewer group showed lower levels of anxiety and higher perceptions of the interviewer than those in the other two groups. This means that the participants in the acquaintance group had the smallest decrease in nasal temperature during presentation. Moreover, their visual attention was focused more on the interviewer.
- The stress caused by the interviewer can be observed through changes in the cerebral blood flow. This indicates that there was more brain activity and a change in cerebral blood flow when the interviewer was seen.

2 Methodology

2.1 Participants

Twenty-one participants (10 females and 11 males, average age:25.3 years old) from the Japan Advanced Institute of Science and Technology participated in our experiment. All participants had experience with video interviews and were randomly assigned to either the control group (stranger group) or one of the experimental groups (acquaintance group, animated character group). Each participant received an honorarium of 1,000 yen.

2.2 Experimental Design

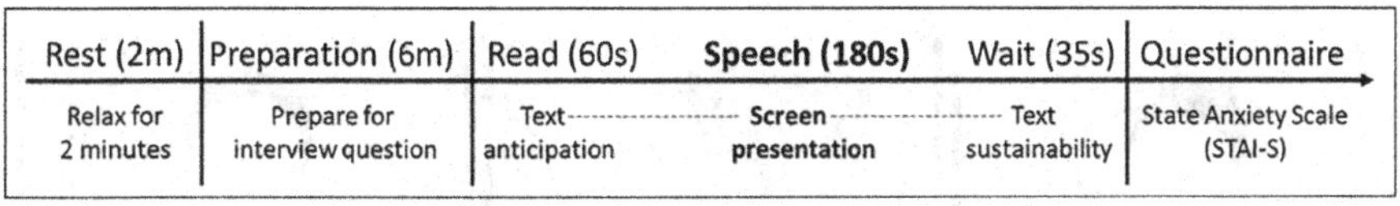

Rest (2m)	Preparation (6m)	Read (60s)	Speech (180s)	Wait (35s)	Questionnaire
Relax for 2 minutes	Prepare for interview question	Text --------- anticipation	Screen --------- presentation	Text --------- sustainability	State Anxiety Scale (STAI-S)

Fig. 1. Flow of Experiment.

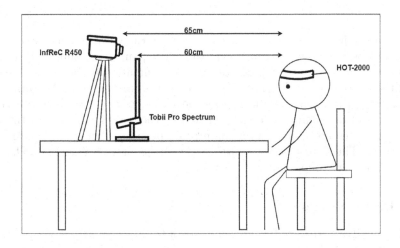

Fig. 2. Layout of the experimental room.

The flow of the experiment is shown in Fig. 1 and the layout of the experimental room is shown in Fig. 2. After understanding the contents of the experiment and becoming acquainted with the procedure, the subjects signed the consent forms. Subsequently, they began using the device (HOT-2000) and adapting to it. The participants had two minutes to close their eyes and relax in a comfortable sitting position, and six minutes to prepare for the interview questions. The interview question required the participants to present a three-minute presentation on their strengths and weaknesses. After calibrating the Tobii Pro Spectrum and informing the participants of the experimental conditions, the implementer exited the room. The participants completed the following tasks according to the different scenes independently:

1. Reading task: 1 min to read the content (experimental procedure) shown on the screen.
2. Speech task: When the interviewer appears, 3 min to present to the interviewer.
3. Wait task: 35 s to wait for the implementer to return to the room.

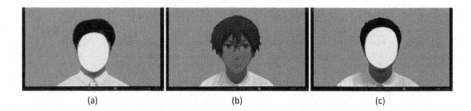

(a)   (b)   (c)

Fig. 3. Screenshots of the monitor.

A realistic interview scenario was set up using the video conference software Webex (https://www.webex.com), and the participants were informed that the interviewer would rate their presentation. The animated character was created using the anime style in Lens Studio[1]. The open-source software Avatarify was used to give the people in the images natural movement [1]. Figure 3 shows screenshots of the computer monitor viewed by the participants during the presentation. Faces are painted over for privacy purposes, but are visible in the experiment. The display screen shows (a) The acquaintance group, (b) The animated character group, and (c) The stranger group.

2.3   Data Collection

STAI State Trait Anxiety Inventor consists of the state anxiety scale (STAI-S), which measures feelings in the present moment, and the trait anxiety scale, which measures general feelings [5]. Higher scores indicate higher levels of anxiety. In our experiment, items from the STAI-S were used to express the current feelings of the participants after completing the presentation. The STAI-S showed solid internal consistency in a previous study [9].

---

[1] Snap Inc.

Infrared Thermal Imaging Camera. At a distance of 1 m from the participants, InfReC R450[2] sampling at 1 frames/s was used to capture facial temperatures. This device has a 480 × 360 pixel array detector. The sensor has a spectral sensitivity ranging from 8 to 14 um. The blackbody was calibrated before recording. The nasal region-of-interest (ROI) was automatically tracked using the open-source project TIPA [7].

Eye Tracking. Tobii Pro Spectrum[3] was used to capture the visual behavior of the participants. Calibration was performed before recording. The live Webex screen was presented by a screen-recording stimulus, and the data were collected in Tobii Studio sampling 25 Hz. The default Tobii I-VT fixation filter was used to detect fixations and saccades.

fNIRS. We used HOT-2000[4], a portable head-mounted device, to measure cerebral blood flow changes. This device has two source-detector (SD) pairs located 1 and 3 cm from the source on the left and right sides of the device, respectively. The device emitted a single wavelength of infrared light (800 nm) and samples 10 Hz. The 3 cm SD is a long separation detector, and its signal reflects blood flow changes associated with neural activity. The 1 cm SD is a short separation detector, which is used to remove scalp contamination from the brain signal measured by 3 cm SD [24].

In HOMER 3 [16], an open-source toolbox from MATLAB[5], we use the general linear model (GLM) with temporally embedded canonical correlation analysis (tCCA) in our data processing to calculate brain activity [19]. The function hmrR_PruneChannels is used to prune bad channels. The raw light intensity signal was converted to optical density using the function hmrR_Intensity2OD. Bandpass filters (functions: hmrR_BandpassFilt: Bandpass_Filter_OpticalDensity, hmrR_BandpassFilt: Bandpass_Filter_Auxilary) are applied to filter the channel data and auxiliary data. The optical density was converted to the total hemoglobin (HbT) concentration using the function hmrR_OD2Conc. Auxiliary data and short separation are used to establish the optimal regressors (function: hmrR_tCCA), and the function hmrR_GLM is applied to observe changes after the event occurred.

3 Results

3.1 Results of Self-Assessment Questionnaires

The results of the STAI-S for the current state of anxiety are shown in Fig. 4. The acquaintance group (average score:39.3) had a more compact distribution of scores and a lower overall score compared to the animated character group

---

[2] Nippon Avionics Co., Ltd.
[3] Tobii Technology Inc.
[4] NeU Crop.
[5] Mathworks.

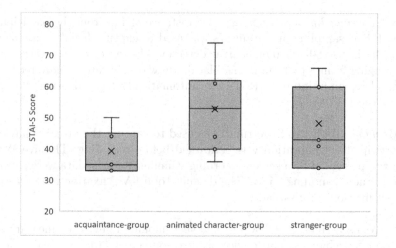

Fig. 4. Result of STAI-S score.

(average score:52.9) and the stranger group (average score:48.3). Higher scores indicate higher anxiety levels in the participants [9]. The results showed a trend towards lower anxiety levels in the acquaintance group than in the animated character and stranger groups.

3.2 Results of Biosignals

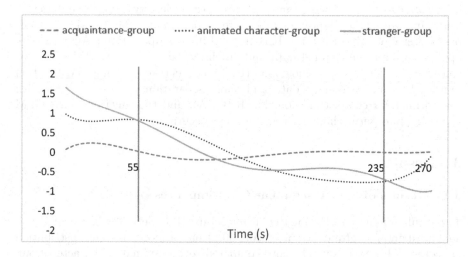

Fig. 5. Change in nose tip temperature.

For the temperature changes of the nose tip, we performed feature scaling (z-score normalization) and polynomials to observe the trend across the timeline.

The results show the trend graphs for the 55 s of the reading task (removal of the first 5 s of reaction time), 180 s of the speech, and the 35 s of the quiet waiting data in the three groups, as shown in Fig. 5. Changes in nose tip temperature have been found to be reliable indicators of stress, with lower temperatures associated with higher stress [11,14,27].

The results of the reading task showed a more pronounced downward trend in the stranger group, which could be explained by the experimental condition informed before the reading task: the stranger interviewer condition was more mentally stressful for participants than the other conditions. In the speech task, we observed that the change in temperature on the nose tip in the acquaintance group was minimal. Midway through the presentation, the animated character group's nasal temperature dropped significantly, which may be related to the difficulty in capturing feedback from the animated character, as described in the comments. In addition, the temperature in the stranger group tended to decrease after the presentation. This result suggests that the experimental conditions also influenced the participants' emotional adjustment afterward, that is, the tension was maintained longer in the stranger group.

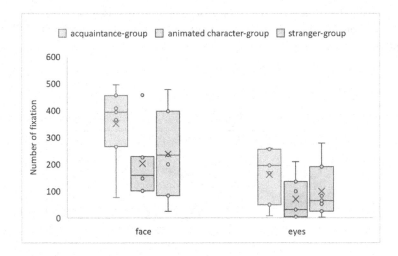

Fig. 6. Number of fixations in AOIs.

For eye movements in areas of interest (AOIs: interviewer's face and eyes) during the speech task, Figs. 6 and 7 show the results for the number and total duration of fixations. Human perception of others diminishes when they are under tension [8,9]. Eye gaze is also an important cue in the interaction; looking directly at the audience makes the speaker appear more convincing and confident [3,15]. Therefore, we chose the interviewer's face and eyes as our AOIs. The results showed that the proposed method influenced the visual behavior of the

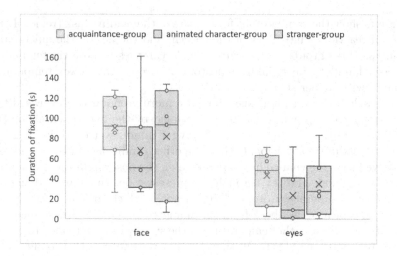

Fig. 7. Total duration of fixations in AOIs.

participants, which means that the participants in the acquaintance group paid more attention to the interviewer and perceived the interviewer with a higher frequency.

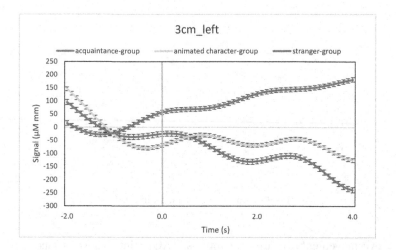

Fig. 8. Neural response time course - left forehead region.

For the average relative hemoglobin concentration, we observed cerebral blood flow activity within 4 s when meeting the interviewer initially ($t = 0$), and the results are shown in Figs. 8 and 9. There was an increase in relative blood flow in the stranger group. This indicates that cerebral blood flow in the PFC

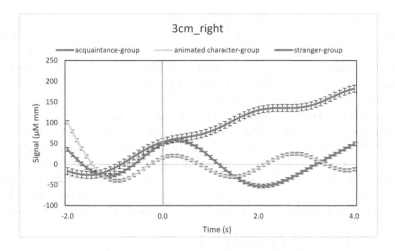

Fig. 9. Neural response time course - right forehead region.

region was activated after meeting the interviewer in the stranger group. Previous studies have shown that the regulation of mental stress in the PFC leads to an increase in cerebral blood flow in this region [23]. In the stranger group, there was a trend of increasing change in cerebral blood flow from 2 s in the anticipation phase to 4 s after meeting the interviewer, but not in the acquaintance and animated character groups. This means that only participants in the stranger group experienced increased anxiety when meeting the interviewer, and the result is consistent with changes in nasal skin temperature over the same period.

4 Discussion

In this study, we compared the effects of the proposed method (acquaintance interviewer) and avatar method (animated character interviewer) on users' emotions and perceptions during the interview by analyzing biological signals and self-evaluation. STAI-S scores were lower in the acquaintance group, implying that participants in the acquaintance group had lower levels of anxiety in their self-evaluation. For the temperature of the nose tip, the changes in the acquaintance group were minor in the speech task compared to the other groups. We chose the interviewer's face and eyes as the AOIs to observe the visual behavior of the participants. The acquaintance group had more gaze counts and longer durations of AOIs than did the animated character group. This result implies that participants from the acquaintance group tended to have lower levels of anxiety and higher perceptions of the interviewer during the presentation than the other two groups.

In this study, we used the HOT-2000 device to investigate whether interview stress affects changes in the total hemoglobin concentration. The average change in cerebral blood flow in the PFC showed an increase on both sides within 4 s of meeting the interviewer only in the stranger group, which means that the brain's function of regulating stress was only activated in the stranger group. The result is consistent with changes in nasal skin temperature over the same period, that is, there was no significant change in nasal tip temperature in the acquaintance and animated character groups around the time of meeting the interviewer, and there was a decreasing trend only in the stranger group.

Anxiety is considered a product of the person (i.e., trait) and situation (i.e., state) [20, 21]. There was a wide range of data distribution in the stranger group, both in terms of ratings of self-state anxiety and biological signals of visual behavior. This result may have been caused by differences in the participants' traits. However, the differences in traits did not result in the dispersion of data in the acquaintance group, which is another feature of the proposed methodology.

Limitations. First, due to the small sample size of the data in this experiment, we did not perform meaningful difference calculations. Therefore, the results of this experiment can only represent possible trends and not significant differences. In future work, we plan to collect data from more participants to demonstrate whether the differences between the groups are significant. We found that the infrared light from the Tobii Pro Spectrum may affect the detector's data in the HOT-2000 device, therefore, we will use Tobii Pro Glasses 3[6] to obtain the participant's eye movement in future experiments. Furthermore, we will analyze the impact of the proposed method on speech performance through subjective (self-evaluation, other evaluation) and objective evaluation (annotation of text content).

Ethics Committee Approval. This research was approved by the Japan Advanced Institute of Science and Technology Life Sciences Committee.

Acknowledgements. We are very grateful to Mr. Teru KAWAKITA for his guidance on the experimental design and to Mr. KECHENG LAI for his advice on the analysis of fNIRS data. We would like to thank Editage (https://www.editage.com/) for English language editing.

References

1. Alievk: Alievk/avatarify-desktop: Successor of avatarify python. https://github.com/alievk/avatarify-desktop
2. Arnsten, A.F.: Stress signalling pathways that impair prefrontal cortex structure and function. Nat. Rev. Neurosci. **10**(6), 410–422 (2009)
3. Bailenson, J.N., Beall, A.C.: Transformed social interaction: exploring the digital plasticity of avatars. In: Avatars at Work and Play: Collaboration and Interaction in Shared Virtual Environments, pp. 1–16 (2006)
4. Boas, D.A., Elwell, C.E., Ferrari, M., Taga, G.: Twenty years of functional near-infrared spectroscopy: introduction for the special issue (2014)

---

[6] Tobii Technology Inc.

5. CD, S.: State-trait anxiety inventory. A comprehensive bibliography (1983)
6. Chan, S.W., Gunasekaran, T.S., Pai, Y.S., Zhang, H., Nanayakkara, S.: Kinvoices: using voices of friends and family in voice interfaces. Proc. ACM Hum.-Comput. Interact. **5**(CSCW2), 1–25 (2021)
7. Cho, Y., Bianchi-Berthouze, N.: Physiological and affective computing through thermal imaging: a survey. arXiv preprint arXiv:1908.10307 (2019)
8. Clark, D.M., Wells, A.: A cognitive model of social phobia. Social phobia: Diagnosis, assessment, and treatment (1995)
9. Craven, M.: Effects of self-focused attention and fear of evaluation on anxiety and perception of speech performance. Ph.D. thesis, Ohio university (2015)
10. De Wachter, J., et al.: Prefrontal cortex oxygenation during endurance performance: a systematic review of functional near-infrared spectroscopy studies. Front. Physiol., 1834 (2021)
11. Engert, V., Merla, A., Grant, J.A., Cardone, D., Tusche, A., Singer, T.: Exploring the use of thermal infrared imaging in human stress research. PloS One **9**(3), e90782 (2014)
12. Ferrari, M., Quaresima, V.: A brief review on the history of human functional near-infrared spectroscopy (fnirs) development and fields of application. Neuroimage **63**(2), 921–935 (2012)
13. Ghanbari, L., Wang, C., Jeon, H.W.: Industrial energy assessment training effectiveness evaluation: An eye-tracking study. Sensors **21**(5), 1584 (2021)
14. Giannakakis, G., Grigoriadis, D., Giannakaki, K., Simantiraki, O., Roniotis, A., Tsiknakis, M.: Review on psychological stress detection using biosignals. IEEE Trans. Affect. Comput. **13**(1), 440–460 (2019)
15. Goldman, M.: Effect of eye contact and distance on the verbal reinforcement of attitude. J. Soc. Psychol. **111**(1), 73–78 (1980)
16. Huppert, T.J., Diamond, S.G., Franceschini, M.A., Boas, D.A.: Homer: a review of time-series analysis methods for near-infrared spectroscopy of the brain. Appl. Opt. **48**(10), D280–D298 (2009)
17. Kaur, A., Smith, C.E., Terveen, L.: Sway together, stay together: visualizing spiritual support networks through the soulgarden prototype. In: Companion Publication of the 2021 Conference on Computer Supported Cooperative Work and Social Computing, pp. 84–88 (2021)
18. Kocur, M., Schauhuber, P., Schwind, V., Wolff, C., Henze, N.: The effects of self- and external perception of avatars on cognitive task performance in virtual reality. In: 26th ACM Symposium on Virtual Reality Software and Technology, pp. 1–11 (2020)
19. von Lühmann, A., Li, X., Müller, K.R., Boas, D.A., Yücel, M.A.: Improved physiological noise regression in fnirs: a multimodal extension of the general linear model using temporally embedded canonical correlation analysis. NeuroImage **208**, 116472 (2020)
20. Martens, R., Vealey, R.S., Burton, D.: Competitive anxiety in sport. Human kinetics (1990)
21. McCarthy, J., Goffin, R.: Measuring job interview anxiety: beyond weak knees and sweaty palms. Pers. Psychol. **57**(3), 607–637 (2004)
22. Mehrabian, A.: Nonverbal betrayal of feeling. J. Exp. Res. Pers. **5**, 64–73 (1971)
23. Murayama, Y., Hu, L., Sakatani, K.: Relation between prefrontal cortex activity and respiratory rate during mental stress tasks: a near-infrared spectroscopic study. In: Luo, Q., Li, L.Z., Harrison, D.K., Shi, H., Bruley, D.F. (eds.) Oxygen Transport to Tissue XXXVIII. AEMB, vol. 923, pp. 209–214. Springer, Cham (2016). https://doi.org/10.1007/978-3-319-38810-6_28

24. Nozawa, T., Sasaki, Y., Sakaki, K., Yokoyama, R., Kawashima, R.: Interpersonal frontopolar neural synchronization in group communication: an exploration toward fnirs hyperscanning of natural interactions. Neuroimage **133**, 484–497 (2016)
25. Tang, X., Liu, Q., Cai, F., Tian, H., Shi, X., Tang, S.: Prevalence of social anxiety disorder and symptoms among chinese children, adolescents and young adults: a systematic review and meta-analysis. Front. Psychol. **13** (2022)
26. Villringer, A., Chance, B.: Non-invasive optical spectroscopy and imaging of human brain function. Trends Neurosci. **20**(10), 435–442 (1997)
27. Vinkers, C.H., et al.: The effect of stress on core and peripheral body temperature in humans. Stress **16**(5), 520–530 (2013)

Don't Think Twice, It's All Right? – An Examination of Commonly Used EEG Indices and Their Sensitivity to Mental Workload

Anneke Hamann$^{(\boxtimes)}$ ⓘ and Nils Carstengerdes ⓘ

Deutsches Zentrum für Luft- und Raumfahrt e.V. (DLR), Institut für Flugführung,
Lilienthalplatz 7, 38108 Braunschweig, Germany
anneke.hamann@dlr.de

Abstract. Physiological monitoring of the operator's current state has gained much attention in aviation research, especially for the development of adaptive assistance systems. In order to tailor the assistance to the human operator's current needs, these systems need to be informed about their operator's state. Physiological data can provide such information objectively, continuously and almost in real-time. Using electroencephalography (EEG) band power analyses, changing cortical activation can be detected and inferences about cognitive states drawn. In addition, the combination of band powers into indices is sometimes used to enhance sensitivity. In the current work, we compared the sensitivity of two indices commonly used for mental workload (MWL) assessment, the Task Load Index (TLI) and the Engagement Index (EI), against each other and with single band powers. We computed the TLI and EI from the datasets of two flight simulator studies that induced MWL while controlling for mental fatigue (MF) ($N = 35$) and vice versa ($N = 31$). We hypothesized that both TLI and EI would increase with MWL, but would not vary with MF. Additionally, according to the literature, TLI and EI should be more sensitive to changes in MWL than single bands. The TLI increased with increasing MWL, but proved less sensitive than theta band power alone. It did not vary with increasing MF. The EI did not vary with MWL, but decreased slightly with MF. We conclude that the usefulness and sensitivity of EEG indices is not universal, but varies considerably across studies and most likely experimental tasks. Therefore, the choice of an EEG feature should be made carefully. Especially in automated systems developed to monitor the operator's state, EEG features should not be used blindly as a seemingly valid data source, but always empirically validated with respect to their sensitivity.

Keywords: EEG · mental workload · physiological monitoring

1 Introduction

In aviation, there has always been a trend towards higher levels of automation. Right from the beginning of powered flight, there have been approaches to automate functions in order to decrease the demand that is put on the pilot. From simple stabilization mechanisms that controlled roll and pitch of the aircraft to automated approaches and landings using an Instrument Landing System (ILS) to fly-by-wire systems that keep the aircraft within its safe operation envelope, this trend has continued all throughout the 20th and 21st century [1, 2]. Today, research and industry work on even more advanced systems that can adapt flexibly to the situation or the needs of the pilot. Such adaptive or even artificial-intelligence based systems could one day replace the co-pilot and enable so-called single pilot operations [2].

Even with the help of automation, flying an aircraft is still a complex, cognitively demanding task. Cognitive resources, however, are limited and pose a boundary to the pilot's capabilities [3]. The extent to which the cognitive resources are occupied by the task is defined as mental workload (MWL) [4]. An easy task that does not require many resources elicits only low MWL, whereas a difficult task elicits higher levels of MWL. Both extremes should be avoided to ensure optimal performance [5]: Too high MWL will drain the limited cognitive resources and lead to performance decline and errors. Too low MWL, on the other hand, will lead to boredom and distraction, and will negatively impact performance just as well. Besides MWL, other factors such as mental fatigue (MF) can have an impact on the pilot's performance. MF results from long periods of task execution, and is characterized by reduced alertness and the unwillingness to expend further effort [6]. If not counteracted in time, MF can transition into sleepiness.

An adaptive or intelligent assistance system could help to keep the pilot's MWL at an optimal level, and could intervene before MF increases to an unwanted extent. The assistance system could for example relieve the pilot of some tasks if they are overloaded, or ask them to take a break and take over completely. It could also give tasks back to manual control if the pilot is underloaded and in danger of getting too distracted. However, there is one problem that still needs to be solved. In order to accurately tailor the assistance to the pilot's current needs, the system needs to be informed about their state. Ideally, this information is valid, objective and available in (near-) real-time. Physiological measurement can provide such data – provided that the measures used are indeed valid indications of the pilot's state.

Especially for cognitive factors such as MWL, electroencephalography (EEG) has been the physiological assessment method of choice [7, 8]. EEG records the electrical activity of the brain via electrodes placed on the scalp. From these raw data, information about the frequencies present in the signal can be extracted. Different frequency bands have been defined and associated with different brain functions and cortical activity (from low to high: delta, theta, alpha, beta, and gamma frequencies). By performing spectral analyses on the gathered data and comparing the composition of the EEG signal between tasks or to a baseline measurement, conclusions can be drawn to the changing cortical activation and cognitive states. For example, increasing MWL usually results in increasing activity in the theta band at frontal cortical areas [9–11], and decreasing activity in the alpha and beta bands at parietal areas [12, 13]. Unfortunately, brain activity is complex and the frequencies captured by the EEG are mere approximations of the underlying processes. Moreover, different frequency bands are associated with more than one function. They thus vary with different influencing factors such as MWL or MF, and interactions between these factors are seldom controlled for [11]. As a result, the sensitivity of the EEG features varies across studies and there is still a lack of consensus on the best EEG features to validly measure each cognitive state.

In addition to the investigation of single band powers, the combination of multiple frequency bands into indices (e.g. by adding or dividing powers of multiple frequency bands and electrodes) is used to enhance the sensitivity of the single band powers. This way, indices are built to emphasize certain trends in the single bands. Although guided by theoretical considerations about the relevant frequency bands and electrode positions, the exact way the EEG features are combined into an index depends entirely on the researchers' choices of frequency bands, electrode positions and formulae to achieve certain value ranges. This leads to a wide variety of different indices [14–19] whose relationships and validity are seldom compared.

In the following, we describe two indices that are widely used to assess MWL and engagement during manual and automated tasks and that therefore, in theory, present two viable candidates for the assessment of pilots' cognitive states: The Task Load Index (TLI) and the Engagement Index (EI).

1.1 Task Load Index (TLI) and Engagement Index (EI)

The TLI is defined as *theta Fz/alpha Pz*. It was originally developed by Smith et al. (2001) to assess changes in EEG with changing task load [17]. In their study, the authors found the most prominent activity in the theta band at 6–7 Hz at electrode Fz, and in the alpha band at 8–12 Hz, further divided into "slow" (8–10 Hz) and "high" (10–12 Hz), at electrode Pz. Thus, the TLI is often computed from these bands and electrodes. It is noteworthy, however, that in the original publication, the authors did not assign a fixed index to all participants. They tested different combinations of alpha and theta power in varying bandwidths and at varying electrode sites, and chose the best combination for each participant. This way they accounted for interindividual variance, and recommended using participant-specific indices instead of a "one size fits all" index [17]. In following studies this approach has largely been abandoned, and the same index is used for all participants. While most researchers now use frontal theta power at Fz and parietal alpha power at Pz to compute the TLI, the definition of the theta and alpha band vary considerably across studies, see Table 1 for an overview of selected studies.

The TLI usually increases with increasing task demands and can therefore be used to assess MWL [12, 19–23]. In some studies, it was more sensitive to task demands than single bands [12, 21, 22], while others find no effect of task demands on the TLI [24]. Finally, in a series of studies using a simulated air traffic control task, the TLI decreased instead of increased with increasing demand [25–27]. Therefore, it is possible that the TLI is task-specific and responds differently to certain aspects of a task.

The EI is defined as *beta/(alpha + theta)*, and each band is averaged over four electrode sites, Cz, Pz, P3 and P4. The EI was originally developed by Pope et al. (1995) to assess an operator's engagement (i.e. alertness/attention) during manual and automated tasks [16]. The idea is that when the index is high, the human operator is engaged in the task and able to monitor it. Thus, more tasks can be automated without the risk that the operator is inattentive and out of the loop. If the index decreases and thus engagement wanes, tasks can be shifted from automated to manual control so that the human operator needs to engage again [16]. The authors initially computed various

Table 1. Overview of studies using the TLI and EI, with respective definitions of the theta, alpha and beta bands. Studies using the inverse EI are marked *.

Studies using TLI and/or EI	TLI (theta Fz/alpha Pz)		EI (beta/(alpha + theta)) over Cz, Pz, P3, P4		
	theta (Hz)	alpha (Hz)	theta (Hz)	alpha (Hz)	beta (Hz)
*D'Anna et al., 2016 [28]	–	–	4–8	8–13	13–30
Figalová et al., 2022 [24]	4–8	8–13	–	–	–
Freeman et al., 1999 [29]	–	–	4–8	8–13	13–22
Hockey et al., 2009 [20]	6–7	8–12	4–8	8–13	13–22
Holm et al., 2009 [12]	4–8	8–12	–	–	–
Jaquess et al., 2018 [21]	4–7	8–13	–	–	–
Kamzanova et al., 2011 [26]	4–8	8–14	4–8	8–14	14–30
Kamzanova et al., 2012 [25]	4–8	8–14	4–8	8–14	14–30
Kamzanova et al., 2014 [27]	4–8	8–14	4–8	8–14	14–30
Matthews et al., 2015 [22]	4–8	9–13	–	–	–
Nickel et al., 2006 [19]	6–7	10–12	4–8	8–13	13–22
Nickel et al., 2007 [30]	6–7	10–12	4–8	8–13	13–22
Nuamah et a., 2020 [23]	4–8	8–12	–	–	–

indices and found the EI to be most sensitive to engagement. However, it was only built upon the data of six participants which may limit the generalizability of the findings. Like the TLI, the EI is subject to varying definitions of the theta, alpha and beta bands used to compute it. In the original version, the bands were set as follows: theta (4–8 Hz), alpha (8–13 Hz) and beta (13–22 Hz). An overview of selected studies and the used bandwidths can be found in Table 1. In addition to the EI, there is an inverse EI that is computed as *(alpha + theta)/beta*. It was proposed by Brookhuis and de Waard (1993) to assess driving performance [31], even before Pope et al.'s EI. It originally consisted only of the electrodes Pz and Oz. There is a recent study [28] that used the inverse EI, but computed over the four electrodes proposed by Pope et al. Therefore, it is only a mathematical inverse of the EI and thus comparable. Hence, we decided to include this study in our work. It is important to keep in mind, however, that the inverse EI decreases with increasing attention, while the EI increases.

While not specifically designed to assess MWL, the EI is often used as an approximation of task demand. It increases in tasks which require more attention, such as manual as compared to automated tasks [28, 29]. However, other studies could not find effects of task demand on the EI [19, 20]. It has been argued that the TLI and EI represent two different aspects of task demand: While the TLI is associated with more or less effort to perform the task, the EI indicates increasing or waning attention and thus fatigue [30]. However, this would imply that the EI is also affected by time on task, which could not be confirmed [25–27].

While TLI and EI are often used together, in the same studies and therefore on the same tasks, no systematic investigation has been made yet of the sensitivity and specificity of the indices to MWL. If the indices indeed are good indications of MWL and attention in demanding tasks, they should only vary with increasing MWL (task difficulty), and not with increasing MF (time on task). If, on the other hand, they indeed represent two different facets of task demand [30], then the TLI would only respond to changing MWL, and the EI only to increasing MF. With this study, we address this problem with an empirical investigation.

1.2 The Current Study

We used data from two previously conducted experiments in which we induced MWL while controlling MF, and vice versa. In both experiments we used the same task, a simulated flight task. In the experiment on MWL, we used four levels of task difficulty, and used randomization and a task duration of max. 45 min to prevent confounding effects of MF. In the experiment on MF, we used only one difficulty level of the simulated flight task to keep MWL constant, but prolonged the task to 90 min to induce MF. This way, we not only controlled for unwanted influences of other cognitive factors, but also for effects of task characteristics.

We computed the TLI and EI for both datasets and compared their behavior with increasing MWL and MF. In order to build the indices, we used the definitions of frequency bands and electrode positions provided in the original publications. We hypothesized that both TLI and EI would increase with increasing MWL, but would not vary with MF. Following the literature on these indices, we also hypothesized that TLI and EI would be more sensitive to changes in MWL than single bands, i.e. differentiate more MWL levels than single band powers could.

2 Method

In this paper, we present a re-analysis of already gathered EEG data from two studies. Here, we give only a brief overview of the experimental tasks and procedures as an explanation of how the data were obtained. Please note that in our previous studies, more data including self-report, performance and functional near-infrared spectroscopy (fNIRS) data have been gathered as well. We performed analyses to ensure that our manipulation of MWL and MF had worked. Results of these analyses as well as further information on the studies can be found in the respective publications [11, 32].

2.1 Sample

The MWL dataset contains data from 35 participants (24 male, 11 female) between 19 and 30 years ($M = 23.7, SD = 2.1$). The MF dataset contains data from 31 participants (20 male, 11 female) between 19 and 33 years ($M = 24.1, SD = 3.4$). All participants were native German-speakers, currently enrolled at a university, right-handed, had normal hearing and normal or corrected-to-normal vision, no pre-existing neurological conditions, no flying experience and held no pilot's or radio telephony licence. All provided written, informed consent and received monetary compensation for participation. Both studies were approved by the ethics commission of the German Psychological Society (DGPs) and conducted in accordance with the declaration of Helsinki.

2.2 Experimental Tasks and Material

Both studies were conducted in an A321 cockpit simulator at the Institute of Flight Guidance, German Aerospace Center (DLR), Braunschweig. The experimental task for both experiments was a simulated flight task that was simplified in a way that it could be learned by novices. Most of the flight parameters were controlled by the autopilot. The participants only had to monitor the altitude of the aircraft and react to deviations (monitoring task), and to change the heading of the aircraft (adapted n-back task). Both tasks were performed in parallel.

In the monitoring task, the altitude of the aircraft was initially set to 20,000 ft. The experimenter could trigger deviations from this altitude, which would lead to slow altitude increases or decreases. The participants were instructed to react if a deviation of more than 40 ft was reached, and to correct the altitude back to the 20,000 ft by setting a vertical speed. In the adapted n-back task, the participants had to memorize and reproduce headings, i.e. courses in degree (for example, an eastward course equals 90°, i.e. a heading of 090). They heard a series of auditory heading commands which they had to follow in line with an instruction adapted from the classical n-back paradigm. In a 0-back condition, the command had to be put in at once and no memorization was necessary. In a 1-, 2-, or 3-back condition, the participants had to memorize one, two or three headings at a time and thus put in the heading one, two or three prior to the one just heard. Thus, the task had four difficulty levels. More information on the flight task can be found in the original publication [11].

2.3 Procedure

Both the MWL and MF study had a within-subject design. The experiments were divided into task blocks (approx. 3–3.5 min) and breaks (2 min). In each block, the monitoring and n-back task were performed in parallel. Per block, the n-back level was kept constant (i.e. instructions did not vary within one block) and one altitude deviation was triggered by the experimenter. In the MWL study, the participants performed each n-back difficulty level (0-, 1-, 2-, 3-back) twice, resulting in eight blocks, and the whole experiment lasted approx. 45 min. In the MF study, only the 1-back level of the task was used, but the experiment was prolonged to 16 blocks, approx. 90 min.

2.4 EEG Data Recording and Pre-processing

EEG data were recorded at 500 Hz with a LiveAmp-32 in BrainVision Recorder 1.24 (Brain Products GmbH, Gilching, Germany). 28 Ag/AgCl active electrodes were positioned according to the 10–20 system with online reference at FCz, see Fig. 1.

Pre-processing was done in BrainVision Analyzer 2.2 (Brain Products GmbH, Gilching, Germany). The data were down-sampled to 256 Hz, re-referenced to average and bandpass-filtered between 0.5–40 Hz using a 4ᵗʰ order IIR filter with an additional 50 Hz notch filter to remove remaining line noise from the unshielded simulator. Motion arte-facts were removed semi-automatically and an independent component analysis was performed for ocular correction. Then, the data were divided into blocks, beginning with the first reaction per block. In the MWL dataset, this resulted in eight blocks (two presentations of 0-back, 1-back, 2-back, 3-back). In the MF dataset, 16 blocks (16 x 1-back, over time) were built. The blocks were segmented into epochs of 2 s with 0.5 s overlap. Power Spectral Density was computed using Fast Fourier Transformation with a Hanning window with 10% overlap. The average per block was exported as raw sum (μV^2/Hz) for the bands and electrodes of interest in both datasets. Following the orig-inal publications, for the TLI, theta power (6–7 Hz) at electrode Fz and alpha power (8–12 Hz) at electrode Pz were exported [17]. For the EI, theta power (4–8 Hz), alpha power (8–13 Hz) and beta power (13–22 Hz) were exported from the four electrodes Cz, Pz, P3 and P4 [16].

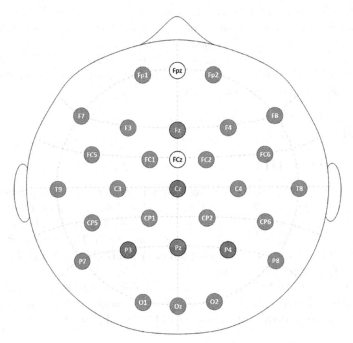

Fig. 1. EEG montage with electrode positions according to the 10–20 system. White = ground and reference electrodes; orange = electrodes used to compute the TLI; blue = electrodes used to compute the EI; grey = all other electrodes. Electrode Pz is part of both TLI and EI.

2.5 Data Analysis

All statistical analyses were conducted in SPSS 26 (IBM Corp., Armonk, NY, USA). Due to skewness, the EEG data were ln-transformed. In the MWL dataset, the two presentations of each n-back level were averaged. In both datasets, missing values were replaced by the mean of the respective variable if necessary. The TLI was computed as *theta Fz/alpha Pz*. The EI was built by first averaging over the four electrodes Cz, Pz, P3 and P4 for each band, then computing *beta/(alpha + theta)*.

For the two indices TLI and EI, separate analyses of variance (ANOVAs) were conducted in each dataset. The sphericity assumption was tested and, in case of violation, corrected using the Greenhouse-Geisser correction. In the MWL dataset, a one-way (4 n-back levels) repeated-measures ANOVA with Bonferroni-corrected post-hoc pairwise comparisons (two-tailed) was computed for each EEG index, i.e. six comparisons. In the MF dataset, a one-way (time on task as 16 blocks) repeated-measures ANOVA was computed for each EEG index. Due to the large number of possible pairwise comparisons, a significant result was followed up with Bonferroni-Holm corrected paired two-tailed t-tests only for the 1st, 4th, 8th, 12th and 16th block (start, ¼, ½, ¾, end of the experiment), i.e. ten comparisons.

Finally, for the comparison of the indices to single bands, we compared the results to those of our previous MWL study [11]. We compared how many MWL levels could be differentiated with which measure, and how large the effect sizes of the respective ANOVAs were. In order to foster comparability with our previous study, in which we had defined the frequency bands slightly differently, we also computed an alternative TLI and alternative EI with the frequency bands from the previous publication: theta (4–8 Hz), alpha (8–12 Hz) and beta (12–30 Hz).

3   Results

3.1   Task Load Index (TLI)

The ANOVA for the MWL dataset showed a significant increase with increasing n-back level, $F(2.26, 76.86) = 15.91$, $p < .001$, $\eta^2_p = .32$, see Fig. 2. Four of the six pairwise comparisons showed a significant difference: 0- vs. 2-back ($p = .004$), 0- vs. 3-back ($p < .001$), 1- vs. 2-back ($p = .033$), 1- vs. 3-back ($p < .001$). The two lowest difficulty levels (0- vs. 1-back) and the two highest difficulty levels (2- vs. 3-back) did not show significant differences, both $ps > .05$.

The ANOVA for the MF dataset showed a significant increase over time, $F(3.52, 105.53) = 2.63$, $p = .045$, $\eta^2_p = .08$, see Fig. 3. The subsequent t-tests did not show any significant difference between any of the tested blocks, all $ps > .05$.

3.2   Engagement Index (EI)

The ANOVA for the MWL dataset did not become significant, $F(3, 103) = 0.51$, $p > .05$, $\eta^2_p = .02$, see Fig. 2. No further tests were carried out.

The ANOVA for the MF dataset showed a significant decrease over time, $F(7.65, 229.52) = 7.05$, $p < .001$, $\eta^2_p = .19$, see Fig. 3. The subsequent t-tests showed significant differences between blocks only for four of the ten comparisons: There were only significant differences between block 1 and the subsequent blocks 4, 8, 12 and 16, all $ps < .001$. No significant differences between any of the later blocks were found.

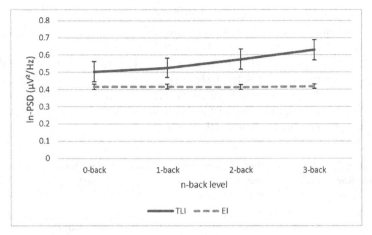

Fig. 2. EEG indices across n-back levels in the MWL dataset. Mean values are shown. Error bars indicate *SE*. EEG data are represented as Power Spectral Density (ln-transformed).

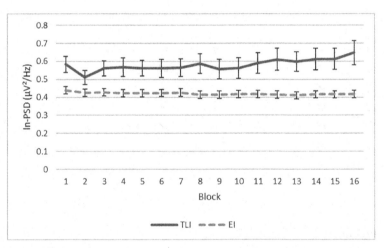

Fig. 3. EEG indices across blocks in the MF dataset. Mean values are shown. Error bars indicate *SE*. EEG data are represented as Power Spectral Density (ln-transformed).

3.3 Comparison to Single EEG Bands

We compared the sensitivity to MWL changes between the indices and single EEG bands. Therefore, we used the results of our previous MWL study on the single band powers for theta Fz, alpha Pz and beta Pz as well as the results from the TLI and EI (computed with the original bandwidths) and alternative TLI and EI (computed with the bandwidths from our previous study). This way, we could analyze if differences were due to the indices per se or variations in the definition of the theta, alpha and beta bands.

For the alternative TLI, the ANOVA showed a significant increase with increasing task difficulty, $F(2.03, 69.04) = 7.57$, $p = .001$, $\eta^2_p = .18$. Two of the six pairwise comparisons showed a significant difference: 0- vs. 3-back ($p = .015$) and 1- vs. 3-back ($p = .012$). No other comparison was significant, all $ps > .05$. For the alternative EI, the ANOVA was not significant, $F(2.05, 69.71) = 0.21$, $p > .05$, $\eta^2_p = .06$.

In our previous research [11], theta Fz was most sensitive to changing MWL. It increased with increasing n-back level, showing a large effect, $F(1.56, 52.87) = 23.91$, $p < .001$, $\eta^2_p = .41$, and differentiated all but the two lowest difficulty levels. We did not find significant changes in alpha Pz and beta Pz. In Table 2 we have contrasted the results of the previous publication and the current analysis.

Table 2. Overview of different EEG features and their ability to discriminate the four n-back levels, including effect sizes of the ANOVAs with significant outcome. Significant differences ($p < .05$, Bonferroni-corrected) marked with ✔.

Pairwise comparisons of different n-back levels		Single band powers (previous study [11])			Indices (current study)			
		theta Fz	alpha Pz	beta Pz	TLI	alternative TLI	EI	alternative EI
0 vs.	1	–	–	–	–	–	–	–
	2	✔	–	–	✔	–	–	–
	3	✔	–	–	✔	✔	–	–
1 vs.	2	✔	–	–	✔	–	–	–
	3	✔	–	–	✔	✔	–	–
2 vs.	3	✔	–	–	–	–	–	–
Effect size η^2_p		.41	–	–	.32	.18	–	–

4 Discussion

In this paper, we tested the sensitivity and specificity of two well-known EEG indices, TLI and EI, to changes in MWL. We analyzed their behavior with increasing MWL and increasing MF, and compared them to single alpha, beta and theta band powers.

The TLI increased substantially with increasing MWL. Using it, we could differentiate all induced MWL levels apart from the two lowest (0- vs. 1-back) and the two highest (2- vs. 3-back). The TLI also increased slightly yet substantially with MF, even if the increase was so weak that no discrimination between blocks was possible. We therefore conclude that the TLI is sensitive to changing MWL, but lacks specificity as it also varies with MF. Moreover, the direction of the variation was the same, i.e. the TLI increased in both datasets. It is therefore not possible to conclude without doubt if the person experiences increasing MWL or MF if only the TLI is used.

Contrary to our expectations, the EI did not vary with MWL and could not be used to discriminate any MWL levels. It did show a slight decrease in the MF dataset, but only between the first and all later blocks. It is unlikely that this is due to MF because of the early onset of the change and the lacking gradual decrease over the time course of the experiment. The observed decrease could be an indication of a learning effect during the first block. With no variation with MWL, we consider the EI not to be sensitive to MWL changes, yet also not sensitive to gradually increasing MF.

When comparing the indices with the single band powers from our previous study regarding sensitivity to MWL, we found that the TLI was more sensitive to MWL changes than only parietal alpha or beta power (which did not vary with MWL at all), but less sensitive than frontal theta band power. This can be seen from both explained variance in the ANOVA and the number of n-back levels it could differentiate. Only single theta band power at Fz was able to differentiate the two highest difficulty levels (2- vs. 3-back). This difference in sensitivity cannot be attributed to varying definitions of the theta band, as can be seen from the alternative TLI: When computed with the same bandwidths as the single band powers, it could only differentiate the highest difficulty level from the two lowest. It was thus less sensitive to MWL changes than both the original TLI and single theta band power. The EI and alternative EI could not differentiate any changes in MWL. In sum, single theta band power at Fz proved most sensitive to changing MWL, followed by the original TLI.

Taken together, when investigated systematically, neither TLI nor EI can be considered ideal measures of MWL. The TLI was sensitive to MWL changes, which aligns with the literature [12, 19–23], but less so than single frontal theta band power. Moreover, the TLI was not specific to MWL as it also varied with MF. The direction of the change, however, was the same: It increased with MWL and with MF. It can therefore be seen as a measure of increasing cognitive demand, regardless of its source. If one wants to pinpoint exactly what causes this increasing demand, the TLI might not be the measure of choice. The EI, to our surprise, was neither sensitive to MWL nor to MF, even though it was designed to capture fluctuations in attention and alertness. We are not the first to conclude this [19, 20, 27], but the first to test it in comparable and controlled experiments on MWL and MF. It is therefore questionable if the EI is a useful measure for any kind of assessment of cognitive demand.

Contrary to earlier work [30], it seems that task demands cannot so easily be split in effort and fatigue, or at least that TLI and EI are not mutually exclusive indices of these facets. When looking at the way the indices are built, however, this is not surprising. Both incorporate parietal alpha and beta band power which vary with a multitude of cognitive factors. They have been shown to decrease with increasing MWL [12, 13] and increase with MF [33–35]. Furthermore, parietal alpha power increases with frequent task switching [10]. Frontal theta band power, which is a part of the TLI, is not exclusive to MWL either. It increases with task demands, both in terms of task difficulty (MWL) [9, 10] and time on task (MF) [33, 36]. If single band powers are subject to variations with different cognitive factors and task characteristics, so are indices that combine them. And the more complex the relationships between bands and influencing factors, the more difficult is the interpretation of the index.

In conclusion, the TLI and EI are two of the most widely known and used EEG indices for assessment of MWL and task engagement. And yet, upon further investigation, their sensitivity and specificity to MWL are not as high as commonly thought, with large variations across studies and experimental tasks. We would therefore like to emphasize the importance of choosing an EEG feature (be it an index or single band) carefully. Ideally, it should be validated for the specific task, application and if possible even tailored to single participants or operators. Especially if the EEG data are meant to be used as a data source for an adaptive or intelligent system that tailors its assistance to the operator's current needs, EEG features should not be trusted blindly. They should always be validated in their sensitivity – and specificity – to indicate the operator's state.

References

1. Billings, C.E.: Toward a human-centered aircraft automation philosophy. Int. J. Aviat. Psychol. **1**, 261–270 (1991). https://doi.org/10.1207/s15327108ijap0104_1
2. Chartered Institute of Ergonomics & Human Factors: The human dimension in tomorrow's aviation system. White Paper (2020)
3. Endsley, M.R.: Situation awareness in aviation systems. In: Garland, D.J. (ed.) Handbook of Aviation Human Factors. Human Factors in Transportation. Erlbaum, Mahwah (1999)
4. O'Donnell, R.D., Eggemeier, F.T.: Workload assessment methodology. In: Boff, K.R., Kaufman, L., Thomas, J.P. (eds.) Handbook of Perception and Human Performance. John Wiley & Sons, New York (1986)
5. Martins, A.P.G.: A review of important cognitive concepts in aviation. Aviation **20**, 65–84 (2016). https://doi.org/10.3846/16487788.2016.1196559
6. Grandjean, E.: Fatigue in industry. Brit. J. Ind. Med. (1979).https://doi.org/10.1136/oem.36.3.175
7. Borghini, G., Astolfi, L., Vecchiato, G., Mattia, D., Babiloni, F.: Measuring neurophysiological signals in aircraft pilots and car drivers for the assessment of mental workload, fatigue and drowsiness. Neurosci. Biobehav. Rev. **44**, 58–75 (2014). https://doi.org/10.1016/j.neubiorev.2012.10.003
8. Charles, R.L., Nixon, J.: Measuring mental workload using physiological measures: a systematic review. Appl. Ergon. **74**, 221–232 (2019). https://doi.org/10.1016/j.apergo.2018.08.028
9. Dussault, C., Jouanin, J.-C., Guezennec, C.-Y.: EEG and ECG changes during selected flight sequences. Aviat. Space Environ. Med. **75**, 889–897 (2004)
10. Puma, S., Matton, N., Paubel, P.-V., Raufaste, É., El-Yagoubi, R.: Using theta and alpha band power to assess cognitive workload in multitasking environments. Int. J. Psychophysiol. Off. J. Int. Organ. Psychophysiol. **123**, 111–120 (2018). https://doi.org/10.1016/j.ijpsycho.2017.10.004
11. Hamann, A., Carstengerdes, N.: Investigating mental workload-induced changes in cortical oxygenation and frontal theta activity during simulated flights. Sci. Rep. **12**, 6449 (2022). https://doi.org/10.1038/s41598-022-10044-y
12. Holm, A., Lukander, K., Korpela, J., Sallinen, M., Müller, K.M.I.: Estimating brain load from the EEG. Sci. World J. **9**, 639–651 (2009). https://doi.org/10.1100/tsw.2009.83
13. Dehais, F., Duprès, A., Blum, S., Drougard, N., Scannella, S., Roy, R.N., Lotte, F.: Monitoring pilot's mental workload using ERPs and spectral power with a six-dry-electrode EEG system in real flight conditions. Sensors (Basel, Switzerland) (2019). https://doi.org/10.3390/s19061324
14. Choi, M.K., Lee, S.M., Ha, J.S., Seong, P.H.: Development of an EEG-based workload measurement method in nuclear power plants. Ann. Nucl. Energy **111**, 595–607 (2018). https://doi.org/10.1016/j.anucene.2017.08.032

15. Freeman, F.G., Mikulka, P.J., Scerbo, M.W., Scott, L.: An evaluation of an adaptive automation system using a cognitive vigilance task. Biol. Psychol. **67**, 283–297 (2004). https://doi.org/10.1016/j.biopsycho.2004.01.002

16. Pope, A.T., Bogart, E.H., Bartolome, D.S.: Biocybernetic system evaluates indices of operator engagement in automated task. Biol. Psychol. **40**, 187–195 (1995). https://doi.org/10.1016/0301-0511(95)05116-3

17. Smith, M.E., Gevins, A., Brown, H., Karnik, A., Du, R.: Monitoring task loading with multivariate EEG measures during complex forms of human-computer interaction. Hum. Fact. **43**, 366–380 (2001). https://doi.org/10.1518/001872001775898287

18. McMahan, T., Parberry, I., Parsons, T.D.: Evaluating electroencephalography engagement indices during video game play. In: Proceedings of the 10th International Conference on the Foundations of Digital Games (FDG 2015). Foundations of Digital Games 2015, Pacific Grove, CA, USA, 22–25 June 2015 (2015)

19. Nickel, P., Hockey, G.R.J., Roberts, A.C., Roberts, M.H.: Markers of high risk operator functional state in adaptive control of process automation. In: Proceedings of IEA 2006, pp. 304–312 (2006)

20. Hockey, G.R.J., Nickel, P., Roberts, A.C., Roberts, M.H.: Sensitivity of candidate markers of psychophysiological strain to cyclical changes in manual control load during simulated process control. Appl. Ergon. **40**, 1011–1018 (2009). https://doi.org/10.1016/j.apergo.2009.04.008

21. Jaquess, K.J., et al.: Changes in mental workload and motor performance throughout multiple practice sessions under various levels of task difficulty. Neuroscience **393**, 305–318 (2018). https://doi.org/10.1016/j.neuroscience.2018.09.019

22. Matthews, G., Reinerman-Jones, L.E., Barber, D.J., Abich, J.: The psychometrics of mental workload: multiple measures are sensitive but divergent. Hum. Fact. **57**, 125–143 (2015). https://doi.org/10.1177/0018720814539505

23. Nuamah, J.K., Seong, Y., Jiang, S., Park, E., Mountjoy, D.: Evaluating effectiveness of information visualizations using cognitive fit theory: a neuroergonomics approach. Appl. Ergon. **88**, 103173 (2020). https://doi.org/10.1016/j.apergo.2020.103173

24. Figalová, N., Chuang, L.L., Pichen, J., Baumann, M., Pollatos, O.: Ambient light conveying reliability improves drivers' takeover performance without increasing mental workload. MTI **6**, 73 (2022). https://doi.org/10.3390/mti6090073

25. Kamzanova, A., Kustubayeva, A., Matthews, G.: Diagnostic monitoring of vigilance decrement using EEG workload indices. In: Proceedings of the Human Factors and Ergonomics Society Annual Meeting (2012).https://doi.org/10.1177/1071181312561019

26. Kamzanova, A.T., Kustubayeva, A.M., Jakupov, S.M.: EEG indices to time-on-task effects and to a workload manipulation (cueing). In: World Academy of Science, Engineering and Technology (2011). https://doi.org/10.5281/zenodo.1071802

27. Kamzanova, A.T., Kustubayeva, A.M., Matthews, G.: Use of EEG workload indices for diagnostic monitoring of vigilance decrement. Hum. Fact. **56**, 1136–1149 (2014). https://doi.org/10.1177/0018720814526617

28. Georgiadis, D., et al.: A robotic cloud ecosystem for elderly care and ageing well: the growmeup approach. In: Kyriacou, E., Christofides, S., Pattichis, C.S. (eds.) XIV Mediterranean Conference on Medical and Biological Engineering and Computing 2016. IP, vol. 57, pp. 913–918. Springer, Cham (2016). https://doi.org/10.1007/978-3-319-32703-7_178

29. Freeman, F.G., Mikulka, P.J., Prinzel, L.J., Scerbo, M.W.: Evaluation of an adaptive automation system using three EEG indices with a visual tracking task. Biol. Psychol. **50**, 61–76 (1999). https://doi.org/10.1016/S0301-0511(99)00002-2

30. Nickel, P., Roberts, A.C., Roberts, M.H., Hockey, G.R.J.: Development of a cyclic loading method for the study of patterns of breakdown in complex performance under high load. In: de Waard, D. (ed.) Human factors issues in complex system performance. Europe Chapter of the Human Factors and Ergonomics Society, Shaker, Maastricht, pp. 325–338 (2007)
31. Brookhuis, K.A., de Waard, D.: The use of psychophysiology to assess driver status. Ergonomics **36**, 1099–1110 (1993). https://doi.org/10.1080/00140139308967981
32. Hamann, A., Carstengerdes, N.: Assessing the development of mental fatigue during simulated flights with concurrent EEG-fNIRS measurement. Sci. Rep. **13**, 4738 (2023). https://doi.org/10.1038/s41598-023-31264-w
33. Dasari, D., Crowe, C., Ling, C., Zhu, M., Ding, L.: EEG pattern analysis for physiological indicators of mental fatigue in simulated air traffic control tasks. In: Proceedings of the Human Factors and Ergonomics Society Annual Meeting (2010).https://doi.org/10.1177/154193121005400304
34. Käthner, I., Wriessnegger, S.C., Müller-Putz, G.R., Kübler, A., Halder, S.: Effects of mental workload and fatigue on the P300, alpha and theta band power during operation of an ERP (P300) brain-computer interface. Biol. Psychol. **102**, 118–129 (2014). https://doi.org/10.1016/j.biopsycho.2014.07.014
35. Nguyen, T., Ahn, S., Jang, H., Jun, S.C., Kim, J.G.: Utilization of a combined EEG/NIRS system to predict driver drowsiness. Sci. Rep. **7**, 43933 (2017). https://doi.org/10.1038/srep43933
36. Roy, R.N., Bonnet, S., Charbonnier, S., Campagne, A.: Mental fatigue and working memory load estimation: Interaction and implications for EEG-based passive BCI. In: Conference Proceedings: Annual International Conference of the IEEE Engineering in Medicine and Biology Society (2013).https://doi.org/10.1109/EMBC.2013.6611070

Generalizability of Mental Workload Prediction Using VACP Scales in Different Fields

Yanrong Huang[1], Nanxi Zhang[2], and Zhizhong Li[1(✉)]

[1] Department of Industrial Engineering, Tsinghua University, Beijing, China
hyr20@mails.tsinghua.edu.cn, zzli@tsinghua.edu.cn
[2] Beijing Aerospace Control Center, Beijing, China

Abstract. Mental workload prediction plays an important role in product design, work organization, task design and assignment in many fields since only with an appropriate mental workload level, could an operator maintain satisfactory task performance. The VACP method was developed for prediction of mental workload that would be induced by a task by calculating a sum score of four independent ratings from visual, auditory, cognitive and psychomotor dimensions, respectively, based on a table of workload component scales. This study aimed to explore the relationship between mental workload scores obtained by the VACP method and NASA-TLX subjective workload ratings, so as to explore the validity of the VACP method applied in different fields. The data with detailed experimental task description and NASA-TLX rating scores were collected from the existing publications, and the predicted mental workload scores were obtained by applying the VACP method for each task described in the publications. By correlation analysis, the results showed that there was a significant correlation between VACP scores and subjective workload ratings. According to the regression models between VACP scores and NASA-TLX ratings in different data groups, there was a significant linear correlation between VACP score and NASA-TLX ratings in most cases. The explicit model of VACP scores and NASA-TLX ratings would contribute to the control of mental workload for different domains and tasks in both product design and operation phases.

Keywords: Mental Workload · NASA-TLX · VACP

1 Introduction

Multitasking becomes very common in real life, which means that people may need to deal with several subtasks concurrently in a limited time, for examples, perform operations while monitoring information changes on multiple screens in a nuclear power plant (NPP). According to the multiple resources theory, each task requires one or more different resources in four dimensions, but the resources available are limited for a person [1]. Thus, multitasking may lead to resource conflicts or resource shortage, which may cause poor performance [2].

Mental workload can be defined as the demands of resources to complete task. Many researches focused on how to predict or measure mental workload of a task. Different level of mental workload may lead to different task performance. Too high or too low mental workload may both lead to poor performance [2], so mental workload prediction plays an important role in product design, work organization, task design and assignment in many fields. Only with an appropriate mental workload level, could an operator maintain satisfactory task performance. There are many ways to measure mental workload, including time-line analysis, information processing studies, operator activation-level studies and subjective effort rating [2]. The measurement method of workload is also summarized as (primary and second) task performance measures, subjective measures and physiological measures [3, 4].

Based on multiple resource theory, the VACP method was developed to predict mental workload that would be induced by a task by calculating a sum score of four independent ratings from visual, auditory, cognitive and psychomotor dimensions, respectively, based on a table of workload component scales. The VACP method was proposed by experts in the field of aviation and has been widely adopted for crew workload prediction in several U.S. Army helicopter design studies [5, 6]. Some other domains also used the VACP method to analyze resource demands of tasks [7, 8]. However, few works have been done to investigate the generalizability of the VACP method. On the other hand, NASA-TLX is one of the common methods to measure the workload. It obtains individual assessment of mental workload from six dimensions, including mental demand, physical demand, temporal demand, effort, performance, and frustration. NASA-TLX has been widely used in different fields, but it is a way for post-hoc self-evaluation, so it can't be used to predict mental workload in the stage of task design and assignment.

Consider the respective advantages and limitations of these two approaches, this study aimed to explore the relationship between mental workload scores obtained by the VACP method and NASA-TLX subjective workload ratings by analyzing the data of task information and NASA-TLX data from the existing researches in different domains, where the NASA-TLX subjective workload ratings as the benchmark. The results would help to validate whether the VACP method can be applied to other application domains and find out the explicit model between VACP scores and NASA-TLX ratings. The model would contribute to the research about the control of mental workload for different domains and tasks in both product design and operation phases.

2 Literature Review

2.1 Mental Workload

Workload is defined as "a set of task demands, as effort, and as activity or accomplishment" [9]. It can be divided into mental workload and physical workload. Mental workload (MWL) reflects the mental demands imposed on operators by tasks they perform, and can be multidimensional and multifaceted [10]. Cain [10] summarized some definitions and perspective of mental workload, and pointed out there was not a commonly accepted and formal definition. Hancock et al. [3] pointed out Resource Theory and Multiple Resource Theory are two of the most prominent theories that construct the bases for the underlying mechanisms of MWL. Van Acker et al. [11] regarded the nature of MWL as a constantly changing and measurable physiological state, it is associated directly with working memory monitoring and allocating resources. Operator will spend the limited cognitive resources to complete the task with different task load, and therefore trigger a subjective experience for the execution of the task [11]. Hancock et al. [3] regarded the definition, "the operator's allocation of limited processing capacity or resources to meet task demands; that is, the balance of internal resources and external demands" [12], be useful to operationalize mental workload. Thus, mental workload is an abstract that reveal the relationship between task demands and operator's capacity or resources, while the relationship is changeable so as to impact on personnel behavior and experience.

Task performance displays the situation and result of the task carried out by operator. The level of mental workload would have an impact on task performance. O'Donnell and Eggemeier [13] indicated that under-load may improve performance and overload may cause a floor effect. Meister [14] divided task demand (mental workload means the task demand impose on person) into three region and drew up the relationship between demand and performance. De Waard [15] expended the Meister's model into six region and indicated that task demand is not the same as mental workload. When task demand is low, operator may have high mental workload since operator will task some compensation behavior to avoid boredom and distraction, which make the mental workload increase and the performance be worse.

In order to keep a satisfactory work performance, it is important to make sure operator stay at the proper mental workload level. Researchers proposed the "red-line" which is the point or region of mental workload that will bring obvious decline in performance if over it [16], it also is the mental model threshold this study focused. According to the model of mental workload and performance, the mental workload threshold for satisfactory performance can be found. Some researchers pointed out the res-line may be located in the location of the transition from region A to region B in the Meister's model [14] or the location of the transition from region A3 to region B in the De Waard's model [15]. This study also explores the mental workload threshold in these two locations. Different task types have different performance indicators, including accuracy, reaction time, completion time and so on. Thus, the uniformity or standardization of performance indicators should be considered when exploring the mental workload threshold.

2.2 Measurements of Mental Workload

Mental model is not directly observable, but it can "be inferred from observation of overt behavior or measurement of psychological and physiological processes" [10, 17]. The current major measuring methods for mental workload include subjective measures, performance measures and physiological measures.

Subjective Measures. Subjective measures is widely used and common evaluation method for mental workload [3], there are five main types: a) Comparison of subjective workload measures, subjective identify which one in the two tasks of workload is higher; b) decision tree subjective workload measures, through a series of discrete problems to achieve a single workload rating; c) set of subscales subjective workload measures, each subscale is used to rate workload from many different aspects; d) a single number subjective workload measures, use a single number to evaluate workload; e) Task-analysis based subjective workload measures, the task is decomposed into subtasks and mission requirements to assess the workload [9].

Subjective measurement has the advantages of low cost, non-invasive, easy to manage, widely used and high face validity [17–19]. But at the same time, subjective measures have some limitations, such as non-real time, post-task rating and subject to personal subjective experience and standards [3, 9, 13].

The current popular subjective MWL measurement scales include NASA Task Load Index (NASA-TLX), Subjective Workload Assessment Technique (SWAT), Cooper-Harper Rating Scale (CH) and so on. Among of them, NASA-TLX is the more common method to measure the workload and can be used in different fields. It makes individual assess mental workload from six dimensions (mental demand, physical demand, temporal demand, effort, performance, and frustration) [9]. And then calculate total scores of subjective workload ratings by two ways: one is crude summation, that is, simply sum up the scores of the six dimensions; the other is weighted summation, and the load of each dimension depends on the selection of fifteen combinations obtained from the pairwise comparison of six dimensions [20].

Performance Measures. Personnel performance in performing tasks can be affected by mental workload, so task performance could be used to measure mental workload. It mainly includes primary task performance measures and second task performance measures [3]. The former measures the ability of operator direct to perform the primary task, while the later measures the ability of operator to perform additional tasks. Since the resource is limited and total fixed, the second task performance can indirectly reflect the situation of primary task performance [3].

Physiological Measures. Physiological measures mainly measure the physiological variables influenced by mental workload to evaluate the change of mental workload. The physiological traits, such as Electrocardiography (ECG), Electroencephalography (EEG), Heart Rate, HRV and so on [3, 10, 21], can reflect the mental load level. This kind of method is the high cost, susceptible to interference, invasive, but can be real time.

2.3 Prediction of Mental Workload Based on Cognitive Resource Demand

Based on multiple resource theory from Wickens [1], VACP method, a subjective measures that provide a convenient way to predictively model the mental workload of a task [10], was proposed. But it is more susceptible to the accuracy of task decomposition and the understanding to the task. Similar to the multiple resource theory, it divides the resources required by a task into four channels: visual, auditory, cognitive and psychomotor, to predict the mental workload. Yee et al. [22] summarized the definition of demand for each channel:

- Visual demand means "the complexity of visual stimuli requiring response"
- Auditory demand means "the complexity of auditory stimuli requiring response"
- Cognitive demand means "the level of thinking required by task executor"

- Psychomotor is defined as "of, relating to, or characterizing movements of the body associated with mental activity", which is the explanation from Collins English-Chinese Dictionary. Then psychomotor demand may mean the complexity of the action in cognitive dimension.

The basic task elements contained in each channel and the explanation and corresponding score for each of them are summarized by the experts. A table of specific workload component scales is formed [5]. The score ranges from 0 to 7 and the most complex task element is 7 points, which indicates 8 points and above are overloaded.

The procedure of VACP method includes three steps: 1) make task decomposition, that is, break down a complex task into several simple subtasks and it is desirable that each subtask contains only one basic task element per channel. 2) complete rating for these subtasks from four channels based on the workload component scales table. According to the understanding of the task description, find the corresponding verbal descriptor in the table and then get the corresponding score as the mental workload score of the channel. 3) calculate VACP score for the task or each subtask. The VACP score of a subtask is a sum score of the independent scores of the four channels, while the VACP score of the total task is obtained by summing the VACP scores of all subtasks.

3   Method

3.1   Data Collection

Using one or any combination of "Mental Workload", "NASA-TLX" and "VACP" as keywords, some existing research articles fit for the study were retrieved in some databases (such as Google Scholar, Web of Science, ScienceDirect and CNKI net). Then the ones containing the detailed task information (which is enough to support task decomposition procedure) and NASA-TLX subjective workload ratings data would be further selected from those articles previously retrieved. At last, the data information, including article title, research domain, the specific task information and corresponding NASA-TLX subjective workload ratings data or the results of other types of mental workload measure and performance (if they are in the articles) were collected from these articles and organized into data sheets for further processing.

3.2   Mental Workload Prediction

VACP method was used to obtain the prediction of mental workload for each specific task or subtask in this study. For the specific task in each article, the task decomposition was made before mental workload prediction. Each task was decomposed into some subtasks with a suitable level of detail, which may only include some basic operations. Then find the mental workload score in visual, auditory, cognitive and psychomotor dimensions respectively for each subtask according to the VACP rating scales [5]. Due to the difference in the number of steps and the length of time for the whole task in the different literature, the VACP score of the whole task averaged by the task time should be adopted as the prediction of mental workload. If the article contained NASA-TLX data of each subtask, then calculate the VACP score for each subtask by directly adding the scores of the four dimensions obtained before as the average VACP score. While if the article only contained the NASA-TLX data of the whole task, sum the VACP scores of all its subtasks as the total VACP score of the task, but it should consider the influence of work time of each subtask. Thus, first estimate the working time of each subtask, the VACP score of each subtask needs to be weighted by the proportion of its working time in the whole task, and then the sum of the VACP score weighted by working time of all subtasks is used as the average VACP score. If time of each subtask can't be estimated exactly, the time of each task step is all regarded as equal weight, in which case the average VACP score should be the average of the total VACP score against the number of task steps.

There were some articles that have already completed the task decomposition and used the VACP method to predict their mental workload. For these articles, the VACP scores could be directly used instead of performing the above process.

3.3 Dependent Variable and Independent Variable

The dependent variable is the NASA-TLX subjective workload ratings directly obtained from articles and the independent variable is the VACP score obtained by the procedure of mental workload prediction as mentioned in Sect. 3.2.

4 Results

4.1 Data Description

A total of 76 pairs of data were obtained, and each pair contained VACP score and NASA-TLX data (as shown in Appendix). The sample size of each field was shown in Table 1. The tasks include:

- Driving: secondary tasks during driving such as calling investigator using a cell phone, texting and so on.
- NPP: emergency operation procedures (EOPs).
- Healthcare: ICT therapy, IPT therapy and IFC therapy.
- Army: some tasks in the TRACKWOLF system.
- Marine: the start turbo alternator procedure.
- Other mix: memory task, simple track task in computer and so on; or the simulated task in VR and simple similar task replacing real tasks (e.g. assembly based on Lego simulation).

The scatter plot of the data is shown in Fig. 1. Most data points are concentrated an increasing trend band between VACP scores and NASA-TLX ratings. From the plots for different fields (see Fig. 2), there are obvious trends between the VACP scores and NASA-TLX data in the driving, healthcare, army and NPP fields can be observed, except in the marine and NPP fields, which only have a small amount of data. The marine and NPP fields are not considered in the subsequent analysis. For the data group of driving, an outlier (27.3, 54.00) was identified and removed.

Table 1. The sample size for each field.

Field	Sample size
Driving	8
NPP	2
Healthcare	23
Army	31
Marine	1
Other mix	11
Total	76

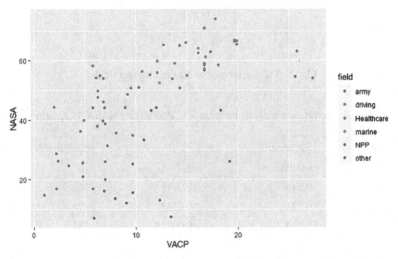

Fig. 1. The scatter plot of all data.

4.2 Correlation Analysis

The correlation between VACP score and subjective workload ratings was analyzed to examine the validity of using the VACP method to predict the mental workload. The normal distribution test was performed for the data of VACP score and NASA-TLX rating. Since most data, except those of driving with a small sample size, did not pass the normality test, the correlation analysis between VACP score and NASA-TLX rating was performed with Spearman correlation coefficient. The results are shown in Table 2.

The correlation of VACP score and NASA-TLX rating was significant for the whole data set ($r = 0.648$, $p < 0.001$), healthcare ($r = 0.763$, $p < 0.001$), and army ($r = 0.684$, $p < 0.001$) fields. After delete an outlier, the driving field ($r = 0.821$, $p = 0.034$) also found the significant correlation between VACP score and NASA-TLX rating. No significant correlation relationship was found for other mix data with a small sample size.

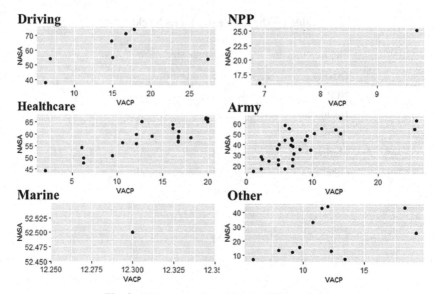

Fig. 2. The scatter plot of data in different fields.

Table 2. Correlation analysis between VACP score and NASA-TLX ratings

Data group	Spearman		Sample size
	Coefficient	Sig.	
All	0.648	<0.001***	76
Driving	0.821	0.034*	7
Healthcare	0.763	<0.001***	23
Army	0.684	<0.001***	31
Other	0.418	0.203	11

4.3 Regression Analysis

The results of regression analysis between VACP scores and NASA-TLX subjective workload ratings are presented in Table 3. The generalized regression model was

$$NASA-TLX\ ratings = \beta_0 + \beta_1(VACP\ score) \tag{1}$$

where β_0 is intercept and β_1 is the coefficient of independent variable.

For the data group of all data, driving, healthcare and army fields, the models and the coefficients were all significant. The regression models (see Fig. 3) are:

$$NASA\text{-}TLX\ rating\ (whole\ data\ set) = 24.666 + 1.781 \cdot VACP\ score \tag{2}$$

$$NASA\text{-}TLX\ rating\ (driving\ data\ set) = 31.472 + 2.119 \cdot VACP\ score \tag{3}$$

NASA-TLX rating (healthcare data set) $= 44.543 + 1.034 \cdot$ VACP score   (4)

NASA-TLX rating (army data set) $= 24.957 + 1.726 \cdot$ VACP score   (5)

Table 3. Regression analysis between VACP score and NASA-TLX ratings

Data group	Intercept		VACP		Model	R^2
	Estimate	Sig.	Estimate	Sig.	Sig.	
All	24.666	0.000***	1.781	0.000***	0.000***	0.340
Driving	31.472	0.014*	2.119	0.016*	0.016*	0.721
Healthcare	44.543	0.000***	1.034	0.000***	0.000***	0.685
Army	24.957	0.000***	1.726	0.000***	0.000***	0.470
Other	2.603	0.852	1.769	0.139	0.139	0.226

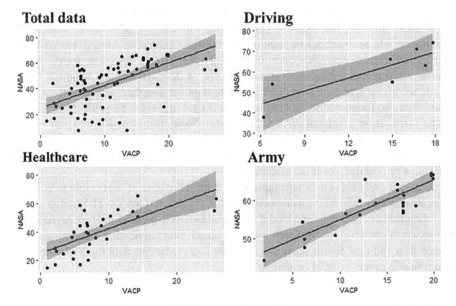

Fig. 3. Regression model

5   Discussion and Conclusion

Establishing models cross application domains is very important for the human factors and ergonomics discipline to play its role in earlier stage of product development and provide analysis tools for systems engineering. This study aimed to explore the relationship between the predicted mental workload by the VACP method and the subjective rated mental workload measured by the NASA-TLX ratings, and to examine the generalizability of the VACP method across different application fields. Through the analysis of the subjective workload ratings data collected from the existing publications and the predicted mental workload data by the VACP method, the results show that their correlations in all data of the selected fields, driving, healthcare, and army fields were significant. The linear regression models between VACP scores and NASA-TLX ratings for the four data sets were also significant. The cross-field linear relationship suggests that the VACP method can be generally used to predict mental workload in different fields. Meanwhile, the explicit model of VACP scores and NASA-TLX ratings makes mental workload control possible at the earlier stage of product and task design. For a given an acceptable level of risk, represented by the subjective mental workload level (NASATLX rating), the general regression model can be used to predict the corresponding acceptable mental workload (VACP score). The VACP score (mental workload threshold) can be used to verify the design, so that a more suitable task process can be finally expected.

Because there are not common performance variables in the selected publications, it is impossible to examine the relationship between subjective mental workload and human performance across different fields. Grier [23] carried out a descriptive analysis of over 1000 global NASA-TLX data to provide a description of distribution for the global workload score, in terms of the whole data set and data sets of different task types. And she found out 58 ($\pm$4) as mean workload (the value 58 is the 70 percentiles in the distribution of global NASA-TLX data). Though this value does not mean a "red-line" because of a lack of research related to performance, maybe the statistical distribution data can help to explore the model of mental workload and performance and determine the mental workload threshold.

A limitation of this study is sample size. With more data, it is possible to get more accurate models of the relationship between VACP score and NASA-TLX ratings. Since the relationship between mental model measured by VACP method and task performance is also worth studying, the next step would be identifying publication containing performance data and task details adequate for workload prediction with the VACP method. The research process would be similar.

6   Appendix

VACP scores and NASA-TLX scores of identified tasks

Literature	Field	Task		VACP	NASA-TLX
[7]	driving	AOSPAN		27.3	54
		PASAT		17.3	63
		Calling		17.8	74
		2-back task		14.9	66
		Texting		16.7	71
		Math arithmetic		15.0	55
		Simple question		6.2	38
		Simple instruction		6.8	54
[24]	other	EOT crane operations in virtual reality		18.3	43.31
[25]	marine	Start turbo alternator procedure		12.3	52.5
[26]	other	Sternberg's Memory Searching Task		13.4	7.44
		Tracking Task		19.2	25.97
[21]	NPP	Low complexity EOP		6.9	16.06
		High complexity EOP		9.7	25.22
[27]	other	Production assembly based on Lego simulation	Low difficulty	10.8	33.3
			Medium difficulty	11.5	43.2
			High difficulty	12	44.3
[28]	other	Memorization 2-pair		12.3	13.12
		Visual-manual task		9.1	12.08
		Menu selection task (search a single digit)		9.7	15.58
[8]	Healthcare	Intermittent Cervical Traction (ICT)	Inquire and check the status of the patient before the treatment	16.7	59.2
			Instruct the patient for an appropriate position and secure halters and harnesses on the patient	16.1	64.1
			Judge and adjust the amount of traction force	19.9	65.5
			Judge and set up the mode and duration of the traction	19.7	66.9
			Explain the nature of the treatment to the patient	6.3	47.7
			Turn on the machine and assure its normality of operation	12.7	65.3

(*continued*)

(continued)

Literature	Field	Task		VACP	NASA-TLX
			Ask and check the status of the patient after starting the machine	16.7	57.1
			After the beep sound of the machine, detach halters and harnesses from the patient and inform the patient about the completion of the treatment	12.1	56.1
[8]	Healthcare	Intermittent Pelvic Traction (IPT) therapies	Inquire and check the status of the patient before the treatment	16.7	56.7
			Instruct the patient for an appropriate position and secure halters and harnesses on the patient	16.1	62.6
			Judge and adjust the amount of traction force	19.9	66.6
			Judge and set up the mode and duration of the traction	19.7	66.4
			Explain the nature of the treatment to the patient	6.3	49.9
			Turn on the machine and assure its normality of operation	12.7	65.3
			Ask and check the status of the patient after starting the machine	16.7	58.5
			After the beep sound of the machine, detach halters and harnesses from the patient and inform the patient about the completion of the treatment	12.1	59.8
[8]	Healthcare	Interferential Current (IFC) therapy	Inquire and check the status of the patient before the treatment	18.1	58.5

(continued)

(*continued*)

Literature	Field	Task		VACP	NASA-TLX
			Prepare suction electrodes	9.5	50.8
			Judge and set up the frequency and intensity of the current, and the amount of suction force. Put the electrodes on the patient's skin	16.8	61.3
			Ask and check the status of the patient	6.1	54.3
			Assure the normality of operation of the machine	13.8	59.1
			After the beep sound of the machine, detach the electrodes from the patient	10.6	56.4
			Inform the patient about the completion of the treatment	2	44.4
[29]	army	05D	Receive a tip	9.7	34.9
			Tune receiver to frequency & locate signal	5.8	17
			Prepare location request & pass to operator	7	38.7
			Take LOBs	2.2	28.7
			Edit LOBs	4.8	21
			Get a fix	2.2	16.9
			Communicate fix to net controller	1	14.7
			Log targets (fixes)	7	26.1
			Communicate targets to traffic analyst	5.8	44.2
			Set up system, including antennas	25.6	54.7
			Perform system check with known targets	7.2	31.5

(*continued*)

(continued)

Literature	Field	Task		VACP	NASA-TLX
			Troubleshoot, correct system & operator errors	25.8	63.1
			Communicate with outstation (to initialize system)	5.8	58.3
[29]	army	05H	Search & locate Morse signal	9.2	48.6
			Listen & copy Morse code	13.6	53.9
			Print traffic file	6.8	46.1
[29]	army	05K	Search &locate non-Morse signal	8.1	35.6
			Set up system for digitizing	2.4	26.3
			Print traffic file (non-Morse)	3.4	24.7
[29]	army	98G	Search & locate voice signal	4.6	36.2
			Determine if signal of interest	4.9	40
			Record signal	4.8	25.7
			Listen, translate, transcribe into report mask	11.4	55.3
			Identify unit & activity with working aids	14.3	65.2
			Transcribe & write Strum report	6.5	55.1
[29]	army	98C	Log traffic from received printout	7	20
			Determine if reportable traffic	6.95	44.2
			Identify unit & activity using working aids	14.3	50.7
			Prepare report	6.75	39.7
			Prepare tasking for all intercept operators	10.3	50.9

(continued)

(*continued*)

Literature	Field	Task		VACP	NASA-TLX
			Update & create working aids	8.95	44.3
[30]	other	To view the image		5.9	7.1
		Search for black spots		8	13.6

References

1. Wickens, C.: Multiple resources and mental workload. Hum. Factors **50**, 449–455 (2008)
2. Moray, N.: Mental Workload: Its Theory and Measurement. Springer, New York (2013). https://doi.org/10.1007/978-1-4757-0884-4
3. Hancock, G.M., Longo, L., Young, M.S., Hancock, P.A.: Mental workload. In: Handbook of Human Factors and Ergonomics, pp. 203–226. Wiley (2021)
4. Meshkati, N., Hancock, P., Rahimi, M., Dawes, S.: Techniques in mental workload assessment. In: Evaluation of Human Work: A Practical Ergonomics Methodology (1995)
5. Bierbaum, C.R., Aldrich, T.B.: Task Analysis of the CH-47D Mission and Decision Rules for Developing a CH-47D Workload Prediction Model, vol. 1. Summary Report (Research Product 90-10a)
6. Bierbaum, C.R., Szabo, S., Aldrich, T.B.: Task Analysis of the UH-60 Mission and Decision Rules for Developing a UH-60 Workload Prediction Model, vol. 1. Summary Report (No. ASI690-302-87) (1989)
7. Chen, W., Sawaragi, T., Horiguchi, Y.: Measurement of driver's mental workload in partial autonomous driving. IFAC-PapersOnLine. **52**, 347–352 (2019)
8. Liang, S.-F.M., Rau, C.-L., Tsai, P.-F., Chen, W.-S.: Validation of a task demand measure for predicting mental workloads of physical therapists. Int. J. Ind. Ergon. **44**, 747–752 (2014)
9. Gawron, V.J.: Human Performance, Workload, and Situational Awareness Measures Handbook, 3rd edn. (2019)
10. Cain, B.: A Review of the Mental Workload Literature. Presented at the July 1 (2007)
11. Van Acker, B.B., Parmentier, D.D., Vlerick, P., Saldien, J.: Understanding mental workload: from a clarifying concept analysis toward an implementable framework. Cogn. Technol. Work **20**(3), 351–365 (2018). https://doi.org/10.1007/s10111-018-0481-3
12. Matthews, G., Reinerman-Jones, L.: Workload assessment: how to diagnose workload issues and enhance performance. Human Factors and Ergonomics Society (2017)
13. O'Donnell, R.D., Eggemeier, F.T.: Workload assessment methodology. In: Handbook of Perception and Human Performance, Cognitive Processes and Performance, vol. 2, pp. 1–49. Wiley, Oxford (1986)
14. Meister, D.: Behavioral Foundations of System Development. Wiley, Oxford (1976)
15. De Waard, D.: The Measurement of Drivers' Mental Workload (1997)
16. Grier, R., et al.: The red-line of workload: theory, research, and design. Presented at the Proceedings of the Human Factors and Ergonomics Society Annual Meeting 1 September (2008)
17. Casali, J.G., Wierwille, W.W.: A comparison of rating scale, secondary-task, physiological, and primary-task workload estimation techniques in a simulated flight task emphasizing communications load. Hum Factors **25**, 623–641 (1983)

18. Wickens, C.D., Helton, W.S., Hollands, J.G., Banbury, S.: Engineering Psychology and Human Performance. Routledge, New York (2021)
19. Wierwille, W.W., Connor, S.A.: Evaluation of 20 workload measures using a psychomotor task in a moving-base aircraft simulator. Hum. Factors **25**, 1–16 (1983)
20. Campoya, F., Hernandez, J., Maldonado, A., González-Muñoz, E.: Development of the NASA-TLX Multi Equation Tool to Assess Workload (2020)
21. Gao, Q., Wang, Y., Song, F., Li, Z., Dong, X.: Mental workload measurement for emergency operating procedures in digital nuclear power plants. Ergonomics **56**, 1070–1085 (2013). https://doi.org/10.1080/00140139.2013.790483
22. Yee, S., Nguyen, L., Green, P., Oberholtzer, J., Miller, B.A.: Visual, auditory, cognitive, and psychomotor demands of real in-vehicle tasks. Presented at the 1 March (2007)
23. Grier, R.A.: How high is high? A meta-analysis of NASA-TLX global workload scores. Proc. Hum. Factors Ergon. Soc. Ann. Meet. **59**, 1727–1731 (2015)
24. Das, S., Maiti, J., Krishna, O.B.: Assessing mental workload in virtual reality based EOT crane operations: a multi-measure approach. Int. J. Ind. Ergon. **80**, 103017 (2020)
25. Yan, S., Wei, Y., Tran, C.C.: Evaluation and prediction mental workload in user interface of maritime operations using eye response. Int. J. Ind. Ergon. **71**, 117–127 (2019)
26. Rubio, S., Diaz, E., Martin, J., Puente, J.M.: Evaluation of subjective mental workload: a comparison of SWAT, NASA-TLX, and workload profile methods. Appl. Psychol. **53**, 61–86 (2004)
27. Yu, Q., Feng, D., Xu, X., Cai, Q., Hu, H.: Measurement of mental workload in assembly based on Lego simulation. Ind. Eng. Manage. **23** (2018)
28. Jo, S., Myung, R., Yoon, D.: Quantitative prediction of mental workload with the ACT-R cognitive architecture. Int. J. Ind. Ergon. **42**, 359–370 (2012)
29. Knapp, B.G., Hall, M.J.: Human performance concerns for the TRACKWOLF System. Army Research Inst for the Behavioral and Social Sciences, Alexandria, VA (1990)
30. Bonnet, C.T., Davin, T., Baudry, S.: Interaction between eye and body movements to perform visual tasks in upright stance. Hum. Mov. Sci. **68**, 102541 (2019)

Research and Application of Fatigue Management of Apron Control in Beijing Daxing International Airport

Aiping Jia[1], He Sun[2(✉)], Yi Liang[1], and Yanxi Qiu[1]

[1] Operation Management Department, Beijing Daxing International Airport, Beijing 100621, China

[2] Air Traffic Management College, Civil Aviation University of China, Tianjin 300300, China

hesun@cauc.edu.cn

Abstract. Managing the risk of air traffic controller fatigue has become a requirement for ensuring the safety of ATC operations and an important means of improving the safety management level. This paper examines apron control fatigue prevention and risk assessment identification methods from both management and technical perspectives, proposes air traffic controller fatigue management programme suitable for apron control in Beijing Daxing International Airport, and makes relevant management recommendations in order to better study the mechanism of apron controller fatigue and provide a theoretical basis for the reasonable arrangement of apron controller shifts.

Keywords: Apron control · Fatigue management · Scheduling

1 Introduction

Air traffic controller fatigue risk management is a basic requirement for the safety of control operations and an important means to improve safety management. As the first airport in China to achieve A-SMGCS Level 4 Lighting Guidance System with omnidirectional runway configuration, CAT IIIB landing and HUD RVR 75m take-off capability, Beijing Daxing International Airport (hereinafter referred to as "Daxing Airport") has thoroughly implemented the document issued by the Civil Aviation Administration of China and followed the guidelines with the full support of civil aviation units at all levels, Daxing Airport is the first airport in China to have an airport management authority independently in charge of apron control since its opening, following the guidelines of "overall planning, efficiency priority, active promotion and smooth operation". Since its smooth operation for three years, it has achieved good results overall.

Due to its special corporate positioning and strategic characteristics, Daxing Airport, as a power source of China's national development, is developing together with Beijing, Tianjin and Hebei province, and continuous improvement of apron control operation efficiency and service level is the only way for future development. As a direct communicator with the crew, the apron controller takes on different command tasks and control

D. Harris and W.-C. Li (Eds.): HCII 2023, LNAI 14017, pp. 95–108, 2023.
https://doi.org/10.1007/978-3-031-35392-5_7

pressure from other first-line positions in the airport, and fatigue, as an important part of aviation human factors, is one of the most common factors causing human error in the air traffic controller's work. About 72%. Therefore, air traffic controllers will be the key factor affecting ATC safety in the long run, and trying to prevent human errors becomes an important way to further improve ATC safety. The international civil aviation community has also conducted a lot of research on air traffic controller human factors [1, 2] and developed some related measures [3, 4]. GAWRON [5] et al. studied the process of controller fatigue generation and analysed that fatigue reduces the ability of air traffic controllers to process information, resolve conflicts and make decisions. Folkard [6] et al. proposed a possible risk of a fatigued state for air traffic controllers on night duty by comparing the levels of sleep deprivation associated with different shift regimes or individuals. Akerstedt [7] confirmed that sleep deprivation is the shift fatigue. Domestic researchers have also proposed methods to monitor fatigue [8, 9] and to optimise air traffic controller scheduling [10]. Wang Jie-Ning [11] constructed an air traffic controller alertness prediction model based on the MCMC model and used PVT to test the change of air traffic controller alertness during work. Wang Jianhui et al. [12] combined the idea of convolutional image classification and proposed a method to introduce an improved speech spectrum map into air traffic controller fatigue detection. Yang Peiyu et al. [13] constructed a air traffic controller shift optimization model and an abnormal shift adjustment model for fatigue management based on biomathematics with the aim of minimizing the maximum fatigue peak and considering the shift constraint problem in the actual work of air traffic controllers. Wang Lili et al. [14] established an air traffic controller fatigue index system, combined fatigue-related indexes to design an experimental scheme, obtained data of each index, calculated the correlation degree of each index based on objective data analysis, and tested the correlation between marker indexes and fatigue, and screened out fatigue marker indexes that could achieve rapid monitoring and direct quantification.

In this paper, by combining the fatigue management system established by ICAO [15] and the contents of the Civil Aviation Administration of China's "Civil Aviation Controller Fatigue Management Reference Study Material", we study the apron controller fatigue prevention and risk assessment identification methods from both management and technical perspectives, propose a apron controller fatigue management plan suitable for apron control in Daxing Airport, and formulate management recommendations.

2   Research Proposal

Daxing Airport apron Control is an operation unit within the Operation Management Department of Daxing Airport. In the form of four shifts, there are 36 first-line apron controllers on duty. In this paper, the fatigue monitoring and data collection of the first-line apron controllers at Daxing Airport were conducted by considering their personal characteristics, sleep characteristics, control load, working environment and duty arrangement. By combining the existing research materials, the objective and subjective evaluation methods are designed, the subjective data are collected by questionnaire survey, and the objective data are collected by scientific and refined experimental methods, and the two are combined to support the subsequent research (Fig. 1).

3   Research Process

Based on the full investigation of the apron control management mode and scheduling situation of Daxing airfield, the study designed a perfect apron controller fatigue test process, during the experiment, the apron controller is wearing a smart wristband throughout the process to collect sleep data; during the change of duty and rest, the PVT test is conducted to record objective fatigue data, and the Stanford sleepiness scale, and the NASA TLX scale are filled out to record subjective fatigue data. The test procedure is shown in Fig. 3.

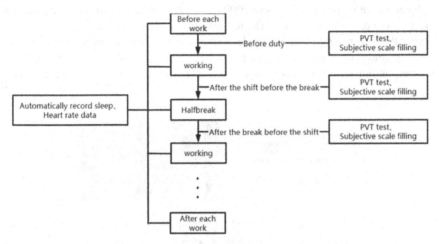

Fig. 1. Apron Control Fatigue Management Study Process

4   Research Methodology

4.1   Objective Assessment

Psychomotor Vigilance Test. In order to measure the fatigue of air traffic controllers before and after duty, this paper tests the level and change of cognitive ability of air traffic controllers before and after duty using the Psychomotor Vigilance Test (PVT). The PVT is essentially a test of the reaction speed of the test taker. The basic model is that a sudden stressor is presented and the time taken to react to it is recorded. The stressor is usually in the form of a screen change, and the respondent's response is usually in the form of a mouse or button click, but in practice the specific form is varied, and the data measured in different forms of the experiment vary widely, so that data from different forms of the experiment are not comparable. In this experiment, a test applet was developed in the form of python+pyqt5 using a custom format. Within this framework, the test applet allows for quick user interaction and a user-friendly interface. Considering the acceptability of the experiment, the application interface is simplified in this paper and only one button is kept and the tester can follow the uniform steps by clicking the mouse. After the test is completed, the detailed data of the subject can be exported, and the fatigue level can be measured under a unified standard.

The specific method of use is: the tester clicks anywhere on the blue start screen to trigger the start signal. From this point on, the background of the screen will always be red when there is no stress, and the background of the screen will suddenly change to green when there is stress. The subject clicks once anywhere on the screen in response to the stress, and the applet automatically records the time difference between the onset of the stress and the stress response. The second and subsequent clicks are considered an early response to the next stress and are also recorded separately. During the full test of approximately 2 min, the stress appears at any time and the interval is randomly distributed in the range of 1000 ms to 5000 ms, so the number of stress appearances in the test is not completely uniform. The test interface is shown in Fig. 2.

After the test is completed, the applet will record and analyse all the raw data. The raw data includes the response time of each click, the marker of the incorrect click and the corresponding time, the mean value of the response time, the relative mean deviation, etc.

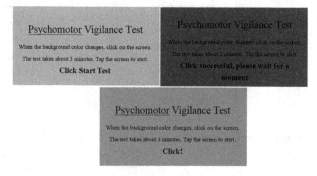

Fig. 2. PVT Test

Sleep Duration Test. The sleep duration test adopts a non-sensory way to obtain the experimental test data, mainly through the smart wristband to collect the apron controller's physiological index data, and through the mobile phone APP to intuitively view the automatic monitoring of sleep. The main experimental test data include: measurement time, deep sleep time, light sleep time, awake time, fall asleep time and wake up time. As shown in Fig. 3.

4.2 Subjective Assessment

Two types of subjective ratings were used in this paper: the Stanford Fatigue Sleepiness Scale and the NASA TLX scale. The subjective rating is based on the collection of personal information, sleep characteristics, fatigue scenarios, fatigue causative factors,

Fig. 3. Bracelet APP Interface

fatigue performance characteristics and fatigue impact characteristics, etc. The subjective fatigue level is obtained by self-scoring on the subjective scale.

Stanford Fatigue Drowsiness Scale. The Stanford Fatigue Drowsiness Scale is a commonly used scale to assess the average level of sleepiness experienced by individuals in their daily lives and can be used to assess the subjective fatigue status of air traffic controllers. It includes 9 levels of fatigue from "1 energetic" to "9 about to fall asleep". As shown in Table 1.

Table 1. Stanford Fatigue Drowsiness Scale

Fatigue level description (1 energetic - 9 will fall asleep immediately)	Current fatigue level
1 - Feeling active, energetic and very alert	
2 - Physical function is at a high level, but not at its peak	
3 - Feeling a bit down in state, alertness starts to decrease	
4 - State can stay awake, not enough alertness, able to respond	
5 - There is a little haziness and a significant drop in status	
6 - Hazy state, still awake but losing interest, body slowed down	
7 - More sleepy, do not want to work	
8 - sleepy, want to lie down, forced to endure this not to fall asleep, dizziness of the head and eyes	
9 - Almost fantasizing, about to fall asleep, hard to stay awake	

NASA-TLX Scale. The NASA-TLX scale, known as the NASA Task Load Index, is a self-assessment by the tester of the load imposed on him or her by the previous phase of work in six areas, including the level of mental demand, the level of physical demand, time demand, task completion, effort and frustration, and proposes a method of integrating the six indicators with each other to evaluate the work load during that period of time. This is shown in Table 2.

(1) There are 6 evaluation items, each of which is divided into 10 ratings (Rating) in the self-assessment, and when the tester considers necessary, half a rating can be used to indicate internal differences. Each rating is recorded as $R_1, R_2, ..., R_6$.

(2) After scoring the 6 indicators separately, the impact of these 6 indicators need to be compared two by two, i.e. $C_6^2 = 15$ times, after each comparison, the more important one will get 1 point of weight (Weight), after all comparisons, the weight of each statistical item is $W_1, W_2, \cdots, W_6$.

(3) Calculate the total workload (Total Workload, TL) of the tester, $TL = \sum_{n=1}^{6} R_n W_n$, where the load of the n item is $R_n W$.

Table 2. NASA-TLX Scale

Dimensions	Score Description	Subjective scores
Level of brain power demand (how much brain power is needed to complete the task?)	Low 1–10 High	
Level of physical demand (how much physical work is required to complete the task?)	Low 1–10 High	
Time requirements (how much urgency is needed to complete the work?)	Slow 1–10 Hurry	
Task completion (what is the level of completion of work tasks?)	Good 1–10 Bad	
Level of effort (level of effort put in to complete the task)	Low 1–10 High	
Frustration level (feelings of insecurity, discouragement, irritation, stress, and annoyance in the work process because the work is not in place)	Low 1–10 High	

The apron controller fatigue scale shown in Table 3 was obtained by combining the two fatigue test scales.

5   Research Analysis

This part analyses the test data to study the relationship between apron controller fatigue and various indicators such as work time, rest time and work load. The factors causing fatigue are studied from an objective point of view to provide a basis for reasonable management proposals.

5.1   Fatigue Variation Analysis Based on PVT

The development of apron controller fatigue can be visually observed through the PVT test values before and after the apron controller's duty. First, this paper counted the

Table 3. Apron controller fatigue scale

Test time	Duty phase	Stanford Fatigue Drowsiness Scale	NASA-TLX Scale
12:30	Before going to work	2 - Physical function is at a high level, but not at its peak	–
15:30	After duty Before the break	4 - State can stay awake, not enough alertness, able to respond	111
18:30	After rest Pre-duty	3 - Feeling a bit down in state, alertness starts to decrease	–
20:30	After Duty Before the break	4 - State can stay awake, not enough alertness, able to respond	111
24:00	After rest Pre-duty	3 - Feeling a bit down in state, alertness starts to decrease	–
06:00	After Duty Before the break	8 - sleepy, want to lie down, forced to endure this not to fall asleep, dizziness of the head and eyes	111
09:30	Before going to work	2 - Physical function is at a high level, but not at its peak	–
12:30	After Duty Before the break	4 - State can stay awake, not enough alertness, able to respond	111
15:30	After rest Pre-duty	3 - Feeling a bit down in state, alertness starts to decrease	–
09:25	After Duty Before the break	5 - There is a little haziness and a significant drop in status	89

average value of PVT change of 6 apron controllers during one day duty in the study cycle, due to the different scheduling situation, the daily duty period is uncertain, in order to better analyse the fatigue change of one day, as much as possible, the situation with more daily duty periods was selected, the average value of each person is calculated as shown in Fig. 4, and the average value of 6 apron controllers is shown in Fig. 5.

After comparison, the change of the test value was consistent with the apron controller's subjective fatigue scale statistics, and the test was valid. Before the morning shift, the apron controller was full of energy, and after 3 h of work, the PVT test value increased significantly and the fatigue was significant; after a period of rest, the PVT value dropped back significantly, indicating that the energy was restored and could continue to work. After the night shift, the PVT value reached its peak, reflecting that the apron controllers were extremely fatigued after the overnight shift and needed to rest as soon as possible. Overall, the PVT test value shows a fluctuating upward trend, which is in line with the law of human fatigue recovery. Therefore, the length of work is the main factor of fatigue generation.

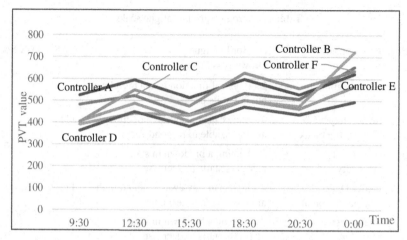

Fig. 4. Relationship between hours of work and level of fatigue of 6 air traffic controllers

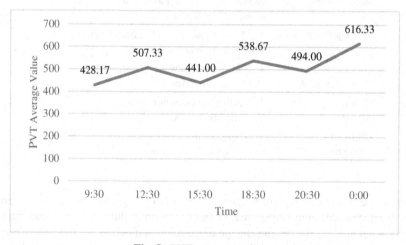

Fig. 5. PVT average statistics

In order to analyze the relationship between working time, rest duration and fatigue level, this paper statistically analyzed the average incremental change of PVT values, the larger the PVT increment, the higher the PVT growth rate. As shown in Table 4.

The analysis showed that the relationship between the increase in apron controller fatigue and the working hours was more obvious, and the absolute value and growth rate of PVT increase significantly increased as the working day progressed, and the degree of recovery also showed a significant decreasing trend, indicating that the closer to the afternoon and night, the more easily fatigued and less easily recovered.

Table 4. Incremental Changes in PVT Measurements

Pre-shift time	Pre-shift PVT value	Post-shift time	Post-shift PVT	PVT Increment	PVT growth rate
09:30	433.57	12:30	506.85	73.28	16.90%
12:30	506.85	15:30	463.51	−43.34	−8.55%
15:30	463.51	18:30	525.22	61.71	13.31%
18:30	525.22	20:30	507.13	−18.09	−3.44%
20:30	507.13	0:00	617.82	110.69	21.83%

5.2 Fatigue Change Analysis Based on Sleep Data

The effect of sleep on fatigue recovery can be further analysed by counting the sleep quality of apron controllers the night before duty. In this paper, the average sleep score and the average pre-duty PVT score of six apron controllers during the study period were calculated. A high sleep score does not necessarily mean a low PVT due to differences in individual physical fitness and other factors. However, by comparing the pattern of change in the same apron controllers over the test period, it can be seen that improving sleep quality has a significant effect on reducing fatigue.

For the data collected from the experiment, this paper analyses the relationship between sleep patterns and apron controllers' cognitive abilities.

(1) After measuring the PVT value after a midday nap and a simple rest in the afternoon, compared with the change in PVT value after the last work, the statistics are shown in Table 11. It can be seen that after the lunch break, the degree of sleep for fatigue recovery is very large, both the absolute value of PVT reduction and the percentage of reduction compared to the incremental PVT are better than in the case of simple rest in the afternoon. This is shown in Table 5.

Table 5. Noon nap vs. afternoon break PVT during pre-shift

Test Item	Noon nap	Afternoon Break
Reduction in PVT value compared to the previous shift	43.34	18.09
Reduction in value as a percentage of the PVT value of the previous shift	8.55%	3.44%
Decrease in value as a percentage of the incremental PVT value of the previous shift	59.14%	29.32%

(2) Sleep is good or bad to consider the length of sleep and sleep quality, individual differences also determine the sleep pattern varies from person to person. Therefore, the sleep recommendation basically requires the apron controller to make a subjective assessment of his cognitive ability state after rest, and the apron controller feels that he can think clearly and react quickly after rest is a good sleep.

(3) There are two dimensions to improving sleep quality. From their own point of view, apron controllers need to speed up the "golden 90 min of sleep" (the 90 min after they start sleeping is the golden time of sleep, which can relieve fatigue extremely effectively), psychologically maintain a relaxed state, regular daily exercise can also improve sleep. From the perspective of the external environment, the scheduling of apron controllers by the control unit should be relatively fixed, try to avoid the situation of overtime shift change, and can provide apron controllers with a comfortable and quiet nap environment, such as the lounge.

5.3 Fatigue Change Analysis Based on Voice Characteristics of Radiotelephony Communication

As a direct output of the control command, the correctness and accuracy of land and air calls are closely related to the apron controller's status. Human fatigue can be analysed by extracting the frequency domain features and establishing the acoustic framework to reflect the apron controller's performance more intuitively from the perspective of control scenes and control processes.

In this paper, we collected the recorded data of apron controllers' land and air calls during their duty period and extracted some voice features for research. Firstly, this paper intercepted the recording files, removed the pilot's voice and kept only the apron controller's voice; secondly, through the self-developed "ATC Land-Air Call Analysis System" software, we extracted the voice features of each minute of the call, including the average value of voice amplitude, the average value of short-time energy and the average value of over-zero rate, which are the basic characteristics of voice signals. These three features are the basic features of speech signals, and according to the preliminary study, their change patterns can reflect the fatigue situation to a certain extent; finally, the apron controller fatigue was analysed by analysing several features worth changing.

As an example, the average of the speech feature data of several apron controllers during the study period is taken. As shown in Figs. 6, 7 and 8.

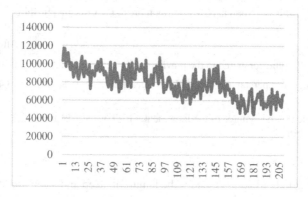

Fig. 6. Mean Value of Speech Amplitude

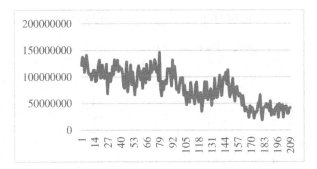

Fig. 7. Speech Short-time Energy Averages

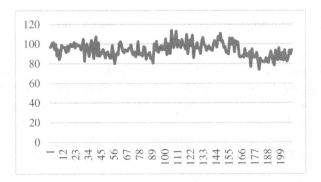

Fig. 8. Mean Value of Voice Over Zero Rate

The pattern of change of these three speech features is basically the same, i.e. when the feature value decreases, it represents an increase in the degree of fatigue. By observing the changes in the above three features, it is easy to see that the speech features show fluctuating changes during the whole three-hour shift, among which the changes in the mean value of speech amplitude and the mean value of speech short-term energy are more obvious. Therefore, the apron controller fatigue status can be estimated by measuring the speech characteristics, and the apron controller fatigue level can be considered to deepen when the indicator continues to decrease.

5.4 Analysis Based on Rest Duration for Recovery of Fatigue Level

As the break time in the middle of each shift was 2 or 3 h, this paper counted the reduction in the PVT test values of the apron controllers before and after the break to further analyse the improvement in fatigue due to the break time. Some of the statistical results are shown in Table 6.

In order to predict the relationship between apron controller rest time and PVT value, this paper assumes that during the rest period the PVT value y is only related to the rest time t, i.e. the two are linearly correlated at once, without considering other factors. A one-dimensional linear regression was performed on the statistical data, and the results

Table 6. Reduction statistics of of PVT by rest time

PVT before break	PVT after rest	PVT Difference	Duration of rest
422.5	341.85	80.65	3
522	436	86	3
534	507	27	2
487	406	81	3
501	462	39	2
439	354	85	3

obtained for the case where the rest time t is not less than 2 h are

$$y = 50.1625t - 67.325$$

If the correlation coefficient is $R^2 = 0.9726 > 0.95$, the correlation can be assumed to hold; if the probability is $p = 0.0003 < 0.5$, the resulting regression model holds.

Calculated according to this equation, the fatigue recovery of the apron controllers at rest is shown in Table 7.

Table 7. Duration of rest and PVT reduction prediction

Duration of rest	PVT reduction
2	33
3	83.1625
4	133.325
5	183.4875
6	233.65
7	283.8125
8	333.975

According to the statistics of the Institute, the incremental PVT of the apron controller after one shift is calculated to be about 107, so in order to return to the state before work, the rest time should be 3.5 h.

6 Recommendations

(1) In absolute terms, the increase in apron controller fatigue is more obviously related to working hours, and the closer the working hours are to the night, the more severe the fatigue. Therefore, it is recommended to increase the overlapping hours between the day and night shifts, and to avoid the rapid form of changeover from the day to the night shift.

(2) Suggestions for apron controllers to improve cognitive performance through sleep.
① Strategies to mitigate sleep inertia. The risk of sleep inertia (sleep inertia refers to the state in which apron controllers awaken from sleep feeling groggy or disoriented) can be reduced by requiring apron controllers to have a period of time to allow sleep inertia to dissipate before returning to their intense duty positions.

Minimise sleep interruptions. The number of times an apron controller's sleep is interrupted during work and non-work periods should be minimised.

Short naps can improve apron controllers' alertness, cognitive performance and work effectiveness, and naps are a valuable linking strategy in fatigue management. It can be divided into three types: pre-work naps, on-duty naps and controlled rest in the lounge. For individuals, it is obvious to ensure the length and improve the quality of sleep to reduce fatigue. It is recommended to sleep scientifically and to schedule naps reasonably during the day, such as a daily one-hour nap at noon, which can effectively and temporarily relieve fatigue. The recovery from fatigue after a midday nap is significantly better than the state of simple rest in the afternoon. However, it is not recommended as a means of extending the duty period, and if a longer rest period is required, appropriate rest facilities shall be provided.

(3) According to the principle of apron control duty arrangement at Daxing Airport, it is recommended that apron controllers should rest for 20 min from 9:00 to 12:00, 45 min from 12:00 to 3:00 and 45 min from 3:00 to 6:00 during the day. Before the apron controller is on night duty, the apron controller should ensure that long uninterrupted sleep can also effectively improve command cognitive power and alertness. Sleep for 180–240 min.

(4) The voice characteristics of land and air calls can reflect the apron controller fatigue status, but the correlation is relatively low and can be used to predict the trend of fatigue change.

7 Conclusion

In this paper, by collecting and analysing some of the apron controllers' physiological indicators and compiling a series of subjective and objective data, such as apron controllers' schedule, voice characteristics of land and air calls, and apron controllers' self-assessment, the apron controllers' fatigue changes during the day were analysed by combining the reaction time before and after apron controllers' duty. The conclusions of the study can provide theoretical support for apron controllers' sleep management and workload management, as well as a reference for apron control scheduling at Daxing Airport. The findings have now been incorporated into the relevant procedures and applied to the daily duty management of apron control at Daxing Airport. After the apron controller test, the feedback is good, which proves that this research method is feasible.

In addition, there are still many issues that need to be further investigated in the application of fatigue management in apron control at Daxing Airport, including the age and gender differences of apron controllers, shift management and operational procedures, the use of complex systems and equipment with HCI, and the control environment, which will be the next direction for further research.

Acknowledgements. The authors are very grateful to the HCII committee and reviewers who provided valuable comments on this paper. And also would like to express special thanks to apron controllers for their contributions to this research.

References

1. Orasanu, J., Parke, B., Kraft, N., et al.: Federal Aviation Administration (FAA) Evaluating the Effectiveness of Schedule Changes for Air Traffic Service (ATS) Providers: Controller Alertness and Fatigue Monitoring Study (2012)
2. Dionisio, A.N.: Air traffic controller fatigue and human error (2010)
3. Zhang, X., Yuan, L., Zhao, M., et al.: Effect of fatigue and stress on air traffic control performance. In: 2019 5th International Conference on Transportation Information and Safety (ICTIS) (2019)
4. Triyanti, V., Azis, H.A., Prasetyawan, Y., et al.: Fatigue in air traffic controller: the work-related factors. In: The 2nd International Conference on Mechanical Engineering Research and Application (2021)
5. Gawron, V.J., Kaminski, M.A., Serber, M.L., et al.: Human Performance and Fatigue Research for Controllers. Federal Aviation Administration, Washington, DC (2011)
6. Folkard, S., Condon, R.: Night shift paralysis in air traffic control officers. Ergonomics **30**(9), 1353–1363 (1987)
7. Akerstedt, T., Knutsson, A., Westerholm, P., et al.: Mental fatigue, work and sleep. J. Psychosom. Res. **57**(5), 427–433 (2004)
8. Zhao, X., Lu, H., Wang, M., et al.: Mental fatigue detection based on heart rate variability. Chin. J. Med. Phys. **35**(5), 6 (2018)
9. Li, Y., Yan, H., Yang, X., et al.: Study of mental fatigue based on heart rate variability. Chin. J. Biomed. Eng. **2010**(1), 6 (2010)
10. Zhang, Y., Yue, T.T., Jin, S.Z., et al.: Intelligent scheduling algorithm for air traffic controllers based on machine learning. J. Civil Aviation **2020**(1), 4 (2020)
11. Wang, J., Zhang, Y., Ji, S.: Controller alert probability prediction based on Markov Monte Carlo. J. Saf. Environ. **20**(04), 1412–1420 (2020)
12. Wang, J., Chen, C., Zhang, S., et al.: Controller fatigue detection method based on spectrogram. Aeronaut. Comput. Technol. **53**(01), 19–23 (2023)
13. Peiyu, Y., Chao, W.: Air traffic controller shift model for fatigue management. J. Saf. Environ. **22**(03), 1394–1399 (2022)
14. Lili, W., Keren, W.: Analysis of controller fatigue indicator based on grey correlation theory. J. Saf. Environ. **22**(02), 810–818 (2022)
15. Schallies, S.: Fatigue in air traffic control: ICAO fatigue risk management task force. Controller **52** (2013)

Pilot Study on Gaze-Based Mental Fatigue Detection During Interactive Image Exploitation

Christian Lengenfelder[(✉)], Jutta Hild[(✉)], Michael Voit, and Elisabeth Peinsipp-Byma

Fraunhofer Institute of Optronics, System Technologies and Image Exploitation IOSB,
76131 Karlsruhe, Germany
{christian.lengenfelder,jutta.hild}@iosb.fraunhofer.de

Abstract. Human mental fatigue occurs during various tasks due to increased load and time-on-task. As it might impair human performance, it could be beneficial detecting it automatically and subsequently implement measures to mitigate fatigue. To accomplish this, mental fatigue has to be detected, preferably as unobtrusive as possible. Recent research proposes that remote eye-tracking could be a promising method. The background of this contribution is interactive image exploitation as it might occur in safety or security applications. We consider wide area motion imagery which typically covers several square kilometers and includes a huge number of tiny vehicles and persons. A human operator has to perform lots of search, zoom and pan operations in order to find relevant objects. We conducted a pilot study (N = 20 non-expert image analysts) where subjects preformed several basic image exploitation tasks. During the sessions, we collected their gaze data using a 500 Hz eye-tracker. From the recorded gaze data protocols, we extracted saccadic and fixational gaze parameters using the I-VT algorithm. Mean and maximum saccadic velocity as well as mean saccadic amplitude decrease over time. This corresponds to findings by the research community in terms of observed gaze behavior under mental fatigue. However, the effects are small and need confirmation by future work.

Keywords: Aerial image analysis · interactive image exploitation · mental fatigue detection · gaze-based user state detection · saccadic velocity · saccadic amplitude · pilot study

1 Introduction

Human mental fatigue occurs during various tasks. It is supposed to be a certain manifestation of physiological fatigue [1]. It arises due to increased cognitive load and time-on-task [2]. Human mental fatigue may result in impaired human performance [3, 4]. Therefore, it could be worthwhile to implement measures supporting the human in order to mitigate fatigue.

In this contribution, we consider interactive image exploitation as a task which is prone to induce fatigue. Typically, it is a human visual task. The main objective is to examine images in order to identify and report task relevant objects, e.g. by framing

D. Harris and W.-C. Li (Eds.): HCII 2023, LNAI 14017, pp. 109–119, 2023.
https://doi.org/10.1007/978-3-031-35392-5_8

or annotating them within the image. Image exploitation occurs in various application domains. For example, a radiologist examines X-ray images to make a diagnosis; a geographer examines aerial images to analyze soil conditions; or a human operator performs traffic control in motion video to find a certain vehicle.

The background of this contribution is interactive image exploitation in wide area motion imagery (WAMI). The considered task is vehicle search as it might occur in safety or security applications. WAMI scenes typically cover several square kilometers and include a huge number of tiny vehicles and persons. When provided on a typical 24-inch desktop monitor, vehicles cover only a few pixels. Reasonably, a human operator has to perform lots of zoom and move operations in order to find relevant objects. The dynamic visual input imposes additional cognitive load. Performed over hours, interactive image exploitation is prone to human mental fatigue.

Hence, in order to prevent exploitation errors, it could be helpful to detect mental fatigue and temporarily adapt the interactive system in a way that makes interaction easier (e.g., provide control elements of the user interface in larger size making them easier selectable). While, users could make such adaptations themselves, automatic system adaptation would be more comfortable.

1.1 Applying Eye-Tracking for Mental Fatigue Detection

A prerequisite for automatic system adaption is the capability to capture the user state. Recently, eye-tracking is establishing as an unobtrusive method to detect mental fatigue [5]. This is partly because only recently lightweight devices are capable to capture eye features in a sufficiently accurate and robust fashion. It is known that eye-tracker data quality is supposed to influence the quality of gaze behavior analysis: Higher sampling rates allow more precise detection of fixations and saccades in the gaze data protocols. Hence, some authors propose to utilize eye-trackers with sampling rates of 250 Hz or higher [6]. Proposed eye features for mental fatigue detection are pupil size, blink frequency, saccades and fixations.

Very popular is *pupil size* which appears to decrease in case of fatigue [7]. Authors utilize the mean or maximum pupil size as well as pupil size variation. Pupil size has been observed to decrease for cognitive tasks [4] as well as for people watching videos [8]. However, pupil size is difficult to utilize if the visual input changes heavily. In this case, the pupillary light reflex induces pupil size variations of several millimeters; this is one order of magnitude more compared to pupil size variations that are induced by mental fatigue [9]. As the dynamic visual input from WAMI data might vary strongly, pupil size is not applicable as a feature for our application task.

Blink frequency increases with mental fatigue. This has been reported, e.g., for cognitive tasks [10] as well as for a driving task [11]. Other blink parameters like mean blink duration or the percentage of eye closure show inconsistent results [12, 13]. Moreover, some authors recommend utilizing blink parameters rather for detection of sleepiness than for detection of fatigue [1]. Hence, blink parameters are also not appropriate for our purposes.

Most promising for detection of mental fatigue appear saccade parameters. For example, mean and peak *saccadic velocity* have been reported to decrease with increasing fatigue. This has been shown for a visual exploration task [14], for a simulated driving task [15], and also for cognitive tasks [5]. *Saccadic amplitude* has been reported to decrease with increasing fatigue as well [16]; the same holds for *saccadic frequency* [17]. *Saccadic duration* shows inconsistent behavior; some authors report increasing duration with increasing fatigue [16]; others report decreasing duration with increasing fatigue [15].

Fixation duration shows inconsistent behavior, too. While Cazzoli et al. [14] report a positive correlation between fixation duration and fatigue for a visual exploration task, Lavine et al. [18] report for a reading task decreasing fixation duration as well as a decreasing number of fixations.

To get first insight whether mental fatigue could be detected using eye features during WAMI exploitation, we conducted an evaluation based on gaze-data which we captured while users performed a number of experimental image exploitation tasks. After that, we extracted saccade and fixation parameters from the gaze data records and analyzed whether the results would indicate fatigue in the way proposed by related work. In the following, Sect. 2 describes the method, and Sect. 3 provides the evaluation results.

2 Method

2.1 Gaze Data Collection

As a data set for mental fatigue detection, we collected gaze data from subjects performing image exploitation. In order to induce fatigue, it is necessary that the subjects are occupied with a mentally stressful task over a sufficiently long time without getting bored. Hence, we designed five experimental image exploitation tasks with differing demands. In general, each single task comprised finding and annotating targets in WAMI data; annotation was accomplished by framing them issuing a left mouse click upon their location in the image.

The experimental tasks included the exploitation of single WAMI frames, in which objects had to be identified as targets (task types 1 and 2, cf. Fig. 1); furthermore, there were tasks, in which the subjects had to observe single objects in an image sequence over a few minutes in order to judge if they would show target behavior (task types 3 and 4, cf. Fig. 2); finally, there were experimental tasks requiring multiple moving object selection in image sequences under time pressure (task type 5, cf. Figs. 3 and 4).

The image data material for the experimental tasks was derived from the WPAFB 2009 data set [19]. It contains about 1,000 images with a size of 30,000 × 23,000 image pixels and ground sampling distance of 0.25 m. Played with a typical data rate of 1 Hz, this results in a data sequence of about 17 min.

Participants performed the experimental tasks using an experimental system equipped with computer mouse and keyboard for interactive exploitation; a remote eye-tracker was integrated into the system for gaze capture (cf. Fig. 5). The experimental system provides typical basic interaction functions that are required to perform basic interactive image exploitation: zooming and panning the image and object annotation.

Mouse input was realized straight forward. Mouse wheel was used for zooming the image in and out; left mouse pressed at mouse movement was used for moving the image;

a left mouse click was used for target framing; a right mouse click was used for deletion of erroneously framed objects. Moreover, the system allowed to display the movement trajectories of moving objects (in short: object tracks) on demand: Left mouse click on an object with the STRG-key pressed displays the object track, right mouse click deletes the object track.

For task presentation, the experimental setup used a 24-inch monitor with a resolution of 1920 × 1200 pixels. Hence, a car with a length of 4 m (corresponding to 16 pixels in the WAMI data) appears on screen with a length of 0.27 mm; this is approximately the size of one pixel. Subjects sat at a distance of 60 cm from the monitor. Key presses were performed using a standard keyboard (105-key DE QWERTZ), and a standard optical mouse was used for mouse input.

On the one hand, eye-tracker data quality is supposed to influence the quality of gaze behavior analysis; on the other hand, it is unclear how much the quality of mental fatigue detection might depend on the sampling rate. Hence, we captured the gaze data with two different eye-trackers. For the eight participants in data collection A, we used the Eyelink 1000 Plus [20] at a 500 Hz sampling rate; and for the twelve participants in data collection B, we used the low-cost eye-tracker Tobii 4C [21] at 90 Hz.

All 20 subjects were colleagues or students from our department. All were experienced desktop and mouse input users. All had normal/corrected to normal vision. The eight subjects in data collection A were 2 females and 8 males (age: two under 30 yrs., five between 30 and 45 yrs., one over 45 yrs.). The twelve subjects in data collection B were two females and ten males (ages: five under 30 yrs., six between 30 and 45 yrs., one over 45 yrs.).

After giving informed consent, a general explanation of the test tasks and an eye-tracker calibration, the subjects learned with three training tasks to get familiar with the interaction functions of the system. After that, each subject performed two sessions I and II of about 30 min of test tasks where their gaze behavior was captured, with a ten-minute break between the two. According to the reference literature, this appears to be an appropriate duration for a mental fatigue experiment [1].

In order to provide different tasks in the two sessions, we designed two task sets. Each session contained 19 experimental tasks including image exploitation in single WAMI frames as well as in short WAMI sequences (durations between about 30 and 90 s). The task instruction specifying vehicles as targets was given right before each trial. The specification included vehicle behavior like parking at a certain spot or exhibiting certain track behavior.

In total, the experimental duration was 2 to 2.5 h. To account for the diurnal rhythm, all data collection appointments started at 9 am or 10 am [2]. To avoid that dim light would induce fatigue [1], we switched on the neon lights in the Lab.

2.2 Extracting Gaze Features from the Gaze Data Protocols

As related work proposed saccadic and fixational gaze parameters as most promising, we considered only those for our evaluation. Gaze data analysis was conducted with a proprietary software tool (Linux/Ubuntu 20.04/Python 3.8/Pandas). The analysis of the gaze data protocols included two steps.

Fig. 1. Example for experimental task type 1. Task instruction: Search and select all vehicles that are parking within the highlighted areas. Task type 2 used a WAMI image section of 9,000 × 4,000 pixels.

First, we detected fixations and saccades applying the I-VT algorithm [22]. Thereby, to avoid results that are impossible from an eye physiological point of view, we applied several thresholds that are reasonable from an eye physiology perspective: minimum fixation duration is 100 ms, maximum saccadic velocity is 1000°/s, minimum saccadic duration was 22 ms, maximum saccadic duration was 100 ms [23, 24].

Second, gaze artefacts were removed. To provide a natural environment, the subjects did not use a chin rest. Thus, interruptions in the gaze data stream occurred due to large head movements, e.g., when the subject looked down at the keyboard. To mitigate effects on the calculated gaze parameters, saccades and fixations directly before and after such an interruption were omitted. Such interruptions appeared as sudden x- or y-movement and mainly affected the computed maximum values.

Finally, based on the resulting fixations/saccades data protocols, we calculated ten saccadic and fixational gaze parameters which are supposed to be affected if mental fatigue occurs:

- Saccadic velocity (maximum and mean) [°/s]
- Saccadic amplitude (maximum and mean) [°]
- Saccadic duration (mean) [s]
- Number of saccades (mean)
- Number of fixations (mean)
- Number of fixations per second
- Fixation duration [s]

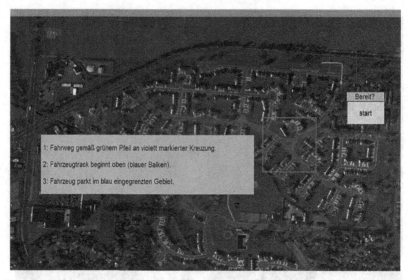

Fig. 2. Example for experimental task type 4. Task instruction: Observe the junction highlighted with a violet frame with the eyes. If a vehicle (1) turns according to the specification (green arrow), it is a potential target. Now, check its track. (2) If the track originates from the image edge specified by the blue bar, follow it with the eyes until the image sequence stops. Select the vehicle as target, if it (3) parks within the specified area. Task type 3 differs in the way that the potential target (which has to be observed) is visually highlighted at the beginning of the image sequence (i.e., criterion (1) is not part of the instruction). (Color figure online)

Fig. 3. Exemplary experimental task. Task instruction: Observe the junction highlighted with a violet frame with the eyes. Any vehicle (1) turning according to the specification (green arrow) is a potential target. Select a vehicle as a target if (2) its track originates from the image edge specified by the blue bar. (Color figure online)

Fig. 4. Cropped image of the exemplary experimental task from Fig. 3 after completion with vehicles selected as target. The vehicle with the lilac-colored object track is no target as the track does not originate from the margin specified by the blue bar. (Color figure online)

3 Results and Conclusion

For fatigue detection, we determined the values of the ten gaze parameters for the sessions I and II separately. Then we determined, how the values differ. Due to the small number of subjects, the results of the present pilot study have to be considered preliminary. The results were as follows.

For the gaze data captured at 90 Hz, none of the considered gaze parameters showed consistent changing behavior, not across task types and some even not across subjects.

For the gaze data captured at 500 Hz, mean and maximum saccadic velocity are lower for the second session. Figure 6 and Fig. 7 show the results for all five task types separately. This corresponds to the findings reported by related work [5, 14, 15] (cf. Sect. 1.1). Moreover, mean saccadic amplitude is lower for the second session as well. This corresponds to the findings reported by related work [16] (cf. Sect. 1.1).

The results for the other gaze parameters did not exhibit consistent tendencies over the five task types.

Overall, it appears that at 500 Hz the gaze parameters saccadic velocity and saccadic amplitude show a tendency that might indicate fatigue. However, the differences between session I and II are small. Possibly, the duration of the experiment was not

Fig. 5. Experimental setup. During the data recording, only one of the eye-trackers was present.

long enough and the tasks were not difficult enough to induce fatigue. Future work will include a refinement of the experimental design and contain a larger number of subjects. Furthermore, it would be interesting to apply classification algorithms, e.g., neural networks, to learn complex dependencies between gaze parameters for mental fatigue detection. Recent research reports that such methods generally outperform traditional threshold-based methods for gaze parameter classification [25].

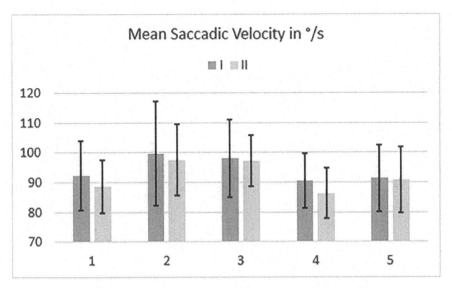

Fig. 6. Results for mean saccadic velocity for data collection with 500 Hz eye-tracker.

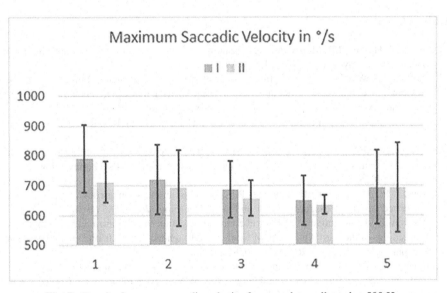

Fig. 7. Results for mean saccadic velocity for gaze data collected at 500 Hz.

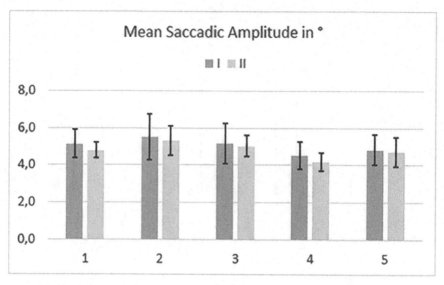

Fig. 8. Results for mean saccadic amplitude for gaze data collected at 500 Hz.

References

1. Bafna, T., Hansen, J.P.: Mental fatigue measurement using eye metrics: a systematic literature review. Psychophysiology **58**(6), e13828 (2021)
2. Balkin, T.J., Wesensten, N.J.: Differentiation of sleepiness and mental fatigue effects. In: Ackerman, P.L. (ed.) Cognitive Fatigue: Multidisciplinary Perspectives on Current Research and Future Applications, pp. 47–66. American Psychological Association (2011)
3. Boksem, M.A., Tops, M.: Mental fatigue: costs and benefits. Brain Res. Rev. **59**(1), 125–139 (2008)
4. Hopstaken, J.F., Van Der Linden, D., Bakker, A.B., Kompier, M.A.: A multifaceted investigation of the link between mental fatigue and task disengagement. Psychophysiology **52**(3), 305–315 (2015)
5. Yoss, R.E., Moyer, N.J., Hollenhorst, R.W.: Pupil size and spontaneous pupillary waves associated with alertness, drowsiness, and sleep. Neurology **20**(6), 545 (1970)
6. Abdulin, E., Komogortsev, O.: User eye fatigue detection via eye movement behavior. In: Proceedings of the 33rd Annual ACM Conference Extended Abstracts on Human Factors in Computing Systems, pp. 1265–1270. ACM (2015)
7. Renata, V., Li, F., Lee, C.H., Chen, C.H.: Investigation on the correlation between eye movement and reaction time under mental fatigue influence. In: 2018 International Conference on Cyberworlds (CW), pp. 207–213. IEEE (2018)
8. Yamada, Y., Kobayashi, M.: Detecting mental fatigue from eye-tracking data gathered while watching video: evaluation in younger and older adults. Artif. Intell. Med. **91**, 39–48 (2018)
9. Eckstein, M.K., Guerra-Carrillo, B., Singley, A.T.M., Bunge, S.A.: Beyond eye gaze: what else can eyetracking reveal about cognition and cognitive development? Dev. Cogn. Neurosci. **25**, 69–91 (2017)
10. Maffei, A., Angrilli, A.: Spontaneous eye blink rate: an index of dopaminergic component of sustained attention and fatigue. Int. J. Psychophysiol. **123**, 58–63 (2018)
11. Di Stasi, L.L., et al.: Effects of driving time on microsaccadic dynamics. Exp. Brain Res. **233**(2), 599–605 (2014). https://doi.org/10.1007/s00221-014-4139-y

12. Li, J., Li, H., Wang, H., Umer, W., Fu, H., Xing, X.: Evaluating the impact of mental fatigue on construction equipment operators' ability to detect hazards using wearable eye-tracking technology. Autom. Constr. **105**, 102835 (2019)
13. Song, J., Wang, R., Zhang, G., Xiong, C., Zhang, L., Sun, C.: Electrooculogram signals analysis for process control operator based on fuzzy c-means. Vectors **1**, 2 (2015)
14. Cazzoli, D., Antoniades, C.A., Kennard, C., Nyffeler, T., Bassetti, C.L., Müri, R.M.: Eye movements discriminate fatigue due to chronotypical factors and time spent on task–a double dissociation. PLoS ONE **9**(1), e87146 (2014)
15. Di Stasi, L.L., Renner, R., Catena, A., Canas, J.J., Velichkovsky, B.M., Pannasch, S.: Towards a driver fatigue test based on the saccadic main sequence: a partial validation by subjective report data. Transp. Res. Part C Emerg. Technol. **21**(1), 122–133 (2012)
16. McGregor, D.K., Stern, J.A.: Time on task and blink effects on saccade duration. Ergonomics **39**(4), 649–660 (1996)
17. Van Orden, K.F., Jung, T.P., Makeig, S.: Combined eye activity measures accurately estimate changes in sustained visual task performance. Biol. Psychol. **52**(3), 221–240 (2000)
18. Lavine, R.A., Sibert, J.L., Gokturk, M., Dickens, B.: Eye-tracking measures and human performance in a vigilance task. Aviat. Space Environ. Med. **73**(4), 367–372 (2002)
19. U.S. Air Force Research Laboratory (AFRL), WPAFB2009 dataset. https://www.sdms.afrl.af.mil/index.php?collection=wpafb2009. Accessed 9 Feb 2023
20. SR Research EyeLink. https://www.sr-research.com/eyelink-1000-plus/. Accessed 8 Feb 2023
21. Tobii Homepage. https://help.tobii.com/hc/en-us/articles/213414285-Specifications-for-the-Tobii-Eye-Tracker-%204C. Accessed 8 Feb 2023
22. Salvucci, D.D., Goldberg, J.H.: Identifying fixations and saccades in eye-tracking protocols. In: Proceedings of the 2000 Symposium on Eye Tracking Research & Applications, pp. 71–78. ACM (2000)
23. Leigh, R.J., Zee, D.S.: The neurology of eye movements. Contemporary Neurology (2015)
24. Holmqvist, K., Nyström, M., Andersson, R., Dewhurst, R., Jarodzka, H., Van de Weijer, J.: Eye Tracking: A Comprehensive Guide to Methods and Measures. OUP, Oxford (2011)
25. Birawo, B., Kasprowski, P.: Review and evaluation of eye movement event detection algorithms. Sensors **22**(22), 8810 (2022)

Using Virtual Reality to Evaluate
the Effect of the Degree of Presence
on Human Working Memory Performance

Majdi Lusta, Cheryl Seals[✉], Susan Teubner-Rhodes,
Sathish Chandra Akula, and Alexicia Richardson

Auburn University, Auburn, USA
{mal0087,sealscd,see0026,sza0096,adr0021}@auburn.edu

Abstract. Background

This research utilizes Virtual Reality as a non-conventional, informal educational setting to measure the impact of presence on human working memory performance. Many researchers have assessed human working memory and working memory performance (WMP) by computerizing a task and calculating the participant's score.

Objective

In this work, we investigate the impact of the degree of presence on working memory performance. First, we evaluate the user's feeling of being in the environment (i.e., presence), and then we investigate the correlation between WMP and presence.

Method

Participants experienced three presence levels (desktop VR (DVR), immersive VR (IVR), and immersive embodied VR (IEVR)) and conducted the same working memory task (N back task) in each environment.

Result

Our results show that the presence level significantly affects participants' mean scores. Likewise, it has a significant impact on the participant response time. Hence, the participant score increases as the presence level increases, and the response time decreases as the feeling of presence increases.

Keywords: Virtual Reality (VR) · Working memory · Head-mounted display (HMD) · Immersive environments · User experience · N-back task · Automated operation span task (Ospan)

1 Introduction

Working Memory: Working memory (WM) is a popular topic in cognitive psychology and neuroscience. Since Baddeley and Hitch introduced the concept of working memory in 1974 [1], there has not been a unanimous agreement on

© The Author(s), under exclusive license to Springer Nature Switzerland AG 2023
D. Harris and W.-C. Li (Eds.): HCII 2023, LNAI 14017, pp. 120–130, 2023.
https://doi.org/10.1007/978-3-031-35392-5_9

the definition of working memory. Working memory is vital for performing multi-faceted tasks that are essential for day-to-day functioning; tasks such as reading an article, calculating numbers, and comparing different features or prices of cars to decide the best to buy usually go through multiple steps with some results in each step needed to be temporarily saved in memory to get the task done [1]. WM is the system that maintains task-relevant information while performing cognitive tasks. In different definitions, WM is a system that temporarily provides access to a set of tasks relevant representations for manipulating information [10]. The traditional definition of short-term memory describes it as a passive storage buffer, while WM refers to an active processing and storage system [12]. WM also has processing and storage functions; it serves as a place of process execution and results storage [9,12]. Reading comprehension can be an excellent example of this, as in reading comprehension, the reader needs to store different types of information from the text and use it. For instance, readers store and reference information presented earlier in the text to make sense of the current input during reading comprehension. However, information can be a part of WM in different ways, such as perceptually encoded from text, retrieved from long-term memory, or the output of a comprehension [4]. Although there is no agreement on the characterization of WM, there is a consensus that the WM has limited capacity, which means that only a limited amount of information can be ready for access at any given time. This limitation of capacity describes the decline in cognitive performance with increasing task complexity [5].

Measuring Working Memory: Theoretically, measuring WMP considers different aspects generally determined by function and content components. Further, each of these two components has three elements. The functional component includes simultaneous storage and manipulation, supervision, and coordination. On the other hand, the content component contains verbal, numerical, and spatial working memory [13].

Simultaneous storage and processing are essential working memory functions [8,18]. For distinguishing working memory from short-term memory, Daneman and Carpenter(1980) [4] proposed that short-term memory temporarily stores this information while working memory holds and processes information at the same time [4]. Transformations are the tasks that need processing and storage of information. A task can be categorized as involving 'processing' when it is required to transform the given information; that is, processing involves more than passive storage and short-term rehearsal. An example of working memory includes, in algebra class, a working memory task involving keeping a formula in mind while using it to solve a math problem simultaneously.

Supervision involves monitoring processing functions and implementing control to select and activate information relevant to the current task. It helps the individual stay on task, and it also inhibits irrelevant information [13]. The prefrontal cortex, which is involved in several higher-level control functions, is believed to implement the supervisory component of working memory [13].

The coordination process requires simultaneous access to distinct stored elements to integrate into their respective roles [13]. Working memory is linked with the responsibility to coordinate information into structures [5,14,17].

Working memory can be theoretically divided into verbal, spatial-figural, and numerical content types. However, the extent to which working memory tasks dissociate between these content types is unclear [13].

Immersive and Less Immersive Environments: The increased usage of VR over the last years increased the focus on user engagement and immersion. In this technology, the level of immersion is referred to as presence. Presence can be defined as the sensation of existing in the virtual sitting [16]. Some research reported that the intensity of emotions users experience is directly impacted by the level of presence [16]. Due to its ability to recall and intensify affective states, VR is referred to as an "affective medium" [16]. Many comparative research pieces investigate the impact of immersive virtual environments against non-immersive environments. Coulter et al. [3] examined the effect of a fully immersive head-mounted display (HMD) and desktop environment. The result showed that the HMD environment significantly positively impacted physical tasks. In contrast, Moreno et al. [11] found no performance difference with either using HMD or desktop-based applications for learning about botany. Juan et al. [7] also found no significant difference between immersive and desktop environments in their study in which students learned about the interior human body.

Researchers have been investigating the impact of immersion and presence in learning environments, showing that this impact varies among environments. However, it is essential to conduct empirical studies on the impact of the level of immersion on working memory performance.

2   System Design

To induce different feelings of presence, we varied the visual and auditory fidelity of the environment. For example, as a knowledge gain among participants in the field of airline safety, Chittaro et al. [2] found that learning outcomes of the HMD immersive environment were better than the traditional card-based learning among passengers. Similarly, Patel et al. [15] found that immersive virtual environments positively impacted participant knowledge gain in physical tasks.

This research compared a fully immersive environment with a 2D video system that tests participants' WMP; the environment varies from an embodied and high level of visual and auditory fidelity to abstract and low fidelity (Fig. 1). The user is immersed in all the environments through a virtual game that utilizes N-Back working memory tasks. In the immersive embodied VR environment (IEVR), the user's working memory performance is scaled through a VR game that immerses the user in an embodied virtual environment. However, in the immersive non-embodied VR (IVR) environment, the game immerses the user into a non-embodied virtual environment. Finally, in the desktop VR (DVR) environment, this game immerses the user in a non-embodied 2D environment (Fig. 3).

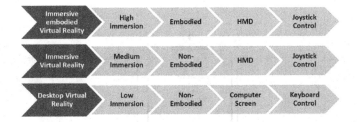

Fig. 1. The different environments with different levels of immersion.

2.1 Immersive Embodied VR (IEVR)

In this environment, the goal is to measure the user's working memory performance through a VR game. This game immerses the user into an embodied virtual game that utilizes the N-Back working memory task. The high-level flow diagram for the Immersive embodied VR Working Memory scale is presented in Fig. 1. The game familiarizes players with either little or no VR experience with the virtual environment through exploration and tutorials. However, the game provides the highest level of immersion, as it provides an immersive embodied virtual reality metaphor that includes sounds, avatar hands, and head-tracking ability. The player views a first-person perspective and controls through the controllers that come with the HMD. Furthermore, the player goes through three levels of the N-Back task, where the difficulty increases at each level. For performance assessment, each achievement is given upon completion of a quest. The user's working memory performance is based on his score (correct answer and response time) (Fig. 2).

2.2 Immersive Non-embodied VR (IVR)

This environment provides a lower level of immersion as the game will immerse the user into a non-embodied (no avatar hands) virtual reality game. This environment also provides a lower level of design fidelity (less realistic design). In addition, no sound is provided in this environment. Otherwise, it has the same features as the IEVR environment.

2.3 Desktop VR (DVR)

This environment provides the lowest level of immersion among the different environments. The environment immerses the user into traditional non-embodied 2D games that offer lower fidelity. The player goes through three levels of the N-Back task, where the difficulty increases at each level. These tasks follow the same approach as the previous environments for score calculation.

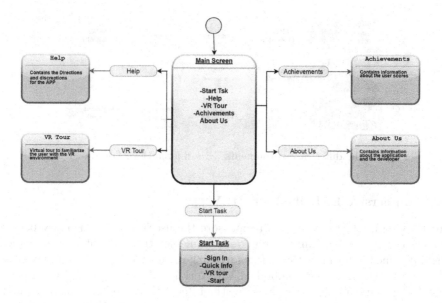

Fig. 2. The different environments with different levels of immersion.

3 Methodology

This research uses the N-Back task (working memory task adopted from Hussey et al. 2017) [6] in different environments that create different levels of immersion and interaction and studies how these circumstances impact WMP. We chose these two WMP tasks based on the following criteria:

1. They are transformable to the computer environment.
2. These tasks include different aspects of WM (transformation, supervision, and coordination).
3. Based on the literature review, these tasks are validated and reliable.

3.1 N-Back Task

This task is adopted from Hussey et al. 2017 [6]. The participant will be asked to recognize the stimulus object that appeared "n" trials earlier. The trial starts with 500 ms of fixation followed by 500 ms of stimulus, then 2 s of inter-stimulus interval. Next, the participant determines whether the displayed object is a "Target" or "Non-target" by pressing one of two keys. Each sequence of items consists of targets, lures, and fillers (6 targets, six lures, and 8+n fillers). Targets are the items repeated in the n position (i.e., that match the object that occurred n trials back), while fillers are items that did not repeat. The lures, however, are objects that repeat in positions n+1, n+2, n−1, and n−2. Non-targets include both lures and fillers. The user score is calculated based on the number of correct answers and the time to choose the correct answers (Fig. 3).

A. n-back task (3-back level example)

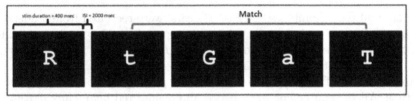

Fig. 3. 3-back Task.

3.2 Questionnaires

The sense of being present in each environment will be evaluated using Witmer and Singer's presence questionnaire [20,21]. Here is a sample of the questionnaire questions:

1. How likely are you to use this system?
2. How involved were you in the virtual environment experience?
3. Waere there moments during the virtual environment experience when you felt completely focused on the task or environment?

A questionnaire will obtain qualitative responses about participants' overall experience, system usability, and satisfaction. This data gives insight into the participant's satisfaction with the design and experience. For example, the participant will be asked questions such as:

1. How much were you able to control events?
2. What would you change in this system?
3. Do you think this immersive experience would help you learn better?

3.3 Experimental Task

The participants did the N-back in three different environments: DVR, IVR, and IEVR. The order was counterbalanced across participants. The task begins with a block of 3-back sequences, followed immediately by a block of 4-back and 5-back sequences. Following each sequence, the subject was provided with the accuracy and the average response time feedback. The participant was provided with practice before the first block in each environment. After the participant had done the N-back task in the three different environments, they were given Witmer and Singer's presence questionnaire [15,16]. Data was gathered after each stage. The experiment is designed as follows:

1. The participant does the N-back WMP task in DVR, IVR, and EIVR environments in counter-balanced order.
2. Recording the score considering the number of correct answers, the number of wrong answers, and reaction time.
3. The exit survey evaluates the participant experience in terms of presence in each environment.

3.4   Experimental Protocol

A total of 20 participants, aged 19 to 23 years, were recruited from students at Auburn University and participated in this experiment after reading the information letter of the research. The total participants included 11 (55%) men and 9 (45%) women with no history of color vision disorders.

In all stages of the experiment, only one participant was in the room at the time. All the equipment was cleaned and disinfected before any participant started any task. The experiment room is tranquil and has no windows to avoid any lightning effect.

Before beginning the experiment, the participant reviewed the information letter approved by the Institutional Review Board (IRB) of Auburn University. The experiment was executed through three environments (DVR, IVR, and IEVR) in a counter-balanced order. For example, if the first participant started with DVR, he will next do IVR and EIVR. Then, however, the second will do IVR, IEVR, and DVR, and the third will do IEVR, DVR, and IVR. At the beginning of the experiment, the user received an explanation about the task. In this explanatory session, the user viewed pictures explaining the task's mechanism.

In each environment, the participant conducted the same series of N-back tasks, consisting of a 3-back, a 4-back, and a 5-back in order of increasing difficulty. Each task takes about one minute, which is three minutes for each environment. In each environment, the participant had one minute to explore and adjust the HMD as needed.

In the DVR environment, the participant sat 60cm away from the screen. Similarly, the letters in the virtual environment (IVR, EIVR) the letters are 0.6 units. As in Unity 3D programming environment, 1 unit equals one perceived distance meter. The font size and font color are unified in all environments.

After the participant finished the three tasks in each environment, they filled out the presence survey that included 32 questions. This survey, on average, takes about 4–5 min (Fig. 4).

3.5   Analysis Method

The aim of this research was to assess the impact of presence on working memory by analyzing the correlation between presence and WMP. The participant score and response time in each task evaluated the WMP. In each environment, the sense of being present was assessed by using a questionnaire.

Witmer and Singer's presence questionnaire [20, 21] is the most cited as it has been cited 3569 times for assessing the presence [19]. Witmer and Singer developed a 32-item presence questionnaire, which they subsequently reduced to 29 items in a study examining the reliability and factor loadings of the questionnaire [20]. The authors identified four sub-scales: Involvement, Adaptation/Immersion, Sensory Fidelity, and Interface Quality. This research adopted this questionnaire due to the way presence elements were categorized, so it can be easy to differentiate and evaluate. In addition, some of the questions were adjusted in a way that can be rated on a 1 (Not) to 7 (Very) scale. Here is a sample of the questionnaire

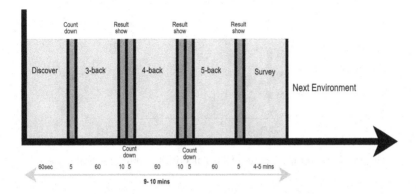

Fig. 4. Protocol Flow.

questions: 1. How much were you able to control events? 2. How involved were you in the virtual environment experience? 3. Were there moments during the virtual environment experience when you felt completely focused on the task or environment?

Since the participants are subjected to three different conditions (DVR vs IVR vs IEVR) and the response to each of these conditions is to be compared, a one-way repeated measures ANOVA and the paired t-test were used to analyze the result.

3.6 Ethics Approval

The experimental protocol was approved by the Institutional Review Board (IRB) of Auburn University (#21-567 EX 2112).

4 Results

The result showed that the level of presence significantly impacts the participant's WMP. Therefore, we first studied the level of presence in each environment and then studied the WMP in each environment. Finally, we study the correlation between the level of presence and the WMP.

The feeling of presence increases from low to medium and high in DVR, IVR, and IEVR. One-way ANOVA test showed a significant difference in the level of presence in each environment $F_{(2,57)} = 102.87$, $p < 0.05$. The paired t-test showed that IEVR has a higher level of presence than the DVR IVR (M = 7.03, SD = 0.67) and DVR (M = 4.47, SD = 1.16); $t(19) = -11.83$, $p < 0.05$. Likewise, t-test showed that IEVR (M = 8.20, SD = 0.30) has a higher level of presence than the IVR(M = 7.03, SD = 0.67); $t(19) = -7.57$, $p < 0.05$. The feeling of presence increases from low to medium and high in DVR, IVR, and IEVR (Fig. 5).

The result also showed that the level of presence significantly impacts participant score $F_{(2,57)} = 60.73$, $p = < 0.05$. The participant score increases as

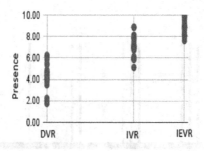

Fig. 5. The average feeling of presence in different environments.

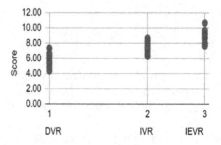

Fig. 6. The score average in different environments.

the level of feeling presence increases. The paired t-test showed that participants obtained higher scores in IEVR (M = 7.42, SD = 0.47) than in DVR (M = 6.00, SD = 0.67; $t(19) = -11.30$, $p < 0.05$. Likewise, the t-test showed that participants obtained higher scores in IEVR (M = 8.75, SD = 0.74) than in IVR (M = 7.42, SD = 0.47; $t(19) = -8.72$, $p < 0.05$. Figure 6 shows the impact of presence on the task score. The score increases as the feeling of presence increases.

In addition, results showed that the presence level significantly impacts the participant response time $F(2,57) = 8.57$, $p = < 0.05$. The response time gets smaller with more feeling of presence. The paired t-test showed that participants have less response time in IEVR (M = 1,119.95, SD = 648,06.56) than in DVR

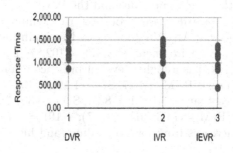

Fig. 7. The response time average in different environments.

Table 1. The correlation between presence and WMP.

	Presence	Score	Response Time
Presence	1.00		
Score	0.67	1.00	
Response Time	−0.29	−0.47	1.00

(M = 1,322.13, SD = 67,357.42; t (19) = 5.69, p ¡ 0.05. Likewise, the t-test showed that participants have less response time in IEVR (M = 947.30, SD = 114,218.53) than in IVR (M = 1,119.95, SD = 64,806.56; t(19) = 6.34, p¡0.05. Figure 7 shows the impact of presence on the response time. The response time decreases as the feeling of presence increases.

Table 1 shows the correlation between the level of presence, participant score, and participants' response time. In other words, increasing the feeling of presence increases the WMP.

5 Discussion and Conclusion

This research investigates the impact of immersion on a user's feeling of presence and user satisfaction when performing a working memory task. The foundational works were prior studies of human working memory capacity using the N-back task methodology. Existing computer applications that measure WM capacity neglect conditions that may affect performance, such as presence. As such, these applications may compromise the experimental validity of the WMP estimate. This project extends former research studies and develops a new measuring system that incorporates other necessary measures to consider dimensions that affect human conditions and user experience. Addressing these considerations and their impact on participant WMP provides greater insight into working memory and the effects of virtual reality. This work discusses the application's design and development plan to measure the WMP in various levels of immersion.

This study shows that a good design improves the feeling of being in the virtual environment (presence). In addition, increasing the presence leads to higher WMP. As a result, the level of presence that the test environment provides significantly affects the user's WMP.

References

1. Baddeley, A.D., Hitch, G.: Working memory. In: Psychology of Learning and Motivation, vol. 8, pp. 47–89. Elsevier (1974)
2. Chittaro, L., Buttussi, F.: Assessing knowledge retention of an immersive serious game vs. a traditional education method in aviation safety. IEEE Trans. Visualization Comput. Graph. **21**(4), 529–538 (2015)
3. Coulter, R., Saland, L., Caudell, T., Goldsmith, T.E., Alverson, D.: The effect of degree of immersion upon learning performance in virtual reality simulations for medical education. Med. Meets Virtual Real. **15**, 155 (2007)

4. Daneman, M., Carpenter, P.A.: Individual differences in working memory and reading. J. Memory Lang. **19**(4), 450 (1980)
5. Halford, G.S., Wilson, W.H., Phillips, S.: Processing capacity defined by relational complexity: implications for comparative, developmental, and cognitive psychology. Behav. Brain Sci. **21**(6), 803–831 (1998)
6. Hussey, E.K., Harbison, J., Teubner-Rhodes, S.E., Mishler, A., Velnoskey, K., Novick, J.M.: Memory and language improvements following cognitive control training. J. Exp. Psychol. Learn. Memory Cogn. **43**(1), 23 (2017)
7. Juan, C., Beatrice, F., Cano, J.: An augmented reality system for learning the interior of the human body. In: 2008 Eighth IEEE International Conference on Advanced Learning Technologies, pp. 186–188. IEEE (2008)
8. Kyllonen, P.C., Christal, R.E.: Reasoning ability is (little more than) working-memory capacity?! Intelligence **14**(4), 389–433 (1990)
9. LaBerge, D., Samuels, S.J.: Toward a theory of automatic information processing in reading. Cogn. Psychol. **6**(2), 293–323 (1974)
10. Miyake, A., Shah, P.: Models of Working Memory: Mechanisms of Active Maintenance and Executive Control. Cambridge University Press, Cambridge (1999)
11. Moreno, R., Mayer, R.E.: Learning science in virtual reality multimedia environments: Role of methods and media. J. Educ. Psychol. **94**(3), 598 (2002)
12. Newell, A.: Production systems: models of control structures. In: Visual Information Processing, pp. 463–526. Elsevier (1973)
13. Oberauer, K., Süß, H.M., Schulze, R., Wilhelm, O., Wittmann, W.W.: Working memory capacity-facets of a cognitive ability construct. Pers. Individ. Differ. **29**(6), 1017–1045 (2000)
14. Oberauer, L., Hagner, C., Raffelt, G., Rieger, E.: Supernova bounds on neutrino radiative decays. Astropart. Phys. **1**(4), 377–386 (1993)
15. Patel, K., Bailenson, J.N., Hack-Jung, S., Diankov, R., Bajcsy, R.: The effects of fully immersive virtual reality on the learning of physical tasks. In: Proceedings of the 9th Annual International Workshop on Presence, Ohio, USA, pp. 87–94 (2006)
16. Riva, G., et al.: Affective interactions using virtual reality: the link between presence and emotions. CyberPsychol. Behav. **10**(1), 45–56 (2007)
17. Robin, N., Holyoak, K.J.: 64 relational complexity and the functions of prefrontal cortex (1995)
18. Salthouse, T.A., Babcock, R.L.: Decomposing adult age differences in working memory. Dev. Psychol. **27**(5), 763 (1991)
19. Schwind, V., Knierim, P., Haas, N., Henze, N.: Using presence questionnaires in virtual reality. In: Proceedings of the 2019 CHI Conference on Human Factors in Computing Systems, pp. 1–12 (2019)
20. Witmer, B.G., Jerome, C.J., Singer, M.J.: The factor structure of the presence questionnaire. Pres. Teleoper. Virt. Environ. **14**(3), 298–312 (2005)
21. Witmer, B.G., Singer, M.J.: Measuring presence in virtual environments: a presence questionnaire. Presence **7**(3), 225–240 (1998)

The Impact of Blue Light and Dark UI on Eye Fatigue and Cognitive Workload

Bilal Mahmood, Fatih Baha Omeroglu, Elahe Abbasi, and Yueqing Li[✉]

Lamar University, Beaumont, TX 77705, USA
{eabbasi,yueqing.li}@lamar.edu

Abstract. The effects of lights from computer screens, specifically the blue light has been a debated research topic in this digital area we are living in. Past research initially has shown the negative effects of blue light on eyestrain, sleep and even focus. However, some recent studies have also shown that blue light might improve the focus and wakefulness of individuals. In addition to blue light usage, dark user interface (UI) themes have become extremely common in our daily usage of technology. Even though, it seems to be a very popular option within users, its effect on cognitive performance is still yet to be researched thoroughly. Some of the past research showed negative effects of dark UI on reading performances. On the other hand, dark UI seemed to cause less eye strain and less fatigue. Based on the past research and some other implications, this research created a custom blue light inspired UI and studied its effects on cognitive workload and eye strain in comparison to dark UI and default UI using EEG and eye trackers. Under each user interface condition, participants performed a hybrid-search task and EEG frequency bands and pupil size measures are collected. As a result of the analysis, statistical trend and individual feedback were gathered however none of the results were significant. It's our belief that, this preliminary study can be the precursor of an improved, well versed usability research with increased sample size and more dependent variables.

Keywords: Usability · User research · User interfaces · EEG · eye tracking · Cognitive workload

1 Introduction

The effects of light from screens and specifically the effects of blue light emitted from these screens have been a longtime subject of discussion in this digital age. It has been proven numerous times that light emitted from computer screens does in fact have some effect on humans, whether good or bad (Blehm et al. 2005). Blue light is one of the topics that is heard a lot when it comes to researching the impact of computer usage on eye strain, eye fatigue, and workload (Sheppard and Wolffsohn 2018).

© The Author(s), under exclusive license to Springer Nature Switzerland AG 2023
D. Harris and W.-C. Li (Eds.): HCII 2023, LNAI 14017, pp. 131–142, 2023.
https://doi.org/10.1007/978-3-031-35392-5_10

1.1 Literature Review

Through the years, there have been many opinions on blue light exposure and about whether it is good or bad for humans. Initial thoughts on blue light where about how harmful blue light can be for humans. Short wavelength blue light exposure has been tied to eyestrain and migraine in some cases and wearing blue light blocking glasses has been shown to reduce critical fusion frequency (CFF) which is related to eye fatigue (Ide et al. 2015). Another risk associated with blue light exposure is the possibility of sleep disorders from over exposure especially at nighttime. A study shows that peak human melatonin suppression occurs from exposure to short wavelength blue light in the range of 420 nm to 480 nm (Baek and Min, 2015). It is widely accepted that the blue light up to 455 nm should be avoided due to its continuous exposure can cause significant eye health problems (Leid 2016). Most reported eye fatigue symptoms are caused by the blue lights emitted from digital devices. There is only one part of the electromagnetic spectrum that is visible to us, and that is this visible light spectrum. As shown in Fig. 2, the visible light spectrum is quite small relative to the rest of the electromagnetic spectrum. The lower limit is generally around 360 to 400 nm, and the upper limit is roughly between 760 and 830 nm (Sliney 2016). Violet color has the shortest wavelength on this range (lowest number area 360–400), while red light has claimed the status of having the longest wavelength in the range (Bell 2003). Most emitted light from our devices are white however the nanometers of these emitted lights are within the category of blue light of 400 to 490 nm wavelength (Wiryawan et al. 2021). Due to excessive use of smartphones, these lights can cause significant eye strain and fatigue symptoms in users (Long et al. 2017) (Fig. 1).

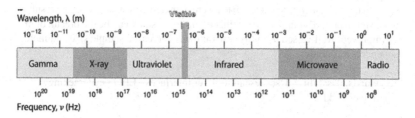

Fig. 1. The Visible Spectrum (Sliney 2016)

However, research also shows that not all blue light is bad, its demonstrated that the blue light above 465 nm can have some beneficial impacts (Leid 2016). For example, one of the seen benefits of blue light is related to our circadian clock, increasing blue light exposure to ourselves during the daytime has also been shown to aid and strengthen our circadian timing system, which would assist us in feeling tired later in the evening for sleep (Holzman 2010). The study of Baek and Min (2015) demonstrates that the exposure to blue light wavelengths beyond 465 nm can help with the sluggishness and tired feelings sometimes obtained after having a lunchtime meal (these feelings are also called post-lunch dip) can be mitigated to some degree. This means that the certain wavelengths of blue light can help individual have more wakefulness. Another study shows that exposure to lights in the workplace that are blue enriched improves alertness and even improves sleep quality later in the day (Viola et al. 2008). This happens because receiving blue light exposure during the daytime helps the brain to fix its circadian rhythm. The human brain associates blue light with daytime and helps to make you more alert (Viola et al. 2008).

Research shows the certain wavelengths of blue light being beneficial that many filter based applications, lenses and special glasses adopts these nanometers utilize the possible benefits of blue light while filtering out the harmful wavelengths. One of the highly commercialized tools blue light glasses are quite popular and these glasses believed to filter out harmful blue light up until 455 nm (Boulton et al. 2001). There are also blue light software and filter applications believed to be eliminating some of these harmful wavelengths by changing the color, and some of these filter applications have shown significant benefits, especially on task performance (Chiu and Liu 2020). Most of these applications were used in the mobile phone setting and not many of them researched with computer usage however their validity of reducing the blue light exposure has been measured in additional research showing that the approach of these filters in fact caused these devices and screens to emit less harmful blue lights (Mitropoulos et al. 2019).

In addition to filter-based research and applications utilizing blue light, dark UI and dark mode interfaces have also gained massive popularity within the users. Dark Mode is simply a user interface option available in many different software in which the interface is simply made darker (Eisfeld and Kristallovich 2020). Even though dark UI has been quite popular and common, scientific research about its effect is still very limited. A study has shown that a dark user interface resulted in lower comprehension scores for text when compared to a lighter theme of fully black text on a full white background, at about a 6% difference (Wang and Chen 2003). This leads us to believe that perhaps on a very dark theme, the human brain struggles slightly more to read the words compared to a regular lighter theme. However, the advantage of dark user interfaces that is of interest to this study is the relation to eye strain and eye fatigue. A lot of users are struggling with visual fatigue and digital eye strain due to overuse of technologies and increased screentime (CooperVision 2018). Dark modes and darkened user interface themes found to reduce eyestrain, especially when looking at screens in darker environments; a study has proven that using dark mode results in significantly lower visual fatigue scores verses when a light mode is used in less bright environments (Erickson et al. 2020).

Overall, this study aims to investigate if it is possible to reduce eye fatigue, and cognitive workload of computer users via enhanced focus from specific wavelengths of blue light exposure incorporated with dark UI while also assessing usability of commonly used dark UI and default UI.

2 Methodology

2.1 Participants

19 (15 males and 4 females) volunteers are participated in this study. The mean age was of age 23.6 and standard deviation was of value roughly 4.45. The participants in these experiments reported no prior mental health conditions and each completed a comprehensive written informed consent document before the start of the experiment. None of the participants were under the effect of any kinds of stimulants or medicines

within 24 h before these experiments. Lastly, this study was fully approved by the International Review Board (IRB) to be conducted on campus.

2.2 Data Acquisition

The G.Tec g.USBamp amplifier was the EEG machine/device used to acquire EEG signals. The software used with the EEG was BCI2000. The g.Gammacap was used with dry electrodes. The positioning of the electrodes for the EEG was based on the 10–20 positioning system. 11 channels were used to measure and obtain the EEG signals according to the 10–20 system; F6, F5, Fz, C4, C3, Cz, Pz, P5, P6, O1, O2, using Ag-AgCl electrodes with the addition of the G.Tec G.GAMMAbox amplifier. The grounding electrode was positioned below and behind the earlobe, on the upper part of the neck. The reference electrode was positioned on the opposite side of the head from the ground electrode at roughly the same height and positioning. The signals from the EEG were sampled at 256 Hz. To clean the lower end noise on the data, the low pass filter was set to a value of 1 Hz. Additionally, to clean out the noise at the high range we set the high pass filter to 40 Hz in the BCI2000 software. Lastly, a notch filter of 50 Hz was applied to the EEG recording. After the experiments, the acquired data was processed offline using EEGlab MATLAB plugin. Independent Component Analysis (ICA) was used in the EEGlab software. The data was then re-referenced using the common average computation. Finally, ocular and movement related artifacts were removed manually from the data. Fast Fourier Transform (FFT) used to extract spectral power density $\mu V2/Hz$ values for theta, alpha and beta bands.

Additionally, a pair of Tobii Pro 2 eye tracking glasses were used to track changes in pupil size. Imotions software is used to record eye tracking responses.

2.3 Creation of Blue Light-Based Custom UI

Computer monitors use only red, green, and blue, which are the additive primary colors (Mishra 2017). With these 3 colors, most colors can be created (roughly 16.7 million possible colors with the modern LED office monitors) by most monitors and graphical display systems. The RGB model can be represented as a cube, with each axis in a 3-dimensional graph representing 1 color, as shown in Fig. 4 (Mihai and Strajescu 2007). Therefore, a point in this 3D space would then reflect a ratio of red, blue, and green.

Hermann Grassman was a German scientist and mathematician who founded the set of 4 laws known as "Grassmann's Laws." These laws together describe a way to mathematically represent light of color (Hardeberg 2001; Koenderink 2010). Grassmann states that for any given color with a spectral distribution power $I(\lambda)$, the RGB coordinates can be calculated using the functions 1, 2, and 3 shown below:

$$Red = \int_{1}^{\infty} I(\lambda)r(\lambda)d\lambda \tag{1}$$

$$Green = \int_{1}^{\infty} I(\lambda)g(\lambda)d\lambda \tag{2}$$

$$Blue = \int_{1}^{\infty} I(\lambda)b(\lambda)d\lambda \tag{3}$$

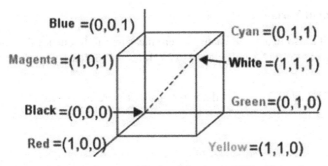

Fig. 2. RGB Color Space System (Mihai and Strajescu 2007). (Color figure online)

Table 1. Wavelength to RGB Chart Based on Previous Formulae (Mihai and Strajescu, 2007)

Wavelength Intervals	R G B
410–440 nm	$R = 0.19 - 0.19\left(\frac{440 - Wavelength}{30}\right)$
	$G = 0$
	$B = 1$
440–490 nm	$R = 0$
	$G = 1 - \left(\frac{490 - Wavelength}{50}\right)$
	$B = 1$

A 2007 study has used these functions from Grassmann's Laws to implement some algorithms to find the red, green, and blue values for the RGB system of any given wavelength in the range of 380 nm to 780 nm (Mihai and Strajescu 2007). The conversion table past studies have used is pictured in Table 1. The same conversion method is also adopted in this study to incorporate blue light wavelength values to transform into a specific color for the custom UI.

Using this table, wavelength from the visible electromagnetic spectrum in the real world can be transformed into value of red, green, and blue to represent the same color on a computer monitor. Based on the literature, 480 nm wavelength is selected to produce the color for our custom UI.

2.4 Independent Variables

User Interface Condition. User interface with 3 different user interface variations were the independent variable with 3 levels in this research: Custom UI, dark UI, and default UI. Custom UI is created with RGB color transformation using the 480 nm of blue light wavelength that has previously shown beneficial effects. Conditions are displayed in Figs. 3, 4, and 5.

2.5 Dependent Variables

Brain Activity. Brain activity changes were measured in frequency domain; Theta (4 to 8 Hz), alpha (8 to 12 Hz) and beta (13 to 30 Hz) wave's relative power spectral density values.

Pupil Size Changes. The pupil diameter changes were measured using eye tracking system.

Fig. 3. Black text on white background (Default UI)

Fig. 4. Light grey text on dark grey background (Dark UI)

2.6 Task

To keep the participants mentally occupied consistently throughout the task, a special hybrid between an information search task and a word search task was implemented. Rather than information search, and word search task, we proposed hybrid-search task which emulated a programmer search or an excel input search within numerous cells. The

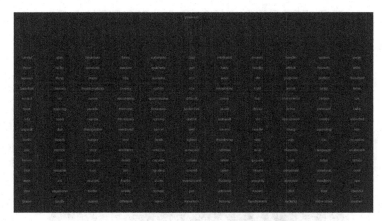

Fig. 5. Light Blue (480 nm) on dark grey background (Custom UI) (Color figure online)

UI conditions consisted of changes in the background color of the screen and changes in the color of the font for the words. All 3 conditions had the same goal of finding a target word in a bank of 165 words on the screen repeatedly until the 15 min ran out. At the end of 15 min, screen showed up to let the participant know that they have entered the rest period.

15 rows and 11 columns of words were also based on the past literature that have implemented similar experiment design using word search tasks. One such study used 15 rows and 13 columns of words for their word search puzzle (Konok et al. 2017). Another had used 15 columns and 11 rows for a jumbles letter matrix search task also (Farley and Yen 1976). Therefore, 15 rows and 11 columns for a total of 165 words were used in our experiment design to ensure the task presented was not too easy. The programs would use a random word bank of 2466 different unique words which were generated through a word generation website. From these 2466 words, 165 words would be randomly chosen by the program to become clickable words on the screen. From the 165 chosen words, a target word would also randomly be chosen and displayed at the top of the screen. Any time a word was clicked on the screen, the program would randomly pull another 165 words from the word bank and a new target word for the new page of words. The tasks in this experiment were all self-programmed from scratch.

2.7 Procedure

The experiments were conducted in a quiet room with no interruptions or distractions show in Fig. 6. The participants were seated at a desk with 1 active computer screen on, in which the stimuli and tasks were presented, as shown below in Fig. 11. The light in the room was kept on during the task to keep the environment steady throughout all conditions. Upon entering the experimentation room and being seated at the desk, participants were then instructed to fill out a demographic questionnaire. The participants were then told to find the most comfortable seating position as they would not be able to move too much so that a cleaner EEG signal would be acquired. After, the EEG headset and eye tracking glasses were equipped. Finally, upon calibrating the eye tracking

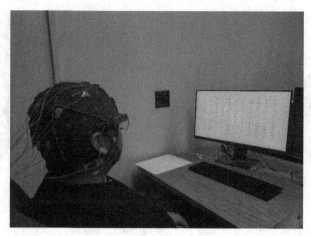

Fig. 6. Participant equipped with EEG and Eye tracking apparatus during the experiment.

glasses, participants would be allowed to commence the task. At the start of each of the trial, task entry screen has the button in the center with the word "START" on it. Once the start button is clicked, timer and the task would start. The order of the 3 UI conditions for the tasks was randomized for every single participant so that being more energetic during the initial tasks and tired for the later tasks can be ruled out. After 15 min, the task would alert the user that they are now in the resting phase. Here participants were offered as much of a break time they need. Most participants stated that the 5-min break was all they needed. After the break, participants continued with the next trial. Between each 15-min task, up to 5 min of rest given with total of 3 different conditions and trial, total experimentation time was roughly around 60 min.

2.8 Data Analysis

To observe the most dominant frequency bands for each of the 3 UI conditions. The relative power spectral density for the Alpha, Beta, and Theta bands were calculated and assessed for the entirety of each task for each participant. 4 participants data had to be excluded from the analysis due to movement related noise occurred during the experiments. Relative PSD values are calculated for each frequency band using the Eq. 4 below.

$$Relative\ PSD(\%) = \frac{Absolute\ Power\ of\ specific\ frequency\ range\ for\ theta,\ alpha\ or\ beta}{Total\ frequency\ band\ (4\ to\ 30\ Hz)}$$

(4)

For the eye tracking measures and pupil size changes, baseline of the pupil sizes were measured before the beginning of each trial and compared to extracted pupil sizes from the last 15 s of each condition.

To observe the significant changes one way analysis of variance (ANOVA) test is conducted for all dependent variables.

3 Results

3.1 Theta Waves (4 to 8 Hz)

The results did not show a significant main effect of UI conditions on relative theta power spectral density values ($F_{2,\,14} = 1.29$, $p = 0.29$). The post hoc test showed that the relative theta power spectral density values during dark UI condition ($M = 0.45$, SD $= 0.089$) were smaller compared to default UI condition ($M = 0.47$, SD $= 0.10$) and custom UI condition ($M = 0.48$, SD $= 0.11$).

3.2 Alpha Waves (8 to 12 Hz)

The results did not show a significant main effect of UI conditions on relative alpha power spectral density values ($F_{2,\,14} = 0.29$, $p = 0.75$). The post hoc test showed that the relative alpha power spectral density values during custom UI condition ($M = 0.25$, SD $= 0.072$) were smaller compared to dark UI condition ($M = 0.26$, SD $= 0.056$) and default UI condition ($M = 0.26$, SD $= 0.055$).

3.3 Beta Waves (13 to 30 Hz)

The results did not show a significant main effect of UI conditions on relative beta power spectrum density values ($F_{2,\,14} = 2.43$, $p = 0.11$). The post hoc test showed that the relative beta power spectral density values during custom UI condition ($M = 0.24$, SD $= 0.07$) were smaller compared to default UI condition ($M = 0.27$, SD $= 0.09$) and dark UI condition ($M = 0.29$, SD $= 0.09$).

3.4 Pupil Size Changes

The results did not show a significant main effect of UI conditions on pupil dilation values ($F_{2,\,19} = 1.28$, $p = 0.29$). The post hoc test showed that the pupil dilation values during custom UI condition ($M = -0.12$, SD $= 0.34$) were larger compared to dark UI ($M = -0.13$, SD $= 0.26$) and default UI condition ($M = -26$, SD $= 0.36$).

4 Discussion

Statistical results did not show any significant effect of UI conditions on user's brain waves and pupil responses. The minimal change between the UI conditions might need a larger sample size to observe significant brain patterns between users. Theta and Alpha waves have been previously linked to mental fatigue, some studies claimed that increase in theta and alpha activity linked to increase in fatigue (Tran et al. 2020). Increase in theta power indicates more theta activity however increase in alpha power indicates less alpha activity due to alpha power having an inverse relationship (Sammler et al. 2007). Previous studies also detected a decrease in beta power values after a fatigue inducing task in users (Tanaka et al. 2012). Even though results were not significant, increase in theta power during custom UI and default UI conditions were detected compared to

Dark UI which might be the indication of default UI and custom UI causing more fatigue in users compared to dark UI. Custom UI also caused more alpha activity compared to default and custom UI. Beta waves were also in parallel with these trends custom UI condition showed more decrease in beta power values compared to default and dark UI conditions.

Decrease in pupil size have been previously linked to increase in mental fatigue in a recent study (Hatsukawa and Ishikawa 2022). Another study also showed pupil constriction can happen due to mental fatigue (Bafna and Hansen 2021). All 3 conditions caused pupil size to reduce when compared to baseline which was the beginning of the task. At the end of the task, all 3 conditions caused pupil size to decrease. Custom UI and dark UI conditions showed the smaller decrease compared to default UI. Past research shows that decrease in pupil size could be due to the visual eye fatigue (Saito et al. 1994). However, the decrease in pupil size could be also due to user interfaces displaying different levels of brightness, since default UI had a lot more white and bright light compared to dark and custom UI. Since emitted light from interface also could be the reason of decrease in pupil size (Winn et al. 1994). Overall, none of these patterns were significantly proven by the statistical analysis, and more experimentation is needed to draw more meaningful conclusions and patterns.

5   Conclusion

In this preliminary study, relationship between different user interface (UI) conditions, eye fatigue, and cognitive workload were investigated. Statistical analysis showed no significant effect of UI conditions on EEG or eye tracking measures. Study contributed the literature with a new hybrid search task, and offered a possible new approach on how blue light color transformation can be implemented in some of the UI designs. Additionally, it also provided some more scientific research about the commonly used dark UI.

Study had a limited sample size and did not incorporate task performance, and some additional workload questionnaires in this phase. EEG measures only considered the changes in whole montage. In the next phase of this research, more localized EEG analysis alongside of task performance measures and questionnaires with increased sample size can really improve the research findings.

References

Baek, H., Min, B.K.: Blue light aids in coping with the post-lunch dip: an EEG study. Ergonomics **58**, 803–810 (2015)
Bafna, T., Hansen, J.P.: Mental fatigue measurement using eye metrics: a systematic literature review. Psychophysiology **58**(6), e13828 (2021)
Bell, R.B.: National Aeronautics and space administration. Space Research, The Office of Biological and Physical Research, Research and Projects, "In Sickness and in Health: Immunity and the Stressed Astronaut" (2003)
Blehm, C., Vishnu, S., Khattak, A., Mitra, S., Yee, R.W.: Computer vision syndrome: a review. Surv. Ophthal. **50**, 253–262 (2005)

Boulton, M., Różanowska, M., Różanowski, B.: Retinal photodamage. J. Photochem. Photobiol. B: Biol. **64**, 144–161 (2001)

Chiu, H.P., Liu, C.H.: The effects of three blue light filter conditions for smartphones on visual fatigue and visual performance. Hum. Factors Ergon. Manuf. Serv. Ind. **30**, 83–90 (2020)

CooperVision. Digital Device Usage and Your Eyes Report (2018). Retrieved from https://cooper vision.com/sites/coopervision.com/files/coopervision-digital-device-usage-and-your-eyes-report.pdf

Eisfeld, H., Kristallovich, F.: The rise of dark mode: a qualitative study of an emerging user interface design trend (2020)

Erickson, A., Kim, K., Bruder, G., Welch, G.F.: Effects of dark mode graphics on visual acuity and fatigue with virtual reality head-mounted displays. In: 2020 IEEE Conference on Virtual Reality and 3D User Interfaces (VR), pp. 434–442 (2020)

Farley, F.H., Yen, S.J.: Arousal and cognition: word arousal and visual search. Percept. Mot. Skills **43**(3), 699–702 (1976)

Hardeberg, J.Y.: Acquisition and Reproduction of Color Images: Colorimetric and Multispectral Approaches. Universal Publishers, Boca Raton (2001)

Hatsukawa, H., Ishikawa, M.: Decreased initial pupil size and shortened constriction latency due to negative mood states and mental fatigue in clinical subacute pain models. Physiol. Behav. **253**, 113850 (2022)

Holzman, D.C.: What's in a color? The unique human health effects of blue light. Environ. Health Perspect. (2010)

Ide, T., Toda, I., Miki, E., Tsubota, K.: Effect of blue light–reducing eye glasses on critical flicker frequency. Asia-Pacific J. Ophthalmol. **4**(2), 80–85 (2015)

Koenderink, J.J.: Color for the Sciences. MIT Press, Cambridge (2010)

Konok, V., Pogány, Á., Miklósi, Á.: Mobile attachment: separation from the mobile phone induces physiological and behavioural stress and attentional bias to separation-related stimuli. Comput. Hum. Behav. **71**, 228–239 (2017)

Leid, J.: Blue light: what are the risks to our eyes? Points de Vue: International Review Ophthalmic Optics, pp. 1–7 (2016)

Long, J., Cheung, R., Duong, S., Paynter, R., Asper, L.: Viewing distance and eyestrain symptoms with prolonged viewing of smartphones. Clin. Exp. Optom. 133–137 (2017)

Mathôt, S.: Pupillometry: psychology, physiology, and function. J. Cogn. **1**(1) (2018)

Mihai, D., Strajescu, E.: From wavelength to RGB Filter. UPB Sci. Bull. Ser. D **69**(2) (2007)

Mitropoulos, S., Tsiantos, V., Americanos, A., Sianoudis, I., Skouroliakou, A.: Blue light reducing software applications for mobile phone screens: measurement of spectral characteristics and biological parameters. In: RAP Conference Proceedings, vol. 4, pp. 220–224 (2019)

Saito, S., Sotoyama, M., Saito, S., Taptagaporn, S.: Physiological indices of visual fatigue due to VDT operation: pupillary reflexes and accommodative responses. Ind. Health **32**(2), 57–66 (1994)

Sammler, D., Grigutsch, M., Fritz, T., Koelsch, S.: Music and emotion: electrophysiological correlates of the processing of pleasant and unpleasant music. Psychophysiology **44**(2), 293–304 (2007)

Sheppard, A.L., Wolffsohn, J.S.: Digital eye strain: prevalence, measurement and amelioration. BMJ Open Ophthalmol. **3**, e000146 (2018)

Sliney, D.H.: What is light? The visible spectrum and beyond. Eye **30**, 222–229 (2016)

Tanaka, M., Shigihara, Y., Ishii, A., Funakura, M., Kanai, E., Watanabe, Y.: Effect of mental fatigue on the central nervous system: an electroencephalography study. Behav. Brain Funct. **8**(1), 1–8 (2012)

Tran, Y., Craig, A., Craig, R., Chai, R., Nguyen, H.: The influence of mental fatigue on brain activity: evidence from a systematic review with meta-analyses. Psychophysiology **57**(5), e13554 (2020)

Viola, A.U., James, L.M., Schlangen, L.J., Dijk, D.J.: Blue-enriched white light in the workplace improves self-reported alertness, performance and sleep quality. Scand. J. Work Environ. Health **34**, 297–306 (2008)

Wang, A.H., Chen, C.H.: Effects of screen type, Chinese typography, text/background color combination, speed, and jump length for VDT leading display on users' reading performance. Int. J. Ind. Ergon. **31**(4), 249–261 (2003)

Winn, B., Whitaker, D., Elliott, D.B., Phillips, N.J.: Factors affecting light-adapted pupil size in normal human subjects. Invest. Ophthalmol. Vis. Sci. **35**(3), 1132–1137 (1994)

Wiryawan, A.V., Maharani, M., Kesoema, T.A., Prihatningtias, R.: The effect of using blue light filter feature on smartphones with Asthenopia occurrence. Diponegoro Int. Med. J. **2**, 30–35 (2021)

The Evaluations of the Impact of the Pilot's Visual Behaviours on the Landing Performance by Using Eye Tracking Technology

Yifan Wang[1] , Lichao Yang[2] , Wojciech Tomasz Korek[3,4] , Yifan Zhao[2] , and Wen-Chin Li[1(✉)]

[1] Safety and Accident Investigation Centre, Cranfield University, Cranfield, UK
Yf.Wang@cranfield.ac.uk
[2] Centre for Life-Cycle Engineering and Management, Cranfield University, Cranfield, UK
[3] Dynamics, Simulation and Control Group, Cranfield University, Cranfield, UK
[4] Faculty of Automatic Control, Electronics and Computer Science, Silesian University of Technology, Gliwice, Poland

Abstract. Introduction. Eye tracking technology can be used to characterise a pilot's visual behaviour as well as to further analyse the workload and status of the pilot, which is crucial for tracking and predicting pilot performance and enhancing flight safety. **Research questions.** This research aims to investigate and identify the visual-related factors that could affect the pilot's landing operation performance (depending on whether the landing was successful or not). **Method.** There are 23 participants who performed the task of landing in the Future system simulator (FSS) while wearing eye trackers. Their eye tracking parameters including proportion of fixation count on primary flight display (PFC on PFD), proportion of fixation count on out the window (PFC on OTW), percentage change in pupil diameter (PCPD) and blink count were trained for classification using XGBoost according to whether they landed successfully or not. **Results & Discussion.** The results demonstrated that eye-movement features can be used to classify and predict a pilot's landing performance with an accuracy of 77.02%. PCPD and PFC on PFD are more crucial for performance classification out of the four features. **Conclusion.** It is practical to classify and predict pilot performance using eye-tracking technologies. The high importance of PCPD and PFC on PFD indicates that there is a correlation between pilots' workload and attention distribution and performance, which has important implications for future predictive and analytical research on performance. The prediction of performance using eye tracking suggests that pilot status monitoring has a useful application in flight deck design.

Keywords: Eye tracking · pilot monitoring · performance classification · future flight deck

1 Introduction

Human factors have always been one of the most important factors that affect flight safety. According to [1], there is approximately 80% of accidents happened due to human factors. Therefore, to enhance flight safety, it is important to effectively evaluate

D. Harris and W.-C. Li (Eds.): HCII 2023, LNAI 14017, pp. 143–153, 2023.
https://doi.org/10.1007/978-3-031-35392-5_11

the status and performance of pilots. Previous research demonstrated that pilots' operating performance could be affected by age, experience, physiological status, workload and how complex the system they were interacting with [2, 3]. Specifically, the complex human-computer interation (HCI) design could pose a challenge for pilots to maintain good performance [4]. Since the modern flight deck is highly information integrated, complex aircraft systems make the pilot status monitoring and a full understanding of the pilot's information acquisition and management processes mandatory requirements for flight deck design. As the most important and common source for information acquisition, vision and visual behaviour analysis have been well-researched in the past few years [5, 6]. Visual behaviour could characterise the human's workload and situational awareness (SA), and further evaluate the working status and capacity [5, 6]. Benefiting from the development of remote and non-intrusive camera-based eye tracking techniques, the pilot's visual behaviour monitoring and analysis have become the main focus of the research recently, which plays an important role in the study of both HCI and pilot information management in flight decks [7]. Many studies have investigated visual patterns and pupil characteristics utilising eye tracking techniques in order to better understand human information processing in different areas, such as cognitive task evaluation [8, 9], scanning behaviours investigation [10], interface evaluation for vehicle [11], and HCI design in flight deck [5, 12]. In the aviation sector, the use of eye tracking could assist researchers to understand the impact of the new flight deck layout on the pilot's SA and performance, and further improve the flight deck design [7]; to understand the differences in monitoring strategies between novice pilots and experienced pilots to improve pilot training efficiency [13]; and even to use eye tracking data as an input so that pilots can manoeuvre the aircraft using their pupil behaviours like blink and gaze [14]. With the further introduction of touchscreen and augmented reality (AR) technologies into flight decks and the need for single-pilot operation, the application of eye tracking technology in flight decks is likely to play an even more important role. In detail, the existing eye tracking research focuses on the investigation of fixation, saccade, pupil diameter and blink. Among these, fixation and saccade are often used in SA-related research, which can effectively describe human attention allocation [15]. In contrast, pupil diameter and blink are considered as physiological parameters to analyse workload and arousal levels [16]. To sum up, these studies have contributed to the exploration of eye behaviour and human cognitive processes and workloads, but it is still a long way for real applicating in the aviation industry.

The implementation of efficient pilot status monitoring is crucial for the future design of the flight deck in order to manage pilot workload and evaluate pilot performance to improve flight safety. Current research on pilot status monitoring has focused on understanding attention distribution and measuring pilot cognitive workload. The researcher found that the distribution of fixation can effectively reflect the distribution of human attention and suggested that this may influence the pilot's decision-making process [12, 17]. Moreover, by examining whether the pilot has a reasonable attention distribution, researchers can evaluate the effectiveness of display designs [18]. The research on evaluating cognitive load by using eye features like pupil diameter and blink rate have been conducted in many application domains [9]. Depending on the tasks performed, the blink rate shows different trends with workload levels. Blink rate rises during high workload tasks such as computation and verbal communication [19], while blink rate is lower during low brain load tasks such as detection and search [20]. Similarly, pupil diameter has been suggested to correlate with workload levels [21]. To verify if subtitle would increase cognitive workload, Kruger et al. measured the pupil diameter of subjects before and halfway through the experiment and introduced the percentage change in pupil diameter (PCPD) as an indicator of cognitive load. They found that subtitle condition in fact created a lower cognitive workload [22]. Furthermore, some research employed the extracted eye features and estimated workload to evaluate the task performance. Coyne et al. claimed that there is an inverted U-shaped relationship between workload and performance [23]. Alhanbali et al. found that a larger pre-stimulus pupil diameter in the digits-in-noise task was associated with lower task performance [24]. Van et al. observed a strong linear relationship between the temporal derivative of pupil diameter and task performance measures [25]. Although the feasibility of using eye features to characterise the human workload and evaluate task performance has been proved in these studies, only a few task circumstances have been examined in studies on the operational performance of pilots based on their visual behaviour and eye features [23]. Moreover, the current analysis of performance using diameter or blink alone still suffers from poor accuracy and is severely limited by the type of task [26]. Eye tracking research that analyses pilot performance stays in the stage of workload evaluation, with fewer studies achieving performance classification and prediction [12]. Achieving accurate classification and prediction of performance is important for the application of eye tracking technology to assist pilot status monitoring in flight decks. Therefore, this study intends to investigate the relationship between eye tracking features and pilot performance in order to implement pilot monitoring in future flight decks. Specifically, this research focuses on the pilot's landing performance (depending on whether the landing was successful or not) and further investigates which pupil parameter has the most potential for evaluating performance during flight. The research questions are as followed.

RQ1: Is it appropriate to categorise pilot performance in landing tasks according to fixation distribution, diameter, and blink?

RQ2: How significant are fixation diameters, distributions, and blinks for performance analysis?

2 Method

2.1 Participant

There were 23 participants invited for this research, age from 22 to 58 years (M = 31.6, SD = 10.3). The participants' fixed-wing experience was from 0 to 300 total flight hours (M = 64.7, SD = 91.0). The data of this paper was gathered from human participants and only for the research purpose, approved by Cranfield University Research Ethics System (CURES/14853/2021). Each participant was presented with the contract before the trial, the experiment was only carried out if they signed the contract and they had the right to end the trial at any stage and delete all data.

2.2 Experiment Design

The study's objective is to employ the Instrument landing system (ILS) landing scenario as a test to investigate the application of eye tracking data for performance classification. Participants weres asked to perform a landing task with the Instrument landing system (ILS) scenario in this simulator with eye tracker glasses on (as shown in Fig. 1). The flight dynamics model of the aircraft is based on a Gulfstream G550 general business aircraft. The aircraft starts in a straight line on Runway 15R at Incheon International Airport (ICAO: RKSI), Seoul, Korea, a distance of 5 miles. The initial speed was 150 knots and the altitude was 1400 feet. Weather conditions were clear and there was no wind influence. The throttle lever, landing gear and autopilot controls are all automatic. All the flight data would be recorded in the simulator automatically. The environment was kept properly illuminated and stable during the experiment to improve the accuracy of the eye tracking data collected. There were two areas of interest (AOI) being discussed in this research, primary flight display (PFD) and out the window (OTW) view.

Before the trial, all participants were provided with the consent form consisted of the experiment and research design. All participants took the following procedures: (1) complete the demographical data including age, gender and flight hours (5 min); (2) briefed the experiment process, simulator and eye tracker used (5 min); (3) seat in the FSS to familiarise the simulator layout (5 min); (4) wearing and setting the eye tracker (10 min); (5) perform the ILS landing scenario (5 min); (6) debriefing and answering questions (5–10 min). It took around 40 min to complete the experiments for each participant (Fig. 2).

Fig. 1. Participant performed the ILS landing scenario in FSS

2.3 Apparatus and Data Pre-processing

This research was conducted using Rolls-Royce Future System Simulator (FSS) at Cranfield university. This simulator was granted the iF DESIGN AWARD in 2021 [27], the FSS is a highly integrated future flight deck simulator with four large reconfigurable touchscreens and two small side screens. This simulator allows pilots and researchers

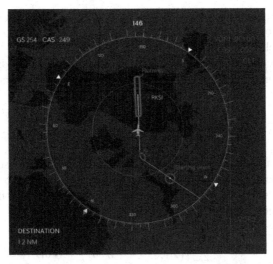

Fig. 2. Landing scenario on navigation display

to explore the best practice for future single-pilot operation flight deck with highly autonomous engine system and new technologies [28, 29].

The Pupil-Labs eye tracker was used in this research for eye tracking data collection. This eye tracker consists of a world camera (for synchronisation of user perspectives) and an eye camera (for monitoring eye characteristics and movement) fixed in a plastic frame. The resolution was 1280*720 pixels with a sample rate of 60 frames per second. The right eye of participants would be tracked by the eye camera to collect the pupil parameters and movements including pupil diameter and blink. In this research, eye fixation was defined as consecutive gaze points that fall into a circle within a radius of 1.5° and duration between 150 ms and 800 ms in line with the previous research [30]. For analysis, the visual parameters including fixation count, pupil diameter and blink were collected while participants performed the landing scenario.

There were four eye tracking parameters selected for this research: proportion of fixation count on PFD (PFC on PFD), proportion of fixation count on OTW (PFC on OTW), percentage change in pupil diameter (PCPD) and blink count. Eye tracking data were recorded throughout the experiment, where PFC on PFD and PFC on OTW were the fixation counts on PFD and OTW divided by the total fixation counts. The PCPD was calculated as the amount of change in participants' pupil diameter in the experimental situation compared to the off-task situation. The off-task state diameter was the average diameter of participants in the steady state for 15 s prior to the experiment.

2.4 Classification Method

As one of the most commonly used algorithms in applied machine learning, XGBoost [31] is employed in this study for performance classification. It is a tree-based ensemble machine learning method, which grows multiple decision trees (weak learner) and combines them together into a prediction model (strong learner). As a kind of gradient-boosted tree method, it grows a new tree in a greedy manner to reduce the residuals of the previous model in each iteration.

The employed dataset has n instances and m features. In this study n = 23 and m = 4. The prediction result $\hat{y}_i$ for an input instance x_i can be written as:

$$\hat{y}_i = \sum_{k=1}^{K} f_k(x_i), f_k \in F \tag{1}$$

where f_k is a function of an independent tree with the specific tree structure and leaf weight. K is the number of the additive functions. F represents the space of the classification and regression trees (CART). The objective function $\mathcal{L}^{(t)}$, at the t-th iteration, that needs to be optimised can be expressed as:

$$\mathcal{L}^{(t)} = \sum_{i=1}^{n} l\left(y_i, \hat{y}_i^{(t-1)} + f_t(x_i)\right) + \Omega(f_t) \tag{2}$$

where l is the loss function that measures the truth y_i and the prediction $\hat{y}_i$, and $\Omega(f_t)$ is the regularisation term that penalizes the complexity of the model to avoid overfitting.

$$\Omega(f) = \gamma T + \frac{1}{2}\lambda\|\omega\|^2 \tag{3}$$

3   Results and Discussion

K-fold cross-validation method was used to evaluate the generalizability performance of the model. In this study, the K was set as 3. Approximately, 66% of data has been used in the train set and 34% of data has been used in the test set. The cross-validation was repeated 5 times for the model performance evaluation. The results are presented in Table 1. It can be seen that the average prediction accuracy and standard deviation of the used method are 77.02% and 4.31%, respectively.

Table 1. 3-fold cross-validation results for model performance evaluation

Accuracy	Repeats					Average
	1	2	3	4	5	
Mean	73.81%	82.74%	74.40%	79.16%	75.00%	77.02%
standard deviation	1.68%	5.52%	8.49%	3.14%	2.70%	4.31%

Figure 3 presents the importance of the evaluated features in the trained classification model. It includes 3 subfigures for a set of 3-fold cross-validation. The F score refers to the number of times that a feature is used to split the data across all trees. From

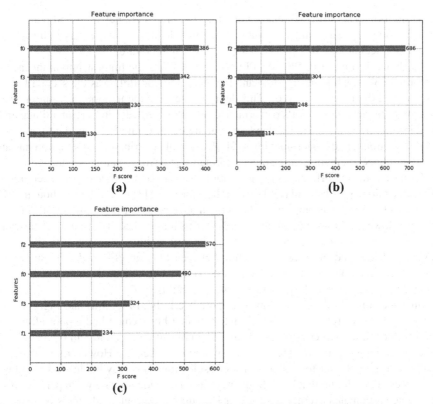

Fig. 3. Feature importance for the classification model. Subfigures (a), (b) and (c) represent the results for each fold in a 3-fold validation set

this figure, it is clear that PCPD (feature 2) and PFC on PFD (feature 0) are used most frequently for growing trees, which are more important for the classification.

The PCPD (feature 2) had the highest importance as shown in Fig. 3(b) and Fig. 3(c) (F $score_2 = 686$, F $score_3 = 570$). It emphasises the diameter variation, which can effectively reflect variations in landing success rate because of its strong association with the workload. Different methods for evaluating diameter have been employed in workload and performance studies using diameter, including baseline diameter, pre-stimulus diameter, PCPD, and derivatives of diameter [24]. Some significant results have been obtained from these studies, for example, baseline diameter and pre-stimulus diameter are both considered to have a correlation with mission completion rate, while the derivative of diameter has a linear relationship with behavioural performance [25]. However, previous studies have commonly used correlation analysis, and the results are influenced by the type of task and load level, yielding different or even contradictory patterns [23]. This study directly employs a machine learning approach to verify the potential of PCPD for landing task classification, which has important implications for further implementation of the classification and evaluation of pilot performance. At the same time, these multiple diameter-related parameters may vary in their validity for performance studies and make practical application inconvenient due to a lack of standardisation. Therefore, comparing and filtering these parameters to find out which is more efficient for analysing performance and workload is also necessary to introduce eye tracking technology into practical applications in the future.

As shown in Fig. 3(a), PFC on PFD (feature 0) was the highest important factor (F score$_1$ = 386), while in Fig. 3(b) and Fig. 3(c), PFC on PFD was the second factor (F score$_2$ = 304, F score$_3$ = 490). This demonstrates that the fixation distribution also has a great impact on the pilot's performance. The PFD provides important altitude and speed information during the ILS landing, making the PFC on PFD important for attention distribution and decision-making [15]. Reasonable distribution of attention has an important impact on maintaining good performance [5]. Additionally, previous research had found significant differences in the fixation distribution between experienced pilots and novice pilots, which could result in a performance gap [32]. However, although PFC on PFD had a significant impact on the performance results, the weighting of PFC on OTW was lower in the case of all three models. This may be because, in the ILS landing scenario, the fixation distribution of participants was highly concentrated in PFD and OTW, which resulted in a high correlation between PFC on PFD and PFC on OTW, thus affecting the importance of PFC on OTW. More rigorous data downscaling may be required in subsequent studies to rule out this possibility.

Unexpectedly, Blink had the lowest importance in both Fig. 3(a) and Fig. 3(b) (F score$_1$ = 130, F score$_2$ = 234), which indicates that blink count had a poor effect on performance. Blink was considered to have a significant correlation with the workload while under a high workload, the blink rate would increase [33]. However, in our study blink was less important for performance classification. This may be due to individual differences, as we found that blink frequency varied considerably between participants, with some participants averaging less than 10 blinks per minute and others perhaps as high as 30–40 blinks per minute. In this study, the blink count over the length of the experiment was used directly, which did not eliminate individual differences. Further research can try to use blink rate of change instead of blink count to obtain better classification results.

As a pilot study, there are some limitations to this study regarding the sample size, the scenarios designed, and the chosen parameters. The sample size selected was relatively small and may not include all levels of pilot experience. However, this research is a proof of concept study and focuses on verifying the feasibility of using eye tracking technology to achieve the pilot's performance classification. Also, the scenario evaluated is limited, which is ILS landing and the complexities of the flight have not been simulated. However, landing, as the task most prone to safety issues during commercial flights, is somewhat generalised as a simulation task and in future research, we will further introduce landing tasks affected by turbulence in order to better simulate complex flight situations. Finally, there were only two parameters related to attention distribution (PFC on PFD and PFC on OTW) and two parameters related to physiological changes and cognitive workload (PCPD and blink count) selected from all eye tracking parameters for performance classification. Parameters such as fixation duration and saccade, which have a correlation with pilot attention allocation, were not selected for this model. In our further research, these parameters will be processed and applied to the model in an appropriate way.

4 Conclusion

This paper investigated the impact of the pilots' visual behaviours on their landing performance. Specifically, the pilots' visual movement has been tracked and characterised by four features, PFC on PFD, PFC on OTW, PCPD and blink count in this study, and the XGboost algorithm has been further employed to achieve the performance classification. The results showed that the pilots' landing performance can be classified and predicted based on eye movement features. The employed method achieves 77.02% accuracy. Moreover, among the four selected features, PCPD and PFC on PFD are more important for performance classification, which suggests there is a significant effect of pilot workload and attention allocation on performance. For future work, the sample size and the number of scenarios used can be further expanded, as well as the different features of eye-tracking data. Such research could provide a further understanding of how pilots' performance is affected by their visual behaviour under different circumstances. In conclusion, the use of eye-tracking technology is feasible to achieve pilots' performance classification and prediction. The prediction of performance through eye tracking indicates that pilot status monitoring has a practical application in flight deck design. Eye tracking will be of greater importance for pilot monitoring in the future flight deck design, which could further promote the efficiency of information acquisition and management, and enhance flight safety.

Acknowledgements. This research is co-financed by the European Union through the European Social Fund (grant number POWR.03.02.00-00-I029). The authors would like to thank the FSS Team in Cranfield, especially Mudassir Lone, for his generous support during the project's development, and Rolls-Royce, particularly Peter Beecroft, for approving the research to be carried out in the Future Systems Simulator.

References

1. Nguyen, T., Lim, C.P., Nguyen, N.D., Gordon-Brown, L., Nahavandi, S.: A review of situation awareness assessment approaches in aviation environments. IEEE Syst. J. **13**(3), 3590–3603 (2019). https://doi.org/10.1109/JSYST.2019.2918283
2. Novak, A., Mrazova, M.: Research of physiological factors affecting pilot performance in flight simulation training device. Commun.-Sci. Lett. Univ. Zilina **17**(3), 103–107 (2015). https://doi.org/10.26552/com.C.2015.3.103-107
3. Lee, K.: Effects of flight factors on pilot performance, workload, and stress at final approach to landing phase of flight. University of Central Florida (2010). Accessed 20 Feb 2023. https://stars.library.ucf.edu/etd/1628
4. Carroll, M., Dahlstrom, N.: Human computer interaction on the modern flight deck. Int. J. Hum.-Comput. Interact. **37**(7), 585–587 (2021). https://doi.org/10.1080/10447318.2021.1890495
5. Li, W.C., Zhang, J., Minh, T.L., Cao, J., Wang, L.: Visual scan patterns reflect to human-computer interactions on processing different types of messages in the flight deck. Int. J. Ind. Ergon. **72**, 54–60 (2019). https://doi.org/10.1016/j.ergon.2019.04.003
6. Stanton, N.A., Plant, K.L., Roberts, A.P., Allison, C.K.: Use of highways in the sky and a virtual pad for landing head up display symbology to enable improved helicopter pilots situation awareness and workload in degraded visual conditions. Ergonomics **62**(2), 255–267 (2017). https://doi.org/10.1080/00140139.2017.1414301

7. Hebbar, P.A., Pashilkar, A.A., Biswas, P.: Using eye tracking system for aircraft design – a flight simulator study. Aviation **26**(1), 11–21 (2022). https://doi.org/10.3846/AVIATION. 2022.16398

8. Ryffel, C.P., Muehlethaler, C.M., Huber, S.M., Elfering, A.: Eye tracking as a debriefing tool in upset prevention and recovery training (UPRT) for general aviation pilots. Ergonomics **62**(2), 319–329 (2019). https://doi.org/10.1080/00140139.2018.1501093

9. Chen, S., Epps, J.: Using task-induced pupil diameter and blink rate to infer cognitive load. Hum. Comput. Interact. **29**, 390–413 (2014). https://doi.org/10.1080/07370024.2014.892428

10. Yang, L., Yu, R., Lin, X., Xie, Y., Ma, L.: Visual search tasks: measurement of dynamic visual lobe and relationship with display movement velocity. Ergonomics **61**(2), 273–283 (2017). https://doi.org/10.1080/00140139.2017.1353138

11. Yahoodik, S., Tahami, H., Unverricht, J., Yamani, Y., Handley, H., Thompson, D.: Blink rate as a measure of driver workload during simulated driving. In: Proceedings of the 2020 HFES 64th International Annual Meeting, vol. 64, no. 1, pp. 1825–1828 (2021). https://doi.org/10. 1177/1071181320641439

12. Li, W.C., Braithwaite, G., Wang, T., Yung, M., Kearney, P.: The benefits of integrated eye tracking with airborne image recorders in the flight deck: a rejected landing case study. Int. J. Ind. Ergon. **78**, 102982 (2020). https://doi.org/10.1016/J.ERGON.2020.102982

13. Neboshynsky, C.M.: Expertise on cognitive workloads and performance during navigation and target detection (2012). Accessed 19 Feb 2023. https://apps.dtic.mil/sti/citations/ADA 561981

14. Biswas, P., Jeevithashree, D.V.: Eye gaze controlled MFD for military aviation. In: International Conference on Intelligent User Interfaces, Proceedings IUI, pp. 79–89 (2018).https:// doi.org/10.1145/3172944.3172973

15. Causse, M., Lancelot, F., Maillant, J., Behrend, J., Cousy, M., Schneider, N.: Encoding decisions and expertise in the operator's eyes: using eye-tracking as input for system adaptation. Int. J. Hum. Comput. Stud. **125**, 55–65 (2019). https://doi.org/10.1016/J.IJHCS.2018.12.010

16. Babu, M.D., JeevithaShree, D.V., Prabhakar, G., Saluja, K.P.S., Pashilkar, A., Biswas, P.: Estimating pilots' cognitive load from ocular parameters through simulation and in-flight studies. J. Eye Mov. Res. **12**(3), 1–16 (2019). https://doi.org/10.16910/JEMR.12.3.3

17. Callaway, F., Rangel, A., Griffiths, T.L.: Fixation patterns in simple choice reflect optimal information sampling. PLoS Comput. Biol. **17**(3), e1008863 (2021). https://doi.org/10.1371/ JOURNAL.PCBI.1008863

18. Li, W.C., Horn, A., Sun, Z., Zhang, J., Braithwaite, G.: Augmented visualization cues on primary flight display facilitating pilot's monitoring performance. Int. J. Hum. Comput. Stud. **135**, 102377 (2020). https://doi.org/10.1016/j.ijhcs.2019.102377

19. Chen, S., Epps, J.: Automatic classification of eye activity for cognitive load measurement with emotion interference. Comput. Methods Programs Biomed. **110**(2), 111–124 (2013). https://doi.org/10.1016/J.CMPB.2012.10.021

20. Chen, S., Epps, J., Ruiz, N., Chen, F.: Eye activity as a measure of human mental effort in HCI. In: International Conference on Intelligent User Interfaces, Proceedings IUI, pp. 315–318 (2011).https://doi.org/10.1145/1943403.1943454

21. Krejtz, K., Duchowski, A.T., Niedzielska, A., Biele, C., Krejtz, I.: Eye tracking cognitive load using pupil diameter and microsaccades with fixed gaze. PLoS ONE **13**(9), e0203629 (2018). https://doi.org/10.1371/JOURNAL.PONE.0203629

22. Kruger, J.L., Hefer, E., Matthew, G.: Measuring the impact of subtitles on cognitive load: eye tracking and dynamic audiovisual texts. In: ACM International Conference Proceeding Series, pp. 62–66 (2013).https://doi.org/10.1145/2509315.2509331

23. Coyne, J.T., Foroughi, C., Sibley, C.: Pupil diameter and performance in a supervisory control task: a measure of effort or individual differences? In: Proceedings of the Human Factors and Ergonomics Society Annual Meeting, pp. 865–869 (2017). https://doi.org/10.1177/154193 1213601689

24. Alhanbali, S., Munro, K.J., Dawes, P., Carolan, P.J., Millman, R.E.: Dimensions of self-reported listening effort and fatigue on a digits-in-noise task, and association with baseline pupil size and performance accuracy. Int. J. Audiol. 60(10), 762–772 (2020). https://doi.org/10.1080/14992027.2020.1853262

25. van den Brink, R.L., Murphy, P.R., Nieuwenhuis, S.: Pupil diameter tracks lapses of attention. PLoS ONE 11(10), e0165274 (2016). https://doi.org/10.1371/JOURNAL.PONE.0165274

26. Appel, T., Scharinger, C., Gerjets, P., Kasneci, E.: Cross-subject workload classification using pupil-related measures. In: Eye Tracking Research and Applications Symposium (ETRA), vol. 18 (2018). https://doi.org/10.1145/3204493.3204531

27. iF Design. Future Systems Simulator (FSS) (2021). https://ifdesign.com/en/winner-ranking/project/future-systems-simulator-fss/314432. Accessed 21 Nov 2022

28. Korek, W.T., Li, W.C., Lu, L., Lone, M.: Investigating pilots' operational behaviours while interacting with different types of inceptors. In: Lecture Notes in Computer Science (including subseries Lecture Notes in Artificial Intelligence and Lecture Notes in Bioinformatics), vol. 13307 LNAI, pp. 314–325 (2022). https://doi.org/10.1007/978-3-031-06086-1_24/COVER

29. Li, W.C., Wang, Y., Korek, W.T.: To be or not to be? assessment on using touchscreen as inceptor in flight operation. Transport. Res. Procedia 66(C), 117–124 (2022). https://doi.org/10.1016/J.TRPRO.2022.12.013

30. Li, W.-C., Moore, P., Zhang, J., Lin, J., Kearney, P.: The impact of out-the-window size on air traffic controllers' visual behaviours and response time on digital tower operations. Int. J. Hum. Comput. Stud. 166, 102880 (2022). https://doi.org/10.1016/J.IJHCS.2022.102880

31. Chen, T., Guestrin, C.: XGBoost: a scalable tree boosting system. In: Proceedings of the ACM SIGKDD International Conference on Knowledge Discovery and Data Mining, 13–17 August 2016, pp. 785–794 (2016). https://doi.org/10.1145/2939672.2939785

32. Ziv, G.: Gaze behavior and visual attention: a review of eye tracking studies in aviation. Int. J. Aviat. Psychol. 26(3–4), 75–104 (2017). https://doi.org/10.1080/10508414.2017.1313096

33. Pfleging, B., Fekety, D.K., Schmidt, A., Kun, A.L.: A model relating pupil diameter to mental workload and lighting conditions. In: Conference on Human Factors in Computing Systems - Proceedings, pp. 5776–5788 (2016). https://doi.org/10.1145/2858036.2858117

How Information Access, Information Volume of Head-Up Display and Work Experience Affect Pilots' Mental Workload During Flight: An EEG Study

Jinchun Wu, Chenhao Li, and Chengqi Xue[✉]

School of Mechanical Engineering, Southeast University, Nanjing 211189, China
ipd_xcq@seu.edu.cn

Abstract. Since the real flight environment for pilots is constantly changing, and existing studies of head-up display (HUD) on flight are often static, the experiment was conducted to simulate the dynamics of flight through Flightgear software to closely match the mental load of pilots in real conditions. To explore the effect of HUD on the flight process in a simulated flight environment, a three-factor experiment was conducted to investigate the change in the pilot's mental workload during flight including two information access (Display1 (integrated HUD and gauge display) vs. Dislpay2 (single gauge display)), two tasks (climb task vs. level flying task) and four visits (Visit2 vs. Visit 3 vs. Visit 4 vs. Visit 5). The information volume was achieved by performing different flight tasks and the work experience is represented by the number of times of flying (visit). From the analysis of NASA-TLX scale, flight performance and EEG data of pilots, it was found that as the number of executions increased, the working memory gradually increased but the mental workload gradually decreased. In addition, we also found that the HUD could assist pilots in cognition and help reduce the workload during flight, and the assistance was most effective when the HUD presented sufficient information.

Keywords: HUD · Mental Workload · EEG · Information Access · Information Volume · Work Experience

1 Introduction

With the increasing automation, integration and intelligence of machines, the amount of information in the system increases geometrically and the cognitive load on the driver increases rather than decreases. Visual displays play the most significant role among human-computer interaction systems and are the most widely utilized [1]. The Head-Up Display (HUD) is one of the main visual displays in the cockpit, and its essential function is to display information. It was originally used in military aircraft to assist pilots in maneuvering the aircraft while obtaining some simple information about the aircraft's flight, and nowadays it has gradually started to be expanded for

D. Harris and W.-C. Li (Eds.): HCII 2023, LNAI 14017, pp. 154–167, 2023.
https://doi.org/10.1007/978-3-031-35392-5_12

civil aviation and automobile traffic. In civil aviation, the biggest advantage of HUD is that it provides pilots with a way to view the aircraft instrument information and the external real environment in the meantime. Some data show that the causes of about 60%-80% of flight accidents involve human factors [2], with long hours of operation and an extremely complicated aircraft cockpit being the major causes of accidents. Many stimuli are present in the cockpit of an aircraft at the same time; these include the instrument panel, the control system, the scenes outside the window, and the information from the command center. Visual displays are the most dominant form of information transmitted from the aircraft to the pilot, who needs to search through the vast amount of information in the cockpit before making decisions during a flight mission. The human brain's cognitive process of information in this process is very sophisticated. Information first enters the perceptual register after stimulating the pilot's senses, and then the brain performs visual processing and makes judgment and decisions based on situational awareness (SA). The whole cognitive process is affected by the allocation of attentional resources, so the pilot's errors are likely to be caused by the uneven allocation of attentional resources [3].

The HUD displays the information necessary for flight centrally on the screen in front of the pilot's flat vision, ensuring that the pilot has a horizon view to obtaining flight information to complete the flight task [2]. Studies have shown that with the use of HUD, the pilot's eyes do not need to switch between the lower-view HUD and the upper-view viewport, reducing the visual load on the pilot [4]. Although pilots' flight performance is higher when using HUDs than using other types of displays [5, 6], which can reduce pilots' mental workload [7], some studies have shown that the degree of performance improvement is not significant [8]. Although the flat-view display system can solve the tricky challenge of limited display of enormous amounts of information, gradually synchronize the information domain with the visual field, and prompt a gradual shift in the pilot's job role from operation to monitoring [9], the HUD is just another way of presenting instrument information, as well as the digital form also represents an extremely high degree of freedom, and the amount of its organization and presentation is difficult to control, resulting in the HUD being highly susceptible to becoming an ecologically imbalanced huge information space, which may cause search difficulties, attention deflection and frequent switching of vision while providing drivers with sufficient information.

The appropriate human-computer interaction can significantly improve work efficiency. The most common form of human-computer interaction in the cockpit is between the HUD and the pilot. The HUD can minimize the safety hazards associated with the sight-switching process, but it can also cause an imbalance in the information ecology. For pilots, there are temporal and logical information requirements and limitations in visual perception capabilities. The amount of information presented on the HUD can directly influence the driver's attention allocation and cognitive efficiency [10], which may cause additional mental workload to the pilot and is not conducive to a long-term flight [11]. In this paper, we discussed the effects of information access, information volume and work experience on pilot mental workload through experiments in detail and discussed the effectiveness of HUD-assisted flighting and the matching degree of HUD information with tasks in a simulated flight environment.

2 Methods

2.1 Participants

Sixteen healthy graduate students (8 females and 8 males, M = 23.24, SD = 2.18) participated in this experiment. All participants were right-handed and met the following conditions: (1) normal or corrected normal vision without any specific physical impairment; (2) no disability in the upper or lower limbs; (3) no neurological issues that would prevent them from performing the task; (4) no previous flight experience.

2.2 Apparatus

The experiments used the LogitechX52 handle for flight operation, and the EEG signal acquisition equipment used the eegoTMmylab all-mobile EEG recording and analysis system developed by ANTNeuro, which included the eegoTM EEG amplifier, waveguardTM 32-channel Ag/AgCl EEG cap, and a laptop with ANT/eego software, as shown in Fig. 1. The position of the electrodes of the EEG cap was according to the international 10–20 system standard, as shown in Fig. 2. Flightgear 2019 software was used for simulating flight and the flight data were recorded using Visual Studio 2019. The distance between the participant and the center of the screen was 550–600 mm and the room was illuminated normally (using 40W fluorescent light) [12].

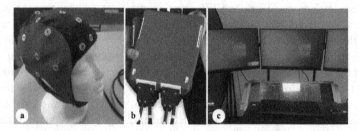

Fig. 1. Experimental apparatus, figure a is the32-channel Ag/AgCl EEG cap, figure b is the eegoTM EEG amplifier and figure c is the experiemnt instruments used in the experiment.

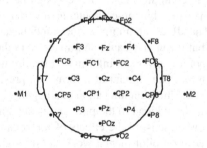

Fig. 2. Electrodes used in the experiment

2.3 The Experimental Variables

In this experiment, there were three independent variables: the way of acquiring flight information, the amount of information required, and the flight experience of the participants. Among them, the amount of required information was achieved by executing different flight tasks (Task1: climb; Task2: level flight). According to the observation of the pilot's flight process and previous studies, when performing a level flight mission, the pilot needs to use the flight information to stabilize the aircraft to smoothly fly to the destination, and when performing a climb mission, it is necessary to pay attention to the climb rate of the aircraft while taking into account the smooth forward flight of the aircraft. Therefore, the information required during the execution of the climb mission includes the amount of information required in the level flight phase. There were two ways to obtain flight information: Display1 (HUD and instrument integrated display), Display2 (single instrument display). The flight experience of the participants was represented by the number of times of flying (Visit), and people would continue to learn and accumulate work experience with repeated executions.

2.4 Experimental Environment

In this paper, Flightgear software was used, and the Cessna127P Skyhawk model was selected to take off from the runway. The time was set to noon in summer, and the weather was uniformly set to a sunny day with no wind and no clouds. In order to further explore whether the matching degree between the information provided by the HUD and the task would affect the pilot's cognition, the HUD was set to present the common information of Task1 and Task2, such as displaying important information such as altitude, airspeed, pitch attitude and heading, as shown in Fig. 3. Therefore, when Task1 was executed in the R1 environment, the matching degree between HUD information and task requirements was not high, while when Task2 executed, the matching degree between HUD information and task requirements was high.

Fig. 3. Flight simulation interface of Flightgear software

2.5 Experimental Procedure

In this experiment, participants were randomly divided into two groups of eight; the first group of participants completed the flight simulation experiment with the combined assistance of the HUD and instruments, and the second group of participants completed the flight simulation experiment with the assistance of the instruments. Before the first experiment, the subjects will be informed of the mission specifics and will be provided with details of all flight information, instruments (e.g., airspeed, vertical, speed, altimeter, etc.), and information presented by the HUD (e.g., airspeed, vertical, speed, altitude, etc.) required for successful execution. A question-and-answer session will also be provided if required.

Before the experiment, the participants mastered the basic operation of flight through learning, and the concrete process of the experiment is shown in Fig. 4. In the experiment, each participant was required to repeat the flight process five times, of which the first time was a practice trial, and the data were not counted. Each flight required the execution of two tasks: take-off climb (Task 1) and level flight (Task 2). In Task 1, a 5-min climb to 2000 ft was required; in Task 2, an altitude of 2000 ft was required to be always maintained. A heading of 45° with a target airspeed of 75 knots was always maintained during the two flight phases. After preparation, participants began the experiment. Each participant in the experiment was required to repeat the flight five times. To ignore the effect of the flight task order, the subjects were randomly selected for the order of the tasks, with six participants in each group performing the take-off climb followed by the cruise level task and six participants performing the cruise level task followed by the take-off climb task. When the task time expires, the task must proceed to the next stage whether it is completed or not. At the end of each mission, participants were required to fill out the NASA-TLX scale and then take a 2-min break.

Task 1 (take off & climb) and Task 2 (cruise & level flight)

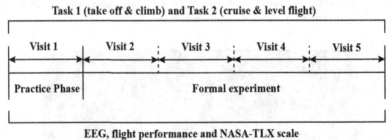

EEG, flight performance and NASA-TLX scale

Fig. 4. Experimental Procedure used in the experiment

As all participants were novice aircraft users, the simulator was programmed to travel at a starting altitude of 1000 ft at 75 knots on a 45-degree heading if a crash occurred in Task 1. In the event of a crash in Task 2, the simulator is programmed to travel at a starting altitude of 2,000 feet at a speed of 75 knots and a heading of 45 degrees. During the entire restart of the software, the timer was kept running so that the entire scenario (including the crash) was maintained for 5 min.

3 Experimental Results and Analysis

3.1 NASA-TLX Scale

A repeated measures ANOVA was performed on the data, which included two within-subject factors and one between-subject factor, the within-subject factors were the number of executions (Visit) and flight tasks (Task 1: climb, Task 2: level flight), and the between-subject factors were information presentation methods (Display 1: integrated display of HUD and instruments, Display 2: instrument). The data all conformed to normal distribution and homogeneity of variance. (1) There were main significant effects of Visit ($p = 0.034 < 0.05$, $\eta_p^2 = 0.122$) and Display ($p = 0.001 < 0.005$, $\eta_p^2 = 0.389$), but no main significant effects of Task was observed ($p = 0.559 > 0.05$). (2) No further significant interaction involving either within-subject or between-subject factors was found.

The main effects analysis of the number of executions revealed that the subjective load in Visit 5 was significantly lower than that in Visit 2 ($p = 0.023 < 0.05$), Visit 3 ($p = 0.044 < 0.05$), and Visit 4 ($p = 0.038 < 0.05$). Therefore, it could be hypothesized that the load showed a decreasing trend as the number of executions increased, which meant that with the increase in the number of operations, the subjective load of the subjects showed a downward tendency. Furthermore, the main effects analysis of the number of executions and information presentation revealed that the subjective load in the condition of Display 1 was significantly lower than the load in the case of Display 2 ($p = 0.001 < 0.005$). It could be hypothesized that the HUD concentrates and projects the information at a parallel line of sight position, which could facilitate the pilot's access to the information more and subjectively reduce the pilot's mental workload.

Although no main effects of the tasks were observed, the estimation of marginal means for the tasks revealed that the load of Task 1 was a little higher than that of Task 2 ($p = 0.559 > 0.05$).Task1 required more information than Task 2, and the complexity of Task1 was a little higher than that of Task 2 in terms of information perception and processing, however, there was no significant difference in the difficulty of the two tasks, therefore, there was a significant difference in subjective feelings, and a load of Task 1 was only slightly higher than that of Task 2.

3.2 Flight Performance

In this paper, the flight data collected during the flight are analyzed to evaluate the flight performance. During the flight, the subject was required to perform the task at 75 knots airspeed and 45 degrees heading. Therefore, the flight data was processed to calculate the percentage of time spent in compliance with the requirements over the entire flight, that is, the correct rate of task completion, which is used to evaluate performance Since this experiment has two indicators: airspeed and heading, both of which are equally important. Therefore, the arithmetic average of the two indexes can be used to measure the performance of the whole flight process. The results of the repeated measures ANOVA revealed that: (1) There was a mian significant effect of Display ($p = 0.000 < 0.005$, $\eta_p^2 = 0.556$). However, both of Task ($p = 0.393 > 0.05$) and Visit ($p = 0.088 > 0.05$) did not achieve significicnace. (2) There were significant interactions between Task and Display (p = 0.003 < 0.005, η_p^2 = 0.339), Task and Visit (p = 0.000 < 0.005, η_p^2 = 0.242). (3) No further significant interaction involving either within-subject or between-subject factors was found.

A simple effect analysis was conducted on the flight mission and information presentation mode, and the results were shown in Fig. 5. The result showed that the correct rate for Task 1 was significantly lower than that for Task 2 in the Display1 case (p = 0.007 < 0.01). When Task 2 was executed, the correct rate in the Display 1 case was significantly higher than that in the Display 2 case (p = 0.000 < 0.001). Thus, it can be speculated that the integrated display of HUD and instruments could help improve flight performance when performing tasks with small information requirements. However, when performing a task with a large amount of information, the HUD could only present partial information, so the assisted effect was not significant.

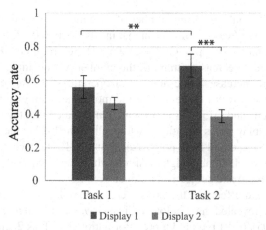

Fig. 5. Flight performance of Task 1 and Task 2 under different information presentation methods

A simple effect analysis was carried out on flight tasks and execution times, and the specific results were shown in Fig. 6, and the result showed that the correct rate of executing Task 2 was significantly higher at Visit 2 than at Task 1 (p = 0.001 < 0.005), and at Visit 4, the correct rate of executing Task 1 was significantly higher than Task 2 (p = 0.034 < 0.05). It indicated that with the increase in the number of executions, the rate of accuracy of Task 1 increases faster than Task 2. In addition, it is found that the correct rate of Visit 2 is significantly lower than Visit 3 (p = 0.001 < 0.005), Visit 4 (p = 0.000 < 0.001) and Visit 5 (p = 0.000 < 0.001). The correct rate of Visit 3 was significantly higher than that of Visit 4 (p = 0.014 < 0.05) and Visit 5 (p = 0.036 < 0.05). In Task 2, however, no significant difference was found between different execution times. Therefore, it could be inferred that when the number of executions is low, the performance of the task with high information demand is significantly lower than the performance of the task with low information demand, but as the number of executions increases, the correct rate in the execution of the task with high information demand increases very fast. It indicated that more work experience was required for information with high information demand. At the time of Visit 2, Task 1's work experience was still insufficient, while Task 2's work experience was sufficient to help complete the task, so a wide performance gap appeared between the two tasks. And when the task was repeated multiple times, Task 1's work experience was accumulated a lot, so the gap between the two gradually narrowed.

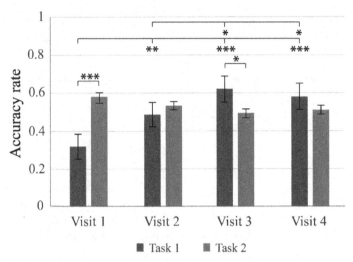

Fig. 6. Flight performance of Task1 and Task2 under different execution times

3.3 EEG Analysis

The acquired EEG signals were first pre-processed using the plug-in EEGlab in Matlab. The electrodes were positioned according to the standard 32-lead format, and two electrodes, M1 and M2, were selected as the new reference electrodes. Next, the brain waves were filtered to retain signals in the 1-40Hz frequency range based on previous experience. Finally, principal component analysis (ICA) was applied to analyze the main components contained in the EEG waves and to filter and eliminate the interfering components, such as blink, EMG and EOG. After the preprocessing of EEG signals is completed, the analysis of EEG signals can begin.

In order to explore the cognitive mechanism of the brain during simulated flight, short-term Fourier calculation was performed on the preprocessed EEG signal to obtain the energy value of each frequency band and plotted into a frequency-energy diagram, as shown in Fig. 7.

By observing the frequency-energy curve, it is found that the energy peaks are concentrated in the 1–13 Hz frequency band, which mainly includes the Delta band, the Theta band and the Alpha band, and the frequency bands where the peaks are located are mostly in the theta wave band. The energy value of the wave crest is analyzed and found that the wave crest under the driving condition with HUD assistance is lower than the wave crest under the condition without HUD assistance. The theta wave is the best indicator of changes in mental workload, and the energy of Theta waves is usually

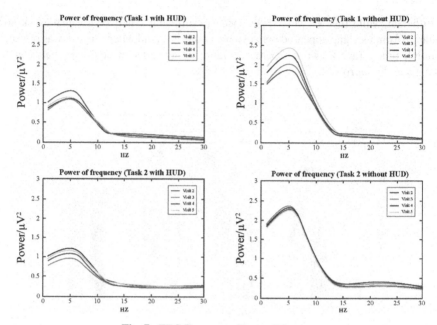

Fig. 7. EEG Frequency-Energy Diagram

proportional to the workload. Thus, Select F3, Fz, F4 to represent the energy of the frontal lobe, select C3, Cz, C4 to represent the energy of the central area, and select P3, Pz, P4 to represent the energy of the parietal lobe. The energy was analyzed by repeated measures analysis of variance. The variables between subjects were different in information presentation (Display1: HUD and instrument integrated display, Display2: instrument display), and the variables within the subjects included flight tasks (Task1: climb, Task2: level flight), number of flights and location of brain regions (Location1: frontal, Location2: central, Location3: parietal). All data were subjected to the Mochiley sphericity test, and the data that did not meet the sphericity test were corrected by Greenhouse-Gellers. The analysis of variance by repeated measurements of Theta waves is showed that: (1) There were significant main effects of Visit ($p = 0.000 < 0.05$, $\eta_p^2 = 0.726$) and Location ($p = 0.000 < 0.05$, $\eta_p^2 = 0.900$). (2) There were significant interactions between Visit and Display ($p = 0.004 < 0.05$, $\eta_p^2 = 0.516$), and Location and Visit ($p = 0.001 < 0.05$, $\eta_p^2 = 0.604$). (3) There was a three-way interaction between Task and Location and Visit ($p = 0.038 < 0.05$, $\eta_p^2 = 0.296$). (4) No further significant interaction involving either within-subject or between-subject factors was found.

First, a simple effect analysis was performed on the task, execution times, and brain region environment. By exploring the effect of brain location on the combination of the flight task and the number of executions, it could be noticed that the differences between brain regions were very significant during Task 1 and Task 2, and the energy of the frontal lobe is much larger than that of the central region and parietal lobe, and the energy of central region is slightly larger than that of the parietal lobe, no matter the number of flight tasks in Task 1 or Task 2. Therefore, it could be inferred that the frontal lobe is the most active region during the flight task, possibly because the frontal lobe is closely related to higher cognitive functions such as attention, memory, and problem-solving.

The effect of execution times on the combination of flight tasks and brain region locations was explored. The results showed that: 1) The analysis results of Task 1 execution are shown in Fig. 8. The energy of Visit 2 is significantly higher than Visit 3 (P = 0.004 < 0.005), Visit 4 (P = 0.003 < 0.005) and Visit 5 (P = 0.003 < 0.005) in the frontal region. The energy of Visit 3 was significantly higher than Visit 5 (P = 0.021 < 0.05). In the central area, Visit 2 energy was significantly higher than Visit 3 energy (P = 0.025 < 0.05), and Visit 3 energy was significantly higher than Visit 4 energy (P = 0.047 < 0.05). In the parietal region, no energy differences were observed between different execution times. 2) The analysis results of Task 2 are shown in Fig. 9. It was found that the energy of Visit 2 in the frontal lobe is significantly higher than that of Visit 4 (P = 0.033 < 0.05) and Visit 5 (P = 0.019 < 0.05). No significant differences between the number of executions were observed in the central and parietal regions. Therefore, it could be inferred that no matter what task was performed, the mental workload showed a downward trend through repeated execution.

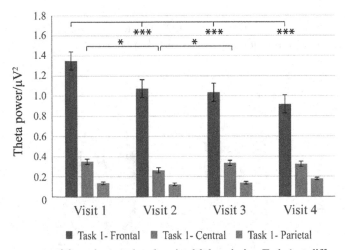

Fig. 8. Theta energy of frontal, central and parietal lobes during Task 1 at different execution times

Exploration of the effects of flight tasks on various combinations of brain area locations and execution times, the results are shown in Fig. 10, and it was found that in Visit 2 in frontal regions, the Theta energy produced by executing Task1 was significantly higher than produced by performing Task 2 (p = 0.027 < 0.05), that is, the load in frontal regions during the execution of Task1 in Visit 2 was Theta energy was significantly higher in Task1 than in Task 2. And no significant difference was observed in other execution times. Therefore, it can be speculated that the load generated by Task 1 was initially higher than Task 2 when the task was first executed, but the gap between them gradually decreased as the number of executions increased. In summary, the energy of the frontal lobe is significantly higher than the central and parietal regions, and the

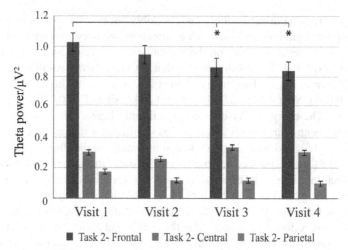

Fig. 9. Theta energy of frontal, central and parietal lobes during Task 2 at different execution times

load of Task 1 is higher than Task 2 in Visit 2. With the increase in execution times, the load decreases gradually, but the load of Task1 decreases faster.

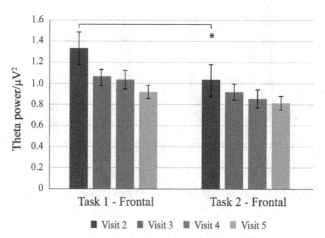

Fig. 10. Theta energy in frontal regions under different tasks

A simple effect analysis was performed on the execution times and information presentation mode, and the results were shown in Fig. 11. The energy of Visit 2 was significantly higher than that of Visit3 ($p = 0.005 < 0.01$), Visit 4 ($p = 0.024 < 0.05$), and Visit 5 ($p = 0.002 < 0.005$) under the condition of Display 1. The energy of Visit 3 was significantly higher than Visit5 ($p = 0.019 < 0.05$), and the energy of Visit 4 was also significantly higher than Visit 5 ($p = 0.011 < 0.05$). Under the condition of Display 2, the energy of Visit 2 is significantly higher than Visit 3 ($p = 0.003 < 0.005$) and Visit4 (p = 0.009 < 0.01). Therefore, it could be concluded that no matter what information presentation mode is, the load will decrease with the increase in execution times.

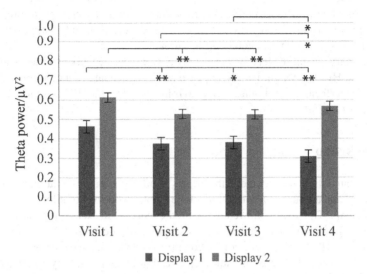

Fig. 11. Theta energy in frontal regions under different information presentation modes

4 Discussion

Based on the above subjective and EEG analysis, it revealed that multiple repetitions of the task could reduce the load during flight. In the cognitive processing of information, a person needs to match external information with memory after perceiving it. When a person has the extensive working experience, there is a large amount of relevant information encoded in memory. If the information can be matched, the information in memory can be called directly, or else it needs to be recoded and stored in memory. When the subjects first performed the task, they were unfamiliar with the information elements of both the instrument and the HUD, and they did not have enough coding information in their memories due to their inexperience and inability, which caused an additional cognitive load. By performing the repeated tasks several times, the subjects could accumulate a large amount of experience and build up relevant memories, which could help cognition during the following task execution, and thus the load would decrease with repeated task execution.

Secondly, it was observed that the combined HUD and instrument display reduced the pilot's mental workload, and the HUD could present the information from the pilot's horizon view, which facilitated the pilot's cognition of the flight information while taking into account the viewport and solved the problem of frequent view switching. Therefore, the HUD presentation could reduce the load during the flight.

In addition, with the combined HUD and instrument display, the load on level flight tasks was less than on climb tasks. The amount of information required for level flight tasks is smaller than that of climb tasks, and it presented by the HUD is fixed. In the level flight phase, the information displayed by the HUD is sufficient for the whole mission, while in the climb phase, the information presented by the HUD does not meet the needs of the mission and requires instrumentation for assistance. Therefore, it could be concluded that the workload when the HUD has sufficient information will be less than the HUD does not have enough information.

In summary, the pilot's load will gradually decrease as the work experience grows. In addition, the HUD can significantly improve performance and reduce workload during flight; flight performance is highest and load is lowest when the HUD provides sufficient mission information.

5 Conclusion

In the simulated flight environment, the effects of information presentation mode, working memory, and amount of information on the mental workload of pilots were explored by experiments. The results showed that with the increase in execution times, the working memory gradually increased and the load gradually decreased. In addition, it was also found that HUD can assist pilots in cognition and help reduce the mental workload during flight. When HUD presents sufficient information, the auxiliary effect is the best.

References

1. Liezhong, G.: Engineering Psychology. East China Normal University Press, Shanghai (2017)
2. Shappell, S., Detwiler, C., Holcomb, K., Hackworth, C., Boquet, A., Wiegmann, D.A.: Human error and commercial aviation accidents: An analysis using the human factors analysis and classification system. Hum. Factors **49**(02), 227–242 (2007)
3. Yonggang, W., Chenliang, F.: Research on relationship between pilots' attention distribution ability and their safety performance. China Safety Sci. J. **31**(8), 8 (2021)
4. Wickens, K., Zhang.: An Introduction to Human factors engineering. East China Normal University Press (2007)
5. Wickens, C.D., Long, J.: Object versus space-based models of visual-attention - implications for the design of head-up displays. J. Exp. Psychol-Appl **1**(3), 179–193 (1995)
6. Fadden, S., Ververs, P.M., Wickens, C.D.: Pathway HUDs: are they viable? Hum. Fact. J. Hum. Factors Ergonom. Soc. **43**(2), 173–193 (2001)
7. Kratchounova, D., Choi, I., Mofle, T C., Miller, L., Stevenson, S., Humphreys, M.: Flight technical error and workload during head-up display localizer guided takeoff. J. Air Trans. 1–7 (2022)
8. Yeh, M., Merlo, J.L., Wickens, C.D., Brandenburg, D.L.: Head up versus head down the costs of imprecision, unreliability, and visual clutter on cue effectiveness for Display signaling. Hum. Factors **45**(3), 390–407 (2003)
9. Anuar, N., Kim, J.: A direct methodology to establish design requirements for the human-system interface (HSI) of automatic systems in nuclear power plants. Ann. Nucl. Energy **63**, 326–338 (2014)
10. Yuan, M.L., Ong, S.K., Nee, A.Y.C.: A generalized registration method for augmented reality systems. Comput. Graph-Uk **29**(6), 980–997 (2005)

11. Zheng, Y., Lu, Y., Jie, Y., Fu, S.: Predicting workload experienced in a flight test by measuring workload in a flight simulator. Aerospace Med. Hum. Perform. **90**(7), 618–623 (2019)
12. Jinchun, W., et al.: Neural mechanisms behind semantic congruity of construction safety signs: An EEG investigation on construction workers. In: Human Factors and Ergonomics in Manufacturing & Service Industries, pp. 1–17 (2022)

A Mental Workload Control Method Based on Human Performance or Safety Risk

Nanxi Zhang[1], Chunye Bao[1], Xin Wang[2], Qiming Han[1], Ye Deng[2], Yijing Zhang[1], and Zhizhong Li[1(✉)]

[1] Department of Industrial Engineering, Tsinghua University, Beijing 100084, China
zzli@tsinghua.edu.cn
[2] China Institute of Marine Technology and Economy, 100081 Beijing, China

Abstract. The prediction of mental workload, as well as the determination of its "redline", is important in Human System Integration (HSI), as it could save time and resources by detecting problems at the early stages of system design. It is also well-recognized as a key issue in safety risk management. Till now, most of the methods in redline determination hold the perspective of a fixed and absolute threshold. However, human operators are inherently flexible and capable of adopting different strategies to maintain their task performance among a range of mental workload. In the present study, mental workload is considered as a more management than technological issue. An idea of risk-based method is proposed to determine the control line of mental workload. The concept of mental workload intensity instead of amount is proposed to establish a relationship between performance or safety risk and mental workload, so that according to the acceptable risk set by the management/administration, the mental workload control line can be determined. The idea was demonstrated with a case study of maritime tasks. The results show that the output of the proposed method is well consistent with expert judgment.

Keywords: Mental Workload · Human System Integration · Safety Risk Management

1 Introduction

Mental workload is defined as "the operator's allocation of limited processing capacity or resources to meet task demands; that is, the balance of internal resources and external demands" [1]. As stated by Young et al. [2], "one of the reasons to study mental workload is to establish a relationship with operator performance". Predicting mental workload is important in two reasons. The one hand is that workload analysis is the basis for function/task allocation and automation level decision during concept formalization and design phases in systems engineering [3]. The other hand is that the earlier the workload analysis in the development progress, the less it would cost to response to human related issues that affect the overall performance of a system [4].

For mental workload management or control, it is desired to establish a safe zone, wherein the resource that could be provided by the operator would meet the demand of the task. Between this zone and the neighboring one wherein the suboptimal mental workload would lead to unacceptable safety risk of human errors is the workload threshold, also known as the "redline" [5–7]. Till now, there are different statements regarding the settlement of this threshold, most of which considering a fixed transient, beyond which the rate of performance is slowed [8, 9] or decreased [5, 6, 10]. Moreover, Parks & Boucek [11], from the perspective of timeline analysis, proposed that the point wherein the time required divided by the time available for the task is lower than 0.8 should be recognized as the redline. However, as noted by Hancock [12] and Smith [13], human beings are flexible enough to adapt their capabilities and strategies to maintain a desired level of performance, until the limits of their flexibility are reached and their performance are catastrophically declined. Therefore, we are hesitating to say if there is a constant objective workload threshold, which makes task operators unable to work satisfactorily. The reason why mental workload should be controlled is that when the workload is too high, the performance of a task operator would be impaired and the likelihood of a human error would rise, finally leading to unexpected consequences [4, 14]. However, it could not be always practical to design a system with low mental workload for human resource, technical (e.g., limited space for crew members), cost and other constraints or difficulties. Therefore, the determination of the mental workload threshold should be based on the trade-off between system requirements and constraints. In other words, mental workload threshold should be recognized as a pool that offer flexibility for system design. For the safety-critical part of a system, the workload threshold should be lowered to ensure an acceptable human error rate. For the less critical part, the workload threshold could be raised to gain efficiency or other benefits. Thus, our opinion is that mental workload should be considered as a more management/control than technological issue.

When predicting mental workload, many studies result in the total amount of resource demand, reflecting the amount of work [15–17]. However, only consider the total amount of work regardless of the time to finish it could hardly delineate the whole picture. Completing a task within one hour would be very different from that within 10 min. Regarding this, the concept of "mental workload intensity" is proposed to refer to the amount of work that completed per unit time. It is the mental workload intensity rather than the amount that would impair human performance. Thus, to consider is mental workload intensity when establishing the relationship with human performance for the management/control purpose. Therefore, this study proposes a risk-based method to determine the control line of mental workload with the concept of mental workload intensity. With such a method, the acceptability of function/task allocation and automation level decision could be evaluated and interactively adjusted at the early stage of system design, and ultimately it can be used to strengthen and optimize the whole human-machine system by contributing to the integration of human factors into systems engineering [18].

2   Method

Holding the idea that mental workload threshold depends on management/control requirement or willingness, mental workload could be controlled in several ways, for example: 1) A performance level (such as human error probability, error rate, or other criteria) could be specified for "redline" control; 2) mental workload can be classified into different regions according to risk levels, then tasks can be controlled by risk level. The second control strategy can be seen as a rough and discrete case of the first one. Thus, only the first control strategy is further explained below and presented in Fig. 1.

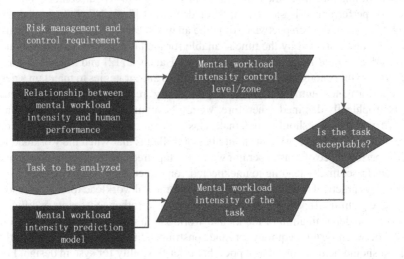

Fig. 1. Human performance based mental workload control method.

First, empirical data should be collected to establish the industry-specific relationship between mental workload intensity (*MWI*) and human performance (*HP*):

$$HP = f_1(MWI) \tag{1}$$

Then the mental workload intensity control line/zone (*MWI$_{ctrl}$*) could be determined according to the requirement *HP$_{req}$* given by the management, i.e.

$$MWI_{ctrl} = f_1^{-1}(HP_{req}) \tag{2}$$

For the task i to be analyzed, a mental workload prediction model such as the Visual/Auditory/Cognitive/Psychomotor model (VACP) [19], the Time-Line Analysis and Prediction (TLAP) [11], and Workload Index (W/INDEX) [20, 21] can be used to predict mental workload amount and then mental workload intensity can be calculated, say MWI_i. By comparing it with the control line/zone, it can be determined whether the task is acceptable, i.e.

if $MWI_i > MWI_{ctrl}$, then task i is not acceptable;

otherwise, task i is acceptable.

The above models support safety risk assessment and control at earlier product development stages.

Furthermore, it would be possible to establish the relationship between subjective mental workload (*MW$_{sub}$*) and objective mental workload intensity, say,

$$MW_{sub} = f_2(MWI) \tag{3}$$

Then it is an optional strategy to control safety risk by specifying an acceptable subjective mental workload rating, which is more straightforward and intuitive. NASA-TLX [22] is one of the classic subjective mental workload rating methods that could be used for this purpose.

3 A Case Study

To validate the above-mentioned method, a maritime use case was adopted and elaborated as below. In this use case, we first established the relationship between Human Error Probability (HEP) and subjective mental workload in maritime domain by a set of empirical data from maritime operation related lab experiment. Then, to predict the workload intensity of the task to be analyzed, a converter was built to convert the subjective mental workload to workload intensity scores based on the VACP scales. The mental workload threshold of the task was determined by the combination of the relationship between HEP and subjective mental workload, and the workload converter. The validity of this threshold was verified by comparing the predicted mental workload intensity and the experts' acceptability judgments.

3.1 Modeling with Experimental Data

Relationship Between Human Error Probability and Subjective Mental Workload
In a lab experiment, 75 male students participated in an experiment of maritime operations to establish the relationship between HEP and mental workload in maritime domain. The tasks used in the lab experiment were combinations of sub-tasks. The sub-tasks included detecting a target, locating a target, checking a target's approaching, searching a specified target, reading information of a target. The combinations were shown in Table 1.

Table 1. Task Combinations used in the lab experiment

Task Combinations
detecting, locating, checking
detecting, locating, searching
detecting, locating, reading
checking, searching
checking, reading
searching, reading

During the experiment, each participant went through all the task combinations in a random order. After each task combination, the participants were asked to finish a NASA-TLX questionnaire to rate their subjective mental workload during the last task combination. Mental workload was manipulated by the variety of task combinations and the number of targets. The duration for each task combination was identical, therefore the subjective mental workload obtained from the NASA-TLX is equivalent to a subjective workload intensity. HEP was calculated as error response rate under each task combination.

Subjective mental workload that measured by the NASA-TLX questionnaire (rating of 0–10 for each of six dimensions, 0 means very low, 10 means very high) was then paired with the HEP. The scores of 6 dimensions of NASA-TLX were summed to get a unified mental workload score MW_{TLX}. The relationship between subjective mental workload and HEP was obtained from this experiment as follows (valid only when $18.0 < MW_{TLX} < 38.5$):

$$HEP = 0.049 * MW_{TLX} - 0.878 \tag{4}$$

$$MW_{TLX} = 20.5 * HEP + 18.0 \tag{5}$$

This formula can be used for management control by subjective mental workload. Say, if the management requires HEP to be no higher than 0.1, then the subjective mental workload control value should be 20.1 (according to Formula 4a, 20.5 * 0.1 + 18.0 = 20.1).

Relationship Between Subjective and Predicted Mental Workload
However, subjective mental workload could only be rated when a system or its prototype has been implemented for human-in-the-loop experiment. For human factors consideration at earlier product development stages, we need another model to predict subjective mental workload.

In another experiment of comprehensive maritime tasks, experimental data were collected to demonstrate the above-mentioned idea. The data included subjective workload and its related predicted workload. The subjective workload (MW_{TLX}) was measured by the TWLQ questionnaire[23], in which the first six dimensions are equivalent to the six dimensions of NASA-TLX. The predicted workload (MWI_{VACP}) was calculated based on a maritime version of VACP scales. To build the maritime version of VACP scales, the typical tasks in the maritime domain were scrutinized and disassembled into general task units (GTUs), which is the basic unit for operators to perform a task. Then the workload scores of visual, auditory, cognitive, and psychomotor channels were analyzed and settled. Examples of GTU and their related workload scores are shown in Table 2.

When predicting mental workload, the task to be analyzed should be disassembled into GTU sequences, with each GTU occupies a period of task duration. MWI_{VACP} is the sum of the workload scores among all the channels divided by the task duration:

$$MWI_{VACP} = \sum ((V_i + A_i + C_i + P_i) * t_i) / T \tag{6}$$

where V_i is the workload score for GTU i in the visual channel, A_i is the workload score for GTU i in the auditory channel, C_i is the workload score for GTU i in the cognitive channel, P_i is the workload score for GTU i in the psychomotor channel, t_i is the duration for GTU i, and T is the duration for the whole task.

Table 2. Examples of maritime GTU and their related workload scores

GTU	Elaboration	Mental Workload Scores			
		Visual	Auditory	Cognitive	Psychomotor
Visually Detecting Target	The operator visually detects a target	1.0	0	1.2	0
Auditorily Detecting Target	The operator auditorily detects a target	0	1.0	1.2	0
Visually Checking Target	The operator visually locates and checks a target	7.0	0	3.7	0
Auditorily Checking Target	The operator auditorily locates and checks a target	0	4.2	1.2	0
Processing Target	The operator interpreting the meaning of the target according to known rules	0	0	5.3	0
Convey Information via Speaking	The operator uses oral method to convey information	0	4.3	5.3	1
Visually Tracing Target	The operator visually tracing the target	5.4	0	1.2	0
Checking targets with mice	The operator uses a mouse to manipulate the target	5.0	0	1.2	4.6
Convey Information via Typing	The operator uses a keyboard to convey information	5.9	0	5.3	7
Idle	The operator does nothing	0	0	0	0

Moreover, factors that influence task process were considered in the predicted mental workload. The ratings of influence factor were obtained from a questionnaire (rating of 1–7, 1 means very low, 7 means very high). Examples of influence factors and their ratings are shown in Table 3.

The upper limit of the influence coefficient is set to 2 (double influence) according to expert opinion (corresponding to rating of 7), while 1 means no influence (corresponding to rating of 1). Supposing each influence factor influences the mental workload independently. Therefore, the overall influence coefficient k can be calculated as:

$$k = \prod \left(\left(I_j - 1 \right) / 6 + 1 \right) \tag{7}$$

Table 3. Examples of influence factors and their ratings

Influence Factor	Rating
Noise	3.8
Vibration	3.6
Insufficient light	3.2
Insufficient training	3.9
Inadequate doctrine	3.7
Inadequate human-machine-interface	3.5
Mental stress	3.9

where I_j is the rating for the influence factor j.

Take all the influence factors into consideration, the predicted mental workload under influence can be calculated as:

$$MWI_{VACP} = \sum(k_i * (V_i + A_i + C_i + P_i) * t_i) /T \tag{8}$$

where k_i is the overall influence coefficient for GTU i.

A software was programmed to assist this procedure (see Fig. 2 for an example of the software interface). The upper line plot delineates the trend of MWI_{VACP} against time, under the circumstance that the task was influenced by noise. The lower bar plot shown that there were two simultaneous tasks that were contributing to the predicted workload shown in the upper plot.).

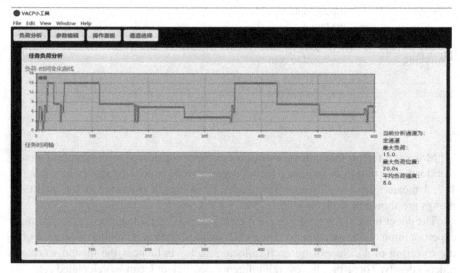

Fig. 2. An example of the maritime workload prediction with VACP scales

The relationship between mental workload intensity and subjective mental workload was established as follows:

$$MW_{TLX} = 2.0 * MWI_{VACP} - 3.5 \tag{9}$$

Establishment of the Mental Workload Threshold Pool

Now we have the relationship between HEP and subjective mental workload (Formula 5) and the relationship between subjective mental workload and predicted mental workload (Formula 8). The relationship between mental workload intensity and HEP could be obtained by combining Formulas 4 and 8 as (valid only when $10.5 < MWI_{VACP} < 20.5$):

$$HEP = 0.098 * MWI_{VACP} - 1.050 \tag{10}$$

$$MWI_{VACP} = 10 * HEP + 10.5 \tag{11}$$

Formula 11 could be regarded as the pool for maritime mental workload management. As an example, for the risk control requirement $HEP \leq 0.1$, MWI_{VACP} in the above-mentioned maritime domain should not exceed 11.5. While for a more strictly risk control requirement $HEP \leq 0.01$, MWI_{VACP} in the above-mentioned maritime domain should not exceed 10.6.

3.2 Validation

For the above comprehensive maritime task experiment, professional users of the system were invited to rate the level of acceptability of the nine task scenarios (rating of 0–10, 0 means totally unacceptable, 10 means very acceptable). With the given management requirement of human error probability control under these circumstances (0.1), the mental workload intensity control line was derived to be 11.5. Then the deviations of the predicted mental workload intensity of the nine task scenarios from the control line were calculated as predicted mental workload acceptability (e.g., a task scenario was predicted to have the mental workload of 5, then the deviation of the predicted mental workload intensity would be $11.5 - 5 = 6.5$. While for another task scenario, if the predicted mental workload was 15, the deviation would be $11.5 - 15 = -3.5$). The Pearson's correlation between the deviations and the experts' acceptability judgments was found to be greater than 0.7, which means that the predicted acceptability obtained from the proposed method is well consistent with expert judgment.

4 Conclusion

In the present study, we propose a risk-based method to determine the control of mental workload with the concept of mental workload intensity. The detail of this method is elaborated. Moreover, the method is demonstrated with a case study of maritime tasks.

With the proposed models, when given a management requirement of human performance (such as human error probability) or subjective workload, the required mental workload intensity threshold can be derived, then a task can be assessed whether it meets the management requirement by comparing its mental workload intensity to the required one. These models can also serve as a tool in the process of system design, wherein human performance-based criteria could be provided for the verification and modification of the function allocation and task design.

References

1. Matthews, G., Reinerman-Jones, L.: Workload assessment: How to diagnose workload issues and enhance performance. Human Factors and Ergonomics Society, Santa Monica, CA (2017)
2. Young, M.S., Brookhuis, K.A., Wickens, C.D., Hancock, P.A.: State of science: mental workload in ergonomics. Ergonomics **58**(1), 1–17 (2015). https://doi.org/10.1080/00140139.2014.956151
3. Kaber, D.B., Riley, J.M.: Adaptive automation of a dynamic control task based on secondary task workload measurement. Int. J. Cogn. Ergon. **3**(3), 169–187 (2010). https://doi.org/10.1207/s15327566ijce0303_1
4. Wickens, C.D.: Mental workload: assessment, prediction and consequences. In: Longo, L., Leva, M.C. (eds.) H-WORKLOAD 2017. CCIS, vol. 726, pp. 18–29. Springer, Cham (2017). https://doi.org/10.1007/978-3-319-61061-0_2
5. Reid, G.B., Colle, H.A.: Critical SWAT values for predicting operator overloadm, 19 edn., p. 1414–8. SAGE Publications Sage CA, Los Angeles, CA (1988)
6. De Waard, D., Brookhuis, K.A.: The measurement of drivers' mental workload. Groningen University, Traffic Research Center Netherlands (1996)
7. Hart, S., Wickens, C.D.: Mental Workload. NASA Human Integration Design Handbook (2008)
8. Rueb, J., Vidulich, M., Hassoun, J.: Establishing workload acceptability: An evaluation of a proposed KC-135 cockpit redesign, 1 edn., pp. 17–21. SAGE Publications Sage CA, Los Angeles, CA (1992)
9. Grier, R., et al.: The red-line of workload: Theory, research, and design. 18 edn, pp. 1204–8. Sage Publications Sage CA: Los Angeles, CA (2008)
10. Meister, D.: Behavioral foundations of system development. Behavioral foundations of system development. Oxford, England: John Wiley & Sons (1976)
11. Parks, D.L., Boucek, G.P.: Workload prediction, diagnosis, and continuing challenges. In: Applications of Human Performance Models to System Design, pp. 47–63. Springer (1989). https://doi.org/10.1007/978-1-4757-9244-7_4
12. Hancock, P.A., Warm, J.S.: A dynamic model of stress and sustained attention. Hum Factors. **31**(5), 519–537 (1989). https://doi.org/10.1177/001872088903100503
13. Smith, K.T.: Observations and issues in the application of cognitive workload modelling for decision making in complex time-critical environments, p. 77–89. Springer (2017). https://doi.org/10.1007/978-3-319-61061-0_5
14. Byrne, A.: Mental workload as an outcome in medical education. In: Longo, L., Leva, M.C. (eds.) H-WORKLOAD 2017. CCIS, vol. 726, pp. 187–197. Springer, Cham (2017). https://doi.org/10.1007/978-3-319-61061-0_12
15. Chen, W., Sawaragi, T., Horiguchi, Y.: Measurement of driver's mental workload in partial autonomous driving. IFAC-PapersOnLine. **52**(19), 347–352 (2019). https://doi.org/10.1016/j.ifacol.2019.12.083
16. Das, S., Maiti, J., Krishna, O.B.: Assessing mental workload in virtual reality based EOT crane operations: A multi-measure approach. Int. J. Ind. Ergon. **80**, 103017 (2020). https://doi.org/10.1016/j.ergon.2020.103017

17. Gao, Q., Wang, Y., Song, F., Li, Z., Dong, X.: Mental workload measurement for emergency operating procedures in digital nuclear power plants. Ergonomics **56**(7), 1070–1085 (2013). https://doi.org/10.1080/00140139.2013.790483
18. Hunn, B.P., Schweitzer, K.M., Cahir, J.A., Finch, M.M.: IMPRINT analysis of an unmanned air system geospatial information process. Army Research Lab Aberdeen Proving Ground Md Human Research and Engineering (2008)
19. Aldrich, T.B., Szabo, S.M., Bierbaum, C.R.: The development and application of models to predict operator workload during system design. In: Applications of Human Performance Models to System Design, pp. 65–80. Springer (1989). https://doi.org/10.1007/978-1-4757-9244-7_5
20. North, R.A., Riley, V.A.: W/INDEX: a predictive model of operator workload. In: McMillan, G.R., Beevis, D., Salas, E., Strub, M.H., Sutton, R., Van Breda, L. (eds.) Applications of Human Performance Models to System Design, pp. 81–89. Springer, US, Boston (1989). https://doi.org/10.1007/978-1-4757-9244-7_6
21. Wickens, C.D.: Multiple resources and performance prediction. Theor. Issues Ergon. Sci. **3**(2), 159–177 (2002). https://doi.org/10.1080/14639220210123806
22. Hart, S.G., Staveland, L.E.: Development of NASA-TLX (Task Load Index): results of empirical and theoretical research. In: Hancock, P.A., Meshkati, N. (eds.) Human Mental Workload, Advances in Psychology, pp. 139–183. North-Holland (1988)
23. Sellers, J., Helton, W.S., Näswall, K., Funke, G.J., Knott, B.A.: Development of the team workload questionnaire (TWLQ). Proc. Human Factors Ergonom. Soc. Annual Meeting **58**(1), 989–993 (2014). https://doi.org/10.1177/1541931214581207

Human Performance and Error Management

Expertise Analysis in Chest X-Rays Diagnosis Based on Eye Tracking Stimulated Retrospections: Effective Diagnosis Strategies in Medical Checkup Condition

Hirotaka Aoki[1]([✉]) [ID], Koji Morishita[2], Marie Takahashi[2], Rea Machida[1],
Atsushi Kudoh[2], Mitsuhiro Kishino[2], and Tsuyoshi Shirai[2]

[1] Tokyo Institute of Technology, Tokyo, Japan
`aoki.h.ad@m.titech.ac.jp`
[2] Tokyo Medical and Dental University, Tokyo, Japan

Abstract. One of the most important differentiators of skills in chest x-rays diagnosis is an effective information acquisition strategy. However, well-experienced doctors frequently find it difficult to explicitly show their own strategies because such strategies are carried out unconsciously. To uncover effective strategies in chest x-rays diagnosis, we performed debriefing stimulate by the doctors' eye movement data. Based on the debriefing data, we elicit effective diagnosis strategies of chest x-ray images under realistic medical checkup conditions.

Keywords: Expertise Analysis · Clinical Reasoning Process · Chest X-Rays · Elicitation of Skilled Diagnosis Strategy

1 Introduction

In the present paper, we apply an effective debriefing procedure aided by eye movement recordings to elicitation of effective clinical reasoning processes during chest x-rays diagnosis under annual medical checkup conditions. In the real medical checkup, when any past image taken from an identical patient is available, the x-ray image as well as the present x-ray image are displayed at the same time to perform a diagnosis of the present state of the patient's chest. First, a doctor performs diagnoses of two images representing present and past states of a patient. Second, he/she conducts comparison between the two images to identify critical changes of chest states along with time. In addition, the diagnosis is performed very rapidly since there are many patients' images that have to be diagnosed in a limited time. This diagnosis condition seems to include much more complicated cognitive processes than that in another condition where a diagnosis of just single image (i.e., one image showing a present state of the patient chest) is conducted.

To uncover the cognitive processes performed under the real medical checkup condition, it seems impossible for us to apply thinking-aloud protocol technique since the processes are too fast to verbalize. Instead, it can be expected that the retrospective

D. Harris and W.-C. Li (Eds.): HCII 2023, LNAI 14017, pp. 181–189, 2023.
https://doi.org/10.1007/978-3-031-35392-5_14

approach where eye movement recordings of a doctor are used as a cue to verbalize his/her cognitive processes allows us to obtain elaborated information regarding hidden cognitive processes [1–5]. Considering the above-mentioned background, the objectives of the study are two folds: to conduct cognitive task analysis based on eye tracking stimulated retrospection, and to elicit effective diagnosis strategies of chest x-ray images under realistic medical checkup conditions.

2 Data Collection

2.1 Participant

Nine expert doctors were recruited. The individual attributes are shown in Table 1. Ethics approval was granted by the Tokyo Institute of Technology Review Board (2020038) and the Tokyo Medical and Dental University Review Board (M2020–103). All participants provided written informed consent prior to the experiment.

2.2 Image Test Set

A test set of four pairs of x-ray images of four patients' chest radiographs were chosen. In selection processes, each radiograph was carefully examined by the third author (radiologist) to identify all of possible symptoms. Additionally, the CT-scan images which were used for final decisions were carefully checked in order to confirm each patient's present status (e.g., cancer). The details of the images are summarized in Table 2.

Table 1. Participant.

Participant	Clinical Department	Experience (year)
D1	Respiratory Medicine	17
D2	Respiratory Medicine	18
D3	Respiratory Medicine	12
D4	Respiratory Medicine	20
D5	Radiology	12
D6	Radiology	12
D7	Radiology	25
D8	Radiology	14
D9	Radiology	10

Table 2. Images used.

X-ray image pair	Patient (age, gender)	Lesion	Diagnosis (present)	Time when past image was taken
1	76, man	Nodule shadow	Lung cancer	7 months ago
2	27, woman	Nodule shadow	Nipple	1 week ago
3	63, man	Infiltrative shadow	Lung cancer	1 month ago
4	62, man	Patchy shadow	Lung cancer	1 and a half year ago

2.3 Task

The experimental task was to perform interpretation of the present x-ray chest image. Each participant was asked to report lesions found and his/her diagnostic decision for each image. Additionally, a participant was asked to give his/her ratings about the followings: how difficult possible lesions/signs could be found, how difficult the case could be diagnosed in Likert five point scale (1: very easy ~ 5: very difficult) and how much the past image was informative for his/her diagnostic decision (1: very informative ~ 5: not at all).

2.4 Procedure

Upon arrival at our experimental site, each participant was briefed on the overall objective of the experiment, the tasks to be conducted, debriefing procedures, calibration procedure of the eye tracker (Tobii X-3 120, Sweden), and questionnaire. Before starting experimental task sessions, a participant completed one practice circuit using an typical example of two images (present and before). After carrying out calibration for the eye tracking system, experimental tasks composed of four image interpretations were started. After interpreting an image, a participant verbally reported his/her findings and diagnostic decision. Then he/she was asked to give rating scores of difficulty perceived, confidence level of his/her decision, and perceived usefulness of the past image for his/her decision. Eye movement data during interpretation task were recorded. The experimental environment during interpretation task is shown in Fig. 1.

After the image interpretation task, a debriefing session where eye movement data were shown to the participant started. In the debriefing session, eye movement data recorded while seeing pairs of images were shown to each participant. By examining the participant's own eye movement data, a series of question were given to the participant in a semi-structured interview style. The questions were developed in order to elicit both holistic and specific diagnosis strategies. The question categories (in total eleven) and their typical questions are summarized in Table 3.

To clearly elicit the participant's pattern which are consciously recognized, we asked each participant to draw his/her typical scanning patterns on an example x-ray image. This was carried out by using an image shown in Fig. 2, and was performed after the debriefing session. This was an important procedure since we could obtain mental

Fig. 1. Experimental environment.

representations of chest structure in addition to the participant's diagnostic routine. In the series of our research [6, 7], we could obtain an intuition that the mental representations of chest structure are different from their anatomical features. As shown in Fig. 2, a participant was asked to draw his/her scanning pattern represented by arcs as well as areas to which much attention is paid. For example, areas indicated by the number five circle they overlap several organs. This means that he/she recognized the areas as a pair of single key area which are different from anatomical organs taxonomy.

In the end of experiment, a participant provided responses to the questionnaire about his/her expertise and experience.

3 Result

3.1 Strategies to Detect Lesions Obtained by Debriefing Sessions

The data analysis has been performed since data collection. In this section, we focus on strategies taken when detecting lesions/giving final decision phase. Using comments to items in question categories 1, 3, 4, 5, 6, 10 and relating comments, we tried to classify comments inductively. Table 4 summarizes the seven classes of strategies inferred. We could also identify that the strategies 1–4 are directly connected with the task execution procedure, and other strategies (5–7) are connected with selection-rule at the final decision phase.

Table 3. Question categories and example items.

Category	Cognitive aspects to be elucidated	Example questions
1	Areas attended first	In what part did you see first? What part attracted your attention first? etc.
2	First impression and its reason	You mentioned that your first impression was positive/negative, why?
3	Lesions detected and its influence to the succeeding reasoning processes	When did you detect the lesions? Was its timing give some influence to your interpretation?
4	How to see the lesions detected	How did you examine the lesions to judge whether it is problematic/not problematic?
5	Holistic interpreting strategy	Throughout the interpretation processes, in what order did you try to see the images?
6	Areas to which much attention are paid intentionally	In addition to the explicit lesions, was there any area to which you paid much attention?
7	How to use the past image	How did you use the past image (if it was useful)? Why didn't you use the past image (if it was not useful)?
8	Influence of the time when the past image was taken	When did you mind the past image while interpreting?
9	Influence of a patient's attributes to reasoning processes	How did you use the patient's information?
10	Critical evidence for the final decision	What was the critical evidence for your final decision?
11	Lessens learnt by seeing own eye movements	Did you find something from your own eye movements?

3.2 Strategies Taken by Expert Doctors

The strategies obtained in our analysis are, as explained before, relating to task execution procedure and selection-rule. Therefore, multiple strategies could be observed for each case for each participant. Table 5 shows the strategies observed for each participant throughout the experiment. The checkmarks represent that the corresponding strategies could be observed. As explained before, all of the participants were experts. One of the most interesting findings is that the doctors' having sufficient knowledge/experiences took different strategies in terms both of the task execution procedure and the selection rules.

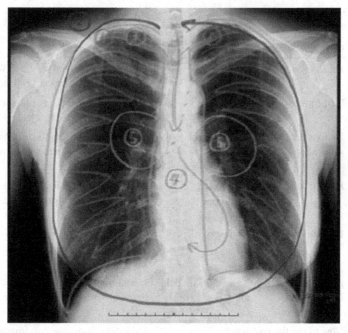

Fig. 2. X-ray image and example description of participant's scanning pattern.

Table 4. Strategies elicited.

	Strategy inferred	Example questions and answers
1	Taking very rational/logical reasoning processes for explicit lesions and relating implicit lesions backed by well-organized and advanced knowledge about lung-related disease	Experimenter: You seemed to see the lesion you first detected very frequently. Why? (question category 4) "I really got confused at that time. The critical evidence for my final decision was the trachea's unnatural curve. I guess that the curve may be caused by two possible reasons. One is just caused by an environmental condition during taking X ray image. Another one is caused by the lesion. If there is some other lesion which make the trachea's unnatural curve. So I could remove one possible disease (relating to the curve)." Experimenter: You seemed to see areas around a heart in the past image, which seemed not directly connected with the present image. Why? (question category 6) "At that time, I was concerned about another possibility. That was an atelectasis. If the patient had an atelectasis, his lung's position was most likely moved to the upper side. I wanted to check this." etc.

(continued)

Table 4. (*continued*)

	Strategy inferred	Example questions and answers
2	Examining organs borders/lines that have to be found	Experimenter: You found various lesions. What was the critical evidence for your final decision? (question category 10) "I could find that the line around the right trachea was lost. This was critical, I guess. This means that some organ was contacting. In principle, this area is always unclear in X ray images. So I strongly suspect that something was wrong." Experimenter: If some shadow exists, is it give some influence to other organs? (additional question) "Yes, sometimes. So I always pay attention to organs borders' position/silhouette. I mean that I check, for example, whether some border/line is lost or not. To examine an unnatural shadow, I check other organs via its line or silhouette." etc.
3	Checking symmetry in a present image	Experimenter: What was the critical evidence for your final decision? (question category 10) "The symmetry between the area in right and left lungs was lost. I guess that the trachea was contacted with something, maybe cancer.'" "The moment I started to see the image, I could find that the symmetry was clearly lost. This was not found in the past image."
4	Checking trend/changes along with time using a past image	Experimenter: What was the critical evidence for your final decision? (question category 10) "The moment I started to see the image, I could find that the symmetry was clearly lost. This was not found in the past image." Experimenter: How did you examine the lesion to judge whether it is problematic/not problematic? (question category 4) "By comparing the images, I could find it in the present image but not in the past image. Considering that the past image was taken eighteen months ago, I could guess that the lesion was problematic." etc.
5	Putting priority on the present image	Experimenter: You mentioned that the patient had had some disease, maybe cancer, based on the past image. And you also indicated the identical one in the present image. What was the critical reason for your final decision? (question category 10) "It is true that the patient should be proceed to CT test. But a doctor might overlook it. So I should give my final decision based on the present status, at any moment." etc.

(*continued*)

Table 4. (*continued*)

Strategy inferred	Example questions and answers
6	Taking a patient's key attributes into account	Experimenter: How did you examine the heart? (question category 4) "The patient is most likely a heavy smoker. This gives a critical influence on a lung. So the most of lesions seemed to be caused by cigarette. Etc.
7	Thinking of the worst	Experimenter: You mentioned that your first impression was negative because of some unnatural shadow (question category 2) "This was a difficult case. The shadow seemed to appear recently. In such difficult case, I choose a worse option. False positive is good for patient safety

Table 5. Differences of strategies.

	Strategy	Participant								
		D1	D2	D3	D4	D5	D6	D7	D8	D9
1	Taking very rational/logical reasoning processes for explicit lesions and relating implicit lesions backed by well-organized and advanced knowledge about lung-related disease	✓	✓	✓			✓	✓	✓	✓
2	Examining organs borders/lines that have to be found	✓	✓				✓		✓	
3	Checking symmetry in a present image	✓	✓		✓	✓	✓	✓	✓	✓
4	Checking trend/changes along with time using a past image	✓	✓	✓	✓	✓	✓	✓	✓	✓
5	Putting priority on the present image	✓	✓							
6	Taking a patient's key attributes into account			✓	✓					
7	Thinking of the worst	✓	✓		✓		✓			

4 Discussion and Conclusion

This paper shows expert doctors' cognitive skill elicitation procedure by application of eye movement data stimulated retrospections. We carried out a series of experiments in which expert medical doctors performed image interpretations and diagnosis under realistic medical checkup condition. In our plan, we will continue analyzing all data obtained in the experiment. We will identify the relations of strategies taken and the effectiveness of the diagnosis in individual levels. In addition, we plan to deploy our approach to educational applications, especially for novice doctors, in order to avoid overlooking [e.g., 8–11]. These analyses will be, we believe, promising to understand detailed skills in image interpretations as well as to contribute to effective training.

References

1. Hansen, J.P.: The use of eye mark recordings to support verbal retrospection in software testing. Acta Physiol. (Oxf) **76**(1), 31–49 (1991)
2. Argelagos, E., Brand-Gruwel, S., Jarodzka, H.M., Pifarré, M.: Unpacking cognitive skills engaged in web-search: how can log files, eye movements, and cued-retrospective reports help? an in-depth qualitative case study. Int. J. Innov. Learn. **24**(2), 152–178 (2018)
3. Elling, S., Lentz, L., De Jong, M.: Retrospective think-aloud method: Using eye movements as an extra cue for participants' verbalizations. In: Proceedings of the 2011 Annual Conference on Human Factors in Computing Systems, pp. 1161–1170. ACM Press, New York (2011)
4. van Gog, T., Paas, F., van Merriënboer, J.J., Witte, P.: Uncovering the problem-solving process: cued retrospective reporting versus concurrent and retrospective reporting. J. Exp. Psychol. Appl. **11**(4), 237–244 (2005)
5. Wu, W., Hall, A.K., Braund, H., Bell, C.R., Szulewski, A.: The development of visual expertise in ECG interpretation: an eye-tracking augmented re situ interview approach. Teach. Learn. Med. **33**(3), 258–269 (2021)
6. Aoki, H., et al.: Elicitation of diagnosis strategy during scanning chest x-rays from eye tracking stimulated retrospections. In: 13th International Conference on Applied Human Factors and Ergonomics (2022)
7. Aoki, H., et al.: Analysis of clinical reasoning processes during scanning chest x-rays based on visual perception patterns. In: Proceedings of the 21st Congress of the International Ergonomics Association, Vancouver, pp. 425–431 (2021)
8. Kok, E., et al.: Re-viewing performance: Showing eye-tracking data as feedback to improve performance monitoring in a complex visual task. J. Comput. Assist. Learn. **38**(4), 1087–1101 (2022)
9. Chisari, L.B., Mockevičiūtė, A., Ruitenburg, S.K., van Vemde, L., Kok, E.M., van Gog, T.: Effects of prior knowledge and joint attention on learning from eye movement modelling examples. J. Comput. Assist. Learn. **36**(4), 569–579 (2020)
10. Donovan, T., Manning, D.J., Crawford, T.: Performance changes in lung nodule detection following perceptual feedback of eye movements. In: Proceedings of the SPIE 6917, Medical Imaging 2008: Image Perception, Observer Performance, and Technology Assessment, p. 9 (2008)
11. Jarodzka, H., et al.: Conveying clinical reasoning based on visual observation via eye-movement modelling examples. Instr. Sci. **40**(5), 813–827 (2012)

An Evaluation Framework on Pilot's Competency-Based Flying Style

Shan Gao⬚, Yuanyuan Xian⬚, and Lei Wang⁽⊠⁾⬚

College of Safety Science and Engineering, Civil Aviation University of China, Tianjin, China
wanglei0564@hotmail.com

Abstract. Like most drivers have their own driving styles, commercial airline pilots also have their own flying styles, referring to a set of individual flying habits that gradually formed with their flying experience. However, little is known about flying style that might affect flight safety. This study aims to develop a framework for evaluating pilots' flying style. Our original evaluation framework was derived from the *"Manual of Evidence-based Training"* issued by the International Civil Aviation Organization (Doc 9995), which outlines eight competencies of commercial airline pilots for observation and evaluation by flight instructors. Furthermore, in the next step, the initial framework can be developed by interviewing evidence-based training (EBT) flight instructors and applying new technologies (e.g., eye-tracking technology and physiological measuring technology). Using the initial framework for flying style, we can evaluate pilots' preferences for flying. In this regard, it is useful for a variety of purposes, including understanding the operational characteristics of pilots, improving flight training, and crew paring in a more rational way.

Keywords: Flying Style · Core Competency · Flight Safety · Evidence-based Training (EBT)

1 Introduction

The safety domain holds promise for the development of transportation. The rapid development of technology coupled with many modes of transportation is expected to make transportation more efficient, safe, and comfortable for users and passengers. Human errors, however, account for the majority of accidents in various transport modes, such as aviation and road transportation [1]. In response to the severity of aviation accidents, researchers have been studying pilots' operations and intentions, as well as their correlations with flight safety 3. Commercial airline pilots are directly responsible for the safety of an aircraft, as they are the direct operators of the aircraft during flight.

People who are accident-prone are more likely to violate laws, take risks, or be involved in accidents or unsafe incidents more often 6. A number of studies and observations have shown that not all pilots behave similarly in the cockpit 7. People who are risky, aggressive, and dissociative may be more likely to be involved in hazardous events than those who are careful, prosocial, and attentive. For example, the concept of

D. Harris and W.-C. Li (Eds.): HCII 2023, LNAI 14017, pp. 190–199, 2023.
https://doi.org/10.1007/978-3-031-35392-5_15

"risky pilots" refers to some pilots with a higher level of psychological risk elements (i.e., risk perception, risk tolerance, and hazardous attitude) than others, and they also account for a larger number of unsafe events [13]. It presents different individual preferences regarding flight operations that have a high correlation to flight safety throughout. Drivers usually have different driving styles, which means they develop a set of individual driving habits over time, such as what speed they choose, when and how they change lanes, and how they interact with other cars [14]. Similarly, pilots have a set of individual flying habits that gradually formed with their flying experience, which consists of technical and non-technical elements. There has been extensive research into drivers' driving styles, but little is known about pilots' flying styles.

As part of the "Manual of Evidence-based Training" [15], pilots were observed and evaluated for their technical and non-technical skills. To fill the research gap, this study first proposes an initial framework of pilots' competency-based flying style (Fig. 1). First, we summarize the literature on drivers' driving styles. Second, we compare the similarities between drivers and pilots. Finally, we propose an initial research framework for pilot's competency-based flying styles. Reviewing flight instructors based on driving styles can provide insight into specific flying styles. The study contributes theoretically to the field of Transdisciplinary Engineering by narrowing the domain specificity between driving and flying. Practically, the findings are expected to offer a predictive avenue for pilots' competency-based flying performance based on driving style.

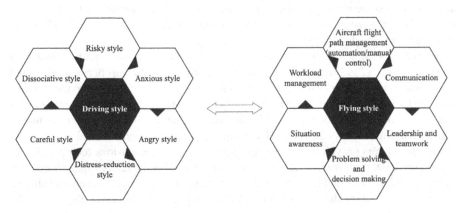

Fig. 1. An initial framework of the competency-based flying style based on driving style.

2   Research on Driving Style

Previous relevant studies have defined driver's driving style differently. Elander et al. [16] defined driving style as the way an individual chooses to drive in a habitual manner. Saad [17] described driving style as a relatively stable characteristic of drivers. According to Ishibashi et al. [18], driving style refers to the attitude and way of thinking when driving. de Groot et al. [19] argued that driving style is influenced by social, neurobehavioral, and biological factors. The driving style of a driver can be summarized as a habitual way of driving, based on these definitions, meaning that a set of individual driving habits, such as the speed at which they drive, when and how they change lanes, and how they interact with other vehicles, varies with driving experience [14].

Several studies have found that driving style and driving behavior significantly predict driving safety performance (e.g., crash risk, see Karimi, Aghabayk, & Moridpour, [20]). Individuals who rated higher scores in violation were prone to driver faster in curve negotiation [21], reported more traffic accidents and worse driving skills [22, 23]. Huo et al. [24] discovered that drivers with angry driving style have shorter lane-changing decision time than others, referring to a higher possibility of collision with vehicles in the target lane. Therefore, to improve road safety, drivers' driving style and behavior have been widely investigated with subjective questionnaires [25] and objective data [26, 27]. To measure driver's driving style, several questionnaires have been developed, including the Aggressive Driving Scale (ADS) [28], the Driver Behavior Questionnaire (DBQ) [29], and the Multidimensional Driving Style Inventory (MDSI) [25, 30]. For example, Van Huysduynen et al. [25] showed that participants' self-reported driving style was modestly correlated with their simulated driving behavior such as average speed, jerk, lateral position, and the distance to preceding vehicles. Using real driving data, Zhu et al. [27] collected 84 human drivers' driving data to quantitate their driving style in Adaptive Cruise Control (ACC) by driving-similarity measuring algorithm; the driving features include speed control, distance control, and the switching rule. Itkonen et al. [26] also captured some driving preferences from 76 individuals' driving data in a motorway, including keeping safety margins (both longitudinal and lateral), lane-changing frequency, and acceleration and speed preference.

However, these scales focus on self-reported abnormal behaviors and intentions with no standard units, and the results may lack objective (i.e., the gap between ideal and real) because participants' subjective ratings may not be comparable due to the distance between their subjective ratings [31, 32]. For example, Molesworth and Chang [33] found that the Implicit Association Test (IAT) showed a greater prediction of pilots' behavior than the Hazardous Attitude Scale (HAS). Although the data from on-road vehicles and driving simulators provide more ecological and objective conclusions (compared with self-reported data), the results largely depend on environmental factors and settings that cannot be fully controlled [34, 35]. In this regard, pilot's flying style is better evaluated and understood from the driving habits behind a pilot's performance than from the behavior itself.

3 Similarity Between Driving and Flying

The similarity between drivers and pilots provides some insights for addressing the above issue. Apart from the prospective research on "flying cars" that integrates drivers and pilots [36], studies that focused on "what can we learn between varying transport modes" also showed the similarities between driving and flying, especially regarding human-automation interaction [37–39]. For example, Trösterer et al. [39] interviewed three pilots about their transitions between manual control and autopilot; they concluded that drivers can gain insight into how to maintain a safe interaction with automation from pilots in many aspects such as situation awareness, training, and calibration of trust. Many users of partially automated vehicles are untrained, and rarely read the owner's manual to learn how to operate the automated features. Casner and Hutchins [37] compared the experience of human-computer interaction between drivers and pilots, and proposed a set of knowledge standards for partially automated vehicles' drivers; they concluded that the successful experience of human-computer interaction in aviation enhances partially automated drivers' operations. Therefore, the findings from driving style may provide a basis for the evaluation of flying style.

4 Research Framework on Flying Style

4.1 PIlot's Core Competency and Evidence-Based Training (EBT)

Competency refers to an individual's characteristics based on expected performance, including knowledge, skill, personal concept, trait, and motivation. To ensure the competency of professional aviation practitioners, it is necessary to predict how they conduct their work and evaluate their performance in selected scenarios. As explained in Chapter N of CCAR-121 and Appendix D and E by the Civil Aviation Administration of China (CAAC) [40], which specifies the requirements for training and inspection for trainee pilots, first officers, and captains with respect to theory, simulators, and aircraft. However, pilots' capability degradation caused by special reasons (e.g., complex weather, special faults, and attention allocation) cannot be effectively remedied by retraining in flight simulators. Furthermore, pilots have strong preparation for retraining, which decreases training effects.

In order to improve flight training quality, the CAAC [41] issued the Guiding Opinions on Comprehensively Deepening the Reform of Flight Training for Transport Airlines on June 21, 2019. It firstly proposed the training idea of "Implementing flight training based on core competencies". In contrast to traditional pilot retraining, evidence-based training (EBT) emphasizes the pilot's core competence, which can be described as a series of abilities regarding how to efficiently conduct specific work and show their skills. Pilot's core competency should include technical and non-technical skills. Technical skills include application of procedures, aircraft flight path management (automation/manual control); non-technical skills include the application of procedures, communication, leadership and teamwork, problem-solving and decision-making, situation awareness, and workload management. The International Civil Aviation Organization [15] provided a description of pilot's core competencies and behavioral indicators (Table 1). EBT instructors developed training courses based on real flight scenarios with the goal of improving pilots' core competencies and offering specific training recommendations. As a result, specific behavioral indicators can be used to assess pilot's core competencies.

Table 1. Pilot's core competencies and description [15].

Competency	Description
Application of procedures	Identifies and applies procedures in accordance with published operating instructions and applicable regulations, using the appropriate knowledge
Communication	Demonstrates effective oral, non-verbal and written communications, in normal and non-normal situations
Leader ship and teamwork	Demonstrates effective leadership and team working
Problem solving and decision making	Accurately identifies risks and resolves problems. Uses the appropriate decision-making processes
Situation awareness	Perceives and comprehends all of the relevant information available and anticipates what could happen that may affect the operation
Workload management	Manages available resources efficiently to prioritize and perform tasks in a timely manner under all circumstances
Aircraft flight path management (automation)	Controls the aircraft flight path through automation, including appropriate use of flight management system(s) and guidance
Aircraft flight path management (manual control)	Controls the aircraft flight path through manual flight, including appropriate use of flight management system(s) and flight guidance systems

4.2 Pilot's Competency-based Flying Style

We have proposed several indicators based on drivers' driving styles that can be reflected pilots' core competencies for a long time (Table 2). Evaluation of competencies, for instance, can reveal a pilot's risky decision-making style. In previous studies, weather-related scenarios were most commonly used. Pilots were observed to make different weather-related decision-making [7–12]. As an example, without visual reference during the final approach, Wang et al. [10] found that some airline pilots chose to go around, while others landed. By capturing this risk proneness, EBT instructors can get a sense of how they solve problems and make decisions.

Table 2. Examples of pilot's flying style.

Risky style
• Inappropriately switching on autopilot
• Enjoying the tension of manual control
• Approaching without a clear visual reference
• Multitasking
Anxiety style
• Preparing to take over the autopilot
• Worrying about flying with unfamiliar partners
• Stressing about plans and prioritization of tasks in flight
Angry style
• Annoying when partner doesn't understand what you are saying
• Not being satisfied with the outcome if things don't go as planned
• Be upset when interruptions, disturbances, changes and breakdowns occur unexpectedly
Distress-reduction style
• Communicating actively with others to relax
• Switching on autopilot to relieve manual control stress
Careful style
• Regularly checking and verifying the instrument parameters
• Keeping good manners at work
Dissociative style
• Trying to turn on the cockpit's air conditioner, but turning on the cabin's
• Disconnecting the autopilot system without noticing

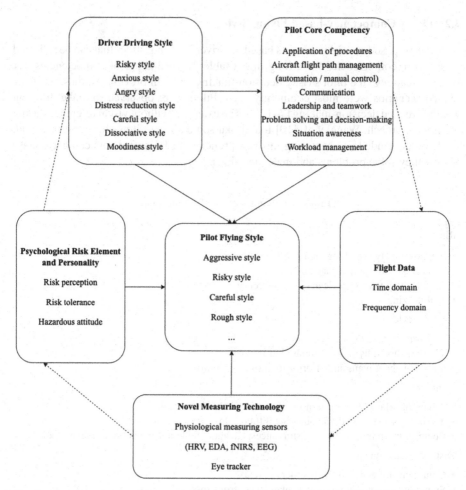

Fig. 2. The research framework of pilot's flying style using multidimensional data in the future.

5 Conclusion

To evaluate pilots' flying style, this study reviewed the relevant studies about driving styles and pointed out the shortages of driving styles measured by self-reported scales and assessed by driving data. By comparing the similarity between driving and flying, we found that flying styles can be evaluated based on their core competencies and driving styles. Finally, we noted that pilots' flying styles should be viewed as performance-based rather than flying operations-based.

It should be noted that the initial framework cannot be used directly to evaluate a pilot's flying style as both the items and the flying style are incomplete. A research framework for defining flying style should be developed by EBT instructors and relevant researchers. Furthermore, the evaluation of flying style should be conducted using a long-term multidimensional data to capture pilots' flying habits, rather than a single evaluation (Fig. 2).

The next step is to collect multidimensional data to evaluate the pilot's flying style. As an example, flight instructors' text regarding pilot's flying styles should be extracted and analyzed to include more flight styles and their specific performance. Furthermore, physiological measurement technology and eye-tracking technology may allow us to more accurately assess some styles not easily reflected by performance (e.g., angry, anxious, and dissociative). And the correlations between the predictive factors should be examined.

Acknowledgments. . The authors would like to appreciate the support of the National Natural Science Foundation of China (grant no. 32071063).

References

1. International Air Transport Association: Safety Report 2021 (2022)
2. National Highway Traffic Safety Administration: Critical reasons for crashes investigated in the national motor vehicle crash causation survey. Washington, DC: US Department of Transportation 2, 1–2 (2015)
3. Ebbatson, M., Harris, D., Huddlestone, J., Sears, R.: The relationship between manual handling performance and recent flying experience in air transport pilots. Ergonomics **53**(2), 268–277 (2010)
4. Wang, L., Ren, Y., Wu, C.: Effects of flare operation on landing safety: a study based on ANOVA of real flight data. Saf. Sci. **102**, 14–25 (2018)
5. Wang, L., Zhang, J., Dong, C., Sun, H., Ren, Y.: A method of applying flight data to evaluate landing operation performance. Ergonomics **62**(2), 171–180 (2019)
6. Greenwood, M.: Accident proneness. Biometrika **37**(1/2), 24–29 (1950)
7. Hunter, D.R., Martinussen, M., Wiggins, M., O'Hare, D.: Situational and personal characteristics associated with adverse weather encounters by pilots. Accid. Anal. Prev. **43**(1), 176–186 (2011)
8. Pauley, K., O'Hare, D., Wiggins, M.: Risk tolerance and pilot involvement in hazardous events and flight into adverse weather. J. Safety Res. **39**(4), 403–411 (2008)
9. Walmsley, S., Gilbey, A.: Applying prospect theory to pilot weather-related decision-making: the impact of monetary and time considerations on risk taking behaviour. Appl. Cogn. Psychol. **34**(3), 685–698 (2020)
10. Wang, L., Gao, S., Tan, W., Zhang, J.: Pilots' mental workload variation when taking a risk in a flight scenario: A study based on flight simulator experiments. Int. J. Occupat. Safety Ergonom. **29**(1), 366–375 (2023)
11. Wiggins, M.W., Azar, D., Hawken, J., Loveday, T., Newman, D.: Cue-utilisation typologies and pilots' pre-flight and in-flight weather decision-making. Saf. Sci. **65**, 118–124 (2014)
12. Wiggins, M.W., Hunter, D.R., O'Hare, D., Martinussen, M.: Characteristics of pilots who report deliberate versus inadvertent visual flight into instrument meteorological conditions. Saf. Sci. **50**(3), 472–477 (2012)
13. Wang, L., Zhang, J.: The effect of psychological risk elements on pilot flight operational performance. Human Factors Ergonom. Manufact. Service Indust. **30**(1), 3–13 (2020)
14. Suzdaleva, E., Nagy, I.: An online estimation of driving style using data-dependent pointer model. Transport. Res. Part C: Emerg. Technol. **86**, 23–36 (2018)

15. International Civil Aviation Organization: Manual of Evidence-based Training (Doc 9995). (2013)
16. Elander, J., West, R., French, D.: Behavioral correlates of individual differences in road-traffic crash risk: An examination of methods and findings. Psychol. Bull. **113**(2), 279–294 (1993)
17. Saad, F.: Behavioural adaptations to new driver support systems: Some critical issues. In: 2004 IEEE International Conference on Systems, Man and Cybernetics (IEEE Cat. No. 04CH37583), pp. 288–293 (2004)
18. Ishibashi, M., Okuwa, M., Doi, S. i., Akamatsu, M.: Indices for characterizing driving style and their relevance to car following behavior. In: SICE Annual Conference 2007, pp. 1132–1137 (2007)
19. de Groot, S., Ricote, F.C., de Winter, J.C.: The effect of tire grip on learning driving skill and driving style: a driving simulator study. Transport. Res. F: Traffic Psychol. Behav. **15**(4), 413–426 (2012)
20. Karimi, S., Aghabayk, K., Moridpour, S.: Impact of driving style, behaviour and anger on crash involvement among Iranian intercity bus drivers. IATSS Research **46**(4), 457–466 (2022)
21. Deng, Z., Chu, D., Wu, C., He, Y., Cui, J.: Curve safe speed model considering driving style based on driver behaviour questionnaire. Transport. Res. F: Traffic Psychol. Behav. **65**, 536–547 (2019)
22. de Winter, J.C., Dodou, D., Stanton, N.A.: A quarter of a century of the DBQ: Some supplementary notes on its validity with regard to accidents. Ergonomics **58**(10), 1745–1769 (2015)
23. Lajunen, T., Sullman, M.J., Gaygısız, E.: Self-assessed driving skills and risky driver behaviour among young drivers: a cross-sectional study. Front. Psychol. **13**, 840269 (2022)
24. Huo, D., Ma, J., Chang, R.: Lane-changing-decision characteristics and the allocation of visual attention of drivers with an angry driving style. Transport. Res. F: Traffic Psychol. Behav. **71**, 62–75 (2020)
25. Van Huysduynen, H.H., Terken, J., Eggen, B.: The relation between self-reported driving style and driving behaviour. A simulator study. Transport. Res. Part F: Traffic Psychol. Behav. **56**, 245–255 (2018)
26. Itkonen, T.H., Lehtonen, E., Selpi.: Characterisation of motorway driving style using naturalistic driving data. Transport. Res. Part F: Traffic Psychol. Behav. **69**, 72–79 (2020)
27. Zhu, B., Jiang, Y., Zhao, J., He, R., Bian, N., Deng, W.: Typical-driving-style-oriented personalized adaptive cruise control design based on human driving data. Transport. Res. Part C: Emerg. Technol. **100**, 274–288 (2019)
28. Krahé, B., Fenske, I.: Predicting aggressive driving behavior: The role of macho personality, age, and power of car. Aggressive Behav. **28**(1), 21–29 (2002)
29. Reason, J., Manstead, A., Stradling, S., Baxter, J., Campbell, K.: Errors and violations on the roads: a real distinction? Ergonomics **33**(10–11), 1315–1332 (1990)
30. Taubman-Ben-Ari, O., Mikulincer, M., Gillath, O.: The multidimensional driving style inventory—scale construct and validation. Accid. Anal. Prev. **36**(3), 323–332 (2004)
31. Casner, S.M., Gore, B.F.: Measuring and evaluating workload: A primer (NASA/TM—2010-216395). NASA Technical Memorandum, 216395 (2010)
32. Mansikka, H., Virtanen, K., Harris, D.: Comparison of NASA-TLX scale, modified Cooper-Harper scale and mean inter-beat interval as measures of pilot mental workload during simulated flight tasks. Ergonomics **62**(2), 246–254 (2019)
33. Molesworth, B.R.C., Chang, B.: Predicting pilots' risk-taking behavior through an implicit association test. Hum. Factors **51**(6), 845–857 (2009)
34. Lu, Y., et al.: Effects of route familiarity on drivers' psychological conditions: Based on driving behavior and driving environment. Transport. Res. F: Traffic Psychol. Behav. **75**, 37–54 (2020)

35. Lyu, N., Wang, Y., Wu, C., Peng, L., Thomas, A.F.: Using naturalistic driving data to identify driving style based on longitudinal driving operation conditions. J. Intell. Connect. Veh. **5**(1), 17–35 (2022)
36. Eker, U., Ahmed, S.S., Fountas, G., Anastasopoulos, P.C.: An exploratory investigation of public perceptions towards safety and security from the future use of flying cars in the United States. Anal. Methods Accident Res. **23**, 100103 (2019)
37. Casner, S.M., Hutchins, E.L.: What do we tell the drivers? Toward minimum driver training standards for partially automated cars. J. Cogn. Eng. Decision Making **13**(2), 55–66 (2019)
38. Papadimitriou, E., Schneider, C., Tello, J.A., Damen, W., Vrouenraets, M.L., Ten Broeke, A.: Transport safety and human factors in the era of automation: what can transport modes learn from each other? Accid. Anal. Prev. **144**, 105656 (2020)
39. Trösterer, S., et al.: What we can learn from pilots for handovers and (de) skilling in semi-autonomous driving: An interview study. In: Proceedings of the 9th International Conference on Automotive User Interfaces and Interactive Vehicular Applications, pp. 173–182 (2017)
40. Civil Aviation Administration of China: Rules for the Certification of the Operation of large Aircraft Public Air Transport Carriers (CCAR-121-R7). (2021). In Chinese
41. Civil Aviation Administration of China: Guidance on Comprehensively Deepening the Reform of Flight Training for Transport Airlines (CAAC No. 39). (2019). In Chinese

Proposing Gaze-Based Interaction and Automated Screening Results for Visual Aerial Image Analysis

Jutta Hild[✉], Lars Sommer, Gerrit Holzbach, Michael Voit,
and Elisabeth Peinsipp-Byma

System Technologies and Image Exploitation IOSB, Fraunhofer Institute of Optronics,
76131 Karlsruhe, Germany
`jutta.hild@iosb.fraunhofer.de`

Abstract. Visual aerial image analysis occurs in various application domains. Recently, high-resolution optical sensors became more and more available. This results in more captured image data and increased workload for the human expert image analysts. In this contribution, we address the situation of a human operator performing a visual screening task in aerial images in order to find certain vehicles. This task is common in the safety and security domain. Based on discussion with expert image analysts about typical image analysis challenges, we implemented an experimental system in order to investigate whether gaze-based interaction and automated image exploitation would provide an appropriate and efficient user interface. The system provides (1) screening results generated from an automated screening algorithm and (2) gaze-based interaction using a low-cost remote eye-tracker and a keyboard for panning/zooming the image as well as for selecting/framing of targets. The results of a pilot study (N = 12 non-expert image analysts) show, that the availability of automated screening results reduces error rates, completion time and perceived workload (NASA-TLX). Ratings of the gaze-based interaction using the ISO 9241–411 questionnaire are good to very good, except for eye strain for users with glasses.

Keywords: Aerial image analysis · multimodal gaze-based interaction · gaze pointing · automated image analysis · user study

1 Introduction

Aerial image analysis occurs as a task in various application domains. Examples are earth sciences like geography or geology, urban planning, cartography, archaeology, agriculture, or safety and security.

Typically, image analysis is a human visual task. A human expert is responsible for the interpretation of the image content by scanning it visually in order to find task relevant issues or objects. This can be very demanding as objects might occur blurred, partly occluded or at unexpected locations. However, missing relevant objects might result in severe consequences and must be prevented.

© The Author(s), under exclusive license to Springer Nature Switzerland AG 2023
D. Harris and W.-C. Li (Eds.): HCII 2023, LNAI 14017, pp. 200–214, 2023.
https://doi.org/10.1007/978-3-031-35392-5_16

In this contribution, we consider the situation of a human expert image analyst performing a visual screening task in aerial images in order to find certain vehicles. This task often occurs in the safety and security domain, e.g., in traffic control or vehicle tracing. If an expert analyst detects a target, they frame it. The annotated image is then given away to other authorities supporting their decision-making processes regarding further response.

For their task, expert analysts typically utilize customized image analysis software provided on a desktop computer equipped with traditional computer mouse and keyboard to frame targets in images. As images often cover a large geographical area, objects might occur at small sizes in the image. This makes the task challenging at various levels. First, it creates perceptive and cognitive load: Detecting targets is cumbersome and error-prone even with a continuously attentive mind (Fig. 1). Second, manual interaction is cumbersome and stressful due to the many required operations for image zooming, panning and object selection. To relieve the human expert analyst, we propose two measures to be included into the image analysis system:

1. In order to reduce misses of relevant target objects, we propose the availability of automated image analysis results as a system function (Fig. 2).
2. In order to reduce manual stress, we propose utilizing gaze-based interaction instead of mouse input for interaction.

The following paragraphs provide related work on automated screening algorithms (cf. Sect. 1.1) and gaze-based interaction (cf. Sect. 1.2), followed by our proposal of an experimental image exploitation system (cf. Sect. 1.3).

1.1 Automated Screening Algorithms

Today's automated image analysis algorithms are quite powerful. The usage of deep learning has led to significant improvement in various domains including object detection in aerial imagery. In particular, detection methods based on Convolutional Neural Networks (CNNs), e.g., Faster R-CNN, SSD and their counterparts, considerably outperformed conventional methods based on hand-crafted features [1, 2]. Applying CNNs as backbone architectures yielded enhanced feature representations, while domain specific adaptations were required to account for the characteristics of aerial imagery, i.e., small object dimensions [3]. An overview about different CNN-based detection methods applied on aerial imagery is given by Zhu et al. [4]. In recent years, novel deep learning methods based on Vision Transformer (ViT) networks further boosted aerial object detection [5], while leveraging inference optimizers allowed real-time capabilities [6].

Today, image exploitation systems like the ABUL system developed by the Fraunhofer Institute of Optronics, System Technologies and Image Exploitation (IOSB) provide a variety of automated image processing and exploitation functions like object detection or screening. Figure 3 shows the ABUL user interface with an automated aircraft screening example.

Discussions with expert image analysts revealed that there would be two ways to utilize automated screening results. Either the human expert performs image analysis at first independently and displays the automated results in a second step to confirm/correct their own findings; or the automated results are displayed from the beginning together

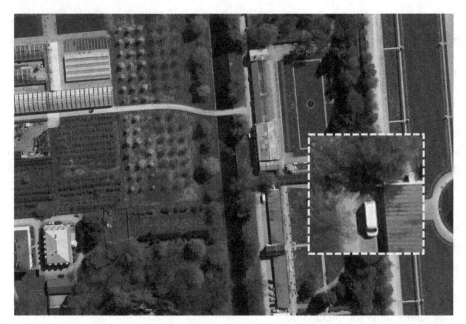

Fig. 1. Aerial image. The target object specification is »Blue car«, target size is 0.7 cm x 0.3 cm. Even with large magnification (close-up), target detection might be difficult.

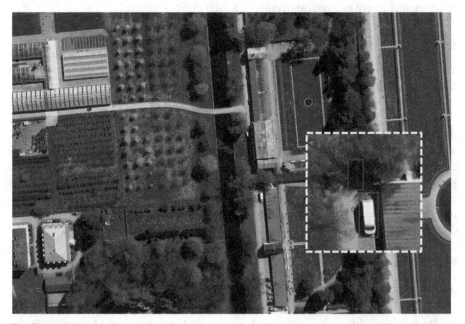

Fig. 2. Aerial image. The target object specification is »Blue car«, target size is 0.7 cm x 0.3 cm. Providing automated screening results as red frames around all vehicles makes target detection much easier.

with the image. The latter way could be beneficial because the automated results direct human attention and, hence, might accelerate the analytic process. On the negative side, display from the beginning could tempt the human expert to fully trust the automat and to omit careful scanning of the remaining image regions.

Fig. 3. Schematic illustration of the automated image exploitation system for unmanned aircraft called ABUL showing an aircraft screening example.

1.2 Gaze-Based Interaction

As image analysis is a visual task, it seems natural to utilize gaze for pointing and thereby provide interaction requiring far fewer manual actions. The key prerequisite when utilizing gaze pointing for human-computer interaction is an eye-tracking device that is able to provide a user's gaze position on screen robustly and in real-time.

However, there are two obstacles to overcome with gaze-based interaction. First, the »Midas Touch« effect [7] occurs as gaze is utilized both for perception and for computer input. Second, limited gaze pointing accuracy occurs due to a combination of eye physiology and the accuracy of current video-based eye-tracking devices allowing free head movement.

Several contributions discussed that multimodal gaze interaction is able to overcome the Midas Touch effect, cf. e.g. Vertegaal [8]. Very popular due to its ease of use, high operational speed and simple technical feasibility is the combination of gaze pointing and manual actuation of a function by hardware key press. For selection operations, authors investigated mostly either the use of a key of the computer keyboard [9–12] or the left mouse button [8, 13]. Several contributions report, that gaze pointing accuracy allows reliable static object selection for object sizes of 2° of visual angle and larger with considerably shorter selection completion time [9, 10]. Such results were mostly achieved with high-end eye-tracking devices. Only recently, there are low-cost eye-tracking devices available which appear to provide similar pointing accuracy [14]. This is a prerequisite for gaze-based interaction to become a commonly used input method.

1.3 Experimental Image Exploitation System

In order to investigate how the two measures would influence human image analysis performance, we implemented an experimental image exploitation system (Python, Windows 10). It provides the basic functions we found when observing military image analysis experts at work during an exercise.

The system is able to display single images and allows zooming and panning the image as well as selecting objects by framing them. Zooming is required to overcome the measurement uncertainty of the eye-tracker's gaze estimation that would not allow to select objects of the typically small size in large images.

Interaction is realized for the traditional mouse input as well as for the gaze-based interaction technique gaze pointing (GP) + key press. Figure 4 shows the keys we utilize for interaction:

- Gaze pointing (GP) + ENTER selects an object by framing it;
- GP + DEL deletes a frame;
- GP + PLUS zooms into the image around the current gaze position;
- GP + MINUS zooms out;
- GP + SPACE moves image position at the current gaze position into the screen center

Mouse input utilizes a left button click for framing an object, and a right button click for deleting a frame; image zoom is performed using the mouse wheel; image pan is performed using the typical method of moving the mouse device while keeping the left mouse button pressed. Moreover, the system includes a mechanism, which is able to display precalculated classification results from an automated vehicle classification algorithm as a screening mask. In order to get first insight, whether such a system would be appreciated by users, we conducted a pilot study, which we describe in the following.

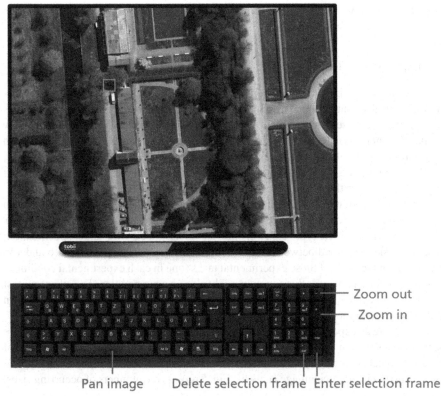

Zoom out
Zoom in

Pan image   Delete selection frame Enter selection frame

Fig. 4. Experimental image exploitation system: Setup and design of the gaze-based interaction. Automated screening results are provided in the image as red frames; target object selection by human operator is displayed as light green frame (framing the »Blue car« from Fig. 1 and 2).

2 Method

In the pilot study, subjects accomplished the task of vehicle search in aerial images. Our focus was on two research questions:

1. Would the availability of automated screening results result in better user performance?
2. How is user satisfaction for the gaze-based interaction rated?

In order to address Q1, we utilize two experimental conditions. In condition A, during vehicle search, automated screening results are provided; in condition B no such results are provided. Condition A presents the screening mask together with the image from the beginning (cf. last paragraph in Sect. 1.1); this way we ensure that all subjects conduct the experimental tasks in a similar manner, which appears to be the more valid approach when it comes to comparison of the performance results of conditions A and B.

To answer Q2, subjects rate their user satisfaction with the gaze-based user interface utilizing the ISO/TS 9241–411 questionnaire [15]. We did not evaluate mouse input against gaze input as this would have resulted in a too long overall session duration for our non-expert subjects. Task design and procedure were realized in close cooperation with military expert image analysts.

2.1 Experimental Tasks

Task design was realized in close cooperation with military expert image analysts. Discussions revealed that a typical task instruction for vehicle search could be more or less specific. In some cases, the instruction specifies an individual search object with many details. In other cases, object specification is only vague, for example, consisting in information about color or brightness together with a coarse vehicle type (e.g., »car«, »truck«). Sometimes, the instruction even tells to find all vehicles – this is in fact what the automated algorithm does.

In total, we designed 26 test tasks and one training task. 22 test tasks (eleven in each experimental condition A and B respectively) used a combination of color/brightness information and a vehicle type, e.g., »White van« or »Dark car« for target specification; those test tasks contained between one and eight target objects and between 6 and 146 distractors. In fact, two of those experimental tasks (one in each experimental condition) contained no target object as this situation might also occur in practice. The other four test tasks (two in each experimental condition) used for target specification the instruction »All vehicles«; target object number was between 14 and 26.

In total, the 26 experimental tasks contained 123 target objects; 28 target objects were located in shadows or under trees and were therefore more difficult to find. The size of the target objects was between 0.3 cm × 0.1 cm and 2.5 cm × 1.0 cm representing typical sizes occurring in practical image analysis; Fig. 5 reports the numbers of occurring sizes.

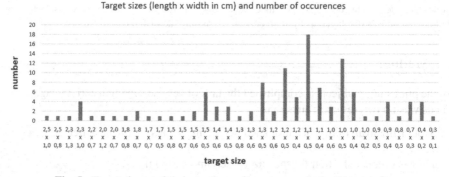

Fig. 5. Target sizes and their numbers of occurrences in the 26 test tasks.

The image data material for the test and trainings tasks was derived from the DLR 3K Munich Vehicle Aerial Image data set [16]. This data set contains twenty aerial images (5616 x 3744 pixels) with a Ground Sampling Distance of 13 cm/pixel. Annotations are only available for the ten images of the train set, which comprises about 4,100 vehicle detections. Hence, the environment of the experimental tasks was either urban, rural, residential neighborhood or industrial area.

As automated screening algorithm for vehicle search, we used a CNN-based SSD detector introduced by Liu et al. [17] and adapted to aerial images by Sommer et al. [1]. The calculated detection results were provided as thin red frames around the vehicles (cf. Fig. 6); they were displayed as image overlay in the experimental condition A (»with support by automated results«).

Fig. 6. Test task with automated vehicle screening results provided as thin red frames. The orange arrow points to a false positive automated result (pole shadow); in all test tasks occurred only seven false positives (six were containers). Task instruction is »Orange van«; the green arrow points to the target (size 1.0 cm × 0.5 cm); the task contains 109 distractors (vehicles that are no targets).

The procedure is the same for each trial. It starts with the instruction presentation on the screen's center (black font on grey background). After reading the instruction, subjects start the trial by selecting the »continue«-button placed beneath the instruction using GP + ENTER (if the gaze is targeted at the button, its color changes from grey to yellow). Immediately, the related image (with or without screening mask) is presented. Now, the subject scans the image and frames the targets. On pressing CTRL + S, the trial ends and the next instruction is presented.

2.2 Experimental Setup

The experimental tasks were presented on a 24″ desktop monitor with a resolution of 1920 x 1200 pixels. The subjects were sitting in front of the monitor with a distance of 65 cm. Gaze Data was recorded using a Tobii 4C remote eye-tracker with a sampling rate of 90 Hz. The manufacturer does not provide information on the accuracy [18];

however, authors reported on average 1° of visual angle without head stabilization [14]. The eye-tracker was connected to the system using RabbitMQ. No chin rest or head stabilization was used during the sessions. The key presses were performed using a standard keyboard.

2.3 Procedure

Twelve subjects (two females, 10 males; average age 28.7 (5.6) years) participated in the pilot study. All subjects had normal or corrected to normal vision (five wore glasses). All were colleagues or students of our department and had no expertise as image analysts. Six subjects had little experience with remote eye tracking for gaze input from another user study.

All subjects performed 26 test tasks of vehicle search in aerial images; 13 with support by automated results (experimental condition A, with a precalculated screening mask displayed; Fig. 2, 6), 13 without such support (experimental condition B; Fig. 1). Half the subjects started with condition A, half with condition B, resulting in a complete counterbalanced within-subjects design.

Each session started with an introduction into the experiment including an explanation of the questionnaires (see below) as well as the task to accomplish. Subjects were instructed to perform as fast and as accurate as possible. After that, they performed the Tobii 4C calibration procedure. Then, each subject performed their first condition, starting with the training task, followed by the 13 test tasks, followed by reporting their subjectively perceived workload using the NASA-TLX [19]. Then, each subject performed their second condition (training task, 13 test tasks, NASA-TLX). Finally, the subjects reported their favorite condition as well as their user satisfaction with the gaze-based interaction using the ISO/TS 9241–411 questionnaire [15]. In order to address eye strain, which is often an issue with gaze-based interaction [20], we added eye fatigue as a feature according to Zhang and MacKenzie [10].

3 Results

As metrics for comparison of the two experimental conditions, we utilized (as proposed by the ISO/TS 9241–411 standard [15]): effectiveness as *error rate* (missed target objects); and efficiency as *completion time.*

In addition, the subjects rated the perceived workload using the NASA-TLX (using a rating scale from 0: no workload to 100: high workload) as well as user satisfaction for the gaze-based interaction. Furthermore, we investigated how the subjects used the zoom function.

The results show that the availability of automated screening results reduces error rates, completion time and perceived workload. *Error rate* was on average (1 Std. Dev.) 8(6) % for condition A (automated screening results available), and 19(12) % for condition B (without automated screening results). The difference is mainly due to the target misses of targets located in shadows or under trees. Figure 7 and Fig. 8 give an example of this issue. In condition A (Fig. 7), all subjects detected the target in the shadow; in condition B (Fig. 8), none of the subjects detected it. Figure 9 shows the content of Fig. 8 together with a heatmap overlay representing the gaze distribution on the image; it is evident that the subject missed the target in the shadow because he or she did not visually fixate it.

The *zoom function* ensured that not a single target was missed because of limited selection accuracy due to eye-tracker measurement uncertainty. Looking at the zoom factors used during target object selection shows that one third of the selections happened without zooming, and 95% of the selections with a zoom factor up to 5.5. Zoom factors did not differ for conditions A and B. Figure 10 shows the zoom factor (median) as a function of target length for all test tasks. The subjects used the zoom function for all target lengths that were smaller than 2 cm (corresponding to about 2° at the viewing distance of 65 cm). The average (zoomed) target size upon target selection was (length x width) 2.2 cm x 0.9 cm (corresponding to 1.95° x 0.80°).

Subjects also made few *false positive selections*, mostly due to a more liberal interpretation of the specification (e.g., selecting dark blue cars for the specification »Black car«). The number of false positive selections varies individually between overall five up to twenty.

Completion time was 40(13) s for condition A (automated screening results available), and 46(15) s for condition B (without automated screening results).

Perceived workload shows a NASA-TLX score of 32 (21) for condition A, and of 41 (25) for condition B.

66% of the subjects preferred using automated screening results (condition A) when performing vehicle search; 33% were not convinced that their performance was better and would prefer to utilize automated results only as a confirmation tool after they performed vehicle search on their own.

Figure 11 shows the ratings of the user satisfaction with the gaze-based interaction on a 7-point scale (7: very good, 1: very bad). The grey bar shows the results for all subjects, the green bar for subjects without glasses, and the orange bar for subject wearing glasses. The results are good to very good and reflect particularly the high operation speed and the little manual stress. Rather mediocre are the ratings for accuracy and eye fatigue. Considering accuracy, the rating may reflect the inherent measurement uncertainty of the eye tracker; however, the availability of the zoom function ensured that not a single object was missed due to limited selection accuracy. Comparing the results for subjects with glasses and subjects without glasses shows differences for the required effort, general comfort and eye fatigue.

Fig. 7. Test task with instruction »Dark car« as presented in condition A (with automated screening results). The subject finds and frames all six target objects, including the car in the shadow at the image center. Target sizes are about 2.3 cm x 1.0 cm.

Fig. 8. Test task with instruction »Dark car« as presented in condition B (without automated screening results). The subject finds and frames five target objects, but misses the car in the shadow.

Fig. 9. Content as in Fig. 8 together with a heatmap representing the subject's gaze distribution. The subject does not fixate the center image region and, therefore, misses the car located in the shadow.

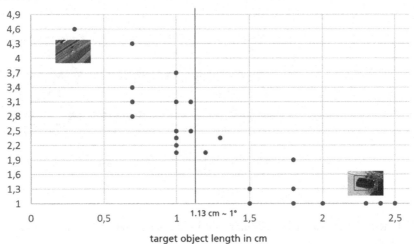

Fig. 10. Zoom factor as a function of target length.

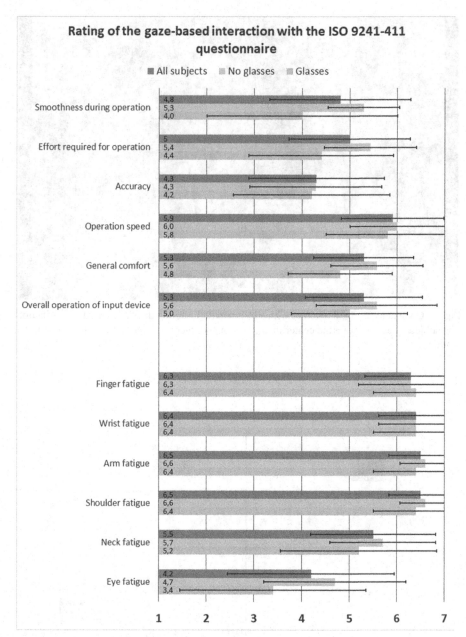

Fig. 11. Rating of user satisfaction for the gaze-based interaction on a 7-point scale (7: very good, 1: very bad).

4   Conclusion and Future Work

The results of our pilot study show that the availability of automated screening results improves user performance for aerial image analysis. Multimodal gaze-based interaction using gaze pointing together with keys from a keyboard for zooming and panning the image and for selecting target objects in the image appears as an appropriate, easy-to-use method. Interestingly, the subjects selected targets on average at a size of about 2°; targets that occurred smaller in the original image were zoomed until they reached this size on the monitor. Prior, 2° had been reported as an object size for robust gaze-based object selection [9, 10].

However, the results have to be considered preliminary due to the small number of subjects. Moreover, the results could be different for expert image analysts.

Future work will address a comparison between gaze input and mouse input considering in particular the results for both for manual stress and eye fatigue. Furthermore, we will consider situations where the automated screening results include some more false positive and false negative results and investigate how this would affect human performance.

References

1. Sommer, L., Schuchert, T., Beyerer, J.: Comprehensive analysis of deep learning-based vehicle detection in aerial images. IEEE Trans. Circuits Syst. Video Technol. **29**(9), 2733–2747 (2018)
2. Acatay, O., Sommer, L., Schumann, A., Beyerer, J.: Comprehensive evaluation of deep learning based detection methods for vehicle detection in aerial imagery. In: IEEE International Conference on Advanced Video and Signal Based Surveillance (AVSS), pp. 1–6. IEEE (2018)
3. Sommer, L., Schuchert, T., Beyerer, J.: Fast deep vehicle detection in aerial images. In: IEEE Winter Conference on Applications of Computer Vision (WACV), pp. 311–319. IEEE (2017)
4. Zhu, P., et al.: VisDrone-DET2018: The Vision Meets Drone Object Detection in Image Challenge Results. In: Leal-Taixé, L., Roth, S. (eds.) ECCV 2018. LNCS, vol. 11133, pp. 437–468. Springer, Cham (2019). https://doi.org/10.1007/978-3-030-11021-5_27
5. Zhang, Z., Lu, X., Cao, G., Yang, Y., Jiao, L., Liu, F.: ViT-YOLO: Transformer-based YOLO for object detection. In: Proceedings of the IEEE/CVF international conference on computer vision, pp. 2799–2808. IEEE (2021)
6. Wolf, S., Sommer, L., Schumann, L.: Fastaer det: fast aerial embedded real-time detection. Remote Sensing **13**(16), 3088 (2021)
7. Jacob, R.J.: What you look at is what you get: eye movement-based interaction techniques. In: Proceedings of the SIGCHI conference on Human factors in computing systems, pp. 11–18. ACM (1990)
8. Vertegaal, R.: A Fitts Law comparison of eye tracking and manual input in the selection of visual targets. In: Proceedings of the 10th international conference on Multimodal interfaces, pp. 241–248. ACM (2008)
9. Ware, C., Mikaelian, H. H.: An evaluation of an eye tracker as a device for computer input2. In: Proceedings of the SIGCHI/GI conference on Human factors in computing systems and graphics interface, pp. 183–188. ACM (1986)
10. Xuan Zhang, I., MacKenzie, S.: Evaluating Eye Tracking with ISO 9241 - Part 9. In: Jacko, J.A. (ed.) HCI 2007. LNCS, vol. 4552, pp. 779–788. Springer, Heidelberg (2007). https://doi.org/10.1007/978-3-540-73110-8_85

11. Kumar, M., Paepcke, A., Winograd, T.: Eyepoint: practical pointing and selection using gaze and keyboard. In: Proceedings of the SIGCHI conference on Human factors in computing systems, pp. 421–430. ACM (2007)

12. Hild, J., Saur, G., Petersen, P., Voit, M., Peinsipp-Byma, E., Beyerer, J.: Evaluating user interfaces supporting change detection in aerial images and aerial image sequences. In: Human Interface and the Management of Information. Information in Applications and Services: 20th International Conference, HIMI 2018, Held as Part of HCI International 2018, pp. 383–402. Springer International Publishing (2018)

13. Bednarik, R., Gowases, T., Tukiainen, M.: Gaze interaction enhances problem solving: effects of dwell-time based, gaze-augmented, and mouse interaction on problem-solving strategies and user experience. J. Eye Movement Res. **3**(1), 1–10 (2009)

14. Hild, J., Peinsipp-Byma, E., Voit, M., Beyerer, J.: Suggesting gaze-based selection for surveillance applications. In: 16th IEEE International Conference on Advanced Video and Signal Based Surveillance (AVSS), pp. 1–8. IEEE (2019)

15. ISO, I. S. O.: 9241–411 Ergonomics of human-system interaction–Part 411: Evaluation methods for the design of physical input devices. International Organization for Standardiza-tion (2012)

16. Liu, K., Mattyus, G.: Fast multiclass vehicle detection on aerial images. IEEE Geosci. Remote Sens. Lett. **12**(9), 1938–1942 (2015)

17. Liu, W., et al.: Ssd: Single shot multibox detector. In: Leibe, B., Matas, J., Sebe, N., Welling, M. (eds.) ECCV 2016. LNCS, vol. 9905, pp. 21–37. Springer, Cham (2016). https://doi.org/10.1007/978-3-319-46448-0_2

18. Tobii Homepage, https://help.tobii.com/hc/en-us/articles/213414285-Specifications-for-the-Tobii-Eye-Tracker-%204C, Accessed 8 Feb 2023

19. Hart, S.G.: NASA-task load index (NASA-TLX); 20 years later. In: Proceedings of the Human Factors and Ergonomics Society Annual Meeting, vol. 50, no. 9, pp. 904–908. Sage CA: Los Angeles, CA: Sage Publications (2006)

20. Hirzle, T., Cordts, M., Rukzio, E., Bulling, A.: A survey of digital eye strain in gaze-based interactive systems. In: ACM Symposium on Eye Tracking Research and Applications, pp. 1–12. ACM (2020)

The Impact Exercise Has on Cognitive Function

Kevin Lee, Fatih Baha Omeroglu, Chukebuka Nwosu, and Yueqing Li[✉]

Department of Industrial and Systems Engineering, Lamar University, Beaumont, TX 77705, USA

Abstract. Improvements of cognitive function and focus have been closely related to long term exercise. Consistent amounts of exercise help cognitive decline in aging adults. Exercise has been used in many ways to improve focus, mood, and energy levels. Different exercise types have been proven to bring cognitive benefits and neurological benefits for those of all ages. This research measures and analyzes the performance of a cognitive task and mental state between those who regularly exercise compared to those who do not.

Keywords: Cognitive function · Exercise · Cognitive Task · EEG · SART

1 Introduction

Exercise is proven to improve mood, energy, memory, and attention [17]. Single workouts will already cause brain changes such as increased levels of neurotransmitters, this leads to an increase in dopamine, serotonin, and noradrenaline [17]. Previous lab results show that after one session exercise can improve your ability to shift and focus attention, whilst improving focus for up to 2 h after the workout, and reaction times. Exercising regularly will impact your hippocampus, which is known to be correlated to your long-term memory. Exercise will actually increase cell production within the hippocampus. Working out 3–4 times a week for at least 30 min from this literature review has been proven to be the optimal amount of exercise to have long lasting cognitive and neurological changes. In this study the authors will be testing cognitive function of participants by utilizing a SART (Sustained Attention to Response Task) test to measure cognitive performance. Authors will also research the immediate short-term effects of aerobic exercise as in previous studies it has shown exercising as little as 10 min will cause neurological changes in the brain [17].

2 Literature Review

According to many studies done by various universities, exercise improves thinking and memory through both direct and indirect means. The benefits of exercise come directly from its ability to reduce insulin resistance, reduce inflammation, and stimulate the release of growth factors—chemicals in the brain that affect the health of brain cells, the growth of new blood vessels in the brain, and even the abundance and survival of

D. Harris and W.-C. Li (Eds.): HCII 2023, LNAI 14017, pp. 215–226, 2023.
https://doi.org/10.1007/978-3-031-35392-5_17

new brain cells. Indirectly, exercise improves mood and sleep, and reduces stress and anxiety. Problems in these areas frequently cause or contribute to cognitive impairment [8]. There have been many studies that show that the prefrontal cortex and the medial temporal cortex [16], which are parts of the brain that control thinking and memory, tend to have greater volume in people who exercise versus people who do not [8]. Our goal is to be able to add more data to further back up this research. EEG will be used to track beta waves, by using this equipment data will be retrieved from each participant and thus be able to find a relationship between exercise and cognitive function. In another journal article by the US National Library of medicine, it was stated that physical exercise is a gene modulator that could prompt structural and functional changes in the brain [20]. According to the article physical exercise also affects neuroplasticity. Neuroplasticity is a feature of the nervous system that can modify itself in response to experience [12]. Exercise has the ability to help the brain adapt quicker to stimuli that the body has experienced before.

Exercise also has some indirect benefits on cognitive function by improving sleep and reducing stress which also impacts cognitive function positively. When stress and anxiety is reduced, cognitive function, memory, and concentration increases [20]. The anaerobic threshold was experimented in another journal and they concluded that by reaching the anaerobic threshold or the lactate threshold this is where cognitive function will be impacted by exercise within the central nervous system. Within the journal they mentioned that the VO2 max for endurance athletes to reach lactate threshold is around 65–75%VO2 max [9]. This is another reason as to why 70% VO2 max was picked for our VO2 threshold for active participants as in this journal neurological changes began occurring at 65–75% of VO2 max for endurance athletes.

In fact, experimental and clinical studies have reported that physical exercise induces structural and functional changes in the brain, determining enormous biological, and psychological benefits [20]. This journal helps determine the fact that physical exercise has both physical and psychological changes to the human, it alters cognition and functional changes to the brain [12]. Cognitive function is our main area of focus in this experiment as it has been proven by previous studies that exercise does alter cognition, our experiment will determine how those who regularly partake in physical exercise performs in relation to those who do not within the SART test, which is a test of cognition and ability to follow a task.

Another literature explains how EEG was used effectively to be able to measure and gather data on the persons Alpha, Beta and Theta waves. This study uses the EEG to gather data on brain waves as participants are exposed to different scenarios with different levels of attention to a learning task. They mentioned that Beta waves are closely related to active thinking and engagement in work [2]. This was one of our chosen factors to measure within our experiment, using the EEG will determine the participants level of focus, in relation to their SART scores. This allows a more in-depth analysis on the participants state of focus, whilst also being able to see their performance levels from SART scores.

Another experiment used augmented reality on operators in process lines to determine their cognitive load. They used both EEG and a NASA task load index to help determine the cognitive load of each of the operators [1]. Using both the EEG and creating our own NASA load task questionnaire to help determine cognitive load for our participants as well. Our simulation task is different however whilst using both these techniques, cognitive load will be able to be measured.

10 min of aerobic exercise will be the aerobic exercise needed to be performed by the participants, in this experiment as from previous articles, it has been shown that your brain changes neurologically instantly from aerobic exercise. 10 min of aerobic exercise is suitable as it provides little to no risk to the participant and enough exercise to allow for a neurological change as mentioned, dopamine, serotonin, and non-adrenaline will flood the brain, and enough to produce a change in performance if there is potentially one [17].

A further study performed by Kassim [10] showed the use of EEG to measure the state and brainwave pattern of active and inactive individuals. Their hypothesis was to see if there was a statistical difference in those who partake in physical activity in comparison to those who do not and their mental well-being from measuring Alpha, Beta, Theta and delta waves from the EEG [10]. From the same journal there was a difference between the active and an inactive person on their ability to focus and concentrate on a task. This is another reason as to why active and inactive people were chosen for the SART test to measure test performance along with brain wave data from EEG. The SART task has been proven to be used in prior experiments to investigate cognitive function. In this journal they established cognitive function as attention, memory, executive function and time to process [1]. The SART task was used to measure cognitive function as it was a task that integrated attention, memory, executive function as well as time to process. This is another reason as to why the authors of this report have chosen the SART task to measure cognitive function.

The experiment that will be conducted by both authors will differ from any past literature or studies. This experiment will investigate the cognitive function of inactive and active lifestyles, EEG equipment will be used as it has been proved to be able to measure an individual's state of mind [2]. Furthermore, this experiment will investigate the instant impact on active participants when exercising, on their cognitive function and ability to follow a task. Although there have been previous studies based on inactive and active participants on focus and concentration [10] this experiment will also focus on whether cognitive function improves after exercise or before, for active participants. The experiment will have 3 dependent variables of EEG data which have been proven to show an individual's current state [10] the experiment will use SART task which is our chosen cognitive task to measure performance, and NASA load task form to measure cognitive load [1]. NASA TLX stands for NASA Task Load Index; it is a measurement of subjective mental workload to assess performance [4].

3 Methodology

3.1 Participants

15 participants were chosen for both the Inactive group (6 females, 9 males), and the Inactive group (5 females, 10 males). Mean ages of the Inactive group were 23.3 (SD = 2.52), whilst the mean ages of the Active group were 21.3 (SD = 0.883). Active group

are separated by those who work out minimum 3 times a week of at least 30 min leading up to the experiment. Inactive participants were those who worked out once or less times in any given week.

3.2 Apparatus

Fitness watches were used to accurately measure when they reach 70% of their VO2 and time them to maintain that level for at least 10 min. For the aerobic exercise a treadmill was used for those partaking in the physical portion of the experiment. There is little risk as participants prepared proper clothing and are physically fit to execute 10 min of aerobic exercise. This is normally an up-tempo walk where the 10 min began once they hit the 70% VO2 threshold. Using Fitbit watches or apple watches to measure heartbeats per minute and accurately know when they have hit the threshold before starting the time. They are also given water and plenty of time to cool down prior to starting the second run of SART experiments. For the EEg equipment the authors used a G.Tec g.USBamp amplifier with BCI2000 software to aid in extracting the EEG signals. To ensure high quality EEG signals the authors used g.Gammacap along with a g.Ladybird wet gel. Then MATLAB was used and the feature EEGlab to help analyze the EEG data. The locations that the electrodes would be placed in was taken from the 10–20 posi-tioning system. Furthermore, there were 11 channels used to obtain and measure EEG signals: F5, F6, Fz, C3, C4, Cz, P5, P6, Pz, O1, O2. By using Ag-AgCl elec-trodes alongside G.Tec G.GAMMAbox amplifier EEG signals can be measured. The EEG signals were sampled at 256 Hz. The EEG signal data was then processed in an EEGlab MATLAB plugin where Independent Component Analysis was utilized. To obtain spectral power density for Alpha, Beta and Theta bands a Fast Fourier Trasnform was used.

3.3 Independent Variable

The frequency of exercise performed in any given week, Active participants had to work out 3 or more times in any given week, Inactive participants had to work out less than once a week in any given week.

3.4 Dependent Variable

Three dependent variables mentioned in this paper: SART scores, EEG data, and NASA-TLX workload.

3.5 Task

Participants will get one trial run on the SART test before beginning the experiment. Inactive group will have 3 attempts, whilst wearing the EEG equipment. Active group will do the same however will be given a 10-min aerobic exercise to perform where they will be at 70% VO2 max or higher for the duration before allowing their heart rate to return to a resting level, before they take another 3 SART test attempts. Participants will be asked to fill out a NASA TLX workload form before and after each run of the SART test.

3.6 Procedure

The experiment will have 15 people for the active group and 15 people for the inactive group. Participants will then come into our experiment location as a suitable time. They will then be asked to fill out questionnaires and NASA TLX workload forms to gain prior information and lifestyle to categorize them into our 2 chosen groups of active and inactive. The EEG equipment will then be equipped onto the participant. To ensure the equipment is working a quick prior calibration of the EEG will be performed before starting the test. Once the equipment is functioning correctly participants will take the SART Test. After initial testing, the authors of this report will then prepare participants for the physical portion of the experiment for the active group. Exercise will be 10 min of moderate to vigorous exercise on a bike/ treadmill of aerobic exercise. After the exercise and until their heart rate has returned to resting heart rate, they will be given the second portion of SART testing again. Participants are in a state of comfort before restarting the exam, the neurological changes will still be in effect even when they return to resting heart rate. (Please see Fig. 1).

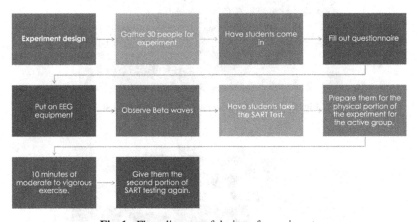

Fig. 1. Flow diagram of design of experiments

The SART test is known for sustained attention to response task [13]. It is a task where there are go numbers and no-go numbers and participants of the experiment have to react to the designated one accordingly. There is also a time window as to when participants will be able to react to the number shown. Participants will get a trial run prior to understanding the task before running the tests. A laptop will be used to set up the various SART tests, and a designated button for the response to the given task of go number and no-go numbers. There is no risk as it involves little to no movement when the EEG is being set up, participants are also required to stay still to get the cleanest signal possible for our data.

Prior studies have shown that with 10 min of aerobic exercise the brain shows signs of neurological changes within the brain and repeated exercise of a minimum of at least 3 times a week of at least 30-min training sessions helps impact the brain's cognitive function, which includes attention and focus [17]. This is why our two main groups will be separated, our active groups for those who exercise a minimum of 3 times a week for at least 30 min for each training session, and the inactive groups for those who do not exercise more than once a week. Another study by Kashihara, Koji [9], shows that as humans approach the anaerobic threshold the human brain will experience neurological changes that impact cognitive function. This was determined at around 60–70% of their VO2 max for athletes that train regularly. This is another reason why 70% VO2 max was chosen for our active participants (See Figs. 2, 3, 4, 5, 6, 7, 9, 10).

Fig. 2. Active participant set up for SART test

Fig. 3. Active participant EEG equipment placement

Fig. 4. Placement of treadmill for Active participants

Fig. 5. Inactive participant experiment setup with only SART test

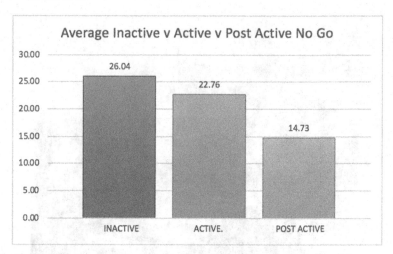

Fig. 6. Graphically comparing Average percentages of attempts participants did not get correct in SART test for Active, Inactive, and Post Active groups.

4   Results and Data

4.1   SART Score Data

The results showed there was no significant difference between Inactive v Active groups ($p = 0.32206$, $t = 1.001$). The mean No Go SART scores showed that the mean SART No Go scores for Inactive participants was higher ($M = 26.044$ $SD = 19.865$) than Active Participants ($M = 22.756$, $SD = 21.214$). The statistical analysis between Active v Post Active group showed significant difference ($p = 0.0163$, $t = 2.497$). The mean No Go SART Scores showed that Active Participants had a significantly higher mean ($M = 22.756$, $SD = 21.214$) when compared to Post Active participants ($M = 15.378$, $SD = 19.277$).

4.2   EEG Data

Statistical analysis on Theta relative power spectrum showed that there was no significant difference between Inactive and Active groups ($p = 0.5584$, $t = 0.6034$). The mean averages also showed the Inactive group had higher theta mean ($M = 0.3867$, $SD = 0.0912$) when compared to Active group ($M = 0.3576$, $SD = 0.1146$). Active and Post active showed no significant difference ($p = 0.2758$, $t = -1.1467$). However, Post Active group had a higher mean ($M = 0.4154$, $SD = 0.1647$) when comparing to Active group ($M = 0.3576$, $SD = 0.1446$).

Statistical analysis on Alpha relative power spectrum showed that there was no significant difference between Inactive and Active groups ($p = 0.3291$, $t = -1.0211$). Inactive group had a lower mean Alpha ($M = 0.2935$, $SD = 0.0669$), compared to Active participants ($M = 0.3258$, $SD = 0.0929$). Active and Post Active analysis showed that the results showed no significant difference ($p = 0.9815$, $t = 0.0237$). With very similar

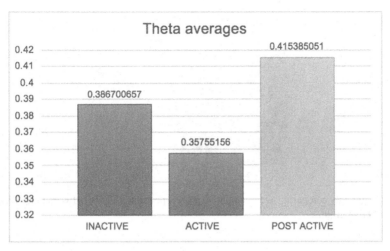

Fig. 7. Graphically comparing average relative power spectrum for Theta between Inactive, Active and Post Active groups

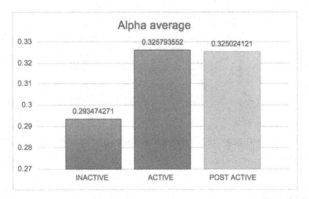

Fig. 8. Graphically comparing average relative power spectrum for Alpha between Inactive, Active and Post Active groups.

mean averages between Active (M = 0.3258, SD = 0.0929) and Post Active (M = 0.325, SD = 0.0874).

Statistical analysis on the Beta relative power spectrum showed there was no significant difference between Inactive and Active groups (p = 0.9273, t = 0.0934). Inactive group had a slightly higher Alpha mean (M = 0.3198, SD = 0.0417) when compared to the active group (M = 0.3167, SD = 0.0938). There was no significant difference between Active and Post active Alpha data (p = 0.1325, t = 1.6247). Post Active group had a lower Beta mean (M = 0.2622, SD = 0.1096) compared to Active group (M = 0.3167, SD = 0.0938).

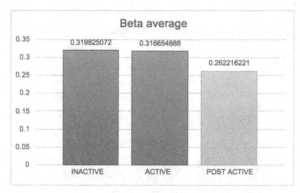

Fig. 9. Graphically comparing average relative power spectrum for Beta between Inactive, Active and Post Active groups.

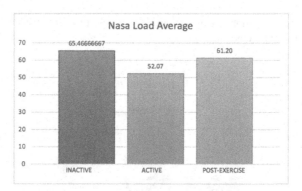

Fig. 10. Graphically comparing average NASA load Index averages between Inactive, Active and Post Active groups.

4.3 NASA Load Index

There was no significant difference between Inactive and Active groups ($p = 0.1032$, $t = 1.7434$). The mean for the Inactive group was higher ($M = 64.467$, $SD = 17.594$) when comparing with Active group ($M = 52.0667$, $SD = 22.817$). When comparing Active and Post Active NASA data it is statistically significant ($p = 0.0162$, $t = -2.732$). The mean for Active group was lower ($M = 52.0667$, $SD = 22.817$) when compared to Post Active group ($M = 61.2$, $SD = 17.64$).

5 Discussion

Theta averages between Inactive and Active groups showed that Active groups had lower theta averages than Inactive group, previous studies showed that theta power is closely correlated with better cognitive functioning [7] which also is supported by SART scores where active participants performed better than inactive participants significantly. Previous studies also showed a relationship between theta power and mental workload, where the higher theta power indicated more workload [18]. As in the results, Active participants showed significantly less fatigue on the NASA TLX workload compared to inactive participants where active participants also had a lower theta power compared to inactive participants. This supports previous studies and claims where they concluded that higher fit males are correlated to better neurocognition functions when compared to low fit males, regardless of age [11]. Even though the EEG results did not show a significant difference in this experiment there is a clear trend between Inactive and Active groups. Active groups SART scores were higher overall. Active participants on average showed less fatigue while also performing better.

Additionally, the Post Active group had a higher mental workload than the Active group, while scoring averagely better in the SART. This relationship could be due to Post Active participants completing a run of SART testing before they perform their last SART test after the aerobic exercise portion, as their physical demand and effort increased. It was noted that participants felt they were getting accustomed to the SART test, however due to how the SART test is set up with minimal time to process before participants must react to the numbers shown on screen, there is no opportunity to predict the numbers preemptively [13].

6   Conclusion

This study evaluated participants' cognitive function using both subjective and quantifiable measures. Previous work has stated there is an impact that exercise has on an individual's physiological state, as well as neural and long-term benefits. This study encompasses this as well as a lesser studied area of the short-term immediate impacts exercise has on cognitive function for those who work out regularly. In conclusion, Active participants on average had performed better on the SART test, and being under less mental workload. This experiment had a small sample size of 30 with active and inactive groups having 15 participants each. To study further, the sample size will need to be increased in the future draw more conclusions. For future recommendations there could be more use of physiological measurements such as EMG to determine physiological markers that give us more insight to an individuals' mental state.

References

1. Atici-Ulusu, H., Ikiz, Y.D., Taskapilioglu, O., Gunduz, T.: Effects of augmented reality glasses on the cognitive load of assembly operators in the automotive industry. Int. J. Comput. Integr. Manufact., J. **34**(5), 487–499 (2021)
2. Chiang, H.-S., Hsiao, K.-L., Liu, L.-C.: EEG-based detection model for evaluating and improving learning attention. J. Med. Biol. Eng. **38**(6), 847–856 (2017). https://doi.org/10.1007/s40846-017-0344-z
3. College of life sciences, https://lifesciences.byu.edu/how-exercise-affects-your-brain, Accessed 3 Dec 2021
4. Colligan, L., Potts, H.W., Finn, C.T., Sinkin, R.A.: Cognitive workload changes for nurses transitioning from a legacy system with paper documentation to a commercial electronic health record. Int. J. Med. Inform., J. **84**(7), 469–476 (2015)

5. Dana Foundation, https://www.dana.org/article/how-does-exercise-affect-the-brain/, Accessed 5 Dec 2021
6. Dustman, R.E., Boswell, R.S., Porter, P.B.: Beta Brain waves as an index of alertness. Sci., J. **137**(3529), 533–534 (1962)
7. Finnigan, S., Robertson, I.H.: Resting EEG theta power correlates with cognitive performance in healthy older adults. Psychophysiol., J. **48**(8), 1083–1087 (2011)
8. Harvard health, https://www.health.harvard.edu/blog/regular-exercise-changes-brain-improve-memory-thinking-skills-201404097110, Accessed 2 Dec 2021
9. Kashihara, K., Maruyama, T., Murota, M., Nakahara, Y.: Positive effects of acute and moderate physical exercise on cognitive function. J. Physiol. Anthropol., J. **28**(4), 155–164 (2019)
10. Kassim, R.A., Ibrahim, A.S., Buniyamin, N., Murat, Z.H.: Analysis of human's brainwave pattern among active and inactive person. In: 2012 International Conference on System Engineering and Technology (ICSET) (2012)
11. Lardon, M.T., Polich, J.: EEG changes from long-term physical exercise. Biol. Psychol. J. **44**(1), 19–30 (1996)
12. Mandolesi, L., et al.: Effects of Physical Exercise on Cognitive Functioning and Wellbeing: Biological and Psychological Benefits. Front. Psychol., J. **9**, (2018)
13. Manly, T.: The absent mind: further investigations of sustained attention to response. Neuropsychol., J. **37**(6), 661–670 (1999)
14. NCBI, https://www.ncbi.nlm.nih.gov/pmc/articles/PMC5934999/, Accessed 6 Dec 2021
15. Robertson, D.A., Savva, G.M., Coen, R.F., Kenny, R.A.: Cognitive function in the prefrailty and frailty syndrome. J. Am. Geriatr. Soc. **62**(11), 2118–2124 (2014)
16. Simons, J.S., Spiers, H.J.: Prefrontal and medial temporal lobe interactions in long-term memory. Nature Rev. Neurosci., J. **4**(8), 637–648 (2003)
17. TED Talks, https://www.ted.com/talks/wendy_suzuki_the_brain_changing_benefits_of_exercise/transcript?language=en, Accessed 5 Dec 2021
18. Tran, Y., Craig, A., Craig, R., Chai, R., Nguyen, H.: The influence of mental fatigue on brain activity: Evidence from a systematic review with meta-analyses. Psychophysiol., J. **57**(5), (2020)
19. Urology of Virginia, https://www.urologyofva.net/articles/category/healthy-living/3330548/08/01/2019/how-exercise-improves-cognitive-function-and-overall-brain-health, Accessed 3 Dec 2021
20. Weinberg, Robert S., Gould, D.: Foundations of sport and exercise psychology, 7E. Human kinetics (2019)

Study on Temperament Characteristics of Air Traffic Controllers Based on BP Neural Network

Tingting Lu[1], Xinyue Liu[1(✉)], Ning Li[2], Wen-Chin Li[3], and Zhaoning Zhang[1]

[1] Air Traffic Management Academy, Civil Aviation University of China, Tianjin 300300, China
1172362329@qq.com
[2] Air Traffic Control Industry Management Office, Civil Aviation Administration of China,
Beijing 100010, China
[3] Safety and Accident Investigation Centre, Cranfield University, Bedfordshire, Cranfield, UK

Abstract. The working characteristics of air traffic controllers are closely related to their temperament type. The selection of controllers, controller posts, and the composition of controller teams should all consider the adapta-bility of temperament. Therefore, it is crucial to study the distribution of temperament types among air traffic controllers to ensure the safety of control system operations and to prevent civil aviation accidents. In this study, we used the Eysenck Personality Questionnaire (EPQ) to conduct a questionnaire survey of air traffic controllers and compared the results to a national norm control group. Our analysis demonstrated that the tem-perament type of air traffic controllers differs significantly from that of ordinary people. We concluded that the most suitable temperament types for control work are polysanguine, mucinous, choleric, and depres-sive, in that order. Finally, we developed a fitting model based on a BP neural network to assess the suitability of individual controllers for spe-cific control positions. We used the questionnaire data to establish a da-ta set and selected the minimum root mean square error as the loss function for back propagation training. The simulation analysis con-firmed the effectiveness of the fitting model.

Keywords: Air Traffic Control · Controller · Temperament Type · Personality · BP Neural Network

1 Introduction

As the executor of air traffic control, air traffic controllers are responsible for ensuring the safe and efficient operation of air traffic flow system. Statistical analyses of unsafe incidents in air traffic control indicate that many unsafe incidents are caused by the unsafe behavior of controllers, which is closely related to their temperament. Temperament, as one of the psychological characteristics of human personality, shows a person's unique psychological style and tendency. Therefore, an objective evaluation of temperament and emotional state of controllers, as well as the screening of temperament characteristics that are suitable for the control environment, are essential for preventing unsafe behavior among controllers.

D. Harris and W.-C. Li (Eds.): HCII 2023, LNAI 14017, pp. 227–237, 2023.
https://doi.org/10.1007/978-3-031-35392-5_18

In psychology, Temperament refers to the typical and stable psychological characteristics of individuals, including the speed of psychological activities (such as language, perception and thinking speed), intensity (such as the strength of emotional experience and willpower), stability (such as the length of attention span) and tendency (such as introversion and extroversion) [1]. Different combinations of these characteristics constitute an individual's temperament type, which is one of the key characteristics of human character. Scholars both at home and abroad have conducted relevant studies on temperament types. For instance, in 1990, Reason posited that human error refers to the failure of people to achieve expected goals or results in a series of planned psychological or physical activities, and such failure cannot be arrtibuted to external factors [2]. In 2000, Grindle et al. analyzed the psychological factors of pilot competency through the psychological tests of pilot selection, and realized the degree of matching between personnel and posts [3]. In 2003, Pal Ulleberg studied the differences in personality, motivation and risk prediction ability of drivers through questionnaires and determined the influence of psychological factors on driving, providing theoretical basis for the selection of drivers [4]. In 2004, Rosenbloom T believed that employees' subjective initiative lies in conscious choice, which has a great impact on behavior choice. Unsafe behavior may be caused by insecure consciousness and negative emotions [5]. In 2006, Daryl Attwood et al. established a model of occupational insecurity event from the perspective of human on the basis of statistical analysis of a large number of insecurity events and conducted evaluation and prediction [6]. In 2011, Remawi H et al. studied and analyzed aviation accidents and unsafe incidents, and found that unsafe behaviors are affected by people's unsafe mentality and unstable emotions [7].

In China, in 2009, Zhang Ying used Eysenck personality questionnaire [8] to investigate and analyze the depressive state of flight cadets and obtained statistically significant results [9]. In 2012, Shi Changyun adopted the method of empirical research and made use of data analysis to explore the inducements of controller burnout, and put forward pre-control countermeasures to prevent and alleviate controller burnout, so as to prevent and control the occurrence of human errors of controllers and effectively improve the level of air traffic safety management [10]. In 2019, Huang Yu proposed optimization suggestions for the selection system of controllers by constructing some commonly used methods in the competency model, based on the work requirements of the International Civil Aviation Organization and Civil Aviation of China for controllers and the characteristics of the competency model, and combined with the actual work characteristics of controllers in Guizhou [11]. It can be seen from the above studies that the current research mainly focuses on temperament types of flight cadets and students majoring in control, the competency and job burnout of controllers, and so on. There are few studies on temperament characteristics of controllers and their relationship with work.

2   Method

2.1   Participants

Some frontline controllers and human factors experts from the Air Traffic Administration in North China, East China and Northeast China participated in the study. Participants ranged in age from 23 to 38 and had between 1 and 16 years of work experience. A total of 360 questionnaires were issued and 356 valid questionnaires were collected. As stated in the consent form, participants are anonymous and have the right to withdraw the data they provide at any time after the data collection is complete.

2.2 Research Framework

The method of EPQ personality survey was adopted to assess the temperament of controllers in the control work by issuing EPQ questionnaires. On this basis, the distribution of temperament characteristics of controllers was obtained by comparing with the results of national norms. Furthermore, a fitting model of EPQ personality questionnaire results and controller adaptability was established based on BP neural netDwork. Finally, simulation analysis was carried out to verify the effectiveness of the model.

2.3 Questionnaire Structure and Processing Method

The ancient Greek physician Hippocrates believed that there are four different liquids in the human body, which come from different organs. The different constitutions of people are due to the different proportions of the four body fluids. Green, a famous Roman biologist and psychologist, started from Hippocrates' humoral theory and founded the temperament theory. He believed that temperament depends on the combination of different properties of substances (or SAP), that is, the mixture ratio of blood, mucus, yellow bile and black bile. On this basis, the theory of temperament continued to develop into the classic four temperaments: polysanguine, choleric, mucinous and melancholic [1]. Pavlov believed that the nervous system has three basic properties, namely the intensity, balance, and flexibility of the excitatory and inhibitory processes. The different combinations of these characteristics constitute the four types of higher neural activity, that is, the strong and unbalanced type is choleric, the strong, balanced and flexible type is polysanguine, the strong, balanced and inflexible type is mucous, and the weak type is depressive [12].

Common temperament assessment methods include psychological observation method, psychological test method, psychological experiment method and questionnaire test. Considering the number of samples, time efficiency, simplicity and other factors, this study used Eysenck Personality Questionnaire to assess controllers to analyze their temperament types, and compared the test results with those of ordinary people.

Aiming at the applicability of the Eysenck Personality Questionnaire, Gong Yaoxian revised it. The revised Eysenck Personality (Adult) Questionnaire (EPQ) included 88 items [7], which was composed of four subscales: extroversion (E), neuroticism (N), psychoticism (P) and concealment (L), among which the L scale was mainly used to analyze whether the subject was concealment. After screening, E, N, P three components to form a three-dimensional coordinate system, three dimensions of different degrees of performance can be composed of four temperament types, namely polyhaematous, mucinous, choleric, depressive.

The specific operation steps of using EPQ to determine the temperament type of controllers are: (1) Use EPQ to measure the controller; (2) The scores of the four scales (the original score and the standard score transformed from the original score -- T score) were counted; (3) Determine the temperament type of the subjects according to the temperament type assessment table.

According to the total score (rough score) obtained by the subjects on each scale, the standard T score (T = 50 + 10*(X-M)/SD) can be converted from the norm to analyze the personality characteristics of the subjects. A T score of 43.3 ~ 56.7 in each scale is the intermediate type, a T score of 38.5 ~ 43.3 or a T score of 56.7 ~ 61.5 is the inclined type, and a T score of 38.5 or above 61.5 is typical [9].

N < M-0.67SD and E > M + 0.67SD are polysanguine;
N < M-0.67SD and E < M + 0.67SD were mucous substance.
N > M-0.67SD and E < M + 0.67SD were depressive substances.
N > M-0.67SD and E > M + 0.67SD were bilious.

2.4 BP Neural Network Procedure

Neural network is a mathematical method with strong nonlinear fitting ability, which can solve some problems that cannot be solved by traditional reasoning model. By extracting, learning and training the hidden pattern in the training data, adjusting the weight of each node, the output value of the neural network approaches to the expected output. Among them, BP neural network has the advantages of simple structure, strong anti-noise and generalization ability, and is used to fit various complex maps. Its main body usually includes input layer, hidden layer and output layer, and the data transmission between the two adjacent layers is carried out in the form of weight transfer. The input data of each neuron is processed by activation function, so each neuron needs to have an appropriate activation function [13]. The structural model of neurons is shown in Fig. 1.

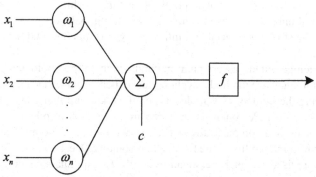

Input   Weight   Threshold   Activation-function   Output

Fig. 1. Neuronal structure diagram

Its mathematical model is:

$$y = f(\sum_{i=1}^{n} x_i \omega_i + c) \tag{1}$$

where, is the ith input of the neuron, is the corresponding weight, b is the threshold, represents the activation function, and y is the output of the neuron. In this paper, Sigmoid function is used as the activation function. Sigmoid function has the advantages of smoothness and easy derivation and has been widely used. The expression is

$$f(x) = \frac{1}{1+e^{-x}} \tag{2}$$

It can be seen from the formula that Sigmoid function can map a function to the interval (0,1) and has good symmetry. Therefore, Sigmoid is used as the activation function in this paper. The output value of each node of the hidden layer and the output layer is calculated in accordance with Eq. (2), that is, the process of forward propagation is completed.

The specific process of back propagation training is as follows [14]: this paper selects the minimum mean square error as the Loss Function, that is, the mean value of the error square between the estimated value and the actual value, expressed as follows:

$$E(y, \hat{y}) = \frac{\sum_{i=1}^{n} (y - \hat{y})^2}{n} \tag{3}$$

where n is the number of samples, y is the output value, and $\hat{y}$ is expected output value can be obtained from the formula. After the error is obtained by subtracting the output value from the expected output value, it is propagated in the network. Taking solving as an example, let the error be, given the learning rate, there is

$$\Delta \omega_{hj} = -\eta \frac{\partial E_k}{\partial \omega_{hj}} \tag{4}$$

where w_{hj} is the weight of the h th neuron and the j th neuron. According to the chain rule, there is

$$\frac{\partial E_k}{\partial \omega_{hj}} = \frac{\partial E_k}{\partial \hat{y}_j^k} \cdot \frac{\partial \hat{y}_j^k}{\partial \beta_j} \cdot \frac{\partial \beta_j}{\partial \omega_{hj}} \tag{5}$$

where β_j is $\sum_{i=1}^{q} x_h \omega_{hj}$, q is the number of hidden layer neurons. According to the definition, obviously there is

$$\frac{\partial \beta_j}{\partial \omega_{hj}} = c_h \tag{6}$$

According to the above formula, there is

$$g_j = f - \frac{\partial E_k}{\partial \hat{y}_j^k} \cdot \frac{\partial \hat{y}_j^k}{\partial \beta_j} = -(\hat{y}_j^k - y_j^k) f'(\beta_j - \theta_j) \tag{7}$$

where θ_j, j is the threshold value of the JTH neuron in the output layer, and w_{hj} is the updated formula of BP algorithm is obtained:

$$\Delta\omega_{hj} = \eta g_j c_h \tag{8}$$

The training process of BP neural network is to optimize the network parameters through the above back propagation, using gradient descent and other algorithms to minimize the sum of squared errors of the above network, and end the training when the root mean square errors of the reference output and actual output of the verification set data meet the requirements.

The implementation flow chart of BP neural network is shown in the Fig. 2.

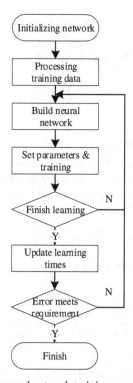

Fig. 2. BP neural network training process diagram

3   Results and Discussion

3.1   Analysis of Test Results for Controllers

Item Analysis and Reliability and Validity Test of the Scale.   To test the validity of the results, a reliability and validity test was conducted first. Most correlation coefficients between each item were between 0.38 and 0.65 (p ≤ 0.01), indicating adequate differentiation. Homogeneity reliability of each subscale ranged from 0.74 to 0.80, splithalf reliability ranged from 0.79 to 0.85, and retest reliability ranged from 0.75 to 0.89. Significant correlation between subscales was observed (p ≤ 0.01), with a correlation coefficient of 0.76 ~ 0.83, indicating good scale validity. The results of this assessment are therefore reliable and can effectively reflect the temperament type of controllers.

Establishment of Controller EPQ Norm and Result Analysis. The three dimensional comparison between the controller assessment results and the enpl component of the national norm [16] is shown in Table 1.

Table 1. Comparison of Scale scores of Controller EPQ with National Norms ($\bar{x} \pm s$)

Group	Number of people	E	N	P	L
Air traffic controllers	356	15.55 ± 3.23	5.96 ± 3 .07	4.78 ± 2 .57	12.50 ± 3.24
National norm	458	9.50 ± 3.2	10.96 ± 4 .3	7.56 ± 3.1	11.52 ± 3.5

According to the statistical results in Table 1, E and N scores of the controller group were statistically different from those of the national norm group (t = 3.97 ~ 8.89, P = 0.002 ~ 0.007), and P scores were significantly lower than those of the national norm (t = 3.77 ~ 8.31, P = 0.001 ~ 0.004). There was no significant difference between L score and national norm (t = 1.28 ~ 1.70, P = 0.111 ~ 0.214). This indicates that only three components of ENP can effectively represent temperament type Fig. 3.

The temperament types of controllers were determined based on the scores of their E/N scale, and the proportions of the four temperament types were: 37.36% for polyhemia, 29.93% for bile, 29.35% for mucinous, and 4.36% for depressive, as illustrated in Fig. 4. The results indicate that the most prevalent temperament type among controllers is sanguine, followed by mucinous and bile. Conversely, the proportion of controllers exhibiting a depressive temperament type is the lowest.

3.2 Analysis of BP Neural Network Simulation Results

According to the analysis of the survey results in the last chapter, the four subscales of EPQ scale, including extroversion (E), neuroticism (N) and psychoticism (P), can effectively reflect the personality characteristics and temperament types of controllers. Therefore, the three dimensional vector composed of E, N and P is selected as the input data of BP neural network. At the same time, the evaluation index value of the measured controller in the air traffic Control Bureau is normalized and used as the reference output data of BP neural network.

Several experiments were conducted to optimize the neural network architecture. The results indicate that increasing the number of hidden layers and nodes does not lead to a reduction in error. Based on these findings, a three layer BP neural network with

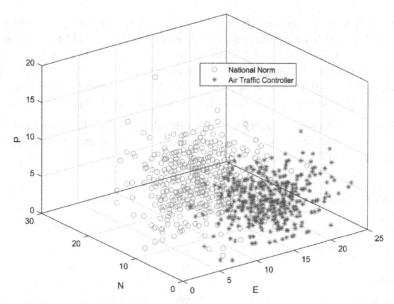

Fig. 3. E, N, P of controllers versus national norms

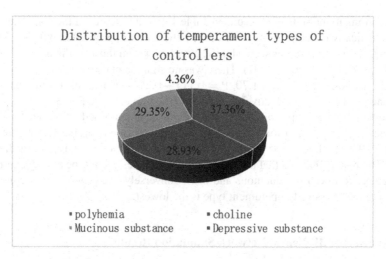

Fig. 4. Distribution of temperament types of controllers

5 nodes in the hidden layer, as shown in Fig. 5, was used. The experimental data was trained using a sample distribution of 70% for the training set, 15% for the verification set, and 15% for the test set.

The experimental simulations were conducted using the MATLAB simulation software. The input vector of the BP neural network comprised the E, N, and P components, as determined from the evaluation of 356 EPQ questionnaires of controllers. The expected output was the evaluation index value of the controller after normalization. To implement

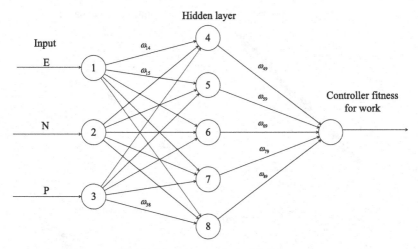

Fig. 5. Neural network model diagram

the neural network, a three layer BP model was employed with a hidden layer consisting of five nodes.

4 Conclusion

The training results of training set, test set and verification set in BP neural network are shown in Fig. 6 and the root mean square error is shown in Fig. 7.

The experimental findings indicate that the BP neural network accurately represents the functional relationship between the E, N, and P components of the controller EPQ scale measurement outcomes and the controller evaluation index. The training, verification, and test sets show a strong correlation with target values: Output = 1Target + 0.0032 (R = 0.997), Output = 0.99Target + 0.0061(R = 0.99674), and Output = 0.99*Target + 0.0041 (R = 0.99718), respectively. The overall correlation for the complete dataset is R = 0.9969, with a final root mean square error of 0.00043133. These results suggest that the BP neural network can quantitatively evaluate the controller's adaptability to the control work based on the controller's EPQ questionnaire test results.

This paper utilized the EPQ questionnaire to investigate controllers and establish EPQ temperament norms for controllers, which were then compared to national norms. The analysis revealed statistically significant differences in the E, N, and P scores of controllers, reflecting their extroversion, emotional stability, and enthusiasm. The study identified sanguine, mucinous, bilious, and melancholic temperament types, ranked in order of suitability for controllers. The study further utilized the BP neural network to fit the questionnaire results and evaluation index data, establishing a functional relationship between the three personality traits and the controller temperament type index. This relationship can be used to evaluate the suitability of EPQ questionnaire testers for control work.

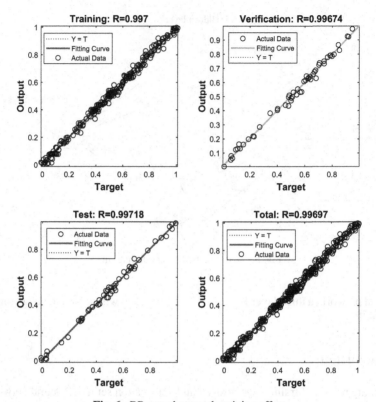

Fig. 6. BP neural network training effect

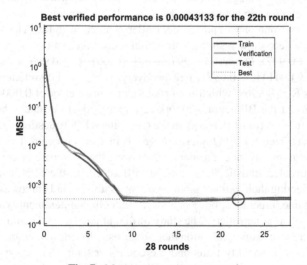

Fig. 7. Mean square sum error graph

Acknowledgements. Authors would like to express special thanks to all frontline controllers for their contributions to this research. Their supports and the enthusiasm of their respective teams were invaluable in facilitating the authors' research efforts.

References

1. Yan, G.L., Li, H.Y.: Types of character and temperament and their identification methods. Tianjin Educ. **12**, 15–18 (1988)
2. Zhang, G.Y.,Li, D.F.,Pan, S.K.: A study on the focused attention of college students with different temperaments. Psychol. Sci. **4**, 819–821(2006)
3. Reason, J.: Human Error. Cambridge University Press, London (1999)
4. Grindle, A.C., Dickinson, A.M., Boettcher, W.: Behavioral safety research in manufacturing settings: A review of the literature. J. Organ. Behav. Manag. **20**(1), 29–68 (2000)
5. Ulleberg, P., Rundmo, T.: Personality, Attitudes and risk perception as predictors of risky driving behavior among young drivers. Saf. Sci. **41**(5), 427–443 (2003)
6. Rosenbloom, T., Dan, N., Barkan, H.: For heaven's sake follow the rules: pedestrians' behavior in an ultra-orthodox and a non-orthodox city. Transport. Res. Part F Traffic Psychol. Behav. **7**(6), 395–404 (2004)
7. Attwood, D., Kha, F., Veitch, B.: Occupational accident models-where have we been and where are we going? J. Loss Prev. Process Ind. **19**(6), 664–682 (2006)
8. Remawi, H., Bates, P., Dix, I.: The relationship between the implementation of a safety management system and the attitudes of employees towards unsafe acts in aviation. Saf. Sci. **49**(5), 625–632 (2011)
9. Gong,Y.X.: Revised Eysenck Personality Questionnaire. Hunan Medical College, Changsha (1981)
10. Zhang, Y.: Study on depression state of flight cadets and analysis of eysenck personality questionnaire. Pract. Prevent. Med. **16**(02), 378–379 (2009)
11. Liu, G.Q., He, Z., Zhao, S.Y.: Eysenck personality questionnaire development model analysis. J. guizhou Normal Univ. **6**, 36–41 (2015)
12. Wang, H.L., Cui, S.: Investigation and analysis of personality characteristics of chinese soldiers. Chinese J. Psych. **30**(3), 179–182 (1997)
13. Garson, D.G.: An introductory guide for social scientists. Sage, London (1998)
14. Liu, C., Wang, J., Fan, S.P., Li, L., Lin, D.F.: Adaptive bias proportional guidance based on BP neural network. Acta Armamentarii **43**(11), 2798–2809 (2022)

The Evaluation Model of Pilot Visual Search with Onboard Context-Sensitive Information System

Wei Tan, Wenqing Wang[(✉)], and Yuan Sun

College of Safety Science and Engineering, Civil Aviation University of China,
Tianjin 300300, China
15263681730@163.com

Abstract. This study is based on the attention allocation to investigate the evaluation model of pilot's visual search performance. Based on the SEEV model of attention allocation, the evaluation model of pilot's visual search performance was determined by three factors: expectancy, value and effort. The eye movement indicators such as fixation duration and numbers of fixation were selected to represent the influencing factors in the model, and the expert scoring method was used to determine the weight coefficient of each factor. Then, the comparative experiment was designed with the level of information systems (context-sensitive information system and electronic flight manuals) as the independent variable and visual search performance as the dependent variable. The eye-tracking data of 20 airline pilots were recorded in the simulator under each experimental scenario. Finally, the data was substituted into the model to verify its effectiveness and feasibility. The results showed that the pilot visual search performance evaluation model can effectively reflect the level of pilot's visual search performance, and the level of pilot visual search performance in critical areas is effectively improved by using context-sensitive information system when handling malfunctions. The model can provide the theoretical reference for the training of standard operating procedures and the optimization of the context-sensitive information system.

Keywords: Context-Sensitive Information System · Visual search Performance · Evaluation Model · Eye-tracking Data · Attention Distribution · Flight Safety

1 Introduction

With the development of aviation science and technology, the aircraft cockpit has also experienced the development process of mechanization and automation, and is now gradually moving towards intelligence [1]. The development of cockpit has brought convenience to the flight crews and also generates some human factor problems. According to statistics, about 70% of major civil aviation accidents are caused by human errors [2], in which human errors of the flight crews accounts for a considerable proportion and become the main consideration of human factors affecting flight safety. One of the main reasons for human errors in flight crews is improper human-computer interaction in the

D. Harris and W.-C. Li (Eds.): HCII 2023, LNAI 14017, pp. 238–252, 2023.
https://doi.org/10.1007/978-3-031-35392-5_19

cockpit. The early cockpit design schemes are mostly determined by the technical feasibility, ignoring human-computer ergonomic issues [3]. With the continuous development of aviation industry technology, the ability to operate has been weakened, while the ability of information processing and decision-making has become increasingly prominent. Therefore, it is necessary to continuously optimize the cockpit human-computer interaction interface, design more human-adapted instruments and equipment, and evaluate them from the perspective of ergonomics, so as to ensure flight safety.

Vision is the most important sensory channel for the pilot to obtain external information. Research shows that in the human-computer interaction process, about 80% of the information is provided to pilots by the visual channel to further information processing [4–7]. The perception and processing of visual information by the pilot are very important during the human-computer interaction between the pilots and the cockpit system. When pilots conduct the flight tasks, most of the system status and parameters are displayed to pilots through the electronic instruments. The pilots have to primarily rely on effective visual perception and visual attention allocation to process various information in the cockpit [8–10], maintain good situation awareness, and make correct decisions and operate it. Therefore, the visual cognitive characteristics of pilots should be considered when designing aircraft cockpit intelligent systems and human-computer interaction interfaces [11].

Visual search is a complex cognitive process, which is an important way for people to obtain external information. The pilot needs to monitor and determine the status and parameters of the aircraft system by visually searching various instruments of the cockpit display interface during the flight, and then conduct correct and effective operations and control the aircraft, especially when the pilot is dealing with malfunctions. The accurate and effective visual search can achieve efficient human-computer interaction behavior, thereby reducing human errors and ensuring flight safety. Therefore, visual search plays a crucial role in flight. In recent years, visual search has been widely studied in the fields of reading [12, 13], car driving [14, 15], interface design [16–19], and a series of research have also been carried out in aviation. Bai et al. [20] showed that unconscious stimuli have a promoting effect on the visual search performance of pilot candidates, and the results showed that under the condition of small-range cues, the correct rate of visual search is highest when the participants receive cues of 35 ms (close to the threshold level), so that the unconscious stimuli have a higher level of processing. Fan et al. [21] concluded that different levels of time pressure and search difficulty have a significant impact on the visual search performance of pilots when monitoring instrument information. Svensson et al. [22] used eye tracking data, i.e. frequency of fixation, as a general indicator of pilot's visual search behavior in their study of the effects of task complexity on pilot's mental workload, situation awareness and performance. Wang et al. [23] explored the visual search characteristics of pilots with different flight experience and ages on the cockpit human-computer interface, and concluded that the ability of eyes to capture and search decreased with age. Lazaro et al. [24] investigated the impact of visual complexity of cockpit displays on pilots' visual search and target detection, and concluded that an increase on visual complexity leads to the increase in visual search time and target detection errors.

Most of the current studies have assessed visual search performance by analyzing subject response time and accuracy, and few studies have been conducted by analyzing eye tracking data and using relatively limited eye-tracking data. Therefore, this study builds a model for assessing pilot's visual search performance based on the attention allocation theory, and investigates the level of visual search performance of pilots using context-sensitive information systems compared with electronic flight manuals to deal with specific scenarios. The context-sensitive information system involved in this paper is one of the products of the development of the intelligent cockpit, and is designed to replace the flight manual in the electronic flight bag. It is not only as a tool for information searching, but also provides pilots with accurate operating procedures and suggestions in the intelligent way in real-time by interacting with flight data, in order to reduce the time of information searching for pilots and improve flight operation efficiency. The electronic flight manuals are stored in the electronic flight bag in the cockpit in a document format, which is used by pilots to read performance charts, aeronautical charts, operating procedures and other information in specific scenarios. This study can provide the theoretical reference for the optimization and update of context-sensitive information system, the ergonomic design of human-computer interaction interface of aircraft cockpits, and the flight training of operating procedures, which is helpful for pilots' recruitment and training, etc.

2 Modeling

Visual search requires people to complete information processing and cognitive processing through a series of fixation, saccades and other behaviors on stimuli [25], so that the relevant research of visual search is mainly studied by analyzing eye-tracking data. Studies have shown that various indicators of eye movement can directly reflect human psychological processes. By analyzing eye movement processes, we can understand how pilots perform visual search, how to allocate attention, and workload status during specific operations. As the basis of cognitive processing of information, attention is the internal drive of visual search behavior and controls some eye movement behaviors in visual search. Human cognitive ability and information processing ability are limited, especially during flight control that requires high concentration. Therefore, the availability of interface information should be fully considered in the cockpit design, and the visual search behavior of pilots can be explored in terms of attention allocation.

2.1 Introduction to the Attention Allocation Model

This study is based on the SEEV attention allocation model to investigate the operational mechanism of pilot's visual search behavior when using the context-sensitive information system and electronic flight manuals, and to construct a model for assessing pilot's visual search performance with eye-tracking data, and then design simulated flight experiments to collect data to verify the effectiveness of the model. The SEEV model states that the pilot's visual search process during a task is driven by four factors [26], namely the

Salience (S) that attracts visual attention by physical attributes; the pilot's expectation of an area of interest, known as expectancy (Ex); The importance of information in an area of interest to the pilot, that is Value (V); and the pilot's effort (Ef) to obtain effective information during the visual search process. By linearly weighting the above four influencing factors and using "a", "b", "c" and "d" respectively to represent the weight coefficients of each influencing factor, the following relationship is finally formed:

$$P = aSalience + bExpectancy + cValue - dEffort \qquad (1)$$

2.2 Build the Pilot's Visual Search Performance Evaluation Model

Flight is a complex task that highly relies on the effective acquisition of visual information and the rational distribution of attention by pilots. With the improvement of aircraft intelligence, the information displayed in the cockpit is increasing, which is crucial to study the visual search behavior and attention allocation of pilots to ensure aviation safety. Eyes can reflect people's physiological and psychological changes, and the study of eye movement is considered to be the most effective tool in visual information processing research. During target search, if the information of the current fixation point is insufficient, the subject will return to the previous fixation point to reacquire the information, which is called retrospective fixation. The generation of these retrospective fixation points results in the subject's total visit duration (denoted by T) being greater than the fixation duration (denoted by F) for a subject in an area of interest, and the total visit time increases as the number of retrospective fixation points increases [27]. Therefore, visual search efficiency can be expressed as the ratio of the subject's fixation duration F to the total visit duration T in a certain area of interest [28]. The percentage of fixation duration in an area of interest refers to the percentage of fixation duration in a certain area of interest to the fixation duration of all areas, reflecting the degree of interest of the subject in the area of interest [29], that is, it can indicate the importance of the area of interest to the subject, and reflect the value of the information in the area of interest to the subject.

In this study, the pilot's visual search performance evaluation model was established based on the SEEV attention allocation theory and related eye-tracking data, and the relational equation is as follows:

$$P = aEx + bV - cEf \qquad (2)$$

where "P" indicates the pilot's visual search performance in a certain area of interest; "Ex" stands for Expectancy, which refers to the pilot's expectation of the area of interest, indicating that the pilot expects to obtain the necessary information in the area of interest, expressed by search efficiency, that is the percentage of fixation duration F to total visit duration T; "V" stands for Value, which refers to the value of information in the area of interest to the pilot, and is the effectiveness of the pilot to obtain information and the user experience, expressed as the percentage of fixation duration; "Ef" stands for Effort, which reflects the effort made by the pilot to observe the instrument interface. "a", "b" and "c" are the weight coefficients, which indicate the degree of influence of " expectancy (Ex)", "value (V)" and "effort (Ef)" on the pilot's visual search performance level, obtained by expert scoring. Since salience is related to the physical attributes of objects in the area of interest, and this study mainly combines eye-tracking data for modeling and experimental analysis, salience is not considered in the evaluation model of pilot's visual searching performance established above.

Where the effort (Ef) in the above relationship is expressed according to the quantitative formula of the crew workload as:

$$Ef = \frac{C*d}{F} \tag{3}$$

where "C" indicates numbers of fixation in a certain area of interest; "d" indicates the degree of influence of the region of interest on the subject's visual search performance, obtained by expert scoring; "F" indicates the fixation duration for the area of interest.

3   Experiment

3.1   Subjects

The subjects were 20 flight pilots, including 6 flight instructors, 4 captains and 10 co-pilots, with a total flight hours range of 2000–18000 h (average flight hours 6771.80 ± 4297.02 h). All subjects were healthy with normal eyesight, well-trained and familiar with flight operations.

3.2   Equipment

The experiment was conducted on the A320 simulator, shown in Fig. 1, which is able to simulate the actual state in the cockpit in a variety of normal and abnormal scenarios. The eye-tracking data acquisition equipment was the Tobii Pro Glasses 2 head-mounted eye tracker, as shown in Fig. 2, the subjects had to wear it throughout the experimental operation, and the equipment can effectively track and collect the subjects' eye-tracking data in real-time. The whole experiment was recorded by the camera.

Fig. 1. A320 cockpit human-computer interaction platform

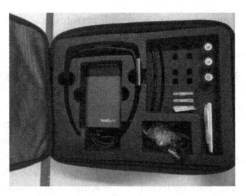

Fig. 2. Tobii Pro Glasses 2 head-mounted eye-tracking glasses

3.3 Experimental Design

Scenario Design. In this experiment, the subjects used the context-sensitive information system and the electronic flight manual to deal with two malfunctions of engine failure and flap locked, as follows:

Scenario 1 engine failure: The aircraft was set to take off from runway 02L, Guangzhou Baiyun Airport. One engine failed (with no damage) during the climb after airborne, and then the subjects responded to the malfunctions according to the standard operating procedures, and landed after successful relight.

Scenario 2 flap locked: During the final approach, when the flaps were set to Configuration 2, the flap jammed malfunction was set on the simulator. The subjects completed the trouble-shooting according to the standard operating procedures, and then landed with this malfunction.

Group Design. The 20 subjects were divided into two groups according to the principle of average distribution of type rating level and flight experience, so that to avoid learning effects. The first group contained 10 subjects who used the context-sensitive information system to deal with the single-engine failure of scenario 1, and then used the electronic flight manual to deal with the flaps locked of scenario 2; The second group contained another 10 subjects used the electronic flight manual to perform tasks of scenario 1, and then used the context-sensitive information system to perform tasks of scenario 2.

Area of Interest Division. According to the characteristics of the experimental scenarios and the human-computer interaction between the subject and the cockpit interface, the data collected by the eye tracker was divided into area of interest (AOI), and finally five areas of interest were delineated, they are: AOI1 Primary Flight Display (PFD), AOI2 Navigation Display (ND), AOI3 Engine/Warning Display (E/ WD), AOI4 System Display (SD), AOI5 Information Area (Context-sensitive information system/Electronic Flight Manuals).

3.4 Data Analysis

In this study, the complete process of handling the two malfunctions of engine failure and flap locked was selected as the research period. The data collected by the eye-tracking glasses was classified and sorted. Extracted the eye-tracking data required for modeling, the relationship of the visual search performance evaluation model can be sort out according to the requirements to analyze the results. The specific calculation process and results are as follows.

Analysis of the Pilot's Visual Search Performance Under Engine Failure. In this experiment, the focus of the two malfunctions was different, which can reflect the differences in the pilot's visual search performance and attention distribution of information in various areas of the cockpit interface under different malfunctions. In scenario 1, pilots needed to pay particular attention to flight parameters and engine parameters distributed on PFD, ND, E/WD, and SD, and also deal with the malfunction according to the standard operating procedures displayed on the E/WD, SD, and information areas. The relevant eye-tracking data collected in this scenario was collated and brought into the model for calculation, and the specific results are as follows.

(1) **Expectancy quantitative value**

According to the pilot's visual searching performance evaluation model, the expectancy was quantified by the percentage of fixation duration F and the total visit duration T in the area of interest. The results are shown in Table 1.

Table 1. Expectancy quantitative value under engine failure.

area of interest	Indicator	AOI1 (PFD)	AOI2 (ND)	AOI3 (E/WD)	AOI4 (SD)	AOI5 (Information Area)
context-sensitive information system	fixation duration	11.502	4.600	19.208	5.508	24.824
	total visit duration	12.996	5.428	27.266	7.302	47.352
	expectancy quantitative value	0.982	0.827	0.701	0.804	0.477
electronic flight manuals	fixation duration	3.446	3.328	35.866	6.556	70.170
	total visit duration	4.388	4.866	50.034	8.176	130.552
	expectancy quantitative value	0.939	0.608	0.676	0.787	0.278

(2) **Value quantitative value**

As can be seen from the model, the value was quantified as a percentage of fixation duration in the area of interest. The results are shown in Table 2.

(3) **Effort quantitative value**

According to formula (3), the quantitative value of effort was related to numbers of fixation, fixation duration and the weight coefficient "d". Among them, the eye-tracking data was collected by the eye tracker, and the weight coefficient was obtained by the

Table 2. Value quantitative value under engine failure.

area of interest	AOI1 (PFD)	AOI2 (ND)	AOI3 (E/WD)	AOI4 (SD)	AOI5 (Information Area)
context-sensitive information system	9.903	4.230	20.232	5.805	24.920
electronic flight manuals	2.287	2.186	26.851	4.068	40.069

expert scoring method (a total of 5 industry experts were consulted, and the results were taken as the average). Table 3 below shows the average score of experts. The relevant eye-tracking data and weight values were substituted into the formula (3) to obtain the quantitative effort values, and the results are shown in Table 4.

Table 3. Expert scoring results for the weighting coefficient "d" under engine failure.

area of interest	AOI1 (PFD)	AOI2 (ND)	AOI3 (E/WD)	AOI4 (SD)	AOI5 (Information Area)
engine failure	0.800	0.640	0.580	0.320	0.760

Note: score range 0–1

Table 4. Effort quantitative value under engine failure.

area of interest	Indicator	AOI1 (PFD)	AOI2 (ND)	AOI3 (E/WD)	AOI4 (SD)	AOI5 (Information Area)
context-sensitive information system	numbers of fixation	39.200	20.000	59.100	20.500	106.900
	Effort quantitative value	2.726	2.783	1.785	1.191	3.273
electronic flight manuals	numbers of fixation	13.600	14.500	82.800	20.400	233.800
	Effort quantitative value	3.157	2.788	1.339	0.996	2.532

(4) Weight value

The weight coefficients "a", "b" and "c" in the model were all scored by experts (a total of 5 industry experts were consulted). Table 5 below shows the average score of experts.

Table 5. Expert scoring results for weighting coefficients "a", "b", "c" under engine failure.

weight coefficient	a	b	c
engine failure	5.200	7.200	6.600

Note: score range 0–10

(5) **Quantitative value of visual search performance**

By substituting the quantitative results of steps (1)–(4) into the relationship Eq. (2), the visual search performance level of pilots using the context-sensitive information system and electronic flight manuals to deal with the engine failure can be obtained, and the specific results are shown in Fig. 3 below.

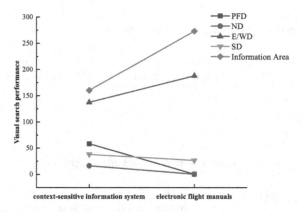

Fig. 3. The pilot's visual search performance under engine failure.

Analysis of the Pilot's Visual Search Performance Under Flap Locked. In scenario 2 flap locked failure, the pilot needed to spend a lot of time on landing performance calculation and operation procedure reading. The relevant information was mainly distributed in the E/WD, SD and information area. At the same time, they also needed to pay attention to the flap status. The information was mainly distributed on PFD, ND, E/WD and SD. The calculation process of the pilot's visual search performance value in this scenario was similar to Scenario 1. The calculation results of each part are shown below.

(1) **Expectancy quantitative value**

The expectancy quantitative value of flap locked is shown in Table 6.

(2) **Value quantitative value**

The value quantitative value of flap locked is shown in Table 7.

Table 6. Expectancy quantitative value under flap locked.

area of interest	Indicator	AOI1 (PFD)	AOI2 (ND)	AOI3 (E/WD)	AOI4 (SD)	AOI5 (Information Area)
context-sensitive information system	fixation duration	3.818	3.052	16.054	1.190	30.650
	total visit duration	4.740	3.860	18.392	1.278	50.440
	Expectancy quantitative value	0.896	0.818	0.815	1.137	0.355
electronic flight manuals	fixation duration	7.792	5.318	12.066	9.770	104.196
	total visit duration	8.322	7.062	16.052	13.910	180.264
	Expectancy quantitative value	0.895	0.452	0.777	0.716	0.500

Table 7. Value quantitative value under flap locked.

area of interest	AOI1 (PFD)	AOI2 (ND)	AOI3 (E/WD)	AOI4 (SD)	AOI5 (Information Area)
context-sensitive information system	5.114	3.864	20.742	1.914	38.212
electronic flight manuals	7.026	3.031	8.729	6.292	59.966

(3) **Effort quantitative value**

The value of "d" and the quantified value of effort under the condition of flap locked are shown in Table 8 and 9.

Table 8. Expert scoring results for the weighting coefficient "d" under flap locked.

area of interest	AOI1 (PFD)	AOI2 (ND)	AOI3 (E/WD)	AOI4 (SD)	AOI5 (Information Area)
flap locked	0.800	0.620	0.640	0.620	0.700

Note: score range 0–1

(4) **Weight value**

The weight coefficients "a", "b" and "c" are shown in Table 10.

Table 9. Effort quantitative value under flap locked.

area of interest	Indicator	AOI1 (PFD)	AOI2 (ND)	AOI3 (E/WD)	AOI4 (SD)	AOI5 (Information Area)
context-sensitive information system	numbers of fixation	13.800	11.200	30.000	3.900	96.000
	effort quantitative value	2.892	2.275	1.196	2.032	2.192
electronic flight manuals	numbers of fixation	24.200	19.800	35.100	29.500	338.100
	effort quantitative value	2.485	2.308	1.862	1.872	2.271

Table 10. Expert scoring results for weighting coefficients "a", "b", "c" under flap locked.

weight coefficient	a	b	c
Flap locked	5.800	7.600	5.000

Note: score range 0–10

(5) Quantitative value of visual search performance

By substituting the quantitative results of steps (1)–(4) into the relational Eq. (2), the visual search performance level of the pilot using the context-sensitive information system and the electronic flight manual to deal with the flap locked can be obtained, and the specific results are shown in Fig. 4 below.

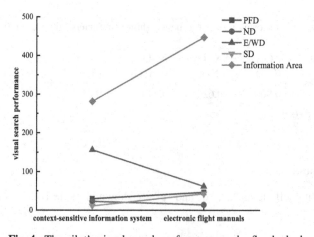

Fig. 4. The pilot's visual search performance under flap locked.

4   Discussion

This study is based on the SEEV attention allocation theory to build a pilot's visual searching performance evaluation model, and carry out experiments to collect eye tracking data into the model to verify the effectiveness and feasibility of the model, and explore the visual search performance level of pilots when using different information systems (context-sensitive information system/electronic flight manuals) to deal with different malfunctions (engine failure/flap locked). The results show that there are significant differences in the eye tracking data and visual search performance of pilots when using different information systems to deal with malfunctions.

In this study, two malfunction scenarios were selected for the experiment. The focus of attention allocation and visual search of pilots in different malfunction scenarios was different. Scenario 1 engine failure occurred in the climb after takeoff, and the pilot needed to obtain relevant flight parameters from AOI1 (PFD) to ensure the stability of flight operation in the critical flight phase, and handled the failure according to the standard operating procedures and recommendations on AOI5 (information area); Scenario 2 flap locked occurred during approach on final flight path. The pilot needed to obtain system information and approach performance data from AOI3 (E/WD), and also checked standard operating procedures and recommendations from AOI5 (information area), so as to quickly carry out landing assessment and implement the operating procedures to complete trouble-shooting.

4.1   Eye-tracking Data

The eye movement indicators selected in this study include fixation duration, the percentage of fixation duration, numbers of fixation and total visit duration. The fixation duration and numbers of fixation are important visual characteristics indicators reflecting information search and information coding [30]. The fixation duration can reflect the difficulty of human cognitive process and the difficulty of extracting information, and numbers of fixation can reflect the importance of AOI [31, 32]. Fewer numbers of fixation and fixation duration indicate a more systematic visual search strategy [33]. The percentage of fixation duration reflects the degree of interest and attention distribution of the subjects in the area of interest, and reflects the importance of the information in the area to the subjects [34]. The longer the total visit time is, the less information the subjects get in this area. The subjects need more time to confirm the information [35].

The results show that there are differences in eye movement indicators when pilots use different information systems to deal with malfunctions. The pilot's fixation duration and the percentage of fixation duration at AOI1 (PFD) and AOI3 (E/WD) for engine failure in scenario 1 and flap locked in scenario 2 were significantly greater than those in the electronic flight manuals; numbers of fixation at AOI1 (PFD) in disposal scenario 1 were significantly greater than those in the electronic flight manuals, and numbers of fixation at AOI3 (E/WD) in disposal scenario 2 were slightly less than those in the electronic flight manuals; The fixation duration, the percentage of fixation duration and numbers of fixation at AOI5 (information area) of the two scenarios were significantly smaller than those in the electronic flight manuals, and the attention distribution of the five AOIs was more uniform than that in the electronic flight manual. This shows that the use of onboard context-sensitive information system helps pilots to allocate their attention to more important areas, which is conducive to improving the visual search performance of this area, so as to quickly handle malfunctions and ensure flight safety.

4.2 Visual Search Performance

The evaluation model of pilot's visual searching performance established in this study is driven by expectation, value and effort. Expectancy represents the pilot's expectancy of information in a certain area of interest, which depends on the effectiveness and efficiency of the pilot's feedback on interactive information. Value represents the importance of information in a certain area of interest to the pilot's handling of the malfunction, which is reflected in the pilot's attention distribution; Effort represents the load that pilots are subjected to when dealing with malfunctions, so it is negatively related to the visual search performance.

The results show that the expectancy quantized values of the four AOIs with the exception of AOI5 (information area) in Scenario 1 and Scenario 2, where the pilot uses the context-sensitive information system to deal with engine failure, are greater than that pilots using the electronic flight manuals; The quantitative values of scenario 1 on AOI1 (PFD), AOI2 (ND), AOI4 (SD) and scenario 2 on AOI2 (ND) and AOI3 (E/WD) are greater than that of the electronic flight manuals; The quantitative values of the effort of scenario 1 on AOI1 (PFD), AOI2 (ND) and scenario 2 on AOI2 (ND), AOI3 (E/WD) and AOI5 (information area) are less than that of the electronic flight manuals; The visual search performance of scenario 1 on AOI1 (PFD), AOI2 (ND), AOI4 (SD) and scenario 2 on AOI3 (E/WD) and AOI2 (ND) is higher than that of the electronic flight manuals. The above results show that the visual searching performance level of pilots using context-sensitive information system to deal with malfunctions in important areas has significantly improved, but the visual searching performance level on AOI5 (information area) has decreased. The reason probably is that the subjects are skilled in searching relevant information from the electronic flight manual when dealing with malfunctions, while the new context-sensitive information system is relatively unfamiliar to them.

5   Conclusion

The eye movement indicators selected in this study can effectively reflect the visual search and attention allocation of pilots when dealing with malfunctions, and can effectively quantify the impact factors in the model.

The evaluation model of pilot's visual searching performance based on the three factors of expectancy, value and effort can effectively quantify the level of pilot visual search performance, and can reflect the attention distribution of pilots on information searching.

The use of context-sensitive information system can effectively improve the visual searching performance of pilots on important display areas when dealing with malfunctions, and allocating attention to more important areas, so as to quickly deal with malfunctions and ensure flight safety.

The further research can use more comprehensive eye-tracking data and physiological data to supplement the visual search performance evaluation model, and design more scenarios with a large number of subjects to verify the effectiveness and feasibility of the model.

Acknowledgments. The authors would like to appreciate the support of the Tianjin Graduate Science and Innovation Research Project (grant no. 2022SKY160). Thanks to Dr. Wang Lei for his supervision and guidance in this research. Thanks to Dr. Feiyin Wang, and Dr. Rong Zhang, who provided us with feedback, suggestions, and comments on this research.

References

1. Xu, W.: User centered design (VII): from automated to intelligent Flight Deck. Chin. J. Appl. Psychol. **28**(04), 291–313 (2022)
2. Human Factors-Harmonization Working Group: Flight Crew Error/Flight Crew Performance Considerations in the Flight Deck Certification Process. Human Factors-HWG Final Report (2004)
3. Liu, W., Yuan, X., Zhuang, D, et al.: Development of a simulated cockpit for synthetic ergonomic evaluation of pilot. China Saf. Sci. J. **13**(11), 13–16 (2003)
4. Gerathewohl, S.: Leitfaden der militärischen Flugpsychologie. Verlag für Wehrwiss (1987)
5. Sun, R., Wang, N.: Visual features of pilot based on Markov chain under flight simulator. J. Beijing Univ. Aeronaut. Astronaut. **39**(07), 897–901 (2013)
6. Wang, N., Yu, S., Xiao, L., et al.: Human-computer interface design considering visual attention. J. Xi'an Technol. Univ. **36**(4), 334–339 (2016)
7. Ge, L., Xu, W.: User Experience: Theory and Practice. China Renmin University Press, Beijing (2020)
8. Liu, Z., Su, H., Lv, S., et al.: Measurement and comparison of situation awareness in air combat environment: evidence from eye movement. Chin. J. Ergon. **21**(6), 17–21 (2015)
9. Li, W.C, Yu, C.S., Braithwaite, G., et al.: Pilots' attention distributions between chasing a moving target and a stationary target. Aerosp. Med. Hum. Perform. **87**(12), 989–995 (2016)
10. Wei, H.-Y., Zhuang, D.-M., Wanyan, X.-R., et al.: An experimental analysis of situation awareness for cockpit display interface evaluation based on flight simulation. Chin. J. Aeronaut. **26**(4), 884–889 (2013)
11. Qu, S., Zhou, Q.: Effects of digital information display time on human and machines monitoring performance. Space Med. Med. Eng. **18**(3), 191–195 (2005)
12. Goonetilleke, R.S., Lau, W.C., Shih, H.M.: Visual search strategies and eye movements when searching Chinese character screens. Int. J. Hum.-Comput. Stud. **57**(6), 447–468 (2002)
13. Ojanp, H., Nasanen, R., Kojo, I.: Eye movements in the visual search of word lists. Vis. Res. **42**(12), 1499–1512 (2002)
14. Christ, S.E., Abrams, R.A.: Abrupt onsets cannot be ignored. Psychon. Bull. Rev. **13**(5), 875–880 (2006)
15. Chu, Y., Qin, H., Ran, L., et. al.: Influence of information layout of vehicle central control screen on visual search performance. Sci. Technol. Eng. **22**(30), 13521–13526 (2022)
16. Chen, X., Huang, L., Li, M.: Visual search performance of intercity logistics APP interface navigation design. Packag. Eng. **42**(08), 198–204 (2021)
17. Qu, Y., Zhu, S., Wang, W., et al.: Research on visual search cognitive characteristics of adaptive interface. Acta Electron. Sinica **49**(02), 338–345 (2021)

18. Li, J., Yu, S., Wu, X.: Effects of shape character encodings in the human-computer interface on visual cognitive performance. J. Comput.-Aided Des. Comput. Graph. **30**(01), 163–172+179 (2018)
19. Lin, C.C.: Effects of screen luminance combination and text color on visual performance with TFT-LCD. Int. J. Ind. Ergon. **35**(3), 229–235 (2005)
20. Bai, S., Huang, Y., Liu, J., et al.: An experimental study of improving visual search performance of pilot candidates by unconscious stimuli. Med. J. Air Force **32**(04), 217–219+223 (2016)
21. Fan, X., Zhou, Q., Liu, Z., et al.: Principle of plane display interface design based on visual search. J. Beijing Univ. Aeronaut. Astronaut. **41**(02), 216–221 (2015)
22. Svensson, E.A.I., Wilson, G.F.: Psychological and psychophysiological models of pilot performance for systems development and mission evaluation. Int. J. Aviat. Psychol. **12**(1), 95–110 (2002)
23. Wang, Y., Guo, X., Liu, Q., et al.: Eye movement characteristics research on pilots of different experience background during aircraft cockpit display image visual search task. In: Long, S., Dhillon, B.S. (eds.) Man–Machine–Environment System Engineering, pp. 85–94. Springer, Singapore (2018). https://doi.org/10.1007/978-981-10-6232-2_11
24. Lazaro, M.J., Kang, Y., Yun, M.H., et al.: The effects of visual complexity and decluttering methods on visual search and target detection in cockpit displays. Int. J. Hum–Comput. Interact. **37**(7), 588–600 (2021)
25. Ren, Y.T., Han, Y.C., Sui, X.: The saccades and its mechanism in the process of visual search. Adv. Psychol. Sci. **14**(3), 340–345 (2006)
26. Wickens, C., McCarley, J., Thomas, L.: Attention-Situation Awareness (A-SA)Model. University of Illinois at Urbana Champaign, Illinois (2003)
27. Zhang, G., Shen, M., Tao, R.: The application of eye tracking in usability tests. J. Ergon. **7**(4), 9–13 (2001)
28. Chen, J., Zhang, S., Zhou, Y., et al.: Availability evaluation of medical device instructions based on eye movement technique. China Health Ind. (5), 35–41 (2016)
29. Liu, Z., Yuan, X., Liu, W., et al.: Quantitative measuring method of pilots' attention allocation. J. Beijing Univ. Aeronaut. Astronaut. **32**(5), 518–520 (2006)
30. Zhang, X.: Modeling and simulation of Pilot's dynamic visual and motion performance in flight deck. Northwestern Polytechnical University (2016)
31. Kotval, X.P., Goldberg, J.H.: Eye movements and interface components grouping: an evaluation method. In: Proceedings of the Human Factors Society 42nd Annual Meeting, pp. 486–490 (1998)
32. Yuan, W.: Study on Car Driver's Dynamic Visual Characters Test on City Road. Chang'an University (2008)
33. Hornof, A.J., Halverson, T.: Cognitive strategies and eye movements for searching hierarchical computer displays. In: Proceedings of the SIGCHI Conference on Human Factors in Computing Systems, pp. 249–256 (2003)
34. Liu, Z., Yuan, X., Liu, W., et al.: Analysis on eye movement indices based on simulated flight task. China Saf. Sci. J. (02), 47–51+145 (2006)
35. Chen, X.: Research on Visual Search Performance Logistics APP Interface Navigation of Intercity Design. Jiangsu University (2020)

The Similarity Recognition of Pilots' Operational Action Sequence Based on Blocked Dynamic Time Warping during a Flight Mission

Huihui Wang, Yanyu Lu[(✉)], and Shan Fu

School of Electronic Information and Electrical Engineering, Shanghai Jiao Tong University,
Shanghai 200240, People's Republic of China
luyanyu@sjtu.edu.cn

Abstract. Human errors are the primary cause of aviation safety accidents. It is necessary to identify the potential operation errors of a crew during a flight task. In this work, we propose a flight mission recognition method using Blocked Dynamic Time Warping (BDTW) to detect the operational errors. DTW is a popular method to calculate the similarity of time series, and can also be used as an effective sequence alignment method for pilots' operational sequence recognition. Traditional DTW has a high computational complexity, and cannot meaningfully align the time series when the outlier exists. In contrast, BDTW based on the encoded representation of time series to reduce calculation time can be applied to the alignment of the operational sequence consisting of a series of the areas of interest (AOI) of pilot's actions. Since the same flight mission has the same operation process, we use BDTW to progressively align multiple AOIs under a mission, and then extract common operations as the pattern. In this way, the interference of noise on recognition is mitigated. The data with 10 flightcrews in 5 different missions was used for test and the results show high recognition accuracy of the proposed method.

Keywords: Aviation Human Factor · Dynamic Time Warping · Operational Series Alignment · Human errors

1 Introduction

Human errors are the main cause of aviation safety accidents, and about 80% of aviation accidents are related to human errors [1]. Human errors cannot be completely eliminated, so the detection of errors in the cabin is important to detect the error and analyze the cause of error and then propose preventive and management measures.

During the flight mission, pilots are required to perform a series of complex operations according to the standard operational procedures (SOP), especially in the emergent conditions. Pilots' deviation from SOP includes action omission, action error, etc. [2]. Therefore, one of the effective ways to detect human errors is to detect whether the pilot's operation deviates from SOP. The traditional method to detect the behavior errors of pilots is to observe the pilots' actions and make a judge by observers. It relies on experienced observers, and the efficiency is low.

The detection and similarity measurement method based on the pilot's operational behavior sequence provides the possibility for automatic and efficient detection of human errors. The sequence of pilot's operation behavior is essentially a time series. Dynamic Time Warping (DTW) [3] is a common method in time series detection and similarity measurement [4–6]. It seeks the optimal alignment of two sequences by warping the time shift. However, DTW-based methods have two main disadvantages: the computational complexity is high and the input data must be clean. Blocked Dynamic Time Warping (BDTW) [7] is an improved DTW algorithm based on encoded sequence. It takes advantage of the sparsity of AOI data and effectively reduces computational complexity.

Due to systematic errors in the process of AOI data extraction and behavior habits of pilots, noises unrelated to the operation procedures will occurs, which are unable to be removed in data preprocessing period by techniques. Because of the randomness of noises, we cannot get a priori information about which is pilot's operation and which is noise. It is necessary to extract clean data from raw data as reference, and then measure the similarity between the reference and tested data using BDTW. AOI data under the same flight mission have the same subsequence which represents discrete operations. The order of these operations is fixed and the time difference between adjacent operations will not change significantly. In this paper, we propose a progressive alignment algorithm based on BDTW, which is effective for the extraction of common subsequences. We select standard data (with no errors) in advance, from which our proposed progressive alignment method can extract clean data that contains only SOP. Finally, we use the obtained clean data as reference to calculate similarity between it and test data for recognition.

2 Related Work

2.1 Acceleration of DTW Algorithm

DTW is a popular time series analysis method, which has been applied to many different research fields [8–11]. One disadvantage of classic DTW algorithm is its high computational cost. A prevalent solution is to use pruning method to avoid unnecessary matching [12–14]. However, owing to existence of a large number of duplicate values in sparse sequence, even if pruning method is used, there is still many redundant calculations. The proposal of AWarp [15] symbolized the rise of encode-based acceleration method [7, 16]. This method works with a special encoded time series, which containing only non-zero observed value and repetitions of zero values. It is a powerful approximate method of DTW. Furthermore, [7] uses a length encoding method which only retains the value and its repetition times, which greatly compresses the length of sparse sequence. Based on this coding method, BDTW proposed by [7] has a more comprehensive scope of application than AWarp. Because it takes into account all values in the sequence, it can adapt to all types of sparse sequences instead of a sequence with a large proportion of zero values. BDTW enormously reduces the operation time and achieves high accuracy in aggregate and freezer power consumption time series. Consequently, we chose it as a means of sequence alignment.

2.2 DTW Applied to Noisy Sequence

Real sequences always have superimposed noise. DTW forces all values in the sequence to be aligned, and the existence of noise will interfere with the warping process, resulting in inaccurate global alignment. Some methods [17, 18] discard outliers in the dynamic programming process by combining DTW and probability model. These methods require abundant training samples. In contrast, our proposed algorithm only needs a small capacity of samples for training.

3 Methodology

3.1 Dynamic Time Warping

DTW is a popular solution to sequence alignment problem. Assumed two time series $X = [x_1, x_2, \cdots, x_m]$ and $Y = [y_1, y_2, \cdots, y_n]$ of length m and n. The matching of two points of X and Y is represented by a cell of a m-by-n matrix M. By dynamic programming, a warp path start from $M(1, 1)$ and end at $M(m, n)$ is generated, which is the optimal alignment of X and Y. The optimal path is calculated by function (1):

$$DTW(x, y) = \sqrt{D_{m,n}} \tag{1}$$

$D_{i,j}$ is defined as:

$$D_{i,j} = (x_i - y_j)^2 + min[D_{i-1,j}, D_{i,j-1}, D_{i-1,j-1}]$$

$$D_{0,0} = 0, D_{1:m,0} = \infty, D(0, 1:n)D_{0,1:n} = \infty \tag{2}$$

$$i \in [1, m], j \in [1, n]$$

Apparently, only adjacent top, left and diagonal cells will be considered when selecting path, and the warp path can not go back in time axis.

3.2 Blocked Dynamic Time Warping

Data Encoding: Sparse time series contains a large amount of duplicate values, so that traditional DTW will lead to a large number of redundant calculations. The encoding method proposed in [5] can effectively compress sparse time series. BDTW algorithm based on this method not only improves the computational efficiency, but also preserves the time domain information of time series.

For example, assumed a time series $T = [1, 1, 1, 2, 2, 3, 3, 3, 3, 4, 4]$, we call each piece of successive repeated values a segment, and extract two types of value from it: the repeated value and the repeat time which indicates the duration of repeated value. The encoding method is defined as follow:

$$X_{encoded} = [[v_1, t_1], [v_2, t_2], \cdots, [v_w, t_w]] \tag{3}$$

where v_i is the repeated value of the ith segment and t_i is the repeat time of the ith segment.

Since the alignment should start with the first value of sequence and end with the last element of sequence, we need to conduct special processing for the beginning and ending of the sequence. If the first value is repeated, we need to divide the value segment into two parts, the segment with run length of one and the next remaining segment. Besides, if the last value is repeated, the second part after splitting is a segment with run length of one, and the first part is the remaining segment. The encoded time series with 4 segments is presented as $T_e = [[1, 1], [1, 2], [2, 2], [3, 4], [4, 1], [4, 1]]$.

From encoded time series, we can restore the initial timestamp which is of great significance for the subsequent constrained method. The initial timestamp of the ith segment is defined as:

$$Time_{init} = \sum_{k=0}^{i-1} t_k \qquad (4)$$

Algorithm Structure: BDTW takes two encoded time series as input. Assumed the encoded length of two time series X_e and Y_e is m' and n', we define a m'-by-n' BDTW matching matrix, where each cell represents the matching pair of two segments of two encoded time series. The cell in the upper left corner of the matrix represents the starting position of alignment, that is the matching of the first segment of two sequences. As well, the cell in the lower right corner of the matrix as the end position of alignment is the matching of the last segment of two sequences.

Then, we build a cost matrix S with the same size as the BDTW cost matrix. Figure 1 shows the traditional DTW cost matrix and BDTW cost matrix for two typical time series. The value of each cell in S is the cumulative distance from the starting position $S(1, 1)$ to this cell. The cumulative distance of the (i, j)th cell $d_{i,j}$ is calculated based on the repeated value $vx_i(vy_j)$, the repeat time $tx_i(ty_j)$ and the.

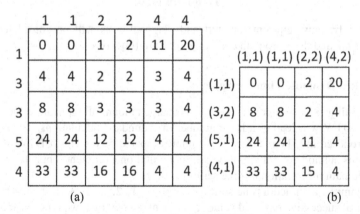

Fig. 1. A comparison between cost matrixs of traditional DTW and BDTW. (a) Traditional DTW cost matrix. (b) BDTW cost matrix.

values of top($d_{i-1,j}$), left($d_{i,j-1}$), diagonal($d_{i-1,j-1}$) cells. The formula for calculation of $d_{i,j}$ is as follows:

$$d_{top} = d_{i-1,j} + tx_i * (vx_i - vy_j)^2$$

$$d_{diagonal} = d_{i-1,j-1} + max[tx_i, ty_j] * (vx_i - vy_j)^2 \tag{5}$$

$$d_{left} = d_{i,j-1} + ty_j * (vx_i - vy_j)^2$$

$$d_{i,j} = min[d_{top}, d_{diagonal}, d_{left}]$$

The cells on the upper left side of the matching matrix will not have top, left and diagonal cells at the same time, so only $S(m', n')$ the existing cell need to be considered in the calculation. As Fig. 2 illustrating, the optimal alignment path is obtained by tracing back from to $S(1, 1)$, the process is expressed as:

$$\text{Previous maching pair} \leftarrow \begin{cases} S(i-1,j) & \text{if } d_{i,j} = top, \\ S(i-1,j-1) & \text{if } d_{i,j} = diagonal, \\ S(i,j-1) & \text{if } d_{i,j} = left. \end{cases} \tag{6}$$

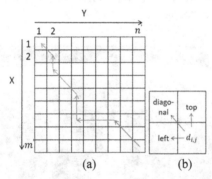

Fig. 2. (a) Optimal alignment path of BDTW, cells on the path are matching pairs. (b) Selection of local optimal path.

Constrained Blocked Dynamic Time Warping: Constrained DTW is used to improve the sequence alignment efficiency. It restricts the process of finding the optimal warping path by adding a self-defined constrained window and makes an element of one sequence only match elements in a certain time range of another sequence. This method has be extended to BDTW. Figure 3 shows a constrained case of BDTW. Assumed segments (vx_i, tx_i) and (vy_j, ty_j) are the ith and jth segment of encoded sequence X and Y respectively. If the absolute difference between start timestamp of two sequence is greater than threshold w, specifically:

$$\left| \sum_{k=0}^{i-1} tx_k - \sum_{k=0}^{j-1} ty_k \right| > w \tag{7}$$

Because in SOP, two operations with the same order will not have a large absolute difference on the timestamp (otherwise there will be an error), this matching will not be considered when selecting the optimal warping path. This method can not only improve the effect of sequence alignment, but also reduce computational complexity.

Fig. 3. A constrained case of BDTW, black cells will not be used in the calculation of the optimal alignment path.

3.3 Progressive Alignment for Reference Data Extraction

Behavior data records the areas of interest (AOI) of pilots' hands during flight. Figure 4 shows the area division of cabin.

Fig. 4. Area division of cabin.

AOI sequence is represented as a one-dimensional time series, and its time range covers the whole mission execution process. The sampling rate is 20 Hz. An example of AOI sequence is shown in Fig. 5. The value of each time point represents the cabin device where pilot's hand is located at that time. The specific corresponding relationship is shown in Table 1.

Each operation performed by the pilot is represented as a continuous value repeat subsequence in the AOI sequence. AOI sequence is a sparse time series, because the

Table 1. Numeric tag of areas where the cabin devices is located.

Areas	Top	FCP	FMS-l	Alert-l	FMS-r	Alert-r	T	ECAM	Out of devices
Numeric Tag	1	2	3	4	5	6	7	8	0

time for pilot to perform operations only accounts for a small part of the total time range. AOI data always contains noises irrelevant to the operation procedure, which cannot be detected in the preprocessing period and will have a negative influence on the sequence alignment process. Therefore, we cannot use the noise sensitive BDTW algorithm to directly calculate the similarity between two tested sequences. Accordingly, it is not always possible to remove these noises. We consider prioritizing the extraction of operational information in the data as a reference for classification by comparing its edited distance to test data. To this end, we proposed a feature extraction method based on a small amount of training samples. The same mission type has the same SOP, which is shown as a series of ordered subsequences in AOI data. As shown in the subsequences marked by red dotted circle in Fig. 5, we regarded these subsequences as the feature of this type of AOI data. For subsequent recognition task, we need clean data without any noise and only features as reference.

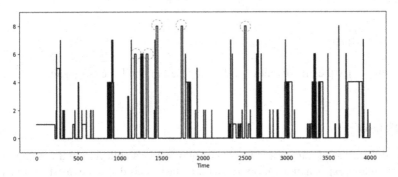

Fig. 5. An example of AOI sequence with red dotted circle signifying the operation procedure.

The progressive alignment method we proposed is an effective method to extract reference data from noise sequences, it only requires a small number of training samples. Figure 6 shows the flow chart of progressive alignment method. Firstly, select two samples from training set and use BDTW algorithm to align the sequences. Each AOI segment in a sequence will be matched to the segment which has the smallest distance to it in the constraint range of another sequence (It may also simultaneous match multiple segments with the smallest distance). Extract all matching pairs with zero distance (with the same AOI value) by backtracking the optimal warping path. For any segment that matches multiple segments at the same time, we took the segment with the smallest difference of start time to form a matching pair.

After getting all the matching pairs, calculate their average timestamp and average duration to form a sequences with a length equal to the length of aligned encoded training

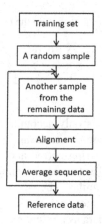

Fig. 6. The flow chart of progressive alignment method.

sequences, which is a sequence with common operations. Then we selected one sample from the remaining training sequences each time, and repeat the alignment process with intermediate output of previous step. After aligned the last data, a reference data is acquired, which contains the common operation of these training samples. Finally, we will establish a reference data set for flight mission recognition.

4 Experiments

In order to verify the effectiveness of the proposed method, we conducted experiments on real data sets.

4.1 Dataset

We used the areas of interest (AOI) data of pilot's hands collected in the A320 MOC8 flight simulator experiments for our recognition task. This data set consists of five flight missions, specifically: Engine Fire, Single Engine Failure after V1, Flap and Slat Jamming Landing, Windshear Go-around, and High Altitude Pressure Relief. Each mission contains AOI data of 11 pilots.

4.2 Preprocessing

By reason of the errors in AOI data extraction process, the AOI segment representing an one-step operation may be divided into multiple close AOI segments with the same value. Moreover, in some cases, even if the pilot does not perform an operation, an AOI segment of this operation will still appear. In either situation, some short segments (value with little repetition times) will appear on sequence. In order to facilitate subsequent recognition, we need to preprocess the encoded data. Consider the clustered short segments as the former case, and merge it into a segment. The isolated short segments are the latter case, and set their value to 0. The preprocessing process is as follows:

(1) Set a threshold $T1$. If the repeat time of the zero value is smaller than $T1$ and the two adjacent segments have the same non-zero value, which is represent as $[\cdots, (v1, t1), (0, t2), (v1, t3), \cdots]$, merge these three segments to a new segment:

$$new\_segment = (v1, t1 + t2 + t3) \qquad if\ t2 < T1 \qquad (8)$$

(2) Set another threshold $T2$ and set value v of non-zero segments with repeat time t smaller than $T2$ to zero:

$$S_{raw} = (v, t)$$

$$S_{filtered} = \begin{cases} (0, t)\ if\ t < T2, \\ S_{raw}\ otherwise. \end{cases} \qquad (9)$$

where S_{raw} represents the raw segment and $S_{filtered}$ represents the filtered segment.

4.3 Results

We selected 4 AOI sequences under each mission as the train set for reference data extraction, and the remaining 7 are used as test data. Constrained BDTW is used to calculate the edited similarities between each test sample and reference data. The definition of the edited similarity is:

$$Similarity = \frac{n_{ref}}{n_{match}} \qquad (10)$$

where n_{ref} is the number of non-zero segments in the reference data and n_{match} is the number of matching pairs with equal AOI values. Test data is classified by the class of reference data when obtaining the maximum similarity, the formula is as follows:

$$Class = argmax\{Similarity_i\} \qquad i \in [1, 5] \qquad (11)$$

The average recognition accuracy and the average CPU time to recognize a test sample are used to evaluate the performance of the proposed method. In our experiment, the value of w in formula (7) is changed after each round of training, and got the maximum accuracy when w = 200. The experimental results are shown in Table 2.

With the increment of the constraint threshold w, the average accuracy rises first and then decreases, and the average CPU time increases by degrees. The reason for the change of accuracy rate is that when w is exceedingly small, BDTW cannot correct the excessive time shift phenomenon, resulting in some segments representing pilot operation cannot be matched. As w increases, it will be more likely to produce mis-matching, resulting in a decline in accuracy. In addition, since the constraint threshold w reduces the space for dynamic normalization when calculating the optimal alignment, the CPU time increases with the increment of w.

Table 2. Experimental results for the proposed method with different granularity *w*.

	Average accuracy	Average CPU time
w = 100	54.29%	3.14 s
w = 200	71.43%	3.14 s
w = 300	60%	3.16 s
w = 400	57.14%	3.17 s
w = 500	51.43%	3.24 s

4.4 Discussion and Limitations

In the AOI data we used, the cabin AOI area was not finely divided, made some different operations be represented by the same AOI value, which is an important cause for recognition errors. In the future, we will subdivide the AOI area into the button level.

Besides, our recognition task only used the pilot's hand AOI data. Although this kind of data can cover most of SOP, it is inevitable to miss some information, such as the pilot's AOI of gaze, speaking and other procedures that do not need to be executed by the hand. The missing procedures from eye movement recorder, speech signal and other data will be considered in the future work. This leads to the problem of multi-dimensional sequences alignment, which makes it necessary to improve BDTW algorithm to adapt to multi-dimensional input.

5 Conclusion

In summary, so as to detect operational errors based on pilot's action sequence, we propose a progressive alignment algorithm based on BDTW to extract common operation procedures as reference data from pilot's action sequences and recognize the incorrect action according to the similarity between reference data and test data. Its great advantage is the reduction of noise interference. Meanwhile, since BDTW realizes low computational complexity, Constrained BDTW further optimizes computational complexity by pruning segments with large timestamp difference. Compared with traditional recognition methods, our method only needs a small capacity of training set. The proposed method also achieved good accuracy in recognizing flight mission represented by the test data.

References

1. Naranji, E.: Reducing human/pilot error in aviation using augmented cognition and automation systems in aircraft cockpit. The George Washington University (2015)
2. Li, W.C., Harris, D.: Pilot error and its relationship with higher organizational levels: HFACS analysis of 523 accidents. Aviat. Space Environ. Med. **77**(10), 1056–1061 (2006)
3. Senin, P.: Dynamic time warping algorithm review. Inf. Comput. Sci. Dept. Univ. Hawaii Manoa Honolulu USA **855**(1–23), 40 (2008)

4. Muda, L., Begam, M., Elamvazuthi, I.: Voice recognition algorithms using Mel frequency cepstral coefficient (MFCC) and dynamic time warping (DTW) techniques. arXiv preprint arXiv:1003.4083 (2010)
5. Huang, M., Shah, N.D., Yao, L.: Evaluating global and local sequence alignment methods for comparing patient medical records. BMC Med. Inform. Decis. Mak. 19(6), 1–13 (2019)
6. Lu, C., Singh, M., Cheng, I., et al.: Efficient video sequences alignment using unbiased bidirectional dynamic time warping. J. Vis. Commun. Image Represent. 22(7), 606–614 (2011)
7. Sharabiani, A., Darabi, H., Harford, S., et al.: Asymptotic dynamic time warping calculation with utilizing value repetition. Knowl. Inf. Syst. 57, 359–388 (2018)
8. Hou, W., Pan, Q., Peng, Q., et al.: A new method to analyze protein sequence similarity using dynamic time warping. Genomics 109(2), 123–130 (2017)
9. Dhingra, S.D., Nijhawan, G., Pandit, P.: Isolated speech recognition using MFCC and DTW. Int. J. Adv. Res. Electric. Electron. Instrum. Eng. 2(8), 4085–4092 (2013)
10. Li, Y., Xue, D., Forrister, E., et al.: Human activity classification based on dynamic time warping of an on-body creeping wave signal. IEEE Trans. Antennas Propag. 64(11), 4901–4905 (2016)
11. Ward, C.R., Obeid, I.: Dynamic time warp distances as feedback for EEG feature density. In: 2015 IEEE Signal Processing in Medicine and Biology Symposium (SPMB), pp. 1–5. IEEE (2015)
12. Silva, D.F., Giusti, R., Keogh, E., et al.: Speeding up similarity search under dynamic time warping by pruning unpromising alignments. Data Min. Knowl. Disc. 32, 988–1016 (2018)
13. Assent, I., Wichterich, M., Krieger, R., et al.: Anticipatory DTW for efficient similarity search in time series databases. Proc. VLDB Endowment 2(1), 826–837 (2009)
14. Tavenard, R., Amsaleg, L.: Improving the efficiency of traditional DTW accelerators. Knowl. Inf. Syst. 42(1), 215–243 (2015)
15. Mueen, A., Chavoshi, N., Abu-El-Rub, N., et al.: Speeding up dynamic time warping distance for sparse time series data. Knowl. Inf. Syst. 54, 237–263 (2018)
16. Ge, L., Chen, S.: Exact dynamic time warping calculation for weak sparse time series. Appl. Soft Comput. 96, 106631 (2020)
17. Lichtenauer, J.F., Hendriks, E.A., Reinders, M.J.T.: Sign language recognition by combining statistical DTW and independent classification. IEEE Trans. Pattern Anal. Mach. Intell. 30(11), 2040–2046 (2008)
18. Chang, Y., et al.: Recovering DTW distance between noise superposed NHPP. In: Yang, Q., Zhou, Z.-H., Gong, Z., Zhang, M.-L., Huang, S.-J. (eds.) PAKDD 2019. LNCS (LNAI), vol. 11440, pp. 229–241. Springer, Cham (2019). https://doi.org/10.1007/978-3-030-16145-3_18
19. Berstein, A.D., Shallom, I.D.: Noise processing DTW algorithms for speech recognition systems. In: 17th Convention of Electrical and Electronics Engineers in Israel, pp. 293–296. IEEE (1991)

Analysis on the Competence Characteristics of Controllers in the Background of Air Traffic Control System with Manmachine Integration

Yonggang Wang and Wenting Ma[✉]

College of Safety Science and Engineering, Civil Aviation University of China, Tianjin, China
mwt13220956832@163.com

Abstract. In order to investigate the competence characteristics required to be a good controller in the context of a new generation of air traffic control system with manmachine integration, based on the competency theory, the controller competency characteristics quality evaluation index system is established by means of questionnaires and workflow analysis, and the mutual influence relationship between the quality characteristics is analyzed according to the DEMATEL-ISM method, and the controller competency quality explanation structure model is constructed. The model is divided into three levels with 12 competence characteristics indicators, reflecting the hierarchical structure and inner connection of air traffic controller competence characteristics. The results show that under the current background of air traffic control system with manmachine integration, spatial awareness, strain response capability, evaluate decision-making capacity, forecast and overall planning capacity, and attention distribution capacity are the core qualities directly related to the effectiveness of control work, and the sense of work responsibility, consciousness of rules and discipline are the basic qualities of control work. The research on the competency model of controllers and the influencing factors between the competency characteristics of controllers can provide a certain reference basis for the construction of personnel qualification and capacity in the safety management of controllers in the context of a new generation of air traffic control system with manmachine integration, and provide a certain reference value for the future recruitment and selection, training and development of controllers.

Keywords: controller · competency · DEMATEL-ISM method

1 Introduction

With the continuous development of Internet technology, the smart air traffic control system proposed at present refers to a system that applies Internet technology to manage aircraft in airspace [1]. By placing sensors with powerful sensing functions in various equipment systems of air traffic control, and then using advanced IT technology to connect them to form a whole air traffic control system, the air traffic control system can be monitored and processed in an all-round way. The controller makes decisions

© The Author(s), under exclusive license to Springer Nature Switzerland AG 2023
D. Harris and W.-C. Li (Eds.): HCII 2023, LNAI 14017, pp. 264–275, 2023.
https://doi.org/10.1007/978-3-031-35392-5_21

based on various information provided by the intelligent air traffic control system to achieve the safe operation of the aircraft. With the continuous development of China's aviation industry, aviation equipment has become more and more advanced, especially after the intelligent air traffic control was proposed, the intelligence of air traffic control system has also been promoted, and the reliability of air traffic control equipment has also been enhanced. However, no matter how intelligent the air traffic control system is, it needs controllers to control and operate it. The investigation results of many years' aviation accident reports also show that three quarters of civil aviation accidents are caused by human factors [2]. As the most adaptable and valuable factor of the aviation air traffic control system, aviation controllers are of great significance to the research of controllers. As a special industry, air traffic control may cause incidents or accidents due to the controller's mistakes or mistakes. The quality and psychology of controllers are increasingly required by the control work. It is particularly important to find suitable personnel for the control work. At present, although some scholars have studied the competency of controllers [3–5], under the current intelligent background, the regulatory environment and conditions have changed for controllers, and because of the complexity of their psychological activities, the behavior of controllers is also changeable and vulnerable to adverse conditions. Therefore, the competency model of controllers under the background of intelligent air traffic control is built, It is of great significance for the selection and training of controllers.

Competency characteristics are the potential deep level characteristics of individuals that can distinguish outstanding and average performers in a job (or organization or culture), including motivation, traits, self-image, attitudes or values, knowledge in a certain field, cognitive or behavioral skills and any other individual characteristics that can be reliably measured or counted and can significantly distinguish excellent and general performance [6]. Competency, as a potential feature of an individual, can deeply prompt the individual's behavioral motivation. The study of competency can improve the overall performance of the system [7]. Competency model refers to the sum of knowledge, skills, abilities and other characteristics that a specific position role should possess. It is a competency structure combined with the requirements of those with excellent performance in this position [8]. At present, there are many researches on competency theory models, among which the iceberg model (as shown in Fig. 1) and onion model (as shown in Fig. 2) are the most representative. The iceberg model and onion model of competency model are similar. The apparent competency elements mainly include knowledge, skills, etc., which are easy to find and cultivate. For in-depth competency elements, they mainly include traits, values, motivation, etc.

The iceberg model divides competency into underwater and above water: Internal drive, values, self-consciousness, personality, Social dynamics, Knowledge and skills.

The onion model believes that the competency elements are distributed from the inside out. Cheetham & Chivers [9] put forward a five dimensional model of competency characteristics on the basis of summing up the previous characteristics of the model elements, and proposed cognitive competency, functional competency, personal competency, values, and meta Competence, Le Deist & Winterton [10] integrated the five dimensional model into a four dimensional model (cognitive competency, functional competency, social competency, meta Competence). The four-dimensional model

Fig. 1. Iceberg Model

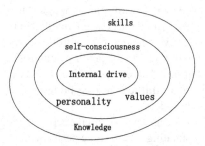

Fig. 2. Onion model

is divided into four quadrants according to the bipolar dimensions of professionalism personalization and conceptualization operability. Yuan Shengren's competency is a personalized conceptual quality, cognitive competency is a professional conceptual quality, social competency is a personalized operational quality, and functional competency is a professional operational quality. At present, the competency four-dimensional model is widely used.

2 Method

2.1 Participants

Participants include qualified controllers of the control branch and relevant experts of the air traffic control bureau. The controllers of the participants are all those who have graduated from three domestic civil aviation colleges and universities in air transportation or have received professional training and qualification in air transportation from three civil aviation colleges and universities, and have met the requirements of induction training. The controller has worked for more than five years. And the participants are anonymous and have the right to terminate the experiment at any time and withdraw the data provided at any time after data collection.

2.2 Research Framework

The objective of this research is to explore the quality characteristics of becoming an excellent controller under the current intelligent background. Based on the competency theory, the competency factors of controllers are initially determined through the preparation of questionnaires such as literature review. The construction of the controller competency model can be determined by the controller competency factors and competency related theories. The controller's competency model is also used as the input result. The analysis of the input result can determine the direct binary relationship between the competency elements by using the DEMATEL-ISM method. DEMATEL method is a method proposed to screen the main elements of complex systems and simplify the process of system structure analysis [12]. ISM (Interactive Structural Modeling) is mainly used to analyze the factors and the direct binary relationship between the factors, and map this conceptual model into a directed graph, decompose the complex system into several subsystem elements in a quantitative way, and finally form a multi-level hierarchical structural model. The integrated DEMATEL-ISM hybrid modeling can not only express the complex influence relationship between the elements of the controller's competency through the hierarchical directed topology, but also determine the importance of each feature element and identify the key competency elements of the controller.

2.3 Scenario

Scenarios include all activities such as writing questionnaires, distributing questionnaires, controllers filling in questionnaires, and data sorting and processing. Combined with the relevant opinions of civil aviation experts and the analysis of the controller work process, the controller competency model is determined.

2.4 Procedure

On the basis of the competency theory, the questionnaire was prepared by reviewing the literature and combining the survey results of controllers in the current smart air traffic control background. The respondents scored the importance of the indicators according to the actual situation. The scoring method was from "1 very unimportant" to "5 very important". 200 questionnaires were distributed to two control sub bureaus, including 64 for Branch A, 66 for Branch B and 70 for Branch C. The distribution object is controllers in three posts of tower, approach and area (excluding trainee controllers), excluding controllers in four posts of flight service, station dispatching, intelligence and operation management. According to the DECIDE model of the controller workflow, as shown in Fig. 3, the model is composed of six parts: detection (D-Detect), estimation (E-Estimate), selection (C-Choose), identification (I-Identify), implementation (D-Do) and evaluation (E-Evaluate). The quality required by the controller in these six workflows is analyzed. Use more specific indicators to replace comprehensive indicators, such as scene awareness is replaced by spatial perception, attention distribution, etc., eliminate the quality with little connection, simplify the quality entries in combination with expert opinions, and determine the final competency evaluation indicator system and the corresponding relationship with the control workflow (Table 1). Judge the competency quality required by the control workflow in combination with the expert opinions of the Air Traffic Control Bureau. "1" means the competency quality required by the control workflow, and "0" means that the control workflow does not need to consider this quality or the impact of this quality on the workflow is small, which can be ignored.

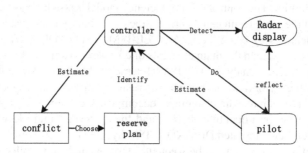

Fig. 3. Air traffic control workflow

Table 1. Evaluation indexes of air traffic controller's competency and their relationship with workflow

	Index	Detect	Estimate	Choose	Identify	Do	Evaluate
X1	Forecast and overall planning capacity	0	1	1	0	0	0
X2	Logical thinking capacity	1	1	1	1	1	1
X3	psychological resilience capacity	1	1	1	0	1	0
X4	Evaluate decision-making capacity	0	0	0	1	0	0
X5	Numerical sensitivity capacity	1	0	0	0	0	0
X6	Strain response capability	0	0	1	0	1	0
X7	Sense of work responsibility	0	0	1	1	1	0
X8	Attention distribution capacity	1	1	0	0	0	0
X9	Spatial awareness	1	0	0	0	0	0
X10	Communication and coordination capacity	0	0	0	0	1	0
X11	Language expression ability	0	0	0	0	1	0
X12	Consciousness of rules and discipline	0	0	0	0	1	0

In this study, 12 elements of controller competency characteristics were identified based on the characteristics of knowledge and skills, driving force and personality in the iceberg model and the relevant regulations of air traffic control as well as the dominant direction and characteristics of the industry for comparison and selection. Based on the special characteristics of air traffic control work, the competencies of controllers are divided into three categories: professional competence, core quality, personality and psychological characteristics, among which professional competence belongs to the upper iceberg characteristics, core quality belongs to the middle iceberg characteristics, while personality and psychological characteristics belong to the lower iceberg characteristics. According to the competency-related theory, the 12 competency elements are classified, and the factor structure is shown in Table 2, and the controller competency characteristics model is shown in Fig. 4.

Table 2. Factor structure of air traffic controller competency model

Level 1 Indicators	Level 2 Indicators	Level 3 Indicators
Explicit Competence Characteristics	Professional Competence	Spatial awareness
		Numerical sensitivity capacity
		Language expression capacity
invisible Competence Characteristics	Core Qualities	Communication and coordination capacity
		Evaluate decision-making capacity
		Forecast and overall planning capacity
		Logical thinking capacity
		Attention distribution capacity
	Personality, psychological characteristics	Psychological resilience capacity
		Strain response capability
		Sense of work responsibility
		Consciousness of rules and discipline

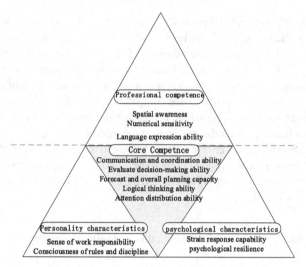

Fig. 4. Air traffic controller competency model

3 Results and Discussion

3.1 DEMATEL-ISM Method

DEMATEL method is a method proposed to screen the main elements of complex systems and simplify the process of system structure analysis [11]. ISM (Interactive Structural Modeling) is mainly used to analyze factors and the direct binary relationship between factors, map this conceptual model into a directed graph, decompose the complex system into several subsystem elements in a quantitative way, and finally form a multi-step structural model [12]. By using the integrated DEMATEL-ISM hybrid modeling, this paper can express the complex influence relationship between the factors of the controller competency features through the hierarchical directed topology, determine the importance of each feature, and identify the key competency factors of the controller. This paper uses DEMATEL-ISM hybrid modeling. According to the competency quality constructed in Table 1, 12 civil aviation experts are invited to score the xij between the competency items of controllers, usually using a 5-point scale to indicate the degree of influence (Table 3).

Table 3. Scale correspond to influence degree

Scale	0	1	2	3	4
Influence degree	nothing	low	medium	high	Very high

Invite the current 12 experts in civil aviation to score xij among the competency items of controllers, determine the final scale by using the score distribution, and obtain the initial direct correlation matrix X.

$$X = \begin{bmatrix} 0&0&1&0&0&2&3&3&0&0&0&1 \\ 1&0&0&0&0&4&4&1&1&3&2&0 \\ 0&0&0&0&2&1&3&3&2&0&3&0 \\ 0&0&0&0&2&0&0&3&1&4&3&0 \\ 0&0&1&4&0&1&2&4&1&3&4&0 \\ 2&0&0&0&2&0&3&3&0&0&2&0 \\ 2&1&1&3&3&2&0&3&2&0&3&2 \\ 3&1&1&1&1&0&0&0&0&0&3&3 \\ 0&0&1&3&3&0&1&3&0&2&3&0 \\ 0&0&0&0&0&3&2&1&0&0&4&3 \\ 0&0&1&1&1&2&0&3&3&2&0&1 \\ 3&2&3&3&3&2&1&4&3&1&3&0 \end{bmatrix}$$

The row sum maximum method is used to normalize the comprehensive impact matrix A

$$A = \begin{bmatrix} 0.046 & 0.017 & 0.063 & 0.044 & 0.056 & 0.105 & 0.142 & 0.182 & 0.035 & 0.025 & 0.078 & 0.072 \\ 0.087 & 0.017 & 0.034 & 0.059 & 0.077 & 0.202 & 0.201 & 0.151 & 0.083 & 0.147 & 0.183 & 0.066 \\ 0.045 & 0.016 & 0.036 & 0.069 & 0.139 & 0.082 & 0.147 & 0.212 & 0.120 & 0.052 & 0.2109 & 0.048 \\ 0.032 & 0.012 & 0.029 & 0.048 & 0.113 & 0.050 & 0.039 & 0.188 & 0.074 & 0.184 & 0.200 & 0.051 \\ 0.053 & 0.019 & 0.076 & 0.205 & 0.082 & 0.100 & 0.123 & 0.272 & 0.098 & 0.177 & 0.279 & 0.069 \\ 0.111 & 0.015 & 0.032 & 0.056 & 0.123 & 0.044 & 0.144 & 0.195 & 0.041 & 0.038 & 0.154 & 0.045 \\ 0.134 & 0.058 & 0.091 & 0.198 & 0.234 & 0.145 & 0.081 & 0.278 & 0.144 & 0.094 & 0.268 & 0.131 \\ 0.143 & 0.051 & 0.073 & 0.085 & 0.090 & 0.056 & 0.053 & 0.106 & 0.052 & 0.050 & 0.189 & 0.140 \\ 0.039 & 0.014 & 0.069 & 0.167 & 0.166 & 0.053 & 0.081 & 0.217 & 0.053 & 0.136 & 0.224 & 0.053 \\ 0.051 & 0.020 & 0.040 & 0.058 & 0.070 & 0.158 & 0.116 & 0.145 & 0.057 & 0.044 & 0.232 & 0.146 \\ 0.042 & 0.015 & 0.067 & 0.090 & 0.097 & 0.112 & 0.049 & 0.202 & 0.143 & 0.117 & 0.107 & 0.079 \\ 0.176 & 0.094 & 0.163 & 0.203 & 0.215 & 0.162 & 0.137 & 0.334 & 0.187 & 0.135 & 0.293 & 0.077 \end{bmatrix}$$

According to the centrality and causation values of each formation factor in the table, use Matlab to draw the influence result diagram of competency factors, as shown in Fig. 5.

Based on the results of the structural matrix division and the interactions between the indicators (Table 4), the hierarchical structure of the model was constructed, i.e. the ISM model of controller competency (Fig. 6). The model is divided into 3 levels and contains 12 controllers' competency indicators.

3.2 Discussion

According to the ISM model of controller competencies: spatial awareness, strain response capability, evaluate decision-making capacity, forecast and overall planning capacity, and attention distribution capacity are located at the top of the structure model,

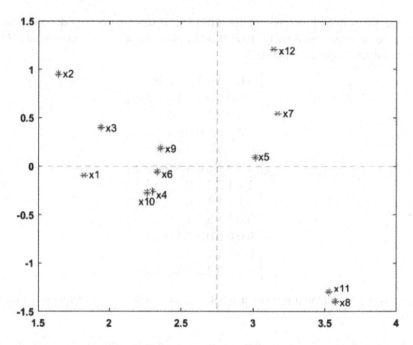

Fig. 5. Competency factors affect results.

Table 4. .

	X1	X2	X3	X4	X5	X6	X7	X8	X9	X10	X11	X12
X1	1	0	0	0	0	0	0	0	0	0	0	0
X2	0	1	0	0	0	1	1	0	0	0	0	0
X3	0	0	1	0	0	0	0	1	0	0	1	0
X4	0	0	0	1	0	0	0	0	0	0	0	0
X5	0	0	0	1	1	0	0	1	0	0	1	0
X6	0	0	0	0	0	1	0	0	0	0	0	0
X7	0	0	0	0	1	0	1	1	0	0	1	0
X8	0	0	0	0	0	0	0	1	0	0	0	0
X9	0	0	0	0	0	0	0	1	1	0	1	0
X10	0	0	0	0	0	0	0	0	0	1	1	0
X11	0	0	0	0	0	0	0	1	0	0	1	0
X12	0	0	0	1	1	0	0	1	0	0	1	0

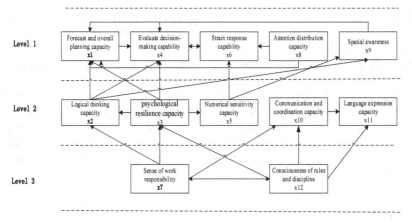

Fig. 6. ISM of air traffic controller's competency

and are the primary qualities to become a good controller in the current context of intelligent air traffic control. The results of control work are directly dependent on the core qualities of controllers: spatial awareness is the basis of information perception in control work situations; forecast and overall planning capacity determine the correctness of information perception; evaluate decision-making capacity influence the correctness of solution direction; and strain response determines the timeliness of work implementation, which together determine the effectiveness of control work. At the same time, this is consistent with the results of DEMATEL's weighting analysis, which also shows the importance of the core qualities of controllers.

Logical thinking ability, psychological resilience capacity, numerical sensitivity, communication and coordination ability, and verbal ability are located at the second level of the structural model. Logical thinking ability refers to the ability to analyze and judge, in order to quickly understand the essence of things and make a reasonable analysis and judgment, you need to master certain logical thinking ability, and logical thinking ability also has an impact on other competency characteristics; the principle of air traffic control work is zero tolerance, but in the work of high load and at any time to face the unexpected situation will bring invisible pressure on the controller, and how to The digital sensitivity is a professional ability of controllers, especially in the context of digital and intelligent air traffic control system, the needs of each work process have been "data-based" to a certain extent [13], so the digital sensitivity of controllers has become particularly important. The ability of communication and coordination refers to the controller's ability to use appropriate information transfer methods, exchange information with others in a timely and accurate manner, and use appropriate interpersonal relationship methods, and have a global thinking about people, the environment, things and other related resources; the ability of language expression refers to the controller's ability to express his or her opinions, views or insights through language, body movements and other means in a fluent manner, and express them clearly and distinctly. The verbal ability refers to the controller's ability to express his or her opinions, views, or insights through language and body movements, and to express his or her intentions or needs clearly and unambiguously. The second level controller competency characteristics are also their basic competency characteristics, and the related competency characteristics interact with each other and influence the formation of various competencies, and are the link between the core quality characteristics and the fundamental competency characteristics.

Awareness of rules and regulations and a sense of work responsibility are the fundamental quality characteristics of controllers, and are fundamental to the formation and development of controllers' quality of competence. Awareness of regulations and discipline or sense of work responsibility is the fundamental guarantee that controllers themselves are suitable for control work and can make excellent work performance in the work.

4   Conclusion

At present, the practical application of intelligent air traffic control is mainly reflected in the data transformation of the needs of each work process, the full materialization of production factors, the informationization of various data resources, and the reflection in the system, so as to achieve sharing [14]. In this context, an iceberg model of controller's competency characteristics was constructed based on the competency iceberg model and related concepts and competency-related theories, and a controller competency ISM model was constructed by combining the DEMATEL-ISM method. ISM model, analyzed its internal structure, and drew the following main conclusions:

1. The model is divided into three levels, containing 12 competency characteristics indicators, and the levels are interconnected and mutually reinforcing, reflecting the progressive order of controller competency characteristics and the mutual intrinsic relationship between the elements.
2. The controller's awareness of regulations and discipline and sense of work responsibility as the fundamental quality of controllers, in the daily training process to continuously strengthen the controller's awareness of regulations and discipline and sense of work responsibility to continuously improve the basic quality of controllers.
3. In the premise of the continuous intelligent development of the air traffic control system, the professional ability of controllers is important, but the development of their quality will also have an important impact on the control work, so in the training of controllers targeted control skills, but also pay attention to the training of other qualities of controllers, in order to improve the overall ability of controllers.

Acknowledgements. Authors would like to express special thanks to all apron controllers for their contributions to this research. Their supports and the enthusiasm of their respective teams were invaluable in facilitating the authors' research efforts.

References

1. Jidong, B.: Intelligent air traffic management system and its application. Sci. Technol. Inform. **12**(20), 22 (2014). https://doi.org/10.16661/j.cnki.1672-3791.2014.20.035

2. Yongkuan, B.: Aviation Accidents and Human Factors. China Civil Aviation Press, Beijing (2002)
3. Wang, D.: Research on the construction of competency model for air traffic controllers in civil aviation. Sci. Technol. Inform. **27**, 851–852 (2011). https://doi.org/10.3969/j.issn.1001-9960.2011.27.672
4. Huo, Z.: Research on fuzzy comprehensive evaluation of overall qualities of air traffic controllers in civil aviation. J. Wuhan Univ. Technol. Soc. Sci. Edn **18**(3), 374–377 (2005). https://doi.org/10.1002/hfm.20827
5. Wang, M.H., Wang, C., Guo, J.: Personality characteristics analysis of air traffic controller by 16PF. **22**, 2098–2099 (2007). https://doi.org/10.3321/j.issn:1000-2790.2007.22.026
6. Spencer, L.M.: Competence at Work, pp. 10–12. Wiley, New York (1993)
7. Okviana, A., Latief, Y.: A method to develop performance indicators based on performance criteria of Indonesian National Occupational Competency Standards (SKKNI) for construction safety technician competency. IOP Conf. Ser. Mater. Sci. Eng. **930**(1), 012010(11pp) (2020). https://doi.org/10.1088/1757-899X/930/1/012010
8. Green, P.C.: Building Robust Competencies: Linking Human Resource Systems to Organizational Strategies, p. 10. Jossey-Bass, NewYork (1999)
9. Cheetham, G., Chivers, G.: Towards a holistic model of professional competence. J. Eur. Ind. Train. **20**(5), 20–30 (1996). https://doi.org/10.1108/03090599610119692
10. Le Deist, F.D., Winterton, J.: What is competence. Hum. Resource Develop. Int. **8**(1), 27–46 (2005). https://doi.org/10.1080/1367886042000338227
11. Attri, R., Dev, N., Sharma, V.: Interpretive structural modeling (ISM) approach: an overview. Res. J. Mange. Sci. **2**(2), 3–8 (2013)
12. Wu, W.-W.: Choosing knowledge management strategies by using a combined ANP and DEMATEL. Appr. Exp. Syst. Appl. **35**(3), 828–835 (2008). https://doi.org/10.1016/j.eswa.2007.07.025
13. Zhong, Y.: Smart air traffic control: open a new era of "digital intelligence control". China Aviat. News (007) (2022). https://doi.org/10.28081/n.cnki.nchqb.2022.001446
14. Sun, R., Zhao, N., Li, J., et al.: Structure analysis of competency model for air traffic controller. China Saf. Sci. J. **24**(10), 8–14 (2014). https://doi.org/10.16265/j.cnki.issn1003-3033.2014.10.019

A Measurement Framework and Method on Airline Transport Pilot's Psychological Competency

Lei Wang(✉), Jiahua Peng, Ying Zou, Mengxi Zhang, and Danfeng Li

College of Safety Science and Engineering, Civil Aviation University of China, Tianjin, China
wanglei0564@hotmail.com

Abstract. Based on the professional characteristics of airline transport pilots and requirements of implementing pilots' Professionalism Lifecycle Management (PLM) system put forward by Civil Aviation Administration of China (CAAC), this study proposes the measurement framework and method on airline transport pilot's psychological competency by consulting the relevant results of psychological competency and psychological assessment of pilots. Firstly, this study points out that the psychological competency of airline transport pilots mainly includes two measurement dimensions: professional adaptability and mental health, covering five measurement modules: general cognitive ability, operational and professional ability, social-interpersonal ability, personality traits and attitude, and mental health. Secondly, this study provides the complete process of psychological competency evaluation for pilots, and the measurement data of the pilot can be obtained through supporting hardware and software devices for evaluation and analysis. Finally, this study designs an index fusion algorithm of pilot's psychological competency, integrates the data obtained by the objective measurement algorithm and the subjective measurement algorithm, and calculates the score value of the pilot's psychological competency after standardized calculation, combined with the psychological competency measurement framework. The research conclusion shows that the measurement framework and method on airline transport pilot's psychological competency proposed in this study have certain applicability, and can be widely applied in the next step, providing direct technical support and input for the development of reliable civil aviation pilot selection, evaluation and training tools.

Keywords: Psychological Competency · Measurement Method · Pilot Selection · Flight Safety

1 Introduction

Over the past 30 years, statistics and analysis of the causes of accidents in the aviation field have shown that human factors account for 60–80% of all accidents, and therefore human factors are widely recognized as a key factor in ensuring flight safety and efficiency [1]. While focusing on the mental activity of pilots, their psychological characteristics and state are two of the most critical human factors. Currently, psychological evaluation has become a necessary step in the selecting and training for pilots all over the world [2].

D. Harris and W.-C. Li (Eds.): HCII 2023, LNAI 14017, pp. 276–285, 2023.
https://doi.org/10.1007/978-3-031-35392-5_22

In 2020, the Civil Aviation Administration of China (CAAC) proposed out a plan of implementing Professionalism Lifecycle Management System (PLM) as a guideline to comprehensively improve the post competency of Chinese civil aviation pilots. In the psychological competency dimension, the need for integration of pilot competency evaluation and mental health evaluation is clearly indicated. Specific contents include professional adaptability and mental health [3]. The PLM system defines professional adaptability is the psychological traits that a person must possess when working as a professional pilot [4], and mental health is an efficient, satisfied and continuous mental state, which are two important modules for selecting and training pilots [3].

In the existing pilot psychological evaluation system research and application of evaluation tools, the evaluation of ability, personality and mental health status is independent of each other, and there is almost no evaluation tool to integrate the evaluation data of psychological characteristics and mental status at the same time. Generally, the ability evaluation is carried out through specific aptitude tests, involving objective measurement methods, and the personality evaluation and mental health evaluation are carried out through questionnaires or scales, involving subjective measurement methods. Psychometric evaluation requires objective and standardized measurement of behavior samples [5], so it is an urgent need to design psychometric data fusion algorithms and develop scientific psychometric tools to conduct quantitative evaluation of pilot's psychological competency.

The aim of this study is to propose out the measurement framework and method on airline transport pilot's psychological competency. Firstly, this study points out the measurement framework and process. Secondly, this study designs a psychological competency index fusion algorithm, integrates the data obtained by the objective measurement algorithm and the subjective measurement algorithm, and calculates the score value of the pilot's psychological competency after standardized calculation, combined with the psychological competency measurement framework. Finally, this study proposes a corresponding evaluation tool, which can provide effective support for selection and training of safer pilots.

2 Measurement Framework and Process

The measurement framework on airline transport pilot's psychological competency is established based on two evaluation dimensions: professional adaptability and mental health.

Professional adaptability is divided into four second-level indexes with corresponding last-level indexes. Namely, general cognitive ability (such as reaction ability, memory ability, attention selection ability, etc.), operational and professional ability (such as spatial orientation ability, hand-eye coordination ability, bimanual coordination ability, etc.), social-interpersonal ability (such as teamwork ability, communication ability, etc.), and personality traits and attitude (such as personality component, personality disorder, risk personality and hazardous attitude) [4].

Mental health is divided into two second-level indexes, and four third-level indexes with corresponding last-level indexes. The second-level indexes include: mental quality and mental state. The third-level indexes include: self-tendency (such as self-esteem, self-efficacy, etc.), adaptability (such as resilience, interpersonal relationship, etc.), negative state (such as depression, anxiety, etc.), and positive state (such as subjective well-being) [3].

The measurement framework of airline transport pilot's psychological competency has five evaluation modules: general cognitive ability, operational and professional ability, social-interpersonal ability, personality traits and attitude, and mental health. The operational and professional ability module can be measured by connecting the peripheral devices of eye tracker and flight control stick, and the personality traits and attitude and mental health can be measured by questionnaires or scales. The final psychological competency score is obtained through the data fusion algorithm of these five modules. The measurement process is shown in Fig. 1.

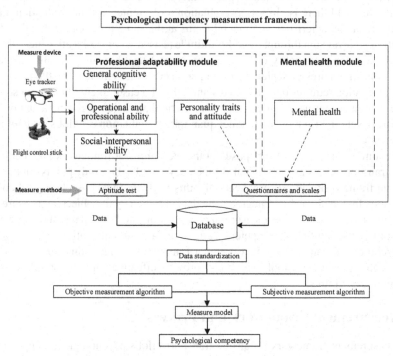

Fig. 1. Measurement framework and process of psychological competency

3 Measurement Method

The psychological competency measurement algorithm is designed according to the principles of objective measurement algorithm and subjective measurement algorithm. The dimension of professional adaptability has four measure modules, which are divided into three measurement modules of ability and one measurement module of personality. And mental health is a separate measurement module.

The evaluation of general cognitive ability, operational and professional ability, and social-interpersonal ability belongs to the category of objective measurement algorithm. Firstly, the initial score x_i is obtained through the aptitude test of each last-level index.

According to the Z-score standardization principle [6], the range of Z value is generally $(-3, 3)$, and the form of $A + BZ$ is used to transform again to obtain Eq. (1), which makes the score interval between $(40,100)$ and avoids the score being a decimal or negative number. The standardized scores of last-level indexes can be obtained by applying Eq. (1).

$$x_{iz} = 70 + 10\frac{x_i - \bar{x}_i}{\sigma_i}, \quad (i = 1, 2, 3, \cdots, n) \tag{1}$$

Among them, x_i is the initial score of the i th index, $\bar{x}_i$ is the mean value of the i th index, σ_i is the standard deviation of the i th index, and x_{iz} is the standardized score of the i th index.

The weight of each last-level indicator can be obtained by the weighting method of expert scoring. Applying Eq. (2), the standardized scores of the last-level indicators are weighted and summed to obtain the measurement value S of the second-level index.

$$S = \sum_{i=1}^{n} x_{iz}w_i, \quad (i = 1, 2, 3, \cdots, n) \tag{2}$$

Among them, w_i is the weight of the i th index.

Finally, we can get the measurement values of S_{CA}, S_{OA} and S_{SA} for each of the three measurement modules of ability by this algorithm.

The evaluation of the personality traits and attitude belongs to the category of subjective measurement algorithms, which is composed of four indexes: personality component, personality disorder, risk personality and hazardous attitude [4]. Firstly, for the measurement of personality component, the internationally authoritative and widely used Big-Five personality questionnaire is selected [7, 8]. There is no good or bad personality component, scoring high or low is just a tendency. However, researches have shown that personality has a predictive effect on job performance in stressful environments [9]. Conscientiousness is positively correlated with job performance [10, 11]. Agreeableness is conducive to better collaboration at work [10]. Extraversion is conducive to interaction at work, but extroverts are more likely to make mistakes at work due to their pursuit of adventure and excitement seeking [12, 13]. Openness is conducive to learning and training, but in the routine work environment where safety and compliance are crucial, open imagination, curiosity and sense of new things will lead to individuals more likely to violate rules [14]. Neuroticism is the strongest single predictor of job stress and an important marker of depression susceptibility. Empirical studies support that neuroticism is negatively correlated with job performance [15, 16]. Drawing on Hunter's meta-analysis [17], Clarke et a l. [14] mined through a wide range of empirical literature and concluded that high scores for extraversion, neuroticism, low conscientiousness, low agreeableness, and openness were associated with high accident rates. Therefore, it is necessary to assign different weights to five personality traits through expert scoring method to measure the personality component.

The score of neuroticism needs to apply Eq. (3) to normalize the inverse index.

$$x_i' = max\{x_i\} - x_i + 1, \quad (i = 1, 2, 3, \cdots, n) \tag{3}$$

Among them, $max\{x_i\}$ is the highest score of the i th question, x_i is the actual score of the i th question, and x_i' is the score after the reverse score is normalized.

The personality component score x_{PC} is obtained by weighting the scores of each dimension of the Big-Five applying Eq. (4).

$$x_{PC} = \frac{w_C x_C + w_N x_N + w_A x_A + w_E x_E + w_O x_O}{M} \times 100\% \tag{4}$$

Among them, x_C, x_N, x_A, x_E and x_O are the actual scores corresponding to the single personality trait, respectively, w_C, w_N, w_A, w_E and x_O are the weights corresponding to single personality trait, respectively, and M is the total score of single personality trait.

Personality Disorder (PD) is a construct used by social and clinical scientists to deal with the complex psychological phenomena that arise when personality is severely dysfunctional [18]. PD will cause serious distress and damage to social and professional fields [19], so the evaluation of personality disorder should be strict and prudent.

The score of personality disorder was calculated using the 0–1 scoring measurement of Eq. (5). In this part, the measurement method is mainly through the personality disorder scale. If the pilot is diagnosed as personality disorder after the scale measurement is equal to or exceeds the critical value (CV), the score of this index will be 0, otherwise, if the diagnosis result is normal, the score will be 1.

$$x_{PD} = f(x) = \begin{cases} 1, x < CV \\ 0, x \geq CV \end{cases} \tag{5}$$

Among them, x_{PD} is the score of PD.

The evaluation of risk personality and hazardous attitude has certain safety margin and tolerance range due to individual differences in perception. The initial score obtained through the questionnaire is in a score range, and the standardized scores x_{RP} and x_{HA} are obtained by applying Eq. (1), respectively.

The final score $S_{P\&A}$ of personality traits and attitude module is obtained by applying Eq. (6):

$$S_{P\&A} = (x_{PC} w_{PC} + x_{RP} w_{RP} + x_{HA} w_{HA}) \times x_{PD} \tag{6}$$

Among them, w_{PC}, w_{RP}, w_{HA} are the weights of personality components, risk personality and hazardous attitude, which are obtained by expert scoring method.

The scores of the four modules were summed by Eq. (7) to obtain the score value P_1 of professional adaptability.

$$P_1 = S_{CA} + S_{OA} + S_{SA} + S_{P\&A} \tag{7}$$

The evaluation of mental health module belongs to the category of subjective measurement algorithm, which is divided into two second-level indexes of mental state and mental quality and the weight is determined by expert scoring method.

As for the measurement of mental state, it can be divided into positive state and negative state. Since human mental state is in the game and balance process of positive or negative state, this part is based on the idea of zero-sum game theory, first of all, applying Eq. (1) to standardize the initial scores of the last-level indexes. Equation (2) is then used for weighting and summation. The score of the positive state in the evaluation is multiplied by 1. Conversely, the score of the negative state is multiplied by −1. The sum is further added to obtain the score of mental state.

As for the measurement of mental quality, Eq. (1) is used to standardize the initial scores of the last-level indexes according to the questionnaires or scales, and then Eq. (2) is used to get the scores of self-tendency and adaptability. These two components are further summed to obtain the score of mental quality.

The score value P_2 of the mental health is obtained by applying Eq. (8).

$$P_2 = S_{MS} + S_{MQ} = S_{PS} - S_{NS} + S_{MQ} \tag{8}$$

Among them, S_{MS} is the mental state score, S_{MQ} is the mental quality score, S_{PS} is the positive state score, and S_{NS} is the negative score.

Finally, the final total score value P_T of pilot's psychological competency is obtained by adding all the score values of professional adaptability and mental health applying Eq. (9).

$$P_T = P_1 + P_2 \tag{9}$$

In the specific implementation in the future, the personality traits and attitude and mental health will involve some immature questionnaires and scales with dichotomous dependent variables, and although these questionnaires and scales have a certain level of reliability and validity, they often involve the problem of not being able to find appropriate diagnostic critical value. Receiver Operating Characteristic (ROC), a scientific and quantitative method, can be applied to solve this problem [20]. By calculating the sensitivity and specificity of the ROC curve, the maximum Youden Index (YI) corresponds to the measure of the diagnostic critical value. The Area Under Curve (AUC) can also be obtained by calculating the area under the ROC curve, so as to compare multiple scales and select a more suitable scale for measurement.

According to the above index fusion algorithm, it can be seen that the evaluation of personality disorder and psychological negative state is very strict. The results of these two items will directly affect the overall score of pilot's psychological competency through the fusion algorithm, and pilots who fail these two items will result in a lower overall score. In particular, when the score of personality traits and attitude measurement module is zero, it means that the subjects have been diagnosed with personality disorder, and this will draw the attention of the administrator to screen out problematic pilots in a timely manner and improve the efficiency of data screening, which has applicability in mass psychological testing for airline transport pilots and pilot candidate selection.

4 Evaluation Tool

According to the PLM system requirements of CAAC, this study refers to pilot psychological selection evaluation basis, combined with measurement framework and method, and puts forward the evaluation tool of psychological competency evaluation system for airline transport pilot.

The evaluation system involves a large amount of information input and output, and is an integrated management system, so it is composed of four subsystems, including the management of operation, information input, measurement and data output. The name and functions of the subsystems are shown in Table 1 below.

Table 1. Evaluation subsystems and functions of psychological competency

Subsystem	Function	Function Introduction
System management subsystem	User registration	Fill in the basic identity information, and register for the system evaluation account
	User login	Enter the account number and password to log in to the evaluation system
	User logout	After canceling the account, leave the system operation
Information management subsystem	User information input	Enter the relevant information, according to the evaluation requirements, including words, numbers, letters, and characters
	User information modification	Modify the personal information, and revise the evaluation score
Measurement subsystem	Test selection	Select the corresponding measurement modules and items according to the evaluation requirements
	Simulation test	To help pilots familiarize themselves with the test program and better complete the test, allow for simulation training before the formal test
	Test reminder	When the pilot conducts wrong operation or enters error information, remind and guide the pilot to make the correct information input according to the specification
Data management subsystem	Evaluation result presentation	After the end of the evaluation, the system presents the measurement scores and evaluation
	Measurement data preservation	After the evaluation, the system automatically saves the measurement data
	Measurement data query	After the evaluation, the user can query the measurement data in the backstage management system, and download the relevant data

(continued)

Table 1. (*continued*)

Subsystem	Function	Function Introduction
	Measurement data upload	After the test, the evaluation system will upload the data to the backstage management system in real time

This study also provides the interface design display of Pilot Psychological Competency Assessment System for Civil Aviation Pilot (PCAS-CAP), which is mainly divided into six basic modules: user login, evaluation introduction and terms of use, evaluation device debugging, entry test, evaluation results and help and feedback. The assessment system interface is shown in Fig. 2.

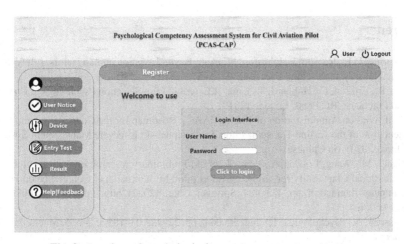

Fig. 2. Interface of psychological competency assessment system

5 Conclusion

Based on the professional characteristics of airline transport pilots and requirements of implementing PLM system put forward by CAAC, this study proposes the measurement framework and method on airline transport pilot's psychological competency by consulting the relevant results of psychological competency and psychological assessment of pilots, which has certain applicability.

Among the five modules of psychological competency measurement framework, the investigation of personality traits and attitude module is primary and principled. Attaching importance to the measurement of personality disorder can help the administrator to select suitable pilot candidates and improve the efficiency of data screening.

The innovation of this study mainly lies in the design of the index fusion algorithm, which integrates the data obtained by objective measurement algorithm and subjective measurement algorithm respectively, and then calculates the psychological competency evaluation scores of pilots by combining the psychological competency measurement framework through standardized calculation.

Finally, the evaluation tool proposed in this study can be used as an example of the implementation of measurement framework and methods. In the next step, a corresponding evaluation tool will be developed and widely promoted for application to airlines to collect pilots test data and determine pilot psychological competency measurement norm through analysis of large sample data, which can provide direct technical support and input for airline transport pilot selection, evaluation and training tools.

Acknowledgments. The authors would like to appreciate the support of the National Natural Science Foundation of China (grant no. 32071063).

References

1. Maurino, D.E., Reason, J., Johnston, N., et al.: Beyond aviation human factors: safety in high technology systems. Hum. Fact. Eng. **3**, 55–57 (1998)
2. Bor, R., Eriksen, C., Hubbard, T., King, R.E. (eds.): Pilot Selection Psychological Principles and Practice. CRC Press, London (2019)
3. Civil Aviation Administration of China (CAAC): Roadmap for the Construction and Implementation of the Airline Transport Pilots Professionalism Lifecycle Management System in China (2020). (in Chinese)
4. Zhang, M., Wang, L., Zou, Y., Peng, J., et al.: Preliminary research on evaluation index of professional adaptability for airline transport pilot. In: International Conference on Human-Computer Interaction, pp. 473–487. Springer, Cham (2022). https://doi.org/10.1007/978-3-031-06086-1_37
5. Anastasi, A.: Psychological Testing, 5th edn., pp. 22–44,103–183,552–555. Macmillan, New York (1982)
6. Qu, C.: The compilation and psychometric analysis of psychological test (in Chinese). Chin. J. Epidemiol. **05**, 451–455 (2006)
7. McCrae, R.R., Costa, P.: Personality in Adulthood. Guilford, New York (1990)
8. Goldberg, L.R.: The structure of phenotypic personality traits. Am. Psychol. **48**, 26–34 (1993)
9. Mosley, E., Laborde, S.: Performing under Pressure. Performance Psychology, pp. 291–314 (2016). https://doi.org/10.1016/b978-0-12-803377-7.00018-1
10. Barrick, M.R., Mount, M.K.: The big five personality dimensions and job performance: a meta-analysis. Pers. Psychol. **44**(1), 1–26 (1991). https://doi.org/10.1111/j.1744-6570.1991.tb00688.x
11. Schmidt, F.L., Hunter, J.E.: The validity and utility of selection methods in personnel psychology: practical and theoretical implications of 85 years of research findings. Psychol. Bull. **124**(2), 262–274 (1998). https://doi.org/10.1037/0033-2909.124.2.262
12. Arthur, W., Graziano, W.G.: The five-factor model, conscientiousness, and driving accident involvement. J. Pers. **63**, 593–618 (1996)
13. Lubner, M.E.: Aviation accidents, incidents, and violations: psychological predictors among United States pilots. Diss. Abstr. Int. **53**, 3003–3004 (1992)

14. Clarke, S., Robertson, I.: A meta-analytic review of the Big Five personality factors and accident involvement in occupational and non-occupational settings. J. Occup. Organ. Psychol. **78**(3), 355–376 (2005). https://doi.org/10.1348/096317905x26183

15. Matthews, G., Dorn, L., Glendon, A.I.: Personality correlates of driver stress. Pers. Individ. Differ. **12**, 535–549 (1991)

16. Kendler, K.S., Gatz, M., Gardner, C.O., Pedersen, N.L.: Personality and major depression: a Swedish longitudinal, population-based twin study. Arch. Gen. Psychiatry **63**(10), 1113–1120 (2006)

17. Hunter, J.E., Schmidt, F.L.: Methods of Meta-Analysis: Correcting Error and Bias in Research Findings. Sage, Newbury Park (1990)

18. Alvarez-Segura, M., Echavarria, M.F., Vitz, P.C.: A psycho-ethical approach to personality disorders: the role of volitionality. New Ideas Psychol. **47**, 49–56 (2017). https://doi.org/10.1016/j.newideapsych.2017.05.003

19. Mosich, Michelle, K.: Reference Module in Neuroscience and Biobehavioral Psychology, Personality Disorders (2018). https://doi.org/10.1016/B978-0-12-809324-5.21226-1

20. Fawcett, T.: An introduction to ROC analysis. **27**(8), 861–874 (2006). https://doi.org/10.1016/j.patrec.2005.10.010

A Study on Real-Time Control Capability Assessment of Approach Controllers

Lili Wang[1], Qiu-Li Gu[2(✉)], and Ke Ren Wang[1]

[1] Air Traffic Management Academy, Civil Aviation University of China, Tianjin 300300, China
[2] College of Computer Science and Technology, Civil Aviation University of China, Tianjin 300300, China
qlgu@cauc.edu.cn

Abstract. In order to evaluate the work capability of approach controllers in real time, further improve the safety of ATC operation and promote the high-quality development of civil aviation. This paper identifies three indicators to assess the real-time capability of approach controllers according to the work characteristics and job requirements: reaction capability, decision-making capability and radar continuous monitoring capability. According to the different traffic volumes of small, medium and large, a controller's real-time capability assessment model was established, and the three indicators were quantified and studied by experimentally using Tobii eye movement instrument to collect controllers' eye movement data, and the weights of the three indicators were determined by using the entropy-CRITIC combination method. The position of approach controller requires the highest reaction capability, followed by radar surveillance capability and decision-making capability. Finally, k-means cluster analysis is used to classify and evaluate the real-time capability of controllers, and the approach controller capability is classified into four levels, with the best capability for Level 1 controllers and the worst capability for Level 4 controllers, and suggestions are given for the capability training of different levels of controllers.

Keywords: Real-time Ability of Controllers · Eye-movement Signals · Entropy-CRITIC Combination Method · K-means Clustering Analysis

1 Introduction

At present, civil aviation of China is in the opening stage of the '14th Five-Year Plan' period. It is one of the main tasks of civil aviation to adhere to the bottom line of flight safety and build a perfect safe and efficient production and operation guarantee system. Air traffic management is an important part of ensuring the safety of civil aviation. With the increasing reliability of air traffic control equipment, the level of capability of air traffic controllers is particularly important for the safety of the ATC system. Therefore, objective, real-time and effective evaluation of controllers' control capability and training for capability shortcomings have important theoretical value and practical significance for continuous improvement of aviation operation safety and efficiency.

By summarizing the research results of domestic and foreign scholars, we found that the current research on air controller competence mainly includes three aspects: controller comprehensive competence, controller competence, and controller safety competence. Foreign scholars mainly focus on the comprehensive competency of controllers. Scholar Petri A M [1] adjusted the traditional competency assessment model in ESARR5 and formed a new hexagonal competency assessment model, including control skills, knowledge, experience, adaptability, pay-driven competency and social competency, and considered social competency to be the most important. S. K. Soldatov [2] summarized the most essential core skills of controllers as: search, detection, situational awareness, and decision-making ability. Domestic scholars have established an assessment system for controller competency based on three models of competency: the four-dimensional model, the iceberg model and the onion model. Scholars Li Jingqiang [3] established a four-dimensional model of meta-competence, cognitive competency, social competency and functional competency. Lu Hantao [4] established a competency iceberg model assessment system based on the iceberg model theory, which consists of seven indicators: job knowledge, general job competence, general cognitive competence, self-perception, job values, good qualities, and achievement motivation. According to the onion theory model, Yang Fan [5] took knowledge and skills as the outer layer factors that are easier to learn and master, and psychological quality, cognitive ability and military political quality as the inner layer factors that are difficult to acquire later in life, which provided an important theoretical basis for the selection mechanism of matching people to jobs in military aviation towers. For the study of controllers' safety competence, scholars Chen Fang [6] firstly defined the connotation of controllers' safety competence, and established a controller safety competence model with three dimensions of physical quality, operational quality and awareness according to the connotation and the work characteristics of controllers. Ma Mengyao [7] proposed a safety competence assessment system for small and medium-sized airport controllers consisting of five first-level indicators: control knowledge and skills, personal traits and cognition, social relationships and actions, control unit operational data and workload, and unit staffing.

Through the above studies, it is found that most of the domestic and foreign scholars' researches on controllers' competencies focus on the construction opinions on the competencies and qualities that controllers should have, and the selection of indicators based on access purpose, job matching purpose and safety operation purpose, without specific analysis on controllers' control competency assessment indicators. In summary, this paper will extract controllers' real-time capability indicators through existing literature and combine with the characteristics of controllers' work, collect controllers' eye movement data by using Tobii eye movement instrument, establish controllers' normal control capability model, and use entropy-CRITIC combination method to determine indicator weights, and use k-means cluster analysis method to classify and evaluate controllers' real-time capability, hoping to provide reference for ATC units to understand the real-time capability of controllers.

2 Method

2.1 Participants

The subjects in this experiment were approach controllers of an air traffic control unit, all of whom were male and right-handed, and there were 40 in total. They ranged in age from 27 to 43, with a mean age of 32.7. All 40 subjects held control licenses, and their service age distribution ranged from 3 to 21 years. Among them, 4 had 3 to 5 years of service and 36 had 6 to 21 years of service. The age and service age distribution of controllers was shown in Fig. 1.

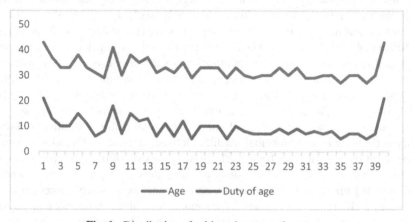

Fig. 1. Distribution of subjects by age and post age

2.2 Research Framework

The position of an air traffic controller requires him or her to have key information in a limited time frame and to make immediate and rational decisions. Therefore, air traffic controllers should have a keen sense of sight and hearing, rigorous logical thinking, clear verbal expression and decisive decision-making ability. The approach control area is the terminal part of the jurisdiction, and is an area prone to dangerous events, which requires a high level of mental state, continuous radar monitoring and coordination.

Therefore, based on the actual work capability requirements of approach controllers, the following indicators were determined for approach control capability assessment.

(1) Reactivity. Refers to the controller's identification, understanding and projection of the aircraft's position, which determines how quickly the controller finds the target when monitoring radar display data, and therefore requires measuring the time interval between the aircraft entry into the jurisdictional area and controller clicks on that aircraft's placard.

(2) Decision-making ability. It refers to the controller's ability to use professional technical knowledge to make a comprehensive assessment of information after identifying

the aircraft and make relevant decisions and plans quickly and accurately, and issue correct instructions to the pilot, which determines the speed of the controller to solve the problem after analysis and judgment, so it is necessary to record the total time interval of aircraft from entering jurisdictional area to leaving.

(3) Continuous radar monitoring capability. The extent to which the controller tracks the aircraft's movement from the time it enters the controller's jurisdiction until it leaves the area.It determines the rationality of controller attention allocation and the probability of potential risk caused by interruption of monitoring without disposition. Therefore, it is necessary to measure the number of controller's eyes on each aircraft.

2.3 Scenario

The scenarios are including all approach activities relevant to departure, arrival, apron activities, abnormal operations and special environment operations. In practice, due to changes in traffic flow, controllers experience certain stress reactions due to different levels of traffic complexity [8]. This leads to fluctuations of different magnitudes in the controller's various abilities. To further quantitatively assess the control capability of controllers under actual traffic flow conditions. The author designed three control capability assessment models for small, medium and large traffic levels, and then synthesized to obtain a real-time control capability assessment model.

2.4   Data Collection Process

Selection of Variables to Assess the Characteristics of Indicators. Based on assessment metrics and data from eye-tracking measurements, determine the measured variables for controllers' responsiveness, decision-making ability, and radar continuous monitoring capability.

(1) Responsiveness.

Mean time to first gaze:

$$\overline{FFD_i} = \frac{1}{N_i} \sum_j \alpha_{ij} \tag{1}$$

(2) Decision-making capacity.

Mean processing time:

$$\overline{TFD_i} = \frac{1}{N_i} \sum_j \beta_{ij} \tag{2}$$

(3) Continuous radar monitoring capability.

Number of visits variance:

$$V_{VC_i} = \sqrt{\frac{(\gamma_{ij} - \frac{1}{N_i} \sum_j \gamma_{ij})^2}{N_i}} \tag{3}$$

where: $i = 1, 2, 3$, represents the small, medium and high traffic levels respectively; j represents the jth aircraft; α_{ij}, β_{ij} and γ_{ij} represent the first gaze time, total gaze time and number of visits of the subject at the appearance of the jth aircraft at the i-th traffic level respectively; N_i represents the number of aircraft appearances at the i-th traffic level.

The first time mean reflects the average length of time it takes for all aircraft to enter their jurisdiction to identify each aircraft during the monitoring of radar data at a certain traffic level. The smaller the mean value, the higher the average level of the controller's response capability. The faster the response time, the better the controller's ability to predict the position of the aircraft in advance. The smaller the mean value, the more effective and accurate the controller's decision making is, and the higher the average level of controller's decision making ability. The variance of the number of visits reflects the fluctuation of the controller's radar continuous monitoring capability, the smaller the variance, the more stable the controller's radar continuous monitoring capability and the more reasonable the allocation of attention. The mean number of visits was not chosen as the average level of radar continuous monitoring capability because each controller has individual habits and patterns of allocating attention, and there is no uniform standard. A smaller value does not indicate that the controller is not paying enough attention to the aircraft, and a larger value does not indicate that the controller is paying too much attention to it, so the variance of visits was chosen to quantify the controller's radar continuous monitoring capability.

Entropy-CRITIC Combination Method of Weight Calculation. The entropy weighting method is an objective assignment that can be used for multiple evaluation schemes and multiple evaluation indicators, where weights are determined by the magnitude of the variation in the indicators [9]. However, when the entropy weights of all indicators are close to 1, small differences can lead to exponential changes in the weight values and be assigned mismatched weights. The CRITIC weighting method is an objective assignment method that combines the weights of indicators based on the strength of contrast of evaluation indicators and the conflict between indicators [10], but does not measure the degree of dispersion between indicators. By solving for the combined weight coefficients, a game-theoretic aggregation model [10, 11] is used to minimize the difference between the combined weights and the weights obtained by the entropy and CRITIC weighting methods respectively. The game-theoretic aggregation model allows the contribution rates of the two aforementioned weighting methods to be determined according to the nature of the indicator data, providing a more objective and accurate method of calculating contribution rates than average or artificial assignments.

The object of evaluation in this paper is the controller, and the values of the evaluation object are the experimental data of the controller's gaze behavior. Therefore, when calculating the weights of each indicator, it is necessary to consider not only the discrete degree between indicators, but also the contrast strength and conflict between indicators. Therefore, the entropy-CRITIC combination method and the game theory assembly model are used to calculate the combination weight coefficients in a more objective way to reflect the indicator weights.

(1) Firstly, the raw data matrix is counted. Assuming that there are m evaluation objects, each with n indicators, construct the raw data matrix R:

$$R = (r_{ij})_{m \times n} \tag{4}$$

Standardize the original matrix R to obtain the new matrix R':

$$R' = (r'_{ij})_{m \times n} \tag{5}$$

where $i = 1, 2, \cdots, m$; $j = 1, 2, \cdots, n$. When the indicator is positive, $r'_{ij} = \frac{r_{ij} - r_{min}}{r_{max} - r_{min}}$. When the indicator is negative, $r'_{ij} = \frac{r_{max} - r_j}{r_{max} - r_{min}}$. r_{max} and r_{min} are the maximum and minimum values of the same indicator for different evaluation objects, respectively.

(2) Define the entropy of the evaluation indicator H_j.

$$H_j = -k \sum_{i=1}^{m} f_{ij} \times \ln f_{ij} \tag{6}$$

where $f_{ij} = \frac{r'_{ij}}{\sum\limits_{i=1}^{m} r'_{ij}}$, $k = \frac{1}{\ln m}$, and $f_{ij} \times \ln f_{ij} = 0$ when $f_{ij} = 0$.

(3) Define the entropy weights of the evaluation indicators ω_j^1.

$$\omega_j^1 = \frac{1 - H_j}{n - \sum\limits_{j=1}^{n} H_j} \tag{7}$$

where $0 \leq \omega_j^1 \leq 1$ and satisfies $\sum\limits_{j=1}^{n} \omega_j^1 = 1$.

(4) Define the variability of the indicator S_j, expressed as a standard deviation.

$$S_j = \sqrt{\frac{\sum\limits_{i=1}^{n} (r'_{ij} - \overline{r'_j})^2}{n - 1}} \tag{8}$$

where $\overline{r'_j} = \frac{1}{m} \sum\limits_{i=1}^{m} r'_{ij}$.

(5) Define the conflicting nature of the indicators δ_j, expressed as a correlation coefficient.

$$\delta_j = \sum_{i=1}^{m} (1 - r'_{ij}) \tag{9}$$

(6) Define the amount of information C_j.

$$C_j = S_j \times \delta_j \tag{10}$$

(7) Define objective weights ω_j^2.

$$\omega_j^2 = \frac{C_j}{\sum\limits_{j=1}^{n} C_j} \tag{11}$$

(8) The weight vector calculated by the entropy weighting method is denoted as W_1^T and The weight vector calculated by the CRITIC assignment method is denoted as W_2^T and W is defined as a linear combination of W_1^T and W_2^T

$$W = \sum_{p=1}^{2} \alpha_p \cdot W_p^T \tag{12}$$

where $p = 1, 2, \alpha_p$ are the combined weighting coefficients,α_1 are the weighting coefficients for the entropy weighting method and α_2 are the weighting coefficients for the CRITIC weighting method.

(9) Define the objective function L based on the principles of the agglomeration model of game theory.

$$L: \min \left\| \sum_{p=1}^{2} \alpha_p \cdot W_p^T - W_i^T \right\| \tag{13}$$

where $i = 1, 2$.

According to the matrix differentiation property, the optimal first order derivative condition is obtained by deriving the above equation as

$$\sum_{p=1}^{2} \alpha_p \cdot W_i \cdot W_p^T = W_i \cdot W_i^T \tag{14}$$

(10) Define a system of linear equations optimized by the objective function and solve for α_p.

$$\begin{pmatrix} W_1 \cdot W_1^T & W_1 \cdot W_2^T & \cdots & W_1 \cdot W_p^T \\ W_2 \cdot W_1^T & W_2 \cdot W_2^T & \cdots & W_2 \cdot W_p^T \\ \vdots & \vdots & \vdots & \vdots \\ W_i \cdot W_1^T & W_i \cdot W_2^T & \cdots & W_i \cdot W_p^T \end{pmatrix} \begin{pmatrix} \alpha_1 \\ \alpha_2 \\ \vdots \\ \alpha_p \end{pmatrix} = \begin{pmatrix} W_1 \cdot W_1^T \\ W_2 \cdot W_2^T \\ \vdots \\ W_i \cdot W_i^T \end{pmatrix} \tag{15}$$

(11) Normalize α_p to obtain α_p' and obtain the final combination weight W'.

$$W' = \sum_{p=1}^{2} \alpha_p' W_p^T \tag{16}$$

3   Results and Discussion

3.1   Model for the Assessment of Approach Control Real-Time Capability

Firstly, the weights of each controller's control ability are calculated for different traffic levels. Then the assessment model of each controller's control ability is derived. Finally, the assessment model of the average level of approach controller's real-time control ability is integrated. The calculation is illustrated by the example of response capability.

(1) Responsiveness

$\overline{FFD}$ is the mean value of the first gaze time for the 40 sample subjects at different flow levels. Build the original data matrix:

$$R = \begin{pmatrix} 0.290 & 0.142 & 0.320 \\ 0.166 & 0.215 & 0.457 \\ \vdots & \vdots & \vdots \\ 0.212 & 0.314 & 0.663 \end{pmatrix}$$

The normalized matrix is obtained according to Eq. (5).

$$R' = \begin{pmatrix} 0.717 & 0.922 & 0.676 \\ 0.888 & 0.821 & 0.487 \\ \vdots & \vdots & \vdots \\ 0.825 & 0.684 & 0.202 \end{pmatrix}$$

The entropy of the reactivity at different flow levels is obtained according to Eq. (6) and is shown in Table 1 below.

Table 1. Entropy of response capacity at different flow levels

Small flow class	Medium flow class	High flow class
0.970	0.950	0.963

The weights calculated by the entropy weighting method can be obtained from Eq. (7).

$$W_1 = (0.229, 0.516, 0.255)$$

The standard deviations of the response capacity at each flow level obtained from Eq. (8) are shown in Table 2 below.

Firstly, SPSS was used to conduct correlation analysis of the standardized observed data of all subjects at each traffic level. And then the correlation coefficient was calculated according to Eq. (9). The results of the analysis are shown in Tables 3 and 4 below, respectively.

Table 2. Standard deviation of response capacity at different flow levels

Small flow class	Medium flow class	High flow class
0.260	0.426	0.314

Table 3. Correlation matrix for responsiveness at different flow levels

	Small flow class	Medium flow class	High flow class
Small flow class	1.000	−0.252	0.000
Medium flow class	−0.252	1.000	0.199
High flow class	0.000	0.199	1.000

Table 4. Correlation coefficients for responsiveness at different flow levels

Small flow class	Medium flow class	High flow rating
2.252	2.053	1.801

The amount of information obtained for the response capacity at each flow level according to Eq. (10) is shown in Table 5 below.

The weights calculated by the CRITIC assignment method can be obtained from Eq. (11).

$$W_2 = (0.504, 0.185, 0.311)$$

Table 5. Amount of information on responsiveness at different flow levels

Small flow class	Medium flow class	High flow class
0.566	0.208	0.349

It can be seen that there are differences in weight assignment between the two methods, so it is necessary to carry out weight integralization. According to the aggregation model (15), it can be written as:

$$\begin{pmatrix} W_1 \cdot W_1^T & W_1 \cdot W_2^T \\ W_2 \cdot W_1^T & W_2 \cdot W_2^T \end{pmatrix} \begin{pmatrix} \alpha_1 \\ \alpha_2 \end{pmatrix} = \begin{pmatrix} W_1 \cdot W_1^T \\ W_2 \cdot W_2^T \end{pmatrix}$$

Using PYTHON software, solve for $\alpha_1 = 0.394$, $\alpha_2 = 0.686$.

From Eq. (16) the optimal weights for the response capacity at different flow levels can be derived as shown in Table 6 below.

Table 6. Optimal weights for responsiveness at different flow levels

Small flow class	Medium flow class	High flow class
0.436	0.330	0.314

This leads to the formula for assessing responsiveness as

$$y_1 = 0.436 \times \overline{FFD_1} + 0.330 \times \overline{FFD_2} + 0.314 \times \overline{FFD_3} \tag{17}$$

(2) Decision-making capacity

The optimal weights for the decision capabilities at different flow levels are shown in Table 7 below.

Table 7. Optimal weights for decision capabilities at different flow levels

Small flow class	Medium flow class	High flow rating
0.435	0.306	0.260

This leads to the formula for assessing decision-making capacity as

$$y_2 = 0.435 \times \overline{TFD_1} + 0.306 \times \overline{TFD_2} + 0.260 \times \overline{TFD_3} \tag{18}$$

(3) Continuous radar monitoring capability

The optimal weights for continuous radar monitoring capability at different traffic levels are shown in Table 8 below.

Table 8. Optimal weights for continuous radar monitoring capability at different traffic levels

Small flow class	Medium flow class	High flow class
0.245	0.454	0.301

This leads to the formula for assessing the continuous monitoring capability of the radar as

$$y_3 = 0.245 \times V_{VC_1} + 0.454 \times V_{VC_2} + 0.301 \times V_{VC_3} \qquad (19)$$

3.2 Model for the Assessment of Approach Control Comprehensive Capability

First, the values of each competency were calculated for all subjects according to the assessment formulae (17)–(19) to obtain the standardized matrix $R' = \begin{pmatrix} 0.590\ 0.549\ 0.912 \\ 0.558\ 0.781\ 0.922 \\ \vdots \quad \vdots \quad \vdots \\ 0.238\ 0.743\ 0.784 \end{pmatrix}$.

The weights $W_1 = (0.421, 0.257, 0.322)$ is calculated by the entropy-CRITIC method can be obtained from Eqs. (6)–(7). The weights $W_2 = (0.440, 0.232, 0.327)$ is calculated by the CRITIC method from Eqs. (8)–(11). It can be seen that although the weights obtained by the two assignment methods are still not identical, the differences are significantly smaller, which proves that the entropy-CRITIC combination method can obtain more objective and accurate weighting results.

The optimal weights for each regulatory capacity were calculated according to Eqs. (12)–(16) and are shown in Table 9 below.

Table 9. Optimal weights for each regulatory capacity

Reactivity	Decision-making capacity	Radar continuous monitoring capability
0.509	0.145	0.346

Thus, the evaluation formula of real-time control capability is as follows.

$$Y_1 = 0.509y_1 + 0.145y_2 + 0.346y_3 \qquad (20)$$

3.3 Clustering Analysis of Real-Time Control Ability of Approach Controllers

One of the defects of k-means algorithm is that it is difficult to determine k value, so k value can be determined objectively and scientifically through elbow diagram [12]. The core indicator of the elbow method is the intra-cluster sum of squares, i.e. the clustering error of all samples, which indicates the degree of clustering effectiveness, expressed as WCSS. The formula for calculating WCSS is as follows.

$$WCSS = \sum_{i=1}^{k} \sum_{x_i \in C_i} |x_i - \mu_k|^2 \tag{21}$$

PYTHON was used for clustering calculation and analysis, and k = 4 was obtained, as shown in Fig. 2.

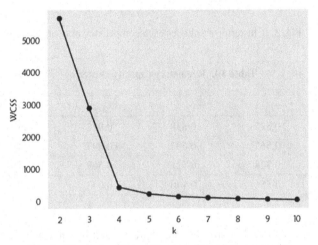

Fig. 2. Clustering elbow diagram of regulatory capacity

The iteration was terminated when the cluster centroids of each cluster converged to the same level. The visualised 3D clustering scatter plot for each ability is shown in Fig. 3 below. The subjects are divided into 4 categories, which are distinguished by 4 symbols: ■▼+X, where ● denotes the cluster centroid of each cluster. The clustering effect is more obvious from the Fig. 3.

The final cluster center results of control capabilities represent the average level of various capabilities of the four types of controllers, as shown in Table 10 below.

The data for category 1 controllers are characterized by the largest values for y_1, y_2 and y_3 compared to the last three categories, and their competence characteristics indicate optimal reaction, decision making and continuous radar monitoring capabilities. The controllers in this category show a high level of sensitivity to the aircraft [13], the ability to quickly and correctly handle the aircraft, and a stable average distribution of attention, which makes the controller less likely to make a human error, and this category has a high overall control capability.

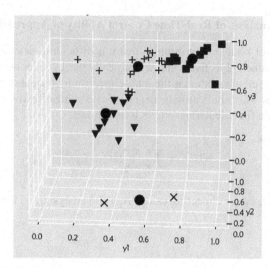

Fig. 3. Clustering results for each competency of controllers

Table 10. Regulatory capacity clustering

Category	y_1	y_2	y_3	Number
1	0.827	0.838	0.922	11
2	0.567	0.692	0.897	4
3	0.328	0.521	0.569	11
4	0.556	0.146	0.033	2

The data for category 2 controllers are characterized by intermediate values for y_1 and y_2 and larger values for y_3. They are characterized by moderate reaction and decision making abilities, but have good continuous radar monitoring. Category 2 controllers are slightly slower to react, take longer to make decisions and are less accurate than category 1 controllers, so training is needed for these two abilities.

The data for category 3 controllers are characterized by the smallest values of y_1 compared to the other three categories, with the values of y_2 and y_3 in the middle of the range. Their competence is characterized by a low level of reactivity and a medium level of decision making and continuous radar monitoring. The slow recognition of aircraft by these controllers indicates a low level of situational awareness. This group of controllers should focus on reaction skills, while training in decision making and continuous radar monitoring should not be relaxed.

The data for the 4 categories of controllers are characterized by intermediate values for y_1, with the smallest values for y_2 and y_3 compared to the previous 3. Their capabilities are characterized by moderate reaction capabilities, with the weakest decision making capabilities and continuous radar monitoring. These controllers are unable to make quick and accurate decisions about aircraft, and their attention to aircraft is unstable, resulting in excessive attention to some aircraft and neglect of others. This category of controller may not only cause congestion in the normal flow of traffic, but may also make human error in missing aircraft, and the distracted attention may cause visual fatigue which may lead to other risks. This category of controller needs to focus on strengthening their decision-making skills and their ability to monitor radar continuously, as well as strengthening their reaction skills.

4 Conclusion

1. In this thesis, three indicators were identified to assess the real-time capability of approach controllers: reaction capability, decision making capability and radar continuous monitoring capability, in response to the work characteristics and requirements of approach controllers. A model for assessing the real-time capability of controllers was established for small, medium and large traffic volumes. The three indicators were quantified and the weight of the three indicators was determined by using the entropy-CRITIC combination method. This indicates that the position of approach controller requires the highest reaction ability, followed by radar surveillance ability and decision making ability.
2. Based on the ability values of the three indicators, k-means cluster analysis was used to classify and evaluate the real-time ability of controllers, and the approach controllers were classified into four levels of ability. Level 1 controllers were the most capable, with the best performance in response, decision making and radar continuous monitoring. The responsiveness and decision-making capacity of level 2 controllers needs to be strengthened. Level 3 controllers are the least responsive and require special training, while the other two capacities also need to be strengthened. Level 4 controllers are the weakest in decision making and continuous radar monitoring, which can easily lead to congestion and safety hazards, and need to strengthen the training intensity of these three skills to reduce safety hazards in control work.
3. The above study only focuses on the assessment of controller capability for different traffic levels under normal conditions, and will continue to study the capability of different controllers under special conditions in the future. It is hoped that the above study can provide reference for the air traffic control units to assess the real-time capability of approach controllers and further enhance the safety and efficiency of aviation operations.

Acknowledgements. The cooperation of air traffic controllers in the study is greatly appreciated, and it is their support that enabled the authors to successfully complete the experimental content and conduct the controller competency assessment study.

References

1. Petri, A.M.: Competence Assessment of Air Traffic Controllers: a transition from Safety-I to Safety-II. Business (2015)

2. Soldatov, S.K.: Professionally important skills of air traffic controllers. Hum. Physiol. **44**(7), 775–778 (2018)
3. Jingqiang, L., Hao, L., Ning, Z., et al.: Competency model and analysis on its influence relationship for air traffic controller. J. Saf. Sci. Technol. **12**(02), 175–180 (2016)
4. Hantao, L., Maolin, Y.: Study on the competency model of controllers in civil aviation guangzhou control center. Oper. Manage. **05**, 86–92 (2021)
5. Yang Fan, Y., Minjian, L.Y., et al.: Research on flight controller job competency under tower command model reform. J. Inf. Eng. Univ. **22**(01), 112–118 (2021)
6. Chen, F., Luo, Y.: Study on Safety Capability Model of Air Traffic Controllers. China Saf. Sci. J. **22**(01), 17–23 (2012)
7. Mengyao, M.: Research on Safety Capability of Small and Medium Airport Controllers Based on Analytic Hierarchy Process-Classification Management Model. Civil Aviation Flight University of China (2020)
8. Yong, Y.: Quantitative Research on Controllers' Situational Awareness. Civil Aviation University of China (2020)
9. Li, F., Li, D.P.: A portfolio evaluation model based on entropy weight method. Inf. Technol. Informatization **09**, 148–150 (2021)
10. Jialiang, C.: Research on the evaluation method of portfolio assignment based on game theory. Fujian Comput. **09**, 15–16 (2003)
11. Libo, H., Baohui, M.: Evaluation of water resources carrying capacity in haine riverbasin based on combinatorial game theory. Water Resour. Power **39**(11), 61–64 (2021)
12. Cui, M.: Introduction to the K-means clustering algorithm based on the elbow method. Acc. Auditing Finance **3**, 9–16 (2020)
13. Yang, J.Z.: Analysis of human factors of flight altitude deviation. J. Civ. Aviat. Flight Acad. China **03**, 16–18 (2000)

A Method for Evaluating Flight Cadets' Operational Performance Based on Simulated Flight Data

Feiyin Wang, Wei Tan[✉], Jintong Yuan, Wenqing Wang, Wenchao Wang,
and Hang Li

College of Safety Science and Engineering, Civil Aviation University of China, Tianjin 300300,
China
weitan2011@outlook.com

Abstract. Building a sound Professionalism Lifecycle Management System for
pilot skills is very necessary and a general trend, among which the evaluation
of pilot cadets' operation performance is an indispensable part. In this paper,
the maneuvering skills of the cadets in the basic flight simulation training of
aircraft are evaluated. The takeoff and landing routes reflect the most basic and
important driving skills, eye, hand and foot coordination ability and attention
distribution ability in flight. In the test, the cadets are designed to simulate the
takeoff and landing routes. Based on the data of simulated flight parameters, the key
characteristic indexes are extracted and the flight control points of take-off, climb,
approach and landing are integrated for the various safety risk events easily caused
in flight. Through programming, the intelligent automatic quantitative evaluation
of the level of evaluation operation indicators achieved by each subject in the
simulated flight is realized. A flight cadets' operational performance evaluation
method based on simulated flight data is proposed to reflect the pilot cadets'
level of handling technology. In addition, based on the above evaluation results
of simulated flight operations, specific and feasible improvement measures are
provided according to the actual flight and training experience of captains of an
airline company for different safety risk events that may be caused by deviation of
each indicator, and a suggestion library for improvement measures is established
to form a closed loop and improve the operation level of flight cadets.

Keywords: Operational Performance · Flight Cadets · Evaluation Method ·
Safety Risk

1   Introduction

Aircraft basic flight simulation training is mainly relying on the flight simulation software
and the manipulation of the built driving wheel, in accordance with the flight plan on
the experimental platform for manual flight, the simulation flight is completed mainly
through the actual flight trajectory displayed on the navigation display as the output of the
flight results. In this whole process, whether the actual flight maneuvering of the flight

student meets the maneuvering requirements of the aircraft type, whether the aircraft has entered the overrun state, and whether there are safety risks in the flight maneuvering cannot be fully and quantitatively reflected. Therefore, it is necessary to quantify the maneuvering behavior of flight students through flight simulation data to truly reflect their flight skills and whether they can master and apply the knowledge of instrument display information, basic flight concepts, flight rules, and aircraft performance.

For the study of flight operation, Zheng Lei [1] et al. based on QAR data started from feature extraction and similarity measure of multivariate time series data of flight parameters, mined flight operation modes by clustering, studied the distribution of relevant QAR monitoring index values for different flight operation modes, and finally quantified the risk levels of different flight operation modes. In the study of flight operations, Sun Ruishan and Xiao Yabing [2] analyzed the pilot's operational behavior based on the psychological principles of operational behavior, combined with the characteristics of the pilot's operational behavior, and formed a complete set of index structure reflecting the pilot's operational characteristics by combining QAR data and relevant monitoring standards. Sun Ruishan and Li Chongfeng [3] used the k-SC time series clustering algorithm and analyzed the relationship between clustering results and unsafe events based on the K-W test. The results showed that there were five different operation modes of the fleet, and there were significant differences in the distribution of landing level drift distance among different operation modes. Sun Ruishan and Liu Yinfu [4] investigated the overall tendency of pilots in flight operations and pilot operating styles and found that there were significant differences in the flight status of aircraft operated by pilots with different operating styles. Wang Lei, Wang Shuai et al. [5] selected wavelet functions to analyze the pilot stick and pitch angle parameters in the landing phase, based on the airborne fast access recorder data and wavelet analysis method, the wavelet analysis method can be combined with flight data for the analysis and evaluation of flight operations. Wang Lei, Dong Chuanting et al. [6] quantitatively evaluated the operational skills of pilots and applied the power spectrum principle to develop a flight skill evaluation model, and finally applied QAR data collected from airlines to verify the practicality and reliability of the model. Wang Lei, Guo Shiguang et al. [7] applied the curve similarity method to quantitatively evaluate the flight landing operation level with real flight data. The validation results showed that the smaller the consistency measure, the higher the similarity between the actual curve and the target curve; the higher the pilot's landing operation level.

In the study of flight risk, Qi Mingliang et al. [8] used flight data from several flights to establish a mathematical model and designed an algorithm based on the golden mean to find out the boundary values of the interval on the operation index, so as to diagnose the high-risk area that may trigger the QAR overrun event and determine the "high-risk subspace" where the flight quality monitoring overrun event occurs in the "space" composed of the pilot's comprehensive operation indicators. Shao Xueyan et al. [9] established a risk analysis model of flight operations by combining the Copula function and Logistic regression and designed an evolutionary algorithm by combining the characteristics of the model to realize the high-risk operations with QAR exceedance through the model-seeking process. Lei Nie et al. [10] used the support vector machine (SVM) to establish an intelligent diagnostic model for the hard landing, analyzed the relevant factors that have an impact on long landing, and finally used sample data for training and validation to prove that the method can effectively determine whether a hard landing has occurred, and the accuracy rate is as high as 92.86%.Lu et al. [11] explored a new autoregressive pre-trained hard landing prediction method that treats QAR data as multivariate time series and processes and converts them into symbolic representations. These landing marker sequences are pre-trained in an autoregressive manner to predict the next landing state based on the previous landing state, and the pre-trained aircraft landing model is fine-tuned on the hard landing training set to predict hard landings. Lv et al. [12] proposed a new method to assess the overrun risk by constructing an overrun hazard line to assess the overrun risk, and three machine learning models were used to examine the association between the overrun risk index and the flight parameters. It was concluded that the most risk factors for overrun events during the landing phase were long grounding distance and premature brake release during the deceleration phase. Lan et al. [13] analyzed the flight data of jet transport aircraft for potential safety issues and organized the filtered data into longitudinal and lateral aerodynamic model data with dynamic ground effects. The model data were refined into numerical models by fuzzy logic algorithms for nonlinear flight dynamics simulations. The results of the nonlinear flight simulations suggest that the vertical winds acting on the aircraft may be mainly updrafts with changing flight paths before landing. The changing updraft appears to make the descent rate more difficult to control, resulting in higher gravity loads at landing. Barry et al. [14] extracted features related to runway excursion feature factors from flight data of Airbus A320 series aircraft and compared the Bayesian search and GTT algorithms in conjunction with meteorological data and other features. Cross-validation of the resulting networks showed that the two algorithms produced networks with similar performance, and subjective analysis concluded that the GTT algorithm was slightly preferable. The resulting networks produce relative probabilities that airlines can use to quantitatively assess the risk of runway deviation under different scenarios, such as different meteorological conditions and unstable approaches. Li et al. [15] developed two cluster-based anomaly detection algorithms, ClusterAD-Flight and ClusterAD-Data Sample, based on flight data recorder (FDR) data and applied cluster analysis to detect anomalous flights, and evaluated the whole detection method using real flight data and domain experts. The results show that both clustering-based detection algorithms outperform existing methods and both are able to identify significant operational anomalies. Wang Lei, Jiang Yin et al. [16] developed the questionnaire of pilot risk portrait index system for airline pilots. As a risk assessment method based on big data theory, the pilot risk portrait can effectively quantify the personal risk of pilots. In order to prevent the risk analysis model of landing over-limit based on QAR data and the Bayesian network, Wang Lei, Sun Jinglu, et al. [17] used the GeNIe3.0 software GTT algorithm for parameter learning to obtain the Bayesian network model of landing over-limit risk, and the study showed that the Bayesian network of landing overrun risk can effectively analyze the causal relationship of landing over-limit events. Zheng et al. [18] conducted a study on fatigue detection of pilots and developed an improved mobile phone-based PVT (Psychomotor Vigilance Task) software to provide data support for rationalizing personnel work and preventing fatigue risk.

At present, there is more research on route flight and less research on flight simulation. The purpose of this paper is to collect flight data of cadets operating the simulator according to the target flight route under the set flight simulation experiment environment, visualize and analyze the key flight parameters, and establish a reasonable flight simulation data evaluation index system and method to analyze and evaluate the mastery of flight cadets' flight simulation maneuvers. At the same time, we propose targeted improvement measures according to different flight maneuvering problems of flight cadets to help flight cadets reach the training standards as soon as possible and improve their competency.

2   Methodology

2.1   Establishment of Simulated Flight Operation Evaluation Index System

When establishing the evaluation index system, due to the characteristics of the simulator, pilot cadets' control performance may be delayed or not directly reflected in the state of the aircraft. Therefore, the evaluation needs to integrate the influencing factors of pilot cadets' control behavior and aircraft performance state. Pilot cadets realize flight by controlling control components, and their driving skills are mainly reflected in the control ability of pilot rod, steering disc or throttle. As different control parts have different characteristics, pilot cadets need to accurately master the characteristics and control methods of each part. Early, late or incorrect control may cause serious consequences. Therefore, flight control needs to be in line with norms, smooth and timely. The control skills of flight cadets are quantified into the following three parts:

(1) **Normative**: In the process of completing the task, it must comply with the legal flight rules, comply with the relevant provisions of the model manual and the operation specifications, such as whether the deceleration plate is not positioned in the approach stage and whether the climb rate meets the regulations;

(2) **Stability**: To measure the degree of consistency, smoothness and stability of pilot cadets' manipulation behavior. For example, the smoothness of the steering lever in the leveling stage and the stability of the take-off direction;

(3) **Timeliness**: Measure whether the pilot cadets have carried out the operation in time, such as the timing of push rod selection, etc.

According to the requirements of flight standard management manual and the event types of airline quality control, a simulated flight control index evaluation system is established for different flight stages, especially approach and landing stages with high accident rate and incident rate.

Referring to the standard operating procedures in the flight crew operation manual and the company operation manual, the established simulated flight maneuver evaluation indicators are shown in Table 1, which also lists the simulated flight parameters involved in the quantification of each indicator in the four phases.

Table 1. Simulated flight operation evaluation indicators and quantification basis

Phases	Indicator codes	Indicator names	Required flight parameters
Take-off phase	T1	Consistency of elevator dimensional control during takeoff	Elevator input
	T2	Consistency of aileron dimensional control during takeoff	Aileron input
	T3	Consistency of rudder dimensional control during takeoff	Rudder input
	T4	Stability of takeoff direction	Heading, engine thrust, air-to-ground switch, wind direction, wind speed
	T5	Lift front wheel speed up to standard	Air speed, ground speed, analytical angle of throttle lever, air-ground switch
	T6	Liftoff Speed up to standard	Air speed, ground speed, air-ground switch, analytical angle of throttle lever
	T7	Liftoff pitch angle up to standard	Pitch angle, air-ground switch, analytical angle of throttle lever, control column position
	T8	Head-up speed up to standard	Pitch angle, air-ground switch, analytical angle of throttle lever
	T9	Takeoff bank angle up to standard	Air-ground switch, radio altitude, roll, left engine N1, right engine N1
Climbing phase	C1	Consistency of elevator dimensional control during climbing	Elevator input
	C2	Consistency of aileron dimensional control during climbing	Aileron input
	C3	Consistency of rudder dimensional control during climbing	Rudder input

(*continued*)

Table 1. (*continued*)

Phases	Indicator codes	Indicator names	Required flight parameters
	C4	Climbing speed up to standard	Air-ground switch, radio altitude, airspeed, left engine N1, right engine N1
	C5	Bank angle up to the standard	Air-ground switch, radio height, roll angle, control column position
	C6	Whether climbing appears to run out of altitude	Air-ground switch, height, left engine N1, right engine N1
Approach phase	A1	Consistency of elevator dimensional control during approach	Elevator input
	A2	Consistency of aileron dimensional control during approach	Aileron input
	A3	Consistency of rudder dimensional control during approach	Rudder input
	A4	Sinkrate 2000–1000 (inclusive) ft	Vertical speed, altitude, air-ground switch
	A5	Sinkrate 1000–500 (inclusive) ft	Vertical speed, altitude, air-ground switch
	A6	Sinkrate 500–50 ft	Vertical speed, altitude, air-ground switch
	A7	Approach bank angle 1500–500 (inclusive) ft	Vertical speed, altitude, air-ground switch
	A8	Low altitude whether to use speed brakes	altitude, speed brake position, left engine N1, right engine N1
	A9	Whether the approaching stage speed brakes are prepositioned	altitude, speed brake position, left engine N1, right engine N1
	A10	Low altitude speed	Airspeed, altitude, left engine N1, right engine N1
	A11	Approach speed	Airspeed, altitude, left engine N1, right engine N1
	A12	Whether the landing flaps are in place late	altitude, flap position, left engine N1, right engine N1

(*continued*)

Table 1. (*continued*)

Phases	Indicator codes	Indicator names	Required flight parameters
Landing phase	L1	Consistency of elevator dimensional control during landing	Elevator input
	L2	Consistency of aileron dimensional control during landing	Aileron input
	L3	Consistency of rudder dimensional control during landing	Rudder input
	L4	Landing bank angle	Altitude,roll angle,air-ground switch, left engine N1, right engine N1
	L5	Landing speed	Altitude, speed, air-ground switch, left engine N1, right engine N1
	L6	Landing pitch angle	Height, pitch angle, air-ground switch, left engine N1, right engine N1, control column position
	L7	Touchdown speed	Air-ground switch, speed, radio altitude, left engine N1, right engine N1
	L8	Directional stability of landing and taxiing	Air-ground switch, left engine N1, right engine N1, magnetic heading
	L9	Whether the landing is overloaded	load factor

2.2 Simulated Flight Operational Performance Evaluation Method Based on the Hierarchical Analysis Method

The operational consistency (OC) in the indicator reflects the consistent and stable level of the flight cadets' operational control input for the three motion dimensions of elevator, aileron and rudder. A high score of this indicator indicates that the driver's manipulation of a certain dimension is accurate and in place, rather than repeatedly adjusting around the standard.

The Mean power frequency (mean power frequency, MPF) is the frequency corresponding to the average energy of the power spectrum, which can reflect the overall frequency of the pilot operation, it is stable and reliable, reflecting more adequate information, and can also be used to describe the overall level of the data itself, and can be used as a standard to measure the differences in the data. The median frequency (MF), which is the point on the power spectrum that makes the left and right sides equal in energy, can reflect where the power is concentrated and can be used as an indicator to compare data differences. These two parameters can be obtained on the basis of Fast Fourier Transform (FFT) of the flight parameter data, which enables data denoising and integration.

The calculation formulas are.

$$OC = \frac{1}{MPF \times w_{MPF} + MF \times w_{MF}} \tag{1}$$

$$MPF = \frac{\int_0^\infty f \cdot p(f)df}{\int_0^\infty p(f)df} \tag{2}$$

$$\int_0^{MF} p(f)df = \int_{MF}^\infty p(f)df \tag{3}$$

f is the frequency, $p(f)$ is the power spectral density function.

The other indicators are quantified as shown in Table 2.

Table 2. Quantification of evaluation indicators for simulated flight operation

Phases	Indicator codes	Indicator names	Evaluation Levels					Remarks
			excellent	good	average	poor	Fail	
Take-off phase	T1	Consistency of elevator dimensional control during takeoff	>20	>15	>10	>5	<=5	The weights are derived from the expert method in the reference
	T2	Consistency of aileron dimensional control during takeoff	>20	>15	>10	>5	<=5	
	T3	Consistency of rudder dimensional control during takeoff	>20	>15	>10	>5	<=5	
	T4	Stability of takeoff direction	No significant deviation	>2, and lasts 1 s or more	>4, and lasts 1 s or more	>3, and lasts 2 s or more	>5, and lasts 2 s or more	Departure from the runway direction before the main wheel leaves the ground

(*continued*)

Table 2. (*continued*)

Phases	Indicator codes	Indicator names	Evaluation Levels					Remarks
			excellent	good	average	poor	Fail	
	T5	Lift front wheel speed up to standard	No significant deviation	>Vr + 5	>Vr + 10	>Vr + 15	>Vr + 20	
			No significant deviation	<Vr	<Vr-1	<Vr-3	<Vr-5	
	T6	Liftoff Speed up to standard	No significant deviation	>V2 + 15	>V2 + 20	>V2 + 25	>V2 + 30	When the main wheel is off the ground
			No significant deviation	<V2	<V2–1	<V2–3	<V2–5	When the main wheel is off the ground
	T7	Liftoff pitch angle up to standard	No significant deviation	>6.6	>7.7	>8.8	>9.9	When the main wheel is off the ground
	T8	Head-up speed up to standard	No significant deviation	>2.5	>3.0	>3.5	>4.0	Lift the front wheel until the main wheel is off the ground
			No significant deviation	<1.9	<1.6	<1.3	<1.0	Lift the front wheel until the main wheel is off the ground
	T9	Takeoff bank angle up to standard	No significant deviation	>3	>4	>5	>6	0–1000(inclusive) ft
Climbing phase	C1	Consistency of elevator dimensional control during climbing	>20	>15	>10	>5	<=5	35-2000ft
	C2	Consistency of aileron dimensional control during climbing	>20	>15	>10	>5	<=5	35-2000ft
	C3	Consistency of rudder dimensional control during climbing	>20	>15	>10	>5	<=5	35-2000ft
	C4	Climbing speed up to standard	No significant deviation	>V2 + 20	>V2 + 25	>V2 + 30	>V2 + 35	35-2000ft
	C5	Bank angle up to the standard	No significant deviation	>7	>10	>20	>30	Climbing above 400ft,below 1500ft
	C6	Whether climbing appears to run out of altitude	No significant deviation	>5	>15	>30	>100	Below 1500ft

(*continued*)

Table 2. (*continued*)

Phases	Indicator codes	Indicator names	Evaluation Levels					Remarks
			excellent	good	average	poor	Fail	
Approach phase	A1	Consistency of elevator dimensional control during approach	>20	>15	>10	>5	<=5	50-2000ft
	A2	Consistency of aileron dimensional control during approach	>20	>15	>10	>5	<=5	50-2000ft
	A3	Consistency of rudder dimensional control during approach	>20	>15	>10	>5	<=5	50-2000ft
	A4	Sinkrate 2000–1000 (inclusive) ft	No significant deviation	>1400	>1500	>1600	>1800	
	A5	Sinkrate 1000–500 (inclusive) ft	No significant deviation	>900	>1000	>1100	>1300	
	A6	500-50ft Sinkrate 500–50 ft	No significant deviation	>800	>900	>1000	>1200	
	A7	Approach bank angle 1500–500 (inclusive) ft	No significant deviation	>6	>7	>8	>10	
	A8	Low altitude whether to use speed brakes	No significant deviation	None	None	None	<1000	
	A9	Whether the approaching stage speed brakes are prepositioned	No significant deviation	None	None	None	Monitored	Below 1500ft
	A10	Low altitude speed	No significant deviation	>210	>220	>230	>250	Below 2500ft
	A11	Approach speed	No significant deviation	>Vref + 15	>Vref + 20	>Vref + 25	>Vref + 30	500–50(inclusive) ft
	A12	Whether the landing flaps are in place late	No significant deviation	<1400	<1300	<1200	<1000	

(*continued*)

Table 2. (*continued*)

Phases	Indicator codes	Indicator names	Evaluation Levels					Remarks
			excellent	good	average	poor	Fail	
Landing phase	L1	Consistency of elevator dimensional control during landing	>20	>15	>10	>5	<=5	Below 50ft
	L2	Consistency of aileron dimensional control during landing	>20	>15	>10	>5	<=5	Below 50ft
	L3	Consistency of rudder dimensional control during landing	>20	>15	>10	>5	<=5	Below 50ft
	L4	Landing bank angle	No significant deviation	>3	>4	>5	>6	50ft to all wheels grounded
	L5	Landing speed	No significant deviation	>Vref + 5	>Vref + 10	>Vref + 15	>Vref + 20	Below 50ft
	L6	Landing pitch angle	No significant deviation	>6	>6.7	>7.4	>8.3	20ft to front wheel ground
			No significant deviation	<2	<1.5	<1	<0.5	10ft to main wheel ground
	L7	Touchdown speed	No significant deviation	<Vref-3	<Vref-5	<Vref-7	<Vref-10	
	L8	Directional stability of landing and taxiing	No significant deviation	>2, and lasts for 1 s and more	>4, and lasts for 1 s and more	>3, and lasts for 2 s and more	>5, and lasts for 2 s and more	Departure from the runway direction after grounding the front wheels
	L9	Whether the landing is overloaded	No significant deviation	>1.2	>1.4	>1.6	>1.8	When the main wheel is grounded

In this paper, analytic hierarchy process method is used to construct the flight maneuvering level evaluation model. After the analysis to determine the maneuvering evaluation indexes, the weights are determined and the weighting method is a subjective weighting method, i.e., expert scoring method. The expert scoring method, as a subjective weighting method, is applicable to the weights where there are many uncertainties and it is difficult to conduct quantitative analysis using other methods. The expert pool is a group of some airline captains, and the importance of the simulated fractal maneuvering indicators is quantified, including 9 indicators in the takeoff phase, 6 indicators in the climb phase, 12 indicators in the approach phase, and 9 indicators in the landing phase, a total of 36 indicators in 4 phases. The total score is:

$$S = w_T \times \sum_{i=1}^{9} (T_i \times w_{Ti}) + w_C \times \sum_{i=1}^{6} (C_i \times w_{Ci}) + w_A \times \sum_{i=1}^{12} (A_i \times w_{Ai}) + w_L \times \sum_{i=1}^{9} (L_i \times w_{Li}) \qquad (4)$$

In addition, the maneuvering level of a single flight simulation can be evaluated by comparing it with the average level of the flight cadet group, the best and worst comparison, and the class grade comparison to identify stubborn operational problems and common problems, and then to provide improvement measures and special training.

2.3 Simulated Flight Operation Improvement Measures Library Construction

According to the evaluation of the flight simulation operation above, the deviation of each evaluation indicator will lead to different risk events, as shown in Table 3, some indicators are one-way deviations, for example, the indicator takeoff direction will lead to the risk event of unstable takeoff direction, while the indicator lift front wheel speed will lead to the risk event of significant lift front wheel speed and small lift front wheel speed. Based on the actual flight and training experience of an airline captain of the same type of aircraft, this paper will develop specific and feasible improvement measures for each risk event and establish a library of suggested improvement measures. The improvement measures given in this paper do not only include suggestions for maneuvering in the opposite direction of the risk event but more importantly, give specific and feasible instructions for the actual operation of the flight cadet in order to improve the operation level of the flight cadet.

For example, in the takeoff phase, for the indicator takeoff direction, which can easily cause the risk event of unstable takeoff direction, the measures to be given in this project are as follows.

1. The line of sight is placed far away and the directional deviation is most easily detected by visual inspection of the far end of the runway.
2. With the seat tuned, the centerline of the runway is pressed against the inner thigh at all times

For indicators that are limited in both directions, for example, during the takeoff phase, for indicators that lift the front wheel speed, two risk events are likely to result, respectively, a large lift front wheel speed and a small lift front wheel speed.

The recommended measures given for lifting the front wheel with large speed are as follows.

(1) PM shouting VR should come with advance.
(2) PF active surveillance VR with gentle lift lever.

The recommended measures given for lifting the front wheel with little speed are as follows.

(1) PM shouting VR should not advance too much.
(2) PF actively monitors VR and steadily waits for the timing of pulling the lever.

3 Experiment

3.1 Subjects

The subjects selected for this experiment were 20 flight cadets majoring in flight technology. All subjects were male, aged 19 to 22 years, with an average age of 20.1 years, and all subjects had normal unaided eye vision or corrected vision, were in good physical and mental condition, and were willing to participate in the experiment as required. The subjects had not consumed alcohol, smoked, caught a cold, or consumed any food or drug prohibited by regulations 24 h prior to the experiment.

3.2 Experimental Instruments

The equipment of this experiment is a set of X-Plane simulation flight platforms, as shown in Fig. 1, the hardware system contains devices such as a simulation control panel, throttle stick, footrest, etc. The view system adopts Prepare 3D, the platform can simulate the cockpit operation of many types of aircraft, including A320, B737, Diamond 42, Cesena 172, and other types of aircraft, and can simulate many airports around the world in different It can control aircraft form, landing gear status, radio altitude, air speed, ground speed, vertical speed, pitch angle, cross roll, etc., and realize the functions of aircraft takeoff, climb, approach, and landing.

The core part of the platform software simulation system is developed based on C standard ISO/IEC 14882:2017, which can handle the simulation events efficiently and quickly, and at the same time can be unitized for different system modules, so that it is convenient to add new system modules. The interface of API can be UDP or C++ dynamic link library with interface documentation, which is convenient for the secondary development of subsequent data processing using program language. The flight quality monitoring data is mainly obtained through the background of the simulator workstation, and the amount of recorded flight data is extremely huge.

Fig. 1. Flight simulation experiment platform

3.3 Design of Simulated Flight Experiment

In the experiment, due to the limitation of time, this paper adopts the takeoff and landing route commonly used in flight training as the planned flight segment of the test by referring to the training system of airlines. Takeoff and landing route is a basic takeoff and landing flight route, which is usually used in the field training and simulator training. It can train the initial pilot or modified pilot on the basic operation of the flight. It includes the most basic and important training of the flight technology, eye and hand coordination and attention allocation. The 5 sides included in the takeoff and landing route in this paper are the key stages of the approach program. The 5 sides represent (1) upwind, (2) crosswind, (3) downwind, (4) base, and (5) final side. The tasks to be completed by flight cadets are as follows.

(1) Upwind: Take off, climb, retract the landing gear, keep the aircraft on the runway extension line, adjust thrust, and increase and retract flaps;
(2) Crosswind: Complete the post-takeoff checklist, continue to climb and turn to confirm approximately 90 degrees to the runway;
(3) Downwind: Set the appropriate thrust, maintain the correct altitude, report to the tower and check before landing, judge whether the distance with the runway is correct, and master the turn time;
(4) Base: Prepare to turn to the runway, do final checks, apply flaps according to aircraft power, maintain normal speed, altitude, and find the right time to turn to the final side;
(5) Final: Make final adjustment, descend at normal descent rate, complete landing checklist, flatten, throttle back, ground and brake.

4 Results

4.1 Simulated Flight Test Results

After 20 test flight cadets performed simulated flight tests, their raw flight data were derived and the main flight parameters were visualized and drawn as shown in Fig. 2. Among them, VIND indicates the indicated airspeed in knots; FLAP indicates the flap position; PITCH indicates pitch, measured by the Euler angle of the fuselage axis; ROLL indicates roll, measured by the Euler angle of the body axis; HDING indicates magnetic heading in degrees; and ALT indicates altitude in feet above the ground.

4.2 Operational Performance Evaluating Results

Operational performance evaluation of the raw flight data derived from the simulated flight test based on the above model yielded the highest and lowest scores of 74.7 and 36.4 for the 20 flight cadets, respectively, with an average score of 54.5, as shown in Table 3. The average scores of the four flight phases were 51.7, 55.8, 54.4, and 55.6, indicating that the degree of looseness of the indicators in each phase did not differ significantly, and the nine indicators in the landing phase were slightly more demanding for the flight cadets overall, while the nine indicators in the takeoff phase were slightly less demanding.

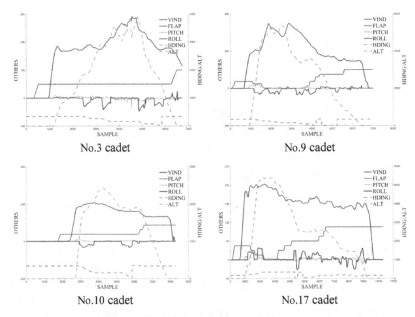

Fig. 2. Raw data of simulated flight test of part of the test flight cadets

Table 3. Operational performance evaluating results in different flight stages.

Score	Total score	Take-off	Climbing	Approach	Landing
Mean	54.5	51.7	55.8	54.4	55.6
Max	74.7	71.1	75.6	73.3	77.8
Min	36.4	33.3	35.6	33.3	42.2

The simulated flight maneuver performance evaluation results for each flight cadet are shown in Fig. 3. Since the weight coefficient of 0.2 for the takeoff and climb phases is lower than 0.3 for the approach and landing phases, the contribution of the takeoff and climb phases to the total performance score is less than the other two phases in the figure.

4.3 Comparative Analysis of Results

The mean, optimal, and worst values of the 36 indicators of the subjects' maneuvering performance were compared and analyzed. Based on the best value, it was found that all participants had landing overload (L9) and inaccurate head-up rate control (T8).

According to the worst value found, the participants were able to grasp the 500-50 ft drop rate (indicator 21) in place.

According to the mean value, the following are found.

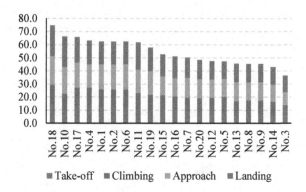

Fig. 3. Results of simulated flight maneuver performance evaluation of test flight cadets.

(1) Satisfactory performance: The participants performed well in takeoff phase directional stability (T4), takeoff slope (T9), climb phase aileron operation consistency (C1), air slope (C5), climb whether to drop altitude (C6), approach phase elevator operation consistency (A1), descent rate (A4-A6), landing phase elevator operation consistency (L1), landing slope (L4), and landing pitch angle (L6).

(2) Key improvements: The cadets need to focus on strengthening their training on the accuracy of front wheel lift speed (T5), the accuracy of head lift rate (T8), consistency of aileron operation during the climb phase (C2), consistency of aileron operation during approach phase (A2), poor landing flap timing (A12), grounding speed (L7), and landing overload (L9).

Corresponding improvement measures are as follows.

T5: ①PM shouting VR should come with advance, but not too much advance; ②PF actively monitors VR, steadily wait for the timing of pulling the lever, and softly pull the lever overhand.

T8: Slowly reduce the rate of the band bar (normal 3 degrees/sec), thus reducing the head-up attitude.

C2: Understand the behavioral indicators of the climb phase, understand the ideal state of the aircraft at this time, and master the precision of lateral operation, soft and consistent.

A2: Understand the behavioral indicators of the approach phase, understand the ideal state of the aircraft at this time, and master the precision, softness, and consistency of lateral operations.

A12 Strengthen speed management, and slow down and release form in advance.

L7: Don't close the throttle too early, and manage the aircraft energy reasonably.

L9: Fly strictly according to the instrument, control the aircraft accurately and gently, maintain stable speed, thrust, attitude, and trajectory; pay attention to the timing of eliminating crossings with the runway.

(3) Second improvements: The next things to be trained are the consistency of elevator, aileron, and rudder operation during the takeoff phase (T1-T3), the accuracy of departure speed (T6), the accuracy of departure elevation angle (T7, consistency of grounded rudder operation during the climb (C3), the accuracy of climb speed (C4), consistency of rudder operation during approach phase (A3), whether the deceleration plate is not prepositioned during approach phase (A9), low altitude speed (A10), app-roach speed (A11) and consistency of aileron and rudder operation during landing phase (L2-L3).

Corresponding improvement measures are as follows.

T1-T3: Understand the behavioral indicators of the takeoff taxiing phase, under-stand the ideal state of the aircraft at this time, master the precision of pitch and lateral operation, and be soft and consistent.

T6: Bring the stick as needed and follow the guidelines; if the speed is largely due to wind shear at the moment of departure from the ground, dispose of it according to the wind shear procedure.

T7: Stabilize the pole and manually reduce the angle of attack.

C3: Understand the behavioral indicators of the climbing phase, understand the ideal state of the aircraft at this time, and master the precision of lateral operation, soft and consistent.

C4: Properly bring the stick; if the attitude is correct and stable, the throttle can be properly closed.

A3: Understand the behavioral indicators of the approach phase, understand the ideal state of the aircraft at this time, and master the precision of lateral operation, soft and consistent.

A9: Strictly follow SOPs; monitor instrument memo information.

A10: Decelerate as soon as possible to establish a landing pattern.

A11: Reduce thrust in a timely manner.

L2-L3: Understand the behavioral indicators of the landing phase, understand the ideal state of the aircraft at this time, and master the precision, softness, and consistency of lateral operations (Fig. 4).

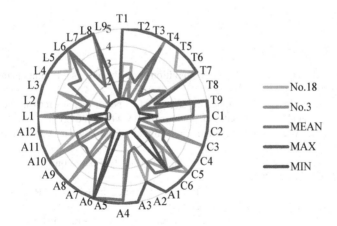

Fig. 4. Comparison of simulated flight operational performance evaluation results.

5   Conclusions

In the simulation flight control evaluation, each index and the corresponding risk are quantified and calculated logically, and the weight of each index is evaluated by the expert scoring method. A simulation flight control performance evaluation method based on analytic hierarchy process is proposed. The case verifies that the degree of tightness of the indexes in each phase does not differ much, and the nine indexes in the landing phase are slightly more demanding for the flight student overall, while the nine indexes in the takeoff phase are slightly less demanding.

The most important thing that flight students need to do is to overcome landing overload and precisely control the head-up rate. Suggested improvement measures include (1) flying strictly according to the instrument, controlling the aircraft accurately and gently, maintaining stable speed, thrust, attitude, and trajectory, and paying attention to eliminate the timing of crossing with the runway to prevent overload; (2) slowly reduce the rate of the band stick (normal 3 degrees/sec), thus reducing the head-up attitude to precisely control the head-up rate. Cadets also need to focus on improving: (1) lifting the front wheel speed accuracy: ① PM shouting VR should come with an amount of advance, but not too much advance; ② PF active monitoring VR, stable waiting for the timing of the lever pull, soft overhand lever pull; (2) climb and approach phase aileron operation consistency: understand the behavioral indicators of the climb and approach phase, understand the ideal state of the aircraft at this time, master the lateral operation accuracy, soft and consistent; (3) landing flap timing: strengthen speed management, early deceleration, and release form; and (4) grounding speed: do not close the throttle too early, reasonable management of aircraft energy.

Acknowledgment. We appreciate the support this work received from the Fundamental Research Funds for the Central Universities (Grant No. 3122019065) and the Civil Aviation Administration of China Security Capacity Construction Fund Project (Grant No. KJZ49420210076).

References

1. Zheng, L., Chi, H., Shao, X.: Pattern recognition and risk analysis for flight operations. Chin. J. Manag. Sci. (10), 10 (2017)
2. Sun, R., Xiao, Y.: Research on indicating structure for operation characteristic of civil aviation pilots based on OAR data. J. Saf. Sci. Technol. **8**(11), 49–54 (2012)
3. Sun, R., Li, C.: Analysis of flight operation patterns and risk based on k-SC clustering. J. Saf. Sci. Technol. **17**(09), 150–155 (2021)
4. Sun, R., Liu, Y.: Research on pilots' flight operation style based on QAR data. China Saf. Sci. J. **32**(12), 63–69 (2022)
5. Wang, L., Wang, S.: Flight operation analysis method based on QAR data and wavelet transformation. Flight Dyn. **38**(5), 7 (2020)
6. Wang, L., Dong, C., Cui, M.: Evaluation method of flight operation skills based on power spectrum. Flight Dyn. **36**(04), 92–96 (2018)
7. Wang, L., Guo, S., Jiang, Y., et al.: A method of landing operation evaluation based on curve similarity. J. Transp. Inf. Saf. **37**(6), 7 (2019)

8. Qi, M.L., Shao, X., Chi, H.: Flight operations risk diagnosis method on quick-access-record exceedance. J. Beijing Univ. Aeron. Astron. **37**(10), 1207–1210 (2011)
9. Shao, X., Chi, H., Gao, M.: Risk analysis of operations in flight based on copula. J. Appl. Stat. Manag. **31**(5), 9 (2012)
10. Nie, L., Huang, S., Shu, P., Wang, X.: Intelligent diagnosis for hard landing of aircraft based on SVM. China Saf. Sci. J. **19**(07), 149–153+181 (2009)
11. Lu, Y., Zhu, T.: Pre-training of autoregressive model for aircraft hard landing prediction based on QAR data. In: 2019 IEEE 31st International Conference on Tools with Artificial Intelligence (ICTAI), pp. 1613–1617. IEEE (2019)
12. Lv, H., Yu, J., Zhu, T.: A novel method of overrun risk measurement and assessment using large scale QAR data. In: 2018 IEEE Fourth International Conference on Big Data Computing Service and Applications (BigDataService), pp. 213–220. IEEE (2018)
13. Lan, C.E., Kaiyuan, W.U., Jiang, Y.U.: Flight characteristics analysis based on QAR data of a jet transport during landing at a high-altitude airport. Chin. J. Aeronaut. **25**(1), 13–24 (2012)
14. Barry, D.J.: Estimating runway veer-off risk using a Bayesian network with flight data. Transp. Res. Part C: Emerg. Technol. **128**, 103180 (2021)
15. Li, L.: Anomaly detection in airline routine operations using flight data recorder data. Massachusetts Institute of Technology (2013)
16. Wang, L., Jiang, Y., Tan, W.: Study on construction of risk portrait index system for airline pilots. China Saf. Sci. J. **30**(11), 9 (2020)
17. Wang, L., Sun, J., Wang, W., Qi, X., Wang, F.: Bayesian network analysis model on landing exceedance risk based on flight QAR data. J. Saf. Environ. **23**(01), 26–34 (2023)
18. Zheng, Z., Sun, J., Zhang, M., et al.: Relationship among fatigue, psychomotor vigilance and physiological index in a flight simulation context (2021)

Applying Multi-source Data to Evaluate Pilots' Flight Safety Style Based on Safety-II Theory

Zixin Wei⬤, Ying Zou⬤, and Lei Wang(✉)⬤

College of Safety Science and Engineering, Civil Aviation University of China, Tianjin, China
weizixin1207@outlook.com, wanglei0564@hotmail.com

Abstract. Different from the traditional safety concept, to make sure things go right is described as Safety-II, which has been used widely in many industries. To describe pilots' stable attitudes and behaviors exhibited by pilots toward flight activities, the definition of flight safety style was proposed. With the aim to quantitatively evaluate airline pilots' flight safety style, a method applying multidimensional data based on the Safety-II theory was proposed. First, based on the literature review, we proposed the definition, intension, and extension of pilots' flight safety style. Second, we analyzed and compared the advantages and disadvantages of different evaluation methods for flight safety attitudes, flight safety behaviors as well as flight safety style. Third, based on the Safety-II theory, we proposed and characterized a quantitative evaluation framework applying multi-source data at implicit and explicit levels, including pilots' hazardous attitudes, operation behaviors, and non-operation behaviors. Finally, we constructed a mathematical model, and thus pilots' flight safety style scores can be calculated and ranked. The collected data were applied to give a case study to validate the method by performing an analysis based on the Safety-II theory. This study shows a data-driven method for the pilots' flight safety style quantitative evaluation based on Safety-II, which can be used to find out the data described as 'as many things as possible go right (Safety-II)' to advance Evidence-based Training (EBT) of flight safety style. It also provides airlines with a more reasonable way to evaluate pilots' flight safety style quantitatively, and further improve flight safety.

Keywords: Flight Safety Style · Safety-II · Flight Safety · Flight Safety Style Evaluation

1 Introduction

The impact of human factors on flight safety has always been a key concern in the field of civil aviation. Research showed that human factors were involved in the causes of up to 70 percent of aviation accidents [1]. A report published by the European Union Aviation Safety Agency (EASA) shows that the number of human factors or human performance-related issues did not reduce with the reduction of the number of accidents and serious incidents in 2020, and the report shows that close to 20 percent of commercial air transport large airplane accidents and serious incidents were related to human factors or human performance [2]. To reduce the threat of human error to aviation safety, and thus ensure aviation safety, the Civil Aviation Administration of China (CAAC) published a guideline on building a long-term safety style for civil aviation safety practitioners in 2021 and revised it in 2022 [3]. Safety style was defined as the stable attitudes and behaviors of safety-related employees of civil aviation during production runs in the guideline. Flight safety is the core priority for aviation safety. To ensure flight safety, the CAAC published the norm of Professional Style of Crew Members in 2022, which further defined and regulated the professional style of crew members [4]. As pilots are the direct operators in the flight deck, and they have extremely crucial responsibilities for flight safety, this study focuses on the stable attitudes and behaviors exhibited by pilots towards flight activities defined as flight safety style, which includes flight safety attitudes and flight safety behaviors. Some airlines have already conducted studies on evaluating flight safety style, but the following problems still exist. Firstly, systematic studies at the theoretical level are lacking. Second, the definition of the boundaries of flight safety style problems needs to be refined. Third, the list of flight safety style problems mainly relies on the observation and evaluation of behaviors by managers, with a distinct lack of investigations on the attitude dimension. Fourth, it is difficult to observe, identify and quantify pilots' flight safety style comprehensively.

With the low accident rate nowadays, it is more achievable to summarize and promote the characteristics of flight safety style of pilots who perform well during regular operations than to draw lessons from accidents, which is similar to the concept of Safety-II proposed by Hollnagel. Safety-II is defined as ensuring that 'as many things as possible go right' [5], while Safety-I focuses on 'what goes wrong' [6]. Therefore, combining the realities of civil aviation operations, the concept of Safety-II can be applied to the evaluation of flight safety style and its application.

In this study, based on Safety-II, a flight safety style evaluation method applying multi-source data was proposed to evaluate pilots' flight safety style quantitatively and thus better ensure flight safety.

2 Literature Review

2.1 State of the Art in Flight Safety Style Evaluation

The CAAC published the "Guideline on the Construction of Long-term Mechanism for Work Style of Civil Aviation Safety Practitioners (Revised Version)" in 2022 [3], which set out specific requirements for quantitative evaluation of safety style: First, civil aviation production and operation agencies should take into account the real situation, adopt effective tools, establish forms related to quantitative management, formulate quantitative scoring criteria by dimension, model, and items, and evaluate safety style based on multi-dimension data. Second, according to the nature and risk level of the style problems, solutions should be formulated based on the quantified results. Thirdly, the quantitative evaluation period can be a combination of single or multiple periods on an annual, quarterly, or monthly basis, with the longest evaluation period being no more than one year. Fourth, civil aviation production and operation units can establish a graded assessment mechanism for safety style issues in conjunction with the hierarchy and functional structure of management. The CAAC Northeast Regional Administration published the "Pilots' Flight Safety Style and Discipline Quantitative Assessment

Management Measures of the Northeast Civil Aviation Transportation Aviation" in 2020 [7], which adopted a scoring system for risk control assessment, based on a quantitative scoring table for flight safety style and discipline and the corresponding deduction items to accumulate points item by item to quantitatively assess and manage pilot's flight safety style. In the "Implementation Guide for the Quantitative Management of Pilots' Flight Safety Style of Transport Airlines in Central and Southern Region" [8] issued by the CAAC Central and Southern Regional Administration in 2020, the assessment of behavior was included as a part of the quantitative pilot style management program, and the "Quantitative Pilots' Flight Safety Style Assessment Standards" and "Pilot's Negative Behaviors Checklist" were adopted as tools for quantitative assessment through cabin sound collection and operational inspection. Data collection can be obtained from cabin sound collection, operational inspections, investigation and verification, Safety Management System (SMS) reports, timely reviews, daily monitoring, information reports, regular statistics, surveillance footage, etc. The Quantitative Evaluation Criteria for Pilot's Behavior, as a quantitative tool for pilot's behavior, classifies and describes pilot's behavior through a framework of "dimension - module - item - subitem", deconstructing pilot behavior into six dimensions: flight safety style, operational style, training style, daily style, management style, and teaching style.

Experts have also focused on the six dimensions of flight safety style. They have also proposed different quantitative assessment methods for flight safety style. Based on the CRM and TEM models, Ji [9] combined the characteristics of modern airline pilots' piloting work and, based on literature, expert opinions, and open-ended questionnaires, screened out the typical crew behavior performance of 12 technical and 27 non-technical skills in airline flying, and composed a multidimensional validity measure for the safety evaluation of technical and non-technical skills respectively, thus a tool for evaluating the normative behavior of airline pilots in a Chinese cultural context was constructed. Gao et al. [10] combined the effectiveness of practice in paramilitary management of trainee pilots and proposed a model of flight safety style assessment based on quantitative management of a point system, which provides a comprehensive quantification of factors related to students' style performance, discipline awareness, compliance awareness, and behavioral discipline ability during their school years. Zhong [11] summarized the main factors affecting flight safety style through expert interviews and literature reviews, used the fuzzy comprehensive evaluation method, combined with the model constructed by DEMATEL/ISM to analyze and assign weights to each indicator, and carried out fuzzy quantification of the indicators with strong subjectivity in flight safety style, to build a more scientific evaluation system and realize the quantitative assessment of pilot's flight safety style. Yu [12] used the advantages of the literature research method, interview research method, and statistical analysis method to integrate and screen the past flight style quantitative assessment behavior samples summarized a set of behavior samples with standardized description, perfect content, and reasonable evaluation, and finally constructed a quantitative flight style assessment standard based on multidimensional validity scale measurement theory. Wei et al. [13] proposed that the evaluation of personal style should be comprehensive considering the behavioral performance of flight and control personnel in different safety production positions, and quantitative evaluation should be conducted from five dimensions: daily, operation, training, teaching, and management. Based on the Daily Negative List, the "harm degree of style behavior" and two indicators of "Hazardousness of Flight Safety Style" and "Quantitative Assessment Score of Flight Safety Style" were calculated and assessed separately according to the Daily Negative List.

2.2 Comparison and Analysis of Evaluation Methods

Based on previous research, it is clear that existing methods for evaluating flight safety style vary. In terms of data sources, there are data obtained through the measurement of self-assessment or other assessment questionnaires and flight data obtained through QAR collection. To make a more objective and accurate comparison of the different evaluation methods, the existing methods were compared and analyzed as follows.

Currently, the use of questionnaires as an assessment tool is widely used both for flight safety attitudes and flight safety behaviors of flight safety style and can be divided into self-rating scales and examiner-rating scales. For example, the Flight Management Attitudes Questionnaire 2.0 (International) developed by Helmreich et al. [14], the Hazardous Attitudes Questionnaire for Airline Pilots developed by Ji et al. [15], and the multidimensional validity measurement system developed by Payne et al. [16] to test the technical skills of pilots are all used to quantify the attitudinal or behavioral aspects of flight style by collecting data from self-rating scales. The examiner-rating scale is a quantitative assessment of the attitudinal or behavioral aspects of flying. The examiner-rating scales were used to assess the behavioral performance of the tested pilot by specialized experts, such as the fuzzy evaluation method based on the flight safety style evaluation system established by Zhong [11], which analyzed the data from the examiner-rating scales to achieve a quantitative flight safety style evaluation. With the continuous optimization of evaluation methods, the combination of self-assessment and other assessment questionnaire scales has also been applied to the assessment of flight style. Ji [9] constructed a tool to assess the normative behavior of airline pilots in the Chinese cultural context, which combines self-rating and examiner-rating scales, allowing for a more objective and comprehensive quantitative assessment of flight safety behaviors of flight safety style.

In addition, the Quantitative Assessment and Management Measures for the Discipline of Pilots of Northeast Civil Aviation Transport Airlines [7] and the Implementation Guide for the Quantitative Management of Pilot's Behavior of Transport Airlines in the Central and Southern Region [8] issued by the CAAC also use data from rating scales to assess flight safety behavior quantitatively. In particular, the Implementation Guide for the Quantitative Management of Pilot Practices of Transport Airlines Central and Southern Region [8] states that data can be collected through cabin sound collection, operational inspections, investigation and verification, SMS reports, timely reviews, daily monitoring, information reports, regular statistics, and surveillance videos, and then scored on a scale. Compared to most flight safety style assessment methods, the "Implementation Guide for Quantitative Management of Pilot Practices in Transport Airlines in the South Central Region" has a more comprehensive range of indicators. However, the overly complicated amount of data can also have an impact on the efficiency of flight safety style assessment.

In addition to the application of questionnaires, the analysis of QAR data has also been widely used in the assessment of flight safety style. Scholars such as Sun [17, 18] and Wang [19–22] have constructed many effective evaluation models based on QAR data to achieve a quantitative assessment of flight safety behaviors of flight safety style.

Compared with the evaluation models built based on QAR data, the data obtained using self-assessment and other-assessment scales are more subjective, with the self-assessment scales being more subjective than the other-assessment scales. However, the range of indicators that can be covered by the self-assessment and other-assessment scales is much larger than that of QAR data. Therefore, in the quantitative assessment of flight style, multi-source data should be combined to make up for the lack of subjectivity of the questionnaire scale by using the objectivity of the QAR data, and to supplement the range of indicators that cannot be covered by the QAR data, so that the quantitative assessment of flight safety style can be more objective and accurate.

Flight safety style includes flight safety attitudes and flight safety behaviors, and therefore the assessment of flight safety style should also be based on a combination of attitudes and behaviors. However, the existing flight safety style evaluation methods aspect of attitude or behavior, and there are few methods that measure both attitudes and behaviors.

2.3 Advantages of Safety-II

In the civil aviation industry, safety management is currently based on the theory of Safety-I, i.e. learning from the experience of unsafe incidents or accidents that have occurred, and reducing the occurrence of unsafe incidents or accidents by minimizing human errors, thereby improving safety in production operations. However, in most cases, unsafe incidents and accidents are relatively rare and therefore how civil aviation flight safety is assessed and safety managed in terms of the incidence of unsafe incidents and accidents should be improved.

The Safety-II theory, which is based on seeking the highest possible number of acceptable outcomes that occur daily, can yield the following advantages in civil aviation safety management and flight safety style evaluation.

First, safety management based on a large number of acceptable outcomes occurring daily can provide a large number of references for analysis and summary of regular work operations. Second, by summarizing excellent flight safety style in daily work operations and promoting it for learning, more pilots will have better work performance before an unsafe incident or accident occurs, thus enhancing flight safety. Therefore, the evaluation of flight safety style based on the theory of Safety-II is potential for application.

3 Flight Safety Style Evaluation Framework Based on Multidimensional Data

To evaluate pilots' flight safety style quantitatively, a flight safety style evaluation method based on multidimensional data is proposed. The assessment of flight safety attitudes and flight safety behaviors are included in this method. The evaluation of pilots' safety style can be more comprehensive and objective by using this method, thus offering a reference for airlines to select and train pilots as well.

Based on Multidimensional data, the flight safety style evaluation framework contains pilots' hazardous attitudes evaluation, pilots' operation behaviors, and pilots' non-operation behaviors.

For a better understanding, the framework of flight safety style evaluation is depicted briefly in Fig. 1.

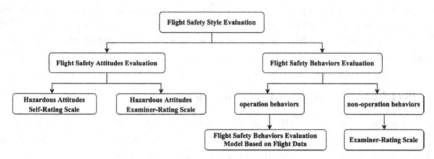

Fig. 1. Flight safety style evaluation framework

3.1 Flight Safety Style Evaluation Based on Hazardous Attitudes

According to the literature review and interview, 10 factors (Macho, Impulsivity, Anti-authority, Escape, Invulnerability, Resignation, Worry, Conceit, Adventurous, and Perfunctory) that have been suggested by previous research as being related to pilots' safety attitudes and safety behaviors were summarized. Based on the above factors, the hazardous attitudes self-rating scale was developed. Through the reliability and validity analysis, the factors were optimized and integrated, and thus 7 factors (Macho, Impulsivity, Anti-authority, Escape, Resignation, Worry, and Conceit) were used to form a formal self-rating scale. Finally, according to the hazardous attitudes self-rating scale, the hazardous attitudes examiner-rating scale was developed. After reliability and validity analysis, invalid questions were eliminated and a formal scale was formed.

To evaluate pilots' flight safety attitudes, two Likert-type scales (hazardous attitudes self-rating scale and hazardous attitudes examiner-rating scale) were established in the context of the flight situation. 28 questions were developed for the self-rating scale of hazardous attitudes and 24 questions for the examiner-rating scale of hazardous attitudes.

3.2 Flight Safety Style Evaluation Based on Operation Behaviors

Based on the Flight Operations Quality Assurance (FOQA) program of Boeing 737–800 aircraft of an airline, 68 unsafe incidents covering the entire phase of the flight were selected. To clarify whether each unsafe incident belongs to competency-based error or flight safety style violation, flight specialists were invited to score the likelihood of each indicator based on their experience. After that, in conjunction with the score of each indicator and the Standard Operating Procedure (SOP), the weight of each indicator belonging to flight safety style violation was confirmed, and thus the flight safety style evaluation model based on flight data was developed through the analysis of the Normal Cloud Model.

3.3 Flight Safety Style Evaluation Based on Non-operation Behaviors

Firstly, based on civil aviation regulations, advisory circulars, and documents from the CAAC, the pilot's flight safety style problems in the pre-flight, flight operation, and post-flight phases were sorted out. The flight safety style evaluation indicators for the pilot's non-operational behavior were initially extracted. After that, an expert questionnaire was prepared and flying experts were invited to evaluate the applicability of the selected evaluation indicators. Through analysis of the data of the questionnaire, unreasonable indicators were eliminated to form a risk of flight safety style evaluation indicator system based on non-operation behavior.

3.4 Pilots' Flight Safety Style Evaluation Model

Pilots' hazardous attitudes self-rating data, hazardous attitudes examiner-rating data, flight data, and non-operation behaviors data are collected through standardization and normalization of multidimensional data, as described in Eq. (1):

$$T_{ji} = (X_{ji} - X_{\min j,i}) / (X_{\max j,i} - X_{\min j,i}) \tag{1}$$

The Criteria Importance Though Intercrieria Correlation (CRITIC) method [23, 24] is utilized to determine the weight of indicators. The flight safety style evaluation model requires inputs in terms of the weight of each index θ related to the amount of information contained in each index C_i, as described in Eq. (2) and Eq. (3):

$$C_i = s_i \sum_{k=1}^{m} (1 - r_{ki}), i = 1, 2, \ldots, m \tag{2}$$

$$\theta_i = C_i \bigg/ \sum_{i=1}^{m} C_i, i = 1, 2, \ldots, m \tag{3}$$

Thus, the weighted rank sum ratio (WRSR) method [25] is used to evaluate pilots' flight safety style based on multidimensional data. M evaluation indexes of N evaluation objects are arranged into the original data table of n rows and m columns, and the rank of each index is assigned to the matrix, as described in Eq. (4):

$$\begin{bmatrix} R_{11} & \cdots & R_{1M} \\ \vdots & \ddots & \vdots \\ R_{N1} & \cdots & R_{NM} \end{bmatrix} \tag{4}$$

The weighted rank sum ratio of each evaluation object can be obtained as described in Eq. (5):

$$WRSR_j = \frac{\sum_{i=1}^{M} \theta_i * R_{ji}}{N} \tag{5}$$

To summarize, pilots' flight safety style can be compared based on WRSR.

4 Case Study

According to the evaluation framework above, there are four input indicators, including the self-rating scores of hazardous attitudes, examiner-rating scores of hazardous attitudes, operation behavior scores, and non-operation behavior scores. Eight pilots were evaluated on their flight safety style. The original scores, normalized data, and the weight of each indicator are shown in Table 1.

Table 1. Scores of pilots

Indicator	Self-rating of hazardous attitudes		Examiner-rating of hazardous attitudes		Operation Behaviors		Non-operation Behaviors	
Weight	0.256		0.204		0.258		0.282	
	Original	Normalized	Original	Normalized	Original	Normalized	Original	Normalized
X1	63	0.739	49	0.667	10.912	0.192	27	1.000
X2	47	0.044	37	0.000	12.611	0.548	26	0.667
X3	64	0.783	42	0.278	9.996	0.000	26	0.667
X4	46	0.000	55	1.000	12.081	0.437	27	1.000
X5	69	1.000	48	0.611	11.471	0.309	27	1.000
X6	67	0.913	38	0.056	14.768	1.000	24	0.000
X7	69	1.000	37	0.000	14.432	0.930	24	0.000
X8	59	0.565	41	0.222	12.317	0.487	24	0.000

Based on the WRSR, the rank and ratio of the flight safety style of each subject to be evaluated were calculated and the pilots' flight safety style was ranked based on the data obtained, with higher scores indicating poorer performance and lower flight safety style ranking. The results of the evaluation are shown in Table 2.

Table 2. Results of flight safety style evaluation

Pilot	WRSR	Ranking
X1	0.618	2
X2	0.454	7
X3	0.479	6
X4	0.612	3
X5	0.737	1
X6	0.597	4
X7	0.574	5
X8	0.430	8

By evaluating the flight safety attitudes and flight safety behavior of 8 pilots, the data related to flight safety style was normalized, weights were determined and the rank sum ratio was calculated to obtain the flight safety style ranking of 8 pilots. A quantitative evaluation of the pilots' flight safety style from multi-dimension has been achieved.

5 Conclusions

Based on the concepts presented in the CAAC documents, the concept of flight safety style, which includes flight safety attitudes and flight safety behaviors, was summarized and proposed. Through a literature review, the evaluation methods of flight safety style, flight safety behaviors, and flight safety attitudes were compared and analyzed, and the characteristics and shortcomings of each method were summarized.

Based on the definition of Safety-II and its core concept, the advantages of Safety-II in civil aviation safety management and flight safety style evaluation were discussed.

This study proposed a multidimensional data-based pilot flight safety style evaluation method to quantitatively assess flight safety style from two dimensions: flight safety attitudes and flight safety behaviors.

The flight style evaluation framework consists of three components: flight safety style evaluation based on hazardous attitudes, flight safety style evaluation based on operation behavior, and flight safety style evaluation based on non-operation behavior.

The data of eight pilots were used to demonstrate the calculations, proving that the multidimensional data-based flight safety style evaluation model proposed in this study is applicable and can provide an effective reference for the selection and training of airline pilots in the future.

As the definition of Safety-II is ensuring that 'as many things as possible go right', the results of pilots' flight safety style comparison can be used to find out some good quality of flight safety attitudes and flight safety behaviors. First, according to the flight safety evaluation results, the characteristic of flight safety attitudes of pilots who show excellent safety performance can be classified and summarized, which can provide references when selecting trainee pilots and developing targeted training for pilots with poor safety performance. Besides, based on pilots' flight safety style evaluation, pilots' operation behaviors performance can be identified and thus the pilots with poor operation behaviors performance can be trained accordingly. In addition, the non-operation behaviors of pilots with excellent flight safety style can be promoted and thus improve flight safety. Moreover, as evidence-based training (EBT) is based on pilot operational data, the data from the quantitative flight safety style evaluation can also provide a reference for EBT, and thus pilots can be trained more efficiently.

Meanwhile, it should be noted that the identification, evaluation, and subsequent training of flight safety style is something that needs to be explored with more effort. Here are some of the topics that need to be further explored based on this research:1) Verify the validity and accuracy of the flight safety style evaluation method through research on the relationship between flight safety style evaluation results and pilots' safety performance.2) Develop a more efficient model to evaluate pilots' flight safety style.3) Find out the way to improve flight safety in the current situation reflected in the results of the flight safety style evaluation.

Acknowledgments. The authors would like to appreciate the support of the National Natural Science Foundation of China (grant no. 32071063).

References

1. Helmreich, R.L.: Managing human error in aviation. Sci. Am. **276**(5), 62–67 (1997)
2. European Union Aviation Safety Agency: Annul Safety Review 2022, Germany (2022)
3. Civil Aviation Administration of China: Guideline for Building a Long-term Mechanism for Civil Aviation Safety Practitioners' Working Style (revised version), Beijing (2022)
4. Civil Aviation Administration of China AC-121-FS-130R1: Guidelines For The Professional Style of Crew Members. CivilAviation Administration of China (2022)
5. Hollnagel, E., Wears, R.L., Braithwaite, J.: From Safety-I to Safety-II: a white paper. The resilient health care net: published simultaneously by the University of Southern Denmark, University of Florida, USA, and Macquarie University, Australia (2015)
6. Patterson, M., Deutsch, E.S.: Safety-I, Safety-II and resilience engineering. Curr. Probl. Pediatr. Adolesc. Health Care **45**(12), 382–389 (2015)
7. CAAC Northeast Regional Administration: Pilots' Flight Safety Style and Discipline Quantitative Assessment Management Measures of the Northeast Civil Aviation Transportation Aviation, Shenyang (2020)
8. CAAC Central and Southern Regional Administration: Implementation Guide for the Quantitative Management of Pilots' Flight Safety Style of Transport Airlines in Central and Southern Region, Guangzhou (2020)
9. Ji, M.: Evaluation of the normative behavior of airline driving based on the Chinese cultural context, Xi'an (2008)
10. Gao, B., Yan, S., Qi, Z.: A study on the assessment of trainee pilots' flight style based on quantitative management of point system. V Mark. China **2018**(12), 129 (2018)
11. Zhong, H.: Quantitative Research on Civil Aviation Flight Discipline. Civil Aviation Flight University of China, Sichuan (2020)
12. Yu, X.: Construction of a Quantitative Evaluation Standard for Flight Discipline Based on a Multi-Dimensional Criterion Measurement System. Civil Aviation Flight University of China, Sichuan (2022)
13. Wei, Y., Zhu, J., Sun, J., et al.: A preliminary study on the evaluation method of ethical conducts of civil aviation employees—a case study of pilots and controllers. Civil Aviat. Manag. **364**(02), 77–81 (2021)
14. Merritt, A., Helmreich, R., Wilhelm, J., Sherman, P.: Flight Management Attitudes Questionnaire 2.0 (International) and 2.19(USA/Anglo). The University of Texas Aerospace Crew Research Project Technical Report, pp. 96–104 (1996)
15. Ji, M., Liu, Z., Yang, S., et al.: A study on the relationship between hazardous attitudes and safe operation behaviors among airline pilots in China. J. Psychol. Sci. **35**(01), 202–207 (2012)
16. Payne, K.H., Harris, D.: A psychometric approach to the development of a multidimensional scale to assess aircraft handling qualities. Int. J. Aviat. Psychol. **10**(4), 343–362 (2000)
17. Sun, R., Xiao, Y.: Research on indicating structure for operation characteristic of civil aviation pilots based on QAR data. J. Saf. Sci. Technol. **8**(11), 49–54 (2012)
18. Sun, R., Yang, Y., Wang, L.: Study on flight safety evaluation based on QAR data. China Saf. Sci. J. **25**(07), 87–92 (2015)
19. Wang, L., Jiang, Y., Tan, W.: Study on construction of risk portrait index system for airline pilots. China Saf. Sci. J. **30**(11), 13–21 (2020)
20. Wang, L., Dong, C., Cui, M.: Evaluation method of flight operation skills based on power spectrum. Flight Dyn. **36**(4), 92–96 (2018)

21. Wang, L., Wang, S.: Flight operation analysis method based on QAR data and wavelet transformation. Flight Dyn. **38**(5), 77–83 (2020)
22. Wang, L., Gao, S., Zhang, J., et al.: Evaluation of the exceedance behaviors of the airline transport pilots based on the QAR data. J. Saf. Environ. **21**(2), 695–700 (2021)
23. Diakoulaki, D., Mavrotas, G., Papayannakis, L.: Determining objective weights in multiple criteria problems: the critic method. Comput. Oper. Res. **22**(7), 763–770 (1995)
24. Zhang, Y., Lu, Y., Yang, G., et al.: Multi-attribute decision making method for node importance metric in complex network. Appl. Sci. **12**(4), 1944 (2022)
25. Wang, Z., Dang, S., Xing, Y., et al.: Applying rank sum ratio (RSR) to the evaluation of feeding practices behaviors, and its associations with infant health risk in Rural Lhasa, Tibet. Int. J. Environ. Res. Public Health **12**(12), 15173–15181 (2015)

Integrated Visual Cognition Performance Evaluation Model of Intelligent Control System Interface

Xiaoli Wu[1,2]([✉]) and Yiyao Zhou[2]

[1] School of Design Art and Medical, Nanjing University of Science and Technology, Nanjing 210094, China
wuxlhhu@163.com

[2] Lab of Human Factors and Information System Interaction and Design, College of Mechanical and Electrical Engineering, Hohai University, Changzhou 213022, China

Abstract. An evaluation model of intelligent control system interface is established to evaluate operator's cognition performance, which is the premise to ensure high-efficient operation of systems. In this paper, in view of intelligent control system interface, the comprehensive cognition performance evaluation indicator system is constructed from the dimension of visual search quality and information processing level. Then, the analytic hierarchy process (AHP) is introduced to weight the indicators; vague set characterization quantitative indicator and TOPSIS method are used to order the designed scheme; and the AHP-VAGUE-TOPSIS combination calculation model is constructed. Finally, an objective quantitative evaluation method is provided by evaluating and improving Trina Solar MES control system and weld interface, for applying the physiological evaluation technologies to evaluate the intelligent control system interface.

Keywords: Cognitive load · Vision physiological evaluation indicator · AHP · Vague · TOPSIS

1 Introduction

With the development of computer technology, the digital man-machine interface expands from Internet technology industry to traditional industry. Due to the rapid expansion of the load carrying capacity of digital interface information, the visual cognitive load has led to a strict request for operator's cognition ability, and demanded higher request for information system designers. Therefore, the cognition performance of control system interface should be improved as much as possible.

Representative research results were first provided by Hess and Plost [1] (1960). Afterwards, the scholars in fields of psychology, pedagogy, and aerospace, began to study the internal mechanism of eye movement indicators and cognitive load. They proved that the eye movement data has a critical role in cognitive load. Just et al. [2] (1993) explored the correlation between pupil diameter variations with the complexity of reading materials. Koufaris M [3] (2002) recorded the eye movement data such as the

© The Author(s), under exclusive license to Springer Nature Switzerland AG 2023
D. Harris and W.-C. Li (Eds.): HCII 2023, LNAI 14017, pp. 331–340, 2023.
https://doi.org/10.1007/978-3-031-35392-5_26

fixation path during browsing web images; and discovered that the scanned path would observe a fixed mode. For example, during user browsing similar images, the scanning paths were similar, that is, the users were used to adopt fixed mode to search the target information. Gerald L. Lohse [4] (2001) compared and analyzed the advertisement effect of different sizes or colors in China Pages according to the recorded eye movement data. Shao-Kang Lo [5] (2004) studied the effects of the layout positions of searching keywords on user searching behaviors by analyzing the eye movement indicators. Anuar [6] (2014) used a visual analysis kit instead of the traditional analytical method of eye movement data, and summarized the searching strategies of user searching information on maps. Hollender [7] (2010) evaluated the user interface design by investigating the eye movement trajectory mode and experience of students while using learning management system. Scott G G [8] (2016) studied the attraction degree of the testees for different visual elements in SNS (social network site) based on eye movement tracking technology. Liu Qing [9] (2010), Chen Xiaojiao [10] (2007), and Zhu Wei [11] (2013) et al., evaluated the interface availability level by constructing eye movement indicator evaluation model. Wang Haibo [12] (2013) started from visual searching quality and information processing level, and used four eye movement indicators, i.e., the times of fixation, the length of fixation path, the times of fixation and time proportion in region of interest, and average fixation time, to construct the man-machine interactive digital interface evaluation system. In the traditional eye movement evaluation system, it is difficult to perform integrated level evaluation for interface due to several indicators and fuzzy definition of interface quality. This paper explores the integrated cognition performance level evaluation method of digital control system interface, and proposes the AHP-VAGUE-TOPSIS combined evaluation system by combing the existing vision cognitive theory and physiological vision response indicators.

2   Evaluation Indicators of Intelligent Control System Interface

2.1   Evaluation Indicator Selection

The mapping relation between cognition performance level evaluation standards and vision physiological evaluation indicators should be analyzed from the two perspectives, i.e., the information acquisition and information processing of visual cognition activities. During the searching process of visual information, a lot of attention resource of operators will be recalled. Shi Zhongzhi [13] (2008) demonstrated that during the searching process of visual information, the experienced experts are more likely to adopt depth searching mode than novices. The searching mode of operators can be determined by the number of fixation points and the length of fixation path; and at the same time a task performance indicator can also be introduced to measure operator's searching efficiency, as shown in Table 1.

The cognition performance level of operator during information processing can be analyzed from the aspect of cognitive resource allocation. When operator's cognitive resources are more concentrated on the processing of target information, the invalid cognitive load will be reduced (Wang Haibo [12]). The cognitive loads generated from information processing are usually effective cognitive loads useful for cognitive activities. Thus, the operator's cognition performance level can be measured by the proportion

Table 1. Mapping mode of cognition performance evaluation standards and physiological vision evaluation indicators

Visual cognition process	Cognition performance level evaluation standards	Vision physiological evaluation indicators
Information searching	Recalled cognitive resource of searching mode	Length of fixation point path
		The times of fixation
	Task performance	The times of fixation
Information processing	Effective cognitive loads	Proportion of fixation time and the times of fixation in region of interest
	Effective cognitive loads	Average fixation time
		Pupil diameter

of effective cognitive loads and the inherent cognitive loads during information processing. Wang Haibo [12] (2013) indicated that during visual cognitive activities, the proportion of effective cognitive loads could be measured by the proportion of the fixation time and the number of fixations in the region of interest. Zhang [14] (2001) found that the longer the fixation time was, the longer it would take for the operator to interpret the visual information representation, indicating that the information processing was more difficult. While studying the relation between cognitive load with pupil diameter, Ahern [15] (1979) found that the pupil diameter had negative correlation with cognitive competence by letting the testees with different cognitive competence to complete the same group of arithmetical operations. Therefore, in this paper, the cognition performance level of information processing in the interface cognitive activities is measured from the aspect of operator's cognitive resource allocation.

2.2 Determination of Indicator Weight

In AHP, in order to determine the weights of each indicator, all indicators in a layer are compared pair-wisely to determine the importance degree of each indicator than others, and the weight coefficients are determined using formula [16].

Table 2. Scale scores of first-level indicators.

	A	B
A	1	3.4
B	0.294	1

According to average value of the results of five expert questionnaires, the scale values of first-level indicators are obtained as shown in Table 2. Moreover, the estimation matrix (1) and Eqs. (2), (3) and (4) are used to obtain the indicator weight values after normalization, as shown in Table 3.

$$A = \begin{bmatrix} 1 & a_{12} & \cdots & a_{1m} \\ a_{21} & 1 & \cdots & a_{2m} \\ \cdots & \cdots & 1 & \cdots \\ a_{n1} & a_{i2} & \cdots & a_{nm} \end{bmatrix} \tag{1}$$

$$W_i = A_{ij} / \sum_{i=1}^{n} A_j \tag{2}$$

$$\overline{W}_i = \sum_{j=1}^{n} \overline{a_{ij}}$$
$$(i = 1, 2, \ldots, n) \tag{3}$$

$$W'_i = \frac{\overline{W}_i}{\sum_{j=1}^{n} \overline{W}_i}$$
$$(i = 1, 2, \ldots, n) \tag{4}$$

Table 3. Weight values of first-level indicators.

Indicator Name	Vision Searching Quality	Information Processing Level
Weight value	0.773	0.227

The consistency ratio of first-level indicators is CR = 0 < 0.1, which passes the consistency test.

Using the same method, all indicators are calculated and arranged, and the obtained weight values of indicators are shown in Table 4.

3 Vague Set-TOPSIS Integrated Preference Sorting Model

3.1 Vague Set Function Calculation

According to Vague theory [17, 18], the target membership matrix is constructed in this paper to obtain the vague value, which is used to measure the degree to which a design satisfies the requirements of the evaluator.

According to the physiological vision evaluation indicator data obtained by experiments, the target membership matrix $\gamma = [\gamma_{ij}]_{m \times n}$ is constructed, where γ_{ij} represents the extent to which the ideal value is reached:

a. For the evaluation indicators that are the smaller the better, such as "searching breadth", "degree of interface convergence", and "physiological effort level", their relative grade-of-membership γ_{ij} can be expressed as:

$$\gamma_{ij} = \begin{cases} 1 - \dfrac{a_{ij}}{a_{jmax}}, & a_{jmin} = 0 \\ \dfrac{a_{jmin}}{a_{ij}}, & a_{jmin} \neq 0 \end{cases} \tag{5}$$

Table 4. Weight values of navigation bar design and integrated cognition performance evaluation indicators.

First-level Indicators	Weight Value	Second-level Indicators	Weight Value	Integrated Weight Value
Vision searching quality	0.773	Searching depth	0.299	0.231
		Searching breadth	0.123	0.095
		Searching efficiency	0.579	0.448
Information processing level	0.227	Interface degree of convergence	0.447	0.101
		Interface divergence degree	0.144	0.033
		Physiological effect degree	0.409	0.093

b. For the evaluation indicators that are the larger the better, such as "searching depth", "searching efficiency", and "degree of interface convergence", their relative grade-of-membership γ_{ij} can be expressed as:

$$\gamma_{ij} = \frac{a_{ij}}{a_{jmax}} \tag{6}$$

Evaluators can define the acceptable data satisfaction degree lower limit λ^U and the allowable dissatisfaction degree upper limit λ^L. By obtaining the matrix value according to matrix γ, it can screen out the design solution's supporting indicators set S, opposing indicators set O, and neural indicators set N [18].

$S_i = \{a_j \in a | \gamma_{ij} \geq \lambda^U\}(i = 1, 2, \cdots, m; j = 1, 2, \cdots, n)$ is the supporting indicators set of the i th evaluation solution, indicating that the j th data in the evaluation solution supports the evaluation solution i.

$O_i = \{a_j \in a | \gamma_{ij} \leq \lambda^L\}(i = 1, 2, \cdots, m; j = 1, 2, \cdots, n)$ is the opposing indicators set of the i th evaluation solution, indicating that the j th data in the evaluation solution opposes the evaluation solution i.

$N_i = \{a_j \in a | \lambda^L \leq \gamma_{ij} \leq \lambda^U\}(i = 1, 2, \cdots, m; j = 1, 2, \cdots, n)$ is the neural indicators set of the i th evaluation solution, indicating that the j th data in the evaluation solution neither supports nor opposes the evaluation solution i.

The VAGUE set evaluation matrix D is constructed by substituting the indicator weight $w = \{w_1, w_2, \cdots, w_n\}$ obtained using the AHP method:

$$D = \begin{vmatrix} [t_1, 1-f_1] \\ [t_2, 1-f_2] \\ \cdots \\ [t_m, 1-f_m] \end{vmatrix} \tag{8}$$

where t_i and f_i represent the degrees to which the solution does and does not satisfy the evaluation indicators, respectively.

The degree v_i to which the solution i satisfies the evaluator's requirement can be expressed by VAGUE number as:

$$v_i = [t_i, 1 - f_i] = \begin{bmatrix} \frac{\sum_{j \in \eta 1} w_j \gamma_{ij}}{\sum_{j=1}^{n} w_j \gamma_{ij}}, \\ 1 - \frac{\sum_{j \in \eta 2} w_j \gamma_{ij}}{\sum_{j=1}^{n} w_j \gamma_{ij}} \end{bmatrix} \tag{9}$$

Where $\eta 1 = \{j | a_j \in S_i\}$, $\eta 2 = \{j | a_j \in O_i\}$; and $i = 1, 2, \cdots, m; j = 1, 2, \cdots, n$.

3.2 TOPSIS Preference Sorting

The idea of TOPSIS preference sorting is to select a positive ideal value and a negative ideal value, and then calculate the proximity of each design to the ideal solution [19]. The larger the proximity, the better the corresponding design will be.

For a group of vague numbers $X (i = 1, 2, \cdots, m)$, the positive and the negative ideal values X^+ and X^- of the vague values of navigation bar design solution are determined:

$$\begin{aligned} X^+ &= \begin{bmatrix} \max_{i=1,2,\cdots,m} t_i, 1 - \min_{i=1,2,\cdots,m} f_i \end{bmatrix} \\ X^- &= \begin{bmatrix} \min_{i=1,2,\cdots,m} t_i, 1 - \max_{i=1,2,\cdots,m} f_i \end{bmatrix} \end{aligned} \tag{10}$$

The distance between the vague value of this design with the positive and the negative ideal values can be calculated by vague distance formula. In the formula, d^+ is the distance between each design's X_i with X^+, while d^- is the distance between each design's X_i with X^-, both can be calculated as below:

$$d_i^+ = d(X_i, X^+) = \sqrt{(t_i - t^+)^2 + (f_i - f^+)^2} \tag{11}$$

$$d_i^- = d(X_i, X^-) = \sqrt{(t_i - t^-)^2 + (f_i - f^-)^2} \tag{12}$$

The relative proximity index from each design's quantitative index value to the ideal value is calculated as:

$$\mu_i = \frac{d^-}{d^+ + d^-} \tag{13}$$

According to the idea of preference method, if a design's X_i approaches to X^+ and deviates from X^-, it indicates that the supporting degree of membership of this design is larger. It also means that if μ_i is larger, the design further approaches to the ideal cognition performance level. Thus, the sorting of preference can be performed for the navigation bar design solutions.

4 Solution Evaluation of Weld Interface Design of MES Control System

4.1 Experimental Design

The MES system's weld interface navigation bar design is taken as example. In order to simulate the real user scenarios as best as possible, the complete interface is adopted and the data processing is performed according to the divisions of regions of interest. Three experiments are performed, i.e., the original interface, the optimized solution based on original interface after considering the navigation bar display size, background, and font information, and the second optimized solution based on the first optimized solution after adding the icon display. The experimental results and the collected eye movement data are shown in Table 5, respectively.

Table 5. Integrated cognition performance physiological evaluation indicators data of navigation bar.

	Vision Searching Quality			Information Processing Level		
	Searching depth	Searching breadth	Searching efficiency	Interface degree of convergence	Interface divergence degree	Physiological effort level
Original interface	0.155	2204.591	0.098	0.052	0.108	3.566
Solution 1	0.211	1260.781	0.133	0.092	0.123	3.715
Solution 2	0.278	1882.378	0.151	0.043	0.112	3.688

4.2 Data Processing and Analysis

According to Eqs. (5) and (6), the six indicators, i.e., "searching depth", "searching breadth", "searching efficiency", "interface degree of convergence", "interface divergence degree", and "physiological effort level", are transformed to a target preference membership matrix $\gamma =$

$$\begin{bmatrix} 0.558 & 0.572 & 0.652 & 0.565 & 1 & 1 \\ 0.759 & 1 & 0.882 & 1 & 0.878 & 0.960 \\ 1 & 0.670 & 1 & 0.467 & 0.964 & 0.967 \end{bmatrix}$$

The satisfaction lower limit $\lambda^U = 0.85$ and the acceptable dissatisfaction upper limit $\lambda^L = 0.7$ are determined and each design's supported, opposed and neutral indicators sets are obtained.

$S_1 = \{a_5, a_6\}, O_1 = \phi, N_1 = \{a_1, a_2, a_3, a_4\};$
$S_2 = \{a_2, a_2, a_4, a_5, a_6\}, O_1 = \phi, N_1 = \{a_1\};$
$S_2 = \{a_1, a_3, a_5, a_6\}, O_1 = \phi, N_1 = \{a_2, a_4\};$

The obtained indicator weight value $W\_i = \{0.231, 0.095, 0.448, 0.101, 0.033, 0.093\}$ are substituted, and Eq. (9) is used to determine the vague values of three solutions.

$$v_i = (0.191, 0.191),$$
$$v_i = (0.802, 1),$$
$$v_i = (0.878, 0.878).$$

Vague set evaluation matrix is constructed.

$$D = \begin{bmatrix} [0.191\ 0.191] \\ [0.802\ 1] \\ [0.878\ 0.878] \end{bmatrix}$$

The solution set's positive ideal value X^+ and negative ideal value X^- are determined.

$$X^+ = [0.878, 1]$$
$$X^- = [0.191, 0.191]$$

According to Eqs. (11) and (12), the distances d_i^+ and d_i^- between X_i with X^+ and X^-, respectively, in each interface navigation bar design solution are calculated.

$$d_1^+ = 1.061, d_1^- = 0$$
$$d_2^+ = 0.077, d_2^- = 1.013,$$
$$d_3^+ = 0.122, d_3^- = 0.972.$$

According to Eq. (13), the proximity of X_i approaching to ideal value in each interface navigation bar design solution is calculated.

$$\mu_1 = 0,$$
$$\mu_2 = 0.930,$$
$$\mu_3 = 0.889.$$

The sorted proximity values are: $X_2 > X_3 > X_1$. The comparison of six evaluation indicators shows that the integrated cognition performance level of navigation bar design 2 approaches to the ideal cognition performance level, which means it is the optimal navigation bar design.

5 Conclusions

1. By using the physiological vision evaluation indicators, the integrated cognition performance evaluation indicators of intelligent control system interface are established from the perspectives of information searching quality and information processing level.
2. By adopting the idea of multi-attribute decision-making, the AHP method is used to weight the indicators and combining the vague set and the TOPSIS preference sorting calculation model, the integrated design evaluation value is presented, which provides objective quantitative data support for interface evaluation.
3. Case analysis indicates that the proposed model has considered reasonable weighting of different indicators and can sort the design solutions according to their integrated preference levels. Thus, the proposed model effectively reduces the subjective evaluation error, and achieves high application value.

Acknowledgments. This work was supported by the National Nature Science Foundation of China (52175469), Jiangsu Province Nature Science Foundation of China (BK20221490), JWKJ Fundamental Strengthen Fundation(JCJQ-JJ-8041), and the Key Fundamental Research Funds for the Central Universities (30920041114).

References

1. Hess, E.H., Polt, J.M.: Pupil size as related to interest value of visual stimuli. Science **132**(3423), 349–350 (1960)
2. Just, M.A., Carpenter, P.A.: The intensity dimension of thought: pupillometric indices of sentence processing. Can J Exp Psychol **47**(2), 310–339 (1993)
3. Koufaris, M.: Applying the technology acceptance model and flow theory to online consumer behavior. Inf. Syst. Res. **13**(2), 205–223 (2002)
4. Lohse, G.L., Wu, D.J.: Eye movement patterns on chinese yellow pages advertising. Electron. Mark. **11**(2), 87–96 (2001). https://doi.org/10.1080/101967801300197007
5. Lo, S.K., Hsieh, A.Y., Chiu, Y.P.: Keyword advertising is not what you think: clicking and eye movement behaviors on keyword advertising. Electron. Commer. Res. Appl. **13**(4), 221–228 (2014)
6. Anuar, N., Kim, J.: A direct methodology to establish design requirements for human–system interface (HSI) of automatic systems in nuclear power plants. Ann. Nucl. Energy **63**(1), 326–338 (2014)
7. Hollender, N., Hofmann, C., Deneke, M., et al.: Integrating cognitive load theory and concepts of human–computer interaction. Comput. Hum. Behav. **26**(6), 1278–1288 (2010)
8. Scott, G.G., Hand, C.J.: Motivation determines Facebook viewing strategy: an eye movement analysis. Comput. Hum. Behav. **56**, 267–280 (2016)
9. Liu, Q., Xue, C., Hoehn, F., et al.: Interface usability evaluation based on eye-tracking technology. J. Southeast Univ. (Nat. Sci. Ed.) **40**(2), 331–334 (2010)
10. Chen, X., Xue, C., Chen, M., et al.: Quality assessment model of digital interface based on eye-tracking experiments. J. Southeast Univ. (Nat. Sci. Ed.) **47**(1), 38–42 (2017)
11. Wang, H., Xue, C., Huang, J., et al.: Design and evaluation of human-computer digital interface based on cognitive load. Electro-Mech. Eng. **29**(5), 57–60 (2013)

12. Wei, Z., Wei, H.: Method of software interface evaluation based on eye-tracking technology. Electro-Mech. Eng. **29**(4), 62–64 (2013)
13. Shi, Z.: Cognition Science. China University of Science and Technology Press, Beijing (2008)
14. .Zhang, G., Shen, M., Tao, R.: The application of eye tracking in usability tests. Chin. Ergon. (04), 9–14+70–71 (2001)
15. Ahern, S.K., Beatty, J.: Pupillary responses during information processing vary with scholastic aptitude test scores. Science **205**(4412), 1289–1292 (1979)
16. Yang, H.: The weight setting and fuzzy evaluation of library service quality evaluation. Inf. Res. (05), 18-20 (2010)
17. Gau, W.L., Buehrer, D.J.: Vague sets. IEEE Trans. Syst. Man Cybern. **23**(2), 610–614 (1993)
18. Geng, X., Chu, X., Zhang, Z.: A new integrated design concept evaluation approach based on vague sets. Expert Syst. Appl. **37**(9), 6629–6638 (2010)
19. Geng, T., Lu, G., Zhang, A.: Group decision-making method for air target threat assessment based on Vague sets. Syst. Eng. Electron. **33**(12), 2686–2690 (2011)

How the Color Level of HUD Affects Users' Search Performance: An Ergonomic Study

Jinchun Wu, Chenhao Li, and Chengqi Xue[✉]

School of Mechanical Engineering, Southeast University, Nanjing 211189, China
ipd_xcq@seu.edu.cn

Abstract. This paper proposed an approach by using the color layering strategy to classify the interface information of HUD, based on the designing of aircraft HUD. The hue attribute of color was used as the breakthrough. The icon search experiment was utilized and the background color in the hue ring was selected every 60° The foreground color is determined according to three color levels, 180°, 120° and 60°, which are different from the background color. We explored the effect of color level on search performance and found the optimal combination of foreground and background colors. The results revealed that the search performance was highest when the background was red, and the foreground was green and yellow.

Keywords: Color Stratification · Search Performance · HUD · Background and Foreground Color Combination

1 Introduction

Pilots receive a plethora of information and different types of information during flight, including flight parameters, navigation parameters, system status information, etc. Complicated information was bound to bring a heavy cognitive load to pilots [1]. The interface information in the HUD is color-coded to distinguish the priority of information, which can reduce the confusion of visual information and help the pilot maintain a fast and efficient cognitive level. Color layering affects the priority allocation of attention resources in the process of information cognition through color coding. Colors with high recognition in the interface could best attract people's attention, guide people's visual behavior, and effectively improve cognitive performance [2]. The current HUD technology has certain limitations. There are instances where the interface's information is obscure and sluggish recognition. Therefore, research into the HUD interface from the perspective of color coding can provide suggestions for improving the HUD interface design, which is of great significance for further enhancing the safety and efficiency of the HUD.

Numerous studies on color layering and HUD interface color design have been undertaken by academics both at home and abroad. Laar [3] studied colors with a higher visual level and using higher-level colors made the user's task prompts more obvious during operation, thus improving the user's work efficiency. Laar [4] et al. conducted search experiments with three different color-coding methods (monochromatic coding,

D. Harris and W.-C. Li (Eds.): HCII 2023, LNAI 14017, pp. 341–353, 2023.
https://doi.org/10.1007/978-3-031-35392-5_27

maximum discriminability coding, and visual hierarchical color coding), and concluded that the visual hierarchical coding method was superior to the other two coding methods. Puhalla [5] pointed out that controlling the contrast between hue, saturation and lightness of colors can significantly improve people's cognitive ability of information. Different combinations of hue, saturation and lightness represent different visual levels, and color combinations at different levels can promote people to rank the importance of information. Ahlstrom et al. [6] designed a set of prototype color swatch systems and applied it to the interface of the air control radar display. This set of color swatches divided the interface information in the display at different levels using color coding, which improved the saliency of important information and maintained good legibility. Li Wei et al. [7] studied the search performance of color characters on a black background and concluded that the search time would decrease with the increase of the color difference between foreground and background. Through the above literature research, it is found that color layering can effectively improve the speed of information search and human cognitive performance, an important means to improve the readability, ease of use and efficiency of digital interfaces. Color difference can be understood as color layering essentially, and different color differences are in different color levels. The influence of color difference on cognitive performance still needs further research.

In terms of HUD interface color design, DereFeldt et al. [8] explored the influence of HUD interface color coding on pilots' visual search and situation awareness through experiments, and the results showed that two-color coding and multicolor coding could improve pilots' search efficiency and situation awareness more than one-color coding. Duanqin Xiong et al. [9] discussed the impact of four-color configurations of HUD interface on flight performance (simulated flight) under day and night conditions, and the result showed that the combined effect of green and magenta was the best. Ling Bai [10] took the HUD display interface of an F-35 fighter jet as the research object, used the ITTI visual saliency model to extract the main color of the actual background pictures such as mountains, snow and mountains, and took the HUD air/air attack - medium and long-range missile interface of a fighter jet as the stimulus interface, and conducted an experimental study on the matching problem between two-color coding and environmental color. It is concluded that the cognitive performance of HUD two-color coding is higher than that of monochromatic coding, and the best two-color matching scheme for different kinds of flight backgrounds is obtained. Xu Xiao et al. [11] proved through experiments that in the color-coding species of HUD, red is better than yellow for abnormal information, and green is not suitable for abnormal information. Wang Haiyan et al. [12] selected 14 kinds of pure color backgrounds, changed the brightness and purity of the foreground character color (the hue is 120 in the HSB color system) to carry out the vernier acuity comparison experiment, and obtained the brightness and purity values with the best recognition in the daytime are (33%, 33%) and (99%, 33%). The best values of brightness and purity were 33% and 66%. Zhang Lei et al. [13] proposed that the combination of background color and target color in the flight interface greatly affects the target recognition of subjects, and the combination of background color and foreground color, namely color coding, will have different effects on cognitive performance due to different mental load and task types. The above literature research found that most domestic and foreign researchers have concluded that two-color coding is better than one-color coding in the study of HUD interface color. When studying the influence of real background on HUD interface design, most of the research experiments are conducted by processing the pictures of the real environment into a solid color background in a certain way.

2 Hue-Based Color Layering Experiments

2.1 Subjects and Experimental Apparatus

In this experiment, 25 subjects (16 females and 9 males, aged from 22 to 29 years old), with corrected visual acuity of more than 1.0, normal vision, and no color blindness or weakness were recruited. The experimental program was compiled with E-prime 2.0, to present the stimulus pictures and record the response times and correctness rates. A 15.4-inch MacBook Pro laptop with a resolution of 2880 * 1800 pixels was used, the same resolution as the stimulus picture. After the experiment, excel was used to sort out the data, and SPSS 26.0 was used to analyze the data.

2.2 Experimental Materials and Experimental Factors

The size of the background image was 2880px by 1800px. A total of 65 kinds of graphics have been designed, all of which are relatively simple and common icons. All icons were drawn on a 50px-by-50px palette in Adobe Illustrator, fine-tuned to make each shape visually the same size (see Fig. 1). They had the same semantic familiarity and were both signs of familiarity.

There were four factors in the experiment. The experimental factor A (information capacity) has three levels: A (1): 16; A (2): 32; and A (3): 64. The number of icons on the page is 16, 32, and 64 (see Fig. 2).

The experimental factor B (the hue of the background color) has six levels: B (1): 60°; B (2): 120°; B (3): 180°; B (4): 240°; B (5): 300°; B (6): 360° (using HSV color system, saturation s and lightness v values are set as 100%) (see Fig. 3).

Experimental factor C (the combination of the two foreground colors) has 10 levels: C (1): high-middle 1; C (2): high - middle 2; C (3): high - low 1; C (4): high - low 2; C (5): middle 1 - middle 2; C (6): middle 1 - low 1; C (7): middle 1 - low 2; C (8): middle 2 - low 1; C (9): middle 2-low 2; C (10): low 1 - low 2.

The experimental factor D (the level of the target figure) has three levels: D (1): in the first foreground color, D (2): in the second foreground color, and D (3): there is no target figure.

2.3 Experimental Procedure

The task of the experiment was an icon search task (see Fig. 4). First, a target figure was presented, and then subjects were asked to find the target figure. There may be a target figure in the interface, and there may not be a target figure. If the target image was on the left side of the interface, the subjects were asked to press the "A" key. Appeared on the right side of the interface and asked the subjects to press the "L" key; If the target

J. Wu et al.

Fig. 1. 65 icons with a hue of 180 degrees

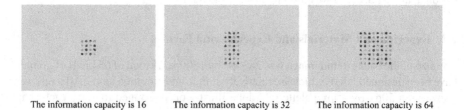

The information capacity is 16   The information capacity is 32   The information capacity is 64

Fig. 2. Chart layout under different information capacities (monochrome)

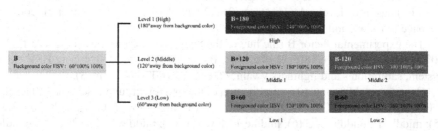

Fig. 3. Division of color hierarchy

graph did not exist, press the Space key. The target figure appeared to the left and right of the interface, and the trial-by-trial cross appeared when no target figure was present. Reaction time and accuracy were all recorded. The total number of tests is 3 * 6* 10 * 3 = 540 times. The subjects first conducted the practice experiment for 20 trials and then proceeded to the formal experiment after familiarity or no errors.

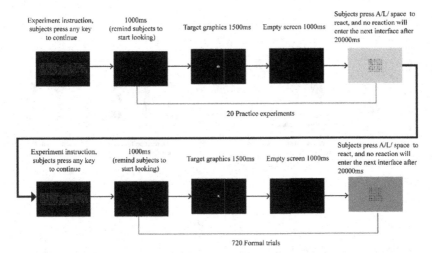

Fig. 4. Experimental procedure

3 Results and Analysis

As shown in Fig. 5, the reaction time among the three levels of information capacity is quite different, and the reaction time increased with the increase of information capacity; for different combinations of background hue and foreground color, the reaction time difference of each level was not very significant; there was almost no difference between the reaction time of the target graphic in the first foreground color and the second foreground color, and the reaction time of the non-existent target graphic was much larger than that of the existing target graphic.

For the reaction time of 25 subjects, 3 (information capacity: 16, 32, 64) × 6 (background hue: 60°, 120°, 180°, 240°, 300°, 360°) × 10 (combination of two foreground colors: High - Medium 1, High - Medium 2, High - low 1, high - low 2, Medium 1 - Medium 2, Medium 1 - low 1, Medium 1 - low 2, medium 2 - low 1, medium 2 - low 2, low 1 - low 2) × 3 (Level of the target graph: the target graph in the first foreground color, the target graph in the second foreground color, and no target graph) four-factor repeated measures ANOVA was performed. According to Table 3-1, (1) Main effect: the main effect of information capacity is significant, $F(2,48) = 4974.476$, $p < 0.001$, $\eta2 = 0.995$; The main effect of background hue was significant, $F(5,120) = 4.630$, $p < 0.001$, $\eta2 = 0.162$; The main effect of foreground color combination was significant, $F(9,216) = 26.623$, $p < 0.001$, $\eta2 = 0.526$; The main effect of the level of the target graph was significant, $F(2,48) = 1883.925$, $p < 0.001$, $\eta2 = 0.987$. (2) Double interaction: the interaction between information capacity and background hue was significant, $F(10,240) = 4.057$, $p < 0.001$, $\eta2 = 0.145$; The interaction between information capacity and foreground color combination was significant, $F(18,432) = 10.045$, $p < 0.001$, $\eta2 = 0.295$; The interaction between information capacity and the level of the target graph was significant $F(4,96) = 402.607$, $p < 0.001$, $\eta2 = 0.944$; The combination of background hue and foreground color had significant interaction, $F(45,1080) = 14.009$, $p < 0.001$, $\eta2 = 0.369$; The interaction between the background hue and the level of the target figure was

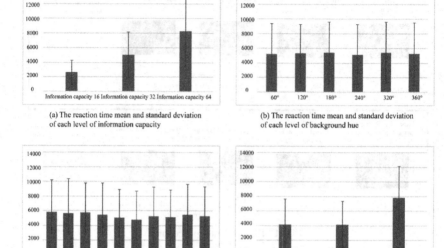

(a) The reaction time mean and standard deviation of each level of information capacity

(b) The reaction time mean and standard deviation of each level of background hue

(c) The reaction time mean and standard deviation of two foreground scenery combinations at each level

(d) The reaction time mean and standard deviation of each level of target graph

Fig. 5. Response time results for each level of the four factors

significant $F(10,240) = 7.505$, $p < 0.001$, $\eta2 = 0.238$; The interaction between the combination of foreground color and the level of the target graph was significant ($F(18,432) = 15.324$, $p < 0.001$, $\eta2 = 0.390$). (3) Triple interaction: the combination of information capacity, background hue and foreground color had significant interaction, $F(90,2160) = 9.682$, $p < 0.001$, $\eta2 = 0.287$; The hierarchical interaction of information capacity, background hue and target figure was significant, $F(20,480) = 13.264$, $p < 0.001$, $\eta2 = 0.356$; The interaction of information capacity, foreground color combination and the level of target graph were significant ($F(36,864) = 13.135$, $p < 0.001$, $\eta2 = 0.354$; The interaction between background hue, foreground color combination and the level of the target figure was significant ($F(90,2160) = 14.525$, $p < 0.001$, $\eta2 = 0.377$). (4) Fourfold interaction: information capacity, background hue, foreground color combination, the level of the target graph interaction was significant, $F(180,4320) = 213.977$, $p < 0.001$, $\eta2 = 0.368$.

According to the experimental purpose, simple simple effect analysis of the information capacity, background hue, and foreground color combination method could obtain the optimal foreground color and background color under different information capacity. The simple simple effect analysis of the combination of background hue, foreground color and the level of the target graph could be concluded which color of the target graph has higher search performance in different background colors and foreground colors. Therefore, the simple simple effect analysis was conducted for the above two groups of factors with significant triple interaction.

In the simple simple effect analysis of the combination of information capacity, background hue, and foreground color, the effect of the combination of foreground color on each level of combined processing of information capacity and background hue was explored. From Table 1, the combination of foreground colors shows a significant difference in the level of combined processing for all levels of information capacity and background hue. Specifically, an LSD post hoc test of the effect of the combination of foreground colors was required to determine which of the 10 levels in the foreground color combination had a significant difference between them.

Table 1. Effect of factor C on the combined treatment of factors A and B

	A(1)B(1)	A(1)B(2)	A(1)B(3)	A(1)B(4)	A(1)B(5)	A(1)B(6)
F	16.10	15.84	4.94	15.75	10.20	10,71
p	.000	.000	.000	.000	.000	.000
	A(2)B(1)	A(2)B(2)	A(2)B(3)	A(2)B(4)	A(2)B(5)	A(2)B(6)
F	5.69	9.42	6.08	20.56	22.79	13.57
p	.000	.000	.000	.000	.000	.000
	A(3)B(1)	A(3)B(2)	A(3)B(3)	A(3)B(4)	A(3)B(5)	A(3)B(6)
F	12.62	7.17	18.22	6.05	11.13	12.24
p	.000	.000	.000	.000	.000	.000

According to Figs. 6, 7 and 8, the ten levels of the foreground color combination method have different trends at various information capacities and background color phases for each level of combined processing. The lowest background and foreground color combinations at response time at each information capacity were further analyzed as follows.

1) When the information capacity was 16, the background color was yellow, the foreground color was cyan or magenta, there was a lower response (A1B1C5), and the results of the post hoc test showed that C5 (1892 ± 83 ms) was not significantly different from C2 (1964 ± 135 ms), C4 (2063 ± 96 ms), and C10 (2064 ± 109 ms), except for the A1B1 condition. Significant differences were found with the other six levels, C1 (4014 ± 244 ms), C3 (3171 ± 188 ms), C6 (2589 ± 121 ms), C7 (2548 ± 128 ms), C8 (2774 ± 316 ms), C9 (2537 ± 119 ms); background color was blue, foreground color was red, cyan and foreground was magenta, cyan There were lower reaction times when the background color was blue (A1B4C7, A1B4C10), and the A1B4 condition, C7 (1785 ± 55 ms) was significantly different from all the other eight levels except for the non-significant difference with C10 (1763 ± 71 ms), C1 (2715 ± 134 ms), C2 (3354 ± 114 ms), C3 (2503 ± 98 ms), C4 (2299 ± 175 ms), C5 (2816 ± 155 ms), C6 (2407 ± 105 ms), C8 (2271 ± 101 ms), C9 (2564 ± 169 ms); there was a lower response time when the background color was red and the foreground color was green and yellow (A1B6C6), and the A1B6 condition, C6 (1859 ± 98 ms), was different from the the the other nine levels were significant, C1 (2226 ± 128 ms), C2 (2640 ± 148 ms), C3 (2739 ± 109 ms), C4 (3156 ± 131 ms), C5 (2254 ± 104 ms), C7 (2730 ± 147 ms), C8 (2118 ± 83 ms), C9 (2459 ± 107 ms), and C10 (2478 ± 76 ms). The combination

of these four groups of background and foreground colors has a lower response time, i.e., the combination of these four groups of background and foreground colors is most beneficial to improve the search performance.

2) When the information capacity was 32, there was a lower response time when the background color was red and the foreground color was green and yellow (A2B6C6), the difference between C6 (3014 ± 137 ms) and the other eight levels in the A2B6 condition was significant except for the non-significant difference with C9 (3480 ± 267 ms), C1 (4381 ± 274 ms), C2 (5095 ± 338 ms), C3 (5588 ± 221 ms), C4 (4460 ± 135 ms), C5 (5988 ± 374 ms), C7 (4588 ± 120 ms), C8 (5262 ± 282 ms), and C10 (5666 ± 291 ms). The background and foreground color combination were most beneficial to increase the search performance.

3) When the information capacity is 64, there was a lower response time when the background color is cyan and the foreground color was magenta and blue (A3B3C6), and the A3B3 condition, C6 (5977 ± 265 ms) was significantly different from the other eight levels except for the non-significant difference with C5 (6782 ± 352 ms), C1 (7457 ± 264 ms), C2 (9688 ± 464 ms), C3 (7522 ± 397 ms), C4 (7832 ± 319 ms), C7 (10644 ± 450 ms), C8 (10251 ± 628 ms), C9 (10494 ± 400 ms), C10 (8002 ± 297 ms); there were lower response times when the background color was red and the foreground color was green and yellow (A3B6C6), and the A3B6 condition was significantly different from the other nine levels for C6 (6067 ± 199 ms), C1 (7640 ± 276 ms), C2 (9885v514 ms), C3 (9006 ± 260 ms), C4 (7763 ± 407 ms), C5 (10339 ± 500 ms), C7 (9404 ± 375 ms), C8 (7367 ± 453 ms), C9 (8290 ± 246 ms), C10 (9360 ± 542 ms); there were lower response times when the background color was yellow and the foreground color was cyan and red (A3B1C7), and the A3B1 condition, C7 (6328 ± 172 ms) was not significantly different from C4 (6831 ± 418 ms) except significant, the differences were significant with the other eight levels, C1 (9315 ± 464 ms), C2 (9097 ± 410 ms), C3 (8227 ± 138 ms), C5 (7422 ± 212 ms), C6 (7025 ± 176 ms), C8 (7706 ± 233 ms), C9 (9194 ± 276 ms), and C10 (8995 ± 356 ms). The combination of these three groups of background and foreground colors had lower response times, indicating that the combination of these three groups of background and foreground colors was most beneficial for improving search performance.

In conclusion, the effect of color level on search performance is affected by information capacity and background hue. The optimal combination of foreground color is different under different information capacities and background hue. Based on the above analysis, A1B6C6, A2B6C6, and A3B6C6 have lower reaction times, indicating that the background color is red under the three information capacities. The foreground color for green and yellow have higher search performance.

Next, the combination mode of background hue, foreground color and the level of the target figure was analyzed to explore the effect of the level of the target figure on the combination mode of background hue and foreground color. The results of simple simple effect analysis showed that the layers of the target graphics showed significant differences in the combination of background hue and foreground color at all levels of combined processing. Specific to the three levels of the level where the target graph was located, the effect of the level where the target graph was located needs to be tested by LSD post hoc test. The post hoc test results showed that there were significant differences

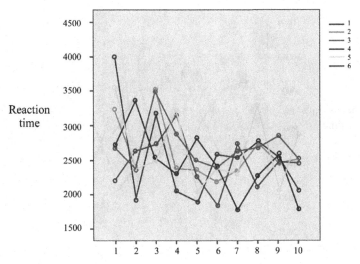

Fig. 6. Mean value of response time at an information capacity of 16

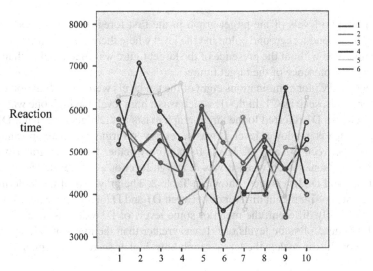

Fig. 7. Mean value of response time at an information capacity of 32

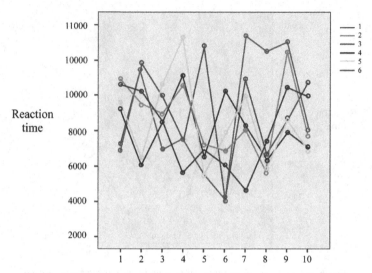

Fig. 8. Mean value of response time at an information capacity of 64

between the two levels of the target graph in the first foreground color and the target graph in the second foreground color and the level where there was no target graph. And the reaction time without the presence of the target figure was much higher than the two levels with the presence of the target figure.

Foreground Color combinations eight of the ten levels were a combination of higher and lower levels, such as C1: high - 1, which was a high level, the high one was lower in the hierarchy, so D1 referred to the target graph exists in the higher level and D2 meant the target shape is in a lower level. It was necessary to further compare and analyze the differences between D1 and D2 levels to explore whether the target graph was more conducive to visual search when it was at a high level or a low level. The differences between D1 and D2 levels were shown in Table 2. The gray part of the table indicated that there was no significant difference between D1 and D2. At levels where D1 and D2 were significantly different, the mean of some levels of D1 was less than the mean of D2, and the mean of some levels of D1 was greater than the mean of D2, so no totally universal conclusion makes the target graph have higher search performance at higher or lower levels.

Table 2. D (1) and D (2) post hoc tests

Mean difference D (1)-D (2)	B (1)	B (2)	B (3)	B (4)	B (5)	B (6)
C (1)	-1901.411*	-183.525	-698.387	358.338	1190.367*	-1826.247*
C (2)	-3098.887*	690.303	-758.415	-1888.785*	-345.203	526.386
C (3)	-753.376*	-1095.207*	195.293	2867.972*	195.405	338.864
C (4)	174.186	-965.889	-2473.699*	620.317	2241.824*	115.604
C (5)	637.419*	2580.492*	-640.417*	-1167.878*	-1197.533*	-1599.114*
C (6)	-1333.811*	662.584	2067.797*	-104.349	-176.540	-433.659*
C (7)	456.505*	-1979.548*	906.793*	415.275	1458.957*	1411.552*
C (8)	1889.856*	-459.965	1391.451*	133.370	-1515.502*	-1503.552*
C (9)	1427.914*	-1139.812*	-1000.267	291.629	-85.770	1962.367*
C (10)	1293.499*	2932.818*	-2654.736*	1596.571*	861.597*	-947.374*

4   Conclusion

The effectiveness of color level on search performance was significantly affected by information capacity and background hue. Under different information capacity and background hue, the optimal foreground color level was very different.

At the low level of information capacity, there are four groups of background and foreground colors with low response time: yellow in the background, cyan-magenta in the foreground, blue in the background, red-cyan in the foreground, blue in the background, magenta-cyan in the foreground, red in the context, green and yellow in the foreground;

at the medium level of information capacity, there was one group of background and foreground colors with low response time: red in the background and foreground view was green-yellow; at the high level of information capacity, there were three groups of background and foreground colors with low response times: cyan in the background, magenta-blue in the foreground, red in the background and green-yellow in the foreground; and yellow in the background and cyan-red in the foreground. A common finding was that the combined background color red and foreground color green yellow had high search performance for all three information volumes.

For the level of the target graph, no universal conclusion was obtained, which made the target graph have higher search efficiency in the higher or lower levels. However, when the background was red and the foreground colors were green and yellow under specific conditions, search performance was higher when the target graph was green than when the target graph was yellow.

Adding a base color to the HUD interface could improve the recognizability of the foreground information. Through this experiment, the best effect was obtained that the red color with a hue of 60 degrees was used as the base color of the HUD interface, and green yellow could be selected for the foreground information at this time. In addition, the information with higher priority could be set to green and the other information to yellow.

References

1. Mohanavelu, K., et al.: Cognitive workload analysis of fighter aircraft pilots in flight simulator environment. Defence Sci. J. **70**, 131–139 (2020)
2. Van Laar, D L.: Colour coding with visual layers can provide performance enhancements in control room displays. In: 2nd International Conference on Human Interfaces in Control Rooms, pp. 228–233. IET Conference Publications, Manchester (2001)
3. Laar, D.L.V.: Psychological and cartographic principles for the production of visual layering effects in computer displays. Displays **22**(4), 125–135 (2001)
4. Laar, D.V., Deshe, O.: Color coding of control room displays: the psychocartography of visual layering effects. Hum. Factors **49**(3), 477–490 (2007)
5. Puhalla, D.M.: Perceiving hierarchy through intrinsic color structure. Vis. Commun. **7**(2), 199–228 (2008)
6. Ahlstrom, U., Arend, L.: Color usability on air traffic control displays. Hum. Factors Ergon. Soc. Ann. Meet. Proc. **49**(1), 93–97 (2005)
7. Wei, L., Yuchun, T.: Characters display the visual benefits of color coding. J. Beijing Inst. Technol. **04**, 485–488 (2000)
8. Derefeldt, G., et al.: Improvement of tactical situation awareness with color-coded horizontal situation displays in combat aircraft. Displays **20**(4), 171–184 (1999)
9. Xiong, Duanqin, Liu, Qingfeng, Guo, Xiaochao, Zhang, Qingjun, Yao, Qin, Bai, Yu., Du, Jian, Wang, Yanyan: The Effect of one-color and multi-color displays with HUD InFormation in aircraft cockpits. In: Long, Shengzhao, Dhillon, Balbir S. (eds.) Man-Machine-Environment System Engineering. LNEE, vol. 406, pp. 389–398. Springer, Singapore (2016). https://doi.org/10.1007/978-981-10-2323-1_44
10. Ling, B., Bo, L., Bingzheng, S., Lingcun, Q., Chengqi, X., YaFeng, N.: A cognitive study of multicolour coding for the Head-up Display (HUD) of fighter aircraft in multiple flight environments. J. Phys. Conf. Ser. **1215**(1), 012032 (2019)

11. Xiao, X., Wanyan, X., Zhuang, D., Wei, Z.: Ergonomic design and evaluation of visual coding for aircraft head-up display. In: 5th International Conference on Biomedical Engineering and Informatics, pp. 748–752. IEEE, Chongqing (2012)

12. Haiyan, W., Jiang, S., Yan, G., Mingwei, S., Ting, B.: Color design of aiming interface for helmet-mounted display. Electron. Opt. Control **23**(06), 64–67, 76 (2016)

13. Lei, Z., Damin, Z.: Color matching of aircraft interface design. J. Beijing Univ. Aeronaut. Astronaut. **35**(08), 1001–1004 (2009)

An Erroneous Behavior Taxonomy for Operation and Maintenance of Network Systems

Zijian Yin[1] ⓘ, Lei Long[2], Jiahao Yu[3], Yijing Zhang[1], and Zhizhong Li[1(✉)] ⓘ

[1] Department of Industrial Engineering, Tsinghua University, Beijing 100084, People's Republic of China
{zhangyijing,zzli}@tsinghua.edu.cn

[2] School of Mechanical and Electrical Engineering, Beijing University of Civil Engineering and Architecture, Beijing 102616, People's Republic of China
2108550020097@stu.bucea.edu.cn

[3] Huawei Technologies Co., Ltd., Shenzhen 518129, People's Republic of China
yujiahao1@huawei.com

Abstract. This paper presents an erroneous behavior taxonomy for network operation and maintenance in the sector of information and communications technology. In this study, through analysis of the procedures of six typical tasks, a generic task type description was first proposed to represent task steps, with three component attributes including operators, objects, and functions. Based on that, four domain experts were invited to make judgments on potential erroneous behaviors when technicians carried out such tasks. Judgment results were analyzed and grouped into a three-level error taxonomy including 10 Level 1 error modes (failures of macro-cognitive functions), 38 Level 2 error modes (general forms of observable erroneous behaviors), and 75 instanced error modes (specific observable erroneous behaviors in specific task steps). The error taxonomy exhibits unique characteristics of the sector of information and communications technology compared with traditional safety-critical domains. Moreover, meaningful insights are gained from this study, including the strength of this three-attribute task type description and the existence of requirements on human understanding in action-type tasks.

Keywords: Human Error · Error Taxonomy · Network Operation and Maintenance

1 Introduction

Communication network systems are crucial infrastructures of information and communications technology (ICT), providing fundamental functions including resource sharing, information transmission and centralized processing, load balancing and distributed processing, and integrated information service [1]. The operation and maintenance of network systems, a common class of tasks in information technology service management (ITSM), are routine but important for guaranteeing that the network system can

D. Harris and W.-C. Li (Eds.): HCII 2023, LNAI 14017, pp. 354–370, 2023.
https://doi.org/10.1007/978-3-031-35392-5_28

meet service requirements and function normally. In general, the network operation and maintenance (NOM) mainly includes hardware resource management (management of electronic labels, CPU, memory, etc.), software resource management (management of license, system software, configuration files, etc.), routine maintenance (to eliminate hidden trouble), and fault handling (to quickly repair arising faults) [1]. Note that in the present study, only software related tasks were our focus. Similar with the tasks in typical sociotechnical systems, NOM tasks are carried out by technicians in the guide of relevant procedures or instructions. Table 1 presents some examples of NOM task steps to demonstrate the characteristics of human-computer interaction (HCI) during the task conduction. The left column of Table 1 presents task steps that require technicians to manipulate through a command-line interface (CLI); this process is somewhat similar with that when we use the Windows CMD.EXE programs in personal computers. In comparison, the right column presents task steps that require technicians to manipulate through a graphical user interface (GUI); in such cases, technicians interact with the computer through graphical widgets rather than command lines. The two types of interactions, as depicted in Fig. 1, are the most used interaction paradigms in NOM tasks.

Table 1. Examples of NOM task steps

Through command-line interface (CLI)	Through graphical user interface (GUI)
① Configure redundancy on ** device, through the commands: MOD CLUSTER: CID=**, ROLE=**; ...... MOD CLUSTER: ****; ② Modify access priority on ** device, through the commands: MOD RLOCATION: RLOCID=**, RMT=**, LP=**; ...... MOD RLOCATION: ****; ③ Configure the remote loading switch, through the commands: MOD INSP: INSPT=**, INSPN=**, INSPV=**, FETYPEN=**; ...... MOD INSP: **;	① Log in the client of standby site. ② In the main menu, click "System > Task list". ③ Check whether the task of data timing synchronization or data forcible synchronization is going on. ④ In the main menu, click "Remote high-availability systems > Manage remote cold backup systems". For the remote cold backup systems to be deleted, click the "Delete" button, and complete the deletion according to notices.

Human errors have been identified as significant contributors to incidents in the ICT sector. According to U.S. Network Reliability Steering Committee (NRSC), the procedural errors, which included problems with documentation, training, supervision, maintenance, or some kind of human error, were the root causes for 33% of telecommunications service outages from 1992 to 1998 [2] with an increasing trend in the frequency of procedural error outages by 2001 [3]. By 2004, the frequency of procedural error outages per year had dropped, but procedural errors were still major contributors to outages [4]. In recent years, there were still procedural errors being reported [5, 6]. The reported

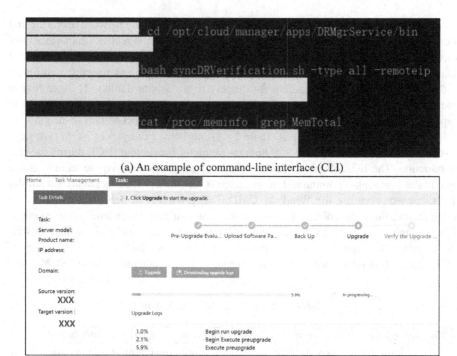

(a) An example of command-line interface (CLI)

(b) An example of graphical user interface (GUI)

Fig. 1. CLI (a) and GUI (b) in NOM tasks

procedural errors have been analyzed by Chang et al. using the IDAC (Information, Decision, and Action in Crew context) model, a simulation model for nuclear power plant (NPP) control room operators [7], and results indicated that important outage-triggering influencing factors included sufficiency of knowledge, level of attention, procedure quality or appropriateness of procedure, motivation/moral/attitude, safety and quality culture, and work process design, taking, and processing [8]. Similarly, statistics in China have revealed that human errors leading to network outages could be grouped into four main categories including misconfigurations, cables/fibers connect errors, poor maintenance or mismanagement, and other operational errors, and the researchers attributed the root cause of misconfigurations to the configuration complexity [9].

An erroneous behavior taxonomy, or error taxonomy, can help us better analyze human errors and understand the underlying mechanisms. Previous researches on human errors establish a solid theoretical foundation which can be referred to in this study. At first sight, errors could be classified based on different behavioral patterns, for example the classification of omission/commission errors [10]. Such behavior-based classifications were criticized for that they failed to reveal underlying mechanisms [11], so cognition-based classifications were developed to better explain human errors. The two different perspectives to classify human errors were also termed as the phenotype and genotype of errors correspondingly by Hollnagel [12]. Towards cognition-based error classifications, both Norman [13] and Reason [14] distinguished slips, i.e., right intentions but wrong actions, and mistakes, i.e., wrong intentions. Such errors could be further categorized; for example, action slips could be categorized into errors in the formation of the intention, faulty activation of schemas, and faulty triggering of active schemas [11]. Rasmussen proposed the SRK framework to categorize human behaviors into three levels, namely skill-based (SB), rule-based (RB), and knowledge-based (KB) [15], and errors could therefore be classified into these three levels accordingly. Reason established a connection between the classifications of slips/mistakes and SRK in his generic error modelling system (GEMS), stating that errors in SB behaviors were slips and lapses, in RB behaviors were RB mistakes, and in KB behaviors were KB mistakes [14]. Another approach to model human performance and errors is the information processing approach, for example the human information processing (HIP) model proposed by Wickens et al. [16]. HIP model identified several stages in the cognition process, such as sensation, perception, response planning, response execution, etc., and the failure of any stages might lead to a human error [17]. These theoretical studies have inspired the developments of relevant error taxonomies in diverse human error identification (HEI) techniques and human reliability analysis (HRA) methods. For example, the Cognitive Reliability Error Analysis Method (CREAM) classified errors according to four cognitive functions, namely observation, interpretation, planning, and execution [18]. Similarly, the Integrated Human Event Analysis System (IDHEAS) classified errors according to five macro-cognitive functions (MCFs), namely detection, understanding, decision-making, action execution, and inter-team coordination [19].

The objective of the present study is to develop an error taxonomy for NOM tasks in the ICT sector. Previous studies have focused on this topic in various safety-critical domains such as nuclear industry [20], aviation [21], healthcare [22, 23], and driving [24], to name a few, while the NOM tasks in the ICT sector are quite different from tasks in traditionally studied sectors with respect to the HCI characteristics as introduced before. As for the perspective of error classification, on one hand, identifying the genotype of human errors has been proved to be a crucial way to understand error mechanisms. But on the other, a purely cognition-based classification seems to be not enough, as the same cognitive failure (e.g., understanding error) can lead to distinct phenotypes (e.g., inputting a wrong command or setting incorrect parameters in a command) which will cause different impacts on the network system. To that end, the present study tried to develop an integrated error taxonomy to combine the two different perspectives. Through such a taxonomy, researchers and ICT practitioners cannot only understand the error mechanisms, but also identify the exact erroneous behavior that will impair the reliability of network systems, so as to design pertinent countermeasures and remedial measures.

2 Methodology

The overall process of the development of the error taxonomy consisted of two phases, as demonstrated in Fig. 2. In the first phase, a generic task type (GTT) description for NOM tasks was developed to represent task steps in a formal structure. Based on that, in the second phase, erroneous behaviors in task steps were collected through expert judgment, and were than categorized into the complete error taxonomy.

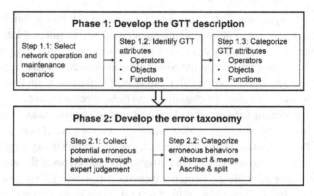

Fig. 2. The overall process of taxonomy development (GTT: generic task type)

2.1 Phase 1: Develop the GTT Description

In this phase, a GTT description was developed to represent task steps in a formal structure. Each GTT in the description is an abstract representation for a class of task steps sharing similar characteristics, such as similarities in familiarity and complexity [25] and in cognitive requirements on human [26, 27]. A standardized GTT description can help us to classify task steps into several groups, so that potential errors in each group can be analyzed. The development of the GTT description was accomplished through the following three steps.

Step 1.1: Select NOM Scenarios

At first, typical NOM scenarios were selected for further analysis. To guarantee that analysis results could represent the characteristics of most NOM tasks, we picked out four most common NOM scenarios, including upgrade, migration, expansion, and proactive change. For each scenario, at least one task was chosen, and all these tasks together covered the two major HCI paradigms (interaction through CLI and GUI). Finally, a total of six tasks were selected, with detailed information presented in Table 2.

Table 2. Selected NOM tasks

Scenarios	Task procedures	CLI	GUI
Upgrade	** upgrade guide	√	√
	** change operations guide	√	√
Migration	** data migration operation guide	√	
Expansion	** expansion operation guide	√	√
Proactive change	** system enhancement guide	√	√
	** redundancy switchover guide	√	

Step 1.2: Identify GTT Attributes

The main objective of a GTT description is to characterize involved human activities (both mental and physical activities), so that potential errors can be identified. It is worth noting that a GTT which solely captures the HCI characteristics can help to analyze errors, but does not aid in analyzing the error consequence, since erroneous operations on different devices can lead to different consequences. Yet, error consequence is an essential index to estimate the risk of errors [28], which can guide the error management and should not be ignored. Therefore, in the present study we proposed three GTT attributes to jointly capture the NOM task steps, namely **operator** (representing the HCI characteristics, such as taking physical actions and evaluating parameters), **object** (representing the target of human operation, such as system configurations and license files), and **function** (representing the type of operation conducted on an object, such as altering and deleting).

Identify Operators

As stated before, the operator was set to characterize technicians' mental and physical activities in HCI. This term was firstly constructed in the GOMS model [29], a well-known model in the discipline of HCI, to represent the action performed in service of a goal [30]. The operators in GOMS were originally designed for human users of interactive computer systems [29], and were therefore suitable for analyzing human activities in the HCI process. Hence, in the present study, the operators provided by GOMSL (hereafter "GOMSL-operator" to distinguish with the operator in this study), an executable notation system for GOMS model [31], were borrowed to analyze required activities in task steps. The second author of this paper, a master student who majored in human factors and ergonomics, completed the identification of involved GOMSL-operators for each task step in selected task procedures, and the results were checked by the first author of this paper, a PhD candidate who focused on human reliability in complex systems.

Identify Objects and Functions

As mentioned, objects in the present study refer to the components of network systems to be manipulated by technicians, and functions refer to the manipulation type. The "function-object" couple describes the exact changes of the network resulting from technicians' operation, for example, "replacing the license file", "modifying the system configuration", "switching the system account", etc. Such objects and functions have already been defined in the technical design of network systems, and there was no need to alter these definitions in this study. Hence, the objects and functions of each task step were identified by simply mapping the item in GTTs into an object and a function according to their technical definitions.

Step 1.3: Categorize GTT Attributes

Categorize Operators

GOMSL-operators specify human activities in a relatively low level, such as pressing a key and clicking the mouse. As illustrated in Table 1, it is obvious that one task step is made up of several GOMSL-operators. In addition, many task steps share the same GOMSL-operators; for instance, those steps in which a command is executed through CLI can all be captured by the same GOMSL-operators (i.e., through pressing a range of keys in the keyboard to input the command). Therefore, those task steps with the same GOMSL-operators shared similar HCI characteristics, and were categorized into one operator in the present study.

Categorize Objects and Functions
Strictly speaking, this process is not a categorizing process, since all objects and functions have been determined in the technical design of network systems. The main work in this step was to standardize all identified items, avoiding potential abuse of terms that caused inconsistent representations. And, if any object was identified as a detailed item, it was abstracted into a general term; for instance, the item "automatic backup function" would be abstracted into "system function".

2.2   Phase 2: Develop the Error Taxonomy

Given the GTT description developed in Phase 1, it was then available to identify potential error modes for the GTTs. Potential errors were first collected through expert judgment, and then categorized into the taxonomy, as introduced below.

Step 2.1: Collect Potential Erroneous Behaviors
This step aimed to identify potential erroneous behaviors when a technician carried out the operators. Four experienced ICT technicians were invited to judge potential erroneous behaviors for each GTT through a questionnaire. The four technicians possessed an average working experience of 7.8 years (SD = 2.3), and could be viewed as domain experts. Table 3 shows an exemplified question for a GTT which is presented to experts for judgement. For each GTT (question), the operator, object, and function of this GTT were presented, alongside with several specific instanced task steps selected from procedures. Experts were required to list potential erroneous behaviors as many as possible on the basis of a total of 120 instanced task steps. Making judgments on the basis of specific instanced task steps allowed experts to contextualize the situations [32], and could therefore improve the judgment quality.

Step 2.2: Categorize Erroneous Behaviors
The erroneous behaviors collected in the last step were then categorized to generate the complete error taxonomy. In the present study, among the three GTT attributes, only operators were used to organize the error modes, since potential error modes mainly depended on the HCI process. As mentioned before, this study aimed to establish an error taxonomy which can characterize erroneous behaviors in NOM tasks in both cognitive and behavioral aspects. For this purpose, a three-level structure was proposed to organize error modes in different levels. The first level, named as "Level 1 error mode", described the underlying cognitive failures of erroneous behaviors, such as "detection error". The second level, named as "Level 2 error mode", described general observable erroneous behaviors, such as "input incorrect parameters". The third level, named as "Instanced error mode", described specific observable erroneous behaviors in specific task steps, such as "input incorrect IP address". This three-level error taxonomy and the operator attribute of GTTs together form an "Operator – Level 1 error mode – Level 2 error mode – Instanced error mode" hierarchy to capture erroneous behaviors in NOM tasks.

Table 3. Exemplified question for expert judgment

Operator	Function	Object	Instanced task steps
Execute operations through CLI	Mod	System function	① Configure redundancy on ** device, through the commands: MOD CLUSTER: CID=**, ROLE=**; ...... MOD CLUSTER: ****; ② Modify access priority on ** device, through the commands: MOD RLOCATION: RLOCID=**, RMT=**, LP=**; ...... MOD RLOCATION: ****; ③ Configure the remote loading switch, through the commands: MOD INSP: INSPT=**, INSPN=**, INSPV=**, FETYPEN=**; ...... MOD INSP: **;

In the present study, the macro-cognition model of IDHEAS [19] was applied as the basic theory, and the failures of five MCFs, i.e., detection, understanding, decision-making, action execution, and inter-team coordination, were adopted as the Level 1 error modes. Besides, the erroneous behaviors collected in the last step were judged by domain experts based on instanced task steps, and therefore agreed with the definition of Instanced error modes. The focus of this step was then to categorize these instanced erroneous behaviors into the Level 2 error modes. This was accomplished by the following two main manipulations.

- Abstract and merge. The Level 2 error modes, which were general error forms that could be applicable to a range of specific task steps, should be abstracted from specific erroneous behaviors of specific task steps (i.e., Instanced error modes). For example, the "Input incorrect IP address" in one task step and the "Input incorrect file name" in another task step should be abstracted and merged into a unified Level 2 error mode "Input incorrect parameters".
- Ascribe and split. It has been broadly recognized that the same observable error mode can be ascribed to diverse cognitive failures. Hence, the underlying cognitive failures of Level 2 error modes should then be identified and attributed to different Level 1 error modes. For example, the "Input incorrect parameters" could be ascribed to both failure of understanding, i.e., that the technician had an incorrect understanding on the parameters, and failure of action execution, i.e., that the technician accidently pressed wrong keys on his/her keyboard.

3   Results

3.1   GTT Description

In total, 6 operators, 14 objects, and 25 functions were identified in the present study, as presented in Table 4, 5 and 6. The permutation of the three attributes would generate a maximum of $6 \times 14 \times 25 = 2100$ different GTTs. However, most cases in the permutation results do not exist for two reasons. On one hand, three out of the six operators, namely Record, Verify, and Decide, would not change the system status, and thus do not have combinations with the 25 functions. On the other, some function-object couples are illegal; for example, the function "Switch" only works on the object "System account", and the combinations of "Switch" and other objects do not exist. Finally, a total of 66 GTTs were obtained via legal combinations of the attributes, which were not presented in this paper due to space limits.

Table 4. GTT attributes: Operators

ID	Operators	GOMSL-operators	Examples
1	Execute operations through CLI	Option 1[1]: ① Type_in *string_of_characters* ② Keystroke *key_name* Option 2: ① Hold_down *mouse_button* ② Point_to *target_object* ③ Double_ Keystroke *key_name+key_name*[2] ④ Keystroke *key_name*	Delete number segment information, through the command: RMV NFRANGEINFO: GRPNAME=**, INDEX=**;
2	Input in CLI according to system notice	Option 1: ① Look_at *object_name* ② Type_in *string_of_characters* ③ Keystroke *key_name* Option 2: ① Look_at *object_name* ② Hold_down *mouse_button* ③ Point_to *target_object* ④ Double_ Keystroke *key_name+key_name* ⑤ Keystroke *key_name*	Select the communication protocol of service plane. The default selection is "http". Input "0" and press "Enter" to select "https". Press "Enter" directly to select "http".
3	Record	① Hold_down *mouse_button* ② Point_to *target_object* ③ Double_ Keystroke *key_name+key_name* ④ Keystroke *key_name*	Record the "management IP address".
4	Execute operations through GUI	① Click *mouse_button* ② Point_to *target_object* (If a keyboard input is required, then the GOMS-operators of Operator 1 are also involved.)[3]	In the main menu, click "Backup and recovery > Configure > Configure timing backup tasks".
5	Verify	① Look_at *object_name* ② Verify *description*	For every node, verify whether the "node status" has been changed to "master/slave".
6	Decide	① Decide *conditional; conditional; ... else-form*	Check the memory size, through the command:[4] -> cat /**/** |grep MemTotal . If the system echoes the following information, the memory size is 16GB. Transfer to Step 4. MemTotal: 15****** kB . Otherwise, skip the remaining steps in this section.

Table 5. GTT attributes: Objects

ID	Objects	ID	Objects
1	System service	8	System data
2	Module	9	System info
3	System	10	System alarm
4	System account	11	Service node
5	System function	12	User data
6	System management function	13	System config
7	System config file	14	System tool

Table 6. GTT attributes: Functions

ID	Functions	ID	Functions
1	Select	14	Set config
2	Select config	15	Delete
3	Mod	16	Delete config
4	Mod config	17	Add config
5	Enter	18	Restart
6	Switch	19	Trans
7	Create	20	Store
8	Display	21	Start
9	Display info	22	Upload
10	Display config	23	Rollback
11	Copy	24	Update
12	Quit	25	Extract
13	Stop		

3.2 Error Taxonomy

Table 7 presents the 10 Level 1 error modes and 38 Level 2 error modes obtained in the present study. There are totally 75 Instanced error modes following the Level 2 error modes, but they are not presented in this paper due to space limits. These Instanced error modes are actually specific appearances of errors in specific task steps. For example, the instanced error modes of the Level 2 error mode "Input an incorrect parameter due to a wrong or inaccurate understanding of it" include "Input an incorrect IP address", "Input an incorrect file name", etc., depending on the parameter type in specific task steps.

Table 7. Error taxonomy (Level 1 and 2)

Operators	Level 1 error modes	Level 2 error modes
Execute operations through CLI	Failure of understanding	Input an incorrect parameter[1] due to a wrong or inaccurate understanding of it
		Input an incorrect template due to a wrong or inaccurate understanding of it
	Failure of action execution	Input an incorrect parameter due to a keystroke or copy/paste error
		Omit to input a parameter
		Input an incorrect template due to a keystroke or copy/paste error
		Input an incorrect character
		Omit to input a character
		Omit to input the space between template, character, and parameter
		Input a repeated command when executing multiple commands
		Input commands with an incorrect order when executing multiple commands
		Omit to input a command when executing multiple commands
		Input an incorrect command due to copying another one command accidently
		The command is executed directly due to copying it with an "Enter" character at the end of the line
		Omit to input a single command
Input in CLI according to system notice	Failure of understanding	Input a value that disagrees with the system notice due to a wrong or inaccurate understanding of the input requirements

(continued)

---

[1] We here take the command "<u>MOD CLUSTER</u>: <u>CID</u> = *XXXX*, <u>ROLE</u> = *XXXX*;" for example to explain related terms in the present study. **Parameters** are those in italics; **templates** are those underlined; **characters** are the remains; the entire sentence is the **command**.

Table 7. (*continued*)

Operators	Level 1 error modes	Level 2 error modes
		Input an incorrect value due to a wrong or inaccurate understanding of the meanings of different values
		Input an incorrect value due to a wrong or inaccurate understanding of the default value
	Failure of action execution	Input an incorrect value or value that disagrees with the system notice due to a keystroke error
		Omit to input a value
		Input a repeated value due to a long response time of the system
Record	Failure of action execution	Record an incorrect value due to a copy/paste error
Execute operations through GUI	Failure of understanding	Select an incorrect function/tool/application due to a wrong or inaccurate understanding of the meaning (unfamiliar with the GUI)
		Execute an incorrect setting/configuring due to a mode confusion of graphical status icons
		Execute an incorrect setting/configuring due to a wrong or inaccurate understanding of the task step
	Failure of action execution	Select an incorrect function/tool/application due to a click error
		Conduct a repeated execution due to a long response time of the system
		Input an incorrect value due to a keystroke or copy/paste error
		Execute an incorrect setting/configuring due to a click error
		Omit to execute

(*continued*)

Table 7. (*continued*)

Operators	Level 1 error modes	Level 2 error modes
Verify	Failure of detection	Omit the detection
		Omit to read part of values
		The time duration or time interval of readings does not meet the requirements
		Read on an incorrect object
		Incorrect reading on the right object
	Failure of understanding	Make an incorrect judgment
		Terminate the data collection prematurely
Decide	Failure of decision-making	Make an incorrect or inappropriate decision due to the ambiguous decision criteria

4 Discussions and Conclusion

The present study demonstrates the development of an error taxonomy for NOM tasks in the ICT sector. The error taxonomy exhibits specific characteristics of NOM tasks compared with the tasks in other sectors. The most salient difference of this error taxonomy compared with those in other sectors is that a range of observable action errors is identified, despite of the underlying cognitive failures. In previous studies, action errors have not been classified in such low-level of granularity. For instance, action errors in THERP (Technique for Human Error Rate Prediction) [10] were classified into commission error and omission error, and in SHERPA (Systematic Human Error Reduction and Prediction Approach) [33], they were classified into ten modes including operation too long/short, operation mistimed, operation in wrong direction, operation too much/little, etc. The difference in the classification of action errors implies the difference between ICT and other sectors in the aspect of manual operation. In traditional safety-critical domains, human operators (or alternatively, pilots, air traffic controllers, etc.) have received plenty of training and are therefore quite familiar with the routine manual operations. In addition, these routine manual operations are relatively simple; for example, NPP operators usually manipulate plant devices (e.g., opening a valve, closing a pump, etc.) through the digital computer interface via simple and regular operations. Previous HRA methods have implied that the error rate of such action errors is very low compared with understanding and decision-making errors (e.g. [34, 35]). As a result, large amount of studies have focused on the understanding and decision-making process (e.g. [36, 37]). However, when it comes to the ICT sector, almost all manual operations on systems are through the input of commands in CLI or the operation on widgets in GUI. These manual operations, though routine, are not that automatic as the SB behaviors. More importantly, there are many details in such actions that are prone to errors. For example, for a command to be executed, any errors in the parameters, the templates, the characters, etc. can lead to an incorrect command. Therefore, there have been various types of observable action errors identified as presented in Table 7. This difference emphasizes the unique characteristics of manual operations in the ICT sector, and is deserved to be furthered studied.

The GTT description in the present study consists of three attributes including operators, objects, and functions. In previous researches, GTT (or named as other terms) usually solely includes the cognitive activities (e.g. [18, 19]) or implicitly includes some objects (e.g. [20, 26]). As Stanton stated, current techniques "do not represent the activity of the device nor the material that the human interacts with in more than a passing manner", and there is a lack of representation of the external environment [38]. This limitation has been partly addressed in the present study. Through this GTT description (operator and the function-object couple), analysts cannot only identify the human activities but also clarify what changes the human activities exert on the system. For example, when using TAFEI (Task Analysis For Error Identification) [39], analysts are convenient to develop the transition matrix to capture the system activities in the light of human activities under the support of such a GTT description. Therefore, such description aligns with the philosophy of systems thinking, enabling the analysis of human error impacts beyond the human error itself.

From Table 7, it is found that some typical action-type operators such as "Execute operations through CLI" and "Execute operations through GUI", can also fail due to the failure of understanding. From Table 4, the GOMSL-operators of these action-type operators only include some physical activities such as pressing keys and clicking the mouse. The dominant cognitive function of such physical actions is usually identified as action execution (e.g. [18, 27]) without the presence of understanding. However, it is argued here that such action-type operators also require the understanding process, at least in the ICT sector. In fact, even if human operators (or alternatively, pilots, air traffic controllers, etc.) conduct their task following the corresponding procedure, there still exist more or less high-level cognitive processes when they carry out action steps. This fact has already been recognized by previous studies. For example, the IDAC model proposed a nested structure, in which the A block still consisted of an I-D-A loop, implying that human operators needed to first make clear the decision of response (I-in-A), then determine how the SB action should be performed (D-in-A), at last physically carry out the action (A-in-A) [7]. O'Hara et al. argued that even with good procedures, human operators needed to perform response planning activities including identifying goals based on situation assessment, selecting appropriate procedures, evaluating the sufficiency of procedure-defined actions, and adapting procedures if necessary [40]. Similarly, Kim et al. identified a cognitive activity "response planning and instruction" for proceduralized task steps to present the process of directing a task step according to the given procedure [20]. Therefore, the understanding, planning, and decision-making process embedded in each procedure step should not be ignored during the task analysis, especially in occasions where procedure steps might need altering according to specific situation, such as in NPP commissioning, NPP maintenance, and the NOM in the present study.

There are several limitations in the present study. According to Xing et al., an error taxonomy should meet four criteria: Completeness, non-overlapping, specificity and sensitivity, and observability [19]. By evaluating this error taxonomy with the criteria, some concerns arise related to the completeness. The error taxonomy was built based on the analysis of selected NOM tasks and expert judgment, and it is possible to identify new Level 2 error modes and Instanced error modes in future practice. Hence, this error taxonomy should be extended and updated in an iterative manner in future practice. Secondly, the cognitive failures in the present taxonomy are only attributed to the failure of MCFs. Previous studies have illustrated that, the relations of the failures of cognitive processors and the observable error modes are many-to-many [41]. To establish a complete taxonomy and clarify the relations among different levels of error modes, more evidences from human factors and psychology experiments and practical experience are essential. At last, the objects and functions have not been applied to group erroneous behaviors, though their meaningfulness has been discussed. The practicable approaches to utilize the two important attributes of GTT to inform the risk assessment of human errors deserve more studies to investigate.

In conclusion, this paper presents an erroneous behavior taxonomy for ICT NOM tasks, which can support analysts to identify the behavioral and cognitive error modes in NOM tasks. The taxonomy exhibits some unique characteristics of the ICT sector compared with traditional safety-critical domains. Besides, several meaningful insights arise from the development of taxonomy with respect to the GTT description and the role of understanding in action-type tasks, which deserve to be noticed and further studied. In future ICT practice, the error taxonomy should be extended and updated in an iterative manner.

References

1. HUAWEI: Construction, Operation and Maintenance of Network System (Junior Level). Springer Singapore, Singapore (2023). https://doi.org/10.1007/978-981-19-3069-0
2. ATIS: Procedural Outage Reduction: Addressing the Human Part. Alliance for Telecommunications Industry Solutions, Washington, DC (1999)
3. ATIS: 2001 NRSC Annual Report. Alliance for Telecommunications Industry Solutions, Washington, DC (2001)
4. ATIS: 2004 NRSC Annual Report. Alliance for Telecommunications Industry Solutions, Washington, DC (2005)
5. ATIS: Network Reliability Steering Committee 2006–2007 Biennial Report. Alliance for Telecommunications Industry Solutions, Washington, DC (2008)
6. ATIS: NRSC Bulletin No. 2012–001: Wireless Outages. Alliance for Telecommunications Industry Solutions, Washington, DC (2012)
7. Chang, Y.H.J., Mosleh, A.: Cognitive modeling and dynamic probabilistic simulation of operating crew response to complex system accidents: Part 1: overview of the IDAC model. Reliab. Eng. Syst. Saf. 92(8), 997–1013 (2007)
8. Chang, Y.H., Mosleh, A., Macwan, A.: Insights from analysis of procedural errors in telecommunications industry. In: Spitzer, C., Schmocker, U., Dang, V.N. (eds.) Probabilistic Safety Assessment and Management (Proceedings of PSAM 7 and ESREL 2004), pp. 656–662. Springer, London (2004). https://doi.org/10.1007/978-0-85729-410-4_107

9. Colwill, C., Chen, A.: Human Factors in Improving Operations Reliability. Paper presented at the 2009 Annual IEEE International Communications Quality and Reliability (CQR) Workshop, Naples, FL, May 12–14 2009
10. Swain, A.D., Guttmann, H.E.: Handbook of Human Reliability Analysis with Emphasis on Nuclear Power Plant Applications. U.S. Nuclear Regulatory Commission, Washington, DC (1983)
11. Norman, D.A.: Categorization of action slips. Psychol. Rev. **88**(1), 1–15 (1981)
12. Hollnagel, E.: The phenotype of erroneous actions. Int. J. Man Mach. Stud. **39**(1), 1–32 (1993). https://doi.org/10.1006/imms.1993.1051
13. Norman, D.: The Design of Everyday Things. Basic Books, New York (2013)
14. Reason, J.: Human error. Cambridge University Press, Cambridge (1990)
15. Rasmussen, J.: Skills, rules, and knowledge; signals, signs, and symbols, and other distinctions in human performance models. IEEE Trans. Syst. Man Cybern. **SMC 13**(3), 257–266 (1983)
16. Wickens, C.D., Hollands, J.G., Banbury, S., Parasuraman, R.: Engineering Psychology and Human Performance, 4th edn. Psychology Press, New York (2013)
17. Liu, P., Zhang, R., Yin, Z., Li, Z.: Human errors and human reliability. In: Salvendy, G., Karwowski, W. (eds.) Handbook of Human Factors and Ergonomics. Wiley, Hoboken (2021)
18. Hollnagel, E.: Cognitive Reliability and Error Analysis Method. Elsevier Science, Oxford (1998)
19. Xing, J., Chang, Y.J., DeJesus Segarra, J.: The General Methodology of An Integrated Human Event Analysis System (IDHEAS-G). U.S. Nuclear Regulatory Commission, Washington, DC (2021)
20. Kim, Y., Park, J., Jung, W.: A classification scheme of erroneous behaviors for human error probability estimations based on simulator data. Reliab. Eng. Syst. Saf. **163**, 1–13 (2017)
21. Shappell, S.A., Wiegmann, D.A.: A human error approach to accident investigation: the taxonomy of unsafe operations. Int. J. Aviat. Psychol. **7**(4), 269–291 (1997). https://doi.org/10.1207/s15327108ijap0704_2
22. Zhang, J., Patel, V.L., Johnson, T.R., Shortliffe, E.H.: A cognitive taxonomy of medical errors. J. Biomed. Inform. **37**(3), 193–204 (2004). https://doi.org/10.1016/j.jbi.2004.04.004
23. Taib, I.A., McIntosh, A.S., Caponecchia, C., Baysari, M.T.: A review of medical error taxonomies: a human factors perspective. Saf. Sci. **49**(5), 607–615 (2011). https://doi.org/10.1016/j.ssci.2010.12.014
24. Stanton, N.A., Salmon, P.M.: Human error taxonomies applied to driving: a generic driver error taxonomy and its implications for intelligent transport systems. Saf. Sci. **47**(2), 227–237 (2009). https://doi.org/10.1016/j.ssci.2008.03.006
25. Williams, J.C.: A data-based method for assessing and reducing human error to improve operational performance. In: Conference Record for 1988 IEEE Fourth Conference on Human Factors and Power Plants, pp. 436–450 (1988)
26. Pandya, D., Podofillini, L., Emert, F., Lomax, A.J., Dang, V.N.: Developing the foundations of a cognition-based human reliability analysis model via mapping task types and performance-influencing factors: Application to radiotherapy. Proc. Inst. Mech. Eng. Part O J. Risk Reliab. **232**(1), 3–37 (2018)
27. Liu, Z., Yin, Z., Yang, D., Li, Z.: Identification of generic task types for nuclear power plant commissioning tasks. In: Xu, Y., Sun, Y., Liu, Y., Gao, F., Gu, P., Liu, Z. (eds.) Nuclear Power Plants: Innovative Technologies for Instrumentation and Control Systems (Proceedings of International Symposium on Software Reliability, Industrial Safety, Cyber Security and Physical Protection for Nuclear Power Plant 2021, ISNPP 2021), pp. 436–450. Springer, Singapore (2022)
28. Kaplan, S., Garrick, B.J.: On the quantitative definition of risk. Risk Anal. **1**(1), 11–27 (1981)
29. Card, S.K., Moran, T.P., Newell, A.: The Psychology of Human-Computer Interaction. Lawrence Erlbaum Associates Inc., Hillsdale (1983)

30. John, B.E., Kieras, D.E.: The GOMS Family of Analysis Techniques: Tools for Design and Evaluation. School of Computer Science, Carnegie Mellon University, Pittsburgh (1994)

31. Kieras, D.: A Guide to GOMS Model Usability Evaluation using GOMSL and GLEAN4. University of Michigan, Ann Arbor (2006)

32. Pandya, D., Podofillini, L., Emert, F., Lomax, A.J., Dang, V.N., Sansavini, G.: Quantification of a human reliability analysis method for radiotherapy applications based on expert judgment aggregation. Reliab. Eng. Syst. Saf. **194**, 106489 (2020)

33. Embrey, D.E.: SHERPA: a systematic human error reduction and prediction approach. In: Proceedings of the International Topical Meeting on Advances in Human Factors in Nuclear Power Systems, pp. 184–193. (1986)

34. Gertman, D., Blackman, H., Marble, J., Byers, J., Smith, C.: The SPAR-H Human Reliability Analysis Method. U.S. Nuclear Regulatory Commission, Washington, DC (2005)

35. Xing, J., Chang, J., DeJesus, J.: Integrated Human Event Analysis System for Event and Condition Assessment (IDHEAS-ECA). U.S. Nuclear Regulatory Commission, Washington, DC (2020)

36. Endsley, M.R.: Toward a theory of situation awareness in dynamic systems. Hum. Fact. **37**(1), 32–64 (1995). https://doi.org/10.1518/001872095779049543

37. Klein, G.A.: Sources of Power: How People Make Decisions. MIT Press, Cambridge (1998)

38. Stanton, N.A.: Human-error identification in human-computer interaction. In: Sears, A., Jacko, J.A. (eds.) Human Computer Interaction: Fundamentals. CRC Press, Boca Raton (2009)

39. Baber, C., Stanton, N.A.: Task analysis for error identification: a methodology for designing error-tolerant consumer products. Ergonomics **37**(11), 1923–1941 (1994). https://doi.org/10.1080/00140139408964958

40. O'Hara, J.M., et al.: Human Factors Considerations with Respect to Emerging Technology in Nuclear Power Plants. U.S. Nuclear Regulatory Commission, Washington, DC (2008)

41. Yin, Z., et al.: Collection of IDHEAS-based human error probability data for nuclear power plant commissioning through expert elicitation. Ann. Nucl. Energy **181**, 109544 (2023). https://doi.org/10.1016/j.anucene.2022.109544

Effects of the Icon Brightness, App Folder Opacity, and Complexity of Mobile Wallpaper on the Search of Thumbnail Icons

Huihui Zhang[1,2], Lingxuan Li[3], Miao He[4], Yanfang Liu[4], and Liang Zhang[1,2(✉)]

[1] Institute of Psychology, Chinese Academy of Sciences, Beijing, China
zhangl@psych.ac.cn
[2] Department of Psychology, University of Chinese Academy of Sciences, Beijing, China
[3] School of Humanities and Social Sciences, Beijing Forestry University, Beijing, China
[4] Huawei Device Co., Ltd., Shenzhen, China

Abstract. In the past ten years, smartphones have gone far beyond communication tools. The average number of apps per capita reached more than eighty, which brings difficulties to the search and recognition of icons. As the number of apps increased, app folders became widely used, which also brought up new problems, i.e., how to search and recognize the apps by their thumbnails icons. Furthermore, those icons are displayed under all kinds of personalized wallpapers. The present study focused on the recognition of thumbnail icons in the folder on wallpapers of different complexity. According to the literature, the contrast between icon and background, and complexity of the wallpaper are two key factors for icon identification. The contrast is determined by the opacity of folder and the brightness of icons. Thus, we studied the effect of the brightness of icons, the opacity of the folder, and the complexity of the wallpapers on icon selecting. Twenty-three users participated in the experiment. The results show interaction effect of wallpaper complexity and folder opacity on search performance and subjective rating. On the complex wallpaper, with the increase of the opacity of the folder background, the search time and the subjective difficulty decreased significantly, the aesthetic and clarity increased significantly. So we recommend high folder opacity for complex wallpaper. On the simple wallpaper, the search time and subjective difficulty does not change with the opacity of the folder background. The aesthetic increased between low level to medium level but decreased at a high level, which imply the folder opacity for simple wallpaper shouldn't be too high.

Keywords: Thumbnail icon recognization · Folder opacity · Wallpaper complexity

1 Introduction

For small screens on handheld devices, graphical icons are widely used. These icons convey sufficient information in a limited space, besides, users are allowed to execute the mobile applications (APP) through simply clicking on the icon of certain application. The data released by China Internet Network Information Center (CNNIC) shown that

D. Harris and W.-C. Li (Eds.): HCII 2023, LNAI 14017, pp. 371–382, 2023.
https://doi.org/10.1007/978-3-031-35392-5_29

average APP number reached 83 per capita by September 2020 [1]. And this increase was universal, online survey found that the average number of installed applications on smart phone increased from 35 in 2016 to 80 in 2018 [2, 3].

In order to facilitates users' icon searching experience, researchers mainly focused on two different aspects to adapt to users' need and preference. Firstly, from the perspective of the recognization of icon itself, important characteristics such as size, design style, and familiarity etc., were studied in the existing researches [4–9]. The minimum identifiable size of icon were given in the international standard [10]. For younger users, flat icons were preferred than skeuomorphic ones [11]. Icon familiarity significantly affected the searching performance [9, 12], which remind us familiarity was an important factor to be controlled in our following study. Besides, how to make an icon attractive and aesthetic was also investigated [13, 14].

Secondly, from the matching of background and icon, previous studies mainly focused on contrast (the degree of difference between the brightness of icon and its background area) and color matching between icons and wallpaper [15, 16]. However, majority of the studies focused on background with a solid color. Based on this simple background, researchers found that the brightness of icon couldn't be too high on dark background, and high color contrast could enhance the efficiency of icon identification [17]. Shen et al. [16] found that medium luminance contrast was better than low or high luminance contrast which could help users find the target stimuli more quickly. Huang [18] explored users' subjective aesthetic preferences for different icon-background color combinations.

However, we only found one study which focused on the icon identification on complex background [19]. This study measured the visual entropy of icon itself and the background. And the researcher designed a 4 * 2 pairs of different entropy level of icon itself and displaying background on the desktop. Under the high entropy background/high entropy icon condition, subjects made more mistakes when selecting certain target.

In actual life, users prefer to choose all kinds of wallpapers which presenting their personality nowadays. So how to improve the icon searching efficiency under complex background is still a remained question. And the designer of mobile interface widely use folders which let icons to be more organized. And users are able to do the adjustment according to personalized need. Consequently, the thumbnail icon will be showed with only one ninth of the original size. And those thumbnail icons are put in the folder on a personalized wallpaper (Fig. 1). The difficulty of searching and recognizing certain application icon is highly increased.

Above all, how to make users quickly locate and identify target thumbnail icons in the folder on a complex wallpaper is still an unsolved problem. Previous researches have shown the effect of luminance contrast on icon identification, which were determined by the icon brightness and background brightness. And the background brightness is determined by the opacity of folder (transparency of folder background) and the wallpaper brightness (which is a fixed value in our study). So the icon brightness, folder opacity and wallpaper complexity were three independent variables. We investigated the impact of these three factors on users' searching performance and subjective ratings.

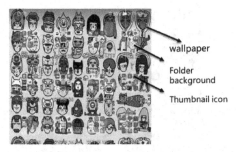

Fig. 1. Thumbnail icons putting in the folder on a complex wallpaper

2 Method

2.1 Participants

A total of 23 subjects (male = 12), aged 20–34 years, with a mean age of 26.6 years (SD = 3.34), participated in the experiment, and 22 subjects' data were analyzed excluding one male with significant lower searching accuracy. All subjects were dextromanual, with normal or corrected visual acuity, without color blindness and color weakness.

2.2 Experimental Device

The experimental device is a mobile phone with 2340 * 1080 pixels screen resolution, 6.47-inch screen size. The experiment was conducted in the laboratory of Institute of Psychology, Chinese Academy of Sciences. The lighting condition of the laboratory was controlled as 500 lx. The screen color temperature was maintained consistently in the experiment.

2.3 Experimental Materials

Two wallpapers of different complexity were selected (shown in Fig. 2). Besides, the brightness of them were almost the same, even every folder areas' brightness of each wallpaper, which allow us to analyze the pure effect of folder opacity.

In the selection of icon materials, 80 icons from a total of 571 icon libraries were selected as the final experimental materials, excluding icons with high familiarity and distinctive features, the main color brightness was calculated as icon brightness.

2.4 The Design of Experiment

2 (wallpaper complexity: complex wallpaper, simple wallpaper) x 5 (background opacity: level 1–5. Level 1 represents the lowest background opacity and level 5 the highest) x 4 (icon brightness: low brightness, medium brightness, high brightness, ultra-high brightness) within-subject design was conducted in this experiment. The dependent variables were searching time, accuracy, and user's subjective evaluation (including searching difficulty, clarity, and aesthetics).

Fig. 2. Complex wallpaper (left); simple wallpaper (right)

2.5 Experimental Procedure

The whole experiment included two tasks: a search task and a subjective evaluation task. In the experiment, participants held the mobile phone in both hands and clicked with right index finger only. The position of mobile phone was fixed.

In the searching task, participants were required to search application icons like usual. Participants began to take the formal experiment with a screen said "click the screen to start", followed by a interface showing the target app for three seconds, after that, a total of 16 thumbnail icons in the folder were shown. In this scenario (the folder cannot be opened), participants need to find and click the folder area where the target icon locates. After finding the target icon, participants rated how difficult they feel on a seven-point scale (1 = very easy, 7 = very difficult). Participants were required to complete the search of the target icon as quickly and accurately as they can. Each condition was repeated 3 times, totally 120 trials were completed.

In the evaluation task of clarity and aesthetics, participants need to compare the differences of clarity and aesthetics between different background opacity under the same icon brightness. After browsing the first screen, participants need to click the screen to switch to the next screen and compare the clarity and aesthetics between these two interfaces. Then they need to do the rating: Which interface do you think is clearer? (First screen, second screen, no difference); Which screen do you think is more beautiful? (First screen, second screen, no difference). The display order was balanced among participants.

3   Result

One participant was excluded because the searching accuracy rate was significantly lower (76.6%) than others (89%–99%). For other participants' (22, including 11 male) data, trials beyond 3 standard deviations of search time's mean value were excluded. SPSS 22.0 was used to conduct the results. The results were analyzed using repeated measured ANOVAs.

3.1 Main Effect of Wallpaper Complexity, Folder Opacity and Icon Brightness on Icon Search Task

The main effect of the wallpaper complexity on the searching time (F (1,21) = 72.09, p < 0.001) and the subjective searching difficulty (F (1,21) = 21.77, p < 0.001, Fig. 3) were significant.

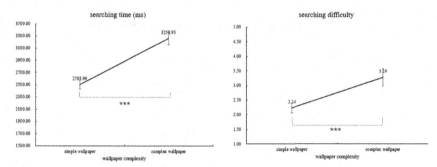

Fig. 3. Searching time and subjective searching difficulty for different wallpaper complexity. (****p < 0.001, **p < 0.01, *p < 0.05, the same below*)

The main effect of folder opacity was also significant for the searching time (F (4, 84) = 7.91, p < 0.001) and the subjective searching difficulty (F (4, 84) = 7.67, p < 0.001, presented in Fig. 4). The searching time was significantly different between level 1 and level 3 (p = 0.015) (which imply that the difference between level 1 and level 4, level 5 were also significant, we omitted to save space), level 2 and level 4 (p = 0.017), and level 3 and level 5 (p = 0.029). The level of subjective searching difficulty at level 2 was significantly higher than at levels 3 (p = 0.029).

The main effect of icon brightness was significant on searching time (F(3, 63) = 21.31, p < 0.001) and the subjective searching difficulty (F (3, 63) = 13.05, p < 0.001, presented in Fig. 5). The searching time was significantly higher in low brightness than in medium brightness (p < 0.001), other levels were not significant. And the subjective searching difficulty was only significantly different between low and medium brightness (p < 0.001).

3.2 The Effect of Folder Opacity and Icon Brightness on Search Task and Evaluation Task: Under Complex Wallpaper

The interaction of wallpaper complexity and folder opacity on searching time (F (4, 84) = 5.74, p < 0.001) and subjective searching difficulty was significant (F (4, 84) = 5.31, p = 0.001). In addition, the interaction of wallpaper complexity and icon brightness on subjective searching difficulty was significant (F (3, 63) = 4.36, p = 0.007). Thus, we demonstrated the result for each wallpaper separately below.

As for complex wallpaper, the main effect of icon brightness is significant for the searching time (F (3, 63) = 11.51, p < 0.001) and the subjective searching difficulty (F (3, 63) = 13.93, p < 0.001, presented in Fig. 6). The searching time and subjective

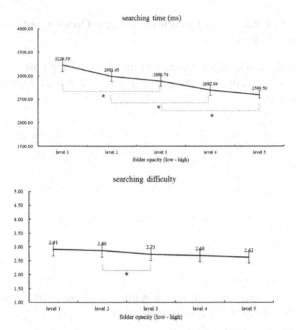

Fig. 4. Searching time and subjective searching difficulty for different folder opacities. *(Only important significant difference were marked to save space, the same below)*

searching difficulty was significantly longer for low icon brightness than other three levels.

The main effect of folder opacity on the searching time ($F(4, 84) = 10.13, p < 0.001$) and the subjective searching difficulty ($F(4, 84) = 10.65, p < 0.001$, presented in Fig. 7) is significant in complex wallpapers. The searching time for level 3 was significantly different from that for level 4 ($p = 0.009$). Moreover, the subjective searching difficulty differs significantly between level 2 and level 3 ($p = 0.034$), and between level 3 and level 5 ($p = 0.034$).

The aesthetics and clarity rating were conducted between different folder opacities. The values for aesthetics and clarity are derived from a two-by-two comparison and we have standardized the values between -2 and 2, higher score means clearer or more aesthetically pleasing. The main effect of folder background opacity on clarity was significant ($F(4, 84) = 314.06, p < 0.001$). Clarity rise significantly with increasing folder background opacity, and there is a significant difference between adjacent levels. The main effect of folder background opacity on aesthetics was significant ($F(4, 84) = 5.46, p < 0.001$, presented in Fig. 8). Aesthetics also rise significantly with increasing folder background opacity, but aesthetics do not improve significantly after level 4.

3.3 The Effect of Folder Opacity and Icon Brightness on Search Task and Evaluation Task: Under Simple Wallpaper

Under simple wallpapers, the main effect of icon brightness is significant for searching time ($F(3, 63) = 10.27, p < 0.001$). The searching time was significantly higher for

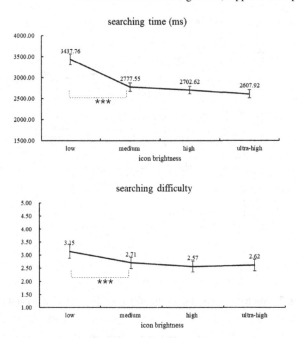

Fig. 5. Searching time and subjective searching difficulty for different icon brightness.

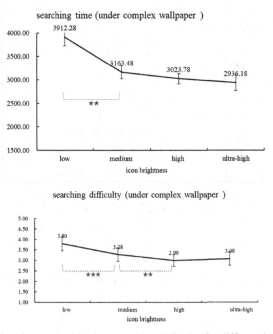

Fig. 6. Searching time and subjective searching difficulty for different icon brightness.

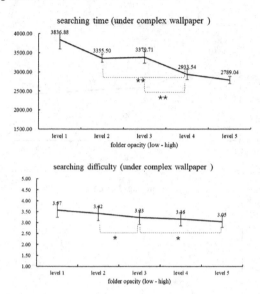

Fig. 7. Subjective searching difficulty for different folder opacities.

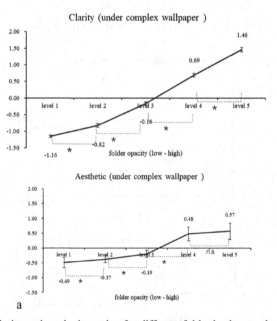

a

Fig. 8. Clarity and aesthetics rating for different folder background opacities.

low icon brightness than for medium brightness (p < 0.001). The main effect of icon brightness on subjective searching difficulty is not significant.

And the main effect of folder background opacity was not significant for searching time and subjective searching difficulty (see Fig. 9).

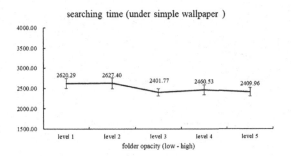

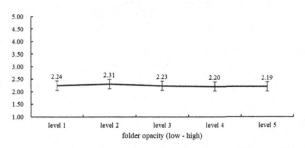

Fig. 9. Searching time and subjective searching difficulty for different folder opacities *(no significant difference)*.

Under simple wallpaper, the main effect of folder background opacity on clarity was significant (F (4, 84) = 107.23, p < 0.001), but not on aesthetics. With the increase of the folder background opacity, the clarity increases significantly, and there is a significant difference between each two adjacent levels. The aesthetics reached peak value when the folder background opacity was at level 3 and then showed a decreasing trend (p = 0.09), illustrated in Fig. 10.

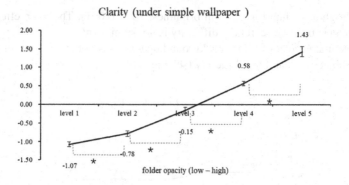

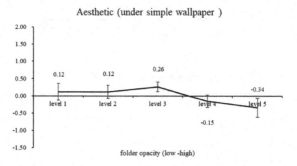

Fig. 10. Clarity and aesthetics rating for different folder background opacities.

4 Discussion

In this study, the effects of mobile phone wallpaper complexity, folder opacity and icon brightness on icon search task and subjective authentic rating were investigated by simulating the daily use of APPs installed on mobile phones. The results show that the above three factors have significant effects on search performance and subjective searching difficulty. Searching difficulty significantly increased under complex wallpaper comparing with the simple wallpaper. And folders of high opacity decreased the area's complexity under icons, which also significantly help users locating certain target. These were consistent with previous studies [19]. And we found that the icons of lowest luminance was the most difficult to locating. And icons of the other three level had no significant difference. The reason for this result was that for low brightness icons, the difference between colors of icon surrounding and the central shape is very small and difficult to distinguish, while in other brightness, the difference will be relatively obvious, making icons much easier to distinguish. Which means that the effect of icons' brightness was probably covered by other features such as the colors and shapes.

So we focused on the effect of folder opacity under each wallpaper. As for the complex wallpaper, with the increase of the folder opacity, search performance and subjective aesthetic feeling increased accordingly. The searching time reduced as the opacity increased until the opacity reaches level 4. The higher the opacity is, the higher the clarity and aesthetic degree is. But the aesthetic degree does not improve significantly after it reaches level 4. Thus, we recommended that the opacity shouldn't be lower than this level. Besides, the increase of opacity reduced the complexity of the background around icons and increased the contrast, which manifest icons and ensure users' recognition.

As for the simple wallpaper, with the increase of the opacity of the folder, the search performance and subjective difficulty did not change significantly. For the subjective evaluation task, the subjective feelings of icons' clarity increased significantly with the increase of folder opacity, while the aesthetic degree reaches the maximum at opacity level 3, and then decreased. If the opacity of the folder on simple wallpaper was too high, the aesthetic degree would decrease. The folder opacity may become an unnecessary element and distract users from the information they really need to focus on. So we recommended that the opacity shouldn't be higher than level 3 for simple wallpaper.

As for contrast, this study did not find correlation between contrast and searching performance. Although many precious studies found the significant relation between them [15, 16]. In those study, they abstracted the factors and all the potential confounding factors were controlled. However, we simulated users' daily usage of icons which brought great difficulty to avoid the effect of many factors like icon richness (hue, graphic features, etc.), icons' differences between them, the color of icon and background etc., which might cover the effect of contrast. The opacity reduced the local complexity of the background, and made the searching more efficient under complex background. However, local complexity has no significant effect on searching time in the simple wallpaper we chose. The reason may be that the complex wallpaper had much more effect on icon identification because the various texture and pattern.

5 Conclusion

In conclusion, we recommended: 1) The identification of thumbnail icons on complex wallpaper were greatly influenced. The mobile phone system designers are able to decrease the complexity using the way of increasing the folder background's opacity. And the opacity should not be lower than level 4. 2) On simple wallpapers, the identification were not significantly affected by the folder opacity. Considering the authentic feeling, we recommended that the folder background opacity should be no higher than level 3.

References

1. The China Internet Network Information Center (CNNIC): 46th Statistical Report on the Development of Internet in China (2020). http://www.gov.cn/xinwen/2020-09/29/content_5 548176.htm
2. Think with Google: How people discover, use, and stay engaged with apps (2016). https://www.thinkwithgoogle.com/advertising-channels/apps/app-marketing-trends-mobile-landscape/
3. Annie, App: 2017 retrospective: a monumental year for the app economy (2018). https://www.appannie.com/cn/insights/market-data/app-annie-2017-retrospective/
4. Huang, K.-C., Chiu, T.-L.: Visual search performance on an LCD monitor: effects of color combination of figure and icon background, shape of icon, and line width of icon border. Percept. Mot. Skills **104**, 562–574 (2007). https://doi.org/10.2466/pms.104.2.562-574

5. Jylhä, H., Hamari, J.: Development of measurement instrument for visual qualities of graphical user interface elements (VISQUAL): a test in the context of mobile game icons. User Model. User-Adap. Inter. **30**(5), 949–982 (2020). https://doi.org/10.1007/s11257-020-09263-7

6. Luo, S., Zhou, Y.: Effects of smartphone icon background shapes and figure/background area ratios on visual search performance and user preferences. Front. Comp. Sci. **9**(5), 751–764 (2014). https://doi.org/10.1007/s11704-014-4155-x

7. Lin, H., Hsieh, Y.C., Wu, F.G.: A study on the relationships between different presentation modes of graphical icons and users' attention **63**, 218–228 (2016)

8. Punchoojit, L., Hongwarittorrn, N.: The influence of icon background colors and icon symbols on menu item selection for smartphone (2018)

9. Smythwood, M., Hadzikadic, M.: The effects of icon characteristics on search time. In: Ahram, T.Z., Falcão, C. (eds.) AHFE 2018. AISC, vol. 794, pp. 57–67. Springer, Cham (2019). https://doi.org/10.1007/978-3-319-94947-5_6

10. ISO 9241-307:2008(en) Ergonomics of human-system interaction—Part 307: Analysis and compliance test methods for electronic visual displays

11. Chen, R., Huang, J., Zhou, J.: Skeuomorphic or flat icons for an efficient visual search by younger and older adults? Appl. Ergon. **85**, 1–16 (2020). https://doi.org/10.1016/j.apergo.2020.103073

12. Shen, Z.G., Zhang, L.H., Xiao, X., Li, R., Liang, R.Y.: Icon familiarity affects the performance of complex cognitive tasks. I-Perception **11**(2) (2020). https://doi.org/10.1177/2041669520910167

13. Ho, C.H., Hou, K.C.: Exploring the attractive factors of app icons. KSII Trans. Internet Inf. Syst. **9**(6), 2251–2270 (2015). https://doi.org/10.3837/tiis.2015.06.016

14. Jylha, H., Hamari, J.: An icon that everyone wants to click: how perceived aesthetic qualities predict app icon successfulness. Int. J. Hum Comput Stud. **130**, 73–85 (2019). https://doi.org/10.1016/j.ijhcs.2019.04.004

15. Näsänen, R., Ojanpää, H.: Effect of image contrast and sharpness on visual search for computer icons. Displays **24**, 137–144 (2003). https://doi.org/10.1016/j.displa.2003.09.003

16. Shen, Z., Zhang, L., Li, R., Hou, J., Liu, C., Hu, W.: The effects of color combinations, luminance contrast, and area ratio on icon visual search performance. Displays **67**, 1–13 (2021). https://doi.org/10.1016/j.displa.2021.101999

17. Shen, Z., Xue, C., Li, J., Zhou, X.: Effect of icon density and color contrast on users' visual perception in human computer interaction. In: Harris, D. (ed.) EPCE 2015. LNCS (LNAI), vol. 9174, pp. 66–76. Springer, Cham (2015). https://doi.org/10.1007/978-3-319-20373-7_7

18. Huang, S.-M.: The rating consistency of aesthetic preferences for icon-background color combinations. Appl. Ergon. **43**(1), 141–150 (2012). https://doi.org/10.1016/j.apergo.2011.04.006

19. Satcharoen, K.: Effect of entropy in icons and background on selection accuracy. In: 2018 3rd International Conference on Computer and Communication Systems (ICCCS) (2018). https://doi.org/10.1109/ccoms.2018.8463324

How the Position Distribution of HUD Information Influences the Driver's Recognition Performance in Different Scenes

Ying Zhou[1,2], Liu Tang[3], Junfeng Huang[3], Yuying Xiang[1], and Yan Ge[1,2(✉)]

[1] CAS Key Laboratory of Behavioural Science, Institute of Psychology,
Chinese Academy of Sciences, Beijing, China
gey@psych.ac.cn

[2] Department of Psychology, University of Chinese Academy of Sciences, Beijing, China

[3] Chongqing Changan Automobile Co., Ltd., Chongqing, China

Abstract. A head-up display (HUD) is a comprehensive electronic display device that projects such information as vehicle status, driving status and navigation to the front of the driver's line of sight, helping the driver to recognize various information. It improves driving safety by preventing drivers from looking down at information and reducing visual deviation on the road. However, visual attention while driving is limited; thus, the HUD information needs to be presented within the driver's field of view for quick recognition. In this study, simulated driving was used to investigate drivers' recognition responses and subjective ratings to stimuli in 77 positions within a field of view of 50° × 50° in different driving scenes. The results showed that as the position deviated from the centre, the driver's recognition response decreased, and the subjective evaluation of the positions in the visible and suitable dimensions also decreased. In the daytime scene, the driver pays more attention to the road than in the nighttime scene, leading to a more noticeable neglect of the surrounding scene. This study provides response time and subjective ratings distribution within a field of view of 50° × 50°, and the results of the test for significant differences at different positions were derived. The results may help designers of head-up displays create better interfaces and avoid disrupting the driver's view and obscuring the road scene.

Keywords: Head-up Display · Field of View · Driving Scenes

1 Introduction

With the arrival of cockpit intelligence, head-up display (HUD) is a new human-computer interaction window. Many studies have shown shorter response times and higher accuracies to information displayed on a HUD than on a traditional in-vehicle display [1–4].

HUD interfaces on the market differ in FOV (field of view), which are shown by the different positions where the HUD is presented in the two-dimensional image of the windshield. The information of the HUD should be within the driver's field of view;

© The Author(s), under exclusive license to Springer Nature Switzerland AG 2023
D. Harris and W.-C. Li (Eds.): HCII 2023, LNAI 14017, pp. 383–395, 2023.
https://doi.org/10.1007/978-3-031-35392-5_30

otherwise, its presentation is meaningless. However, the information on the HUD should not prevent peripheral event recognition and vehicle control, which rely mainly on visual attention [5]. Poorly designed HUDs can increase the number of issues that affect driving safety, such as information overload, attention capture and cognitive tunnel-ling effects [5, 6]. Therefore, it is necessary to determine a position that is best suited for presenting the information and design a user-friendly HUD to enable low access and response times [7].

Many studies have indicated that the lowest response times are at 0° and the surrounding areas. Zhao divided the HUD interface into 15 equal parts, and each part was filled with numbers in one region at a time [8]. The results showed that the areas with the shortest reaction times were the visual centre and the four surrounding areas, while the average reaction times of the peripheral areas were all relatively long and differed significantly from those of the central areas. Yang separated the driver's field of view of 20° × 10° evenly into 15 positions [9]. The results indicated that the reaction times were significantly shorter in the central part (0°, 0°) and the four surrounding parts. Other researchers have used more refined measurements that produced more detailed results. Topliss et al. investigated 48 HUD positions and 3 HDD (head-down display) positions [10]. Horizontally, as the displayed image got closer to the lead vehicle, the lane exceedances were fewer and the times of the first lane departure were longer. However, the chances of unsafe driving became higher. Vertically, as the displayed image was located at the lower centre rather than the higher centre, first lane departure times were longer. Haeuslschmid et al. measured the response times at 17 positions within an extended field of view of 35° × 15° [7]. It was found that the reaction times increase significantly when the horizontal field of view is greater than 15°. It was validated that the lowest response times are not mandato-rily at 0° and rather shifted 5° to the right. Hagino et al. enlarged the appearance area of the stimulus to ±50° horizontally and +5° to −7.5° vertically [11]. With the use of the three-dimensional display and the driving simulator, researchers noted that drivers reacted more quickly to stimuli that were located at +10° to −5° horizontally, which also showed right bias, and +5° to −5° vertically when longitudinal and lateral controls were both automated. It is essential to investigate response times outside of the area that has been tested thus far because research and development now intends to enlarge the size of the HUD [7].

In addition, studies have shown that response times vary in different environments. HMDs (Helmet Mounted Display system) used by pilots are the predecessors of in-vehicle HUD. Shao divided HMDs into a reality layer and an augmented reality layer [12]. In the reality layer, the natural environment, human environment and driving status are the three factors that affect pilots' cognitive load, which affects pilots' reactions. It is easy to assume that the outside environment and the HUD interface could interact with each other, which further affects the driver's response time and accuracy. A video-based study demonstrated that the driver's ability to detect targets in the periphery was reduced during night-time driving as a result of HUD system use [13]. However, this phenomenon did not appear during dusk-time driving. Thus, the author posited that it was due to the greater contrast of the HUD to the background view. Similarly, Haeuslschmid et al. noted that response times increase for lower contrast between stimuli and background [7]. Furthermore, Liu explored how drivers performed differently when they switched their attention from a HUD presentation to the road scene [14]. As a result of processing information displayed on the HUD as opposed to on the road, response times to speed limit signs decreased, indicating evidence of attention capacity. According to the study's findings, this effect tended to be alleviated with a high driving workload. Diverse driving environments lead to greater contrast and thus easier recognition of changes in response time.

Hence, the purpose of the study was to find the suitable position for HUD presentation and the maximum FOV acceptable to drivers. A previous study suggested that the horizontal field of view is mostly $-20°$ to $10°$, and the vertical field of view is mostly $-10°$ to $20°$ [15]. The setting range of the FOV in this study is further expanded to look for turning points, so the FOV range designed in this study is $-20°$ to $30°$ horizontally and $-20°-30°$ vertically. This study explored the influence of the position distribution of head-up display information on drivers' recognition during driving. Meanwhile, 2 (day/night) $\times$ 2 (surrounding traffic flow/no traffic flow) driving scenes were designed to explore the effect of outside environments on the information displayed by the HUD.

2   Method

2.1 Participants

Thirty-one participants were voluntarily recruited through online posters. All participants were above 18 years old (mean $= 30.480$, SD $= 4.032$). In total, 28 were male (90%), and 3 were female (10%). Participants had held a driving licence for more than three years. All participants self-reported that they had previously known about the use of HUDs in cars and that they would not feel dizziness or discomfort during the virtual game.

2.2 Apparatus

This experiment was conducted in the laboratory of the R&D Center of Changan Automobile Company in Chongqing, China. The basic experimental environment is shown in Fig. 1. Virtual Test Drive (VTD) software is used to simulate the road environment. The simulated driving road was designed as a two-way 4-lane road with a width of 3.5 m on one side. The total length is 50 km, consisting of 7 curves, including 3 left turns and 4 right turns, all having the same curvature. The driving simulator also included a Logitech G29 steering wheel with buttons, a gas pedal, and a brake pedal. The simulated scene was projected on a 6.15 m $\times$ 5.5 m circular screen. The display area measures 1900 $\times$ 1600 px. The Logitech steering wheel was fixed on a 0.8 m high table, which was 3 m away from the circular screen and aligned with the centerline. The code for the recognition task was compiled using VS Code so that when running the VTD simulation scene, the stimulus can be displayed in the scene at the designed time and position. Each stimulus was presented for 1.5 s, and the next appeared at a random interval of 5 to 12 s. The figure height was 3.7 cm.

Fig. 1. Experiment environment (a participant was performing the experimental task).

2.3 Task

Driving Task. The subject was asked to keep driving in the same lane and to control the driving speed at 80 km/h as much as possible. There would be a beep when the speed exceeded ±10 km/h.

Figure-Recognition Task. During the driving task, subjects were asked to recognize the figures that appeared in the driving scene and to respond by pressing the relative button on the wheel, pressing the left button when 60 was recognized and pressing the right button when 90 was recognized. Subjects were informed in advance that the position of the figure displayed was random. The stimulus was chosen to be figure because the important information provided to the driver while driving is usually in figure form, such as speed. 60 and 90 were chosen because they are similar and require little effort to recognize. Taking into account the previous results illustrating the high visibility of purple in AR simulation scenes [16] and the specific presentation effect, the figures are set to purple, making them visible at every position. The response time and correct rate were recorded.

Subjective Rating Task. Participants were asked to rate each position marked in the driving scene on a 7-point Likert scale for 2 questions: (1) Visible: Whether the figure is easily visible when presented at the position (1 - very difficult, 7 - very easy); (2) Suitable: Whether you think it would be suitable if the HUD information was presented in this position (1 - very unlikely, 7 - very suitable).

2.4 Design and Procedure

A within-subject design was used. Independent variables: (1) Position, the visual angle at which a stimulus appears (11 horizontal positions and 11 vertical positions). A total of 77 positions within an extended field of view of 50° × 50° were investigated (see Fig. 2). (2) Scene complexity: a 2 (day/night) × 2 (surrounding with vehicle/no vehicle) driving scene was designed to explore the effect of outside environments on the information displayed by the HUD.

The subjects were required to first adjust the seat height to make the line of sight 1.2 m (so that the subjects' sight would be at 0°). After the introduction by the experimenter, the subjects practised the simulated driving task and recognition task for approximately 5 min to ensure that they understood the task and operation. After the formal experiment started, each subject needed to complete the tasks in 4 driving scenes. Each scene lasted approximately 22 min, and 154 figure stimuli were presented (2 times in each position, 60 for once 90 for once, presented pseudorandomly). Subjects took a 5-min break to complete a scene. The sequence of the scenes for subjects was counterbalanced. Each participant signed an informed consent form before the experiment and received CNY 160 for their participation.

Fig. 2. 77 positions within an extended field of view of 50° × 50°, the marked yellow circles are the studied visual angles. (Color figure online)

3 Results

Preprocessing of the response time based on the statistical outlier ($\geq 3\sigma$). We integrated the results of all subjects and drew the distributions of response time (see Fig. 3), correct rate (see Fig. 4) and subjective ratings (see Fig. 5 and Fig. 6) by position. The response time distribution and correct rate distribution could visually reflect the subjects' visual cognitive responses to stimuli presented at different visual angles. The visible and suitable rating distributions could show the participants' subjective attitude towards HUD information displayed in different positions. The dependent variables were analysed. The correct-response time and correct-response rate were tested using two-way repeated-measures ANOVA ("horizontal position" × "scene complexity"; and "vertical position" × "scene complexity") and post hoc Fischer's least significant difference (LSD) test. The visible rating and suitable rating were tested using one-way repeated-measures ANOVA ("horizontal position" and "vertical position"), and post hoc Fischer's least significant difference (LSD) test was used. The analyses were performed at the 5% significance level using SPSS Statistics Version 27 (IBM Corp, Armonk, NY, United States).

3.1 Response Time

Horizontal Position × Scene Complexity. The main effect of horizontal position was significant ($F(10,300) = 10.044$, $p < 0.001$, $\eta_p^2 = 0.251$). The response times on $-20°$

(M = 1.018, SD = 0.017) and -10° (M = 1.022, SD = 0.018) were significantly lower than those on −15° (M = 1.055, SD = 0.021), −5° (M = 1.049, SD = 0.02) and 0° (M = 1.044, SD = 0.02). The response times at 25° (M = 1.102, SD = 0.025) and 30° (M = 1.085, SD = 0.021) were significantly higher than those at 0°, 10° (M = 1.015, SD = 0.018), 15° (M = 1.019, SD = 0.02) and 20° (M = 1.017, SD = 0.018).

The interaction of horizontal position × scene complexity was significant (F(30, 900) = 5.114, $p < 0.001$, $\eta_p^2 = 0.146$). On -20° in horizontal, the response time in the scene of Night & Veh (M = 1.073, SD = 0.025) was significantly higher than in Day & noVeh (0.993, SD = 0.019), Day & Veh (M = 1.013, SD = 0.021), and Night & noVeh (M = 1.023, SD = 0.018). On −10° in the horizontal direction, the response times in the Night & Veh (M = 1.080, SD = 0.025) and Night & noVeh (M = 1.092, SD = 0.030) conditions were significantly higher than those in the Day & NoVeh (0.978, SD = 0.026) and Day & Veh (M = 0.974, SD = 0.018) conditions. On −5° in the horizontal direction, the response times in the Night & Veh (M = 1.107, SD = 0.035) and Night & NoVeh (M = 1.121, SD = 0.026) conditions were significantly higher than those in the Day & NoVeh (0.990, SD = 0.017) and Day & Veh (M = 1.012, SD = 0.021) conditions.

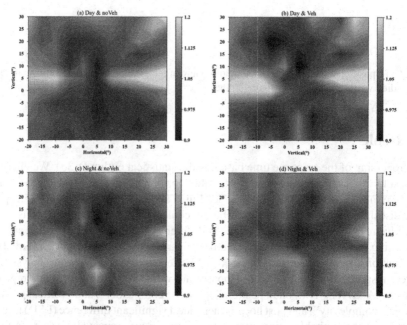

Fig. 3. Response time distribution (s). (a), (b), (c) and (d) each represent scenes of different complexity.

Vertical Position × Scene Complexity. The main effect of vertical position was significant (F(10,300) = 21.853, $p < 0.001$, $\eta_p^2 = 0.421$). The response times on −20° (M = 1.092, SD = 0.020) and −10° (M = 1.054, SD = 0.017) were significantly higher than those on −5° (M = 1.021, SD = 0.019) and 0° (M = 1.019, SD = 0.018). The response time on 15° (M = 1.027, SD = 0.018) was significantly higher than that on 10° (M = 0.994, SD = 0.019). The response times on 25° (M = 1.158, SD = 0.032) and 30° (M = 1.092, SD = 0.018) were significantly higher than those on 15°.

3.2 Correct Rate

The analysis of correct rate did not show any significant effect.

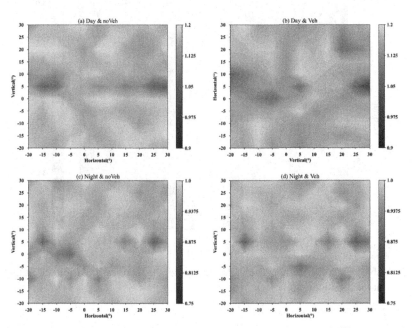

Fig. 4. Correct rate distribution. (a), (b), (c) and (d) each represent scenes of different complexity.

3.3 Visible Rating

Horizontal Position. The main effect of horizontal position was significant (F(10,300) = 58.769, p < 0.001, η_p^2 = 0.662). The rating on −10° (M = 4.742, SD = 0.229) was significantly higher than on −15° (M = 3.452, SD = 0.286), and −20° (M = 3.423, SD = 0.270) was significantly lower than on −5° (M = 5.306, SD = 0.184). The rating on −5° was significantly lower than on 0° (M = 5.591, SD = 0.151). The rating on 5° (M = 5.931, SD = 0.119) was significantly higher than on 0° and 10° (M = 5.798, SD = 0.133). The rating on 10° was significantly higher than on 15° (M = 4.72, SD = 0.235) and 10°. The rating at 25° (M = 4.621, SD = 0.197) was significantly higher than that at 30° (M = 3.672, SD = 0.282).

Vertical Position. The main effect of vertical position was significant (F(10,300) = 18.719, p < 0.001, η_p^2 = 0.384). The ratings on −20° (M = 4.416, SD = 1.634) and −

15° (M = 3.828, SD = 1.655) were significantly lower than those on −10° (M = 5.323, SD = 1.111), −5° (M = 5.468, SD = 1.028) and 0° (M = 5.147, SD = 0.966). The rating on 15° (M = 3.914, SD = 1.803) was significantly lower than on 0°, 5° (M = 5.080, SD = 1.248) and 10° (M = 5.270, SD = 1.068) but significantly higher than on 25° (M = 3.030, SD = 1.853). The ratings at 25° and 30° (M = 3.823, SD = 1.645) were significantly lower than those at 20° (M = 3.030, SD = 1.853).

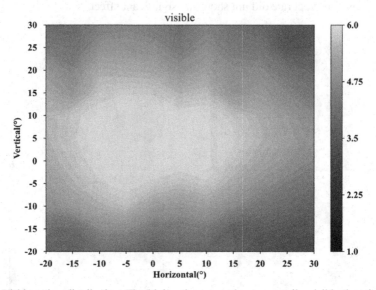

Fig. 5. Visble rating distribution. The higher the score, the more easily visible the stimulus is displayed at that position.

3.4 Suitable Rating

Horizontal Position. The main effect of horizontal position was significant (F(10,300) = 38.458, p < 0.001, ηp2 = 0.562). The rating on −10° (M = 4.431, SD = 1.436) was significantly higher than on −15° (M = 3.194, SD = 1.517), and −20° (M = 3.075, SD = 1.381) was significantly lower than on −5° (M = 4.802, SD = 1.200). The rating on −5° was significantly lower than on 0° (M = 5.024, SD = 1.068). The rating on 5° (M = 5.214, SD = 1.093) was significantly higher than on 0° and 10° (M = 5.129, SD = 1.050). The rating on 10° was significantly higher than on 15° (M = 4.226, SD = 1.467) and 10°. The rating at 25° (M = 4.112, SD = 1.167) was significantly higher than that at 30° (M = 3.296, SD = 1.520).

Vertical Position. The main effect of vertical position was significant (F(10,300) = 20.542, p < 0.001, ηp2 = 0.406). The ratings on −20° (M = 4.442, SD = 1.677) and -15° (M = 3.656, SD = 1.679) were significantly lower than those on −10° (M = 4.827, SD = 1.333). The rating on 15° (M = 3.183, SD = 1.475) was significantly lower than on 0° (M = 4.631, SD = 1.475), 5° (M = 4.797, SD = 1.598) and 10° (M = 4.698, SD

= 1.450) but significantly higher than on 25° (M = 2.390, SD = 1.647). The ratings at 25° and 30° (M = 3.117, SD = 1.640) were significantly lower than those at 20° (M = 3.919, SD = 1.487).

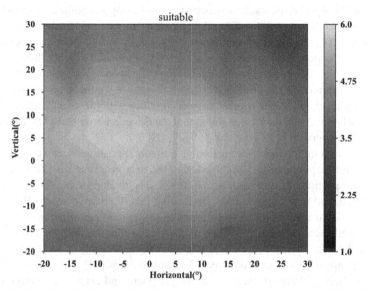

Fig. 6. Suitable rating distribution. The higher the score, the more suitable the HUD information is displayed at that position.

4 Discussion

This study investigated the driver's visual cognitive ability to respond to stimuli appearing from different visual angles during driving, as well as the driver's subjective evaluation of different positions. It was hoped that the experimental results could be used to find the range of FOVs in which HUD information is appropriate to be presented and to make recommendations for the FOV settings for HUD. Previous studies have also explored driver recognition of HUD information in a certain FOV range [11, 17]. The present study has expanded the range of the FOV and increased it to 77 positions and specifically analysed 11 horizontal and 11 vertical positions. The difference in recognition response is expected to give recommendations for HUD development size, in addition to suggestions for the position of the presented HUD information. Future development should aim to enlarge the size of the HUD. Based on driving time and traffic flow, the complexity of the scene was defined, and the differences in drivers' visual recognition responses in different complex scenes were investigated. The study focused not only on the results of recognition responses but also on the subjective perceptions of the drivers, which were studied in multiple dimensions.

The results of response time and subjective ratings showed that the greater the deviation from 0° in the horizontal direction, the longer the response time and the lower the subjective ratings. In the vertical direction, the lower or higher the position was from 0°, the longer the response time and the lower the subjective ratings, which is consistent with the findings of Tsimhoni [18]. The distribution of drivers' visual fixation points decreases from the centre to the periphery [19, 20]. Drivers focus most of their attention directly on the front of the road, only occasionally paying attention to both sides of the road [21]. In the horizontal direction, the response time at $-15°$ is significantly higher than that at $-10°$, and the response time at 25° is significantly higher than that at 20°. In the vertical direction, the response time at $-10°$ is significantly higher than that at $-5°$, and that at 25° and 30* is significantly higher than that at 15°. According to the results, it could be considered that the driver's recognition response would be better in the range of -10 to 20 and -5 to 15. The results are in accordance with the visual characteristics of the driver when driving, and it was found that the driver's horizontal FOV is distributed within 30° and vertical FOV is within 15° [22, 23].

It was also found that the interaction of horizontal position*scene complexity was significant for response time. Combined with the response time distribution, it is also clear that the portion of faster responses (<0.975 s) is greater for Day&noVeh, followed by Day&Veh, and then Night&noVeh, indicating that the more complex the scene, the weaker the visual recognition. The complexity of the road environment can affect the driver's visual attention span [24]. Time of day could influence both the severity and the rate of crashes [25]. The problems with night driving are mainly due to visual problems and low visibility, which lead to increased response times [26]. It was found that compared to nighttime, the response times at the periphery and centre of the daytime scene differed significantly, with the periphery being longer. Leibowitz and Owens considered that "focal" vision would be weakened when driving at night [27].

This study also has some limitations. First, the experiments were conducted in a simulated driving environment. However, even the most advanced driving simulators cannot fully reproduce real driving. In addition, stimuli in different backgrounds are perceived differently due to the contrast, colour and brightness. We selected a specific colour to ensure that the stimuli were easily visible at each position in the scenes during the static state. Once a suitable head-up display prototype exists, future practical research should be evaluated. Second, this study only explored the recognition of individual stimuli. The presentation corresponds more to the reality of the alarm information. The results of this study show faster responses and higher suitability ratings for HUD information in the centre position. However, it is important to note that this result should also and only apply to alarm information. The HUD would also set constant information, including multiple information such as driving status and vehicle status. This information would be presented in front of the driver's view all the time; thus, it might not be suitable to be placed in the centre, which might cause obstruction to the road ahead, increasing the driving danger. The third is the restriction of the sample. Due to laboratory access constraints, most of the participants recruited were male, and the participants were approximately 30 years old. With increasing age, the structure of the eyes degenerates, eyesight weakens, and visual acuity decreases [28, 29]. Nocturnal visual cognitive ability decreases with age [30]. It was found that increasing age leads to poor readability of the night vision of traffic signs, which is the result of visual acuity deficits [31]. Additionally, differences in visual attention were found across drivers of different genders. Female drivers were found to exhibit greater visual attentional bias than male drivers in turning scenarios [32]. Yang observed that male drivers focus their attention on a smaller area and have deficits in peripheral vision when performing audiovisual dual tasks while driving [33]. Therefore, drivers of different ages and genders have differences in visual attention when driving. Future research should pay more attention to the specific differences between drivers of different ages and genders.

5 Conclusion

The focus of this study is driver recognition of HUD information, especially the position of information presentation. The results showed that as the position deviated from the centre, the driver's recognition response decreased, and the subjective evaluation of the positions in the visible and suitable dimensions also decreased. In addition, the simpler the driving scene, the more areas will be quickly recognized. Compared to the night scenes, in the daytime scenes, the driver pays more attention to the road, and there is a greater difference between the periphery and the centre in response. According to the results of the difference significance test between different positions, it could be considered that the driver's recognition response is better in the range of $-10°$ to $20°$ and $-5°$ to $15°$. The results could provide a reference for the size of HUD development in the future. At the same time, designers could refer to the distributions to select the position of HUD alarm information.

Acknowledgement. The authors would like to thank Chongqing Changan Automobile Co., Ltd. For project support.

References

1. Green, P., Williams, M.: Perspective in orientation/navigation displays: a human factors test. In: The 3rd International Conference on Vehicle Navigation and Information Systems, pp. 221–226. IEEE (1992)
2. Ablaßmeier, M., Poitschke, T., Wallhoff, F., Bengler, K., Rigoll, G.: Eye gaze studies comparing head-up and head-down displays in vehicles. In: 2007 IEEE International Conference on Multimedia and Expo, pp. 2250–2252. IEEE (2007)
3. James, C., Ehret, B., Philips, B., James, W.S., Alicandri, E.: Effects of rotation and location on advanced traveler information system displays. In: Proceedings of the Human Factors and Ergonomics Society Annual Meeting, pp. 1077–1081. SAGE Publications Sage CA, Los Angeles (1995)
4. Vashitz, G., Shinar, D., Blum, Y.: In-vehicle information systems to improve traffic safety in road tunnels. Transport. Res. F: Traffic Psychol. Behav. **11**, 61–74 (2008)
5. Donkor, G.: Evaluating the impact of Head-Up Display complexity on peripheral detection performance: a driving simulator study. In: Advances in TRANSPORTATION studies (2012)
6. Park, J., Park, W.: A review on the interface design of automotive head-up displays for communicating safety-related information. In: Proceedings of the Human Factors and Ergonomics Society Annual Meeting, pp. 2016–2017. SAGE Publications Sage CA, Los Angeles (2019)

7. Haeuslschmid, R., Schnurr, L., Wagner, J., Butz, A.: Contact-analog warnings on windshield displays promote monitoring the road scene. In: Proceedings of the 7th International Conference on Automotive User Interfaces and Interactive Vehicular Applications, pp. 64–71 (2015)
8. Zhao, J.: In-vehicle HUD interface based on visual cognitive load Design optimization study (translated), vol. Master. Nangjing University of Science & Technology, Nangjing, China (2019)
9. Yang, F.: Interface design study of in-vehicle navigation system (translated), vol. Master. Tongji University, Shanghai, China (2009)
10. Hannah Topliss, B., Harvey, C., Burnett, G.: How long can a driver look? exploring time thresholds to evaluate head-up display imagery. In: 12th International Conference on Automotive User Interfaces and Interactive Vehicular Applications, pp. 9–18 (2020)
11. Hagino, M., Miura, H., Kimura, N., Watanuki, K.: Driver's recognition of head-up display (HUD) as information provision system (2015)
12. Shao, J.: Research on the information encoding method of helmet mounted display system interface based on visual perception theory (translated), vol. Doctor. Southeast University, Nanjing, China (2016)
13. Bossi, L.L., Ward, N.J., Parkes, A.M., Howarth, P.A.: The effect of vision enhancement systems on driver peripheral visual performance. In: Ergonomics and Safety of Intelligent Driver Interfaces, pp. 239–260. CRC Press (2020)
14. Liu, Y.-C.: Effects of using head-up display in automobile context on attention demand and driving performance. Displays 24, 157–165 (2003)
15. Yuan, W.: Study on car driver's dynamic visual characters test on city road (translated), vol. Doctor. Chang'an University, Xi'an, China (2008)
16. Thomas, B., Close, B., Donoghue, J., Squires, J., Bondi, P.D., Piekarski, W.: First person indoor/outdoor augmented reality application: ARQuake. Pers. Ubiquit. Comput. 6, 75–86 (2002)
17. Häuslschmid, R., Forster, S., Vierheilig, K., Buschek, D., Butz, A.: Recognition of Text and Shapes on a Large-Sized Head-Up Display (2017)
18. Tsimhoni, O., Green, P., Watanabe, H.: Detecting and Reading Text on HUDs: Effects of Driving Workload and Message Location (2022)
19. Chapman, P.R., Underwood, G.: Visual search of driving situations: danger and experience. Perception 27, 951–964 (1998)
20. Konstantopoulos, P., Chapman, P., Crundall, D.: Driver's visual attention as a function of driving experience and visibility: using a driving simulator to explore drivers' eye movements in day, night and rain driving. Accid. Anal. Prev. 42, 827–834 (2010)
21. Ko, M., Higgins, L., Chrysler, S.T., Lord, D.: Effect of driving environment on drivers' eye movements: Re-analyzing previously collected eye-tracker data (2010)
22. Wilson, M., Chattington, M., Marple-Horvat, D.E.: Eye movements drive steering: reduced eye movement distribution impairs steering and driving performance. J. Mot. Behav. 40, 190–202 (2008)
23. Meng, N.: The Analysis on driver's fixation process in different traffic environment road, vol. Master. Chang'an University, Xi'an, China (2009)
24. Ma, J., Chang, R., Chen, X.: Effects of cognitive distraction on driving safety and moderating factors (translated). Chin. J. Ergon. 20, 92–95 (2014)
25. Clarke, D.D., Ward, P., Bartle, C., Truman, W.: Young driver accidents in the UK: the influence of age, experience, and time of day. Accid. Anal. Prev. 38, 871–878 (2006)
26. Plainis, S., Murray, I.: Reaction times as an index of visual conspicuity when driving at night. Ophthalmic Physiol. Opt. 22, 409–415 (2002)
27. Leibowitz, H., Owens, D.: Nighttime driving accidents and selective visual degradation. Science 197, 422–423 (1977)

28. Schieber, F.: Vision and aging. In: Handbook of the Psychology of Aging, pp. 129–161. Elsevier, Amsterdam (2006)
29. Pitts, D.G.: The effects of aging on selected visual functions: dark adaptation, visual acuity, stereopsis, and brightness contrast. Aging and human visual function (1982)
30. Wood, J.M.: Nighttime driving: visual, lighting and visibility challenges. Ophthalmic Physiol. Opt. **40**, 187–201 (2020)
31. Sivak, M., Olson, P.L., Pastalan, L.A.: Effect of driver's age on nighttime legibility of highway signs. Hum. Factors **23**, 59–64 (1981)
32. Guo, Y., Wang, X., Xu, Q., Liu, F., Liu, Y., Xia, Y.: Change-point analysis of eye movement characteristics for female drivers in anxiety. Int. J. Environ. Res. Public Health **16**, 1236 (2019)
33. Yang, Y., Wong, A., McDonald, M.: Does gender make a difference to performing in-vehicle tasks? IET Intel. Transport Syst. **9**, 359–365 (2015)

Resilience and Performance
in Demanding Contexts

A 7-Day Space Habitat Simulated Task: Using a Projection-Based Natural Environment to Improve Psychological Health in Short-Term Isolation Confinement

Xinyu He[1,3] and Ao Jiang[2,3(✉)]

[1] Zhejiang A&F University, Hangzhou, China
[2] Imperial College London, London, UK
aojohn928@gmail.com
[3] EuroMoonMars ILEWG at ESA, Amsterdam, Netherlands

Abstract. Due to prolonged missions in isolated, enclosed, and extreme (ICE) environments, astronauts are exposed to complex stressors that can easily negatively impact psychological states, increase the risk of undesirable behaviors, and jeopardize mission success. Yet long-term journeys will limit the use of existing psychological countermeasures. We are concerned about the long-term mental health of astronauts, and for this reason, we conducted a 7-day controlled experiment in Xiangtan Central Hospital, conducting an isolation simulation to compare the effectiveness of a projection-based virtual natural environment for psychological interventions. 20 participants (10 males and 10 females) were randomized into two groups: the intervention group was exposed to an environment with virtual natural environment projections, and the control group maintained a monotonous indoor environment. Changes in participants' anxiety levels before and after the experiment, as well as their positive and negative emotional states on days 1, 4, and 7, were recorded. The results of the study showed that negative emotions and anxiety continued to increase and positive emotions decreased over time for all participants. However, differences between groups suggest that a natural environment based on projections can be effective in reducing negative mental states in solitary confinement states. This paper will help inform habitat habitability design and psychological responses in future long-term missions.

Keywords: Isolation and confinement · Virtual natural environment · Psychological health · Astronaut

1 Introduction

As humans continue to explore the solar system, long-term missions (LDEMs) are on the agenda and will bring new knowledge and opportunities to Earth [1, 2]. However, Technological limitations are no longer the only concern for space missions, human factors including the physiological and psychological elements become particularly critical. On the one hand, prolonged space flight makes the crew more vulnerable to radiation and

© The Author(s), under exclusive license to Springer Nature Switzerland AG 2023
D. Harris and W.-C. Li (Eds.): HCII 2023, LNAI 14017, pp. 399–414, 2023.
https://doi.org/10.1007/978-3-031-35392-5_31

microgravity, with some physiological effects being even more severe and persistent [3, 4]. On the other hand, one of the largest challenges is that astronauts will experience more complex psychological difficulties because of their extended isolated and confined extreme (ICE) environments [5–7]. The most serious issues humans encounter during extended space travel, according to Oleg Atkov (Russian cosmonaut), are psychosocial and psychological issues [3].

Lazarus views stress as a multifaceted, complicated, interactive state process that arises from how an individual interacts with their environment [8]. Complex stresses may cause negative psychological states in astronauts when they are in an ICE environment, which can harm their behavioral health, impair their cognitive functioning, and threaten mission success [8–11]. Long-term exploration missions pose a more serious challenge: due to the distance from Earth, it will become difficult for astronauts to be supported by the Earth-based psychological strategies that were previously used in near-orbit missions [7, 12]. For example, in previous flight experiences, observing Earth from the ISS was considered to have psychological benefits [13]; contact with family can also benefit mission performance [14]. Therefore, in the face of long communication delays and "Earth out-of-view" phenomena [5, 15], more severe homesickness and anxiety generated by the unknown of deep space exploration should be a concern [7, 16]. Furthermore, in the absence of Earth-based emergency supply and rescue missions, more autonomy and off-mission free time may exacerbate perceived monotony and further boredom, predisposing to disruptive behaviors [12, 17]. To prevent, minimize and manage psychological risks and maintain astronauts' long-term psychological well-being in the face of increasing challenges, new psychological countermeasures must be investigated [18].

Many studies have shown that nature-based exposure, whether direct, indirect or alternative experiences [19], is beneficial for mental health [20]. More specifically, it benefits mental states and cognitive functioning by reducing stress and anxiety, minimizing negative and enhancing positive emotions, and restoring attention [21–25]. The restorative effects occur in natural exposure induced by visual perception, soundscape, and olfaction [26–29]. Vision is the sensory function with the highest information processing capacity [30], making the visual experience the most studied aspect of natural experience [31].

Several theories have explained the benefit of natural exposure: the biophilia hypothesis posits that people have a natural inclination to connect with nature and that the "discord" environment caused by nature deprivation is detrimental to human health [32, 33]. Restorative environmental theories (Attention Restoration Theory and Stress Reduction Theory) offer two different explanations for the psychological benefits of nature [22, 34], and have been supported by empirical studies [35−37]. In addition, with the onset of Covid-19, the isolation of the general population has brought more attention to the benefits of nature experiences in isolation for humans [29, 38, 39]. For the study of human factors in the ICE environment of space, the isolation of this "ICE-like environment" serves as a reference [40]. The research on more general populations, as opposed to the extremely strict physical and psycholog-ical selection of populations now participating in space missions [41], has specific significance for future space travel and habitation initiatives accessible to a wider audience [40, 42].

The unique environment of space includes lower gravity, increased radiation rates, the lack of light sources, and space constraints, which limit astronauts' contact with nature [43–46]. However, many anecdotes from previous flights have revealed the astronauts' affinity for natural plants. For example, during the Salute mission (1971–82), astronauts "designed" greenhouses for the experimental plants to be viewed [45]; similarly, during the Shuttle-Mir mission, plant experiments were an "inspiring" activity for astronaut Mike Foale [47]. In addition to this, related studies have pointed out that activities associated with nature contact (e.g., gardening, cultivation, plant experiments) not only benefit physiological health, such as providing fresher food supplies and diversifying the nutritional structure of astronauts but also have a great potential to provide psychological benefits [46–51]. For example, the colors, tastes, and smells of plants provide a richer sensory experience, and observing or caring for plants can produce feelings like companionship or connection to Earth, providing psychological comfort and alleviating nostalgia [47, 52, 53].

With the development of visualization techniques [54], psychological conditioning based on technological interventions has shown great potential as a non-invasive method to maintain psychological well-being in space habitats [55]. Although there is little relevant research currently available, it is being proposed by an increasing number of researchers that by offering natural alternative experiences, the negative psychological effects of space ICE environments can be reduced and psychological benefits promoted [12, 56–59]. For instance, in the 2016 Mars-500 project simulation experiment, it was discovered that digital nature experiences based on virtual reality technology had a positive psychological effect to elicit memories of the earth [60]; For participants in the 2019 HI-SEAS analog habitat project, nature scenes based on virtual reality (VR) were employed to produce virtual nature experiences provide independent psychological support for confinement and isolation [58]. Notably, participants in a study based on three aerospace simulation missions were asked to rate their preferences for the virtual reality nature scenes used in the missions. The most popular content was scenes with more dynamics, and positive descriptions of nature scene content frequently included wildlife [61].

There are some gaps in the existing research: compared to the acute stress that astronauts may encounter [62], the stress faced under prolonged confinement is more likely to induce further "vicious circles" [8]. In addition, stress is often accompanied by anxiety, depression, and sleep disorders, and long-term stress can easily produce negative psychological effects and lead to stress-related diseases. There are potential negative elements of the immune system [8], and it is more important to provide psychological countermeasures that are conducive to the prevention of negative effects caused by long-term stress. Virtual reality (VR) has received a lot of attention due to its undeniable benefits [12, 57, 60], particularly for its ability to deliver a more autonomous virtual experience and to create a more immersive multisensory collaborative experience that has the potential to be a highly successful psychological strategy in ICE environments [63]. However, providing dynamic and unobtrusive visual stimuli in public areas of the habitat is more appropriate to positively influence astronauts' perception of the environment [55]. Future space habitats with "biophilic human-driven design" based on visual technologies could therefore lessen the initial stressors of confinement and monotony, prevent negative psychological effects, and even mitigate the negative psychological effects experienced by astronauts, especially in environments lacking natural contact [55, 59, 64].

Focusing on the interaction between human and environmental elements, this study aims to explore whether short-term sustained exposure to a projection-based digital natural habitat affects people's emotional state and anxiety in isolation. This study will guide the design of future habitats that are habitable and for psychological safeguards that will keep astronauts' long-term psychological well-being. To this end, we designed and conducted a 7-day isolation task simulation study with a self-assessment questionnaire and personal interviews to assess the effects of having a projection-based digital natural habitat intervention on people's emotional experiences as well as anxiety in isolation.

The main hypotheses of this study were that: (1) a projection-based digital natural environment setting would affect participants' mood states and anxiety during short-term isolation; (2) short-term sustained exposure to a projection-based natural alternative experience of the environment would improve mood states and anxiety in the isolation incarceration state, especially in the context of the monotonous environment of isolation and the lack of direct natural contact; and (3) as the duration of isolation continued to increase, the effect of the projection on mood state improvement would plateau or even wane in the intervention group.

2   Materials and Methods

2.1   Participants and Inclusion Criteria

This study was conducted at Xiangtan Central Hospital, China, and approved by the Ethics Review Committee of Xiangtan Central Hospital, China. We recruited and invited participants to participate in a study to assess mental health in isolation through a web-based platform as well as snowball sampling, and the requirements for participants were good general health, with the following inclusion criteria.

a) Pass a medical blindness test (Ishihara) and be free of color blindness [65].
b) Passing a psychiatric examination and no adverse substance use.
c) ≥18 years of age.
d) Women cannot be pregnant or breastfeeding.
e) Able to give written consent and sign an informed consent form;
f) No isolation within one week before the start of the experiment.

Participants were initiated into participation in the experiment after verbal and written consent was obtained.

Twenty participants (10 male, 10 female) ultimately participated in the experiment. All participants completed the Basic Demographic Questionnaire and the STAI (State-Trait Anxiety Inventory) Questionnaire after recruitment to collect baseline data. Participants were initiated into the isolation experiment after verbal and written consent was reached.

The average age of the final participants was 23.1 ± 2.8 years. All participants were students pursuing science and technology degrees at Xiangtan University and had varying degrees of experience with isolation. This experiment was conducted as a longitudinal controlled experiment and questionnaire from month to day in 2022. Participants were randomly assigned equally to either the experimental or control group using a random number generator from Excel (Microsoft Corporation, Redmond, Washington, USA) to minimize selection bias. In this, the number of males and females in each group was balanced. All participants were unaware of the specific study protocol, the grouping, and the isolation of information from each other during the experiment to prevent any inter or intra-group dependence.

2.2   Materials and Equipment

Projection Equipment and Stimulus Materials. The Epson CO-W01 projector (Epson America Inc, Long Beach, CA) was used in the intervention group to provide a digital nature experience. The projection system in each room could be controlled wirelessly and remotely, and the projection conditions were set to the same brightness and ensured that it would present clear images despite the room lighting. The projection was covered on a 3.5 m * 2.2 m wall in the middle area of the isolated room, which was the main area of the participants' daily visual range, to ensure that the participants could be visually affected by the projection during most of their daily activities. The projection's center was placed above eye level at a projection distance of approximately 2.75 m, and its dimension was 135 * 215 cm (100'').

The BBC Blue Planet BBC Blue Planet is a series of documentaries on marine life produced by the BBC Natural History Unit (NHU) [66, 67]. The series is of public interest as it addresses animal behavior, natural history, anthropogenic impacts, and conservation information, and has been used to provide visuals of positive emotional impact in a study of restorative virtual nature experiences [68, 69]. For the experimental group, we selected "Blue Planet" as the source material. We silenced and edited it so that the edited content was finalized to cover the theme of pristine nature but did not include environmental protection information or relevant information about anthropogenic impacts on the marine environment. The final visual material on which the experiment was conducted was a film featuring silent blue footage of dynamic scenes including the daily activities of multiple biomes in their habitats, lasting 50 min. (see Fig. 1).

Self-Report Questionnaires. This study focused on participants' positive and negative emotional states and sleep during isolation. Measurements included demographic questionnaires, the STAI scale administered at baseline conditions and the end of the study [70], and the PANAS scale administered daily [71].

To assess changes in participants' anxiety mood states before and after isolation, we used The State-Trait Anxiety Inventory (STAI) scale [70]. The STAI-Y is a widely used anxiety measurement scale consisting of a state anxiety measure (STAI-Y1) and a trait anxiety measure (STAI-Y2). The STAI-Y1 contains items describing the current anxiety the individual felt at the time of the assessment.STAI-Y2 contains items related to general anxiety tendencies or situational anxiety. A total of 40 items are included, each measured on a Likert scale, with a score of 1 indicating "not at all" and 4 indicating "always". For each subscale, scores may range from 20 to 80, with higher scores indicating higher levels of anxiety.

Fig. 1. Example stills from the stimulus materials of exposure conditions.

The Positive and Negative Affect Schedule (PANAS) scale was used to evaluate people's daily emotional states while they were isolated [71]. It has been demonstrated that the PANAS, a self-report tool for assessing current or short-term state mood, has good validity and reliability for spotting mood swings. There are 20 items on affect used to evaluate the PANAS, including 10 positive emotion items and 10 negative emotion items, all on a 5-point Likert-type scale with response options ranging from 1 (very mild or never) to 5 (extreme), and participants were asked to indicate the extent to which they felt each emotion.

Scene Setting. The experiment was conducted in 20 isolation wards in Xiangtan Central Hospital. These wards were all 3.5 m long, 3 m wide, and 2.2 m high. The interior of the rooms was all set up in white, gray, and beige to minimize the effect of the colors of the environment on the experiment. Each room was windowless and had a separate bathroom. The walls, ceilings, and floors of the environment were predominantly white and beige and were configured with wood-colored, gray chairs and tables. In the room with the digital habitat group, the projection equipment was a ceiling-mounted projector with an Epson CO-W01 projector (Epson America Inc, Long Beach, CA), while the room without the digital habitat group maintained a monotonous environment with no additional settings added. The temperature in the wards was stable at 25° Celsius. The room was located on the 3rd floor of an interior multi-story building with minimal variation in temperature and humidity throughout the year. (see Fig. 2).

Fig. 2. Computer recreation of the simulated isolation environment.

Procedure. This is a longitudinal observational study. Before the trial, both verbal and written agreements were given by participants. The investigator merely described the substance and meaning of the experimental questionnaire to ensure that each participant could completely grasp the questions of each questionnaire, but all participants were unaware of the study protocol. The study began with a baseline assessment conducted on January 1, 2022, and participants were asked to complete a demographic questionnaire and the STAI scale before entering the isolation phase. During the isolation period, they woke up at 8:00 a.m. and went to bed at 11:00 p.m. daily. Three standardized meals were provided at 8:30 a.m., 11:30 a.m., and 6:00 p.m. respectively to ensure that the participants ate properly. Every day from 8:30 a.m. to 8:30 p.m., participants in the intervention group were exposed to a projection stimulus that presented a silent video loop but was not constrained by viewing requirements for duration or time. The control group was exposed to an internal environment that was monotonous and unstimulated. During seclusion, participants in both groups were required to take a daily round of the PANAS scale at 8:40 p.m. to self-assess their emotional state at that time. At the end of the isolation, all participants were required to take the STAI scale for a self-assessment of their current anxiety state. This was followed by a 5–10 min personal interview, the content of which is subsequently recorded for subsequent transcription and qualitative analysis, a method widely used in longitudinal isolation surveys [72]. (see Fig. 3).

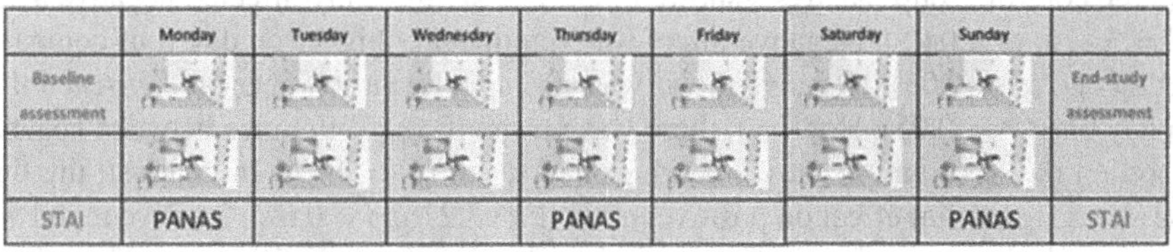

Fig. 3. Experimental design for 7-day isolation

Statistical Analysis. Data collected by the daily conducted PANAS were tested for variables using chi-square tests. The effect of isolation on emotional experience was measured using the General Linear Model Repeated Measures Method (GLM-RM). Daily mood state was used as the repeated measures outcome variable. In addition, a post hoc test of the least significant difference was used to detect differences between the intervention and control groups. Differences in STAI conducted before and after 1 week were then calculated using a paired samples t-test. All analyses were performed using SPSS version 25.0.

3 Result

Self-reported emotions are summarized in Table 1. Emotion in the virtual scene group and the control group on the three test days. The PANAS showed good internal consistency. Cronbach's alpha calculation showed that positive emotions $= 0.95$ and negative emotions $= 0.93$ on day one, 16 (80%) participants each reported at least a little negative emotion, and 15 (75%) reported at least a little positive emotion. On day four, all participants (100%) reported at least a little negative emotion, with three participants (15%) producing a considerable amount of negative emotion; four participants (20%) reported at least a little positive emotion. On Day 7, all participants (100%) reported at least a little negative emotion, and one participant (5%) produced a considerable amount of negative emotion; eight (40%) participants reported at least a little positive emotion. On day one, there was no significant difference between the virtual scene group and the control group in terms of negative mood, positive mood, and anxiety ($p = 0.63$), but there was a significant difference in terms of negative mood and anxiety ($p = 0.038 < 0.05$). No significant differences were found in positive mood on days four and seven (P $= 0.82$) (Table 1).

Regarding STAI, there were no significant differences between pre-and post-experiment (Table 2).

Figure 4 summarizes the changes in PANAS over time for the virtual scenario group and the control group. Analysis showed that time significantly affected negative affect ($F = 3.276$, $p < 0.05$). Negative affect was significantly higher on day four compared to day one ($p < 0.05$). Negative mood was also significantly higher on day seven than on day one ($P < 0.05$). However, there was no significant difference between negative mood on day four and negative mood on day seven ($p = 0.39$). In contrast, the time has also a significant effect on positive mood ($F = 3.276$, $p < 0.05$). Positive mood was significantly lower on day four compared to day one ($p < 0.05$). Positive mood was also significantly lower on day seven than on day one ($p < 0.05$). However, there was no significant difference between positive mood on day four and day seven ($P = 0.63$). Furthermore, as the duration of isolation increased, there was a significant difference between the virtual scene group and the control group in terms of negative mood ($F = 5.13$, $p < 0.05$), but not in terms of positive mood ($F = 3.66$, $p = 0.195$). As the differences were found to be significant after multiple comparisons, a post hoc analysis was also conducted. The results showed that negative emotions were significantly lower in the virtual scenario group compared to the control group ($p < 0.05$).

Table 1. Emotion in the virtual scene group and the control group on the three test days

Participant characteristics	Total	Virtual Scene Group	Control group	Z/t/χ2	P value
PANAS					
First day					
Negative emotions (median, IQR)	17(13–21)	16(13–19)	18.5(15–22)	1.183	0.374
Positive emotions (median, IQR)	27(24–30)	27.5(25–30)	28(26–30)	1.254	0.432
Fourth day					
Negative emotions (median, IQR)	29 (24–34)	28(26–30)	31(28–34)	2.035	0.033
Positive emotions (median, IQR)	16.5(13–30)	15.5(14–17)	14(13–15)	1.159	0.602
Seventh day					
Negative emotions (median, IQR)	28.5(24–33)	27(24–30)	32(31–33)	1.631	0.57
Positive emotions (median, IQR)	13(11–15)	13.5(13–14)	11.5(11–12)	0.724	0.055

Table 2. Anxiety in the virtual scene group and the control group before and after the experiment

Measure	Condition	One-Week Pre-Post Value Mean (sd, Range)	T value	P
STAI	Control Group	39.5 (13.1, 21–62) – 41.1 (13.3, 22–72)	0.18	0.577
	Virtual Scene Group	40.4 (10.6, 21–68) – 41.8 (11.4, 21–69)	0.11	0.764

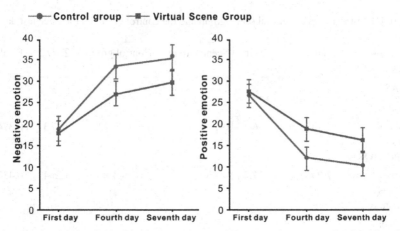

Fig. 4. Emotion levels of the virtual scene group and the control group on the first, fourth, and seventh days (error bars indicate standard errors of the variables).

4 Discussion

This study aims to assess the feasibility of a projection-based virtual nature scene as a tool for providing mental health support in an ICE environment, with applications in aerospace or other nature-deprived industrial scenarios. In addition, it provides an exploratory purpose to inform the design of future habitats.

The results of the study showed that the participants in the virtual habitat group had significantly lower negative emotions compared to the control group. The PANAS data showed that during the seven days of isolation, both the control group and the intervention group showed a gradual increase in the overall level of negative emotions, with the increase decreasing after the fourth day. In contrast, the positive mood levels of both groups showed an overall decreasing trend, with a decreasing trend after the fourth day. Considering that as time increases, the participants' level of adaptation to the environment and their anticipation of the end of the experiment can have an impact on mood. Therefore, the trend in the control group may be the result of recovery from the participants' regulation. However, the between-group differences in positive and negative mood support our initial hypothesis that the increased virtual nature scenes significantly positively affected emotional responses and reduced the negative effect. In contrast to positive versus negative mood changes, no significant anxiety mood changes were observed in this experiment, possibly because the detection of the effects of isolation on anxiety mood was more pronounced in the long-term task (≥ 15 days).

Consistent with previous hypotheses, the positive effects of virtual nature scenes on psychological states in the intervention group diminished over time. Previous research surfaces that differences in immersion experience will influence the effects of natural recovery [73], and when asked in the experimental interviews about the level of immersion and attention to virtual nature scenes, most participants in the intervention group indicated that attention and immersion experience to the virtual scenes decreased with increasing time, possibly due to adaptation to the content of the recurring images. In addition, many participants expressed a desire for richer scene variations to be provided, some expressed a desire to be able to interact with the scenes, and some expressed a desire to add other sensory stimuli to the images, such as sound. One of the participants expressed slight boredom with the recurring scene content as time increased.

Most participants reported that the loss of social contact made people miss their friends and family more and produced more negative emotions of depression, anxiety, and loneliness, especially during the first four days of isolation. Some participants in the virtual habitat group reported that the movement of the marine animals and the blue images made them feel calm and distracted from the negative emotions. Other participants reported that the wildlife scenes provided companionship and reduced feelings of isolation. This is consistent with previous related studies. Previous studies of aerospace simulation showed a higher preference for natural scenes provided by virtual reality, both for more dynamic change scenes and for scenes associated with wildlife [61]. In addition, contact with natural blue elements (sky or water) is beneficial for stress relaxation and emotional relief [74], and in another study, pictures of aquatic environments were suggested to be potentially attractive and restorative in terms of visual properties [75].

Being in a place with limited light and activity and consequent psychological impacts is thought to be linked to the phenomena of circadian rhythm disruption in people in solitary locations [76]. This is one of the potential problems during the long-term journey in spaceflight. Interestingly, we noted that more than half of the participants in the interviews on the first day of the experiment reported difficulty falling asleep and some participants experienced insomnia, which could be an effect of adaptation to the new environment on the participants. In subsequent isolation observations, difficulty falling asleep, and insomnia gradually decreased in overall numbers.

There are many limitations to the present experimental study. First, facing the challenges of future long-term missions, astronauts will not only need to face isolated confinement of a single stressor; the complex stressors of long-term space flight conditions cannot be replicated in the short-term isolation environment provided by the present experiment. Second, it has been found that a person's experience of scenarios is influenced by past experiences and individual preferences and that different natural scenarios do not have the same degree of psychological impact on an individual [61]. However, in the present study, participants' natural scenario preferences were not investigated, and it was not possible to determine how participants' preferences for scenarios and to what extent preferences influenced the experimental results. Furthermore, it has been shown that population variability affects the likelihood of the emergence of negative emotions. However, in the current experiment, the restricted number of participants prevented us from obtaining information about the effect of population variability on the experimental results. Finally, some studies have indicated that exposure to higher color temperatures at bedtime is prone to sleep problems compared to light environments with low color temperatures. This may be related to the suppression of melatonin production [77]. Sleep quality can have an impact on negative mood changes, however, the color temperature change in the environment produced by the projection was not investigated in this experiment to determine if the projection of blue images had an impact on the sleep status of the participants in the intervention group.

5 Conclusion

This study supports the fact that short-term exposure to a natural alternative experience based on projection improves mood states and anxiety in isolation incarceration, and the positive effects on mood states were most pronounced in the first four days of isolation. In addition, we observed participants' sleep and, in interviews, their desire for more varied scene content and multisensory experiences, in addition to the noteworthy need for scene interactivity. However, there are two main limitations of our study. First, simulations of short-term isolated environments are difficult to replicate in realistic long-term spaceflight environments. Therefore, future research could conduct simulated experiments for long-term missions. Second, we did not investigate the individual preferences of the scenarios. This can be investigated and supplemented in future studies. Therefore, in future long-term explorations, in addition to existing psychological countermeasures in the face of severe natural deprivation of the ICE environment, psychological interventions using virtual natural scenes with interactivity and variability could be considered in public areas to reduce negative emotions and anxiety. The present experiment provides a reference value for this purpose.

References

1. Messina, P., Vennemann, D.: The European space exploration programme: current status of ESA's plans for Moon and Mars exploration. Acta Astronaut. **57**(2), 156–160 (2005)
2. Board, S.S., Council, N.R.: Vision and voyages for planetary science in the decade 2013–2022. National Academies Press (2012)
3. Morphew, E.: Psychological and human factors in long duration spaceflight. McGill J. Med. 6(1) (2001)
4. Zwart, S.R., et al.: The role of nutrition in space exploration: Implications for sensorimotor, cognition, behavior and the cerebral changes due to the exposure to radiation, altered gravity, and isolation/confinement hazards of spaceflight. Neurosci. Biobehav. Rev. **127**, 307–331 (2021)
5. Kanas, N., Manzey, D.: Space Psychology and Psychiatry, vol. 16. Springer, Heidelberg (2008). https://doi.org/10.1007/978-1-4020-6770-9
6. Ball, J.R., Evans Jr., C.H.: Medicine IO: Safe Passage: Astronaut Care for Exploration Missions, VOL. 317. The National Academies Press, Washington, DC (2001)
7. Vakoch, D.A.: On Orbit and Beyond: Psychological Perspectives on Human Spaceflight. Springer, Heidelberg (2013). https://doi.org/10.1007/978-3-642-30583-2
8. Geuna, S., Brunelli, F., Perino, M.A.: Stressors, stress and stress consequences during long-duration manned space missions: a descriptive model. Acta Astronaut. **36**(6), 347–356 (1995)
9. Chouker, A.: Stress Challenges and Immunity in Space. Springer, Heidelberg (2012). https://doi.org/10.1007/978-3-030-16996-1
10. Palinkas, L.A.: Psychosocial issues in long-term space flight: overview. Gravit Space Biol Bull **14**(2), 25–33 (2001)
11. Landon, L.B.: Risk of Performance and Behavioral Health Decrements Due to Inadequate Cooperation, Coordination, and Psychosocial Adaptions within a Team (2022)
12. Salamon, N., et al.: Application of virtual reality for crew mental health in extended-duration space missions. Acta Astronaut. **146**, 117–122 (2018)
13. Robinson, J.A., et al.: Patterns in crew-initiated photography of Earth from the ISS: Is earth observation a salutogenic experience? In: On orbit and Beyond, pp. 51–68. Springer, Heidelberg (2013). https://doi.org/10.1007/978-3-642-30583-2_3

14. Kelly, A.D., Kanas, N.: Communication between space crews and ground personnel: a survey of astronauts and cosmonauts. In: Aviation, Space, and Environmental Medicine (1993)
15. Jiang, A.O.: Effects of colour environment on spaceflight cognitive abilities during short-term simulations of three gravity states (Doctoral dissertation, University of Leeds) (2022)
16. Sandal, G.M., et al., Psychological reactions during polar expeditions and isolation in hyperbaric chambers. Aviation, Space, and Environmental Medicine, 1996
17. Peldszus, R., et al.: The perfect boring situation—addressing the experience of monotony during crewed deep space missions through habitability design. Acta Astronaut. **94**(1), 262–276 (2014)
18. Gatti, M., et al.: Affective health and countermeasures in long-duration space exploration. Heliyon **8**(5), e09414 (2022)
19. Kahn Jr, P.H., Kellert, S.R.: Children and Nature: Psychological, Sociocultural, and Evolutionary Investigations. MIT press, Cambridge (2002)
20. Gong, Y., et al: Effects of intensity of short-wavelength light on the eeg and performance of astronauts during target tracking. In: Harris, D., Li, W.-C. (eds.) Engineering Psychology and Cognitive Ergonomics: 19th International Conference, EPCE 2022, Held as Part of the 24th HCI International Conference, HCII 2022, Virtual Event, June 26 – July 1, 2022, Proceedings, pp. 279–289. Springer International Publishing, Cham (2022). https://doi.org/10.1007/978-3-031-06086-1_21
21. Berto, R.: The role of nature in coping with psycho-physiological stress: a literature review on restorativeness. Behav. Sci. **4**(4), 394–409 (2014)
22. Kaplan, S.: The restorative benefits of nature: toward an integrative framework. J. Environ. Psychol. **15**(3), 169–182 (1995)
23. Ulrich, C., Nadkarni, N.M.: Sustainability research and practices in enforced residential institutions: collaborations of ecologists and prisoners. Environ. Dev. Sustain. **11**(4), 815–832 (2009)
24. Jiang, A., et al.: Short-term virtual reality simulation of the effects of space station colour and microgravity and lunar gravity on cognitive task performance and emotion. Build. Environ. **227**, 109789 (2023)
25. Jiang, A., Yao, X., Westland, S., Hemingray, C., Foing, B., Lin, J.: The effect of correlated colour temperature on physiological, emotional and subjective satisfaction in the hygiene area of a space station. Int. J. Environ. Res. Public Health **19**(15), 9090 (2022)
26. Ratcliffe, E.: Sound and soundscape in restorative natural environments: a narrative literature review. Front. Psychol. **12**, 963 (2021)
27. Jiang, A., et al.: Space Habitat Astronautics: Multicolour Lighting Psychology in a 7-Day Simulated Habitat. Space: Science & Technology (2022)
28. Beery, T., Jørgensen, K.A.: Children in nature: sensory engagement and the experience of biodiversity. Environ. Educ. Res. **24**(1), 13–25 (2018)
29. Qiu, M., Sha, J., Utomo, S.: Listening to forests: comparing the perceived restorative characteristics of natural soundscapes before and after the COVID-19 Pandemic. Sustainability **13**(1), 293 (2020)
30. Zimmermann, M.: The nervous system in the context of information theory, in human physiology. In: Schmidt, R.F., Thews, G. (eds.) Human Physiology, pp. 166–173. Springer, Heidelberg (1989). https://doi.org/10.1007/978-3-642-73831-9_7
31. Franco, L.S., Shanahan, D.F., Fuller, R.A.: A review of the benefits of nature experiences: more than meets the eye. Int. J. Environ. Res. Public Health **14**(8), 864 (2017)
32. Kun, Y., Jiang, A., Zeng, X., Wang, J., Yao, X., Chen, Y.: Colour design method of ship centralized control cabin. In: Stanton, N. (ed.) AHFE 2021. LNNS, vol. 270, pp. 495–502. Springer, Cham (2021). https://doi.org/10.1007/978-3-030-80012-3_57
33. Grinde, B., Patil, G.G.: Biophilia: does visual contact with nature impact on health and well-being? Int. J. Environ. Res. Public Health **6**(9), 2332–2343 (2009)

34. Ulrich, R.S., et al.: Stress recovery during exposure to natural and urban environments. J. Environ. Psychol. **11**(3), 201–230 (1991)
35. Nadkarni, N.M., et al.: Impacts of nature imagery on people in severely nature-deprived environments. Front. Ecol. Environ. **15**(7), 395–403 (2017)
36. Kun, Y., Jiang, A., Wang, J., Zeng, X., Yao, X., Chen, Y.: Construction of crew visual behaviour mechanism in ship centralized control cabin. In: Stanton, N. (ed.) Advances in Human Aspects of Transportation: Proceedings of the AHFE 2021 Virtual Conference on Human Aspects of Transportation, July 25-29, 2021, USA, pp. 503–510. Springer International Publishing, Cham (2021). https://doi.org/10.1007/978-3-030-80012-3_58
37. Lohr, V.I., Pearson-Mims, C.H., Goodwin, G.K.: Interior plants may improve worker productivity and reduce stress in a windowless environment. J. Environ. Hortic. **14**(2), 97–100 (1996)
38. Soga, M., et al.: A room with a green view: the importance of nearby nature for mental health during the COVID-19 pandemic. Ecol. Appl. **31**(2), e2248 (2021)
39. Shizhu, L., et al.: Effects and challenges of operational lighting illuminance in spacecraft on human visual acuity. In: Stanton, N. (ed.) AHFE 2021. LNNS, vol. 270, pp. 582–588. Springer, Cham (2021). https://doi.org/10.1007/978-3-030-80012-3_67
40. Arquilla, K., Webb, A.K., Anderson, A.P.: Isolation and confinement due to the COVID-19 pandemic: lessons for human spaceflight. Acta Astronaut. **196**, 282–289 (2022)
41. Rivolier, J., Bachelard, C., Cazes, G.: Crew selection for an Antarctic-based space simulator. In: Harrison, A.A., Clearwater, Y.A., McKay, C.P. (eds.) From Antarctica to outer space, pp. 291–296. Springer, New York, NY (1991). https://doi.org/10.1007/978-1-4612-3012-0_27
42. Webber, D.: Space tourism–essential step in human settlement of space. In: 63rd International Astronautical Congress (2012)
43. Jiang, A., Yao, X., Hemingray, C., Westland, S.: Young people's colour preference and the arousal level of small apartments. Color. Res. Appl. **47**(3), 783–795 (2022)
44. Ruyters, G., Braun, M.: Plant biology in space: recent accomplishments and recommendations for future research. Plant Biol. **16**, 4–11 (2014)
45. Porterfield, D.M., et al.: Spaceflight hardware for conducting plant growth experiments in space: the early years 1960–2000. Adv. Space Res. **31**(1), 183–193 (2003)
46. Koçkaya, E.S., Cemal, U.: Life of plants in space: a challenging mission for tiny greens in an everlasting darkness. Havacılık ve Uzay Çalışmaları Dergisi **2**(2), 1–23 (2022)
47. Jiang, A., Foing, B.H., Schlacht, I.L., Yao, X., Cheung, V., Rhodes, P.A.: Colour schemes to reduce stress response in the hygiene area of a space station: a Delphi study. Appl. Ergon. **98**, 103573 (2022)
48. Meinen, E., et al.: Growing fresh food on future space missions: environmental conditions and crop management. Sci. Hortic. **235**, 270–278 (2018)
49. Oluwafemi, F.A., et al.: Space food and nutrition in a long term manned mission. Adv. Astron. Sci. Technol. **1**(1), 1–21 (2018)
50. Dueck, T., et al. Choosing crops for cultivation in space. In: 46th International Conference on Environmental Systems (2016)
51. Zabel, P., et al.: Review and analysis of over 40 years of space plant growth systems. Life Sci. Space Res. **10**, 1–16 (2016)
52. Haeuplik-Meusburger, S., et al.: Greenhouses and their humanizing synergies. Acta Astronaut. **96**, 138–150 (2014)
53. Jiang, A., Yao, X., Schlacht, I.L., Musso, G., Tang, T., Westland, S.: Habitability study on space station colour design. In: Stanton, N. (ed.) AHFE 2020. AISC, vol. 1212, pp. 507–514. Springer, Cham (2020). https://doi.org/10.1007/978-3-030-50943-9_64
54. Valtchanov, D., Barton, K.R., Ellard, C.: Restorative effects of virtual nature settings. Cyberpsychol. Behav. Soc. Netw. **13**(5), 503–512 (2010)

55. Bannova, O., Camba, J.D., Bishop, S.: Projection-based visualization technology and its design implications in space habitats. Acta Astronaut. **160**, 310–316 (2019)

56. Nukarinen, T., et al.: Measures and modalities in restorative virtual natural environments: an integrative narrative review. Comput. Hum. Behav. **126**, 107008 (2022)

57. Lockard, E., Kaufman,: Bringing nature into space: the restorative potential of virtual environments for long term space travel. In: 49th International Conference on Environmental Systems (2019)

58. Lyons, K.D., et al.: Autonomous psychological support for isolation and confinement. Aeros. Med. Hum. Perf. **91**(11), 876–885 (2020)

59. Bishop, S., et al.: The bionomic design and mixed reality as passive countermeasures in terrestrial analogs and extraterrestrial habitats. In: 2020 International Conference on Environmental Systems (2020)

60. Botella, C., et al.: Psychological countermeasures in manned space missions: "EARTH" system for the Mars-500 project. Comput. Hum. Behav. **55**, 898–908 (2016)

61. Anderson, A., et al.: Natural scene virtual reality as a behavioral health countermeasure in isolated, confined, and extreme environments: three isolated, confined, extreme analog case studies. In: Human Factors, p. 00187208221100693 (2022)

62. Abbott, R., Diaz-Artiles, A.: The impact of digital scents on behavioral health in a restorative virtual reality environment. Acta Astronaut. **197**, 145–153 (2022)

63. Gushin, V., et al.: Prospects for psychological support in interplanetary expeditions. Front. Physiol. **12**, 750414 (2021). https://doi.org/10.3389/fphys.2021.750414

64. Bishop, S., et al.: Bionomic design countermeasures for enhancing cognitive and psychological functioning and crew performance in isolated and confined habitats. In: 46th International Conference on Environmental Systems (2016)

65. Ishihara, S.: Test for colour-blindness. Kanehara Tokyo, Japan (1987)

66. Jiang, A., Zhu, Y., Yao, X., Foing, B.H., Westland, S., Hemingray, C.: The effect of three body positions on colour preference: an exploration of microgravity and lunar gravity simulations. Acta Astronaut. **204**, 1–10 (2023)

67. Honeyborne, J., Brownlow, M.: Blue planet II. Random House (2017)

68. Dunn, M.E., Mills, M., Veríssimo, D.: Evaluating the impact of the documentary series Blue Planet II on viewers' plastic consumption behaviors. Conser. Sci. Pract. **2**(10), e280 (2020)

69. Yeo, N.L., et al.: What is the best way of delivering virtual nature for improving mood? an experimental comparison of high definition TV, 360 degrees video, and computer generated virtual reality. J Environ Psychol **72**, 101500 (2020)

70. Spielberger, C., et al.: Manual for the Stait-Trait Anxiety Inventory Consulting. Psychologists Press, Palo Alto (1983)

71. Watson, D., Clark, L.A., Tellegen, A.: Development and validation of brief measures of positive and negative affect: the PANAS scales. J. Pers. Soc. Psychol. **54**(6), 1063 (1988)

72. Missions, C.D.L.-D.S. and M. Kanas, PSYCHOLOGY AND CULTURE DURING LONG-DURATION SPACE MISSIONS. 2007

73. de Kort, Y.A.W., et al.: What's wrong with virtual trees? restoring from stress in a mediated environment. J. Environ. Psychol. **26**(4), 309–320 (2006)

74. Amirbeiki, F., Ghasr, A.K.: Investigating the effects of exposure to natural blue elements on the psychological restoration of university studentsity students. Iran Univ. Sci. Technol. **30**(1), 1–10 (2020)

75. White, M., et al.: Blue space: the importance of water for preference, affect, and restorativeness ratings of natural and built scenes. J. Environ. Psychol. **30**(4), 482–493 (2010)

76. Tao, S., et al.: Associations of circadian rhythm abnormalities caused by home quarantine during the COVID-19 outbreak and mental health in Chinese undergraduates: evidence from a nationwide school-based survey. Available at SSRN 3582851 (2020)
77. Hashimoto, S., et al.: Melatonin rhythm is not shifted by lights that suppress nocturnal melatonin in humans under entrainment. Am. J. Physiol.-Regulat. Integr. Compar. Physiol. **270**(5), R1073–R1077 (1996)

Emerging Challenges – How Pilot Students Remained Resilient During the Pandemic?

Chien-Tsung Lu[1]([⊠]), Xinyu Lu[1], Ming Cheng[2], Haoruo Fu[1], and Zhenglei Ji[1]

[1] School of Aviation and Transportation Technology, Purdue University, West Lafayette, USA
{Ctlu,Lu910,Fu361,Ji188}@purdue.edu

[2] College of Safety Science and Engineering, Civil Aviation University of China, Tianjin, People's Republic of China

Abstract. Due to the low volume of passenger services between March 2020 and May 2022, manpower demand was dwindled by airlines and simultaneously shape undesirable or appalling moods among flight students due to the unpredictable timeline of business recovery. To realize the psychological impact and understand how they coped with the challenges generated by COVID-19, this follow-up study surveyed flight schools in the United States (U.S.) and compared respondents' perception of health protocols, flight training, human factors, psychological issues, and safety culture to that of Chinese respondents. Cronbach's alpha, Spearman correlation coefficients, and Wilcoxon-Mann-Whitney t-test were used to coin instrument consistency, data validity, and correlation among questions before testing perceptional differences. The result discovered that "Stress" "Pressure", and "Fatigue" were the three dominant Human Factors, where "Stress" and "Uncertainty" were the two top psychological issues affecting U.S. respondents during the pandemic time. Moreover, U.S. flight schools were less supportive to wear a face mask in the cockpit but showed a stronger motivation to seek mental/psychological health support and were more willing to adapt to new safety and health standards. China's flight schools encountered more disrupted scheduled flight training and check-rides and decreased flight skills due to the stricter health protocols, but flight schools tried as diligently as possible to offer refresher courses during the pandemic.

Keywords: psychological impact · human factors · flight schools · wilcoxon-Mann-Whitney

1 Introduction

This is a follow-up study of a previous project that surveyed two Chinese flight schools, between May and September 2022, regarding how COVID-19 affected their flight training in addition to mental threats that may have been quietly shaped that changed pilot students' daily operations. The researchers' previous study showed that Chinese Civil Aviation Regulation (CCAR) Part 141 flight schools precisely followed strict pandemic policies and protocols, as well as initiated internal guidelines to comply with the government's rules. Most respondents gave constructive suggestions and supported stringent guidelines but hoped for more operational flexibility. Despite frequent advocates, health and safety protocols were met in the cockpit. Pilots received more polymerase chain reaction (PCR) tests to buttress a COVID-free operational environment. While the "Dynamic COVID-Zero" policy is active in China, Chinese flight schools enforce a temporary lockdown or increase the frequency of mandatory PCR tests accordingly [1]. Respondents of the previous study revealed that their training proficiency had been influenced by COVID-19, yet, flight schools worked diligently to maintain pilot students' skill competency by providing refresher courses as much as realistically possible. It is worth noting that Chinese airlines outsource flight training to CCAR Part 141 flight schools worldwide and therefore close communication, monitoring, curriculum development, and quality assurance must stay effective. Even if COVID-19 has slowed down flight training, the pilot delivery schedule is decided by the sponsoring employers, namely airlines [1].

2   Background

In the authors' previous study, "Pressure", "Fatigue", and "Distraction" were the three top Human Factors perceived by Chinese respondents [1]. During COVID-19, Chinese pilot students lived in a confined space for an extended period and perceived long-lasting concerns, stress, and worry leading to fatigue and pressure. Flight schools in China adopted the closed-campus or lockdown strategy to manage campus activities. That said, pilot students must live within the campus perimeters unless with the school's administrator's permit but it was very unlikely. The campus administration managed the flow of faculty members and pilot students' arrival at or departure from the training base to decrease the likelihood of cross-infection [2]. Nonetheless, a few months of isolation could lead to severe mental impacts on students [3]. A study showed that a strict closure of universities in China could lead to students' depression and social life inconvenience [2].

Furthermore, in Lu's study concerning psychological issues, respondents chose "Uncertainty" as their leading psychological problem followed by "Stress", "Anxiety" and "Worry" due to the unpredictable development of the COVID-19 pandemic. While the global aviation and travel industry are both slowly recovering, Chinese aviation is still under strict governmental control. Lu's finding of "Anxiety" from Chinese pilot students echoed Wang and Zhao's research outcome that university students in China had higher anxiety than that of the public after the outbreak of COVID-19 [4].

Flight schools in China provided mental/psychological health consultant services to pilot students that assisted students in solving urgent mental needs, strengthening students' confidence, integrity, and self-esteem, and to continue achieving their career goals [5, 6]. Students believed that getting consultation services was beneficial, and most preferred to visit psychological consultants soon or hoped that their flight training institutes would provide a similar service [1].

Maintaining flight safety performance during COVID-19 was more challenging than usual due to limited operation, revenue reduction, salient Human Factors, and students' psychological status. However, flight training organizations in China persistently reiterated safety by hosting safety meetings, training, and briefings, and collecting hazard reports to continue supporting the all-inclusive safety management systems (SMS).

Reporting, informed, just, and learning cultures had been well-maintained and deeply accentuated in every flight student's mind [7]. Top management's commitment to invest valuable resources and assets in maintaining safety performance and improving safety culture had been promised.

2.1 Bibliographic Qualitative Analysis

To better understand the impact of the pandemic to pilot students, a bibliographical qualitative analysis was conducted. Documentations were found through Elsevier's Scopus where VOSviewer, a software tool for constructing bibliometric networks, was used for the analysis and data visualization. Two keywords, "student pilot" and "COVID-19", were used to identify 510 articles and five (5) color-coded clusters were generated as provided in Fig. 1.

During the documentation search, there were 102 keywords repeatedly mentioned more than ten (10) times in 510 documents. When looking into the "student" keyword, it linked to two clusters - new innovative learning channels and psychological impact during the pandemic (see Fig. 2), which partially reflected our previous study focused on understanding Chinese pilot students' perception of health protocols, flight training interference, human factors, psychological impact, and safety culture during the pandemic.

To better understand pilot students' psychological impact during the pandemic, the terms "student pilot" and "psychological impact" were used for the second VOSviewer analysis. Elsevier's Scopus showed 304 documents related to the selected terms. A total of 79 keywords were repeatedly mentioned more than 10 times in the archived documentation. Four clusters were listed in the VOSviewer result and "stress" was tightly connected to other factors. Our previous studies listed common emotions, such as "stress" and "anxiety," which can significantly impact pilots' performance (see Fig. 3).

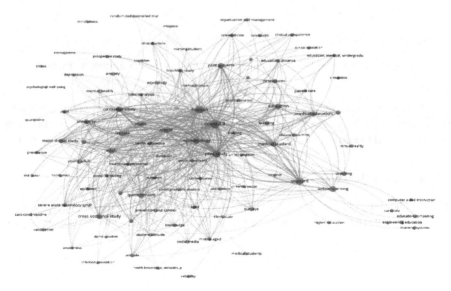

Fig. 1. VOSviewer Visualization: Student Pilot, COVID-19.

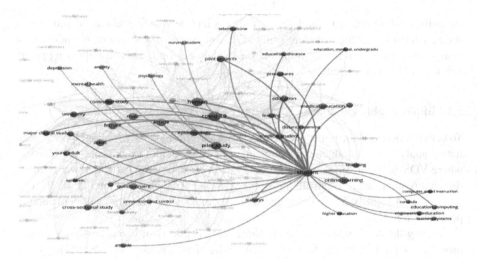

Fig. 2. VOSviewer Visualization: Student Pilot, COVID-19. "student" connections

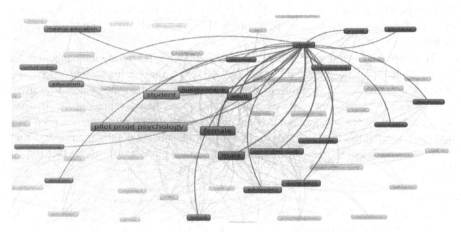

Fig. 3. VOSviewer Visualization: Student Pilot, Psychological Impact: Stress

In addition, the sub-cluster of psychological education included medical education, policy, and prevention methodology, which were also recommended in our previous study designed to understand Chinese pilot students during the pandemic (see Fig. 4).

2.2 Research Questions

To continue, the purpose of this follow-up study was twofold: 1) to discover U.S. pilot students' perception of health protocols, flight training, human factors, psychological

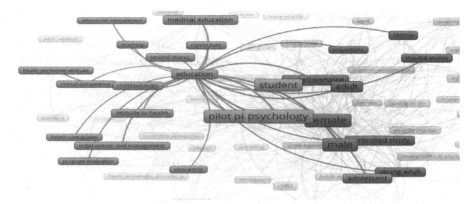

Fig. 4. VOSviewer Visualization: Student Pilot, Psychological Impact: Education Centered

issues, and safety culture; and 2) to compare collected data between respondents of Part 141 flight schools in the U.S. and China. There were two primary research questions:

Q1. How have pilot students in the China and United States (U.S.) responded to the COVID-19 pandemic in terms of health policies, flight schedules, and safety culture? Q2. What human factors and psychological issues were perceived at flight schools in China and the United States during the pandemic?

3 Methodology

This study surveyed two U.S-based FAA FAR Part 141 flight schools to retrieve inputs from pilot students and instructors reflecting on their perception of the pandemic impact including training schedule interference, emerging human factors and psychological issues, and safety culture. Researchers used close-ended questions and corresponding Likert Scale (1: Strongly Disagree and 5: Strongly Agree) as well as open-ended questions to collect subjective inputs. Cronbach's alpha was used to benchmark instrument consistency, while the Wilcoxon-Mann-Whitney t-test was calculated for outcome comparison. The same research questions were answered by two Chinese flight schools between March and August 2022, while data collection for this study was conducted between June 2022 and completed in September 2022.

4 Findings

4.1 Descriptive Statistics

Most U.S. respondents were male aged between 18 and 24, including 37 percent senior and 31 percent junior students with 15 percent respondents at a graduate school level. 91 percent of respondents hold a certified flight instructor (CFI), commercial pilot license (CPL), or at least a private pilot license (PPL).

4.2 Awareness of Pandemic Protocol at Flight Schools

The first section measured COVID-19 health protocols/rules at U.S. Part 141 flight schools based on the guidelines of COVID-19 pandemic prevention. There were six (6) close-ended questions (Likert Scale, where "1" represents Strongly Disagree and "5" for Strongly Agree) and one open-ended question. Cronbach's alpha value was 0.768 showing a high internal consistency, which provided a further analysis. Table 1 delivers the *Descriptive Analysis of Survey Questions on Health Protocols.*

Table 1. Descriptive Analysis of Survey Questions – Health Protocol (Bar Charts)

It is necessary to wear a mask in the cockpit during flight training	20.99%*
My flight department has special health protocols/checklists for flight training during COVID-19	72.84%
I am familiar with special COVID-19 protocols/checklists (symptoms, quarantine policy, personal hygiene, etc.) related to flight training	79.01%
I prefer to fly with the same instructors to prevent the virus spread	58.03%
I have a clear understanding of the health risks associated with flight operations during COVID-19	84.95%
The COVID-19 prevention protocols at my flight training institute have been successful	76.54%

* Both Agree or Strongly Agree

Researchers conducted a Spearman Correlation Coefficient test to find correlative attitudes among questions from U.S. respondents. The result is shown in Table 2 and Fig. 5 below:

Table 2. Spearman Correlation Coefficient Matrix - Health Protocol Questions

	Q. No.					
Q. No.	1.1	1.2	1.3	1.4	1.5	1.6
1.1 Wearing a face mask	1					
1.2 Pandemic protocols in place	0.295	1				
1.3 Familiarity with protocols	0.202	0.638	1			
1.4 Flying w/the same instructor	0.509	0.227	0.223	1		
1.5 Understanding risk	0.198	0.419	0.660	5.6	1	
1.6 Successful protocols	0.145	0.510	0.582	0.237	0.632	1

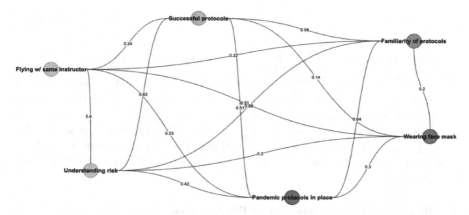

Fig. 5. Spearman Correlation Coefficient Matrix - Health Protocol Section

As shown in Fig. 5 above, those who supported the protocol of wearing a face mask in the cockpit were also in favor of flying with the same instructor due to the high correlation coefficient, 0.509. Moreover, the correlation coefficient of 0.638 between Q1.2 and Q1.3 showed that flight students who were aware of COVID-19 guidelines were also familiar with the mandatory details. The Correlation Coefficient between Q1.3 and Q1.5 was 0.66, which meant that the respondents were familiar with the CDC's, local government, and flight schools' policies who also clearly understood the pandemic risks during COVID-19. The correlation between Q1.3 and Q1.6 was 0.582, which meant that those who perceived that flight schools' prevention protocols seemed adequate, they also indicated the success of the policies. Overall, most questions in the Health Protocol section possessed a moderated correlation, indicating that flight schools had enforced comprehensive measures against pandemic risk. Some weak Correlation Coefficient indexes (between 0.15 to 0.35) reflected that flight schools' health protocol still required more pandemic protocol promotion to flight students.

The respondents also provided specific comments about the health protocols or policies and most indicated positive perceptions regarding health protocols during the COVID-19 pandemic. Positive comments include:

- "Operations were never shut down and the infection rates remained low throughout my freshman year because our department did excellent jog on temperature screening, PCR test and all student pairing with the health protocols"

However, these respondents argued the effectiveness of wearing a facemask in the cockpit. When asked for their perception of protection protocols or safety screenings, they responded:

- "I believe wearing masks in an aircraft during a flight is non-effective. If the pilots are practically touching shoulders, the virus will spread regardless of if you are wearing a mask or not."
- "Besides, you are bringing the same air with your instructor for 2–3 h or maybe even more."

- "It can also create safety risks, like when using [g]oggles for the simulated instrument."

Other comments related to health protocols are listed as the following:

- "I feel that the current protocols are well equipped for COVID. However, I had an instructor who was feeling ill and very sick and decided to continue with our lesson and I caught COVID from them."
- "Protocols were very strict and thus very effective at first, but now, there are very few restrictions which increases the risk of contamination. The restrictions were relaxed as most students are now vaccinated, but it has not stopped the spread these last 2 semesters."

4.3 Impact on Flight Training Due to the Pandemic

The second part of the survey assessed the COVID-19 influences on flight training progress, including challenges such as training interruption, scheduled check rides, and medical examination delays. The Cronbach's alpha was 0.763 by the F-distribution, which showed a high internal consistency. Table 3 presents a descriptive analysis of close-ended questions regarding the impact on flight training from COVID-19.

I had financial challenges during my flight training during COVID-19

Table 3. Descriptive Analysis of Close-ended Questions – Flight Training (Histogram and Pie Charts)

I had financial challenges during my flight training during COVID-19	48.15%*
My flight training progress was disrupted during COVID-19	74.07%
My check ride was disrupted during COVID-19	43.21%
I successfully got my FAA medical exam during COVID-19	61.73%
I got less training during COVID-19	58.02%
YES	58.02%
I think my flight skills decreased due to the reduction of flight training	35.80%
I spent extra time refreshing my knowledge and skills before returning to flight training during COVID-19	55.55%

* Both Agree or Strongly Agree

Researchers conducted a Spearman Correlation Coefficient test to find correlative attitudes among questions from respondents. The result is shown in Table 4 and Fig. 6 below:

The correlation coefficient between Q2.4 (Decreased skills) and Q2.5 (Refresher courses) was the strongest, 0.674, which meant that respondents were eager to receive refresher courses to reinstate and restore their decreased flight skills during the pandemic. The correlation coefficient between Q2.1 (financial hardship) and Q2.2 (training interference) showed a strong correlation of 0.468. The correlation between Q2.2 (training

Table 4. Spearman Correlation Coefficient Matrix - Flight Training Questions

Q. No.	Q. No.				
	2.1	2.2	2.3	2.4	2.5
2.1 Financial hardship	1				
2.2 Training interference	0.468	1			
2.3 Check ride interference	0.401	0.425	1		
2.4 Decreased skills	0.286	0.344	0.412	1	
2.5 Needing refresher course	0.199	0.432	0.312	0.674	1

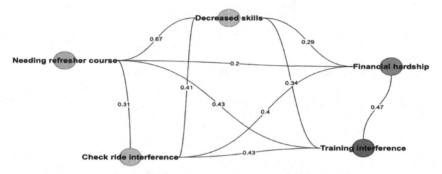

Fig. 6. Spearman Correlation Coefficient Matrix - Flight Training Section

interference) and Q2.3 (check ride interference) was 0.425, which meant that respondents indicated their training schedule had been interrupted as well as scheduled check rides.

4.4 Human Factors that Surfaced During the Pandemic

Respondents selected specific Human Factors they had encountered, perceived, or observed during COVID-19 time. The result shows that "stress" (57/81, 70.37%), "pressure" (50/81, 61.73%), and "fatigue" (30/81, 37.04%) were the three dominant Human Factors during COVID-19 time, followed by "lack of communication" (28/81, 34.57%), "norm/safety culture" (27/81, 33.33%) and "distraction" (24/81, 29.63%) (See Fig. 7).

Stress was the most relentless factor that U.S. respondents were concerned about. The respondent's stress was from various sources such as family issues, academic course interferences, and financial hardship that could also lead to lacking rest, irregular training shifts, and work-life imbalance, and ultimately formed a deceptive forerunner of fatigue. Not surprisingly, the result indicated that fatigue could lead to pilot distraction, which consequently caused poor operations or erroneous decisions in the cockpit. Respondents' concerns on "lack of communication" and "norm/safety culture" also translated into a sound understanding of crew resource management and risk assessment.

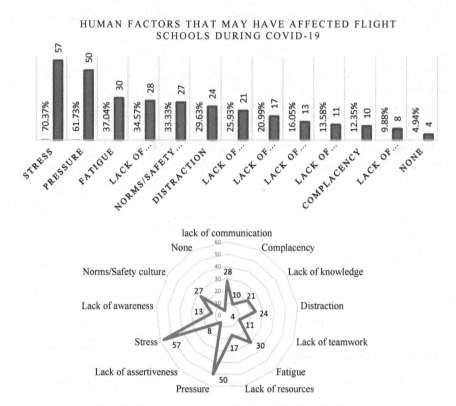

Fig. 7. Human Factor Issues Surfaced during COVID-19

4.5 Psychological Impact During the Pandemic

Questions in the 4th section were designed to obtain respondents' psychological and mental health status during COVID-19. Respondents selected "Stress" (57/81, 70.38%) and "Uncertainty" (52/81, 64.2%) were two prevalent psychological factors they had perceived (see Fig. 2). Additionally, many respondents expressed their feeling of "Worry" (44/81, 54.32%), "Pressure" (41/81, 50.61%), "Frustration" (39/81, 48.15%), "Longlines" (39/81, 48.15%) followed by "Fatigue" (33/81, 40.74%). The "Poor Social Relationship" (30/81, 37.04%) indicated respondents required more social activities at training bases/airports (See Fig. 8).

While some respondents skipped the following questions, it is informative to provide some insights as well:

- My flight program provides mental health consultants, 41 (Yes), 11 (No), and 27 (Not Sure).
- I have been to mental health consultant service during COVID-19, 11 (Yes), 35 (No).
- I think my flight department needs to have a comprehensive mental health consultant service, 14 (Strong Agree), 12 (Agree), 6 (Neutral), and 3 (Disagree).
- I think the consultant service is useful, 3 (Strong Agree), 7 (Agree), and 1 (Neutral).

PSYCHOLOGICAL ISSUES THAT FLIGHT SCHOOLS
HAVE PERCEIVED DURING COVID-19

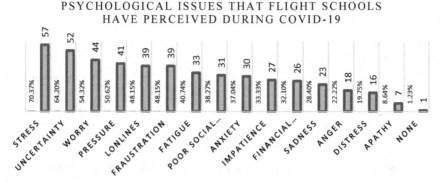

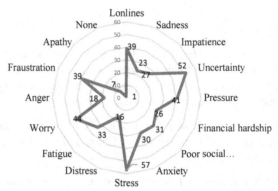

Fig. 8. Psychological Issues Perceived during COVID-19

- It is important to seek mental/psychological health support/consultant if there is a need, 49 (Strong Agree), 20 (Agree), 7 (Neutral), 1 (Disagree), and 4 (Strongly Disagree).

4.6 Safety Culture

The last section of this survey was designed to measure safety culture during the COVID-19 pandemic. The Cronbach's alpha value was 0.876 per F-distribution. The high internal consistency among questions helped researchers further develop a comprehensive understanding of safety cultures at the participating U.S. flight schools.

According to the collected data, most surveyed respondents had indicated a positive safety culture during the COVID-19 pandemic time, while a small number of respondents had demonstrated concerns. To further analyze the collected data, Spearman's Correlation Coefficient was conducted showing strong correlations among questions (perception of safety priority, safety meeting, reporting culture, just culture, informed culture, learning culture, and safety commitment) (See Fig. 9). However, the "refresher courses" item possessed a low correlation to all other questions. This situation revealed that respondents focused on safety items instead of an outlier (refresher courses) in this section that simultaneously verified the validity of the result.

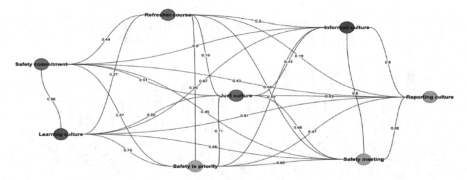

Fig. 9. Spearman Correlation Coefficient of Likert Scale questions in Safety Culture Section.

4.7 Discussion

Health Protocols – Statistical Hypothesis Testing. In the previous study, the researchers surveyed two Chinese flight schools and archived data can be used to compare to that of U.S.-based flight schools. Using parametric analysis, the following tables showed the result of each survey question. A tabulated list is provided:

An unequal samples Wilcoxon-Mann-Whitney t-test was conducted to compare respondents' perception of flight schools in China and the U.S. A quick summary is presented as follows:

- Reject H_0 – *"It is necessary to wear a mask in the cockpit during flight training."* There was a significant difference in the scores between China (M = 3.453, SD = 1.198) and the USA (M = 2.370, SD = 0.943) where t(174) = 4.979, p < 0.05. These results suggested that U.S. pilot students were less supportive to wear a face mask in the cockpit, which was also reflected in their opposing comments.
- Accept H_0 – *"My flight department has special health protocols/checklists for flight training during COVID-19."*
- Accept H_0 – *"I am familiar with special COVID-19 protocols/checklists (symptoms, quarantine policy, personal hygiene, etc.) related to flight training."*
- Accept H_0 – *"I prefer to fly with the same instructors to prevent the virus spread."*
- Accept H_0 – *"I have a clear understanding of health risks associated with flight operations during COVID-19."*
- Accept H_0 – *"The COVID-19 prevention protocols at my flight training institute have been successful."*

Flight Training Impact – Statistical Hypothesis Testing. For the questions surveying respondents at Chinses and U.S. flight schools regarding flight training interference during the pandemic time, the Wilcoxon-Mann-Whitney t-test result comparing two sample means of each question is provided as the following tabulated list:

- Accept H_0 – *"I had financial challenges during my flight training during COVID-19."*
- Accept H_0 – *"My flight training progress was disrupted during COVID-19."*

- Reject H$_0$ – *"My check ride was disrupted during COVID-19"*. There was a significant difference in the scores between China (M = 3.547, SD = 1.42) and the USA (M = 2.936, SD = 1.651) where t(159) = 2.48, p < 0.05. These results indicated that China's flight schools showed a stronger feeling of disrupted scheduled check rides during COVID-19.
- Reject H$_0$ – "I *think my flight skills were decreased due to a reduction of flight training.*". There was a significant difference in the scores between China (M = 3.284, SD = 1.287) and the USA (M = 2.926, SD = 1.412) where t(164) = 1.737, p < 0.05. These results indicated that China's flight schools showed a stronger feeling regarding decreased flight skills due to the reduction of flight training even though the overall perception of reduced skills" was not strong.
- Accept H$_0$ – *"I spent extra time to refresh my knowledge and skills before returning to flight training during COVID-19."*

Emerging Human Factors. For the perceived human factors, both China and U.S. respondents indicated high pressure, but U.S. respondents suffered more from stress (70.37%). (see Fig. 10). For U.S. respondents, "Stress", "Pressure", "Fatigue", "Lack of Communication" and "Culture" were the top five human factors selected. For Chinese respondents, "Pressure", "Fatigue", "Distraction", "Stress" and "Lack of Communication" were the top five reported human factors. The overall impact of human factors on U.S. respondents was more significant than that of the Chinese respondents.

Fig. 10. Human Factors that may have affected flight schools During COVID-19 (China vs U.S.)

Psychological Impact – Statistical Hypothesis Testing. For the perception between respondents from China and U.S., only two Likert Scale questions were tested. The finding showed that:

- Reject H_0 – *"It is important to seek mental/psychological health support/consultant if there is a need."* There was a significant difference in the scores between China (M = 4.053, SD = 1.268) and the USA (M = 4.346, SD = 1.032) where t(174) = −1.68, p < 0.05. These results indicated that U.S. respondents perceived a stronger motivation regarding the importance of seeking mental/psychological health support if there was a need.
- Accept H_0 – There is no difference between respondents from China and U.S. flight schools regarding their overall mental health. However, the scores were relatively discouraging as they were between 3.674 and 3.852.

Figure 11 below demonstrated the perceived psychological issues from respondents indicated "Stress", "Uncertainty", "Worry", "Frustration", and "Loneliness" were the top five psychological issues where Chinese respondents selected "Uncertainty", Stress", "Worry", "Fatigue" as the top four issues and 18.95 percent chose "None" as the answer.

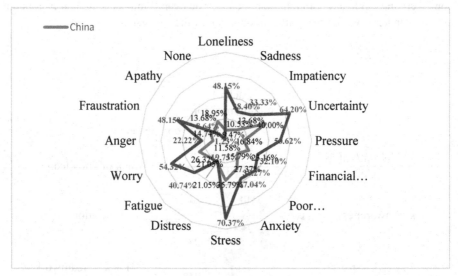

Fig. 11. Psychological issues that may have affected pilot students during COVID-19 (China vs U.S.)

As seen in Fig. 4 above, the overall perceived psychological issues were less significant on the Chinese students' side. This is simply because most Chinese pilot students were paid by airlines to go through flight training. Although they felt uncertain about flight training progress, they were less worried and more confident about future career development. Figure 4 possesses valuable information for the mental health department to determine the priority of psychological/mental health problems and provide adequate services.

Safety Culture – Statistical Hypothesis Testing. For the safety culture measurement, the researchers provided the following table to show the testing results. A tabulated result comparing both sample means is provided below:

- Accept H_0 – *"Safety remained the core value at my flight training institute during COVID-19."*
- Accept H_0 – *"My flight training program conducted safety meetings periodically or whenever necessary during COVID-19."*
- Accept H_0 – *"I have been willing to report hazards regardless of COVID-19."*
- Accept H_0 – *"I trust that the review of a hazard report has been effective and fair."*
- Accept H_0 – *"My institute has routinely informed me of the safety status regardless of COVID-19."*
- Reject H_0 – *"I can adapt to new safety standards and changes regardless of COVID-19."* There was a significant difference in the scores between China (M = 3.968, SD = 1.244) and the USA (M = 4.321, SD = 0.844) where $t(166) = -2.214$, $p < 0.05$. These results indicated that U.S.-based flight schools showed a stronger willingness when adapting to new safety standards and changes due to COVID-19.
- Reject H_0 - There was a significant difference in the scores between China (M = 3.853, SD = 1.239) and the USA (M = 3.346, SD = 1.326) where $t(165) = 2.59$, $p < 0.05$. These results indicated that China-based flight schools had a stronger need for refresher courses if they have not operated aircraft for an extended time.
- Accept H_0 – *"The top executives of my institute showed strong support to safety during COVID-19."*

5 Conclusion

This study surveyed flight schools in China and U.S.A. and compared respondents' perceptions of selected research areas concerning health protocols, scheduled flight training, human factors, psychological issues, and safety culture. The descriptive statistics of U.S.-based flight schools were provided where Cronbach's alpha and correlation coefficients among questions were calculated to coin instrument consistency and data validity. The result shows that "stress" "pressure", and "fatigue" were the three dominant Human Factors, where "Stress" and "Uncertainty" were the two top psychological issues affecting respondents during the pandemic time. Following the descriptive statistics, the researchers revisited previous studies on China's flight schools to obtain two datasets and compared them. Using two sample Wilcoxon-Mann-Whitney t-test (unequal variances) among collected data of each section, the result showed that U.S. flights schools: 1) were more supportive to wear a face mask in the cockpit regardless of the narrative comments, 2) showed a stronger motivation regarding seeking mental/psychological health support if there was a need, and 3) were more willing to adapt to new safety and health standards. On the other hand, respondents of China's flight schools showed a perception of 1) more disrupted scheduled check rides, 2) decreased flight skills due to the reduction of flight training, and 3) available refresher courses during the COVID-19 pandemic time.

References

1. Lu, C.-T., Cheng, M., Lu, X.: Multifaceted pandemic impact on pilot students – perspectives of chinese part 141 flight schools (2022). While Paper, Purdue University. https://purr.purdue.edu/projects/psychologicalimpact/files/browse?subdir=Psychologicalimpactpart1
2. Zhang, X., Tian, X.: The challenges of Chinese university leaders during the COVID-19 pandemic period: a case study approach. Front. Psychol. (2022). https://doi.org/10.3389/fpsyg.2022.881969
3. Wang, C., Cheng, Z., Yue, X., McAleer, M.: Risk management of COVID-19 by universities in China. J. Risk Finan. Manag. 13(36), 1–6 (2020). https://doi.org/10.3390/jrfm13020036
4. Wang, C., Zhao, H.: The impact of COVID-19 on anxiety in Chinese universities students. Front. Psychol. 11, 1–8 (2020). https://doi.org/10.3389/fpsyg.2020.01168
5. Carleton, R.N., Norton, P., Asmundson, G.J.G.: Fearing the unknown: a short version of the intolerance of uncertainty scale. J. Anxiety Disord. 21(1), 105–117 (2007). https://doi.org/10.1016/j.janxdis.2006.03.014
6. Cox, J.L., Holden, J.M., Sagovsky, R.: Detection of postnatal depression: development of the 10-item edinburgh postnatal depression scale. Brit. J. Psychiat. 150(6), 782–786 (1987). https://pubmed.ncbi.nlm.nih.gov/3651732/
7. Reason, J.: Managing the Risks of Organizational Accidents. Ashgate, London (1997)

A Study on Civil Aviation Pilots Vigilance Change on Ultra-Long-Range Routes

Min Luo[1(✉)], Chunyang Zhang[1], Xingyu Liu[1], and Lin Zhang[2]

[1] China Academy of Civil Aviation Science and Technology (Engineering and Technical, Research Center of Civil Aviation Safety Analysis and Prevention of Beijing), Beijing, China
luomin@sina.com
[2] Civil Aviation Medicine Center, Beijing, China

Abstract. With the start of the COVID-19 on 2020, in order to protect the flight crew who are operating in ultra-long-range routes, the Civil Aviation Administration of China has implemented temporary deviation approval for the flight time restrictions of some airlines. That is, multiple sets of crew members are allowed to fly back and forth in the form of rest on the plane without getting off the plane after landing overseas. This type of flight has been questioned by local regulators. China civil aviation was required to provide the proof of safety in this operation mode. Therefore, this study uses NASA TLX workloads scale and alertness monitoring tools to collect and analyze subjective and objective data of pilots in one airline of China. The study compares the data including before, during and after the flight duty to prove the feasibility of China current ultra-long-range flight. It found that the appropriate shift work can limit the perception of fatigue and workloads.

Keywords: fatigue · alertness · workloads · ultra-long-range routes

1 Background

Pilots fatigue seriously affects the safety of aviation. As early as 1988, the Ames Research Center of the National Aeronautics and Space Administration (NASA) started the earliest and most authoritative flight fatigue research in the world. They have completed several research programs on flight fatigue, such as "Flight Fatigue and Jet Lag Research Program", "Flight Fatigue Prevention and Control Measures Research Program", and finally choose a variety of different flight environments to conduct comprehensive research on fatigue. This long-term, large-scale survey study found that fatigue is closely related to three factors: flight plan, sleep status and workload [1].

In 2009, an aircraft of Colgan Air crashed in Buffalo. The investigation report [2] pointed out that the aircraft had no known mechanical or computer failures, but the pilot errors, including the "confused" reactions of the captain, were the major causes of the accident. The underlying root was concluded to be the increased workloads and weakened vigilance accompanied by long duty periods. Then the accident drove Federal Aviation Administration (FAA) to legislate for fatigue risks. In 2013, FAA launched Fatigue Risk Management Systems (FRMS) for Aviation Safety (AC 120-103A) [3], which explicitly stated that "fatigue is objectively observed as changes in many aspects of performance, including increased reaction time, lapses in attention (e.g., reaction times greater than 500 ms), reduced speed of cognitive tasks, reduced situational awareness, and reduced motivation." In 2011, 2016 and 2018, International Civil Aviation Organization (ICAO) published three editions of Fatigue Risk Management System Oversight Manual (DOC 9966) [4], which provided the definitions, contributing factors and mitigation measures for flight fatigue. Meanwhile, the manual recommended the establishment of FRMS to gradually replace the traditional fatigue management based on the duty hours.

Before 2020, with the rapid development of international aviation business, the fatigue problem of pilots due to long, irregular night flights and long-distance flights across time zones has become increasingly prominent. From the beginning of 2020 to the present, with the start of the COVID-19, in order to protect the flight crew who are operating ultra-long-range routes, the Civil Aviation Administration of China (CAAC) has implemented temporary deviation approval for the work restrictions of some airlines in accordance with the CCAR-121 regulations. That is, multiple sets of crew members are allowed to fly back and forth in the form of rest on the plane without getting off the plane after landing overseas. This type of flight has been questioned by local regulators. China civil aviation was required to provide the proof of this operation mode.

Therefore, this study uses workloads and alertness monitoring tools to collect and analyze subjective and objective data of pilots in one China's domestic airline. The study compares the data including before, during and after the flight duty to prove the feasibility of China current ultra-long-range flight.

2 Experiment Methods

2.1 Route Selection

Considering factors such as the departures, destinations, aircraft types, flight time of each flight segment, turnaround time, number of cross-time zones, and multi-group operation methods, the research has chosen a westward ultra-long route, operated by 3 pairs of flight crew (6 people) on A330 or A350. The route crosses 6 time zones, with the turnaround time being 3 h and the total roundtrip flight time being 19 h. The departure time of the outbound leg is 10:00am and the departure time of the inbound leg is 11:00 pm.

2.2 Measurement Methods and Tools

The project adopts subjective and objective methods to measure alertness and workloads.

Objective Measurement. The objective tools adopted in the research is the psychomotor vigilance task (PVT). PVT is a widely used tool to test the attention, arousal and vigilance of the subjects [5–7]. It measures the consistency with which subjects respond to a prominent signal to evaluate their sustained attention. The research observes the changes in different indicators, including reaction time, reaction speed, the 10% shortest and longest reaction time, reaction variations and error rates.

The research adopts the PVT test on the mobile phone developed by the Civil Aviation Medicine Center of CAAC (shown in Fig. 1) to analyze the vigilance of pilots at different time points of roundtrip flights (including: before taxi-out, before the first entry into the cockpit, after leaving the cockpit for the first time, before the second entry into the cockpit and after landing). The PVT requires the pilots to react as quickly as possible to a visual stimulus, and the reaction time is used to measure the vigilance, with shorter reaction time indicating higher vigilance.

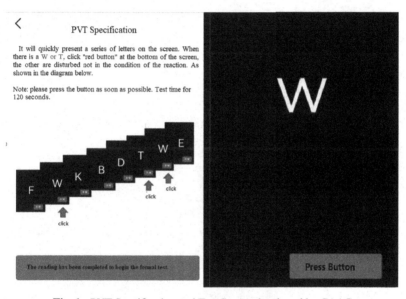

Fig. 1. PVT Specification and Test Screen developed by CAAC

Subjective Measurement. The subjective tools adopted the NASA-Task Load Index scale (NASA-TLX) and Karolinska Sleepiness Scale (KSS) on the mobile phone to evaluate the workloads and alertness of the pilots on duty.

NASA-TLX (shown in Fig. 2) evaluates workloads from different dimensions including mental demand, physical demand, temporal demand, performance, efforts and frustration, with each dimension scored between 0 to 100. The average score of all dimensions represents the overall workloads, with the higher score indicating more workloads [8–10]. The test is conducted on pilots after the landing of both inbound and outbound flights.

KSS (shown in Fig. 3) assesses subjective fatigue on a scale from 1 to 9, with higher scores representing greater subjective alertness. For each time point during the pilot's duty process, including preparation point, before taxiing out, before entering the cockpit for the first time, after exiting the cockpit for the first time, before entering the cockpit for the second time and after landing, the test is conducted on pilots.

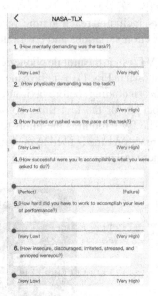

Fig. 2. NASA-TLX Test

Fig. 3. Karolinska Sleepiness Scale (KSS)

2.3 Data Collection Situation

According to the flight plan, the research collects the data from pilots in 9 roundtrip flights from January 28th to March 11th. The data of 39 pilots in total are collected, with 21 on outbound flights and 18 on inbound flights.

3 Data Analysis

Analysis of Alertness Change

Vigilance on Outbound Flights. The descriptive statistics of the PVT results on outbound flights are presented in Table 1. It is demonstrated that the reaction time averages below 600 ms.

The results show that the flight crews remain highly vigilant from the taxi-out to the taxi-in of outbound flights.

Table 1. Descriptive statistics of reaction time on outbound flights

Variables	N	Mean	Standard Deviations	Minimum Value	Maximum Value
Before take-off	36	581.51	56.17	483.0	707.5
Before the first entry into the cockpit	35	574.64	58.91	483.0	782.0
After leaving the cockpit for the first time	29	584.64	65.30	484.0	766.5
Before the second entry into the cockpit	8	592.06	57.34	517.5	690.5
After the landing	31	577.32	45.23	481.0	674.5

The ranges of reaction time on outbound flights are shown in Fig. 4. As the variations to reaction time are limited to a small range, it is proved that mitigation measures such as onboard shift work and onboard napping can keep crew members vigilant during the whole duty period.

Specifically, the reaction time of pilots after they leave the cockpit for the first time is longer than that before the first entry into the cockpit, which indicating that the vigilance is slightly weakened by the workloads of the flight tasks.

The crew members who enter the cockpit for the second time take more flight tasks and have fewer rest time. Therefore, they have longer reaction time due to the fatigue accompanied by more workloads.

The reaction time is decreased after landing, which indicates that crew members increase their vigilance due to mitigation measures such as appropriate shift work and onboard napping.

Vigilance on inbound flights. The descriptive statistics of the PVT results on inbound flights are presented in Table 2. It is demonstrated that the reaction time averages around 600 ms, slightly higher than that on outbound flights.

The results show that though the reaction time is slightly extended by the accumulated task loads and circadian rhythm, the flight crew still remains relatively vigilant on inbound flights.

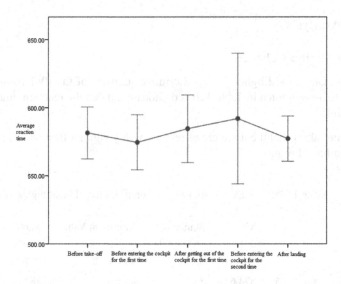

Fig. 4. The variations to reaction time on outbound flights

Table 2. Descriptive statistics of reaction time on inbound flights

Variables	N	Mean	Standard Deviations	Minimum Value	Maximum Value
Before take-off	28	581.45	61.85	484.5	698.5
Before the first entry into the cockpit	24	587.85	73.74	468.0	750.0
After leaving the cockpit for the first time	26	596.58	61.45	499.5	723.0
Before the second entry into the cockpit	6	601.17	34.25	565.0	650.5
After the landing	15	566.83	41.63	513.5	634.0

The ranges of reaction time on inbound flights are shown in Fig. 5. The variations to reaction time duty are limited to a small range.

Specifically, the reaction time at three time points demonstrates a slight upward trend: before take-off, before the first entry into the cockpit and before the second entry into the cockpit.

The upward trend indicates a slight decrease in vigilance due to workloads. Similar to the results on outbound legs, the reaction time before the second entry into the cockpit is the longest.

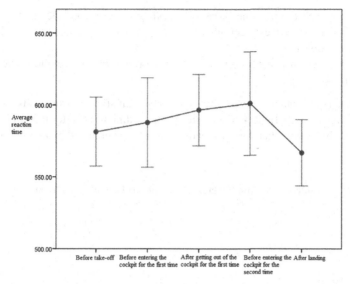

Fig. 5. The variations to reaction time on inbound flights

The reaction time is decreased after landing, indicating that crew members increase their vigilance due to mitigation measures such as appropriate shift work and onboard napping.

Analysis of Workload Change

Workloads on outbound flights. The descriptive statistics of workloads on outbound flights are presented in Table 3. The scores for each dimension after outbound flights are all below 40, indicating that the workloads subjectively perceived by flight crew from departures to destinations are modest.

Table 3. Descriptive statistics of workloads on outbound flights

Variables	N	Mean	Standard Deviations	Minimum Value	Maximum Value
Mental demand	18	36.11	20.90	5	80
Physical demand	18	31.94	15.54	10	65
Temporal demand	18	30.56	18.46	5	65
Performance	18	20.83	17.26	0	65
Efforts	18	31.11	17.20	10	60
Frustration	18	19.44	11.87	0	40
Average score	18	28.33	13.69	9.17	52.5

In regard to different dimensions of workloads, the mental demand is the most important in the subjective perception of flight crew, and has more heterogeneity among different individuals.

The dimension of frustration is the least important with the smallest heterogeneity among different individuals.

Workloads on Inbound Flights.   The descriptive statistics of workloads on inbound flights are presented in Table 4. The scores for each dimension after inbound flights are all below 35, indicating that the workloads subjectively perceived by flight crew are also modest.

Table 4. Descriptive statistics of workloads on inbound flights

Variables	N	Mean	Standard Deviations	Minimum Value	Maximum Value
Mental demand	18	27.50	16.91	0	65
Physical demand	18	32.22	18.73	10	75
Temporal demand	18	26.11	16.76	0	60
Performance	18	20.28	15.00	0	60
Efforts	18	31.39	18.85	0	65
Frustration	18	12.50	13.31	0	45
Average score	18	25.00	13.10	4.17	52.5

In regard to different dimensions of workloads, the dimensions of physical demand and efforts are more important in the subjective perception of flight crew, and have more heterogeneity among different individuals.

Also, the dimension of frustration is the least important with the smallest heterogeneity among different individuals.

Analysis of Subjective Fatigue Fluctuation

Subjective Fatigue on Outbound Flight.   The project conducted descriptive statistics on the subjective fatigue on the outbound flight. The results (Table 5) showed that the average subjective fatigue of the flight crew was between 4 and 6 points, that is, the flight crew was preparing for the outbound flight and landing on the ground. After entering, the subjective fatigue is within the controllable range.

By analyzing the fluctuation of subjective fatigue during the flight crew on duty on the outbound flight, the results (Fig. 6) show that there is a small range of fluctuations in subjective fatigue during the flight crew's on-duty process, indicating that through multiple sets of on-board rotation and on-board naps and other fatigue mitigation measures to make the subjective fatigue of the flight crew controllable during the on-duty process.

Table 5. Descriptive statistics of subjective fatigue on outbound routes

Variables	N	Mean	Standard Deviations	Minimum Value	Maximum Value
Get ready time	16	4.31	1.08	2	5
Before sliding out	16	4.19	1.11	2	5
Before entering the cockpit for the first time	14	5.14	1.17	2	6
After getting out of the cockpit for the first time	18	4.47	1.27	1	6
Before entering the cockpit for the second time	6	4.83	1.60	3	7
After landing	17	4.82	1.07	3	7

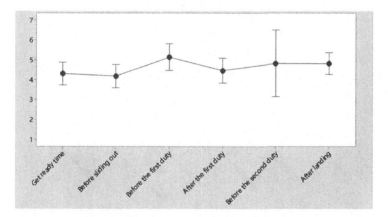

Fig. 6. Fluctuation of subjective fatigue on outbound flight routes

Subjective Fatigue on Inbound flight. The project conducted descriptive statistics on the subjective fatigue during the return flight. The results (Table 6) showed that the average subjective fatigue of the flight crew was between 3 and 5 points, that is, the flight crew made the direct preparation to the return flight after landing and sliding in. The subjective fatigue is within the controllable range.

By analyzing the fluctuation of subjective fatigue during the return flight crew on duty, the results (Fig. 7) show that there is a small range of fluctuations in subjective fatigue during the flight crew duty process.

The fluctuation of subjective fatigue is always below 5 points, indicating that the subjective fatigue of the flight crew is controllable during the on-duty process through multiple sets of fatigue mitigation measures such as on-board rotation and on-board naps.

Table 6. Descriptive statistics of subjective fatigue on inbound flight

Variables	N	Mean	Standard Deviations	Minimum Value	Maximum Value
Get ready time	15	3.73	1.22	2	6
Before sliding out	11	3.91	1.30	2	6
Before entering the cockpit for the first time	14	4.43	1.70	2	8
After getting out of the cockpit for the first time	1	3.00	-	3	3
Before entering the cockpit for the second time	15	4.53	1.25	3	7
After landing	15	3.73	1.22	2	6

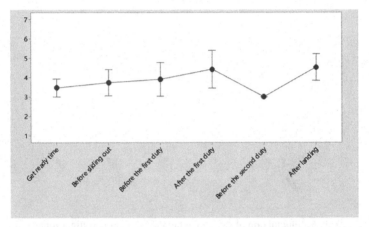

Fig. 7. Fluctuation of subjective fatigue on inbound flight routes

4   Conclusions

The flight crews remain highly alertness during the ultra-long routes, with the reaction time averaging 600ms. The variations to the reaction time during the duty period indicate that workloads, circadian rhythm, time differences and onboard rest impact the level of alertness.

Moreover, the subjective ratings of flight crew in regard to the workloads on ultra-long-haul flights are modest. Judging from the results, the average scores of workloads are below 40, demonstrating that the appropriate shift work and nap strategy can limit the perception of fatigue and workloads.

In addition, flight crews are subjectively alert while on duty on ultra-long-haul flights.

The research will continue collecting and analyzing the data of alertness and workloads on other ultra-long routes, and will adopt more method and tools to subjectively and objectively measure fatigue risks and contributing factors, so as to help airlines establish their FRMS.

References

1. Gregoy, K.B., Connell, L.J., Graeber, R.C., Miller, D.L., Rosekind, M.A.: Flight crewfatigue IV: overnight cargo operations. Aviat. Space Environ. Med. **69**, B26–B36 (1998)
2. http://www.ntsb.gov/publictn/A_Acc1.htm. NTSB/AAR-10/01 (2019)
3. http://www.faa.gov/regulations_polocies/advisory_circulars/index.cfm/go/document.inform ation/documentID/1021088.(2019)
4. International Civil Aviation Organization. Manual for the Oversight of Fatigue Management Approaches (DOC 9966) (2018)
5. Wei, J., Jing, P.: Feng yanzhong. Development and psychometric analysis of cognitive aptitude battery for chinese ab-initio pilots in civil aviation. J. Preven. Med. Chin. People's Liberation Army **32**(2), 122–124 (2014)
6. Heather, M., Hartman-Hall David, A.F.: Haaga.content analysis of cognitive bias: development of a standardized measure. J. Rational Emotive Cogn. Behav. Therapy **17**(2), 105–114(1999)
7. Lei, W., Zheng, H., Zhang, Z.: Research on self-test system of fatigue degree based on vigilance. Space Med. Med. Eng. **33**(3), 228–232 (2020)
8. Susan, G., Hill, H.P., Iavecchia, Byers, J.C.: comparison of four subjective workload rating scales. Hum. Fact. J. Hum. Fact. Ergon. Soc. 34(4), 429–439 (1992)
9. Zhang, Z.: Role of subjective assessment technique in pilot mental workload measurement. Chin. J. Aerospace Med. **05**(1), 57–59 (1994)
10. Xiao, Y., Wang, Z., Zhen, W.: The appraisal of reliability and validity of subjective workload assessment technique and NASA-task load index. Chin. J. Indus. Hygiene Occup. Dis. **23**(3), 178–181 (2005)

Short Time Algorithms for Screening Examinations of the Collective and Personal Stress Resilience

Sergey Lytaev[✉] [iD]

St. Petersburg State Pediatric Medical University, St. Petersburg 194100, Russia
physiology@gpmu.org

Abstract. The article discusses the search for clinical, psychological and neurophysiological markers of stress resilience when examining large groups in a limited time. Stress resilience is determined by stress factors, working conditions in professional teams, occupational health of subjects, awareness, etc. In the limited time (25–40 min) for diagnosing stress resilience, a research algorithm was tested, consisting of a clinical-psychological and neurophysiological study (EEG) with traditional tests and analysis of indices and power spectra. Groups of healthy subjects (over 100 people) and neuropsychiatric outpatients (38 people) were examined. The emphasis in the analysis of the results of the study is on the data of secondary (integrative) indicators, both for psychological tests (correlation analysis) and for EEG (factorial analysis). In particular, the integrative indicator SCL-90-R - "general severity index" has a high statistical significance ($p < 0.05$) both in healthy individuals and in neuropsychiatric outpatients. The effectiveness of Mini-Mult is shown by the scales of hypochondria, depression, hysteria, paranoia, psychasthenia, schizoidness and hypomania ($p < 0.05$). A number of logical thinking techniques were also used. EEG power indicators and spectra in theta, delta, and alpha frequency ranges are an effective reflection of cognitive status. The article discusses the existing testing algorithm as an option for assessing neurocognitive status in screening studies.

Keywords: Stressors · Time deficit · Cognitive functions · Activation factors · EEG · Psychological testing

1 Introduction

The physiological consequences of psychological stress depend on a number of factors, among which we highlight the awareness of the subject about the environment, as well as the level of professional health, consisting of mental, physical and clinical components. Against this background, human perception of stress suggests the integration of physiological systems [20, 23]. Firstly, these are sensory systems, where visual and auditory systems occupy a leading place in terms of the volume of processed information. Undoubtedly, other sensory systems (skin, vestibular, pain awareness, etc.) also perform their functions in a variety of impressions. Sensory systems process incoming

© The Author(s), under exclusive license to Springer Nature Switzerland AG 2023
D. Harris and W.-C. Li (Eds.): HCII 2023, LNAI 14017, pp. 442–458, 2023.
https://doi.org/10.1007/978-3-031-35392-5_34

information, comparing stressful conditions with the current state and previous experience of perceiving stress. Secondly, the focus of stress in the cerebral cortex activates the hypothalamus, the highest center of autonomic regulation, which then launches the sympathetic-adreno-medullary chain, which is accompanied by a rapid release of catecholamines (mediator and hormone) – norepinephrine and adrenaline. Thirdly, the hypothalamic-pituitary-adrenal integration is simultaneously activated, which significantly increases the concentration of glucocorticoids and cortisol in a person in the blood [3, 27, 29, 38]. Thus, the perception of stressful conditions and factors is directly carried out through sensory systems, but then specific chains of stress reactions are triggered.

The biggest methodological problem in diagnosing stress indicators is the comparison of direct and indirect measurements with the assessment of fluctuations in professional performance [19, 21, 24]. An entity doing excellent work on direct measures may reflect marked fluctuations in proxy measures. The price of such behavioral reactions is excessively high, and the nature of the information obtained because of measurements can be misleading about a high level of performance [31].

There are known stress factors and conditions such as crises, disasters, financial problems, toxic team leadership, etc. This list is endless. Against this background, in the last 10–20 years, new ones have been added to the list of professions associated with stress. For example, the use of artificial intelligence technologies makes a significant contribution to the formation of new stress factors. This also includes new working conditions for medical personal, athletes, etc. [14, 16, 30].

The dynamics of a person's functional state during a stressful period can vary from eustress to distress, which directly affects labor performance [1, 5]. Efficiency decreases sharply when the level of physiological stress fatigue during arousal is reached. At the same time, the level of fatigue in different people is different and depends on the state of professional health (physical, mental, clinical), awareness of ongoing events, as well as awareness. During an increase in arousal, no one pays attention to a decrease in performance, but certain symptoms associated with exhaustion appear, such as headaches and migraines, and even a complete "lack" of strength. Therefore, the idea was formed that the definition of stress should include both eustress ("good" stress) and distress ("bad" stress) [1, 9, 34].

Artificial intelligence (AI) technologies are developed and created in order to progress in various areas of professional activity, including to improve social well-being between subjects [12]. However, research in this area suggests that AI also generates unpredictable ethical dilemmas in decision making. Among the problems are algorithmic discrimination, data bias, reduction (blurring) of the level of responsibility of both managers and staff. Technological uncertainty, incomplete data, and management errors are major sources of ethical risk in AI decision making. Thus, the intervention of risk management elements can effectively block social risks arising from algorithmic, technological and data-related risks. Based on the theory of rooting, two main categories have been obtained: "technical risk identification" and "managerial risk identification". Technical risk identification includes algorithm risk, data risk and technology risk, which occupies 36.5% of the first level nodes. Management risk identification includes both "management risk" and "risk management" [10].

Executive functions (EF) include operative memory, inhibition of conditioned reflex activity, cognitive adaptability, etc. The assessments of sports experts indicate, on the one hand, outstanding physical abilities, and, on the other hand, unique mechanisms of motor control, perception, information processing, and, in general, about cognitive functioning [21, 22]. Existing EF tests describe the cognitive abilities of the subject. These neuropsychological examinations are an in-depth assessment of skills and abilities such as attentional ability, problem solving, memory, IQ, visuospatial awareness associated with specific brain functions. A number of researchers [3, 27] consider the measurement of EF as a cognitive part of the diagnostics of working capacity. Also describes the age function of the development of EF [11]. This means that it is difficult to distinguish and demarcate different developmental processes between individuals. The age of the participants is a significant factor in every analysis of adolescents, since significant changes in EF scores are observed at this age [23]. Thus, the use of EF is justified for describing the cognitive abilities of athletes. Against the background of the fact that athletes have excellent cognitive abilities [6], and impairments can significantly affect their athletic performance [30], in contact game sports, EF may be a predictor of concussion [12].

Recently, the criteria for assessing medical activity have lost their differentiation. The assessment depends on the opinions of experts, which are often heterogeneous and contradictory. The absence of a specific legislative framework related to the issues of "medical error" and "responsibility of doctors" makes it necessary to develop and formulate clear diagnostic and treatment algorithms. In this regard, health systems face the fundamental challenge of adapting to changes in health service structures that require technological and scientific innovation. The speed of multiple and interconnected problems puts additional strain on healthcare professionals and reduces their ability to innovate. It has been established that there is a partial mediation (without the participation of sensory systems) of health between eustress and innovative work behavior, while supervisor support does not mediate eustress and health. In addition, the results show that distress is negatively associated with innovative behavior. At the same time, it is even possible that two opposite emotions (eustress and distress) appear in the innovative work behavior of employees. The presence of eustress ("good" stress) exacerbates the detrimental effects of a disaster. That is, if we are not sure that distress has been eliminated, eustress can do more harm than good, especially for medical workers who are particularly susceptible to diseases [2, 3, 16, 31].

Thus, professional and life stress factors affect both individual subjects and teams. In this regard, the problem of resistance to adverse (stressful) situations becomes relevant. Resilience can be defined as the successful and positive ability of a person to endure, recover, or return to the state they were in before the stressful situation. This activates the mechanisms of adaptation to changing conditions of significant and severe levels of stress, trauma, and adversity; the ability to thrive and survive despite their hardships. Specifically, in psychology, resilience is defined in three ways. First, resilience is the positive ability of people to cope with major adversity, trauma, tragedy, threat or major source of stress and disaster. The second is the ability to return to physiological levels of functioning without the help of doctors and psychologists. Finally, resilience is an adaptive information system that uses sensory information about stressful conditions to provide resilience to future negative events.

Based on the peculiarities of the action of stress activation factors, the state of the subject's executive cognitive functions, the study was aimed at the psychological and neurophysiological substantiation of approaches to screening algorithms for assessing cognitive functions and stress tolerance under time pressure.

2 Materials and Methods

For the assessment of cognitive functions, two methodological approaches were applied. The first of them was a complex of psychological testing, and the second – EEG with subsequent computer processing of the big data. The full range of examination took up to 40 min with the subsequent reduction to 15–25 min. The complex of psychological testing included six tests – the questionnaire of the severity of psychopathological symptoms SCL-90-R, the method of clinical and psychological research of the personality structure "Mini-Mult", as well as a block of logical methods: "Isolation of essential features", "Exclusion of unnecessary", "Simple analogies" and "Understanding the figurative meaning of proverbs and metaphors".

The SCL-90-R test results were used to assess nine main scales of symptomatic disorders: somatization, obsessive-compulsiveness, interpersonal anxiety, hostility, depressiveness, anxiety, phobia, paranoia, and psychotism. In addition, three second-order SCL-90-R scales were analyzed: Present Symptomatic Distress Index (PSDI), General Severity Index (GSI), and Total Positive Responses (TPR). The function of each of them is to bring the level and depth of personal psychopathology to a single scale. GSI is an indicator of the current state and depth of the disorder. PSDI is solely a measure of the intensity of the condition, corresponding to the number of symptoms. TPR is simply a count of the number of symptoms to which the patient gives positive responses – that is, the number of statements for which the subject marks at least some level above zero.

Mini-Mult is an abbreviated version of the Minnesota Multiphasic Personality Inventory (MMPI test, 556 questions) and consists of 71 questions and 11 scales, of which 3 are evaluative [40]. In the present study, we analyzed the rating scales of lie, reliability and correction, which affect the mathematical calculation of thematic scales. In addition, basic scales were considered – hypochondria, hysteria, psychopathy, paranoia, psychoasthenia, schizoidness, and hypomania.

EEG at rest with the performance of traditional functional tests in eight bipolar leads: Fp1 – C3, Fp2 – C4, C3 – O1, C4 – O2, O1 – T3, O2 – T4, T3 – Fp1, T4 – Fp2, according to the international 10/20 system was recorded. Biosignal processing was carried out using the WinEEG software package by counting EEG indices and power spectra in 5 frequency bands (theta, delta, alpha, beta1, beta2). The location of the electrodes can be shown by considering the results of the indices and spectra below (see Fig. 5).

To select the most valid indicators under time constraints, the following algorithm for assessing biosignals was chosen. After dividing the EEG recording interval into segments (analysis epochs), calculations for each channel are performed separately. First of all, for each segment of the EEG recording, the parameters of the polynomial trend are calculated, and this trend is compensated. The order of the polynomial trend is set by the corresponding parameter, and we chose the value equal to 0, that is, only the constant component was eliminated during the calculation. To suppress the leakage of energy through the side maxima, each segment is smoothed out by a time window. Bartlett, Khann and Welch time windows can be used. During our work, we chose to use the Hann time window. Further, using the "fast Fourier transform" the power spectrum (periodogram) is calculated.

The results of the study using the statistical program SPSS for Windows according to the following algorithm were analyzed. Initially, each sample was checked for compliance with the normal distribution (Gaussian) visually using the construction of a histogram and using the Kolmogorov-Smirnov criterion. The data obeying the laws of normal distribution were analyzed for reliability using Student's t-test. Data for which compliance with the normal distribution could not be proved were analyzed using the Wald-Wolfowitz and Mann-Whitney test. As a result, indicators were selected that were statistically different in the studied groups [13, 25].

As part of analytical statistics, a multivariate analysis was performed to assess the dependence of one quantitative trait on several other traits when predicting the value of one trait based on the value of several traits. Since the dependent and independent features are quantitative, we chose the method of multiple linear regression analysis, in which each of the studied features was consistently evaluated.

Using the described methodological techniques a study for three groups of subjects was performed. Study group I consisted of 102 healthy volunteers (18–35 years) who underwent psychological testing. For neurophysiological research, study group II was formed, which consisted of 102 healthy subjects (18–60 years) who underwent a planned psychiatric examination for professional purposes. To compare the data of healthy subjects, group III was formed, which consisted of 38 outpatients of a neuropsychiatric clinic [25].

3 Outcomes

3.1 Clinical Psychological Research

When considering the results of the study, it is not planned to dwell on the details of the primary digital parameters and scales that were published earlier [25]. Here, secondary indicators, a number of correlation features and statistical significance will be presented, both for clinical-psychological testing and for EEG analysis.

Below is a summary of the statistical significance of differences in the study groups I and III (Table 1). The table shows the significance level "p", determined by the criteria of Wald-Wolfowitz and Mann-Whitney. It is noteworthy that according to the SCL-90-R data, the differences are significant only on the "depressiveness" scale. While when testing the Mini-Mult, the differences are significant on most scales with the exception of reliability, correction, and psychasthenia. The significance of differences on the secondary scales SCL-90-R is more noticeable – the overall severity index, the total number of affirmative answers. Characteristically, for all 4 tests for logical thinking, noticeable differences are recorded ($p < 0.01$).

The resulting regression equations also indicate a correlation between different scales not only within the same methodology, but also with other tests used, which is illustrated in Table 2.

Table 1. Comparative reliability of the results of psychological testing according to SCL-90-R, Mini-Mult and a block of methods for assessing logical thinking

SCL-90-R		Mini-Mult	
Scales	p	Scales	p
Somatization		Lie	p < 0,05
Obsessive-Compulsive		Reliability	
Interpersonal anxiety		Correction	
Depression	p < 0,05	Hypochondria	p < 0,05
Anxiety		Depression	p < 0,05
Hostility		Hysteria	p < 0,05
Phobia		Psychopathy	p < 0,05
Paranoia		Paranoia	p < 0,05
Psychoticism		Psychasthenia	
General Severity Index	p < 0,05	Schizoid	p < 0,05
Symptomatic Distress Index		Hypomania	p < 0,05
Total Number of Affirmative Answers	p < 0,05		
Logic Methods			
Identification of essential features			p < 0,01
Exclusion of superfluous			p < 0,01
Simple analogies			p < 0,01
Understanding the figurative meaning of proverbs and metaphors			p < 0,01

Note. At p > 0.05, the significance level is not given

Table 2. Correlation between different method scales

Scales	Dependent indicators according to linear regression equations, in order of decreasing standard regression coefficients
Somatization	General severity index (S), hypochondria (M), psychopathy (I), interpersonal anxiety (S)
Obsessive-compulsive	Scales of the second order (S) and the method of "figurative meaning"
Interpersonal anxiety	General index of severity (S), somatization (S), anxiety (S), phobias (S)
Depression	General severity index (S), depression (M), symptomatic distress index (S), interpersonal anxiety (S)

(continued)

Table 2. (*continued*)

Scales	Dependent indicators according to linear regression equations, in order of decreasing standard regression coefficients
Anxiety	General index of severity (S), hostility (S), phobias (S), interpersonal anxiety (S)
Hostility	Anxiety (S), "exclusion of unnecessary" technique, symptomatic distress index (S)
Phobias	General severity index (S), anxiety (S), interpersonal anxiety (S), symptomatic distress index (S)
Paranoia	Total number of affirmative answers (S) Psychoticism (S), hysteria (M)
Ppsychoticism	General severity index (S), paranoia (S), schizoid (M), hostility (S)
General Severity Index	Anxiety (S), psychotism (S), other secondary scales (S)
Total number of affirmative answers	Other scales of the second order (S), obsessive-compulsive (S), paranoid (S)
Present Symptomatic Distress Index	Other scales of the second order (S), depression (S), somatization (S)

Note. In parentheses, the belonging of a particular scale to the method "S" - SCL-90-R "M" - Mini-Mult

In Table 3 shows the detailed results of constructing regression lines for the indicators of the scales of the Mini-Mult methodology.

Table 3. Results of constructing regression lines for indicators scales of the Mini-Mult

Scales	Dependent indicators according to linear regression equations, in order of decreasing standard regression coefficients, scales related to the SCL-90-R methodology are marked with the code (S)
Hypochondria	Hysteria, technique, essential features, somatization (S)
Depression	Hysteria, psychasthenia, lies, psychopathy
Hysteria	Depression, hypochondria, method, essential features, symptomatic distress index (S)
Psychopathy	Schizoid, technique, essential features, symptomatic distress index (S), depression

(*continued*)

Table 3. (*continued*)

Scales	Dependent indicators according to linear regression equations, in order of decreasing standard regression coefficients, scales related to the SCL-90-R methodology are marked with the code (S)
Paranoia	Schizoid, correction, index of present symptomatic distress (S), method of exclusion of excess
Psychasthenia	Schizoid, depression, confidence, interpersonal anxiety (S)
Schizoid	Psychasthenia, reliability, correction, paranoia
Hypomania	Reliability, correction, schizoidness, total number of affirmative answers (S)

As can be seen from Table 3, many scales of the Mini-Mult technique have a regression dependence on the second-order scale, the SCL-90-R symptomatic distress index, for example, the psychopathy scale (Fig. 1).

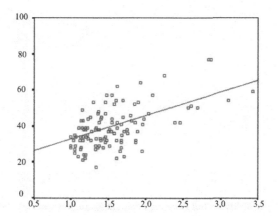

Fig. 1. Scatterplot for psychopathy (ordinate scale, points) and PSDI (abscissa scale, points).

With the help of multiple linear regression analysis, the test results were also analyzed according to the methods of "exclusion of superfluous", "simple analogies", "essential features" and "figurative meaning". For three methods at once, the dependent factor with the maximum standard regression coefficient is the "figurative meaning" method. On Fig. 2 shows a scatterplot with regression lines for the results of the Simple Analogies and Figurative Sense methods.

In addition, three out of four methods correlate with small regression coefficients with the Mini-Mult psychopathy scale. For example, in Fig. 3 shows a scatterplot with regression lines for the results of the "Essential Features" method and the results of the Mini-Mult hysteria scale.

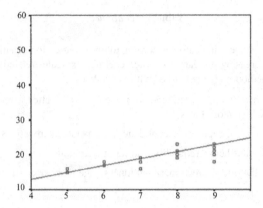

Fig. 2. Scatterplot for the "Simple Analogies" (ordinate scale, points) and "Figurative Sense" (abscissa scale, points) methods.

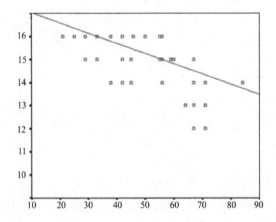

Fig. 3. Scatterplot for the "Essential Features" method (ordinate scale, points) and the HS Mini-Mult (abscissa scale, points).

3.2 Neurophysiological Research

On Fig. 4 shows an EEG fragment and a topogram of the spectral power of the same 10 s EEG fragment of a 23-year-old patient diagnosed with epilepsy with personality changes, which is shown as an example of a pathological EEG. On the EEG, diffuse disturbances of the bioelectrical activity of the brain are formed with severe diffuse irritation of the cortex, irritation of the hypothalomo-diencephalic structures, paroxysmal activity starting from the deep parts of the left hemisphere and generalization, interest in the mediobasal parts of the left temporal region.

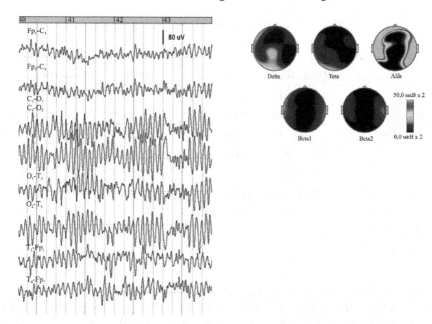

Fig. 4. EEG (left) and spectral power topogram (right). Patient aged 23, epilepsy. **Note.** Fp_1-C_3, Fp_2-C_4, C_3-O_1, C_4-O_2, O_1-T_3, $_2$-T_4, T_3-Fp_1, T_4-Fp_2 – EEG bipolar sites; 40 – 43 s.

In Table 4 shows the average values in the studied groups II and III, obtained by calculating the EEG indices in the Delta and Teta bands.

Table 4. EEG indices in Delta and Theta bands

Bipolar sites, 10/20	Delta		Teta	
	Group II	Group III	Group II	Group III
$Fp_1 - C_3$	30,05 ± 1,1	25,66 ± 3,0	11,54 ± 0,6	26,07 ± 2,4**
$Fp_2 - C_4$	28,48 ± 1,1	22,91 ± 4,2*	12,74 ± 0,6	27,86 ± 2,0**
$C_3 - O_1$	19,45 ± 1,1	17,77 ± 3,3	10,63 ± 0,6	26,16 ± 2,7**
$C_4 - O_2$	17,94 ± 1,1	20,66 ± 3,3	10,67 ± 0,6	24,58 ± 2,4**
$O_1 - T_3$	19,73 ± 1,2	19,13 ± 3,2	10,34 ± 0,5	27,37 ± 2,4**
$O_2 - T_4$	18,16 ± 1,2	19,65 ± 3,2	11,04 ± 0,6	25,30 ± 2,7**
$T_3 - Fp_1$	29,76 ± 1,0	23,16 ± 4,1*	14,25 ± 0,6	28,73 ± 2,2**
$T_4 - Fp_2$	31,31 ± 1,2	20,85 ± 4,0*	13,81 ± 0,6	29,26 ± 2,4**

Note. * – $p < 0,05$; ** – $p < 0,01$

In Table 5 shows the average values in groups II and III, obtained by calculating the EEG power spectra in the Delta and Teta bands.

Table 5. EEG power spectra in Delta and Theta bands

Bipolar sites, 10/20	Delta		Teta	
	Group II	Group III	Group II	Group III
$Fp_1 - C_3$	$14,72 \pm 0,9$	$13,45 \pm 2,4$	$10,38 \pm 0,5$	$16,32 \pm 2,2**$
$Fp_2 - C_4$	$13,18 \pm 0,8$	$13,80 \pm 2,8$	$10,28 \pm 0,6$	$16,93 \pm 2,4**$
$C_3 - O_1$	$7,30 \pm 0,6$	$11,40 \pm 2,0$	$6,16 \pm 0,4$	$17,49 \pm 2,9**$
$C_4 - O_2$	$6,60 \pm 0,5*$	$11,95 \pm 2,1$	$6,31 \pm 0,4$	$17,63 \pm 2,9**$
$O_1 - T_3$	$9,60 \pm 1,3$	$12,60 \pm 2,3$	$6,02 \pm 0,4$	$16,74 \pm 2,5**$
$O_2 - T_4$	$7,52 \pm 0,5*$	$12,83 \pm 1,7$	$6,12 \pm 0,4$	$17,79 \pm 2,8**$
$T_3 - Fp_1$	$14,25 \pm 0,9$	$12,70 \pm 2,2$	$10,46 \pm 0,5$	$18,63 \pm 2,7**$
$T_4 - Fp_2$	$13,66 \pm 0,8$	$13,22 \pm 1,7$	$11,17 \pm 0,6$	$18,72 \pm 2,3**$

Note. See Table 4

When analyzing the statistical significance of the difference in indices and EEG power spectra in the studied groups II and III, the following results were obtained. Statistically significant difference in indicators in the base and second groups with an error level $p < 0.01$ for the Teta band was obtained in all bipolar leads for indices and for EEG power spectra. In addition, a statistically significant difference with an error level $p < 0.05$ was obtained for the EEG indices and spectra in some bipolar leads in the Alfa, Delta and Beta ranges.

In order to reduce the dimension of multidimensional features and select the most informative indicators, a factor analysis was performed. Of all the factors selected by the software, based on the scatter plot (Fig. 5), only those whose values exceeded one were selected. Such a diagram serves to separate unimportant factors from the most significant factors.

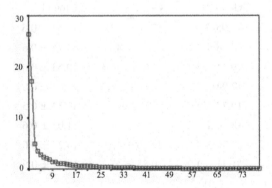

Fig. 5. Scatter plot of factor analysis. Ordinate scale – the factor's value; abscissa scale – factor number.

These significant factors form a "slope" on the chart – a part of the line with a steep rise. In the above diagram, a steep rise is observed in the region of the first five factors. These five factors are chosen as the basis of the model at the beginning of the factor analysis. At the next stage of factor analysis, factor loadings for each of the selected factors are considered. As a result, the following definitions of factors were obtained:

Factor 1 – Indices and spectra in Delta and Alfa ranges.
Factor 2 – Indices in the Beta1 and Beta2 ranges.
Factor 3 – Spectra in the Beta1 range.
Factor 4 – Power spectra in the Beta2 range.
Factor 5 – Indices and spectra in the Teta range in the frontal and temporal leads.

A statistically significant difference with $p < 0.01$ according to the Walda-Wolfowitz and Mann-Whitney tests was proven for factors 1 and 5.

4 Discussion

There is no doubt that a perfectly healthy person is under the influence of stress factors of various strengths with various manifestations. At the same time, mental or even psychosomatic disorders are not always formed. As a rule, a person (or a professional team) develops stress resistance – the ability to adapt to stress factors [4, 8].

Sensory perception forms a "psychological situation" – an individual internal reflection, which is considered critical for determining the level of functioning against a background of stress. In the course of the primary "cognitive assessment", a judgment is formed about the significance of the event as stressful – positive, controlled, provocative or inadequate, followed by an assessment of one's resources and survival opportunities. The secondary assessment is accompanied by the activation of mnestic processes about a potential reaction to a threat and its overcoming as a process of realizing this reaction [22, 24]. "Cognitive assessment" can proceed differently in the conditions of time pressure – lack of time.

From the physiological point of view, in studies on the mechanisms of regulation of sensory signals of various intensities entering the brain, a connection is made with the processes of activation/inhibition in the CNS [23, 41]. From the point of view of classical psychophysics, the nature of the response depends on the threshold sensitivity of sensory systems. Low sensitivity, i.e., an initially high threshold of absolute sensory sensitivity, increases the severity of the reaction to an increase in the intensity of the stimulus. On the contrary, a system with high sensitivity, that is, with a low absolute sensory threshold, launches a "program" that protects against "overload", and, despite an increase in stimulus intensity, a reduced evoked response is obtained [21, 23].

It is believed that the most informative indicator of SCL-90-R is the second-order indicator - the index of the presence of symptomatic distress, the effectiveness of which has been shown to quickly assess subjects in a number of studies [17, 26, 28]. Other studies have proven the statistical significance of all integrative indicators and points on the anxiety scale [17, 36]. For example, when testing the SCL-90-R of students who spend a lot of time online, significant differences were recorded compared with the control group on all thematic scales [40]. Of course, SCL-90-R is more effective in examining patients with various psychosomatic diseases [4]. In the present study, the SCL-90-R was found to have the highest second-order integrative indicators, the overall symptom severity index (GSI) and the present symptomatic distress index (PSDI). An analysis of the results of individual scales found that only one of the nine scales (depression) was independently statistically significant. Similar results have also been obtained by a number of authors, for example, to assess the response to stress in college students. According to researchers, the most informative is the second-order GSI, which can be used to quickly assess subjects [2]. Some studies emphasize the statistical significance of integrative indicators and indicators on the anxiety scale [35]. In general, SCL-90-R reflects the stress-reactivity of the individual, allows you to assess the severity of psychopathological symptoms, or in other words, the individual specificity of the reaction to the stress factors of the surrounding world. At the same time, integral indicators, including unfavorable combinations of high values obtained, such as the overall symptom severity index and the symptomatic distress index, turned out to be more sensitive when comparing subjects from different study groups. A number of authors also describe the high reliability of the integrative indicators of SCL-90-R [17, 26, 28, 32].

The results of Mini-Multi-Testing showed significantly greater statistical significance on a number of scales – hypochondria, depression, hysteria, psychopathy, paranoia, schizoidness and hypomania. Only the psychasthenia scale did not show a statistically significant difference. There is a point of view about the lack of validity of the abbreviated version of the Mini-Mult personality structure study compared to the "full version" of MMPI. In particular, this is shown for mental patients [39], when examining parents with problems in raising children [7, 39]. Other studies, on the contrary, show convincing results using Mini-Mult. The effectiveness of Mini-Multi-testing in psychiatric patients is noted, namely, under time pressure, which was of fundamental importance in our work [15]. Like the SCL-90-R, the Mini-Mult test is also successfully used in clinical medical practice, for example, in assessing the mental status of patients with the consequences of acute myocardial infarction [33]. Thus, Mini-Mult allows you to evaluate the structure of personality on a number of scales. At the same time, we concluded that, apparently, this test allows us to analyze deeper and more permanent components of executive functions, in contrast to the SCL-90-R test, where sensations and perceptions are actualized right now, right at the time of the study. A healthy person, even under normal conditions, can be in a state of daily stress. Therefore, conducting a medical (psychiatric) examination does not always give him positive emotions. However, psychopathology is not actualized if the ability to switch from negative to positive components is activated, that is, to reach a new level of mobility of mental processes. That is, when a stable dominant (nervous and mental processes) is formed, which exists not only today and now, but also long before the study due to the duration of their manifestation, the subject's personal qualities are better diagnosed by the Mini-Mult. The effectiveness of Mini-Mult testing for assessing mental status is also confirmed by literature data [33].

Tests for assessing logical thinking made it possible to obtain high results (the level of statistical error $p < 0.01$ according to the Mann-Whitney and Wald-Wolfowitz criteria) according to the logical tests "exclusion of superfluous", "simple analogies", "essential features", "interpretation of the figurative meanings of proverbs and sayings". Psychological tests that assess logical thinking in different variations are widely described in the literature, their effectiveness in complex studies is especially emphasized [18, 37]. In present research during conducting a multiple linear regression analysis of the test results using the "exclusion of unnecessary", "simple analogies", "essential features" and "figurative meaning" methods, it was found that for three methods at once, the dependent factor with the maximum standard regression coefficient is the method "interpretation of the figurative meaning of proverbs and sayings". The effectiveness of this test also has been demonstrated in a line of studies; it is described that subjects with diseases of the central nervous system often cannot understand the figurative meaning of proverbs and metaphors [25].

In the present study it was found that the EEG indices and power spectra in the same brain areas within the same range correlate with each other. It is known that the percentage of indices and power spectra reflects the "degree of presence" in the total activity of waves of a particular range. The dependence between the indicators of "neighboring sites" is also recorded, since in the case of bipolar EEG recording, the dipole reflects the algebraic sum of the oscillations of the electric potential between the two electrodes. Thus, one of the two components of the algebraic sum for each of the pair of "neighboring points" turns out to be common. In addition, in some cases (this is shown for delta-, beta-1 and beta-2 ranges) there is a regression relationship between "paired electrodes" for the same leads in different hemispheres.

The analysis of the obtained outcomes allowed us to make the following theses. Indices and power spectra at the same points for the same range, despite the significant difference in the algorithms for their determination, are usually interconnected. It has been established that EEG indices and power spectra at different angles characterize the same indicators of total severity. Indices and power spectra reflect a certain "degree of presence" in the total fluctuations of a particular EEG frequency range. In most of the studied indices and spectra, there is a dependence between the indicators at "neighboring points", since with bipolar registration the total electric dipole reflects the algebraic sum of oscillations between two points of registration. As a result, one of the two components of the algebraic sum for each pair of "neighboring sites" turns out to be common. Sometimes, which is relevant for the delta-, beta-1 and beta-2 ranges of the EEG, it is possible to establish a regression relationship between "paired electrodes" in the same leads of different hemispheres. It has been suggested that the total expression (in %) of delta and beta oscillations is symmetrical in both hemispheres.

These approaches can be used to develop new efficient systems for automatic EEG classification [6, 13, 23]. For example, it is possible to develop a technology that makes it possible to distinguish a normal EEG from a pathological one, as well as to classify different types of pathology and different types of human functional states caused by stressors and sensory stimuli. The 30-s EEG data, combined with a small amount of other data, can be easily sent to remote computers for quick analysis and results, which can be critical for a timely conclusion [21, 34].

5 Conclusion

Thus, the search for markers of stress resistance is determined by a number of factors and conditions. Among the main ones, we can identify stress factors, working conditions in professional teams, the level of staff awareness, and a direct applied set of methodological techniques. For a quick screening analysis (25–40 min) for diagnosing stress resilience, a research algorithm is proposed that evaluates clinical and psychological scales, logical thinking, as well as EEG with traditional tests and analysis of indicators and spectra.

SCL-90-R and Mini-Mult are universal tests for evaluating clinical psychological scales. The effectiveness of using Mini-Mult in conditions of time pressure is determined by the data on the scales of hypochondria, depression, hysteria, paranoia, psychasthenia, schizoidness and hypomania ($p < 0.05$ when comparing healthy and neuropsychiatric patients). High values (> 70) on any of the Mini-Mult scales require an extended examination. Integrative index SCL-90-R – "general index of severity of symptoms" in healthy individuals has an average value of 0.73 ± 0.04, in the group of neuropsychiatric outpatients, the average value was 1.08 ± 0.12 ($p < 0.05$). Such testing (15 – 25 min) can be used as a standard for assessing neurocognitive status in screening studies of large groups.

The high statistical significance of methods for assessing logical thinking ($p < 0.01$) was shown, first of all, this test "understanding the figurative meaning of proverbs and metaphors" – the average value in the group of healthy subjects was 8.99 ± 0.01, in the group of neuropsychiatric outpatients – 7.55 ± 0.3.

EEG indicators and power spectra in slow wave (theta-, delta-), as well as alpha-bands are an effective reflection of the cognitive status. Power indicators and EEG spectra steadily correlate with each other in bipolar leads in all frequency ranges, with correlation dependence regression coefficients in the range of $0.6 – 0.8$. Data indices and power spectra in the theta range are highly reliable ($p < 0.01$) in assessing the neurophysiological status.

References

1. Albort-Morant, G., Ariza-Montes, A., Leal-Rodríguez, A., Giorgi, G.: How does positive work-related stress affect the degree of innovation development? Int. J. Environ. Res. Public Health **17**(2), 520 (2020)
2. Anjum, A., Anjum, A., Anjum, U., Ming, X.: An empirical study exploring the determinants of stress among medical healthcare professionals. Afr. Health Sci. **19**, 3091–3099 (2020)
3. Anjum, A., Zhao, Y.: The impact of stress on innovative work behavior among medical healthcare professionals. Behav. Sci. **12**, 340 (2022)
4. Arrindell, W.A., Barelds, D.P., Janssen, I.C.: Invariance of SCL-90-R dimensions of symptom distress in patients with peri partum pelvic pain (PPPP) syndrome. Br. J. Clin. Psychol. **45**, 377–391 (2006)
5. Buchanan, T.: Self-report measures of executive function problems correlate with personality, not performance-based executive function measures, non-clinical samples. Psychol. Assess. **28**, 372–385 (2016)
6. De Groot, T., De Heer, J., Htynkiewicz, R., et al.: Evaluation of real-time assessment of human operator workload during a simulated crisis situation, using EEG and PPG. In: Ayaz, H. (ed.) Neuroergonomics and Cognitive Engineering. AHFE International Conference. NY, USA, AHFE Open Access, vol. 42, pp. 50–56 (2022)
7. Finch, A.J., Edwards, G.L., Griffin, J.L.: Utility of the mini-mult with parents of emotionally disturbed children. J. Pers. Assess. **39**, 146–150 (1975)
8. Grande, T.L., Newmeyer, M.D., Underwood, L.A., Williams, C.R.: Path analysis of the SCL-90-R: exploring use in outpatient assessment. Meas. Eval. Couns. Dev. **47**, 271–290 (2014)

9. Grawitch, M.J., Barber, L.K., Leiter, M.P., et al.: Editorial: stress and stress management—pushing back against existing paradigms. Front. Psychol. **13**, 859660 (2022)
10. Guan, H., Dong, L., Zhao, A.: Ethical risk factors and mechanisms in artificial intelligence decision making. Behav. Sci. **12**, 343 (2022)
11. Heilmann, F.: Self-report versus neuropsychological tests for examining executive functions in youth soccer athletes – a cross-sectional study. Behav. Sci. **12**, 346 (2022)
12. Jian, G.: Artificial intelligence in healthcare and medicine: promises, ethical challenges and governance. Chin. Med. Sci. J. **34**, 76–83 (2019)
13. Khil'ko, V.A., Shostak, V.I., Khlunovskiĭ, A.N., et al.: Topograficheskoe kartirovanie vyzvannoĭ bioélektricheskoĭ aktivnosti i drugie metody funktsional'noĭ neĭrovizualizatsii mozga [The topographic mapping of evoked bioelectrical activity and other methods for the functional neural visualization of the brain]. Vestn Ross Akad Med Nauk **3**, 36–41 (1993)
14. Langer, K., Wolf, O.T., Jentsch, V.L.: Delayed effects of acute stress on cognitive emotion regulation. Psychoneuroendocrinology **125**, 105101 (2021)
15. Larry, P.: Comparison of the MMPI and the mini-mult in a psychiatric outpatient clinic. J. Consult. Clin. Psychol. **44**, 495–497 (2006)
16. Lever-van Milligen, B.A., Lamers, F., Smit, J.H., et al.: Physiological stress markers, mental health and objective physical function. J. Psychosom. Res. **133**, 109996 (2020)
17. Lucht, M., Jahn, U., Barnow, S., et al.: The use of a symptom checklist (SCL-90-R) as an easy method to estimate the relapse risk after alcoholism detoxification. Eur. Addict. Res. **8**, 190–194 (2002)
18. Luna-Guevara, J.R., Silva, F.D.M., López-Regalado, O.: Logical thinking in the educational context. ASEAN J. Psychiat. **22**, 1–11 (2021)
19. Lytaev, S., Aleksandrov, M., Ulitin, A.: Psychophysiological and intraoperative AEPs and SEPs monitoring for perception, attention and cognition. Commun. Comput. Inf. Sci. **713**, 229–236 (2017)
20. Lytaev, S., Belskaya, K.: Integration and disintegration of auditory images perception. In: Schmorrow, D.D., Fidopiastis, C.M. (eds.) AC 2015. LNCS (LNAI), vol. 9183, pp. 470–480. Springer, Cham (2015). https://doi.org/10.1007/978-3-319-20816-9_45
21. Lytaev, S., Aleksandrov, M., Popovich, T., et al.: Auditory evoked potentials and PET-scan: early and late mechanisms of selective attention. Adv. Intel. Sys. Comput. **775**, 169–178 (2019)
22. Lytaev, S., Vatamaniuk, I.: Physiological and medico-social research trends of the Wave P300 and more late components of visual event-related potentials. Brain Sci. **11**, 125 (2021)
23. Lytaev, S.: Modern neurophysiological research of the human brain in clinic and psychophysiology. In: Rojas, I., Castillo-Secilla, D., Herrera, L.J., Pomares, H. (eds.) BIOMESIP 2021. LNCS, vol. 12940, pp. 231–241. Springer, Cham (2021). https://doi.org/10.1007/978-3-030-88163-4_21
24. Lytaev, S.: Long-latency event-related potentials (300–1000 ms) of the visual insight. Sensors **22**, 1323 (2022)
25. Lytaev, S.: Psychological and neurophysiological screening investigation of the collective and personal stress resilience. Behav. Sci. **13**, 258 (2023)
26. Martinez, S., Stillerman, L., Waldo, M.: Reliability and validity of the SCL-90-R with hispanic college students. Hisp. J. Behav. Sci. **27**, 254–264 (2005)
27. McGregor, B.A., Murphy, K.M., Albano, D.L., et al.: Stress, cortisol, and b lymphocytes: a novel approach to understanding academic stress and immune function. Stress **19**, 185–191 (2016)
28. Noelle, E.C.: Reliability and validity of the SCL-90-R PTSD subscale. J. Interpers. Violence **23**, 1162–1176 (2008)
29. Noushad, S., Ahmed, S., Ansari, B., et al.: Physiological biomarkers of chronic stress: a systematic review. Int. J. Health Sci. **15**, 46 (2021)

30. O'Connor, D.B., Thayer, J.F., Vedhara, K.: Stress and health: a review of psychobiological processes. Annu. Rev. Psychol. **72**, 663–688 (2020)

31. Orel, V., et al.: Ways of economical production in medical institution risk management. Presented at the (2022). https://doi.org/10.1007/978-3-031-06018-2_17

32. Paap, M.C., Meijer, R.R., Van Bebber, J., et al.: A study of the dimensionality and measurement precision of the SCL-90-R using item response theory. Int. J. Methods Psychiatr. Res. **20**, 39–55 (2011)

33. Palmer, A.B.: Psychodiagnosis: personality inventories and other measure: a comparison of the MMPI and Mini-Mult in a sample of state mental hospital patients. J. Clin. Psychol. **29**, 484–485 (2006)

34. Sakalidis, K.E., Burns, J., van Biesen, D., et al.: The impact of cognitive functions and intellectual impairment on pacing and performance in sports. Psychol. Sport Exerc. **52**, 101840 (2021)

35. Scharfen, H.-E., Memmert, D.: Measurement of cognitive functions in experts and elite athletes: a meta-analytic review. Appl. Cogn. Psychol. **33**, 843–860 (2019)

36. Schmitz, N., Hartkamp, N., Franke, G.H.: Assessing clinically significant change: application to the SCL-90-R. Psychol. Rep. **86**, 263–274 (2000)

37. Sezen, N., Bülbül, A.: A scale on logical thinking abilities. Procedia Soc. Behav. Sci. **15**, 2476–2480 (2011)

38. Špiljak, B., Vilibić, M., Glavina, A., et al.: A review of psychological stress among students and its assessment using salivary biomarkers. Behav. Sci. **12**, 400 (2022)

39. Thornton, I.S., Finch, A.J., Griffin, J.L.: The mini-mult with criminal psychiatric patients. J. Pers. Assess. **39**, 394–396 (1975)

40. Yang, C.-K., Choe, B.-M., Baity, M.: SCL-90-R and 16PF profiles of senior high school students with excessive internet use. Can. J. Psychiatry **50**, 407–414 (2005)

41. Yerkes, R.M., Dodson, J.D.: The relation of strength of stimulus to rapidity of habit-formation. J. Comp. Neurol. Psychol. **18**, 459–482 (1908)

An Exploratory Study into Resilience Engineering and the Applicability to the Private Jet Environment

Heather McCann[✉] and Anastasios Plioutsias

Coventry University, Coventry, UK
mccannh2@uni.coventry.ac.uk

Abstract. Resilience Engineering (often abbreviated to resilience) has gained increasing prominence in the training and operating environment. According to the European Union Aviation Safety Agency (EASA), resilience is the ability of a crew member to recognize, absorb and adapt to disruptions (Malinge 2021). Private jet operations range from single pilot light jets owned and operated by one pilot to very sophisticated ultra-long-range jets. This study is focused primarily on the Fractional side of private jets. Fractional is a type of jet ownership that allows a corporation or very high net worth individual to buy a share of an aircraft. For the crews, the operation is high tempo with multiple sectors a day with many changes.

Previous studies on resilience have focused on airline pilots and military pilots, in particular, how they handle abnormal situations. To date, there has been no known study on resilience conducted on private jet pilots operating in a high tempo environment. Therefore, this research was based around a mixed method online survey involving pilots who were new to the private jet environment compared to the behaviours of the experienced private jet pilots. Behaviours explored involve how work is done, technology use and the uptake of activity and mindfulness.

Keywords: Resilience · Resilience Engineering · private jet pilots · business jet pilots · Human Factors

1 Introduction

1.1 Overview

Resilience Engineering (RE), also known as Resilience, in simple terms is the ability of an individual, group, or organisation to recognise, adapt and absorb variations, changes, disturbances, and surprises especially when the disruption falls outside the system design remit. Previously, it was viewed that pilots are the weak link in the safety chain but with understanding that humans (pilots) are adaptable the new viewpoint is that pilots are an integral and proactive part of the safety process.

The European Union Aviation Safety Agency (EASA) defines resilience as "the ability of a flight crew member to recognize, absorb and adapt to disruptions" (Malinge

2021). According to Airbus (Malinge 2021) resilience is built on two pillars: confidence and competence. Therefore, training needs to be such that variety of scenarios can be utilised to develop resilience through the ability to adapt to changing situations. Disruptions do not have to be an abnormal or an emergency situation, simply a change of runway or type of approach requires pilots to quickly adapt to the new situation.

A Private Jet pilot usually has no fixed schedule and can be called on to work with very little notice. A Fractional Jet pilot will have a roster but will often fly multiple sectors that can change during the day, if not inflight. Compared to an airline pilot, the Fractional and private jet pilot must contend with a lot more variables and distractions. These can include late passengers and/or demanding passengers, luggage, and catering as well as the many different airports they may encounter. The potential for error and/or stress is high.

This research aims to identify what behaviours have evolved in experienced Private/Fractional Jet pilots. By understanding how pilots use tools to get the work done, this can direct IT and Training departments to better design application software and training programs that will further develop resilience and competence. Finally, assessing activity/exercise uptake within the pilot group as well as mindfulness uptake in the pilot group.

1.2 Background

Business or private jet operations have increased in popularity over the past couple of decades. Business aviation boomed during the recent COVID pandemic because the airlines stopped flying (Malinge 2021). Fractional business jet operations are a subset, albeit a rather large part of the private aviation world.

Business (also known as private) jets often fly to Category C airfields (such as airports in mountainous areas) that require specific simulator training and while airline pilots do this too, their schedule is known well in advance while the private jet pilots may just get an hour or two's notice to review the procedures. This is where understanding of human factors such as CRM (Crew Resource Management), is invaluable. Human factors encompass such topics as ergonomics, physiology, health, stress and fatigue, cognitive psychology, communication, and leadership. CRM brings together elements of human factors to facilitate team building and working within teams. (Harris 2011, p. 2).

CRM (Crew Resource Management) and the requirement for pilots to realize that they need to learn to work more effectively in teams came after several high-profile crashes in the 1970s. The worst being the Tenerife crash where two Boeing 747s collided on the runway. It was found that there were no mechanical failures or failures of controlling the aircraft, but the deficiencies in performance came from information management, decision making, leadership and cooperation (Dahlström et al. 2017). So, CRM was developed initially to reduce incidences of "pilot error" (Helmreich et al. 1999). CRM was introduced several decades ago as a way to train crews to use all of the available resources such as equipment, people (crew, cabin crew, Air Traffic Control and so on) and information by using effective communication and coordination as a team (Salas et al. 2001).

Therefore, effective CRM and resilience is important for individuals and crews to be able to absorb the many changes and challenges that they may face during the day's operation and continue to operate safely and efficiently (Harris 2011, p5). The purpose of competency-based training is to train the pilot to be prepared for an infinite number of abnormal or changing situations by training the pilot in developing a core set of competencies that can be adapted to the situation at hand (Malinge 2021).

1.3 Research Problem

At the time of writing, very little research has been conducted on Private Jet pilots and the skillsets required to operate in such a dynamic operational environment. Coupled with the many changes to the daily schedule and as well as meeting the expectations of demanding passengers while maintaining a calm and pleasant demeanour. This requires the ability to rapidly process information as well as remain reasonably calm and unflustered.

Therefore, the research questions centred about 3 main areas:

RQ1. What skills and techniques do the pilot group utilise?
RQ2. Do the tools provided by management (IT and Training) assist or hinder the pilots.
RQ3. Is there a link between RE and health practices such as yoga, exercise and mindfulness?

1.4 Study Limitations

A significant limitation in the study was the unevenness of the two pilot populations under study. The Less than 1-year group only had 9 participants whereas the Greater than 1-year group had 47 participants. Therefore, a total of 56 participants.

Another limitation is that there is no control group. All the pilots surveyed had extensive experience in the commercial aviation industry prior to joining their current employer. Finally, many respondents are not native English speakers, therefore, there may have been errors in question interpretation.

Finally, the qualitative section of the survey did not utilise a "Likert" format and so hindered the type of statistical analysis that could be conducted. However, given the poor turn out in numbers it was fortunate that a thematic analysis was possible on the open questions.

2 Literary Review

Given the lack of research published on Private Jet pilots, the search was expanded to capture the relevant topics of resilience, crew resource management in multi-pilot operations, stress and mindfulness.

Resilience has many applications, ranging from the individual, organizations to industries and societies (Hollnagel 2011, p. xxxvii). For this study, the focus will be on individual pilots and, to a lesser extent, the two-pilot flight deck.

The focus of civil airline pilot resilience research has been on resolving abnormal situations (Malinge 2021) (FAA 2009, p.1–3). It must be noted that the training program suggested by EASA and Airbus (Malinge 2021) to enhance a pilot's confidence and competence has in large, been adopted by the larger private jet companies.

Given that it is not unusual in the Fractional or private business jet environment to have plans changed during the day or even during the flight, being able to maintain high situational awareness (Endsley and Garland 2000, p. 16) and flexibility is vital for not only the safe operation but also for the pilot's stress management and mental well-being.

Being able to make sound decisions in a timely manner is very important, especially in a dynamic environment. It has been suggested that inflight decision errors are relevant in 69% of all accidents (Li and Harris 2008, cited in Li et al. 2011). Time pressure may lead to a shift in how cognitive resources are allocated. That is, shift away from the decision-making process to stress coping processes (Li et al. 2011). Understanding the situation whether it is developed from training and or experience is essential to developing the crew's situational awareness which in turn, is vital for all aspects of decision making (Li et al. 2011).

Therefore, the investigation will focus on what resilience engineering is acquired amongst the experienced pilot group (FAA 2009, p. 1–30). What tools do the pilots find helpful, or do the tools provided by the pilots' company, in fact hinder the way the pilots would naturally work, an example of "work as imagined versus work as done" (Dekker 2006, p. 86).

Finally, activities such as regular cardio activities and/or mindfulness (Berger and Owen (1992), as cited in Berger and Motl 2000) (Meland et al. 2015) assist in developing resilience engineering and stress management. Mood or emotion being related to physical health and well-being has been well known for a few years now. Physical activity can bring about positive changes to mood (Berger and Motl 2000) and so if a pilot has had a challenging day or tour, being able to partake in some physical activity will facilitate a return to a positive state. A study conducted on Norwegian military pilots found that mindfulness training was found to be beneficial in attention regulation and arousal (that is, alertness) regulation. Also, the pilots reported less anxiousness and stress over performance assessments (Meland et al. 2015).

3 Methodology

3.1 Online Survey

The purpose of the study was to begin to explore resilience in private jet pilots as, to date, no research had targeted this group of pilots. An online survey, accessible anonymously was made available to all pilots working for a large Fractional jet company both in the USA and Europe. As numbers were limited, this was expanded to permit former employees of the European company. Whilst all the pilots were experienced, the groups were divided into those who had been in the current company for less than 1 year and those who had been employed by the company for greater than a year. The survey was online because the pilots operate remotely from the operations centre.

3.2 Mixed Method Survey

Both qualitative and quantitative methods were used, in part to get an overview of what pilot behaviour is happening but to also to allow the participants to expand on their answers (Coolican 2019, p. 274). The data was collected through an online survey utilising both open and closed questions (Coolican 2019, p. 293).

Thematic Analysis. This proved useful given the low participation rate. Thematic analysis (TA) was chosen as the method for analyzing the rich data because of its flexibility (Braun and Clarke 2006). Given that this is novel research, it was felt that TA would permit freedom in identifying, analyzing and reporting patterns (or themes) within the data. It is important to be clear that the researcher is a Fractional jet pilot herself and thus could understand the nuances of the participant replies without needing further explanation. In this case, PDFs of the answers were manually processed and keywords such as "anticipation" and "learning" were highlighted.

Statistical Analysis. A chi-squared test of independence was conducted on four of the survey questions. This test was appropriate for this analysis as the design of the experiment was between groups and the variables categorical (Coolican 2019, p. 523). The two groups were the new hires or pilots with less than 1 year in their current employer and the experienced pilots, who had been in their company for greater than a year. The questions were selected to explore whether experience made between the results of the two groups.
Given the lack of participants, the statistical data had to be grouped together to increase the power of the chi-square test.

4   Results

The original study included both statistical and free answers. Given the previously stated limitations of the statistical answers, this paper will concentrate on what was learned from experienced pilot responses. To recap the objectives.

The first objective is to identify any evidence of resilience within the pilot group. This will be done through the identification of operational behaviours that reflect Hollnagel's (2011) four cornerstones of resilience.

Evaluation of the tools available to the pilots and the effectiveness of the training, especially for special airports will be conducted. The purpose of this is to identify what is working for the pilots on the line. The reasoning being is that time spent searching for relevant information can be a distraction.

Resilience is not purely mental; a healthy body can better absorb the stresses of the day. Hence the inquiry into the amount of physical activity. Mindfulness is a relatively new concept but is particularly important in emotional control which is essential when dealing with the multiple challenges of private aviation.

4.1   Operational Behaviours

All four cornerstones of RE; Anticipation, Responding, Monitoring and Learning (Hollnagel 2011) featured highly amongst the experienced Private Jet pilots. Many responses expanded on the importance of anticipating. Many referenced their experiences of changes and/or previous exposure to situations that modified how they approached the new day. Therefore, this means that learning had taken place, and thus the pilot had gained experience enabling greater resilience when the pilot reencountered a similar situation. Several responses highlighted that change is a constant in private jet operations. Simply knowing that the day's plan is likely to change can lessen the impact of the possible change when it happens. This highlights the adaptability required from the pilots.

"... with our type of operations, being independent is very important."

"I anticipate there WILL be change (it's the nature of the business)."

From experience, the pilots have focussed on where the potential issues can occur. Planning where to uplift fuel can save some time in other areas, time being a premium when preparing for the day. Some airports are notoriously difficult to get fuel during peak times. Therefore, it is best to have planned for that.

Having the fuel onboard can allow the crew to take meal breaks and short "time outs". To tanker fuel means to carry enough fuel for 2 or more flights.

"is there enough time for a meal [...] respond to potential time pressure [...] could be to refuel ahead of time [...] tankering where possible"

Many pilots responded that with experience, having the capacity to monitor and respond was essential. Some pilots noted that stress levels were influenced by their mental attitude to how the day/tour was going. For example, a participant mentioned that:

"How I respond can affect my health/stress level [...] "roll with the punches""

Others suggested that knowing where the issues could appear and thus preparing for them was essential to keep an even temperament.

"secret to a smooth day"

One pilot said it very well. This pilot has demonstrated a high degree of self-awareness and where errors and mistakes can occur.

"it's better to actually slow down [...] manage fatigue and potential mistakes"

Overall, by the responses, most pilots have acknowledged that Resilience comes from experience and learning from it. Sharing one's experience through safety reports was mentioned once. One pilot acknowledged that learning could come from successes as well and highlighted the importance of a team debrief at the end of the day. The debrief allows the aircrew team to openly share their thoughts of the day for learning to occur.

"it is important to debrief and try and highlight what went well and why and what could be improved and how."

Several pilots noted that looking after their mental attitude and health is essential. Several commented that getting appropriate nutrition breaks was important for mood and managing fatigue. Several suggested no point in over planning the day as the plan will probably change.

"one can anticipate but often I find my assumptions are wrong and my 'new' plan is inappropriate as the plan has changed again."

Fatigue management were significant to the pilots with respect to resilience.

"The more tired u (sic) are the less acceptable you are to change"

Unsurprisingly, the new (to the job) pilots needed more time on average than the experienced pilots. Given the quantity of esoteric items that need to be checked and assessed, compared to a routine airline operation, this was not a revelation. There was evidence of adaptation as some of the new pilots were checking what the passenger needs were. However, the quantity of items assessed were less, this could also be down to the rank of the respective pilots. The new hires (less than 1 year) were all First Officers, while the majority of the experienced pilots were Captains (Table 1).

Table 1. Time Taken Before Official Start Show) Time.

Condition	Less than 15 min	Greater than 15 min	Total
Less than 1 year	2	7	9
Greater than 1 year	28	19	47

The chi-square statistic is 4.2371. The p-value is .03955. The result is significant at p < .05. Many pilots do not have enough time to prepare for the flight within the allocated show time.

A chi-square test of independence was performed to examine the relation between pilots' experience level and extra time required before the show for flight preparation. 78% of the new hires needed more time than the experienced pilots, 40%. The relation between these variables was significant, $X2 (1, N = 56) = 4.23$, $p = .040$. New hires were more likely than experienced pilots to require more flight preparation time.

However, what the experienced pilots reviewed is far more extensive than the inexperienced pilots. Passenger profiles/demands and catering feature often, as it did with the inexperienced pilots but considerations such as the duty legality, airport notes and special procedures, handling and FBO and where the fuel savings can be made were all highlighted.

The experience gained over the years has taught the experienced pilots where the issues can arise and do not rely on operations to pick up all the issues.

This does tie in with the ResilienceEngineering "anticipation" cornerstone. By assessing these issues and developing a plan, the pilot's stress levels are reduced, and the impact on the operation and passenger experience is minimised.

91.5% of the respondents said they do flight preparations before the official show time. Weather is the most often cited item reviewed. Then the day's plan and any unique items that need attention.

4.2 Tools, "Apps" and Training

The rationale behind this line of enquiry was that pilots need to utilise tools and internet applications on their company issued phones and iPads to rapidly access weather, flight packages, flight details such as catering and owner needs. The various companies have supplied some Apps but many have reduced functionality because they are the "free" versions.

The documentation included Operations Manual A (general company and flight operations), B (type specific Standard Operating Procedures) and C, (special airports and route specific information). Paper documentation such as airport charts are now electronic, one example is Jeppview and one example of performance tools is iPreflight. This has the weight and balance as well as the operational speeds and expected performance.

The results revealed that a large majority of the pilots surveyed used their own devices with paid for "Apps" to obtain the relevant information pertinent to flight. Since this survey was completed, one company has now issued to the pilots an app that lets them check for flight delays. Note, this was not only in the pilot's interest, it has also freed up the Dispatchers (people who prepare, check and submit flight plans) in office to concentrate on creating flight plans instead of emailing the pilots with information about slots and delays.

Most of the captains will be rated on upwards of five to seven special airports that require simulator training. So therefore, the ability to rapidly and accurate pick out the salient points from the documentation, recall from experience and the relevant daily information is vital to ensure a safe and trouble-free flight.

Some pilots suggested that the key points should be more visible. Some observed that the special airport briefings conflict with other airspace users, creating an inflight hazard. Therefore, better communications with all stakeholders at particular demanding airports would be of benefit when designing procedures to operate there.

"the company needs to consult with local ATC (Air Traffic Control) before developing their own procedures. At Lake Tahoe (USA) one of their procedures puts you in the way of heavy glider and parachute activity. ATC is not aware of our procedures"

4.3 Attitudes, Mental and Physical Activity

The remaining questions focussed on mental attitudes and communication and exploring physical activity and mindfulness uptake. Flying is a mentally and physically demanding occupation. To avoid distractions from tiredness and emotionally draining attitudes, a degree of physical fitness is required (thus the medical assesses weight and blood pressure, amongst other items) to be handle passenger luggage as well as the length of the duty day. Emotional stability is desired so as not to be distracted by arguments with colleagues.

Fortunately, the majority of pilots surveyed were not unduly affected by the changes in their schedule. Most took it in their stride and viewed it as a positive challenge. This was true amongst both groups of pilots. It could be argued that the pilots who did not like or enjoy the constant changes had already left this part of the industry (Table 2).

Table 2. Pilot response to a change in plan.

Condition	Annoyed	Challenge	Total
Less than 1 year	3	6	9
Greater than 1 year	15	32	47

The chi-square statistic is 0.007. The p-value is .933475. *Not* significant at $p < .05$. The null hypothesis is accepted. The schedule change does not affect the pilot's mental outlook.

Awareness of fatigue and tiredness was high amongst both groups of pilots and so made conscious efforts to manage their activity and rest schedules. Forms of activity were walking or hotel gym if there was one there. Again, the experienced pilots acknowledged that they were not as young as they were and thus, modified their behaviour to reflect that.

The new hire group's self-awareness of fatigue was high, relying on being aware of missing items and calls.

" levels of fatigue. If I noticed I start to miss things, then yes."

The caveat is that the fatigued pilot may not be aware that they are missing calls and checks (Dekker, 2014, p98); therefore, they may rely on a colleague to identify missed items/calls. Notably, one pilot suggested that their feelings are unimportant to their company.

"Does my opinion/feeling matter to the company?"

This starkly contrasted the general theme of positivity throughout the participants' answers.

Overall, the experienced pilots recognized that rest was important but did acknowledge the insidious nature of commercial pressure and how it can influence a pilot's decision to continue.

Fatigue awareness was highlighted with a few responses, also the acknowledgment that as the population gets older, rest becomes paramount. Several pilots suggested that whether they continue is dependent on how difficult the flight is and how their colleague is feeling. A few pilots acknowledged that there is commercial pressure.

" but now (as I get older) make sure that I really get enough rest (no booze [...])"

"... how I feel but the pressure often makes a decision which is not wanted but better for the company. Not wanted to be the pilot who says no..."

All participants acknowledged that adequate sleep is essential. All acknowledged that the job/tour could make getting good quality sleep essential to managing fatigue.

It was highlighted that getting good quality sleep as well as maintaining some form of regular exercise was difficult on tour. Many highlighted the need to partake in regular forms of exercise on tour. The use of caffeine was mentioned as a short-term fix as well as good nutrition to maintain adequate energy levels.

"try to sleep at least 8 hours a night."

It was noted that consuming only moderate levels of alcohol was essential to manage rest.

"Avoid alcohol, like a maximum a casual beer to relax…"

Being able to relax at the end of the day was important to conclude the day's work.

"… to relax at the end of the day with a chat with the crew."

There was an excellent awareness of what was required physiologically to cope with the day and tour from the experienced group. Rest or sleep was mentioned several times, as was eating appropriately to ensure a good chance of falling asleep quickly. Nutrition during the day was mentioned often to keep energy levels up during the day.8 (17%) pilots answered "it depends" regarding tiredness, and accepting duty expanded their answers. Two have learned that managing rest is essential, especially as they have gotten older.

"… But I now (as I get older) make sure that I really get enough rest"

Coffee and caffeinated drinks are featured as part of the energy management strategy. A few pilots did think that caffeine intake should be managed to not interfere with sleep.

"Chocolate and coffee at TOD to provide adequate blood sugar for […] landing"

Physical activity during the day, such as getting up to check on the passengers, was used by a few pilots as a strategy to keep engaged with the day's duty. A few pilots mentioned partaking in some exercise during the tour if possible.

"Do daily exercise"

Limiting the consumption of alcohol as it can disturb the quality of sleep was mentioned several times.

"Almost no alcohol on tour any longer since it disturbs my sleep"

Both internal and commercial pressure was mentioned. Several pilots commented on not being rushed by commercial pressure and assessing fatigue levels within the team. Several pilots said they used methods such as crossword puzzles or reading magazines to keep mentally stimulated. Others suggested having interesting conversations with colleagues to generate some mental activity. One pilot mentioned that it could be tiring if they do not have a good relationship with your colleague.

"Humor helps. Also, if you are with a colleague who has a personality like a black hole, that's when its extra challenging."

4.4 Exercise and Mindfulness

All participants seemed to be aware of the need for some form of exercise/activity whilst on tour and on their days off. It was acknowledged that the rest location and facilities can make exercise difficult as well as the lateness of arrival. However, by and large, the majority of the pilots were regularly partaking in some exercise.

Mindfulness uptake however, was significantly different. Given that mindfulness is a comparatively new concept for pilots, it was expected that not many were practising mindfulness or yoga regularly. Of the two groups surveyed, only 9% of the experienced group participated in any form of mental relaxation and no one in the inexperienced groups did.

5 Discussion

This work focussed on the fractional and private jet operations in normal circumstances. The purpose of resilience is to enable the pilot to be able to handle the changes without being negatively affected themselves or the operation. The objectives of this research were to determine that resilience was being demonstrated and what experienced pilots were doing differently to plan for the day and its inevitable changes, what tools and applications were useful to the pilots and whether physical activities and mindfulness activities were contributing to the pilot's resilience.

Overall, the pilots are using not only the company applications but also commercially available applications to make gathering relevant information more accessible and faster. 100% of the new hires and 81% of the experienced pilots used commercially available applications.

Finally, mental health, communications and personal care were considered. Concepts like Crew Resource Management are not new and are utilised to significant effect within the pilot groups. However, some of the experienced pilots displayed a sense of cynicism. Overall, the team dynamic appears to be working well in countering the changes of the day and handling individual pressures. Generally, both pilot groups are looking after their physical health reasonably well, but there is an opportunity for more pilots to explore mindfulness activities to manage stress better.

5.1 Operational Behaviours

The first questions in the survey focussed on whether the pilot understood what resilience means in an aviation setting and then probed the pilot for evidence of efficient and effective behaviours. There were opportunities for the respondents to expand their answers. Both pilot groups revealed a high degree of understanding of what resilience is, even though many had not heard the term 'Resilience Engineering' in an aviation setting before.

Within pilot initial training and recurrent training (Malinge 2021) CRM and Human Factors (HF) concepts are taught, assessed, and refreshed (Malinge 2021) (FAA 2009). A key cornerstone of HF is the understanding of Situational Awareness (SA) (Endsley and Garland2000) part to facilitate effective decision-making, whether it be via a structured form or Naturalistic Decision Making (FAA 2009) (Klein, 2015). The acquisition of pertinent information is vital to be able to update the pilot's mental model and SA (Endsley and Garland2000) which will in turn, increase the likelihood of a correct decision being made. The pilots in the survey highlighted anticipation and monitoring as two key components that are essential for a successful day's flying. Such examples can be found with runway changes and distance to fly changes. The negative impact could be an unstable approach which leads to a go around and another attempt (Pariès 2011).

Effective preparation or pre-flight planning revealed differences between the two pilot groups. The experienced pilots on average took less time before the official show time compared to the new hires. Also, what was looked for was different between the two groups. As many of the new hires had come from the airline industry, a lot of the issues that can cause an impact on the flight are not a pilot's concern in airline operations. By understanding the impact such items like parking permissions can have, this can influence how the day will go and thus may need to proactive in finding solutions or work arounds. Nearly all pilots used their own time before show time (official start time) suggests that the time allocated by the companies is not enough for all the items to be checked and processed, especially by the new hires. This does highlight one of the issues that people remote from the pilot workforce do not fully understand the work required to get everything squared away before the flight commences (Dekker 2006).

5.2   Use of Applications, Tools, and Training.

The second group of questions relates to Dekker's (2006) Work as imagined versus Work as done.

They do link in with the above group of questions in that the less time a pilot needs to search for the pertinent information, the more time they have on strategic planning. Jeppview is one such programme installed on the company issued iPad. The pilot can load up the flight plan onto a map and overlay weather information thus giving them Situational Awareness about turbulence, as an example. A lot of the review stage can occur well before arrival at the aircraft, thus giving the pilots capacity to assess any changes that arise.

However, not everything can be done electronically. Hence the need to get items required for the flight printed through the handling agent (a representative at the airport). Many pilots use commercially available and paid for applications to facilitate the timely acquisition of these items. The key here is time management.

Apps that inform the pilots about airport slots and airway slots featured heavily too. An experienced pilot will be able to manage the passenger handling to ensure they are comfortable and informed but also, are in the right place if there is an improvement. The variables a private jet pilot need to contend with include security screening, distance to the aeroplane, ease of access and the type of the aircraft. In many cases, it is more comfortable to remain in the lounge than wait on the aircraft with no air conditioning.

Often there is little notice that a crew will be flying to a special airport, therefore, to be able to pick out the pertinent points in a timely manner is essential. By utilising experience and training the pilots can minimise the time and effort taken to do this. Both pilot groups highlighted possible issues with the competency-based training (Malinge

2021) and potentially failing to build an adequate mental model of the airport in question. An accurate mental model is required to build situational awareness (Endsley and Garland2000).

This was a real difference in the behaviours of the two groups. The experienced pilots knew what was relevant to that flight and so could navigate their way around the various documents necessary to plan a safe departure or arrival.

5.3 Attitudes, Mental and Physical Activity

The first of this series of questions explored the mood of the pilots after a significant schedule change. Overall, when the pilots were asked about how they felt after a destination change, most viewed that change as a positive, a challenge to embrace. It must be noted that if a pilot did not enjoy that challenge of constant change, it was quite likely that they had already resigned. The new hires were all still enjoying the variety of flying that private jet operations bring, it must be reminded that none were fresh out of flight school, all had come from demanding airline operations in Europe and the Middle East.

"I anticipate there WILL be change (it's the nature of the business)."

Getting sufficient rest and maintaining appropriate energy levels is essential for a busy tour. Fatigue can have a profound effect on a pilot's ability to cope with multiple changes and distractions (Meland et al. 2015) (Endsley and Garland2000). One pilot noted that if s/he was tired, then s/he noticed s/he missed items. The experienced pilots who were more likely to be captains (PICs) also considered their colleague's energy levels as well. This is particularly important to maintain the integrity of the team.

The final two questions in this section relate to exercise and mindfulness participation. Depending on their age, a pilot must undergo a medical every 6 to 12 months. One of the items monitored is weight. Physical activity is one way of maintaining a healthy body weight, but it also has positive benefits on mood (Meland et al. 2015) (NHS National Health Service) (APA American Psychological Association). Mood or emotional control is a key to being a resilient pilot. Not reacting negatively to a schedule change retains capacity to process that change. Maintaining a positive outlook enhances the crew dynamic as the colleague's feel able to talk to the crew member but as one experienced pilot observed:

Being active and partaking in exercise was used as often as possible by the crews when on tour as a means of unwinding. This would suggest that exercise is used by the pilots for mental relaxation as well (Berger and Motl 2000). This may well explain the lack of participation in mindfulness type activities such as yoga as they may feel they get enough mental care.

The results show that both pilot groups are getting sufficient physical activity for sustained health.

It is accepted that on a busy tour, there may not be sufficient time to comply with the guidelines set out by the NHS but doing what one can is better than nothing.

Mindfulness activities on the other hand did not have a high participation rate.

No new hires partook in any mindfulness activities whereas only 19% of the experienced pilots did.

Given the positive effect mindfulness has on emotion regulation and attention control, this is a missed opportunity to manage stress and to practice mental health activities. The study on the Norwegian pilots by Meland et al. (2015) went to great lengths to adapt the programme to make it palatable to pilots but even they experienced some dropouts citing boredom.

If it possible to summarise the positive benefits of a resilient pilot and having the capacity to manage the day well, it is captured by a quote from an experienced pilot.

"Chaos consumes energy"

6 Conclusion

This research explored resilience development in private jet pilots. The pool of pilots was taken from a large Fractional business jet company operating in Europe and USA, as well as a couple of former employees now operating as contract pilots. They were divided by length of service in their current job; less than one year (9 participants) and greater than one year (47 participants). Whilst the nine new hires had only been employed for less than a year, all were very experienced airline or military pilots. What is also now known is trying to get pilots to do a survey is like trying to herd cats.

Overall, both pilot groups displayed resilient behaviours while the experienced group displayed a more efficient use of their time before signing on and sought out different items that could impact the smooth running of the day. This has probably been developed through experience rather than through training programs.

Both pilot groups utilized the tools provided by the company as well as relying on commercially available products. Again, the experienced pilot group were more selective in the data acquired thus making better use of the time available to prepare for the task ahead. The experienced pilots expressed concern that training on special (that is, demanding) airports could prevent effective mental models from being developed by the new hires. This could be countered by streamlining the information presented in the official documents.

Sound Crew Resource Management principles were utilised for effective communication and team building. Resilience per se may be viewed as a novel development however, how the pilots described their behaviours and mood during programme changes, and how they self-managed their energy levels and their colleagues would suggest that the pilots are displaying resilient behaviour. Physical activity was well embraced as a means of maintaining physical health but also, to a degree, mental health. It is possible that the experienced pilots who could not readily tolerate the changes and demands peculiar to private jet operations have already left and returned to airline operations.

The maintenance of mental health is an area to be explored further. To find a way to make mindfulness accessible to a busy pilot is a challenge yet to be taken up.

References

Berger, B.G., Motl, R.W.: Exercise and mood: a selective review and synthesis of research employing the profile of mood states. J. Appl. Sport Psychol. **12**(1), 69–92 (2000). https://doi.org/10.1080/10413200008404214

Braun, V., Clarke, V.: Using thematic analysis in psychology. Qual. Res. Psychol. **3**(2), 77–101 (2006). https://doi.org/10.1191/1478088706qp063oa

Coolican, H.: Research Methods and Statistics in Psychology. Psychology Press, London (2019)

Dekker, S.D.: Resilience engineering: chronicling the emergence of confused consensus. In Resilience Engineering: Concepts and Precepts, pp. 77–93. CRC Press (2017)

Dahlström, N., Laursen, J., Bergström, J.: Crew resource management, threat and error and assessment of CRM skills – current situation and development of knowledge, methods and practice. Swedish APA (2008)

Endsley, M.R., Garland, D.J.: Situation awareness analysis and measurement. CRC Press, Boca Raton (2000)

Federal Aviation Administration FAA. Risk management handbook (FAA-H-8083-2). FAA Aviation Supplies & Academics (2009)

Harris, D.: Human Performance on the Flight Deck. CRC Press, Boca Raton (2011)

Helmreich, R.L., Merritt, A.C., Wilhelm, J.A.: The evolution of crew resource management training in commercial aviation. Int. J. Aviat. Psychol. **9**(1), 19–32 (1999)

Hollnagel, E., Pariès, J., Woods, D.D., Wreathall, J.: Resilience Engineering in Practice: A Guidebook. Ashgate Publishing Company, Farnham (2011)

Klein, G.: A naturalistic decision making perspective on studying intuitive decision making. J. Appl. Res. Mem. Cogn. **4**(3), 164–168 (2015). https://doi.org/10.1016/j.jarmac.2015.07.001

Li, W.-C., Harris, D., Hsu Y.-L., Wang, T.: Understanding pilots' cognitive processes for making in-flight decisions under stress. In: Proceedings of the 42nd Annual International Seminar: Investigation a Shared Process. International Society of Air Safety Investigators (2011)

Malinge, Y.. Training pilots for resilience. Safety First. The Airbus Safety magazine (2021)

Meland, A., Fonne, V., Wagstaff, A., Pensgaard, A.M.: Mindfulness-based mental training in a high-performance combat aviation population: a one-year intervention study and two-year follow-up. Int. J. Aviat. Psychol. **25**(1), 48–61 (2015). https://doi.org/10.1080/10508414.2015.995572

Mindfulness meditation: A research-proven way to reduce stress. PsycEXTRA Dataset (2019). http://www.apa.org/topics/mindfulness/meditation

National Health Service NHS. Physical activity guidelines for adults aged 19 to 64 (2021). https://www.nhs.uk/live-well/exercise/exercise-guidelines/physical-activity-guidelines-for-adults-aged-19-to-64/

Pariès, J., Wreathall, J.: Resilience Engineering in Practice: A Guidebook. CRC Press, Boca Raton (2011)

Salas, E.C., Burke, S., Bowers, C.A., Wilson, K.: Team training in the skies: does crew resource management (CRM) training work? Hum. Factors **43**(4), 641–674 (2001)

U.S Department of Health and Human Services. Physical activity guidelines for Americans (2). Physical Activity Guidelines Advisory Committee (2018)

Working out boosts brain health. PsycEXTRA Dataset (2020). http://www.apa.org/topics/exercise-fitness/stress

Resilience Engineering's Synergy with Threat and Error Management – An Operationalised Model

Andrew Mizzi[1]([⊠]) [iD] and Pete McCarthy[2] [iD]

[1] Griffith University, Nathan, QLD, Australia
`andrew.mizzi@griffithuni.edu.au`
[2] Cranfield University, Cranfield, UK
`pete.mccarthy@cranfield.ac.uk`

Abstract. As air travel continuously becomes safer, airlines continue to evolve their focus in managing flight safety. Part of flight safety's success has been the evolution of Crew Resource Management and Threat and Error Management (TEM) techniques. TEM has been thoroughly adopted throughout the industry and its success reflected in training syllabuses and demonstrated through the Line Oriented Safety Audit program (LOSA). However most recently, airlines have begun to adopt Safety-II and Resilience Engineering principles to further develop its frontline safety. Whilst TEM's focus is on the prevention of undesired outcomes, a resilience focus is on the reinforcement of success. This paper firstly presents the contributions that the Threat and Error Management model has made to flight safety. Resilience Engineering and the concept of the resilient potentials are then presented, and recent regulatory changes in resilience training debated. The synergistic attributes between the threat and error management model, and the resilient potentials are discussed, which is then demonstrated with a crew briefing model which operationalises these concepts as a tool for flight crew. Future applications of Safety-II and Resilience Engineering are discussed, presenting how a combined focus of threat and error management and resilient potentials can help airlines further improve flight safety.

Keywords: flight crew · briefing · resilience engineering · capacity · team cognition · aviation

1 Introduction

Recently, recognition of the variability of work in complex systems and its influence on human performance has been published in a guidance manual by the International Civil Aviation Organization, which drives state aviation regulations [1]. Additionally, new regulatory requirements around Crew Resource Management (CRM) have been introduced requiring training into resilience by the supranational regulator in Europe [2]. These improvements to the understanding of human influence within socio-technical systems require improved models to operationalise the theory. The discipline of Resilience

Engineering has adopted four potentials required for resilience in an organisation, first presented by Hollnagel. They are described as the potential to anticipate, to monitor, to respond and to learn [3]. Whilst the incorporation of resilience in pilot training is only emerging, the Threat and Error Management (TEM) model has been widely adopted throughout the industry [4]. It has three basic concepts: the anticipation of threats, the recognition of errors and recovery from unintended aircraft states [5]. The constant identification and mitigation of threats by the flight crew engages a sense of unease which fosters resilience and prevents complacency. However, despite its wide adoption, confusion can exist in the way that TEM is integrated into CRM training, and how crew can use TEM tools in practice [6]. This paper investigates the synergy which is present between the resilient potentials of anticipate, monitor, and respond [7] and Threat and Error Management. A briefing model concept is presented which can extend operational resilience by engaging crews' capacity to *anticipate* threats and errors, *monitor* for errors and *respond* with countermeasures, so to recover from errors and undesired aircraft states.

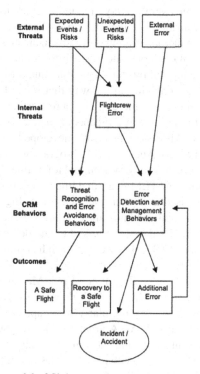

Fig. 1. The model of flight crew threat and error management [8]

2 Threat and Error Management

Threat and error management (TEM) is a proactive approach to safety in the aviation industry. The TEM model (Fig. 1, [8]) is based on the premise that threats and errors are inevitable on any flight, and that it is important to have processes in place to detect and correct these before they lead to an incident or accident. Through applying the TEM framework, crew are compelled first to identify potential threats to the safe operation of a flight and implement strategies to mitigate those threats. If those threats aren't managed or are mismanaged, errors can occur which require detection and management to resolve. If errors are led to continue an undesired aircraft state can occur, leading to an incident or accident. There are several strategies that can be used to manage threats and errors in aviation. These include the proactive implementation of strategies to mitigate against anticipated threats such as weather, the use of checklists and standard operating procedures to counter latent threats, the use of automation to reduce the workload on pilots, and the execution of go-arounds or diversions when the situation require recovery actions. By implementing these strategies, it is possible to significantly reduce the risk of accidents and improve the overall safety of aviation operations.

There are several applications of the TEM model in practice. It has become the foundation of many human factors training programs in airlines. The International Civil Aviation Organization (ICAO) adopted the model into its human factors curriculum [9], prompting to the further adoption by state regulators and airlines. However, MacLeod has mentioned that there is confusion in the way that it can be deeply integrated into CRM training [6], by arguing that there is no 'pure' airline training implementation of TEM aside from mentioning its key concepts of threat, errors, and outcomes. Deep integration of TEM into workflows can be further developed, as further explained in this paper. The Line Oriented Safety Audit (LOSA) program was developed in conjunction with TEM and provides a systemic observation tool for airlines [10]. A behavioural audit methodology studies flight crew TEM in normal line flight operations which has proven successful [11] and recognised as a proactive measure of flight safety [12]. The TEM model has also been operationalised into safety reporting. The United States' Aviation Safety Action Program (ASAP) identifies parts of the model to describe the event at the level of threats and errors, and a TEM based approach has shown to increase the quality of reports [13].

It is important to recognise that Threat and Error Management principles focus is based on a model of error management which doesn't account for the complexity of systems involved in its application, particularly when applied in incident investigation (ASAP) and safety assurance (LOSA). A greater focus in systems thinking is needed. As the industry's journey into applying the fundamentals of Safety-II continues, the utilisation of the mature TEM model with newer modes of thinking is needed to achieve further improvement in flight safety. Resilience engineering provides needed guidance.

3 Resilient Potentials

Resilience engineering is a field of study that focuses on improving safety by helping people cope with complexity to achieve success [14]. The goal of resilience engineering is to design systems that can adapt and recover quickly when faced with unexpected challenges or failures. Resilience is achieved by the system, in this case the flight crew and aircraft state, sustaining its required operation in both expected and unexpected conditions [7]. Nemeth and Herrera [15] describe three core values of resilience engineering: finding resilience, assessing resilience, and creating resilience. The topic of creating resilience has remained foundational to the term resilience *engineering*, thus finding ways to operationalise the capacities which remerge in resilient work is key to future development.

There are several key potentials developed by Woods and Hollnagel and modelled in Fig. 2 [16] that contribute to the resilience of a system. The first potential is the ability to *anticipate* and prepare for potential failures. This requires having attention in place to identify and assess potential threats, and planning strategies to mitigate or prevent those threats from occurring. The next potential is the ability to *monitor* for signals of system degradation, in order to adapt and recover from failures when they do occur. This then requires having systems and processes in place to quickly identify and *respond* to failures, as well as having the necessary resources and capabilities to address degraded systems or recover from undesired aircraft states. In addition to these technical capacities, resilience engineering also recognises the importance of human factors in the resilience of a system. This includes the need for effective communication and collaboration among crew, as well as the need for clear roles and responsibilities to ensure that everyone knows their part in the response to a failure. By understanding and improving these capacities, it is possible to significantly improve the resilience of complex systems.

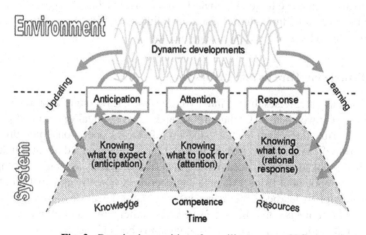

Fig. 2. Required capacities of a resilient system [16]

The requirement for team training in resilience is emerging in aviation. The European Aviation Safety Agency (EASA) has modified its regulatory framework in Crew Resource Management (CRM) to include 'Resilience Development' [2]. Training topics required under the regulations involve mental flexibility and performance adaptation, requiring crew to draw the right conclusions from both positive and negative experiences.

The normative language involved in the regulations however may see these training categorisations turned into levels of accountability, in a similar vein as CRM [17, 18]. As argued by Dekker and Bergström [19], "the language responsibilities pilots not only for the performance of the system, but in a sense even for their beliefs in resilience theory". It's therefore key for airlines to develop ways to encompass it wisely and ethically into their training, policies, and procedures, and for regulators to follow ICAO guidance on human performance [1]. Utilising the synergistic attributes between the resilient potentials and TEM may provide the required assistance to galvanise these regulations into practice.

4 Discussion: Synergistic Attributes

In design, the threat and error management model's actions can be closely aligned to the resilient potentials, allowing for the two concepts to be operationalised into flight decks and every-day work with greater ease (Fig. 3). One important way that TEM contributes to resilience is through its focus on proactive identification and assessment of potential threats. These two actions call upon the crews' capacity to learn and anticipate. By identifying and assessing potential threats in advance, it is possible to implement strategies to mitigate or prevent those threats from occurring. This proactive approach helps to broaden the crew's capacity and acceptable boundaries in dealing with disturbances to their flight, which in turn increases the overall resilience of the system. Another way in which TEM enhances resilience is through its focus on error detection and correction. By having processes in place to quickly identify and correct errors, it is possible to prevent those errors from cascading into more serious failures and disturbances to the flight are quickly recovered back to a crews' acceptable norm.

4.1 Anticipate for Threats and Errors

The TEM model categorises threats into two categories. Environmental threats are associated to adverse weather, ATC, the airport, and environmental operational pressures. Conversely, airline threats are related to the aircraft, airline operational pressures, cabin, dispatch, ground, maintenance, and documentation. A mismanaged threat is defined "as a threat that is linked to or induces flight crew error" [5]. This associates strongly into the anticipation potential from resilience engineering, where the anticipation of threats (based on previously learned experience and information) is made to mitigate and monitor. Hollnagel delineates the difference between anticipation and monitoring [20] by explaining that anticipation deals with that which is beyond the immediate event horizon, either something that lies further into the future or something that has no immediate relation or impact on the flight.

4.2 Monitor Errors and Responding Actions

Monitoring then, according to Hollnagel is about observing whether the flight state is changing in a way that requires a response or an intervention. This can be monitoring for threats which were first anticipated, or where TEM actions to manage subsequently led

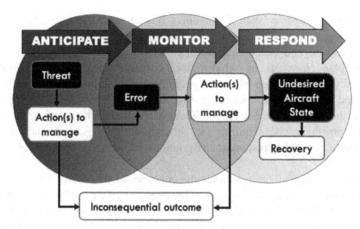

Fig. 3. The TEM model (simplified flow diagram) overlaid with the Resilient Potentials (Venn diagram)

to an error. Errors are actions (or inactions) which lead to a deviation from intentions or expectations. Errors are categorised into aircraft handling errors, procedural errors, and communication errors. Klinect et al. [5] explain that threats come 'at' the crew - which crew can work to anticipate, whereas errors come 'from' the crew - which crew should monitor for. The development of monitoring cues is essential for resilient performance in everyday work.

Error management is a driving force behind TEM and subsequently, the resilient potentials encompass error anticipation and monitoring, whilst response potential manages error 'capture' actions.

4.3   Respond with Actions to Errors and Undesired Aircraft States

The response to errors, if successful may lead to an inconsequential outcome. However, if the response is insufficient or absent, can result in an undesired aircraft state. These are categorised into aircraft handling, ground handling and incorrect aircraft configurations. The response potential is crucial in resilient performance for being able to handle disturbances to the flight.

It should also be strongly noted that whilst the TEM model is linear, the capacity for crew to learn should take place throughout, allowing new experience gained to be further disseminated, creating new understanding and anticipation of threats.

5   Example Application

An example of how Threat and Error Management can be deeply integrated into pilots' work is through planning and briefing models. An example is the '*STC*' briefing model [21], which is constructed around a foundation of the resilient potentials of 'anticipate', 'monitor' and 'respond'. The briefing is broken into four segments or steps. The '*situation*' is a pre-briefed segment conducted prior to the main '*strategic*' plan (**S**), '*tactical*' plan (**T**), and '*contingency*' plan (**C**) modules. It is designed to identify threats-first and foster crew communication through a framework of briefing an overview of 'where we are' (the situation*)*, and then a more detailed 'what our plan is' (*strategic)*, 'how we'll execute the plan' (*tactical)* and 'what we'll do outside the plan' (*contingency)* (Fig. 4). The three key resilient potentials are structured as integral pillars to the brief with the *situation* and *strategic* modules **anticipating** threats and establishing a broad strategic plan. Then, the *strategic* and *tactical* modules establishing the boundaries of the strategic plan, and **monitoring** cues requiring tactical intervention. Lastly, the tactical and contingency modules priming **responses** in deviations outside the boundaries of anticipated work.

The *STC* briefing model combines the concepts of threat and error management with the potentials needed for resilience. However, as depicted in Fig. 4, it's recognised that each of the three core modules of the *STC* brief does not align solely with the three resilient potentials of anticipate, monitor, and respond. Instead, there is an overlap between the three resilient potentials and the four briefing modules. Through the briefing process, the crew anticipate threats and strategy with their *strategic* plan, which sets monitoring cues and boundaries through the *strategic* and *tactical* plans. This builds upon the crews' capacity to respond through the *tactical* and *contingency* plan. An improved conversational flow is developed between each module, strengthening resilient potentials. It maintains foundational strength of the resilient potentials, particularly where the *strategic* and *tactical* modules are foundationally constructed of two resilient potentials whilst the *situation* is anticipated, and *contingencies* responded with.

This example of how the resilient potentials can be applied directly into the every-day work of pilots could show improvements to threat awareness and mitigation strategies and improve communication between crew. This is particularly important as airlines recover from the COVID-19 pandemic and re-train their flight crew [22]. This concept of work directly operationalises Carroll & Malmquist's recommendation that the attributes of resilience performance be operationalised directly into flight crews' procedures [23].

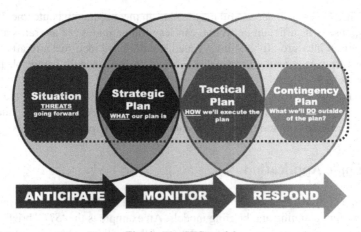

Fig. 4. The STC model

6 Future Development

The future for resilience engineering in aviation is strong. Supra-national regulators such as EASA are implementing early editions of regulation requiring training into resilience. Future evolutions of this regulation, plus from other regulators are anticipated.

Given the widespread adoption of threat and error management in aviation, future research, and development into how the resilient potentials can be operationalised into training, procedures and practices would assist airlines in meeting their regulatory obligations along with fostering resilient performance amongst their flight crew. This is particularly needed in training evaluation, such as competency based training and evidence based training.

An exciting evolution of resilience has been made by American Airlines' Learning and Improvement Team (LIT) [24, 25]. They have utilised the success of their Line Oriented Safety Audit program as a vehicle to develop a Safety-II audit program. LIT proficiencies were developed from the resilient potentials specific to the program's needs and a series of observations and interviews conducted to gather data. LIT offers evolutionary development from Safety-I's TEM and LOSA approach into Safety-II flight safety auditing. One further example of this shift to a Safety II approach is the Learning Review Safety Audit [26]. Flight crew performance in a normal line environment is disclosed by the flight crew, facilitated by individuals who have been specially selected and trained to conduct Operational Learning Reviews (OLRs) – these facilitators utilise TEM and systems thinking to identify resilient behaviours from the context being provided by the flight crew – this can then be analysed alongside data sources such as flight data, creating a much wider understanding of "work as done" in the operation.

7 Conclusion

TEM largely contributes to the resilience of a system through its emphasis on human factors. By training and supporting crew members to effectively anticipate, monitor and respond to threats and errors, TEM's synergy with the resilient potentials helps to improve the overall performance and decision-making skills of flight crews. This improved performance can be critical in the response to an undesired aircraft state, as it helps to ensure that corrective actions are taken at the appropriate time to lead to inconsequential outcomes or minimise their impact in recovery. Future development and integration between the two concepts of TEM and resilience is recommended to regulators and airlines, and Safety-II audit programs encouraged to develop into maturity and widespread use.

References

1. ICAO: Manual on Human Performance (HP) for Regulators (2021). https://www.icao.int/safety/OPS/OPS-Section/Documents/Advance-unedited.Doc.10151.alltext.en.pdf
2. European Aviation Safety Agency: Annex II to Decision 2015/022/R (2015). https://www.easa.europa.eu/en/downloads/19874/en

3. Hollnagel, E.: The four cornerstones of resilience engineering. In: Nameth, C., Hollnagel, E., Dekker, S. (eds.) Resilience Engineering Perspectives: Preparation and Restoration, pp. 117–133. Ashgate, Hampshire (2009). https://doi.org/10.1201/9781315244389-7

4. Dekker, S., Lundström, J.: From threat and error management (TEM) to resilience. Hum. Factors Aerosp. Safety **6**(3), 261–273 (2006)

5. Klinect, J., Merritt, A.: Defensive flying for pilots: an introduction to threat and error management (2006)

6. MacLeod, N.: Crew Resource Management Training: A Competence-based Approach for Airline Pilots. CRC Press, Boca Raton (2021). https://doi.org/10.1201/9781003138839

7. Hollnagel, E.: Epilogue: RAG. The resilience analysis grid. In: Pariès, J., Wreathall, J., Hollnagel, E., Woods, D.D. (eds.) Resilience Engineering in Practice, pp. 275–296. Ashgate, Hampshire (2011). https://doi.org/10.1201/9781317065265

8. Helmreich, R., Klinect, J., Wilhelm, J.: Models of threat, error, and CRM in flight operations. In: Proceedings of the Tenth International Symposium on Aviation Psychology, Columbus, Ohio (1999)

9. ICAO: Human Factors Training Manual (1998). https://elibrary.icao.int/

10. Klinect, J., Murray, P., Merritt, A., Helmreich, R.: Line operations safety audit - definition and operating characteristics. In: Proceedings of the 12th International Symposium on Aviation Psychology, Dayton, pp. 663–668 (2003)

11. Klinect, J.: Line Operations Safety Audit - A Cockpit Observation Methodology for Monitoring Commercial Airline Safety Performance (2005)

12. Dismukes, R.K., Berman, B.A., Loukopoulos, L.: The Limits of Expertise. Ashgate, Hampshire (2007). https://doi.org/10.4324/9781315238654

13. Harper, M.: The aviation safety action program: assessment of the threat and error management model for improving the quantity and quality of reported information (2011). http://hdl.handle.net/2152/ETD-UT-2011-05-3061

14. Woods, D.D., Hollnagel, E.: Prologue: resilience engineering concepts. In: Hollnagel, E., Woods, D.D., Leveson, N. (eds.) Resilience Engineering: Concepts and Precepts (2006). https://doi.org/10.1201/9781315605685

15. Nemeth, C.P., Herrera, I.: Building change: resilience engineering after ten years. Reliab. Eng. Syst. Safe. **141**, 1–4 (2015). https://doi.org/10.1016/j.ress.2015.04.006

16. Woods, D.D., Hollnagel, E.: Epilogue: resilience engineering precepts. In: Hollnagel, E., Woods, D.D., Leveson, N. (eds.) Resilience Engineering: Concepts and Precepts, pp. 347–358 (2006). https://doi.org/10.1201/9781315605685-30

17. Cook, R.I., Nemeth, C.P.: "Those found responsible have been sacked": Some observations on the usefulness of error. Cogn. Technol. Work **12**, 87–93 (2010). https://doi.org/10.1007/s10111-010-0149-0

18. Dekker, S.W.A., Nyce, J.M., Myers, D.J.: The little engine who could not: "rehabilitating" the individual in safety research. Cogn. Technol. Work **15**, 277–282 (2013). https://doi.org/10.1007/s10111-012-0228-5

19. Dekker, S.: Foundations of Safety Science. CRC Press, Boca Raton (2019). https://doi.org/10.4324/9781351059794

20. Hollnagel, E.: Safety-II in Practice. Routledge, New York (2018). https://doi.org/10.4324/9781315201023

21. Mizzi, A., McCarthy, P.: Flight crew briefings with resilience engineering capacities - the STC model. Pre-Print ResearchGate (2023). https://doi.org/10.13140/RG.2.2.13499.08480

22. Mizzi, A., Lohmann, G., Junior, G.C.: The role of self-study in addressing competency decline among airline pilots during the COVID-19 pandemic. Hum. Factors 00187208221113614 (2022). https://doi.org/10.1177/00187208221113614

23. Carroll, M., Malmquist, S.: Resilient performance in aviation. In: Nemeth, C.P., Hollnagel, E. (eds.) Advancing Resilient Performance, pp. 85–95. Springer, Cham (2022). https://doi.org/10.1007/978-3-030-74689-6_7
24. American Airlines: Trailblazers into Safety - II: American Airlines' Learning and Improvement Team (2020). https://www.skybrary.aero/sites/default/files/bookshelf/5964.pdf
25. American Airlines: Charting a New Approach: What Goes Well and Why at American Airlines (2021). https://skybrary.aero/sites/default/files/bookshelf/AA%20LIT%20White%20Paper%20II%20-%20SEP%202021.pdf
26. McCarthy, P.: The application of safety II in commercial aviation – the operational learning review (OLR). In: Harris, D., Li, W.-C. (eds.) HCII 2020. LNCS (LNAI), vol. 12187, pp. 368–383. Springer, Cham (2020). https://doi.org/10.1007/978-3-030-49183-3_29

A Preparedness Drill Scenario Development and System Safety Competency Assessment Based on the STAMP Model

Apostolos Zeleskidis, Stavroula Charalampidou[✉], Ioannis M. Dokas, and Basil Papadopoulos

Democritus University of Thrace, 69100 Xanthi, Greece
{azeleski,stcharal}@civil.duth.gr

Abstract. This paper proposes an approach for generating operational preparedness drill scenarios accompanied by a safety competency evaluation process. The approach combines the "Engineering for Humans" extension of the STPA (Systems Theoretic Process Analysis) hazard analysis introduced by France (2017) to identify causal scenarios incorporating human behavior and human-computer interaction to any unsafe control actions performed by the human operators in the processes of the Risk and Resilience Assessment Centre of the Region of Eastern Macedonia and Thrace. The safety requirements identified via the STPA extension will be utilized then to generate preparedness drill scenarios and, at the same time, will be used to set up the Real-Time Safety Level (RealTSL) calculation methodology to assess the safety level of the process during preparedness drills. The paper will also present results of operational scenarios and how these scenarios are used in the initial steps of RealTSL to be applied effectively during future preparedness drills to assess the safety competency of the system under study.

Keywords: Preparedness Drills · Safety Competency · Human Factors · STPA · RealTSL

1 Introduction

Due to the rising frequency of natural disaster events in recent years on a global scale, there is a need to effectively support decision-making in all aspects of the risk management cycle. The Risk and Resilience Assessment Centre (RiskAC) of the Eastern Macedonia and Thrace Region (REMTh) in Greece is a new research infrastructure aiming at supporting decision-making in the phases of repression and prevention of risks that may occur. The Centre comprises of ten research teams that work together to collect and analyze data, to produce libraries of hazard maps, and assessments about the magnitude and effects of possible natural and disastrous technological scenarios that may occur in the geographical limits of REMTh.

Hazardous scenarios and assessments about the magnitude and effects of earthquakes, forest fires, floods, landslides, rockfalls, earth liquefaction, and accidents involving dangerous substances in factories located in REMTh are some types of outputs that

© The Author(s), under exclusive license to Springer Nature Switzerland AG 2023
D. Harris and W.-C. Li (Eds.): HCII 2023, LNAI 14017, pp. 484–500, 2023.
https://doi.org/10.1007/978-3-031-35392-5_37

the Centre can produce for decision support, thanks to the research teams of the Centre, given that each one is specialized into a specific type of hazard.

The novelty of the Centre is the holistic approach of its produced hazard maps and assessments, meaning that a potential hazard, depending on its characteristics and context of occurrence, may be a contributing factor to another hazard in terms of time and space. For example, a forest fire in a specific geographical location may contribute to the occurrence of a flood after some period in the same or a nearby geographic location.

The Centre has three operational modes. The idle, the operational, and the evaluation mode. During idle mode, the Centre's main activity is to generate new hazard maps and assessments to enrich its libraries with possible future hazardous scenarios. In the case of hazard occurrence, the Centre shifts its mode from idle to operational. Suppose the hazard has been analyzed, and its assessments are available in the Centre's libraries. In that case, analyses are passed on, upon request, to the decision makers to have, as early as possible, a sense of the progression of the adverse effects of the hazard over time or its expected magnitude.

Suppose the hazard has not been analyzed; then, depending on the nature and characteristics of the event, the Centre can collect data from the affected area, create hazard maps, and assess the event's magnitude and effect. In that case, the decision-makers will receive the outputs after several hours or days. During the assessment mode, the research teams evaluate the Centre's performance during its operational mode and collect data to validate the assessments submitted to decision-makers. The teams can then recommend suggestions for improvement and identify lessons learned to improve the performance of the Centre in the future.

One critical subsystem during the idle and operational modes of the Centre is the Environmental Monitoring and Scanning (EMS) subsystem. Its main responsibility is to scan the wider environment of REMTh for data and information indicating events or disturbances, which may indicate the occurrence of a hazard or signs and information indicating that a hazard has occurred. Another responsibility of the EMS subsystem is to receive and process any request from decision makers, such as Regional Civil Protection officials, to the Centre and then forward the request to the appropriate expert groups based on hazard characteristics and type to be processed further.

There is a need to train those involved in the EMS subsystem via periodic preparedness drills to enhance its safe and continuous operation and assess its safety competency, since observations through adequate data collection from these exercises make it possible to monitor situations closer to reality and analyze the resilience of team performance (Gomes et al. 2014). The problem however is that disaster exercise evaluation is lacking analytical methodologies presented together with evidence of their use, as well as methodologies based on systems thinking as per the literature review by Beerens and Tehler (2016). To solve this problem de Carvalho et al. (2018) proposed an ethnographic based approach to find and discuss gaps between the instructions and the activities carried out during the exercise, highlighting the differences between work as done (WAD) and work as imagined (WAI), as it was instantiated in the prescriptions of standard operating procedures.

The aim of this paper is to investigate whether the Systems-Theoretic Accident Model and Processes (STAMP) model and its tools can provide a useful approach for the development of preparedness drills in sociotechnical systems and assess their safety competency. Up to date STAMP tools were utilized by Khastgir et al. (2021) to generate testing scenarios for automated driving systems. Kafoutis and Dokas (2021) incorporated STAMP tools to evaluate emergency response plans but, to this day STAMP tools have not been utilized on the topic of preparedness drills.

This paper will present a novel approach for generating preparedness drills using human factors and STAMP, evaluating these drills, and identifing the training needed for the operators of the EMS subsystem of the RiskAC infrastructure. This is the first time STAMP tools have been utilized in the domain of preparedness drills generation and evaluation. The proposed approach is demonstrated using the EMS subsystem of RiskAC and the evaluation of such drills is demonstrated using a drill for a technological disaster event.

2 Methods

2.1 Requirements

From the point of view of RiskAC the following requirements of such an approach must be fulfilled.

1. Generate challenging periodic drills.
2. Generate material to train the actors and enhance their safety competency over time.
3. Evaluate the competency of actors involved in the drills in terms of safety.

In response to the above requirements, STPA and its "Engineering for Humans" extension are proposed as tools for generating periodic drills. The EWaSAP analysis is utilized to satisfy the second requirement, namely the generation of training material for the actors involved in the EMS subsystem of RiskAC. Lastly, RealTSL is utilized to evaluate the competency of the actors of EMS in terms of safety after the drills have concluded. These methods will be described briefly in the following section.

2.2 STAMP, STPA and "Engineering for Humans" Extension of STPA

STAMP. The STAMP accident model was created by Leveson (2004). The goal of the accident model is to enhance systems safety by utilizing systems thinking principles. According to the STAMP accident model, safety should be viewed as an emergent property of systems. STAMP provides the foundation of toolsets for defining safety constraints that determine potential hazardous states and interactions in given system contexts that ideally should not occur during its operation phase.

Based on STAMP a system must be modeled using feedback control loops. A model of a feedback control loop is depicted in Fig. 1. It is comprised of a controlled process that receives inputs and produces outputs, a controller who, by utilizing a control algorithm and mental/process model, is in charge of maintaining the safe and productive operation of the controlled process, actuators that enforce the actions taken by the controller to affect the control process and finally sensors that provide the information needed by the controller to maintain the controlled process to acceptable levels effectively.

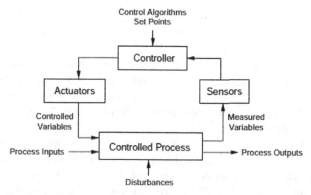

Fig. 1. A standard system feedback control loop (Leveson 2004)

STPA. The Systems Theoretic Process Analysis (STPA) (Leveson and Thomas 2018) is the hazard analysis approach based on STAMP. With STPA analysts can identify, among other things, under which operational circumstances and contexts the controllers in the system could enforce unsafe control actions. The term "unsafe" here refers to the occurrence of losses at a system level, including loss of life, injuries, financial losses, productivity losses, etc.

STPA is comprised of the following steps:

1. This step aims at identifying the system boundaries, the events that constitute system losses, and the system states called hazards, which, when paired with the most detrimental to environmental safety conditions, will lead to those losses, and lastly, the system-level safety constraints that are generated from those hazards.
2. The aim then is to create a model of the system using feedback control loops in a comprehensive, hierarchical safety control structure with all the appropriate controllers, control algorithms, process models, actuators, sensors, and controlled processes.
3. The identification of unsafe control actions follows. In this step, the analyst identifies system states or operational contexts in which control actions that may be enforced, not enforced provided too early/late, out of order, stopped too soon, or applied too long by a controller may lead to hazards.
4. The identification of the loss scenarios (also referred to as causal scenarios) that would lead to control actions being improperly executed or unsafe control actions occurring.

"Engineering for Humans". Extension of STPA. The "Engineering for Humans" extension of STPA was introduced by France (2017). The extension implements human factors research to STPA by expanding the identification of loss scenarios in the 4th step of STPA. This is achieved by implementing three additional parts to the modeling of human controllers, as well as introducing new questions that can be used to identify additional loss scenarios.

The three parts are as follows: 1) Control action selection, 2) Mental models which include process state, process behavior and environment and 3) Mental model updates.

The control action selection part refers to the control algorithm of the human controller and aims at identifying why a particular control action was chosen. The questions recommended for the control action selection part are: "How did the controller choose which control action to perform?", "What were his goals?", "How experienced was he in operating the system or similar systems" etc.

The mental models part refers to the cognitive understanding of the system and its environment by the operator. The mental models are divided into mentals model of process state, mental models of process behavior and mental model of the environment. The questions recommended for the mental models part are: "What does the operator know or believe about the system?", "Does the operator know the current state of the system?", "What causes the system to change states?", "How will the system behave in its current state?", "Does the operator know what he can do in the current state of the system?", "Does the operator know his actions affect system behavior?", "Is the operator familiar with this environment?", "What does the operator believe other operators in the environment will do" etc.

The mental model updates part refers to the process by which new elements of the operating environment are incorporated into the mental model of the operator. The questions recommended for the mental model updates part are: "How does the operator have their current beliefs and knowledge?", "What training or experience does the operator have?" etc.

2.3 EWaSAP

EWaSAP (Dokas et al. 2013) is an STPA extension for identifying early warning signs based on the STAMP accident model that indicates the violation of the safety constraints (Leveson 2016). It is focused, among other things, on the identification of the appropriate sensors that should be installed in the system, together with the data (i.e., signs) that should be collected by its controllers to comprehend which system states identified by STPA hazard analysis occurred or not in a given time moment. The steps of the EWaSAP analysis are shown below:

1. The first step of EWaSAP takes place during the definition of system boundaries by STPA, and it aims at identifying entities outside of the system boundaries (e.g.., local authorities, first responders, company managers, etc.), who should be informed about the occurrence or progression of hazardous events in the system. This step is most important when dealing with safety critical systems where accidents significantly affect society (e.g., Seveso establishments, power plants, airports, etc.). This step helps to minimize the potential consequences of those hazardous events by lowering response times and delays due to information distribution.
2. The second step of EWaSAP consists of identifying the data (i.e., the warning signs) that the controllers need to perceive to be able to comprehend the occurrence of unsafe system states described by STPA (losses, hazards, UCA's, loss scenarios), the violation of safety constraints derived by those states and the violation of the assumptions made during the analysis. Next, it identifies the sensory equipment (e.g., proximity sensors, surveillance systems, etc.) that the system must have to collect that data.
3. The third step of EWaSAP has the goal of employing "awareness actions," namely the transmission of appropriately coded warnings and alert messages, which must be

perceived by controllers at a higher level of system hierarchy or by other controllers outside of the boundaries of the system under study, to make them aware of the migration of the system under study from a safe to an unsafe state.

2.4 RealTSL

RealTSL is a methodology that combines the above analyses (STPA, EWaSAP) under the STAMP accident model and, together with a non-stochastic mathematical model. It aims at providing a real-time assessment of the safety level of systems. The safety level is defined in RealTSL as "the ordered set of the most detrimental to safety sequences of unsafe system states that result in an accident and are ordered according to the severity of their resulting accident" (Zeleskidis et al. 2022). To calculate this the two phases of RealTSL should be executed. The first is the preparation phase, where the inputs of the methodology are collected, and the mathematical model is calibrated based on them. The second phase is the execution phase, where real-time data from the system are used in conjunction with the calibrated mathematical model to calculate its safety level.

The inputs of the preparation phase and their use are shown below:

1. Losses, Hazards, Unsafe Control Actions, and Loss Scenarios: These are system states that are causally connected via the STPA analysis. They are used to form an acyclic diagram that is the basis for the RealTSL mathematical model. The RealTSL acyclic diagram is, in essence, a transformation of the STPA hazard analysis results into a form that the mathematics of RealTSL can use.
2. Time ranges: The time ranges indicate the possible range of time (minimum to maximum) that it would take for the system to transition from one unsafe system state to another, as described in the STPA analysis. They are used to populate the RealTSL acyclic diagram with time information for every connection between two states, as described in the STPA analysis.
3. Mathematical operation: Mathematical operations are, for example, minimum (MIN), maximum (MAX), mean-average (MEAN), etc. The mathematical operation aims at narrowing the time ranges to single values for every connection between system states. The operation is selected by those responsible for applying RealTSL in the system under study.
4. EWaSAP outputs: The data that must be perceived during the operation phase by the controllers in the system to comprehend whether the system states identified by the STPA analysis have occurred or are occurring. The early warning signs defined by EWaSAP provide the set of data that must be perceived by the sensors of the systems to be aware of the existence of unsafe states, according to STPA.

During the execution phase of RealTSL, the system operates as designed. The sensors transmit data indicating if and when a system state identified by the STPA analysis has occurred. RealTSL utilizes the sensor data to comprehend to what extent the system is in a hazardous state. To do this, RealTSL is using the acyclic diagram and its parameters to calculate the most detrimental to safety sequences of unsafe system state transitions according to a) the time left until the accident occurs, b) the progress of the sequence in terms of system state hierarchy (losses > hazards > UCAs > loss scenarios) and c) the severity of the resulting accidents.

For more details about the methodology and an in-depth analysis of its mathematical model, the reader is referred to the work by Zeleskidis et al. (2022).

3   The Environmental Monitoring and Scanning Subsystem

The EMS subsystem of RiskAC has the responsibility of constantly observing the social media, news outlets etc. of the REMTh region for signs of potentially hazardous events. The main goal of the subsystem is to make RiskAC aware of hazardous events before an official request is made from decision makers.

The EMS subsystem is composed of multiple human controllers, which in essence are selected RiskAC employees with specific training in identifying the appropriate signs that indicate the existence of potential or ongoing hazardous events, verifying those signs and producing detailed awareness actions, namely warnings and alerts. The "Warning" awareness action is meant for events that are of lower severity, events that require more monitoring to determine all their parameters and events that will potentially take some amount of time before becoming hazardous (i.e. groundwater contamination). The "Alert" awareness action is meant for events that require immediate attention from the scientific teams of RiskAC, e.g., large forest fires near populated areas, industrial accidents etc.

Those will be transmitted to the RiskAC coordinator who will coordinate and consult the appropriate teams of RiskAC in conducting the appropriate analyses. Another responsibility of the human controllers in the subsystem is to receive a hazard analysis request of an event occurring in the Region from Official Agencies, such as the Civil Protection Agency, collect relevant information about the event and transmit those to the RiskAC coordinator.

4   Demonstration

4.1   Applying STPA and its Extension to Generate Challenging Periodic Drills

The "Engineering for Humans" extension of STPA requires the application of STPA to the system, beginning with the definition of the losses and system level hazards for the EMS subsystem. The results are shown in Table 1. The symbolism in the hazard row identifies if the system state is a loss (L) or hazard (H) as well as any connections this system state has with other system states in brackets [].

Following that, the control structure of the system is presented. The controllers in this system are the human controllers of the EMS subsystem. The "controlled" process is the REMTh environment. The aim of the EMS subsystem is to provide the function of environmental scanning of REMTh. Thus, the EMS controllers do not provide control actions as per the STPA analysis to control the behavior of REMTh (i.e., the controlled process) but as per EWaSAP, they do provide awareness actions to controllers in parallel or higher levels of the RiskAC system hierarchy. The EMS controller thus has mental models of their environment and the process that they are monitoring, a control algorithm that helps them determine the type of awareness action to provide, actuators to provide

Table 1. Losses and System Level Hazards

Losses		Hazards	
L-1	Loss trust by the public and stakeholders	H-1	The RiskAC coordinator is not made aware of the existence of a hazardous event going on in the region by the EMS subsystem. [L-1, L-2, L-3]
L-2	Loss of resources	H-2	The EMS subsystem notifies the RiskAC coordinator, while there is no hazardous event present. [L-2]
L-3	Loss of mission	H-3	The RiskAC coordinator is notified about the occurrence of an event by a formal request made to RiskAC. [L-2, L-3]

these awareness actions and sensors to receive feedback about the process they are monitoring.

There are two distinct feedback mechanisms for the controller, one being the feedback streams (news outlets, visual observations, social media and RiskAC sensors) and the second being requests from agencies, industries, and the public. While there are no control actions given by the controller, the controller provides two awareness actions: "warning" and "alert". The control structure of the EMS subsystem is shown in Fig. 2.

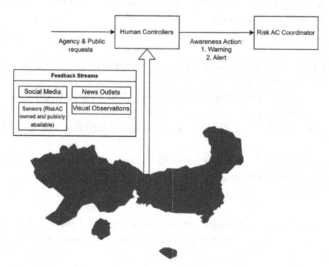

Fig. 2. Safety control structure of the EMS subsystem of RiskAC.

Some of the UCAs that were generated for the awareness actions "Alert" and "Warning" are:

1. UCA-1: Controller provides the awareness action "warning" while they should have provided the awareness action "alert" [H-2].
2. UCA-2: Controller provides the awareness action "alert", while there is no hazard or a preparedness drill occurring. Which leads to hazard [H-2].
3. UCA-8: Controller does not give the awareness action "warning" while there are records indicating a hazardous event in the REMTh. Which leads to hazard [H-1].

The application of the STPA analysis concludes with the generation of the loss scenarios (i.e., Step 4 of STPA). In the proposed approach, this step is replaced by the "Engineering for Humans" extension of STPA. Some scenarios derived by the STPA extension, with their corresponding UCAs, are presented below. These scenarios were generated using the questions provided by the "Engineering for Humans" extension STPA and as such are categorized according to the three parts of human controllers identified by the extension.

UCA-1: Controller provides the awareness action "warning" while they should have provided the awareness action "alert"

Awareness action selection

Scenario 1, for UCA-1: They were provided with irrelevant information.
Scenario 2, for UCA-1: Between the time needed to validate the information, new data came in that required the "alert" control action.
Scenario 3, for UCA-1: They were not properly trained in giving the control actions "warning" and "alert", they were not experienced enough in similar types of events, or they did not have the guidelines of the correct usage of "warning" or "alert".
Scenario 4, for UCA-1: They were tired or stressed.

Mental models

Scenario 5, for UCA-1: They did not want to burden RiskAC more, due to it actively monitoring other events.
Scenario 6, for UCA-1: The information was not clear enough to differentiate whether to use "alert" or "warning".
Scenario 7, for UCA-1: They believed that another controller would give the control action "alert".
Scenario 8, for UCA-1: They don't know how the RiskAC operates, and they believe that the "alert" and the "warning" action generate the same response.

Model updates

Scenario 9, for UCA-1: They were not able to monitor all the feedback streams and they missed necessary information that escalated the event to require the control action "alert".
Scenario 10, for UCA-1: They received information concerning an event but did not register it appropriately.

UCA-8: Controller does not provide the awareness action "warning" while there are records indicating a hazardous event in the REMTh.

Awareness action selection

Scenario 36, for UCA-8: They are not pleased with their work, and they want to get fired or cause disturbances.

Scenario 37, for UCA-8: They were not available when the event occurred (they were asleep, they had time off or were on break).

Mental models

Scenario 38, for UCA-8: During the validation process they concluded that the event was not real.

Scenario 39, for UCA-8: They did not recognize the event, due to them being preoccupied with other events.

Scenario 40, for UCA-8: They did not have the necessary knowledge or training to be able to associate the information with an existing event.

Scenario 41, for UCA-8: Correct information about the event came from untrustworthy sources.

Scenario 42, for UCA-8: They believed that the RiskAC was already analyzing this event.

Model updates

Scenario 43, for UCA-8: They were incorrectly ordered to cease monitoring.

Scenario 44, for UCA-8: They believed that the event occurred outside of the REMTh boundaries.

Scenario 45, for UCA-8: They did not know the spatial and temporal interactions between different hazards.

Scenario 46, for UCA-8: They had data about the event, but they lost it and decided to not inform RiskAC.

Scenario 47, for UCA-8: The event happened during a shift change.

The safety constraints generated in the different steps of the STPA analysis are not utilized by the RealTSL methodology and will not be presented in this work.

The loss scenarios presented above are used as stimuli for identifying disturbances to be included in a periodic drill scenario. Based on the context of the drill, the disturbances can be grouped and integrated to form the periodic drill scenario. For example, the stimuli from Scenario 1 "The controllers were provided with irrelevant information", can generate the disturbance "the controller, after the initial information of event occurrence will be given some irrelevant information in order to prompt them to provide the wrong type of awareness action" into a drill scenario.

When multiple scenarios are grouped, a complete drill exercise can be created. Using the Scenarios 1, 4 and 9 the following drill can be deduced: during the end of the human controllers shift, at a time they will most likely be tired, a sum of information is going to manually be provided by drill coordinators through the various feedback streams that human controllers use to monitor the region that a technological disaster has occurred. In this case, the technological disaster is a fire in a SEVESO categorized facility in the REMTh region. The information provided to the controllers contains some irrelevant information, for instance multiple phone calls to distract the controllers attention from the actual event and some information that will help the controller to categorize it as an event requiring an "alert" awareness action (e.g., that first responders to the event are experiencing breathing problems which means that evacuation of the greater area might be needed).

4.2 Applying EWaSAP to Generate Training Material for Actors

The EWaSAP analysis was conducted on the system states identified by STPA. Table 2 presents some of the EWaSAP outputs created, namely the sensory equipment and the identifying signs of unsafe system states described by STPA shown in the above section. Specifically, each row in Table 2 represents a system state determined by STPA. The first column shows the symbolism that identifies if the system state is a loss (L), hazard (H), Unsafe control action (UCA), or Loss Scenario (LS) and its identifying number. The second column shows the description of the analyzed system state as well as any connections this system state has with other system states in brackets []. The third column shows the sensory equipment needed to be present in the system to identify the occurrence of the system state. The fourth and final column presents the signs that would indicate the occurrence of the system state by the sensory equipment of the last column.

Table 2. Indicative outputs of the EWaSAP analysis applied on the EMS subsystem.

Symbols	Description	Sensory System	Identifying Sings
UCA 1	Controller provides the awareness action "warning" while they should have provided the control action "alert"	Visual checks, perception of abnormal system behavior via oral, visual, and audio channels, social media, written and verbal communication systems	Comparison of the description of the warning message with the description of the hazard on sources
UCA 8	Controller does not provide the awareness action "warning" while there are records indicating a hazardous event in the REMTh	Social media, written and verbal communication systems	Written and verbal complaints

UCA-1: Controller provides the control action "warning" while they should have provided the control action "alert"

Symbols	Description	Sensory System	Identifying Sings
LS-1	They were provided with irrelevant information	Visual checks, perception of abnormal system behavior via oral, visual and audio channels, social media, written and verbal communication systems	Suspicious website or text of the source, biased narrative of the source, contradicting information, absence of detailed descriptions, photos etc. Omission of active monitoring service during validation

(continued)

Table 2. (*continued*)

Symbols	Description	Sensory System	Identifying Sings
LS-4	They were tired or stressed	Visual checks, perception of abnormal system behavior via oral, visual and audio channels, social media, written and verbal communication systems	Active work hours, number of available coworkers, number of worker complaints
LS-6	The information was not clear enough to differentiate whether to use "alert" or "warning"	Visual checks, perception of abnormal system behavior via oral, visual and audio channels, social media, written and verbal communication systems	Discrepancy, unclear website or text of the source, biased narrative of the source, contradicting information. Absence of detailed descriptions, photos etc. Communication noise, blurry images

UCA 8: Controller does not give the control action "warning" while there are records indicating a hazardous event in the REMTh

Symbols	Description	Sensory System	Identifying Sings
LS-37	They were not available when the event occurred (they were asleep, they had time off or were on break)	Visual checks, perception of abnormal system behavior via oral, visual and audio channels, social media, written and verbal communication systems	Worker availability, inactive worker in discord server etc
LS-38	During the validation process they concluded that the event was not real	Visual checks, perception of abnormal system behavior via oral, visual and audio channels, social media, written and verbal communication systems	Collected contradicting information, validation process started
LS-40	They did not have the necessary knowledge or training to be able to associate the information with an existing event	Training records	Hours in training, hours of work experience in the position, number of guidelines available
LS-41	Correct information about the event came from untrustworthy sources	Visual checks, perception of abnormal system behavior via oral, visual and audio channels, social media, written and verbal communication systems	Collected contradicting information, validation process started

(*continued*)

Table 2. (*continued*)

Symbols	Description	Sensory System	Identifying Sings
LS-42	They believed that the RiskAC was already analyzing this event	Visual checks, perception of abnormal system behavior via oral, visual and audio channels, social media, written and verbal communication systems	Discrepancy between the state of the RiskAC and the comprehension of the state by the controller
LS-43	They were incorrectly ordered to cease monitoring	Visual checks, perception of abnormal system behavior via oral, visual and audio channels, social media, written and verbal communication systems	Discrepancy between the state of the controller and the comprehension of the state by the RiskAC
LS-44	They believed that the event occurred outside of the REMTh boundaries	Training records/ interviews	Discrepancy of the perception of the REMTh boundaries
LS-45	They did not know the spatial and temporal interactions between different hazards	Training records	Hours in training, hours of work experience in the position, number of guidelines available
LS-47	The event happened during a shift change	Shifts records	Comparison between the time of the shift change and the time the hazard occurred

With the information produced by EWaSAP one can create procedures or checklists that can be used to train the human controllers. For example, from scenario 40: "They were incorrectly ordered to cease environmental monitoring and scanning." derived from UCA-8: "Controller does not give the control action "warning" while there are records indicating a hazardous event in REMTh.", the need for proper training of the human controllers is highlighted, based on the following signs: Discrepancy between the state of the controller and the comprehension of the state by RiskAC.

This can be interpreted as a need to expand the knowledge of the controllers to be able to identify these signs and prevent the occurrence of the loss scenario.

4.3 Using RealTSL to Evaluate the Safety Competency of the EMS System via Periodic Drills

To evaluate the safety competency of the system, simulated drill exercises must be organized and executed. Before each drill, data collection via proper equipment (e.g., cameras, log files, recording of interactions etc.) must be ensured. The data to be collected and the proper equipment are identified by the EWaSAP analysis applied to the system.

After the execution of the drills the collected data are analyzed based on the RealTSL methodology.

When applying RealTSL the outputs of STPA analysis with its extension and the outputs of EWaSAP are translated to create the RealTSL acyclic graph, a portion of which is shown in Fig. 3.

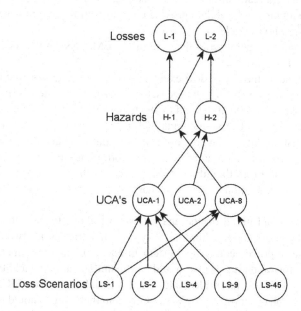

Fig. 3. Portion of the acyclic diagram for the EMS system as created by RealTSL.

During debriefing, the recorded data of the drill can be utilized to present to the actors the time duration from one unsafe system state to another with the use of the acyclic diagram. Then the actors can discuss the aspects that contributed to the migration of the system to the unsafe system states over time and to provide a first assessment of the possible time ranges which RealTSL needs to calculate the safety level of the system. The following drills are utilized then to refine the time ranges of the system state transitions, which in turn can be used as an indicator of safety competency of the actors and their performance over their participation in the drills.

The drill scenario generated in Sect. 4.1 is used as a demonstrative example of the safety competency evaluation of the approach. The drill scenario was conducted in the RiskAC system in late spring of 2022. Data logs and camera feeds were collected, stored and analyzed. A brief timeline of events taking place during the drill is presented in the following paragraph.

The virtual hazardous event took place at the end of the second shift (23:00) of the EMS controllers which takes place from 16:00 to 00:00. Five minutes later (23:05) information was planted in the feedback streams of the controllers. The human controllers identified the information concerning the event 15 min later (23:20). The controllers left a detailed report and notified the controllers of the next shift to validate and collect information about the event which took them around 5 h (05:00). At that time (05:00) the RiskAC coordinator was notified about the event and the controllers were actively scanning for additional information about the event. For this type of event official agencies will take about 15 h to provide RiskAC with a formal request for analysis of the hazard, so when at 14:00 a simulated formal request was made from civil protection, the RiskAC teams were already informed about the event and had the necessary time needed to analyze the situation to be able to provide civil protection with potential solutions by the time the request was made.

The mathematical operation in the case of the EMS system was decided to be the minimum (MIN).

In the timeline of the above drill exercise the system state described in scenario 4 (Sect. 4.1) occurred at 23:00, that state ceased to exist at 00:10 when the new shift started and occurred again at 07:00 at the end of the new shift. Scenario 47 occurred at 00:00 due to the shift change. The system state described in UCA 8 occurred at 24:00 and continued to exist till 05:00 when the event was validated by the human controllers, the alert awareness action was prepared with the appropriate information and sent to the RiskAC coordinator. From the information above it is shown that the time duration of the system state to transition between Scenario 4 and UCA 8 is 6 h, Scenario 47 and UCA 8 is 5 h.

At the debrief and based on the analysis shown above to the actors utilizing the RealTSL acyclic graph and the duration of system state transitions, two decisions were made about the improvement of the system in terms of safety competency. Namely, that procedures for validating events should be streamlined utilizing additional feedback streams directly with first responders and officials to reduce the time UCA 8 was active (in this drill 5 h) and secondly for the RiskAC system that efforts should be made to aim at developing memorandum of cooperation with first responders and the civil protection agency to reduce the time it will take to make requests to RiskAC about ongoing events.

5 Conclusions

This paper presented a novel methodology with the aim of producing periodic drill scenarios for systems, training material for the actors involved, and evaluating the safety competency of the system in these drills after their completion. With the proposed methodology, STAMP tools were combined in a novel manner to achieve these aims. Specifically, STPA and its "Engineering for Humans" extension were used to provide stimuli and identify disturbances that were then grouped and integrated to form drill scenarios, EWaSAP was used to determine procedures under which the actors involved in the system can be trained to prevent unsafe system states from occurring and finally, RealTSL was implemented to provide an evaluation of the systems' safety competency during the drills created by STPA and its extension.

This novel methodology was demonstrated on the EMS critical subsystem of the RiskAC infrastructure by producing and evaluating a drill scenario as well as producing training procedures for its controllers. Another novelty of this approach is that the usefulness of the EWaSAP methodology was highlighted when applied to systems whose purpose is environmental monitoring and scanning.

Based on the above it can be concluded that STAMP based tools can be utilized in this manner, for this purpose.

However, there are limitations to this methodology and additional work needs to be conducted before organizations can be familiarized with those tools. Initially, while some organizations might be familiar with the STPA analysis, the "Engineering for Humans" extension of STPA, the EWaSAP analysis and the RealTSL methodology are not widespread, and their application might be flawed due to lack of experience in their use. Also, the application of those tools to complex sociotechnical systems will take a significant amount of time and resources, due to the need of incorporation of the required sensors and data collection systems needed to conduct safety capability evaluation with the RealTSL methodology. Future works aiming at enhancing the smoother and effortless integration of the methods presented in this paper will be valuable.

Acknowledgments. We acknowledge support of this work by the project "Risk and Resilience Assessment Center –Prefecture of East Macedonia and Thrace -Greece." (MIS 5047293) which is implemented under the Action "Reinforcement of the Research and Innovation Infrastructure", funded by the Operational Programme "Competitiveness, Entrepreneurship and Innovation" (NSRF 2014–2020) and co-financed by Greece and the European Union (European Regional Development Fund).

Co-financed by Greece and the European Union

References

Beerens, R.J.J., Tehler, H.: Scoping the field of disaster exercise evaluation-a literature overview and analysis. Int. J. Disast. Risk Reduct. **19**, 413–446 (2016)

de Carvalho, P.V.R., Righi, A.W., Huber, G.J., Lemos, C.D.F., Jatoba, A., Gomes, J.O.: Reflections on work as done (WAD) and work as imagined (WAI) in an emergency response organization: a study on firefighters training exercises. Appl. Ergon. **68**, 28–41 (2018)

Gomes, J.O., Borges, M.R., Huber, G.J., Carvalho, P.V.R.: Analysis of the resilience of team performance during a nuclear emergency response exercise. Appl. Ergon. **45**(3), 780–788 (2014)

Kafoutis, G.C.E., Dokas, I.M.: MIND-VERSA: a new methodology for IdentifyiNg and determining loopholes and the completeness value of emergency ResponSe plAns. Saf. Sci. **136**, 105154 (2021)

Khastgir, S., Brewerton, S., Thomas, J., Jennings, P.: Systems approach to creating test scenarios for automated driving systems. Reliab. Eng. Syst. Saf. **215**, 107610 (2021)

Leveson, N.G.: Engineering a Safer World: Systems Thinking Applied to Safet, p. 560. The MIT Press, Cambridge (2016)

Leveson, N.G., Thomas, J.P.: STPA Handbook. Cambridge, MA, USA (2018)

Zeleskidis, A., Dokas, I.M., Papadopoulos, B.K.: Knowing the safety level of a system in real-time: an extended mathematical model of the STAMP-based RealTSL methodology. Saf. Sci. **152**, 105739 (2022)

Study of Psychological Stress Among Air Traffic Controllers

Zhaoning Zhang[1], Zhuochen Shi[1(✉)], Ning Li[2], Yiyang Zhang[3], and Xiangrong Xu[4]

[1] Air Traffic Management Academy, Civil Aviation University of China, Tianjin 300300, China
786870452@qq.com
[2] Air Traffic Control Industry Management Office, Civil Aviation Administration of China, Beijing 100010, China
[3] College of Arts and Sciences, Embry-Riddle Aeronautical University, Daytona Beach, FL 32114, USA
[4] Zhejiang Low-Altitude Flight Service Center Co., Ltd., Hangzhou 311600, China

Abstract. This study aims to investigate the psychological stress experienced by air traffic controllers in order to improve their well-being and ensure safe and efficient air transportation. The research approach consists of three main steps. Firstly, the daily work content of controllers is analyzed and divided into three categories: work factors, management factors, and personal factors. Based on this analysis, an index system is developed comprising 12 factor indicators that can influence controller psychological stress. Secondly, a questionnaire is designed based on the Occupational Stress Indicator (OSI) and the controller's psychological stress influence factor index. The questionnaire includes two parts: a test to determine the level of psychological stress and a ranking of the importance of each factor indicator. Finally, a questionnaire survey is conducted among air traffic controllers, and the collected data is analyzed to identify patterns and trends. The results show that 92% of air traffic controllers experience some level of psychological stress, with stress levels increasing with age and working time. Based on the findings, the paper proposes measures to mitigate the negative effects of psychological stress on air traffic controllers.

Keywords: Air Traffic Management · Controller · Psychological Stress · Index System · Human Factors

1 Introduction

The work of air traffic controllers is critical for ensuring safe and efficient air transportation. Given the high-pressure nature of their job, controllers are subject to various stresses that can impact the quality of their work. Among these stresses, psychological stress is of particular importance since it can have a significant influence on controllers' performance. Addressing controllers' psychological stress is thus essential to enhancing their work attitude and the quality of their services. To this end, it is imperative to undertake a thorough investigation of the sources of psychological stress affecting controllers. This research can identify effective management strategies and work environment improvements that can enhance control safety and efficiency.

© The Author(s), under exclusive license to Springer Nature Switzerland AG 2023
D. Harris and W.-C. Li (Eds.): HCII 2023, LNAI 14017, pp. 501–519, 2023.
https://doi.org/10.1007/978-3-031-35392-5_38

Foreign scholars have a lot of achievements in the study of controllers' stress. As early as 1978, Rose et al. [1] described the main variables assessed in all participating controllers, including differences in endocrine, cardiovascular, and behavioral responses to work, occurrence of major life events, work attitudes and morale, availability of psychological support, usefulness, work commitment, and performance. In 1988, Cooper et al. [2] proposed the Occupational Stress Indicator (Occupational stress Indicator, OSI) to measure occupational stress and then classified it into 6 domains based on 167 items. In 1993, Rose et al. [3] used random regression models to assess individual differences in behavioral, cardiovascular, and endocrine responses to different workloads in 381 air traffic controllers. In 1997, Rodahl K et al. [4] assessed work stress by continuously recording the heart rate of 31 air traffic controllers at seven airports in Norway and showed that the work stress of all types of air traffic controllers was within reasonable limits. 2022, Špiljak Bruno et al. [5] concluded from a study of the involvement of neuroimmune factors in the complex response of the organism to psychological stress that the measurement of academic measurement of stress levels during stress can improve our understanding of the nature and impact of stressful events in the student population and prevent adverse reactions to long-term stress, such as reduced immune response and increased anxiety. In 2022, Liu Cong et al. [6] constructed a system of risk indicators by analyzing the causes of human resource attrition, and established a PLS structural equation of risk evaluation model for employee psychological stress and analyzed with corresponding cases. In China, in 2015, Liu Qiang [7] analyzed and studied the stress and behavioral errors of air traffic controllers, specifically in several aspects such as work stress, psychological stress and occupational risk stress. In the same year, Xu Hongjia et al. [8] used whole-group sampling to investigate controllers' occupational stress and obtained the conclusion that there was a correlation between air traffic controllers' occupational stress and burnout through logistic regression analysis, and controllers with occupational stress had a stronger sense of burnout. In 2021, Lin Yanfei et al. [9] collected four physiological signals from 21 university students in school. In 2021, Zheng Xiaoyu [10] studied and analyzed the physiological fatigue and psychological fatigue indices of air traffic controllers in different age groups through simulation experiments and proposed corresponding prevention as well as mitigation measures.

Previous studies on air traffic controllers' stress, both domestically and internationally, have mainly focused on exploring the relationship between controller stress and specific influencing factors or simply assessing controller stress levels. Although there have been studies on methods and models for assessing psychological stress in other fields, research specifically focused on measuring and analyzing controller psychological stress remains scarce. In this paper, we seek to address this gap by establishing a comprehensive index system for measuring controller psychological stress from multiple perspectives. Using a psychological test assessment method, we also develop a questionnaire that ranks the importance of factors and indicators affecting controller psychological stress. The findings of this research can aid in the identification of effective improvement measures to mitigate the negative effects of psychological stress on air traffic controllers.

2 Method

Psychological stress, also known as mental stress, can be defined as a dynamic equilibrium 'system' in which biological, psychological and social factors, such as life events, cognitive evaluations, coping styles, social support, personality traits and psychosomatic reactions of an individual, interact with each other, and when the system is out of balance for some reason, it is psychological stress [11]. By analogy to the psychological stress of controllers, it can be understood as the process of stress caused by various factors in the work of controllers.

On the premise of exploring the causes of psychological stress among air traffic controllers, a system of indicators of psychological stress among air traffic controllers is considered from multiple perspectives, and a questionnaire is developed based on the factor indicators in the indicator system to assess the controllers' psychological tests. At the same time, the importance of each factor indicator in the index system is ranked and the more important factor indicators are obtained.

The work of air traffic controllers has some special characteristics, and the causes of their psychological stress are mainly the following.

1) Psychological aspects of personnel

The psychological pressure of air traffic controllers mainly comes from their personal mental problems. It can be explored from two aspects: family and society.

For the family, due to the nature of the work of air traffic controllers, their working hours need to be reversed day and night, which will lead to certain negligence in the care of the family. In the long run, this may lead to family conflicts and increase the psychological pressure on air traffic controllers.

For the community, the tense working atmosphere of air traffic controllers is very different from the relaxed working atmosphere of their friends around them, which will make them have a certain degree of psychological gap, which will also cause them a certain degree of psychological pressure.

2) Work content

On the one hand, air traffic controllers need to maintain a high state of mental concentration in their daily work, which can easily produce fatigue and form a huge psychological pressure. On the other hand, due to the working hours against the normal biological clock, air traffic controllers will also generate a certain degree of stress when they do not have enough sleep.

3) Management assessment aspect

Since the control work is extremely important, the selection of air traffic controllers is also more stringent. The relevant units will regularly hold some tests to check the ability and quality of air traffic controllers in all aspects, and if any air traffic controllers are found to be unqualified, they will be eliminated. In the case of fierce competition, controllers will also be under psychological pressure.

2.1   Participants

The participants mainly target frontline controllers of 7 regional air traffic authorities in China, namely North China, East China, Northeast China, South Central China, Northwest China, Southwest China and Xinjiang, where frontline controllers include approach controllers, regional controllers, airport controllers and ramp controllers. There were no requirements for participants' age or work experience, and both release controllers and trainee controllers were eligible. In order to prevent the findings from creating a bias against female employment, gender was not studied in this paper. A total of 300 questionnaires were distributed and 245 valid questionnaires were collected. As stated in the consent form, participants were anonymous and had the right to withdraw the data they provided.

2.2   Research Framework

Firstly, the controller's psychological stress index system is established by analyzing the controller's work. Secondly, the controller's psychological stress is assessed by distributing questionnaires according to the content of the index system using the survey method of the improved OSI. On this basis, controllers are asked to rank the importance of the indicators. Finally, the distribution of controllers' psychological stress levels and the ranking of the importance of each indicator were obtained by comparing the results with the standard norms.

2.3   Questionnaire Structure and Processing Method

The methods of testing psychological stress are physical test method and the psychological test assessment method.

Physical testing methods, now commonly used in psychiatric hospitals, such as testing neurological function, there is physical stress, psychological stress physical measurement of the instrument, through the instrument to determine the size of the pressure at this time. Although these methods can directly give the degree of stress, none of them can accurately describe the source of stress, and because of the special nature of the control work, there are certain difficulties in the implementation of physical testing methods on a large scale, and the results may also have some deviation from the actual situation of psychological stress.

The principle of the psychological test assessment method is to determine the psychological stress situation of an individual based on authoritative psychological test questions. Not only can the source of stress be given, but also the degree of psychological stress of the individual can be assessed.

In summary, this paper uses the psychological test assessment method to test and analyze the psychological stress of controllers, which can not only get the source of psychological stress but also make the implementation of the method easier.

The OSI (Occupational stress Indicator), also known as the Occupational Stress Indicator, was proposed by Cooper et al. in 1988 [2], and its purpose is to measure occupational stress, of which 140 questions can be divided into six domains, namely: job satisfaction, health, Type A behaviors (including life attitudes, behavioral styles, and

Aspirations), control points (including organizational forces, management processes, and personal influences), sources of stress, and coping strategies. The OSI is now widely used in existing studies of job stressors in various industries. In order to increase the applicability of the questionnaire to controllers' psychological stress, some modifications were made to the OSI to test controllers' psychological stress.

According to the content and nature of controllers' daily work, a controller psychological stress index system is established from three aspects: work factors, management factors and personal factors, in which environmental factors are included, so we will not elaborate too much. As shown in Fig. 1.

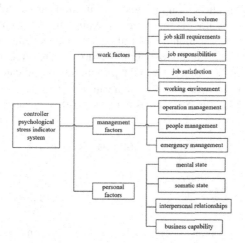

Fig. 1. Controller psychological stress indicator system

Among them, control task refers to the workload of controllers in the work, such as flight popularity, etc.; job skill requirements refer to the job skill requirements that controllers have, such as control license, English level, etc.; job responsibility refers to the responsibility that controllers take when performing control work; job satisfaction refers to the controller's recognition of control work or feedback on whether they are suitable for the position of controller. Work environment refers to the condition of the environment in which the controller works; operation management refers to the coordination of various departments when the controller performs control work; personnel management refers to the management of the controller by the control unit, such as duty arrangements; emergency management refers to the emergency response capability of the control unit in the event of an emergency; psychological state refers to the psychological state of the controller at work; physical state refers to the physical health of the controller during daily work Interpersonal relationship refers to the controller's interpersonal relationship with colleagues and family; operational ability refers to the controller's proficiency and flexibility in performing daily control work.

A description of the questionnaire design with modifications to some of the questions in the OSI based on this indicator system is as follows.

The questionnaire is divided into two parts. The first part is a test of the controller's psychological stress level, in which the controller selects the corresponding options and scores them according to the questions on the questionnaire, and finally makes a judgment on the current stress situation according to the total score. The second part of the questionnaire is based on the established controller psychological stress index system, which allows controllers to rank the indexes in order of importance, and then get the more important influencing factors index.

There are 120 questions in the questionnaire, and the specific contents of the questionnaire are shown in Table 1. Among the 120 questions, there are both positive and negative questions, and the questions marked with '*' are negative questions. The meanings of '0, 1, 2, 3, 4' in the scoring of positive questions are as follows: '0' means no symptoms in the past month; '1' means fewer symptoms in the past month; '2' means fewer symptoms in the past month. Less often; '2' means symptoms occurred sometimes in the past month; '3' means symptoms occurred more often in the past month; '4' means symptoms occurred frequently in the past month. 4' indicates that the symptoms occurred frequently in the past month. The meanings of '0, 1, 2, 3, 4' in the scoring of the reverse questions are the exact opposite of the positive questions.

Table 1. Questionnaire content

Issue Properties	Questionnaire questions	Options
Basic Information	Age	Fill in the specific age (unit: years)
	Working hours	Fill in the specific work time (unit: years)
Work Factors	In the control work, I was required to complete several tasks in a short period	No/Less often/Sometimes/More often/Often
	I feel that my job responsibilities are increasing	No/Less often/Sometimes/More often/Often
	Placing me on tasks for which I have never been trained	No/Less often/Sometimes/More often/Often
	Too many tasks, I had to take my work home to do	No/Less often/Sometimes/More often/Often
	*I have the ability to get the job done	No/Less often/Sometimes/More often/Often
	*I am good at controlling work	No/Less often/Sometimes/More often/Often
	I have a very tight work schedule	No/Less often/Sometimes/More often/Often
	*I would like to get more help to do my job better	No/Less often/Sometimes/More often/Often

(*continued*)

Table 1. (*continued*)

Issue Properties	Questionnaire questions	Options
	Requires me to work in several equally important areas at the same time	No/Less often/Sometimes/More often/Often
	Asking me to complete an overload of work	No/Less often/Sometimes/More often/Often
	*I think the emergency management procedures in my working environment are comprehensive	No/Less often/Sometimes/More often/Often
	*I think the unit's emergency management manual is comprehensive	No/Less often/Sometimes/More often/Often
	*I am well aware of the possible contingencies of my position	No/Less often/Sometimes/More often/Often
	I am worried about my ability to handle unexpected situations during my shift	No/Less often/Sometimes/More often/Often
	*Unit-designated emergency procedures are implemented to be effective in dealing with emergencies	No/Less often/Sometimes/More often/Often
	*Units frequently organize emergency drills	No/Less often/Sometimes/More often/Often
	*Emergency training frequently organized by the unit	No/Less often/Sometimes/More often/Often
	*In the event of an emergency, I am clear that the immediate leader in charge	No/Less often/Sometimes/More often/Often
	The possibility of emergencies in my position	No/Less often/Sometimes/More often/Often
	*In case of emergencies, my colleagues and I have the ability to work together to deal with them reasonably	No/Less often/Sometimes/More often/Often
	There are too many people to deal with at work every day	No/Less often/Sometimes/More often/Often
	I have to spend some time at work to consider the issues raised by others	No/Less often/Sometimes/More often/Often

(*continued*)

Table 1. (*continued*)

Issue Properties	Questionnaire questions	Options
	I am responsible for the welfare of employees	No/Less often/Sometimes/More often/Often
	Colleagues see me as a leader	No/Less often/Sometimes/More often/Often
	I am responsible for what others do at work	No/Less often/Sometimes/More often/Often
	I worry about how well my colleagues will do their jobs	No/Less often/Sometimes/More often/Often
	My job requires me to make big decisions	No/Less often/Sometimes/More often/Often
	If I make a mistake in my work, it will have serious consequences for others	No/Less often/Sometimes/More often/Often
	I am concerned about the responsibility of my work	No/Less often/Sometimes/More often/Often
	*I like my colleagues	No/Less often/Sometimes/More often/Often
	*My career is progressing significantly	No/Less often/Sometimes/More often/Often
	*My job suits my skills and interests	No/Less often/Sometimes/More often/Often
	I am tired of my profession	No/Less often/Sometimes/More often/Often
	I feel a great responsibility for my work	No/Less often/Sometimes/More often/Often
	*My talent is put to work	No/Less often/Sometimes/More often/Often
	*I have good job prospects	No/Less often/Sometimes/More often/Often
	*I am satisfied with my work performance	No/Less often/Sometimes/More often/Often
	*I think I am perfectly capable of doing the job	No/Less often/Sometimes/More often/Often
	*I can learn new skills at work	No/Less often/Sometimes/More often/Often
	*I can do what I can do	No/Less often/Sometimes/More often/Often
	High noise level in the working environment	No/Less often/Sometimes/More often/Often

(*continued*)

Table 1. (*continued*)

Issue Properties	Questionnaire questions	Options
	Very humid in the working environment	No/Less often/Sometimes/More often/Often
	High dust concentration in the working environment	No/Less often/Sometimes/More often/Often
	High temperature in the working environment	No/Less often/Sometimes/More often/Often
	Excessive light in the working environment	No/Less often/Sometimes/More often/Often
	My job is dangerous	No/Less often/Sometimes/More often/Often
	My working hours change a lot	No/Less often/Sometimes/More often/Often
	I work independently	No/Less often/Sometimes/More often/Often
	Unpleasant odor in the working environment	No/Less often/Sometimes/More often/Often
	The presence of toxic substances in the working environment	No/Less often/Sometimes/More often/Often
Management Factors	There is a conflict between what leadership expects me to do and what I think I should do	No/Less often/Sometimes/More often/Often
	In my work, I feel caught in the conflict between factions	No/Less often/Sometimes/More often/Often
	At work, I have multiple people telling me what to do	No/Less often/Sometimes/More often/Often
	*I know exactly where I stand in the unit (position)	No/Less often/Sometimes/More often/Often
	*I am satisfied with the work I have done	No/Less often/Sometimes/More often/Often
	The leaders have different views on what I should do	No/Less often/Sometimes/More often/Often
	My work requires the cooperation of many departments to accomplish	No/Less often/Sometimes/More often/Often
	*I know exactly who is running the show at work	No/Less often/Sometimes/More often/Often
	I'm not so responsible for my work	No/Less often/Sometimes/More often/Often
	I often disagree with people in other departments at work	No/Less often/Sometimes/More often/Often

(*continued*)

Table 1. (*continued*)

Issue Properties	Questionnaire questions	Options
	When I need to take a vacation, I can take a vacation	No/Less often/Sometimes/More often/Often
	During my free time, I can do what I want to do	No/Less often/Sometimes/More often/Often
	On weekends, I do what I like best	No/Less often/Sometimes/More often/Often
	I hardly ever watch TV	No/Less often/Sometimes/More often/Often
	Most of my spare time I go to some performances (e.g. sporting events, opera, movies and concerts)	No/Less often/Sometimes/More often/Often
	I spend a lot of my spare time participating in activities (such as woodworking and sewing)	No/Less often/Sometimes/More often/Often
	I use some time to do what I like to do	No/Less often/Sometimes/More often/Often
	*When I take a break, I still often think about work	No/Less often/Sometimes/More often/Often
	I spend a lot of time on recreational activities to satisfy my interests and hobbies	No/Less often/Sometimes/More often/Often
	*I spend a lot of my spare time on hobbies (such as collecting various items)	No/Less often/Sometimes/More often/Often
	*I think my English level is easy to cope with the current control work	No/Less often/Sometimes/More often/Often
	*The control directive I issued is well understood	No/Less often/Sometimes/More often/Often
	My language for land and air calls is not standard	No/Less often/Sometimes/More often/Often
	*It was easy for me to get the license required for the control position	No/Less often/Sometimes/More often/Often
	*The various systems for control seats in our units work well	No/Less often/Sometimes/More often/Often
	I can't adapt to the new control system related software installed by the unit	No/Less often/Sometimes/More often/Often

(*continued*)

Table 1. (*continued*)

Issue Properties	Questionnaire questions	Options
	*I am always excited to command a plane	No/Less often/Sometimes/More often/Often
	I'm not sure about the safety spacing between planes	No/Less often/Sometimes/More often/Often
	*I know the airspace or airports in my control area	No/Less often/Sometimes/More often/Often
	I find it difficult when it comes to coordinating issues with the Air Force	No/Less often/Sometimes/More often/Often
Personal factors	Lately, I am prone to anger	No/Less often/Sometimes/More often/Often
	Lately, I feel depressed	No/Less often/Sometimes/More often/Often
	Lately, I feel anxious	No/Less often/Sometimes/More often/Often
	*Lately, I feel happy	No/Less often/Sometimes/More often/Often
	When I go to sleep at night, I am often troubled by thoughts that make it difficult to sleep	No/Less often/Sometimes/More often/Often
	Lately, I've been very poor at coping with difficult situations	No/Less often/Sometimes/More often/Often
	I find myself complaining about the little things	No/Less often/Sometimes/More often/Often
	Recently, I have been upset	No/Less often/Sometimes/More often/Often
	*I speak with a sense of humor	No/Less often/Sometimes/More often/Often
	*I found that everything was going well	No/Less often/Sometimes/More often/Often
	My unexpected weight gain	No/Less often/Sometimes/More often/Often
	My eating habits are not regular	No/Less often/Sometimes/More often/Often
	Recently, I drink a lot of alcohol	No/Less often/Sometimes/More often/Often
	Lately, I feel tired	No/Less often/Sometimes/More often/Often
	I feel nervous	No/Less often/Sometimes/More often/Often

(*continued*)

Table 1. (*continued*)

Issue Properties	Questionnaire questions	Options
	I have trouble falling asleep and staying asleep	No/Less often/Sometimes/More often/Often
	I feel some indescribable pain	No/Less often/Sometimes/More often/Often
	I consume some unhygienic food	No/Less often/Sometimes/More often/Often
	*I feel good	No/Less often/Sometimes/More often/Often
	*Lately I've had a lot of energy	No/Less often/Sometimes/More often/Often
	I wish I had more time to spend with good friends	No/Less often/Sometimes/More often/Often
	I often have arguments with people close to me	No/Less often/Sometimes/More often/Often
	I often argue with my friends	No/Less often/Sometimes/More often/Often
	*I am happy with my spouse	No/Less often/Sometimes/More often/Often
	Lately, I do everything myself	No/Less often/Sometimes/More often/Often
	I had an argument with my family	No/Less often/Sometimes/More often/Often
	*Lately I've been doing well with people	No/Less often/Sometimes/More often/Often
	I think it takes time to work out my own problems	No/Less often/Sometimes/More often/Often
	Lately, I'm worried about what my colleagues think of me	No/Less often/Sometimes/More often/Often
	Lately I don't want to be in contact with people	No/Less often/Sometimes/More often/Often
	I feel like I can't get a lot of work done	No/Less often/Sometimes/More often/Often
	Lately, I am afraid to go to work	No/Less often/Sometimes/More often/Often
	I'm bored with my job	No/Less often/Sometimes/More often/Often
	Lately, I feel I am behind in my work	No/Less often/Sometimes/More often/Often

(*continued*)

Table 1. (*continued*)

Issue Properties	Questionnaire questions	Options
	Recently there have been accidents at work	No/Less often/Sometimes/More often/Often
	*The quality of my work is good	No/Less often/Sometimes/More often/Often
	I've been absent from work a lot lately	No/Less often/Sometimes/More often/Often
	*I feel that my work is meaningful and inspiring	No/Less often/Sometimes/More often/Often
	*I can concentrate on my work	No/Less often/Sometimes/More often/Often
	I caused some mistakes in my work	No/Less often/Sometimes/More often/Often

Among the 120 questions, different questions reflect different problem attributes, among which, questions 1–50 reflect the psychological stress caused by work factors; questions 51–80 reflect the psychological stress caused by management factors; questions 81–120 reflect the psychological stress caused by personal factors. The specific refinement analysis is shown in Table 2.

The maximum total score is 480, '0–96' is no pressure, '97–192' is very light pressure, '193–288' is medium pressure, '289–384' is high pressure, and '385–480' is very high pressure. Since there are more questions and larger scores, the total score values are uniformly reduced by a factor of 6 in this paper for better visualization.

Considering that the psychological stress of controllers is closely related to the age and working hours of controllers, this information was added to the test paper. The specific psychological stress level criteria are shown in Table 3.

2.4 Data Collection and Processing

According to the designed questionnaires, front-line controllers in seven regional administrations were randomly distributed, and the collected questionnaires were analyzed for validity and credibility before data processing. The correlation coefficient method was used for data processing, which is a statistical indicator first devised by the statistician Carl Pearson and is a quantity that studies the degree of linear correlation between variables, generally denoted by the letter r. There are various ways of defining the correlation coefficient, such as simple correlation coefficient, complex correlation coefficient and typical correlation coefficient, due to the different objects of study, and the simple correlation coefficient is utilized in this paper [13]. Its formula is as follow

$$\gamma(X, Y) = \frac{Cov(X, Y)}{\sqrt{Var[X]Var[Y]}} \tag{1}$$

Table 2. Questionnaire questions corresponding to the three-level indicator description

Indicators	Corresponding title	Indicators	Corresponding title
control task volume	1–10	people management	61–70
job skill requirements	11–20	emergency management	71–80
job responsibilities	21–30	mental state	81–90
job satisfaction	31–40	somatic state	91–100
working environment	41–50	interpersonal relationships	101–110
operation management	51–60	business capability	111–120

Table 3. Psychological stress level criteria

Total Score	0–16	17–32	33–48	49–64	65–80
pressure rating	No pressure	Very light pressure	Medium pressure	Higher pressure	Extremely stressful

The results of the questionnaire test can be analyzed from three aspects: the distribution of controllers' psychological stress, the psychological stress of controllers in different age groups and the psychological stress of controllers during different working hours, using the correlation coefficient in statistics to more accurately illustrate the relationship between them, as well as to obtain the ranking of the importance of each factor indicator.

3 Results and Discussion

3.1 Validity of the Questionnaire

The validity of a questionnaire is the extent to which it reflects the theoretical concept it is measuring. Based on the above theoretical study, practical research was conducted and 300 questionnaires were distributed to the frontline controllers of the ATC, who were required to complete and submit the questionnaires within 7 days. The requirements for a valid questionnaire were as follows: 1. The questionnaire was submitted within the specified time; 2. All questions in the submitted questionnaire were to be completed; 3. The options in the questionnaire could not all be the same. According to the screening of the validity criteria, 245 questionnaires were collected.

3.2 Credibility of the Questionnaire

The reliability of a questionnaire refers to the degree of consistency or stability that the questionnaire results have. The Kuder-Richardson reliability (Kuder & Richardson) calculation and the Cronbach (Cronbach) alpha coefficient have often been used to estimate internal consistency reliability [12].

In this paper, the Cronbach coefficient is used. It is generally considered that a more reasonable confidence result should be between 0 and 1, and its formula is shown below.

$$\alpha = \frac{K}{K-1}(1 - \frac{\sum_{i=1}^{k} S_i^2}{S_t^2})$$
(2)

where, 'K' is the number of questionnaire items; 'S_i^2' is the variance of the score of the 'i' question; 'S_t^2' is the variance of the total score. The reliability of the questionnaire was calculated to be 0.625, which shows that the reliability of the questionnaire is within a reasonable range.

3.3 Questionnaire Analysis Methods and Results

Controllers' Psychological Stress Distribution. According to the statistical results of the questionnaire, Regarding the overall psychological stress level of controllers, 3 out of 245 questionnaires had no stress, 10 had very low stress, 110 had medium stress, 115 had high stress, and 7 had very high stress. It can be seen that most of the controllers' psychological stress is moderate and high, and a small proportion of controllers' psychological stress is no stress, low stress and high stress. The specific distribution is shown in Fig. 2.

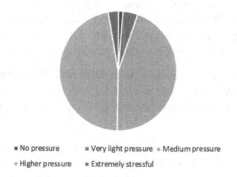

■ No pressure   ■ Very light pressure ■ Medium pressure
■ Higher pressure   ■ Extremely stressful

Fig. 2. Controllers' psychological stress level distribution chart

In summary, according to the questionnaire data, 92% of controllers have some psychological stress problems, so it is necessary to analyze and solve the psychological stress problems of controllers. According to the obtained important impact, indicators should be proposed as corresponding solution measures.

Psychological Stress of Controllers in Different Age Groups. Among the returned questionnaires, 35 controllers were aged 22–25 (including 25); 88 controllers were aged

26–30 (including 30); 81 controllers were aged 31–35 (including 35); 31 controllers were aged 36–40 (including 40); and 10 controllers were aged 40 or older.

According to the formula in Eq. (2), the correlation coefficient between controllers' age and controllers' psychological stress level can be calculated as 0.764, so it can be seen that the older controllers are positively correlated with controllers' psychological stress level, and the correlation is larger. The specific correlation line graph is shown in Fig. 3.

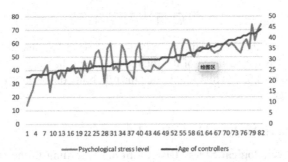

Fig. 3. The relationship between controller age and psychological stress level

In summary, as controllers get older, the psychological pressure on controllers increases. On the one hand, as controllers grow older, their sources of stress are much more than work pressure, their children's lives, parents' health and personal family's daily life are all sources of their stress, so under the pressure of many aspects, controllers' psychological stress will increase. On the other hand, when the controller's age increases, their physical functions will also be weaker than before, such as memory, reaction ability and physical recovery ability, etc. These factors more or less affect their work, so the older controllers will also have more psychological pressure.

Psychological Stress of Controllers with Different Working hours. Among the returned questionnaires, 35 people worked for less than 3 years (including 3 years); 113 people worked for 4 to 10 years (including 10 years) and 97 people worked for more than 10 years.

According to the formula in Eq. (2), we can calculate that the correlation coefficient between controllers' working hours and controllers' psychological stress is 0.785, so it can be seen that controllers' working hours are positively correlated with controllers' psychological stress, which means that the longer controllers' working hours are, the greater the psychological stress generated by controllers will be, and the specific correlation scatter diagram is shown in Fig. 4.

In conclusion, as the working hours of controllers increase, controllers understand more about the nature of control work and their responsibilities, plus they see more examples in their daily work, and their psychological stress will increase to a certain extent.

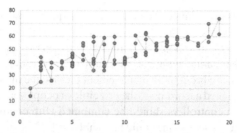

Fig. 4. The relationship between the working hours of controllers and the level of psychological stress

From the above three aspects, we can get that most of the controllers in China have certain psychological stress, and their psychological stress will increase with the increase of age and working hours, which is positively correlated.

3.4 Ranking the Importance of Each Factor Indicator

The index system used to rank the factors that affect controllers' psychological stress comprises 12 indicators. Through the use of a questionnaire, the controllers ranked the importance of each factor indicator, which was then used to obtain the final ranking of the importance of each indicator. The indicators were ordered by importance, with job responsibility, control task volume, and emergency management ranking highest, followed by job skill requirements, work environment, operation management, personnel management, interpersonal relationship, business ability, psychological state, physical state, and job satisfaction, as depicted in Fig. 5.

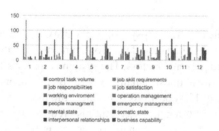

Fig. 5. Ranking of indicators for each factor

The horizontal coordinate is the ranking number and the vertical coordinate is the questionnaire data of different indicators on that ranking number.

3.5 Optimization Suggestions

The results of the psychological questionnaire and importance of the indicators were analyzed to provide the following optimization recommendations. First, to alleviate the psychological pressure brought by personal factors, four aspects should be strengthened. Professional skills training and self-confidence training can improve the safety of air transport operations and enhance the psychological quality and tolerance of air traffic controllers. Stress relief methods and good habits of life can also be taught to reduce tension and stress. Efficient teams should be built and managed to provide appropriate counseling, consultation, encouragement, and motivation to controllers. Second, to alleviate the psychological pressure brought by management factors, the management system and norms should be formulated according to the principle of people-oriented. The work characteristics of air traffic controllers should be combined with continuous improvement, and a perfect emergency rescue plan should be established. Third, to alleviate the psychological pressure brought by work factors, four aspects should be considered. The working environment should be comfortable and efficient with complete logistical support. Relevant departments should focus on the skills training of controllers, including overseas training, simulator training, and regular evaluations to increase decision-making ability and proficiency. Duty time should be reasonably adjusted, and effective supervision and management of the "double post system" is essential. The incentive mechanism and career planning should also be improved to relieve the pressure. Fourth, for the age of controllers, care and sympathy should be given to those around the age of 35 who face pressure from both work and family. A healthy lifestyle can ease the pressure. As controllers age, they should be withdrawn from front-line work before they reach the upper age limit. Fifth, relevant organizations should set up psychological counseling departments to provide counseling to controllers who work in the front line for a long time. Organizing regular medical checkups can also help controllers reduce psychological pressure.

Based on the analysis of the results of the psychological questionnaire and the importance of the indicators, the following optimization recommendations are given.

4   Conclusion

An index system for measuring the psychological stress experienced by air traffic controllers was established based on their daily work content and nature, taking into account work, management, and personal factors. The system comprises 12 indicators. To gather data, a psychological stress questionnaire was designed according to the established index system, containing 120 questions that reflect the psychological stress induced by different factors. The questionnaire was administered to 300 frontline controllers, of which 245 were valid. The data was analyzed, taking into account the controllers' age and working hours, and it was found that as these factors increased, so did the psychological stress experienced by the controllers. This underscores the importance of addressing psychological stress among controllers. Additionally, the 12 indicators were ranked by the controllers in order of importance. Based on these findings, it is recommended that appropriate measures be developed to reduce psychological stress among controllers, to enhance the safety and efficiency of air transportation.

Acknowledgements. Authors would like to express special thanks to all members for their contributions to this research. Their supports and the enthusiasm of their respective teams were invaluable in facilitating the authors' research efforts.

References

1. Rose, R.M., Jenkins, D.C., Hurst, M.W.: Health change in air traffic controllers: a prospective study I. Background and description. Psychosom. Med. **40**(2), 142–165 (1978)
2. Cooper, C.L., Sloan, S.J., Williams, S.: Occupational Stress Indicator Management Guide. NFER-Nelson Press, Windsor UK (1988)
3. Rose, R.M., Fogg, L.F.: Definition of a responder: analysis of behavioral, cardiovascular, and endocrine responses to varied workload in air traffic controllers. Psychosom. Med. **55**(4), 325–38 (1993). https://doi.org/10.1097/00006842-199307000-00001. PMID: 8416083
4. Rodahl, K., Mundal, R., Bjørklund, R.A.: Stress hos flygeledere [Stress among air traffic controllers]. Tidsskr Nor Laegeforen. **117**(22), 3234–3237 (1997). Norwegian. PMID: 9411865
5. Špiljak, B., Vilibić, M., Glavina, A., Crnković, M., Šešerko, A., LugovićMihić, L.: A review of psychological stress among students and its assessment using salivary biomarkers. Behav. Sci. **12**(10), 400 (2022)
6. Cong, L., Wenqing, M.: The role of employee psychological stress assessment in reducing human resource turnover in enterprises. Front. Psychol. **13**, 1005716 (2022)
7. Qiang, L.: Stress analysis and behavioral error analysis of air traffic controllers. Technol. Econ. Market (04), 87 (2015)
8. Xu, H., Yao, S., Liu, H., Tang, L., Wang, Z.: Study on the relationship between occupational stress and burnout among air traffic controllers. Environ. Occup. Med. **32**(12), 1102–1106 (2015). https://doi.org/10.13213/j.cnki.jeom.2015.15303
9. Lin, Y., Long, Y., Zhang, H., Liu, Z., Zhang, Z.: Multiple physiological signals based on XGBoost method for assessing psychological stress levels. J. Beijing Univ. Technol. **42**(08), 871–880 (2022). https://doi.org/10.15918/j.tbit1001-0645.2021.195
10. Zheng, X.: Physiological fatigue and psychological fatigue of air traffic controllers. J. Civil Aviat. Flight Acad. Chin **32**(01), 14–16 (2021)
11. Yao, S., Yang, Y.: Medical Psychology. 7th edn., pp. 96–99. People's Health Publishing House, Beijing (2018)
12. Peng, R.Z.: On the analysis method of questionnaire survey reliability calculation. J. Xinjiang Radio Telev. Univ. **15**(01), 46–50 (2011)
13. He, C., Long, W., Zhu, F.: Probability Theory and Mathematical Statistics, p. 79. Higher Education Press, Beijing (2012)
14. Li, W.-C., Zhang, J., Kearney, P.: Psychophysiological coherence training to moderate air traffic controllers' fatigue on rotating roster. Risk Anal. **43**(2), 391–404. https://doi.org/10.1111/risa.13899
15. Huang, Y.T., Zhou, L.S., Abdillah, H.: Progress of research on the assessment and influencing factors of psychological stress in early childhood. Evid. Based Nurs. **8**(24), 3314–3317 (2022)
16. Hui, X.: A study on stress management of air traffic controllers. Sci. Technol. Innov. Appl. **27**, 280 (2015)
17. Tang, W., Zeng, B., Sun, W., Wu, R.: Analysis of controller stress impact based on accident tree. J. Civil Aviat. Flight Acad. Chin. **33**(02), 16–21 (2022)

Author Index

Printed in the United States
by Baker & Taylor Publisher Services